Nurturing Future
GENERATIONS

Nurturing Future GENERATIONS

Promoting Resilience in Children and Adolescents

Through Social, Emotional and Cognitive Skills,

SECOND EDITION

Rosemary A. Thompson

Routledge
Taylor & Francis Group
New York   London

Published in 2006 by
Routledge
Taylor & Francis Group
270 Madison Avenue
New York, NY 10016

International Standard Book Number-10: 0-415-95096-1 (Hardcover) 0-415-95097-X (Softcover)
International Standard Book Number-13: 978-0415-95096-1 (Hardcover) 978-0-4159-5097-8 (Softcover)

Taylor & Francis Group
is the Academic Division of Informa plc.

Visit the Taylor & Francis Web site at
http://www.taylorandfrancis.com

and the Routledge Web site at
http://www.routledge-ny.com

Contents

Preface

Each day in America among all children

- 1 mother dies in childbirth.
- 4 children are killed by abuse or neglect.
- 5 children or teens commit suicide.
- 8 children or teens are killed by firearms.
- 76 babies die before their first birthday.
- 182 children are arrested for violent crimes.
- 366 children are arrested for drug abuse.
- 390 babies are born to mothers who received late or no prenatal care.
- 860 babies are born at low birth weight.
- 1,186 babies are born to teen mothers
- 1,707 babies are born without health insurance.
- 1,887 public school students are corporally punished.
- 2,171 babies are born into poverty.
- 2,539 high school students drop out.
- 3,742 babies are born to unmarried mothers.
- 4,440 children are arrested.
- 17,072 public school students are suspended.
- 2,867 children and teens die from gunfire.

Based on calculations per school day (180 days of 7 hours each).
From *Each Day in America among All Children*, by Children's Defense Fund, 2004, Washington, DC: Author. Copyright 2004 by Children's Defense Fund. Reprinted with permission.

Acknowledgments

A number of individuals have influenced the development of this book. First and foremost are the children—the children whom I have taught, counseled, or nurtured over the years who have overcome insurmountable odds and who have become successful despite preconceived notions about their potential. We are reminded every day that our children are struggling with more stressors than ever before and these are concurrent with serious social, emotional, and cognitive deficits. In terms of relationships, children and adolescents have fewer social, emotional, and cognitive interactions with fewer people than at any time in our history. Yet, we are also armed with the knowledge that protective factors exist that buffer children against risks; these factors include collaborative prevention and intervention initiatives among the school, the family, and the entire community, which must work in tandem to nurture youth.

I am most grateful to the late Dr. Joseph Hollis, former publisher of Accelerated Development, who launched my writing career two decades ago. His guidance, support, and suggestions through the years were invaluable. Other significant professional influences have been the school counselors of Chesapeake Public Schools, Chesapeake, Virginia, and the extraordinary leadership of Dr. W. Randolph Nichols. Through the years, Dr. Nichols has had the wisdom to provide me with many professional experiences with children that reflected the full spectrum of their diverse needs—from those in extreme poverty to those with the most intellectual gifts. Dr. Patricia Powers, Assistant Superintendent for Curriculum and Instruction, is also acknowledged for her support of the school counseling initiatives for Chesapeake Public Schools.

Appreciation is also extended to the graduate and undergraduate students at Old Dominion University, Norfolk, Virginia; the graduate students at Regent University, Virginia Beach, Virginia; and the students who gather annually in Vermont for the New England School Professionals Institute. All provide fresh perspectives and invaluable knowledge from the diversity of their professional experiences.

I would be remiss if I did not mention the support of the exceptional staff at Routledge—Behavioral Sciences, Taylor and Francis Group, most notably Emily Epstein-Loeb, Dana Bliss, Jay S. Whitney, and Rachael Panthier; their steadfast support from the beginning to the end of this project has been unprecedented.

Finally, I am most indebted to my husband Charles and to our two children, Jessica and Ryan. They unconditionally gave their love, patience, understanding, and support to make my writing ventures a reality.

Introduction

Indicators of troubled youth are all too familiar: school dropouts, gang involvement, alcohol and other drug abuse, unintended pregnancy, crime, violence, homicide, and suicide. Reams of research have punctuated these demographics and have circulated through government agencies, organizational think tanks, national school boards, and community agencies. An estimated 9.2 million to 15.8 million children are considered "at risk" in this country. Typically, youth considered at risk are more vulnerable to becoming pregnant, using alcohol and other drugs, dropping out of school, being unemployed, engaging in violence or other high-risk behaviors, and facing an increased propensity to develop a host of mental health problems

Executive summaries that attempt to capture the nature of the problem have been drafted by the U.S. Department of Education, the U.S. Department of Health and Human Services, the Centers for Disease Control and Prevention, the U.S. Department of Justice, the U.S. Bureau of the Census, the Office the U.S. Surgeon General, and the National Institute of Mental Health. Professional organizations such as the National Association of Elementary, Middle and Secondary School Principals; the American School Counselors Association; the American School Psychologists Association; and the American School Board Association, among others, have extrapolated the demographics and promoted initiatives for youth risk prevention.

Most research initiatives have focused on youth through a deficit lens. Some of those deficits or risk factors as provided by the U.S. Census Bureau (Kominski, Jamieson, & Martinez, 2001), are as follows:

1

- **Risk factor 1: Poverty.** Twenty-one percent of American children under age 18 live in families with incomes below the poverty level. Today one in five lives in poverty in the critical preschool years. Three of the richest countries in the world, America, Britain and Italy, have some of the highest levels of child poverty, according to an international study published in 2000 (Duckworth, 2000). The U.S. ranks second with a rate of 26.3%; Britain is third at 21.3%, while Italy comes in only slightly behind this at 21.2%. (Duckworth, 2000). The survey of child poverty across the industrialized world, which is the first to use fully comparable figures, reveals hardly any deprivation among children in the Nordic countries. The poverty rate among America's single mothes is also the highest in the world, with 59% raising children or incomes which are less than half the typical national income.

- **Risk factor 2: Welfare dependence.** Approximately 15% of the nation's children were in households receiving case assistance or food stamps. The percentage of children whose families participate in these programs has increased as the percentage of children in poverty has risen.

- **Risk factor 3: Both parents absent.** Children are slightly more likely than in the past to live in a home with neither parent. Some lived with grandparents or other relatives; others lived with nonrelatives, such as foster parents. The number of children living with grandparents (i.e., "skip generation parents") rose from fewer than 1 million in 1990 to more than to more than 1.4 million in 1996.

- **Risk factor 4: Single-parent families.** In 1996, 28% of children lived in single-parent families. Although the number of single mothers (9.8 million) has remained constant over the past 3 years, the number of single fathers has grown 25%, from 1.7 million in 1995 to 2.1 million in 1998, according to tabulations released today by the U.S. Commerce Department's Census Bureau. Men now comprise one sixth of the nation's 11.9 million single parents.

- **Risk factor 5: Unwed mothers or unintended pregnancies.** In 1996, 9% of children lived with a never-married mother. Each year in America, almost 500,000 teenagers give birth. The preliminary U.S. birth rate for teenagers in 1996 was 54.7 live births per 1,000 women aged 15 to 19, down 4% from 1995 and 12% from 1991, when the rate was 62.1. These recent declines reverse the 24% rise in the teenage birth rate from 1986 to 1991. There has been success in lowering the birth rate for both young and older teens, with rates for those 15 to 17 years of age down 12% between 1991 and 1996, and the rate for those 18 and 19 down 8%.

- **Risk factor 6: Parents who have not graduated from high school.** In 1996, 19% of children lived with a parent or guardian who had not graduated from high school.
- **Risk factor 7: Gun violence.** An average of eight children or teenagers are killed by firearms each day. An American child is 12 times more likely to die from gunfire than a child in any other industrial country (Goldstein & Eckstein, 2003; 2005).

Risks and Resiliency

One of the most trusted keepers of the data on the maladies of youth is the Centers for Disease Control and Prevention and its annual Youth Risk Behavior Surveillance of the United States (2002). The Youth Risk Behavior Surveillance System (YRBSS) monitors six categories of priority high-risk behaviors among youth and young adults: behaviors that contribute to unintentional injuries and violence; tobacco use; alcohol and other drug use; sexual behaviors that contribute to unintended pregnancies and sexually transmitted diseases (STDs), including human immunodeficiency virus (HIV) infections; unhealthy dietary behaviors; and physical inactivity. To monitor priority health-risk behaviors in these categories, the CDC developed the *Youth Risk Behavior Surveillance System* (Kolbe, Kann, & Collins, 1993). The YRBSS includes national, state, territorial, and local school-based surveys of students in grades 9 through 12. National surveys were conducted in 1991, 1993, 1995, 1997, 1999, and 2001. Readers should use caution regarding one aspect of the survey: it does not reflect the population of youth (however small) who have already dropped out of school. The YRBSS (2002) revealed the following about high-risk behavior:

- Riding with a driver who had been drinking alcohol:
  - Nationwide, 30.7% of students had ridden with a driver who had been drinking alcohol.
- Driving after drinking alcohol:
  - Nationwide, 13.3% students had driven a car or other vehicle after drinking alcohol.
- Carrying a weapon:
  - Nationwide, 17.4% of students had carried a weapon such as a gun or a knife.
- Physical fighting:
  - Among students nationwide, 33.2% had been in a physical fight.
- Dating violence and forced sexual intercourse:

- Nationwide, 9.5% of students had been hit, slapped, or physically hurt on purpose by their boyfriend or girlfriend.
- Nationwide, 7.7% of students had been forced to have sexual intercourse when they did not want to engage in sexual relations.
- School-related violence:
  - Nationwide, 6.6% of students had missed a day of school because they felt unsafe at school or on their way to or from school; 8.9% of students had been threatened or injured with a weapon on school property.
- Sadness and suicide ideation and attempts:
  - Nationwide, 28.3% of students had felt sad or hopeless almost every day for 2 weeks in a row; 19% of students had seriously considered attempting suicide; 14.8% of students had made a suicidal plan; and 8.8% of students had attempted suicide.
- Current tobacco use:
  - Nationwide, 33% of students had reported current cigarette use, current smokeless tobacco use, or current cigar use.
- Alcohol and other drug use:
  - Nationwide, 78.2% of students had reported alcohol use; Hispanic and White students (80.8% and 80.1%, respectively) were significantly more likely than Black students (69.1%) to report alcohol use.
  - Nationwide, 42.4% of students had reported marijuana use.
  - Nationwide, 9.4% of students had used some form of cocaine.
  - Nationwide, 14.7% students had used inhalants, such as sniffing glue, breathing the contents of aerosol spray cans, or inhaling paints or sprays, to get high.
  - Nationwide, 3.1% of students had used heroin, 9.8% of students had used methamphetamines, and 5% had used illegal steroids.
- Sexual behaviors that contribute to unintended pregnancy and sexually transmitted diseases (STDs), including HIV infection:
  - Nationwide, 46% of students had had sexual intercourse; among the 33.4% of currently sexually active students, 57.9% reported that either they or their partner had used a condom during intercourse; 25.6% had used alcohol or drugs during intercourse.
  - Nationwide, 4.7% of students reported that they had been pregnant or had gotten someone else pregnant; 89% of students reported being taught in school about acquired immunodeficiency syndrome (AIDS) or HIV infection.
- Mental health disorders:

- Mental disorders fall into a number of broad categories, most of which apply not just to children but across the entire life span: anxiety disorders; attention-deficit and disruptive behavior disorders; autism and other pervasive developmental disorders; eating disorders (e.g., anorexia nervosa); elimination disorders (e.g., enuresis, encopresis); learning and communication disorders; mood disorders (e.g., major depressive disorder, bipolar disorder); schizophrenia; and tic disorders (e.g., Tourette's disorder). The YRBSS demonstrated that numerous children and adolescents engage in behaviors that increase their likelihood for developmental risks, such as experimenting with alcohol and other drugs by the age of 13, carrying a weapon, drinking and driving, having unintended pregnancies, attempting suicide, or HIV infection. Trend analysis of selected risk factors indicated increases and decreases in some behaviors. Additional research is needed to assess the effect of specific educational, socioeconomic, cultural, and racial and ethnic factors on the prevalence of health-risk behaviors among youth (CDC, 2002).

Essentially, the preceding data reflect the harm that troubled and dysfunctional families, communities, and societies can inflict on children and adolescents through a deficit lens. Our society has been consumed by labels framing the demise of youth as "Generation X," "coming from a dysfunctional home," "having developmental deficits," " being disabled," and so on. This perspective is one of hopelessness, depicting children as passive victims without choices or the ability to help themselves. Essentially, labels are disabling and stigmatize children and adolescents. Traditionally, the fields of education, prevention, and therapy for children and adolescents who struggle with hardship have been dominated by an at-risk paradigm.

Concurrently, there is a growing movement that is studying resiliency in children. The underlying hypothesis examines how children and adolescents "make it" when their development is threatened by poverty, neglect, maltreatment, or war with caregivers whose "care giving" is hindered because of incarceration or mental or physical illness. The resiliency model breaks with a long tradition of research and practice that emphasized problems and vulnerabilities in children, families, communities, and institutions burdened by adversity. The research on resiliency (children succeeding in spite of serious challenges to their development) emerged over two decades ago, when pioneering researchers kept uncovering examples of successful development in their studies of children at risk

(Masten, Best, & Garmezy, 1990). These investigators realized that we did not understand how good outcomes are achieved and that this information was critical for improving the odds of these high-risk children for productive lives (Egeland, Carlson, & Stroufe, 1993; Garmezy & Masten, 1994; Masten & Wright, 1997). This resiliency model empowers youth with the strength and the potential to recover and bounce back from hardship (Wolin & Wolin, 1993). It fosters their power to help themselves and casts professionals as partners, rather than authority figures who direct the change process.

Three Case Studies of Resilience: Against All Odds

What follows are three case studies that fall under the deficit lenses of underachievement, unintended pregnancy, and loss. These children did not succumb to labels that would chain them to a less-than-fruitful life.

Underachievement: The Case of Rosie

Her elementary school report card echoed what might have been a life sentence: "Has ability, but lacks effort." Easy summons for the school counselor to "write off": *...no time to work with this student...parents don't have a clue, anyway. The mother is an immigrant and the father is an absentee career soldier. They surely wouldn't be invested in their child's education.* By the time Rosie reached high school, she was well known in the social circuit of her peers but not in the academic arena of her teachers. She spent time in detention, usually for such infractions as talking in class or passing notes to a friend. During her junior year, Rosie went to visit her school counselor to get some information on the SAT. Her counselor, Mr. Allen, quickly brought it to her attention—and the attention of everyone within earshot in the counseling suite—that Rosie was "not college material." Rosie was so embarrassed, she felt sure that even the principal knew she "wasn't college material"—and what if he was on the public address system and now the whole school (especially her trusted peers) knew she "wasn't college material!" Mr. Allen hadn't noticed that Rosie was taking college preparatory classes. Neither had he met her mother, who was determined that her daughter was going to college. Rosie's mother left her family and the war-torn ravages of Nazi Germany to come to America to make a better life.

Rosie was befriended by the head counselor, Mrs. Vaughn, who overheard the "not college material" dialogue and gradually encouraged Rosie to go into teaching. Mrs. Vaughn called Radford University personally.

Both counselors struck a deal that if Rosie worked hard her senior year, they would give her a second look.

Today, Rosemary has her doctorate in counseling and educational administration from the College of William and Mary. She has published numerous books, consults nationally, is an adjunct professor at three local universities, and is currently a school administrator who supervises school counselors, kindergarten through twelfth grade, in a large school division in Virginia.

Unintended Pregnancy: the Case of Becky

Becky had an unintended pregnancy at age 16, during the height of the prochoice movement. Her brother tried to convince her to get rid of her unborn child because it would "ruin her life forever." He even offered to pay for the abortion. Becky insisted on having her child, went out of state to get married, and had another child 2 years later.

Becky began taking courses at the local community college, in the evenings, before her children entered preschool. Like collecting green stamps at the grocery store, her credits started adding up. When Becky's children entered elementary school, she went back to work full time at the local Wal-Mart. By then her marriage was over. Becky didn't mind working retail and was even tapped to pursue the management track. Her real dream, however, was to become a nurse. She wanted to have a more meaningful relationship with the people she encountered. She pursued her LPN at the community college, then received her RN through distance learning at Old Dominion University. She married twice more during this time, once to a physically abusive man and the other to an alcoholic.

Rebecca was determined. She became an emergency room nurse at a prestigious children's hospital, put both her children through college and, at age 41, has returned to the university to pursue her bachelor's degree, maintaining a 3.9 GPA while working full time. She finally met a wonderful man and is now married for the fourth time.

Grief and Loss: The Case of Danny

Danny was a disheveled, neglected third grader who came to school dirty, sometimes wearing the same clothes for days. His mother had recently died of cancer; he and his father were devastated. His academic performance was suffering, and he was slated to go to the Child Study Committee to receive special education services. His teacher, Miss Dodson, was convinced that Danny was learning disabled and needed special services she didn't have the time to provide.

At the classroom Christmas party, Danny gave Miss Dodson a present. She was surprised because she felt sure that Danny was poor, neglected, and, she suspected, subjected to some form of child abuse. She had even referred him to the nurse because she suspected head lice. He seemed to be one of those kids that even a mother couldn't love.

She opened the present: a rhinestone bracelet and a half a bottle of cheap perfume. After the classroom Christmas party, Danny lingered and told Miss Dodson that she looked nice in his mom's bracelet, and she smelled like her, too.

Touched by his thoughtfulness and taking the time to learn more about Danny's background, Miss Dodson was embarrassed that she had stereotyped the boy. When Miss Dodson returned in January, she worked hard to help Danny catch up with his classmates. He began to thrive academically, and she pulled his referral to the Child Study Committee. Danny became salutatorian of his graduating class, went to college, and continued to medical school.

Today, Daniel is a pediatrician on the medical board of a regional hospital. He is founder of the Grieving Center for Children and Families.

The Construct Global of Resilience

A multitude of constructs relate to invulnerability, such as resilience, hardiness, adaptation, adjustment, mastery, plasticity, person–environment fit, or social buffering (Losel, Bliesener, & Koferl, 1989, p. 187). Wolin and Wolin (1993) defined resilience as the capacity to bounce back: to withstand hardship and repair oneself. The constellation of strengths identified among individuals in this study includes the following:

- Insight
- Independence
- Relationships
- Initiative
- Creativity and humor
- Morality

Flach (1988) termed resiliency as the strengths humans require to master cycles of disruption and reintegration throughout the life cycle. He maintained that the makeup of a resilient personality would include the following:

- A sense of self esteem.
- Independent thoughts and actions.

- The ability to compromise in interactions with others and a well-established network of friends.
- A high level of discipline and a sense of responsibility.
- Acknowledgment of one's own special gifts and talents.
- Open-mindedness and willingness to explore new ideas.
- A willingness to dream.
- A broad range of interests.
- A sharp sense of humor.
- Insight into one's own feelings and those of others and the ability to communicate these feelings effectively.
- A high endurance of distress.
- Focus, a commitment to life, and a philosophical structure in which personal encounters can be represented with meaning and hope, even at the most despairing times of life.

Best Practices

Best practices initiatives are programs or services that empirically demonstrate that they reduce self-defeating behaviors among youth. The most articulated and implemented program models are those that employ the following principles: "holistic approaches that promote youth development; collaborative efforts among different agencies that provide services for youth risk prevention; integration of family peers and the community in treatment; enhanced adult and youth interaction through such program initiatives such as mentoring, work-based learning, and links to the private sector; and community-service and service-learning activities" (National Governors Association Center for Best Practices, 2000, p.1).

This new youth development approach has evolved as a movement "from remediation to prevention; from targeting at-risk youth to building on the strengths of youth; from addressing single problems to addressing a broad array of youth needs; from one agency/one discipline approaches to interagency/interdisciplinary strategies; and from treating youth outside the context of the community to working with youth in the context of their own environment" (National Governors Association for Best Practices, 2000, p. 1).

With the emerging research on resiliency and best practices in prevention research, this second edition of *Nurturing an Endangered Generation: Empowering Youth with Critical Social, Emotional, and Cognitive Skills* will focus on the positive aspects of youth development. Its new title, *Nurturing Future Generations, Second Edition: Promoting Resilience in Children and Adolescents through Social, Emotional, and Cognitive Skills* illustrates a focus on assets—not deficits—when trying to apply best practices to youth development.

Part I (Chapter 1 through Chapter 3) introduces the text, providing both a rationale and a theoretical framework for the intervention strategies that follow. Resiliency, protective factors, and developmental assets are introduced. Chapter 1 focuses on social, emotional, and cognitive deficits that emerge in children's and adolescents' self-defeating behavior. A unique addition to Chapter 1 is an outline of the developmental tasks for children and adolescents in the domains of thinking (cognitive skills), feeling (emotional skills), and relating (social skills), which remains the cornerstone of this book. Inherently, children, adolescents, as well as adults all need to enhance their social, emotional, and cognitive skills to "foster better relationships." Chapter 2 focuses on the quest for resilient youth, outlining the concept of resiliency, listing risks and threats to resiliency in children and adolescents, and emphasizing protective factors. Chapter 3 details the value of implementing psychoeducational groups in school, community, and institutional settings and outlines the structured six-step model that can be implemented in any setting with populations across the lifespan. This chapter also outlines the efficacy of small-group counseling with selected structured group exercises. Through the mutual sharing of anxieties and problem-solving strategies in a secure environment, children and adolescents discover a commonality of fears, stressors, ambitions, goals, and aspirations and learn successful ways to prevent and solve problems. Problems are no longer unique but are universal and shared by others.

Part II (Chapter 4 through Chapter 10) focuses on specific categories of child and adolescent self-defeating behavior that require structured intervention: Chapter 4 focuses on alcohol and drug abuse; Chapter 5 on unintended teenage pregnancy and high-risk sexual activity; Chapter 6 on depression, suicide, and self-injury; Chapter 7 on violence, delinquency, gangs, and bullying behavior; Chapter 8 on alienation, underachievement and dropping out; Chapter 9 on isolation, victimization and abuse; and Chapter 10 on gay, lesbian, bisexual, transgendered, and questioning (GLBTQ) youth. Chapter 10 is a new chapter to this second edition. All of these issues have been growing concerns among helping professionals.

Therapeutic initiatives concentrate on counseling session plans that focus on specific techniques and multimodal treatment plans. These are followed by collective initiatives, which collectively focus on the developmental needs of children and adolescents and critical social, emotional, and cognitive skills, following the psychoeducation life skill intervention model.

Part III (Chapter 11) focuses on empowering youth, families, institutions, and agencies from the perspective that it takes a whole community to nurture a healthy child. The book's intent is to identify critical social, emotional, and cognitive skills that can enhance the well-being of children and adolescents. Multiple strategies and multidisciplinary teams of helping professionals can organize to reduce risk factors and to enhance protective factors for this imperiled generation of young people. This final chapter focuses on the importance of school, community, and agency interaction to foster the developmental assets that are critical for youth risk prevention. Today, the most successful program initiatives embrace the following principles: holistic approaches that promote youth development; collaborative efforts among different agencies that promote services for youth risk prevention; and integration of family, peers, and the community in treatment and intervention.

This book can be used in schools, community agencies, youth service organizations, and faith communities. It is intended for counselors, teachers, social workers, probation officers, school psychologists, human service workers, and other helping professionals who work with children and adolescents. However, social, emotional, and cognitive skills are utilized across the life span, so this aspect of the book is appropriate to all populations.

Rationale and Theoretical Framework

CHAPTER 1

Social, Emotional, and Cognitive Deficits from a Developmental Perspective

It appears we have lost sight of some of the fundamental goals of our educational system: namely, to foster the development of human relationships (National Education Association, Educational Policies Commission, 1938) and to teach respect for other persons, develop insights into ethical values and principles, and strengthen our children's ability to live and to work cooperatively with others. (National Education Association, Educational Policies Commission, 1952)

Dinkmeyer (1971) stated that the lack of a required, sequentially developmental program in self-understanding and human behavior testifies to an educational paradox: "We have taught children almost everything in school except to understand and accept themselves and to function more effectively in human relations" (p. 62). Rogers (1980) asserted, "I deplore the manner in which from early years, the child's education splits him or her: the mind can come to school and the body is permitted peripherally to tag along, but the feelings and emotions can live freely and expressively only outside the school" (p. 263). We have been schooled for years to stress only the cognitive, to avoid any feeling connected to learning. Rogers

(1980) maintained "if we are truly aware, we can hear the silent screams of denied feelings echoing off every classroom wall" (p. 251). In 1990, the Carnegie Foundation released a report entitled *Turning Point: Preparing American Youth for the 21st Century*, which concluded that half of America's youth were "extremely vulnerable to multiple high-risk behaviors and school failures" or were "at moderate risk, but remain ... a cause for serious concern" (p. 36). The perpetual neglect of the importance of nurturing emotional learning and the implications of developing and maintaining meaningful relationships have existed for decades.

High-Risk Behaviors

Growing evidence of predictors for high-risk behaviors can be found in many sources. In the United States, 70.8% of all deaths among youth and young adults aged 10 to 24 years result from only four causes: motor-vehicle crashes (32.3%), other unintentional injuries (11.7%), homicide (15.1%), and suicide (11.7%) The Youth Risk Behavior Surveillance System (2004) monitors six categories of priority health-risk behaviors among youth and young adults, that is, behaviors that contribute to unintentional injuries and violence; tobacco use; alcohol and other drug use; sexual behaviors that contribute to unintended pregnancy and sexually transmitted diseases (STDs), including human immunodeficiency virus (HIV) infection; unhealthy dietary behaviors; and physical inactivity. YRBSS (2004) includes a national school-based survey conducted by CDC as well as state and local school-based surveys conducted by education and health agencies. This report summarizes results from the national survey, 32 state surveys, and 18 local surveys conducted among students in grades 9 through 12 during February through December 2003. Selected health risk behaviors include the following:

- **Failed to use seat belt.** Nationwide, 18.2% of students had rarely or never worn seat belts when riding in a car driven by someone else.
- **Failed to use bicycle helmet.** Among the 62.3% of students nationwide who had ridden a bicycle during the 12 months preceding the survey, 85.9% had rarely or never worn a bicycle helmet.
- **Rode with a driver who had been drinking alcohol.** During the 30 days preceding the survey, 30.2% of students nationwide had ridden in a car or other vehicle one or more times with a driver who had been drinking alcohol.
- **Drove after drinking alcohol.** During the 30 days preceding the survey, 12.1% of students nationwide had driven a car or other vehicle one or more times after drinking alcohol.

- **Carried a weapon.** Nationwide, 17.1% of students had carried a weapon (e.g., a gun, knife, or club) on one or more of the 30 days preceding the survey.
- **Carried a gun.** Nationwide, 6.1% of students had carried a gun on one or more of the 30 days preceding the survey.
- **Involved in physical fighting.** Nationwide, 33.0% of students had been in a physical fight one or more times during the 12 months preceding the survey.
- **Injured in a physical fight.** Among students nationwide, 4.2% had been in a physical fight, that resulted in injuries that had to be treated by a doctor or nurse, one or more times during the 12 months preceding the survey.
- **Experienced dating violence.** During the 12 months preceding the survey, 8.9% of students nationwide had been hit, slapped, or physically hurt on purpose by a boyfriend or girlfriend.
- **Experienced forced sexual intercourse.** Nationwide, 9.0% of students had been physically forced to have sexual intercourse when they did not want to.
- **Carried a weapon on school property.** Nationwide, 6.1% of students carried a weapon (e.g., a gun, knife, or club) on school property on one or more of the 30 days preceding the survey.
- **Threatened or injured with a weapon on school property.** During the 12 months preceding the survey, 9.2% of students nationwide had been threatened or injured with a weapon (e.g., a gun, knife, or club) on school property one or more times.
- **Involved in a physical fight on school property.** Nationwide, 12.8% of students had been in a physical fight on school property one or more times during the 12 months preceding the survey.
- **Did not go to school because of safety concerns.** Among students nationwide, 5.4% had not gone to school on one or more of the 30 days preceding the survey because they felt unsafe at school or on their way to or from school.
- **Property stolen or damaged on school property.** Nationwide, 29.8% of students had had their property (e.g., car, clothing, or books) stolen or deliberately damaged on school property one or more times during the 12 months preceding the survey.
- **Felt sad or hopeless.** During the 12 months preceding the survey, 28.6% of students nationwide had felt so sad or hopeless almost every day for two or more weeks in a row that they stopped doing some usual activities.

- **Seriously considered attempting suicide.** Nationwide, 16.9% of students had seriously considered attempting suicide during the 12 months preceding the survey.
- **Made a suicide plan.** During the 12 months preceding the survey, 16.5% of students nationwide had made a plan to attempt suicide.
- **Attempted suicide.** Nationwide, 8.5% of students had actually attempted suicide one or more times during the 12 months preceding the survey.
- **Attempted suicide and required medical attention.** During the 12 months preceding the survey, 2.9% of students nationwide had made a suicide attempt that resulted in an injury, poisoning, or overdose that had to be treated by a doctor or nurse.
- **Used tobacco.** Nationwide, 58.4% of students had tried cigarette smoking (even one or two puffs) at some point during their lifetime. Nationwide, 15.8% of students had smoked one or more cigarettes every day for 30 days at some point during their lifetime.
- **Currently using smokeless tobacco.** Nationwide, 6.7% of students had used smokeless tobacco (e.g., chewing tobacco, snuff, or dip) on one or more of the 30 days preceding the survey.
- **Used alcohol or other drug.** Approximately three-fourths (74.9%) of students nationwide had had one or more drinks of alcohol on one or more days during their lifetime. Nationwide, 44.9% of students had had one or more drinks of alcohol on one or more of the 30 days preceding the survey.
- **Did episodic heavy drinking.** Nationwide, 28.3% of students had done episodic heavy drinking: five or more drinks of alcohol in a row (i.e., within a couple of hours) on one or more of the 30 days preceding the survey.
- **Used marijuana.** Nationwide, 40.2% of students had used marijuana one or more times during their lifetime. Nationwide, 22.4% of students had used marijuana one or more times during the 30 days preceding the survey.
- **Used cocaine.** Nationwide, 8.7% of students had used a form of cocaine (e.g., powder, "crack," or "freebase") one or more times during their lifetime.
- **Currently using cocaine.** Nationwide, 4.1% of students had used a form of cocaine one or more times during the 30 days preceding the survey.
- **Used illegal injection drugs.** Nationwide, 3.2% of students had used a needle to inject any illegal drug into their body one or more times during their lifetime.

- **Used inhalants.** Nationwide, 12.1% of student had sniffed glue, breathed the contents of aerosol spray cans, or inhaled paints or sprays to get high one or more times during their lifetime.
- **Currently using inhalants.** Nationwide, 3.9% of students had used inhalants one or more times during the 30 days preceding the survey.
- **Used illegal steroids.** Nationwide, 6.1% of students had taken steroid pills or shots without a doctor's prescription one or more times during their lifetime.
- **Used heroin.** Nationwide, 3.3% of students had used heroin one or more times during their lifetime.
- **Used methamphetamines.** Nationwide, 7.6% of students had used methamphetamines one or more times during their lifetime.
- **Used ecstasy.** Nationwide, 11.1% of students had used ecstasy one or more times during their lifetime.
- **Participated in sexual intercourse.** Nationwide, 46.7% of students had had sexual intercourse during their lifetime.
- **Participated in sexual intercourse before age 13.** Nationwide, 7.4% of students had sexual intercourse for the first time before the age of 13 years.
- **Currently sexually active.** Approximately one-third (34.3%) of students nationwide had had sexual intercourse during the 3 months preceding the survey.
- **Used a condom during last sexual intercourse.** Among the 34.3% of currently sexually active students nationwide, 63.0% reported that either they or their partner had used a condom during last sexual intercourse.
- **Used birth control pills before last sexual intercourse.** Among the 34.3% of currently sexually active students nationwide, 17.0% reported either they or their partner had used birth control pills to prevent pregnancy before their last sexual intercourse.
- **Used alcohol or drugs before last sexual intercourse.** Among the 34.3% of currently sexually active students nationwide, 25.4% had drunk alcohol or used drugs before their last sexual intercourse.
- **Became pregnant or caused pregnancy.** Nationwide, 4.2% of students had been pregnant or had gotten someone pregnant.
- **Received AIDS or HIV-infection education.** Nationwide, 87.9% of students had been taught in school about acquired immunodeficiency syndrome (AIDS) or HIV infection.

The findings in this report are subject to multiple limitations. First, these data applies only to youth who attend school and, therefore, are not representative of all persons in this age group. Second, nationwide, of persons aged 16 to 17 years, approximately 5% were not enrolled in a high school program and had not completed high school (Kaufman, Alt, & Chapman, 2001).

Further, Growald (1994) maintained

> Our children are getting lost in a sea of uncensored images. They see X-rated pictures of love, and lose their childhood before the age of 10. Along with the images go the disappearance of confidence in self that can only develop with adequate nurturance and parenting, but are no longer available where we formally found them... I believe that one of the roots for the rise in crime throughout our nation is the screaming plea to be seen, heard, and loved. If children can't get positive attention, they seek the negative. Without love the soul shrivels and the body atrophies. (p. 3)

The United States has the highest murder rate for 12- to 24-year-olds of any industrialized nation (Viadero, 1993). Marian Wright Edelman, president of the Children's Defense Fund, recently gave a graphic illustration of the reality of violence that directly confronts our children: "Our worst nightmares are coming true, after years of family disintegration, the crisis of children having children has been eclipsed by the greater crisis of children killing children" (Edelman, 1994, p. 7). Between 1979 and 2002, nearly 95,761 children and teens under the age of 19 were killed by firearms in America (Goldstein & Eckstein, 2005). Firearms are the second leading cause of death among 10- to 19-year-olds, second only to motor-vehicle accidents (Goldstein & Eckstein, 2005).

Not coincidentally, the number of juvenile arrests for weapons possession and murder also has increased. The number of juveniles arrested for murder and manslaughter climbed 93% from 1982 to 1991, while the number of adults arrested for the same crimes rose only 11%. Snyder & Sickmund (1999) found:

- The rate of juvenile violent crime arrests—after peaking in 1994—has consistenly decreased over the past several years. However, it has yet to return to the 1988 level, the year in which dramatic increases in juvenile crime arrests were first seen;
- Between 1980 and 1997, nearly 38,000 juveniles were murdered in the United States;

- The increase in juvenile homicides is tied to firearm use by nonfamily offenders;
- The proportion of juvenile murders that involved a juvenile offender increased from 21% in 1980 to 33% in 1994—the peak year for all murders by juveniles—and by 1997 declined to the lowest level since 1986;
- Fewer than half of serious violent crimes by juveniles are reported to law enforcement. This number has not changed significantly in 20 years; and
- U.S. child homicide and suicide rates exceed rates for other industrialized countries.

Columnist William Raspberry (1994) perhaps summarized our nation's mission most succinctly:

A top priority should be a movement to rescue our children. An astounding number of children are being lost: to drugs, to hopelessness, to violence, to death. They fail at school, become parents before they are grown-ups, and reach adulthood without acquiring the education or skills to earn a living. Our young women suffer debilitating effects of low self-esteem, and our young men, who ought to be the strength of their communities, are more likely to terrorize them. (p. 24)

The long-range implications of such behavior are just beginning to emerge. For example, 66% of college freshmen admit to having cheated in high school. Cheating by college students has reached epidemic porportions. According to the Center for Academic Integrity's Integrity Assessment Project, over 70% of students on most campuses admit to cheating (McCabe, 2005). Technology has impacted this pervasive problem. Programmable calculators, cell phones, pagers, text messaging and other portable electronic devices, make it possible to communicate with people both inside the clasroom or remotely to get help with answers on examinations

One in four college women has been the victim of rape or attempted rape, most often by an acquaintance (Viadero, 1993). Women ages 16 to 24 experience rape at rates four times higher than the assault rate of all women, making the college (and high school) years the most vulnerable for women (Abbey, Thomson, McDuggie & McAuslan, 1996). College women are more at risk for rape and other forms of sexual assault than women the same age but not in college (Benson, Charton & Goodhart, 1992). It is estimaed that almost 25% of college women have been victims of rape or attempted rape (Bernstein, 1996). In addition, a disquieting number of young adults do not bother to vote, are unprepared to join in public policy debates, or are unwilling to take part in community-building activities that are the central components of civic participation and responsibility (O'Neil, 1991).

The litany of statistics on violent crime, racial and ethnic discrimination, gang violence, school dropouts, post–high school unemployment, teenage pregnancy, teenage suicide, drug and alcohol abuse, and general social maladaption has contributed to a sense of national emergency of unprecedented proportions (Gates, 1988; Orr, 1987; Soderberg, 1988; Thompson, 1992; Harrell, 2005). Social, emotional, and cognitive skills are commonly viewed as being in critically short supply, which leads to the dysfunctional behavior of contemporary youth.

Dangerous Deficits

Social Skill Deficits

Basic social skills essential for constructive interpersonal interactions—which, in turn, are linked to community, social, family, and career adjustment—are significantly lacking for many of today's youth (Gresham & Elliot, 1984; LeCroy, 1983). In response, many educators, researchers, helping professionals, and advocates for youth are proclaiming the need to develop social literacy skills in today's children and adolescents. Nurturing social literacy in children and adolescents gives them advantages in their cognitive abilities, in their interpersonal adjustment, and in their resiliency skills during stressful life events. The concept of social literacy is not new. It first evolved in the 1970s under the cloak of deliberate psychological education, affective education, or values clarification, then reemerged in the theoretical framework of Howard Gardner's model of multiple intelligences.

In his book *Frames of Mind*, Gardner (1983) revealed seven major domains of intellectual performance and academic competence. Traditional education addresses only two domains: mathematical and linguistic (both left-brain dominated). Two other intelligences are intrapersonal (the ability to know one's own feelings and inner experiences and manage them well) and interpersonal (the capacity for handling relationships skillfully). Key abilities in these areas include being able to monitor and manage one's own feelings, being able to empathize and handle personal relationships, and being able to harness emotions for positive motivation in performing cognitive tasks, including problem solving and creative thinking. The other three intelligences (Gardner, 1983) include the following:

- Visual–spatial intelligence, which relies on the sense of sight and the ability to visualize an object, such as creating internal mental images.
- Body–kinesthetic intelligence, which relates to physical movement, motion, and awareness.
- Music–rhythmic intelligence, which recognizes tonal patterns, sensitivity to rhythm and beats, and environmental surroundings.

Cawelti (1989) maintained that "to be successful socially and professionally, people need to complement their cognitive knowledge with good interpersonal skills, a strong value base, and a positive view of self." These skills are neither systematically taught in schools or in the community nor adequately nurtured in many homes (Greenberger & Steinberg, 1987).

David Hamburg, president of the Carnegie Corporation (1990), also stressed the importance of teaching basic skills such as "sharing, taking turns, learning to cooperate, and helping others." It used to be assumed that children received such training outside of school. This was never a sound assumption, and it is less so now than before.

The need for social literacy has been further documented by recent studies showing a correlation between delinquent behaviors and certain experiences of adolescents in their development, including these: poor performance in school, negative labeling, poor peer relations, multiple health problems (e.g., speech, vision, motor, hearing, or neurological impairment), attention deficits, learning disabilities, alcohol and other drug abuse, violence, and increased involvement with law enforcement and juvenile and domestic courts. Concurrently, Stellas (1992) found that violent adolescents (as well as adult offenders) often were missing one or more of the following six social skills or characteristics:

- **Assertiveness.** The ability to speak up appropriately for oneself. (Offenders often swing between passivity and aggression.)
- **Decision-making skills.** The ability to anticipate consequences.
- **Social support and meaningful contacts.** The ability to use community systems.
- **Empathy.** The ability to identify with the felt experiences of someone else.
- **Impulse-control and problem-solving skills.** Self-control and the ability to find and use solutions.
- **Anger management.** The ability to deal with frustration without violating the rights of others.

Further, many criminologists are now finding a common psychological fault line in rapists, child molesters, and perpetrators of family violence:

Perpetrators are incapable of empathy, one of the fundamentals of emotional intelligence (Goleman, 1994). This inability to feel a victim's pain provokes a proclivity toward violent or aggressive acts. For example, an adolescent gang member may show little remorse for killing someone in a dispute over drug turf, or an elementary student may be insensitive to another child's feelings about his possession as he destroys it.

Armstrong and McPherson (1991) maintained that social skills promote successful interactions with peers and adults. According to social validity definition (Gresham, 1981), social skills are those behaviors that, within a given situation, predict important social outcomes such as the following:

- Peer acceptance or popularity.
- Significant others' judgments of behavior.
- Other behaviors known to correlate consistently with peer acceptance or significant others' judgments.

Kain, Downs, and Black (1988) described social skills as "life tools needed to successfully survive in society." When these skills are absent, there is an increase in the likelihood that a child's behavior will be labeled disabling, deviant, or antisocial. According to many researchers (Armstrong & McPherson, 1991; Goldstein, Sprafkin, Gershaw, & Klein, 1982; L'Abate & Milan, 1985; Larson, 1984), social skills fall into several categories, including these:

- Being kind, cooperative, and compliant to reduce defiance, aggression, and antisocial behavior.
- Showing interest in people and socializing successfully to reduce behavior problems associated with withdrawal, depression, and fearfulness.
- Possessing the language skills to increase expressive vocabulary to allow for interesting conversation with peers and adults.
- Possessing critical thinking skills and peer-pressure refusal skills to cope with peer and media pressure to take dangerous risks.
- Establishing and maintaining realistic goals for health, wellness education, leisure pursuits, and career development.

Other researchers have demonstrated the value of integrating social skills across community and institutional settings. Thompson, Bundy, and Boncheau (1995) found that adolescents could learn and retain cognitive information basic to assertion skills. Social-skills training for adolescents has been associated with positive outcomes, such as improved self-esteem, increased problem-solving skills, refusal of alcohol and other drugs, and refusal of premarital sex.

Cognitive Skills Deficits

A number of researchers have identified several cognitive skills that today's delinquent youth lack, with implications for educators and helping professionals. Here are some of their findings:

- Many delinquents are *externally oriented*. They believe what happens to them depends on fate, chance, or luck. They believe that they are powerless and are controlled by people and circumstances (Ross & Ross, 1989, p. 126). External locus of control also is prevalent in the behavior of underachievers and teenage mothers (Thompson, 1986).
- Many delinquents are "quite concrete in their thinking, and their lack of *abstract reasoning* makes it difficult for them to understand their world and the reasons for rules and laws" (Ross & Ross, 1989, p. 126).
- Many antisocial individuals have deficits in interpersonal functioning, problem-solving, and cognitive skills, which are required for decision making and interacting with people. A delinquent's lack of awareness of or sensitivity to other people's thoughts or feelings severely impairs his or her ability to form acceptable relationships with people. (Baggs & Spence, 1990; Botvin, Baker, Filazzola & Botvin, 1990; Fabiano, Porporino, Robinson, 1991; Serin & Kuriychuk, 1994; Rose, 1998).

A lack of cognitive skills places individuals at a distinct disadvantage academically, vocationally, and socially, making such individuals more vulnerable to criminal influences and to self-destructive and self-defeating behavior. This trend can be reversed, however, by converting strategies into teachable psychoeducational skills that are systematically integrated into a cognitive skills curriculum.

Cognitive skills fall into categories, such as knowing how to *solve problems, describe, associate, conceptualize, classify, evaluate,* and *think critically.* Cognitive psychologists advocate teaching at-risk youth a repertoire of cognitive and metacognitive strategies using *graphic organizers, organizational patterns, monitoring, self-questioning, verbal self-instruction, self-regulation,* and *study skills.* Social, emotional, and cognitive skills can be taught and cultivated, giving youth advantages in their interpersonal adjustment and their academic or vocational success, as well as enhancing their resiliency through life's ultimate challenges.

Emotional Skills Deficits

> America's children are desperately in need of lessons in how to handle their emotions and settle disagreements, in caring, and just plain getting along. Institutions and communities across the United States are experiencing a new kind of deficit in youth behavior, one that is, in many ways, more alarming than a cognitive skills deficit: Today's youth demonstrate an emotional skills deficit. The results of this deficiency are seen in the increase in incidents of violence and the sharp rises in the numbers of teenage suicides, homicides, and abusive and violent acts in the last decade. (Goleman, 1994, p. 2)

Goleman (1994) "poignantly revealed that we pay the price for emotional illiteracy in failed marriages and troubled families, in stunted social and work lives, in deteriorating physical health and mental anguish, and in tragedies such as random acts of violence. Our social nets for the emotionally illiterate are prisons, safe houses for abused wives and families, shelters for the homeless, mental hospitals, and the psychotherapist's office" (p. 2).

Goleman (1994) also maintained that a single intervention will not cover the full range of emotional skills that a proactive mental health program should provide. He proposed the following emotional literacy curriculum:

- **Self-awareness.** Building a vocabulary for feelings; knowing the relationship between thoughts, feelings, and reactions; knowing whether thought or feeling is ruling an action.
- **Decision making.** Examining actions and knowing their consequences; a self-reflective view of what goes into decisions; applying this to issues such as sex, alcohol, and drugs.
- **Managing feelings.** Monitoring "self-talk" to catch negative messages such as internal put-downs; realizing what is behind a feeling (e.g., the hurt that underlies anger).
- **Self-concept.** Establishing a firm sense of identity and feeling esteem and acceptance of oneself.
- **Handling stress.** Learning the value of exercise, guided imagery, and relaxation methods.
- **Communications.** Sending "I" messages instead of blame; being a good listener.
- **Group dynamics.** Learning the value of teamwork, collaboration, and cooperation; knowing when and how to lead, and when to follow.

- **Conflict resolution.** "Learning to resolve conflicts with peers, with parents, and with teachers; learning the win–win model for negotiating compromise" (pp. 7–8).

Many schools and institutions and business and community initiatives assume that social, emotional, and cognitive skills will develop as a natural consequence of maturation and development. It has become increasingly apparent that this is an erroneous assumption. Goleman (1995) aptly stated in his treatise on emotional IQ that "IQ will get you hired, but emotional EQ will get you promoted" (p. 35). Other researchers who have examined the importance of emotional skills include: (Bar-On & Parker, 2000; Cohen, 1999; Cooper & Sawaf, 1996; Salovey & Sluyter, 1997; and Salovey, Bedell, Detweiler & Mayer, 1999).

The foundation of emotional literacy includes being able to monitor and manage one's own feelings, empathize and handle personal relationships, and manage emotions for positive motivation (Goleman, 1995)—and there is a definite link between emotional skills and cognitive skills. Young people who are experiencing emotional discord and who harbor hurt feelings, anger, depression, or anxiety have difficulty attending, processing, and remembering new information. Emotional literacy actually promotes cognitive well-being and can act as a crucial inoculation against obstacles that impede development. Emotional and social skills can be cultivated, giving young people advantages in their cognitive abilities, their interpersonal adjustment, and their resiliency through life's challenges.

Table 1.1 Developmental Tasks for Children and Adolescents in the Domains of Thinking, Feeling, and Relating

Early school age (4 to 6 years of age)		
Thinking (cognitive)	**Feeling (emotional)**	**Relating (social)**
• Beliefs and practices followed at home will come under scrutiny at school and be challenged by community norms and values.	• Children are aware of sex-typed expectations for dress, play, and career aspirations (Martin, 1989).	• Children are most likely to interact with same-sex friends (Maccoby, 1988).
• Personal hopes and aspirations that parents have for their children will be tempered by the reality of school performance.	• Significant conceptual and emotional changes give sex role a greater degree of clarity and highlight the relevance of one's sex in overall self-concept. Major aspects of sex-role identification are an understanding of gender, sex-role standards, identification with parents, and sex-role preference (Baumrind, 1982; Martin, 1989; Spence, 1982).	• Preferences for sex-typed play activities and same-sex play companions have been observed among preschoolers, as well as older children (Caldera, Huston, & O'Brien, 1989; Maccoby, 1988).
• Family, school, peer group, neighborhood, and television will all influence the child's self concept.		• Girls and boys establish peer friendship groups with members of the same sex and may reject or compete with members of the opposite sex (Maccoby, 1988).
• Early-school-age children exhibit wide-ranging curiosity about all aspects of life.	• Within a family, children are likely to have personality characteristics similar to those of the more dominant parent. (Hetherington, 1967).	• Children are influenced by the social groups that immediately surround them (Rosenberg, 1979).
	• Children behave like their parents in order to increase the perceived similarity between them, valuing characteristics such as physical size, good looks, special competences, power, success, and respect.	
• A child's sex-role identity becomes a major cognitive structure that influences a child's interpretation of experiences, developing expectations about what toys, interests, behaviors, dispositions, and occupations are appropriate for each sex (Bem, 1981; Martin, 1989).	• Early-school-age children can use the social circumstances that may have produced a child's emotional responses, especially responses of anger and distress, to understand and empathize with another child's feelings (Fabes, Eisenberg, McCormick, & Wilson, 1988; Hoffner & Badzinski, 1989).	• Early-school-age children are aware of the importance of acceptance by adults and peers outside the family, especially teachers and classmates (Weinstein, Marshall, Sharp, & Botkin, 1987).

- Learning the moral code of family and the community begins to guide behavior.

- Under conditions of peer competition, children begin to experience anxiety about their performance and about the way their abilities will be evaluated in comparison with others (Butler, 1989).

- Children's ability to form close relationships becomes highly dependent on their social skills, which include an ability to interpret and understand other children's nonverbal cues, such as body language and pitch of voice; an ability to respond to what other children say; use of eye contact; frequent mention of the other child's name; and the possible use of touch to get attention. If the child wants to do something that another child opposes, they can articulate why their plan is a good one. They can suppress their own wishes and desires to reach a compromise with other children and be willing to change. When they are with a group of children they do not know, they are quiet but observant until they have a feeling for the structure and dynamics of the group (Coie & Kuperschmidt, 1983; Dodge, 1983; Putallaz, 1983; Dodge & Feldman, 1990; Kagan & Gall, 1998).

- Behaviors that are linked to moral principles, such as telling the truth and being respectful of authority figures, become integrated into the child's concepts of right and wrong (Carroll & Rest, 1982, 1983; Damon, 1980; Gibbs, 1979; Kolberg, 1976; Rest, Narvaez, Thomas, Bebeau, 2000).

- Open peer criticism tends to outnumber compliments, and boys tend more than girls to be critical of their peers' work (Frey & Ruble, 1987).

- Children who lack social skills tend to be rejected by other children. Commonly, they are withdrawn, do not listen well, and offer few if any reasons for their wishes; they rarely praise others and find it difficult to join in cooperative activities (Dodge, 1983). They often exhibit features of oppositional defiant or conduct disorder, such as regular fighting, dominating, pushing others around, or being spiteful (Dodge, Bates, & Pettit, 1990).

– continued

Table 1.1 *(continued)* Developmental Tasks for Children and Adolescents in the Domains of Thinking, Feeling, and Relating

	Early school age (4 to 6 years of age)	
Thinking (cognitive)	**Feeling (emotional)**	**Relating (social)**
• Young girls are better able to resist temptation than boys and show patterns of decreasng moral transressions from the toddler years to the earlier school years (Mischel, Shoda, & Rodriguez, 1989).	• Friendship relations in early-school-age children are based on concrete goods, that is, friendships can be broken by the taking of a toy, hitting, or name-calling (Damon, 1977).	• It is essential to begin developing prosocial attitudes and behaviors in children at a very young age because unremedied aggression in young children nearly always leads to later acts of delinquency (Yoshikawa, 1995).
	• Friendship groups are segregated by sex; boys and girls grow up in quite distinctive peer environ-ments and use different strategies to achieve dominance or leadership in their groups. Boys tend to use physical assertiveness and direct demands; girls tend to use verbal persuasion and polite suggestions (Maccoby, 1988; Maccoby & Jacklin, 1987).	• The specific antisocial behaviors that young children engage in are learned "through specific and alterable processes of socialization and development" (Slaby, Roedell, Asrezzo, & Kendrix, 1995, p. 2).
	• Some traits of temperament, such as attention span, goal orientation, lack of distractibility, and curiosity, can affect cognitive functioning because the more pronounced these traits are, the better the child will learn (Campos, Barrett, Lamb Goldsmith, & Stenberg, 1983).	• The most critical factor in promoting children's social development may well be bonding with positive, nurturing adults: teachers who offer unconditional acceptance and support, model prosocial behavior, live according to positive values, and convey the importance of these values to an individual's well-being (Gregg, 1996).

- Some researchers think that external stimuli, such as love and nurturing, can affect brain chemistry to the extent that seemingly innate negative personality characteristics can be reversed (Embry & Flannery, 1999).

- Securely attached children "demonstrate an expectation of an empathic response," whereas insecurely attached children tend to be anxious, fearful, or clingy and see the world and other people as threatening (Fonagy, Steele, Steele, Higgitt, & Target, 1994, p. 235).

- Resilient children have a strong ability to make and keep good friends. They are very good at choosing a couple of friends who stick with them, sometimes from kindergarten through middle age (Werner, 1996).

Table 1.2 Developmental Tasks for Children and Adolescents in the Domains of Thinking, Feeling, and Relating

	Middle school age (6 to 12 years)	
Thinking (cognitive)	Feeling (emotional)	Relating (social)
• The behavior of well-adjusted, competent children is maintained in part by a number of important cognitive abilities, such as social perspective taking, interpersonal problem solving, and information processing. These cognitive abilities foster a child's entry into successful peer relations (Asarnow & Callan, 1985; Chalmers & Townsend, 1990; Dodge, Murphy, & Buschsbaum, 1984; Dodge, Petit, McClaskey, & Brown, 1986; Downey & Walker, 1989; Elias, Beier, & Gara, 1989; Patterson, 1982; French, 1988; Pellegrini, 1984; Renshaw & Asher, 1982).	• The need for peer approval becomes a powerful force toward conformity (Ames, Ilg, & Baker, 1988; Pepitone, Loeb, & Murdock, 1977); the peer group establishes norms for acceptance and rejection; children learn to dress, talk, and joke in ways that are acceptable to peers. With the increased emphasis on peer acceptance and conformity comes the risk of peer rejection and feelings of loneliness. The stresses once identified with adolescence have now become prevalent in the lives of children (Ames, Ilg, & Baker, 1988; Nelson and Crawford, 1990). Increase in stress also increases anxiety, depression, and suicide ideation (Herring, 1990). In childhood, the manifestations of depression occur along with a broader array of behaviors, such as aggression, school failure, anxiety, antisocial behavior, and poor peer relations, making the diagnosis of depression in childhood difficult (Weiner, 1980).	• Children describe close friends as people who like the same activities, share common interests, enjoy each other's company, and can count on each other for help: friendships provide social and developmental advantages (Ainsworth, 1989; Hartup and Stevens, 1999; Youniss, 1980).

- Peers have an important influence on diminishing one another's self-centered outlooks (Piaget, 1932, 1948).

- Adults, particularly teachers, lose some of their power to influence children's behavior. Children often play to their peers in class instead of responding to the teacher. Roles of class clown, class snob, Joe Cool, and so on serve as ways to gain approval from the peer group. The need for peer approval becomes a powerful force toward conformity (Pepitone, Loeb, & Murdock, 1977); perceived pressure to conform seems stronger in the fifth and sixth grades than later (Gavin & Furman, 1989).

- The structure of the school influences friendship formation. Close friends connect in classes and at extracurricular activities (Epstein & culliman, 1987; Hallinan, 1979). Close friendships appear to be influenced by attractiveness, intelligence, and classroom social status (Clark & Ayers, 1988).

–continued

- Many children express loneliness, social dissatisfaction, and difficulty in making friends (Asher, Hymel, & Renshaw, 1984). Being oneself, showing enthusiasm and concern for others, and showing self-confidence but not conceit are among the characteristics that lead to popularity (Hartup and Stevens, 1999).

- These are the years children have best friends; early same-sex friendships become building blocks for adult relationships (Berndt, 1981; Sullivan, 1953). Children learn to discriminate among different types of peer relationships: best friends, social friends, activity partners, acquaintances, and strangers (Oden, 1987).

- Middle school-age years focus on self-evaluation; children receive feedback from others about the quality of their performance. At around 6 or 7, children's thoughts and those of their peers clearly conflict and they begin to accommodate others; egocentric thought begins to give way to social pressure (Wadsworth, 1989).

- At age 6 or 7, a new stage of intellectual development evolves as *concrete operational thought* in which rules of logic could be applied to observable or manipulative physical relations (Piaget & Inhelder, 1969).

- Children enjoy classifying and ordering the environment. Addition, subtraction, multiplication, and division are all learned during this stage. Children's performances on tests of cognitive maturity are likely to be inconsistent.

- Children develop metacognition (i.e., "thinking about their thinking") as a means of assessing and monitoring knowledge. They begin to distinguish those answers about which they are confident from those answers they doubt; they are able to review various strategies for approaching a problem to reach the best solution; and they can select strategies to increase their comprehension of a concept (Butterfield, Nelson, & Peck, 1988; Carr, Kurtz, Schneider, Turner, & Borkowski, 1989; Cross & Paris, 1988).

Table 1.2 *(continued)* Developmental Tasks for Children and Adolescents in the Domains of Thinking, Feeling, and Relating

	Middle school age (6 to 12 years)	
Thinking (cognitive)	**Feeling (emotional)**	**Relating (social)**
• Children can learn study techniques that will enhance their ability to organize and recall information. They are also amenable to training, both at home and school. They can master the principles of classification and causality, manipulate techniques for measurement, understand exploratory hypothesis and evaluate evidence, and consider events that happened long ago. They strive to match their achievements to internalized goals and external standards.	• By age 11, children are able to differentiate specific areas of competence that contribute to overall self-evaluation, particularly the domains of cognitive, physical, and social competence and their contributions to self-satisfaction in different ways (Harter, 1982; Stigler, Smith, & Mao, 1985).	• The peer group joins the adult world as a source of both criticism and approval. Pressures toward conformity, competition, and the need for approval feed into the evaluation process; peers identify one another's skills and begin to generate profiles of one another.
• A high IQ is a powerful predictor of academic competence (Masten, Garmezy, Tellegren, Pellegrini, Larkin, & Larsen, 1988; Pellegrini, Masten, Garmezy, & Ferrarese, 1987). In addition, academic performance has been associated with fewer behavior problems, social competence, and successful judgment in general (Garmezy, 1985; Madge & Tigard, 1981).	• Children approach their process of self-evaluation from a framework of either self-confidence or self-doubt.	• Children who relate aggressively with others have a high probability of being rejected by peers, whereas children who withdraw have a high probability of being neglected by peers (Dodge, 1983).

• Self-efficacy, a person's sense of confidence, is increased with successful experience, and decreased with repeated failure. Children who have a low sense of self-efficacy tend to give up in the face of difficulty because they attribute their failure to a basic lack of ability (Bandura, 1982; Bandura & Schunck, 1981; Brown & Inouye, 1978; McAuley, Duncan, & McElroy, 1989; Skaalvik & Hagtvet, 1990).

• Children who have a low sense of self-esteem are more likely to experience intense anxiety about losing in a competitive situation (Brustad, 1988).

• To assess their own abilities, children tend to rely on many external sources of evaluation, including grades, teachers' comments, parental approval, and peer approval (Crooks, 1988). By the middle school-age years, parents develop expectations of how they think their children will behave, and children develop similar expectations of their parents. Parents and children tend to label each other in broad categories (e.g., a parent is likely to label his or her child as "smart" or "dumb," "introverted" or "extroverted," "mannerly" or "unruly," "lazy" or "a hard worker"). The child is likely to label his or her parent as "cold" or "warm," "understanding and easy to talk to," or "not understanding and difficult to talk to," or "too stern" or "too permissive" (Hess, 1981; Maccoby, 1984; Maccoby & Martin, 1983).

• Social expectations contribute to children's expectations about their own abilities and behaviors. Evaluative feedback that is associated with intellectual ability or skills reinforces children's conceptualization of their own competence. The pattern of expectations appears to crystallize during the second and third grades. By the end of fifth grade, children are very aware of their teachers' expectations for their performance, and they are likely to reflect those expectations in their own academic achievement (Alexander & Entwisle, 1988; Entwisle, Alexander, Pallas, & Cadigan, 1987; Harris & Rosenthal, 1985; Weinstein, Marshall, Shaarp, & Botkin, 1987).

–continued

Table 1.2 *(continued)* Developmental Tasks for Children and Adolescents in the Domains of Thinking, Feeling, and Relating

	Middle school age (6 to 12 years)	
Thinking (cognitive)	**Feeling (emotional)**	**Relating (social)**
	• A child's attitude toward work and need to achieve is established by the end of this stage (Atkinson & Birch, 1978; Erikson, 1963).	• A new dimension of play is added to the quality of child's play — team play. Children learn to subordinate personal goals to group goals; they learn the principles of the division of labor and elements of competition (Klint & Weiss, 1987).
	• Children who are not capable of mastering certain skills will experience feelings of inferiority and inadequacy.	• Involvement in social activities seems to be as important as academic programs for youth development. Social activities help foster personality development and socialization (Holland & Andre, 1987). Participation in different social activities is related to low incidence of behavior problems (Rae-Grant, Thomas, Offord, & Boyle, 1989).
		• The social environment stimulates feelings of inferiority through the negative value it places on any kind of failure. Failure in school and the public ridicule that it brings have been shown to play a central role in the establishment of a negative self-image (Calhoun & Morse, 1977). In general, girls tend to have lower levels of aspiration, more anxiety about failing, and a stronger tendency to avoid risking failure and to be more likely to accept failure than boys (Dweck & Elliot, 1983; Parsons, Ruble, Hodges, & Small, 1976; Stein & Baily, 1973).

- Peer relationships contribute to a child's social and cognitive development and socialization. Children directly learn attitudes, values, and skills through peer modeling and reinforcement. Peers contribute significantly to one's moral development, because the child "needs opportunities to see rules of society not only as dictates from figures of authority but also as products that emerge from group agreement" (Segal & Segal, 1986, p. 16).

- In peer interactions, children "learn to share, to help, to comfort, to empathize with others. Empathy (or perspective taking) is one of the most critical competencies for cognitive and social development" (Bernard, 1990, p. 2). In peer resource groups, children learn impulse control, communication skills, creative and critical thinking, and relationship skills. Lack of these skills is a "powerful well-proven early predictor of later substance abuse, delinquency, and mental health problems, social competence is a predictor of life success" (p. 2).

- Positive peer relationships are strongly correlated with liking school, higher school attendance rates, and higher academic performance. Peer relationships exert a powerful influence on a child's development of identity and autonomy. It is through peer relationships that a frame of reference for perceiving oneself is developed.

Table 1.3 Developmental Tasks for Children and Adolescents in the Domains of Thinking, Feeling, and Relating

| Thinking (cognitive) | Early adolescence (12 to 18 years) | |
	Feeling (emotional)	Relating (social)
• Thinking becomes more abstract. The final stage of cognitive development evolves, characterized by reasoning, hypothesis generating, and hypothesis testing (Chapman, 1988; Inhelder & Piaget, 1958; Piaget, 1970, 1972). Improved ability to use speech to express oneself also occurs.	• Early adolescence is characterized by rapid physical changes heightened sensitivity to peer relations and a struggle between identity vs. alienation (Erikson, 1963), autonomy from the family, and the development of a personal identity.	• Adolescents struggle with identity.
• Adolescents learn to manipulate more than two categories of variables simultaneously, think about changes that come with time, hypothesize logical sequences of events, foresee consequences of actions, detect logical consistency or inconsistency in a set of statements, and think in realistic ways about self, others, and the world (Acredolo, Adams, & Schmid, 1984; Demetrious & Efklides, 1985; Flavell, 1963; Inhelder & Piaget, 1958; Neimark, 1975, 1982; Siegler, Liebert, & Liebert, 1973).	• Generally, girls are more dissatisfied than boys with their physical appearance and overall body image (Peterson, Schulenberg, Abramowitz, Offer, & Jarcho, 1984).	• With respect to the psychological meaning of bodily changes for males and females, the changes influence the adolescent's identification with the role of man or woman. Adolescents become more egocentric and self-involved; the changes produce ambivalence about new aspects of self and, if not supported, negative feelings and conflicts can result. (Flavel, 1963)
• The gains in conceptual skill made during adolescence are enhanced by active involvement in a more complex and differentiated academic environment (Kuhn, Amsel, & O'Loughlin, 1988; Linn, Clement, Pulos, & Sullivan, 1989; Rafinowitz, 1988).	• Boys who mature later than their age mates experience considerable psychological stress and develop a negative self-image (Blyth, Bulcroft, & Simmons, 1981; Clausen, 1975); Early-maturing girls experience increased stress resulting in heightened self-consciousness and anxiety; Early-maturing girls are more likely to be identified as behavior problems in school (Blyth, Bulcroft, & Simmons, 1981).	• The peer group becomes more structured and organized, with distinct subgroups (Newman, 1982). Peer group friendships, especially for girls, provide opportunities for emotional intimacy, support, self-disclosure, and companionship (Berndt, 1982; Raffaelli & Duckett, 1989.)

- The focus of the adolescent's abstract thinking is on gaining a deeper and more profound self-awareness (Hacker, 1994).

- Adolescent behavior can be viewed as a defense mechanism in response to conflict arising from the existential concerns of isolation, death, meaningless, and choice (Hacker, 1994).

- Adolescents have fewer daily experiences of overt joy and more experiences of the mildly negative emotions perceived as moodiness or apathy (Larson & Lampman-Petratis, 1989). The most troublesome of these emotions are anxiety, shame, embarrassment, guilt, shyness, depression, and anger (Adelson & Doehrman, 1980; Garrison, Schoenbach, & Kaplan, 1984; Magg, Rutherford, & Parks, 1988; Robertson & Simmons, 1989). Adolescent girls are likely to have heightened awareness of new levels of negative emotions that focus inward, such as shame, guilt, and depression. Adolescent boys are likely to have a heightened

- awareness of new levels of negative emotions that focus on others, such as contempt and aggression (Costello, 1990; Ostrov, Offer, & Howard, 1989; Stapley & Haviland, 1989; Tuma, 1989; Zill & Schoenborn, 1990). A major development task is to sustain a tolerance for one's emotionality. Anxiety and overcontrol of emotions is manifested in such self-destructive behaviors as anorexia nervosa (Yates, 1989).

- Popularity and acceptance into a peer group at the high-school level is based on attractiveness; athletic ability; social class; academic performance; future goals; affiliation with a religious, racial, or ethnic group; and special talents.

- Beginning in seventh grade, adolescents perceive their relationships with friends as more intimate than those with parents. Mothers are perceived as remaining at a constant level of intimacy across all ages. Intimacy between a child and his or her mother during the middle school years provides a basis for establishing close, affectionate relationships with adolescent friends (Gold & Yanof, 1985; Hunter & Youniss, 1985). Fathers were perceived as declining in intimacy from seventh to tenth grade and as remaining constant in intimacy from tenth grade through college.

– continued

Table 1.3 Developmental Tasks for Children and Adolescents in the Domains of Thinking, Feeling, and Relating *(continued)*

| Thinking (cognitive) | Early adolescence (12 to 18 years) | |
	Feeling (emotional)	Relating (social)
	• As adolescents make their transition from childhood to adolescence, they must resolve the conflict of group identification vs. alienation. The absence of peer social support that can result from a negative resolution of this crisis can have significant implications for adjustment in school, self-efficacy, and related psychosocial development. Chronic conflict from one's inability to integrate into a meaningful reference group can lead to lifelong difficulties in areas of personal health and well-being, work satisfaction, and the formation of intimate family bonds (Allen, Weissberg, & Hawkins, 1989; East, Hess, & Lerner, 1987; Spencer, 1982, 1988).	• Over the age ranges 12 to 13 and 14 to 15, adolescents discuss academic–vocational, social–ethical and family relations topics more often with their parents than their friends. They discuss peer relations more with their friends (Hunter, 1985).
		• Parental values, educational expectations, the capacity of parents to exercise appropriate control over their child's social and school activities, and the norms of the peer group all play important roles in a young person's willingness to become sexually active (Brooks-Gunn & Furstenberg, 1989; Hanson, Myers, & Ginsburg, 1987; Newcomber & Udry, 1987).

- Adolescents with high self-esteem seldom use avoidance strategies and prefer problem-solving strategies (Dumont & Provost, 1999). Self-esteem is positively correlated with involvement in the community, family, and neighborhood (Dumont & Provost, 1999).

- Adolescents who do not have a high self-esteem are more likely to use avoidant coping strategies (Dumont & Provost, 1999). Involvement in negative social or illegal activities (stealing, bullying, illegal use of alcohol or drugs) is positively correlated with depression and stress (Patterson, McCubbin, & Neede, 1983).

- Overly socially competent adolescents reported increased levels of depression, anxiety, and self-criticism, much more than competent children from low-stress backgrounds (Luthar, 1991; Luthar & Zigler, 1991).

Fundamentally, emotional deficits manifest themselves in increased incidents of violence, suicide, and homicide. Emotional skills are intrapersonal skills, such as managing emotions, recognizing a feeling as it happens, motivating oneself to attain goals, delaying gratification, maintaining self-control, and making mood connections (metamood). Cognitive deficits place youth at a disadvantage academically, making them more vulnerable to criminal influences. Cognitive skills are thinking skills, such as knowing how to solve problems, describe, associate, conceptualize, classify, analyze, make inferences, and think critically. Cognitive skills encourage metacognition (i.e., thinking about what one is thinking). Social deficits manifest themselves with poor peer relations and an inability to resolve conflicts and manage anger. Social skills are interpersonal skills essential for meaningful relationships with others. They fall into categories such as being kind, cooperative, and compliant to reduce defiance, aggression, and conflict.

The Importance of Self-Esteem

The universal solution researchers offer to the crisis of our youth is *enhanced self-esteem*, especially for high-risk adolescents. Studies have identified two factors that seem to foster positive self-esteem:

- Unconditional love and acceptance from a primary caregiver, which provide an internal sense of value and worth.
- Social competence, which is the successful management of one's social milieu.

Marton, Golombek, Stein, and Korenblum (1988) found that self-esteem is related to adaptive skills and the ability to reflect a sense of self and a sense of significant attachment to another adult. Further, when stressful events do not overwhelm an individual's ability to cope, the triumph over adversity fosters a sense of self-competence.

"When people are socially competent, their worth is not dependent on someone else's opinion of them but rather on their skills to affect their environment in the way they choose" (Stellas, 1992, p. 25). Children learn through physical and emotional rewards and punishments, which can be negative or positive. A negative self-concept generates an ongoing cycle of academic failure, lower self-esteem, and a diminished willingness to risk failure—in other words, an unmotivated and distracted learner—all of which perpetuates failure.

People achieve social competence by learning and utilizing the skills listed earlier: assertiveness, decision making, social support contacts, empathy, impulse control, problem solving, and anger management. These skills should be taught to all children. That means, as a nation, we must place as much importance on social literacy as we do on academic literacy. The result could well be an environment in which the norm is cooperation, respect, and nonviolence instead of alienation, aggression, and exploitation.

To build self-esteem in children and adolescents, it is important to help them develop a sense of security by defining expectations and boundaries. It also is important to help them see themselves as having potential and success in a specific area, as well as a sense of belonging and purpose. Fortunately, self-concept has the capacity to continually change and develop. Through psychoeducational groups, we can perhaps begin to address our young people's emotional and cognitive skills deficits and reduce self-destructive and self-defeating behavior. Table 1.4 shows a partial spectrum of the critical deficits affecting our young people today.

Educators, researchers, and helping professionals often feel compelled to create a comprehensive initiative to remediate the broad spectrum of threats to the physical, intellectual, emotional, and social well-being of contemporary youth. The growing concern over adolescent subpopulations who are at risk demonstrates the critical need for responsible adults to establish close, helping relationships with young people. What is needed is a comprehensive, integrated curriculum to help young people master daily problem-solving skills, such as self-competency, enhancement of interpersonal relationships, communication, values, and the awareness of rules, attitudes, and motivation (Worrell & Stilwell, 1981).

Interpersonal and personal development should become an integral part of systematic intervention and prevention programs. The effect of such programs is to make counseling and learning available on a larger scale to the many people who need help but are not currently receiving it. Life-skills training could provide children and adolescents with support services to help with social, emotional, and cognitive problems. Students with any of the following difficulties would benefit from such a systematic delivery of skills:

- **School-Behavior Difficulties.** Students experiencing school-behavior difficulties might exhibit the following behaviors:
  - Recent behaviors "unlike" the student's typical behavior.
  - Disruptive behavior in the class or in the building.
  - Fear of attending school, unusual phobic or anxiety reactions.
  - Beginning truancy, tardiness, or cutting classes.
  - An unusually negative attitude toward school.
  - A resistance to school rules.
  - Frequent suspensions.

- **Personality Difficulties.** Students with personality difficulties might display the following behaviors:
  - Recent depression.
  - Age-inappropriate behavior.
  - Recent isolation and withdrawal.
  - Negative change in self-perception or self-esteem.
  - Psychosomatic complaints.
- **Social Difficulties.** Students with social difficulties might display the following behaviors:
  - Increase in peer conflict or poor peer relations.
  - Conflicts with authority.
  - Increase in physical aggression.
  - Increase in verbal aggression.
- **Educational Difficulties.** Students with educational difficulties might display the following behaviors:
  - Evidence of knowledge gaps.
  - Lack of interest in work.
  - Inconsistent and erratic performance.
  - A drop in grades.
  - Inability to concentrate.
  - Unwillingness to finish work.
  - Alienation from the classroom.

Education and counseling in life skills can be delivered as a comprehensive system to facilitate effective functioning throughout an individual's life span. Woody, Hanson, and Rossberg (1989) explained that counseling focuses on a cooperative relationship that encourages self-exploration and self-understanding and provides the opportunity for people to practice appropriate behaviors. Successful counseling produces a working alliance and creates opportunities for the client to restructure emotional experiences, develop self-confidence, and internalize the therapeutic relationship. The following life skills reflect the full spectrum of program components. When integrated into prevention and intervention programs, such social, emotional, and cognitive skills will have long-term implications for future well-being:

- **Interpersonal communication and human relations.** Skills necessary for effective verbal and nonverbal communication (e.g., attitudes of empathy, genuineness, clearly expressing ideas and opinions); giving and receiving feedback; assertiveness and peer-pressure refusal skills.

- **Problem solving and decision making.** Skills of seeking, assessing, and analyzing information; problem solving; responsible decision making; assessment of goal attainment.
- **Identity development and purpose in life.** Skills that contribute to the ongoing development of personal identity, enhance self-esteem, and ease life transitions.
- **Physical fitness and health maintenance.** Skills necessary for nutrition, stress management, and wellness; skills in reducing high-risk sexual activity.
- **Career awareness.** Skills in obtaining and maintaining desired career goals; opportunities to practice these skills.
- **Conflict resolution and conflict mediation.** Skills in effective problem-solving techniques; skills to build more effective interpersonal skills.
- **Study skills.** Skills to improve academic work by developing greater academic mastery and enhancing cognitive skills.
- **Family concerns.** "Skills to improve communication with parents, step-parents, and siblings to bring about a more harmonious family life" (Stellas, 1992, p. 53).
- **Anxiety coping skills.** Skills to promote emotional well-being and relaxation and stress inoculation.

Today, young people suffer from deficits in more than one life skill. Helping them develop life skills requires a psychoeducational intervention. Developmentally appropriate instruction is critical in such areas as interpersonal communication, making thoughtful choices, setting manageable goals, and refusing peer pressure. Social and emotional skill development is critical in building character, enhancing emotional intelligence, promoting social competence, and preventing high-risk behaviors.

McWhirter, McWhirter, McWhirter, and McWhirter (1994) isolated five basic skill strengths or skill deficits that mark a critical difference between low-risk and high-risk youth. The researchers called these characteristics the *Five Cs of Competency*. They are

1. critical school competencies,
2. concept of self and self-esteem,
3. communication skills,
4. coping ability, and
5. control.

Enhancing children's and adolescents' strengths in these areas enhances their well-being during the storms and stresses of emerging adulthood.

Nurturing Hope

Hope is defined as the process of thinking about one's goals, in tandem with the motivation to move toward those goals (agency) and the ways to achieve them (pathways). Goal-directed thoughts are the impetus for human learning and coping. Snyder (1995) delineated two necessary components to goal-directed cognitions:

1. The cognitive will power or energy to move toward one's goal (the agency component).
2. The perceived ability to generate routes to get somewhere (the pathways component).

To think about goals, individuals inherently perform a cognitive analysis of their agency and pathways (i.e., both the will and the way).

The dichotomy of low and high hope can be further delineated. Higher hope reflects an elevated sense of mental energy and pathways for goals. Snyder (1995, p. 355) defined hope as "a cognitive set that is based on a reciprocally derived sense of successful (a) agency (goal-directed determination) and (b) pathways (planning of ways to meet goals)."

Hope depends on the cognitive appraisal of one's goal-related capabilities. Low-hope individuals approach goals with negative expectations, a sense of ambivalence, and a focus on failure rather than success. In contrast, high-hope hope individuals approach their goals with the expectation of succeeding rather than failing, the perception that they will reach their goals, and a positive emotional state.

Table 1.4 The Hope Scale

Directions: Read each item carefully. Using the scale shown below, please select the number that best describes you and put that number in the blank provided.

1 = Definitely false, 2 = Mostly false, 3 = Mostly true, 4 = Definitely true

_____	1. I can think of many ways to get out of a jam.
_____	2. I energetically pursue my goals.
_____	3. I feel tired most of the time.
_____	4. There are lots of ways around any problem.
_____	5. I am easily downed in an argument.
_____	6. I can think of many ways to get the things in life that are most important to me.
_____	7. I worry about my health.

Table 1.4 The Hope Scale

____	8. Even when others get discouraged, I know I can find a way to solve the problem.
____	9. My past experiences have prepared me well for my future.
____	10. I've been pretty successful in life.
____	11. I usually find myself worrying about something.
____	12. I meet the goals that I set for myself

When administering the scale, it is labeled the Future Scale.

Source: From "Conceptualizing, Measuring, and Nurturing Hope," by C. R. Snyder, 1995, *Journal of Counseling and Development, 73*(30), p. 355–360. Copyright 1995 by the American Counseling Association. Reprinted with permission. No further reproduction is authorized without written permission of the American Counseling Association.

Scoring and Norms for the Hope Scale

The Hope scale, shown in Table 1.4, was developed by Snyder (1995) to measure aspects of hope. The agency subscale score is derived by adding items, 2, 9, 10, and 12; the pathways subscale score is derived by adding items 1, 4, 6, and 8. The total score is derived by adding the four agency and the four pathways items. (Items 3, 5, 7, and 11 were added as distracters, to make the content of the scale less obvious.)

The highest possible Hope scale score is 32, and the lowest is 8. "The average score for college and noncollege samples of people was 24, with significantly lower scores for people who are seeking psychological help and in-patients at psychiatric hospitals" (Snyder, 1995, p. 356).

Synder (1995) revealed that hope can be nurtured. Agency- and pathway-enhancing lessons include the following strategies:

- Learning self-talk about succeeding.
- Reframing difficulties as the result of using the wrong strategy rather than of a lack of talent or skill.
- Thinking of setbacks as challenges, not failures.
- Recalling past successes.
- Identifying role models.
- Cultivating goal-directed friends.
- Adjusting and modifying goals, and rewarding subgoals.

Hope theory proponents suggest that counselors and therapists can understand emotions by looking at how effective people are in the pursuit of their goals. Enhancing agency and pathways has the potential to produce more positive interactions between parents and children, psychotherapists and clients, managers and employees, coaches and athletes, teachers and students, and partners in relationships (Snyder, 1989, 1994, 1995).

From the perspective of emotional intelligence, having hope means that one will not give in to overwhelming anxiety, a defeatist attitude, or depression in the face of difficult challenges and setbacks. Indeed, "people who are hopeful evidence less depression than others as they maneuver through life in pursuit of their goals, are less anxious in general, and have fewer emotional distresses" (Goleman, 1995, p. 87).

Empowering Youth

Empowerment—defined as "nurturing belief in capability or competence, or assisting others in gaining a sense of personal power or control over their lives" (Ashcroft, 1987, p. 143)—is central to helping children and adolescents. The paramount goal of empowerment is to help people live in a way that maximizes their potential for developing a positive and satisfying lifestyle. One of the major assumptions underlying the empowerment process is the need to recognize and foster strengths and competencies.

Empowerment promotes autonomy rather than dependency, and an internal rather than external locus of control. Empowerment is helping people develop the resources to cope constructively with the forces that undermine or hinder coping and to achieve some reasonable control over their destiny. Empowerment is rooted in attitude and behavior, and is defined as the ability to promote one's own abilities, interests, rights, and needs both in interpersonal relationships and within the broader realm of school, community, and work settings. If young people perceive their role in the empowerment process as active and important, they are more likely to assume ownership of positive outcomes and continue the intervention on their own.

For youth, empowerment means critical life-skills development. For example, life-skills training in decision making, problem solving, assertiveness, and conflict resolution contributes to increased control over self and the environment. These skills enable students to make realistic self-appraisals, to network within the school and community, to brainstorm alternatives, and to reframe problem situations. Empowerment focuses on self-responsibility and on the need to be assertive in creating one's own lifestyle, rather than passively reacting to circumstances.

For educators and helping professionals, empowerment is universal in all institutional and community intervention strategies. Casas (1990) stressed that problem analysis within the school and the community is empowering when responsibility for the problem is shared between youth and helping professionals.

Life-Skills Training Model

Essentially, life skills are those that involve behaviors and attitudes necessary for coping with academic challenges, communicating with others, improving relationships, and developing strategies for social, emotional, and cognitive well-being.

When teaching a life-skill session, it helps to follow a six-step model:

1. Instruction (teach an overview of the skill).
2. Modeling (model the skill for participants).
3. Discussion (discuss the skill that has been modeled to show how it can be used in daily life).
4. Role-play (practice the skill by role-playing).
5. Feedback (reinforce positive aspects of the role play).
6. Ownwork (apply the skill outside the group setting).

These steps, when used with situational logs and homework assignments, reinforce desired behaviors.

The instructional techniques for skills training have evolved from social learning and typically consist of verbal instructions, modeling the desired behavior, role-playing, and performance feedback. Skill training can cover one skill in one or two sessions, with the goal of learning and transfer (McWhirter, McWhirter, & McWhirter, 1993). Helping professionals in school and community settings can reinforce coping skills and teach or model behaviors that enhance self-management skills. Rak and Patterson (1996) proposed that helping professionals focus on building transferable skills with the following selected techniques:

- Role-playing to help youth improve their self-expression.
- Conflict-resolution techniques that help youth work through their interpersonal struggles at home, in school, and in the community.
- A nurturing stance that conveys unconditional positive regard, encouragement, positive reinforcement, and genuine hope.
- Modeling the principles of a healthy self-concept.
- Establishing peer support models, such as peer-counseling programs.
- Empowering self-awareness through journaling, positive imagery, and bibliotherapy.

A more in-depth explanation of this intervention strategy is included in Chapter 3.

Conclusion

Children and adolescents universally need the critical skills of communication, cooperation, conflict resolution, self-confidence, clear thinking, and managing distressing or self-destructive feelings. The challenge for helping professionals is to integrate these skills into prevention and intervention programs. Life-skills programs that focus on social, emotional, and cognitive deficits can enhance the efforts of schools across the nation.

Today's youth show serious deficits in cognitive, social, and emotional skills—deficits that impair their chances for social, emotional, and intellectual success. In addition, there is a critical need in this country to create just and caring educational communities and to ensure that *all* youth are valued, have a safe and secure learning environment, and receive opportunities to experience a sense of belonging, respect for their rights, and freedom from violence and abuse.

Table 1.5 Selected Social, Cognitive, and Emotional Skill Deficits

Social skill deficits	Cognitive skill deficits	Emotional skill deficits
Assertiveness	External locus of control	Self-awareness
Decision making	Concrete thinking	Managing feelings
Social support contacts	Critical thinking	Stress management
Impulse control	Academic organization skills	Sensitivity to others
Problem solving	Probable consequences	Coping skills
Anger management	Comparing, contrasting, predicting	Giving feedback
Conflict resolution	Evaluating actions	Giving empathy
Cooperating	Creative problem solving	Confronting
Self-acceptance	Brainstorming	Relating to others
Communicating	Attention deficits	Self-esteem

CHAPTER 2

The Quest for Resilient Youth

No longer can we compartmentalize youth and isolate the relevance of family, peers, school, work settings, and community.

Karen Bogenschneider, Stephen Small, and David Riley, 1993

Vulnerable Children

An estimated 9.2 million children are considered "at-risk" in the United States (The Annie E. Casey Foundation, 1999). In today's society, children and adolescents experience a tremendous amount of stress, much of which is not within their control. In an extensive study, Sandler and Ramsay (1980) found that loss events (e.g., death of a parent, sibling, or friend; divorce; and separation) were the primary promoters of crisis reactions in children and adolescents, followed by family troubles (e.g., abuse, neglect, loss of job). Lower on the scale were environmental changes (e.g., moving or attending a new school), sibling difficulties, physical harm (e.g., illness, accidents, and violence), and disasters (e.g., fire, floods, hurricanes, or earthquakes). Kashani and Simonds (1979) maintained, "the life stresses for children are probably different from those for adults and center mainly around the behavior of significant adults" (p. 149).

Children and adolescents can respond to these stresses with adaptive or maladaptive behaviors, either of which can have critical implications for long-term functioning. Children in crisis or under constant and extreme stress manifest pervasive feelings of anxiety, confusion, failure, and entrapment. They frequently are sick, isolated, unable to concentrate, and noncommunicative. They can be uncooperative, negative, defensive, easily angered, and unable to see the resources in others. Further, acute stressors (such as failing a final exam, losing a close friend, or breaking up with a boyfriend or girlfriend) may precipitate depression or an impulsive suicide attempt. Zitzow (1992) provided an overview of the multiplicity, intensity, and commonality of the stress experienced by adolescents. His study revealed the stress indicators listed in Table 2.1.

Table 2.1 Assessing Stress in Youth

Rank	Stress item
1	Death of a brother or sister
2	Death of a parent
3	Being responsible for an unwanted pregnancy
4	Being suspended from school or on probation
5	Having parents who are separated or divorced
6	Receiving a D or an F on a test
7	Being physically hurt by others while in school
8	Giving a speech in class
9	Feeling that much of my life is worthless
10	Being teased or made fun of
11	Feeling guilty about things I've done in the past
12	Pressure to get an A or a B in a course
13	Pressure from friends to use alcohol or other drugs
14	Fear of pregnancy
15	Failure to live up to family expectations
16	Feelings of anxiousness or general tension
17	Pressure to have sex
18	Feeling like I don't fit in
19	Fear of being physically hurt by other students
20	Past or present sexual contact with a family member

Source: Reprinted from "Assessing Student Stress: School Adjustment Rating by Self-Report," by D. Zitzow, 1992, *The School Counselor, 40*(1), p. 23. Copyright 1992 by the American Counseling Association. Reprinted with permission. No further reproduction is authorized without written permission of the American Counseling Association.

Zitzow (1992) claimed that the data support marshalling resources within systems such as schools, communities, agencies, churches, synagogues, and youth organizations, and maintained that priorities should be established to respond to issues such as child and adolescent grief (e.g., family death, separation, and divorce); sexual dilemmas (e.g., unintended pregnancies, fear of pregnancies and sexually transmitted diseases, pressure to have sex, and abuse and incest); academic pressures (e.g., underachievement, lack of study skills, performance anxiety, and cognitive skill deficits); and psychosocial stressors (e.g., anxiety and guilt, alcohol and other drug abuse, feelings of worthlessness, low self-esteem, and dealing with failure). Conversely, protective factors—such as positive, open relationships with parents or significant adults and perceived competence due to scholastic, athletic, or public service achievements—may help youth cope more effectively with stressful events.

Psychosocial Stressors and Coping Skill Deficits

Psychosocial stressors interact with personal dispositions and support factors in one's social environment. Stress management, stress reduction, and stress relief are key intervention strategies for both children and adolescents, as well as for the adults who care for them. Debilitating stress and vulnerability intensify an individual's risk. Risk is diminished if an individual possesses reliable coping skills, has a positive sense of self, and feels social support in his or her immediate environment. To assess risk factors, Albee (1982) provided the following equation for the individual and a population:

Individual Risk Factors:

$$\text{Incidence of behavioral and emotional disorder} = \frac{\text{stressors} + \text{physical vulnerability}}{\text{coping skill} + \text{social support} + \text{self-esteem}}$$

There is an environmental-centered analogue to this equation that focuses on risk of psychopathology for a *population*:

$$\text{Likelihood of disorder in a population} = \frac{\text{stressors} + \text{risk factors in the environment}}{\text{socialization} + \text{social support} + \text{opportunities}}$$
$$\text{practices} \quad \text{resources} \quad \text{for connectedness}$$

Figure 2.1   Risk factors for individual versus population risk factors.

Psychosocial stressors are less likely to occur in a population if there are socialization practices that teach and promote social competence, create supportive resources, and provide opportunities for people to form positive social bonds and identities connected with the mainstream of society. Both equations are interdependent and reflect the paramount need for stress-related interventions that are multidimensional (Elias, 1989).

Risk and Protective Factors

Concurrently, there has been growing research interest in the concept of resilience and identifying factors that enable individuals to achieve adaptive developmental outcomes despite adversity. This interest has been spawned by two divergent perspectives: risk versus resiliency. Studies of risk factors emphasize negative features, whereas studies of resilience emphasize positive features. As a result, resilience research differs fundamentally from risk research because the focus of resilience research is on the more positive aspects of human development (Davis, 1999; Werner & Smith, 1992). This more optimistic perspective on youth development is also being incorporated into models of program development that emphasize the need for school and community programs to build on individual, family, or community strengths rather than focusing on individual, family, or community deficits or risk factors (Werner & Smith, 1992). Resilience reflects the developmental process by which children acquire the fundamental ability to use both their internal and external resources to achieve a more positive adaptation despite prior adversity. Resilience is not an outcome in and of itself; rather, resilience is a dynamic developmental process that cannot be dissociated from the child's developmental history. The fundamental goal of resilience research is to focus on identifying protective factors that enhance adjustment.

The Origins and Construct of Resilience Research

Researchers have typically emphasized the pathology of disadvantage by cataloging risk factors and documenting their adverse effects on healthy adolescent development (Dryfoos, 1990; Hawkins, Catalano, & Miller, 1992; Newcomb & Felix-Ortiz, 1992). They intensively studied risk factors for psychopathology, alcohol and drug abuse, and delinquency. Problem behavior therapy (Jessor & Jessor, 1977), stage theory of adolescent drug use (Kandel, 1975), and social influence models (Barnes & Welte, 1986; Dishion & Loeber, 1985; Huba & Bentler, 1980) have all focused on risk factors associated with negative outcomes of adolescence. This approach has focused on childhood vulnerability. The pioneering work of Garmezy, Rutter, and Werner has launched the more optimistic study of childhood resiliency (Garmezy, 1991, 1993; Rutter, 1985, 1987; Werner, 1993). The study of resilience evolved from research devoted to identifying risk factors (i.e., "those variables that directly increase the likelihood of a maladaptive outcome") and risk processes (i.e., "interactive operations that enhance the potency of a given risk dosage for an individual and thus increase the likelihood of the expression of a bad outcome") (Rolf & Johnson, 1990, p. 387).

Resilience is a set of qualities that foster the process of successful adaptation and transformation, despite risk and adversity. Losel, Bliesener, and Koferl (1989) revealed, "There are a multitude of constructs that relate to invulnerability, such as resilience, hardiness, adaptation, adjustment, mastery, plasticity, person–environmental fit, or social buffering" (p. 187). Rutter (1990) defined resilience as a "positive pole of ubiquitous phenomenon demonstrating individual differences in people's responses to stress and adversity" (p. 181). Wolin and Wolin (1993) defined resilience as the capacity to bounce back: to withstand hardship and repair yourself. Flach (1988) terms resiliencies as the strengths humans require to master cycles of disruption and reintegration throughout the life cycle. In his work, he organized a set of resilient attributes that make up a resilient personality. These include the following:

- A sense of self-esteem.
- Independent thoughts and actions.
- The ability to compromise in interactions with others and a well-established network of friends.
- A high level of discipline and a sense of responsibility.
- Acknowledgment of one's own special gifts and talents.
- Open-mindedness and willingness to explore new ideas.
- A willingness to dream.
- A broad range of interests.
- A sharp sense of humor.
- Insight into one's own feelings and those of others, and the ability to effectively communicate these.
- A high endurance of distress.
- Focus, a commitment to life and hope for the future even at the most despairing time of life.

Masten and Coatsworth (1998) defined resilience as "manifested competence in the context of significant challenges to adaptation and development" (p. 206).

"Resiliency research broadens the focus of social and behavioral science research to include not just risk, deficit, and pathology but also empowering the *self-righting capacities*, that is, the strengths people, families, schools and communities call upon to promote health, healing, and well-being" (Werner & Smith, 1992, p. 202). Werner (1996) found that high risk status generally includes factors such as these:

- Chronic poverty.
- Mother with little education.
- Moderate to severe perinatal complication.
- Genetic abnormalities.
- Parental pathology.

She lists the other sources of stress in children and adolescents as follows:

- Prolonged separation from primary caregiver during first year.
- Birth of younger siblings within 2 years after a child's birth.
- Serious or repeated childhood illness.
- Chronic parental illness.
- Parental mental illness.
- Sibling with a handicap, learning, or behavior problem.
- Chronic family discord.
- Absent father.
- Loss of job or sporadic unemployment of parents.
- Change of residence.
- Change of school.
- Divorce of parents.
- Remarriage and entry of stepparent into household.
- Departure or death of older sibling or close friend.
- Placement in a foster home.

Resiliency research consists of a body of international crosscultural, lifespan development studies that followed children born into seriously high-risk conditions, such as families where parents were mentally ill, alcohol abusive, or criminal or in communities there were poverty stricken or war torn. Results revealed that 50% to 70% of youth growing up in these debilitating conditions were able to develop social competence, despite exposure to severe stress, and overcome the detrimental odds to lead successful lives. Resiliency research, supported by research on child development, family dynamics, school effectiveness, community development, and ethnographic studies, documented the characteristics of family, school, and community environments that elicit and foster the natural resiliency in children. Resiliency research validates prior theoretical models of human development, including those of Erik Erickson, Urie Bronfenbrenner,

Jean Piaget, Lawrence Kohlberg, Carol Gilligan, Rudolf Steiner, Abraham Maslow, and Joseph Chilton Pierce. Although these earlier models focused on different components of human development (e.g., psychosocial, moral, spiritual, and cognitive), the fundamental assumption of each approach is the biological imperative of growth and development that unfolds naturally in the presence of certain environmental attributes. Masten captured the idea succinctly: "When adversity is relieved and basic human needs are restored, then resilience has a chance to be restored" (1994, p. 202).

Premature birth, poverty, mental illness in a parent, divorce, war, maltreatment, and many other forms of adversity experienced by children have been studied by researchers of risk and resilience (Haggerty, Sherrod, Garmezy, & Rutter, 1994; Luthar, Burack, Cicchetti, & Weisz, 1997; Rolf, Masten, Cicchetti, Nuechterlein, & Weintraub, 1990). In addition, a sequence of stressful experiences, rather than a single event, often accumulates in the lives of children over time (Garmezy & Masten, 1994; Rolf et al., 1990; Sameroff & Seifer, 1983). Collectively, there has been a paradigm shift in the way educators and helping professionals evaluate the relative outcome of at-risk children that reflects the influence of many researchers in development and prevention sciences, including resilience investigators, prevention researchers, and developmental psychologists (Cicchetti, Rappaport, Sandler, & Weissberg, 2000; Cowen, 2000; Luthar & Cicchetti, 2000; Masten, 2001). Educators, helping professionals, and laypeople are beginning to realize that some children survive against the worst odds. Thus, the title of this second edition has taken on a new perspective. Rather than *Nurturing an Endangered Generation: Empowering Youth with Critical Social, Emotional, and Cognitive Skills*, this second edition is entitled *Nurturing Future Generations, Second Edition: Promoting Resilience in Children and Adolescents Through Social, Emotional, and Cognitive Skills* to reflect hope and optimism about the future generation of current youth. The theoretical orientation is a shift from being risk focused to becoming asset focused. Prevention and intervention strategies can be accomplished by providing youth with structured training in social, emotional, and cognitive skills such as self-monitoring, mediation, anger management, and other self-regulation skills.

Illuminating prevention interventions and social policies that could improve the lives of vulnerable children and families is critical (Luthar & Cicchetti, 2000; Luthar, Cicchetti, & Becker, 2000; Masten, 2001). The multiplicity of risks that predispose youth to maladaptive and pathological outcomes include pervasive genetic and biological predispositions, assaults on development associated with inadequate caregiving, traumatic occurrences in the home, and exposure to community violence, to name a few. Ten environmental risk factors that have been documented in the literature to have a demonstrated detrimental effects on a child's developmental history are:

1. history of maternal mental illness;
2. high maternal anxiety or depression;
3. parental beliefs that reflected rigidity in the attitudes, beliefs, and values that mothers had in regard to their child's development;
4. few positive interactions with the child during infancy;
5. head of household in an unskilled occupation;
6. minimal or no maternal education;
7. disadvantaged minority status;
8. single parenthood;
9. stressful life events; and
10. large family size (Damon & Eisenberg, 1998; Sameroff, Lewis, & Miller, 2000; Zeanah, 2000).

Masten & Curtis (2000) emphasized the importance of examining protective factors in high-risk populations, laying the groundwork for contemporary investigations in the area of resilience. Essentially, the construct of resilience has the potential to affirm, challenge, and expand existing developmental theory; to suggest useful avenues for preventive interventions to promote competent functioning and resilient adaptation; and to foster the implementation of social policies that could decrease the vast erosion of human potential that mental disorder, maladaptive functioning, and economic misery engender (Luther & Cicchetti, 2000; Luther et al., 2000).

Resilience is defined as a dynamic developmental process reflecting evidence of positive adaptation despite significant life adversity (Egeland, Carlson, & Stroufe, 1993; Luther et al., 2000; Masten, 2001). Resilience is a phenomenon that manifests in an individual who functions competently despite experiencing significant adversity (Luther et al., 2000; Masten & Coatsworth, 1995).

Many kinds of adversity experienced by children have been studied by researchers on risk and resiliency such as the detrimental effects of premature birth, mental illness of the parent, divorce, poverty, and maltreatment (Haggerty, Sherrod, Garmazy, & Rutter, 1994; Luthar, Burack, Cicchetti, & Weisz, 1997; Rolf, Masten, Cicchetti, Nuechterlein, & Weintraub, 1990). Resilience research has the potential of integrating what we know about developmental theory and knowledge into theory and research designs concerned with the etiology and prevention of psychopathology; as well as

Table 2.2   Examples of Attributes of Individuals and Their Contexts Often Associated with Resilience

Individual differences
Cognitive abilities (IQ scores, attentional skills, executive functioning skills)
Self-perceptions of competence, worth, confidence (self-efficacy, self-esteem)
Temperament and personality (adaptability, sociability)
Self-regulation skills (impulse control, affect and arousal regulation)
Positive outlook on life (hopefulness, belief that life has meaning, faith)
Relationships
Parenting quality (including warmth, structure and monitoring, expectations)
Close relationships with competent adults (parents, relatives, mentors)
Connections to prosocial and rule-abiding peers (among older children)
Community resources and opportunities
Good schools
Connections to prosocial organizations (such as clubs and religious groups)
Neighborhood quality (public safety, collective supervision, libraries, recreation centers)
Quality of social service and health care

Source: From *Resilience and Vulnerability: Adaptation in the Context of Childhood Adversities*, by S. S. Luthar, 2003, New York: Cambridge University Press. Copyright 2003 by Suniya S. Luthar. Reprinted with permission.

the with the promotion of self-sufficiency and competence. Luthar (2003) outlines important individual qualities of resilience in Table 2.2.

Threats to the Development of Resilience: Risk and Adversity

Risk and Adversity: Depression

It is well established that depression runs in families and is related to a variety of negative or maladaptive outcomes. However, to date, there is no consensus on whether more severe forms of depression are especially likely to be genetically related (Hammen, Shih, Altman, Tamara, & Brennan, 2003; Kendler, Gardner, & Prescott, 1999; Lyons, Eisen, Goldber, True, Lin, Meyer, Toomey, Faraone, Merla-Ramos, & Tsuang, 1998; McGuffin, Katz, Watkins, & Rutherford, 1996). Depression often co-occurs with or follows anxiety disorders, eating disorders, attention deficit disorders, and schizophrenia. Mothers who are hostile and depressed are more likely to use inconsistent, permissive, harsh, and punitive or coercive discipline (Gelfand & Teti, 1990) and neglect their parenting responsibilities (Osofsky & Thompson, 2000).

Maternal depression is associated with lower maternal sensitivity and insecure infant attachment (Hipwell, Goosens, Melhuish, & Kuman, 2000), which often makes children at risk for early conduct problems (Shaw & Vondra, 1993). Yet, highly stressed, depressed mothers participating in a home-visiting intervention are less likely to have children with disorganized attachment or with insecure attachment (Lyons-Ruth, Connell, Grunebaum, & Botein, 1990). Negative emotionality and attachment insecurity in tandem appear to be predictors of behavior problems as the result of maternal depression. Hostile behavior in school and at home is more frequent in children whose mothers have consistent depression in the first years of a child's life (Alpern & Lyons-Ruth, 1993). Intensive approaches over time are required to produce meaningful interventions and outcomes that focus on parent–child and family systems (Cicchetti, Toth, & Rogosch 1999; Olds, Eckenrode, Henderson, Kitzman, Powers, Cole, Sidora, Morris, Pettitt, & Luckey, 1997). Children of depressed mothers are at risk for maladjustment, with 65% to 80% of those in clinical samples of mothers developing at least one psychiatric disorder by the age of 18 years (Hammen, 2003; McGuffin, Katz, Watkins, & Rutherford, 1996). Variables potentially implicated in risk transmission include hereditary and biological factors, disturbances in dimensions of parenting, marital conflict, and other stressful life events.

Parental depression is associated with an eight-fold increase in childhood onset of depression and with a five-fold increase in early adult–onset depression. Rates of other disorders are also significantly elevated, such as anxiety disorders, disruptive behavioral disorders, and substance use disorders (Hammen, Burge, Burney, & Adrian, 1990; Weissman, Warner, Wickramaratne, Moreau, & Olfson, 1997). Infants of depressed mothers may be born with or acquire through maladaptive parenting and stress exposure dysfunctional neuroregulatory processes essential to emotional regulation (Goodman & Gotlib, 1999). Currently, there is no consensus on whether more severe forms of depression are likely to be genetically related (Kendler, Gardner, & Prescott, 1999; Lyons et al., 1998), nor is it clear how depression across generations may be transmitted. Could depression occur because of abnormal biological stress responses, negative affect, poor temperament, or deficits in emotional regulation? Goodman and Gotlib (1999) maintain that environmental variables that increase children's risk for depression, such as parenting quality, life stressors, and marital conflict, may be transgenerational. However, numerous biological processes, such as abnormalities in brain structure and function, neurotransmitter processes, neurohormonal processes, and the role of stress on the developing brain, could be a factor in developing depression (Goodman & Gotlib,

1999). Abnormal processes of cortisol and other neurohormones of the hypothalamic–pituitary–adrenal axis may serve as risk markers for dysfunction in response to stressful events and depressive reactions (Ladd, Huot, Thrivikraman, Nemeroff, Meaney, & Plotsky, 2000; Plotsky, Owens, & Nemeroff, 1998).

Protective Factors for Depression

Intelligence, a positive self-concept, cognitive and behavioral coping skills, good school functioning, positive social relationships or friendships, and supportive adult relationships may serve as protective factors for the child (Conrad & Hammen, 1993). Hammen (1991) defined seven variables as potentially protective for children of risk for mood disorders:

1. Positive self-concept.
2. Social competence.
3. Good academic performance.
4. Low current maternal depression.
5. Low chronic stress in the family.
6. Absence of paternal diagnosis.
7. Non-ill father present in the home.

Risk and Adversity: Alcoholism

Children of alcoholics (COAs) are at a significantly elevated risk for alcoholism in adulthood (Goodman, 1987; Russell, 1990). Behavioral and cognitive deficits have also been recognized as more common in this population (Fitzgerald, Sullivan, Ham, Zucker, Bruckel, & Schneider, 1993; Sher, 1991; West & Prinz, 1987) and could be possible predictors of later alcohol abuse and alcoholism. A number of childhood characteristics have also been associated with an increased risk for alcoholism, such as risky temperament involving hyperactivity, emotionality, impulsivity, and low attention span (Jansen, Fitzgerald, Ham, & Zucker, 1995; Windle, 1991; Wong, Zucker, Puttler, & Fitzgerald, 1999); conduct disorders (Henry, Feehan, McGee, Stanton, Moffitt, & Silva, 1993); and a combination of negative mood and behavioral undercontrol (Chassin, 1994; Hussong & Chassin, 1994). In addition, fathers who are alcoholic and depressed are likely to engage in insensitive parenting (Das Eiden, Cavez, & Leonard, 1999). Externalizing behavior is known to be a predictor for early substance abuse and for precocious abuse (Zucker, 2000; Zucker, Chermack, & Curran, 2000). High levels of internalizing behavior are also known to precipitate substance abuse, especially if the behavior continues into adolescence (Caspi, Moffitt, Newman, & Silva, 1996).

Protective Factors for Alcoholism

Protective factors would include an affectionate and nurturing relationship in early life, lower life stress, an affectionate temperament, internal locus of control, and one parent in the household who condemns irresponsible alcoholic behavior. For example, when the mother was supportive of the father and his drinking, alcoholism was more likely among offspring. Berlin and Davis (1989) revealed the critical nature of the mother's support and nurturance as a factor leading to a nonalcoholic outcome in adulthood. Resilient children are significantly lower in internalizing symptoms than vulnerable children. Resilient children also scored highest in intellectual functioning, showed less emotional reactivity, had better reading skills, and were less likely to show conduct problems. The concept of resilience has implications for psychosocial functioning, cognitive development, and academic achievement.

Risk and Adversity: Mental Illness

The well-established risks for children with mentally ill parents include difficulties in school and problems with social adjustment, which often manifest themselves in delinquent behavior. Depression in combination with other factors predicts attachment. Maternal depression is associated with lower maternal sensitivity and more insecure infant attachment (Hipwell, Goosens, Melhuish, & Kumar, 2000). Stability of attachment patterns seems to be related to depression. Weinfield, Stroufe, and Egeland (2000) found that children are more likely to shift from a secure to a more insecure demeanor when living in poverty, experiencing maltreatment, or living with maternal depression. In a longitudinal study of low-income families, Shaw and Vondra (1995) found that negative emotionality and attachment insecurity both appear to manifest as predictors of behavior problems in the context of risk due to maternal depression. Maternal depression and insensitive parenting are associated with poorer child cognitive functioning at 18 months and at 5 years of age (Murray, Fioru-Cowley, Hooper, & Cooper, 1996; Murray, Hipwill, Hooper, & Stein, 1996). Hostile behavior in school and at home is more frequent in children whose mothers have consistent depression versus those whose symptoms have been resolved (Alpern & Lyons-Ruth, 1993). Parental depression is associated with childhood-onset depression and with increased rates of other disorders, such as anxiety disorders, disruptive behavioral disorders, substance use disorders, and impaired social and other role functioning (Hammen et al., 1990; Weissman et al., 1997).

Protective Factors for Mental Illness

Protective factors include child temperament, parenting behavior, family functioning, marital functioning, and parental course of illness. Highly stressed, depressed mothers participating in home-visiting intervention are less likely to have children with disorganized attachment or with insecure attachment (Lyons-Ruth et al., 1990). Children of depressed mothers who maintain positive emotional states will be more likely to have more positive social and behavioral adjustment. Parenting sensitivity also functions more as a protective process. Protective factors that promote the resilience process in young children of mentally ill parents include economic resources, social supports, few risks, positive emotions, secure attachment, positive thoughts, positive feelings, and self-efficacy (Seifer, 2003).

Risk and Adversity: Dysfunctional Parenting

Multiple, developmentally specific consequences of dysfunctional parenting can contribute to maladjustment in children and adolescents. Negative or disengaged interactions between children and parents may inhibit the acquisition of important interpersonal skills and problem-solving abilities, which may leave children and adolescents with poor coping skills and dysfunctional perceptions about themselves and others and eventually lead to impaired social functioning and interpersonal relations (Goodman & Gotlib, 1999). Insensitive caregiving is associated with negative conduct, attention deficits, and other behavioral problems in later childhood (Egeland, Pianta, & O'Brien, 1993). Inconsistent, insensitive, inattentive caregiving can distort the child's developing perceptions of trust, self-worth, and relationships involving mutual exchange (Anthony, 1987).

Protective Factors for Dysfunctional Parenting

A responsive, supportive, structured, and emotionally stimulating environment in early childhood contributes to children's feelings of self-worth, empathic responses to others, social competence, self-confidence, curiosity, and positive emotional expression (Englund, Levy, Hyson, & Sroufe, 2000). Prevention and intervention programs designed to promote resilience must begin in the early years of a child's development and should involve attachment-oriented interventions (Egeland, Weinfield, Bosquet, & Cheng, 2000). Programs that promote secure attachment-related behavior and that enhance parental sensitivity, maternal empathy, and goal-directed partnerships are promising approaches (Cicchetti et al., 1999; Lieberman, Weston, & Pawl, 1991). Successful intervention efforts should target the parent–child attachment relationship in the context of a family-focused, multipronged, interdisciplinary program model (Black & Krishnakumar, 1998; Rolf & Johnson, 1999). Fundamentally, parent intervention programs serving high-risk families with parenting issues should include medical, mental health, social, and chemical dependency services to meet the unique needs of each family system (Egeland et al., 2000).

Risk and Adversity: Child Maltreatment

Child maltreatment leads to poor adaptation across the lifespan. To grow into a competent, productive, self-sufficient adult, a child must learn through the relationship with his or her primary caregiver to regulate his or her emotions and behavior; to develop a congruent, positive sense of self; and to form and maintain meaningful relationships with other people. Maltreatment by caregivers predisposes children to a variety of difficulties in adjustment and adaptation (Cicchetti & Lynch, 1995; Scarr, 1992). Maltreatment during childhood is associated with depression and anxiety (Lynch & Cicchetti, 1998; McGee, Wolfe, & Wilson, 1997); aggression, delinquency, and antisocial behavior (Herrenkohl, Egolf, & Herrenkohl, 1997); more difficulties in developing autonomy and self-esteem (Egeland, Sroufe, & Erickson, 1983); and more difficulties in developing meaningful relationships with others, including peers (Salzinger, Feldman, Hammer, & Rosario, 1993). Chronic maltreatment in particular is associated with poor peer relationships and rejection by peers (Bolger & Patterson, 2001a). Maltreated children also demonstrated a tendency to internalize problems based on reports of anxiety, depression, withdrawal, and somatic complaints (Bolger & Patterson 2001b).

Protective Factors for Child Maltreatment

Resilience may be rare among maltreated children because of the lack of protective factors in the child's environment. Yet some maltreated children achieve higher levels of adaptive functioning than others (Cicchetti & Rogosch, 1997). Better adjusted children were exposed to fewer stressors. Protective factors, such as personality characteristics, positive relationships with alternate caregivers, or attitudes that foster a more optimistic view of life, enable some children to achieve positive adaptation despite high risk (Masten & Coatsworth, 1998; Werner & Smith, 1992). Another protective factor is perceived internal control, that is, the belief that one's own actions create one's own successes or failures. Perceived control as a protective factor is especially important to individuals exposed to high levels of psychosocial stress (Luthar, 1991). Ego resilience, ego control, and self-esteem also led to more positive outcomes (Cicchetti & Rogosch, 1997;

Cicchetti, Rogosch, Lynch, & Holt, 1993). Positive friendships and support-ive personal relationships were also found to foster resiliency (Egeland, Jacobvitz, & Sroufe, 1998; Werner & Smith, 1992). Personal friendships have a unique contribution to a child's social adjustment and sense of well-being (Hartup & Stevens, 1999; Parker & Asher, 1993). Positive, reciprocal, and stable friendships may enhance children's sense of emotional security (Cicchetti, Lynch, Shonk, & Manly, 1992) and play a pivotal role in provid-ing the milieu to learn and practice social skills.

Promising strategies to deter the detrimental effects of child maltreat-ment include home visiting (Olds & Kitzmann, 1993); therapeutic foster care (Fisher, Gunnar, Chamberlain, & Reid, 2000); group-based, relation-ship-oriented interventions (Luthar & Suchman, 2000); programs that match children with adult mentors who provide a supportive, consistent relationship outside the family (Grossman & Tierney, 1998); and pairing maltreated children with well-functioning peers to increase positive inter-active peer play (Fantuzzo, Sutton-Smith, Atkins, Stevenson, Coolahan, Weiss, & Manz, 1996).

Risk and Adversity: Divorce

Marriage as an institution has become less permanent. Marriage is being delayed; rates of marital formation are decreasing; and divorce, births to single mothers, and cohabitation have increased (Hetherington & Elmore, 2003). Approximately 45% of contemporary marriages are expected to fail (Teachman, Tedrow, & Crowder, 2000; U.S. Bureau of Census, 1998). Cohabitation has become an increasingly common antecedent or alter-native to marriage and remarriage (Seltzer, 2001). Almost one third of adults have cohabited before a first marriage and 75% before a remarriage. Children in divorced and remarried families are at an increased risk of developing psychological, behavioral, social, and academic problems when compared to children in two-parent nondivorced families (Amato, 2001; Emery, 1999; Hetherington, Bridges, & Insabella, 1998). Preado-lescent children in divorced families showed increased aggression, con-duct disorders, noncompliance, disobedience, decreased self-regulation, poorer classroom conduct and academic performance, and an increase in the frequency of school suspensions (Amato, 2001; Bray, 1999; Emery, 1999). Further, children's relationships with parents, siblings, and peers are adversely affected by their parents' marital instability and are charac-terized by increased negativity, conflict, aggression, and coercion (Amato, 2001; Simon & Associates, 1996).

Adolescents from divorced or step families demonstrate an increased risk for psychological and behavioral problems, including the risk of dropping out of school, early sexual activity, having children out of wed-lock, unemployment, substance abuse, delinquent activities, and involve-ment with antisocial peer groups (Amato, 2000, 2001; McLanahan, 1999). Children who have low self-efficacy and an external locus of control (Kim, Sandler, & Jenn-Yun, 1997) or who blame themselves for the divorce (Bus-sell, 1995) are more likely to exhibit a wide range of problems such as low self-esteem and internalizing and externalizing disorders. Conflict with parents regarding most issues is associated with a wide range of detri-mental outcomes for children, such as higher levels of depression, anxi-ety, externalizing behaviors, lower levels of self-esteem, and lower levels of social and academic competence (Amato, 2001; Bray, 1999; Hetherington, 1999). Adolescents from divorced and remarried families are less socially competent (Hetherington & Clingempeel, 1992) and more vulnerable to negative peer influence (Hetherington, 1993; Hetherington & Jodl, 1994).

Protective Factors for Divorce

Supportive relationships outside of the family with peers and other individ-uals, such as teachers, coaches, parents of friends, and extended family, may protect older children from the negative outcomes associated with divorce. Further, academic, social, artistic, athletic, and extracurricular achievements and activities may serve to buffer children from the adverse consequences of divorce (Hetherington & Elmore, 2003). Many girls from divorced, mater-nal head-of-household arrangements often emerge as exceptionally resilient by taking on the challenges and responsibilities that follow divorce, when those girls have the support of a competent, caring adult (Hetherington & Kelly, 2002). Personality characteristics also play a role in child adjustment. Children with an easy temperament, physical attractiveness, above-average intelligence, high self-esteem, and a sense of humor are better able to adapt to the stresses and challenges associated with divorce (Amato, 2001; Werner, 1999). Shared parenting with a minimal amount of conflict and support-ive, cooperative parenting based on mutual consent, trust, and open com-munication would be a protective factor if divorced parents could form this rapport. Boys are more likely than girls to benefit from the presence of a stepfather; these boys show increased achievement and decreased antisocial behavior in comparison to boys in a divorced, maternal head-of-household family configuration (Amato & Keith, 1991; Hetherington & Jodl, 1994).

Risk and Adversity: Poverty

In 1999, about one in five infants and preschool-aged children in the United States lived in families whose income fell below the poverty threshold (U.S. Census Bureau, 2000). Poverty is considered a pervasive and nonspecific stressor. Low-income families are disproportionately affected by parental depression and substance abuse disorders (Belle, 1990). "Poverty and economic loss diminish the capacity for supportive, consistent, and involved parenting" (McLoyd, 1990, p. 312; McLoyd, 1998). Poverty and the associated debilitating or frustrating life experiences contribute to poor parental emotional well-being; insufficient child-directed attention; and harsh, intrusive, and punitive parenting (Brooks-Gunn, Duncan, & Maritato, 1997; Sampson & Lamb, 1994). Economically disadvantaged infants are subject to less stable, erratic caregiving patterns and daily routines (Halpern, 1993), which may foster a perception that the world is frightening, unstable, and unpredictable, rather than a perception of optimism and hope for the future. The detrimental outcomes of living in poverty include poor physical health (Pollitt, 1994); lower intellectual attainment and subsequent poor academic performance (Guo, 1998); and the increased propensity for social, emotional, and behavioral problems (Dubow & Ippolito, 1994).

Socioeconomic disadvantage has a detrimental impact on children's cognitive, social, and emotional development. Children and adolescents raised in poverty perform below their higher-income counterparts on assessments of cognitive development, physical health, academic achievement, and emotional well-being (Brooks-Gunn et al., 1997; Halpern, 1993). Academically, poverty increases the likelihood of placement in special education (Egeland & Abery, 1991), grade retention (Jimerson, Carlson, Rotert, Egeland, & Sroufe, 1997), school dropout (Jimerson, Egeland, Sroufe, & Carlson, 2000), psychiatric disorders (Costello, Farmer, Angold, Burns, & Erkanli, 1997), and behavioral and emotional problems (Bolger, Patterson, Thompson, & Kupersmidt, 1995; McLeod & Shanahan, 1993).

Protective Factors for Poverty

Fortunately, a significant proportion of impoverished youth manage to achieve adaptive developmental outcomes and become successful in the midst of adversity (Luthar, Cicchetti, & Becker, 2000). Resources that serve to protect children from adversity come from three domains:

1. Child characteristics.
2. Family characteristics.
3. Community characteristics (Garmezy, 1991; Masten, Best, & Garmezy, 1990; Werner & Smith, 1992).

Children who are able to develop flexible coping strategies and a locus of control that allows them the capacity to value their own strengths, assets, and abilities fare better in the face of adversity (Luther, 1991; Werner, 1995). Intelligence and a sense of humor are also associated with flexible problem-solving skills and with academic and social competence (Masten, Hubbard, Gest, Tellegen, Garmezy, & Ramirez, 1999; Werner, 1990). Thriving under adversity requires resilient children to be socially responsive and to have the ability to elicit positive regard and warmth from their caregivers (Werner, 1993). The ability to regulate emotional arousal and maintain self-control is critical for social and emotional intelligence, which tends to foster academic and social competence (Eisenberg, Guthrie, Fabes, Reiser, Murphy, Holgren, Maszk, & Losoya, 1997; Rubin, Coplan, Fox, & Calkins, 1995). Other protective factors include cohesive intrafamilial relationships (Cowen, Wyman, Work, & Parker, 1990), nurturing and attentive teacher–child relationships (Brooks, 1994; Werner, 1995), safe housing and communities (Brooks-Gunn, 1995), and adult role models, such as adults who mentor youth (Freedman, 1993). Children who surpass adversity have developmental histories of interaction that instill in them an expectation that adults will be available to them to provide nurturance, support, and guidance and to meet their needs (Sameroff, 2000).

Risk and Adversity: Witnessing Community Violence

Witnessing violence in the community has a detrimental effect on healthy child development (Cooley-Quill, Boyd, Franz, & Walsh, 2001; Gorman-Smith & Tolan, 1998). Community violence comes in many forms, including murder, shootings, physical assault, rape, robbery, and drive-by shootings. Approximately 50% to 96% of urban children have witnessed community violence in their lifetimes (Gorman-Smith & Tolan, 1998; Miller, Wasserman, Neugebauer, Gorman-Smith, & Kamboukos, 1999). Children exposed to community violence are at risk for a variety psychological, social, emotional, behavioral, and academic problems (Kliewer, Leport, Oskin, & Johnson, 1998), as well as difficulty concentrating, impaired memory, post-traumatic stress, anxious attachment to caregivers, and aggressive behavior (Garbarino, Dubrow, Kostelny, & Pardo, 1992).

Some studies have linked violence exposure to anxiety, depression, dissociation, fears, internalizing behavior, and negative life experiences (Cooley-Quille et al., 2001). Jenkins and Bell (1994) found that females who witnessed violence were more vulnerable to drinking alcohol, using drugs, carrying guns and knives, and having difficulty in school. Males who witnessed violence were more likely to carry a weapon, fight in school, and experience difficulty in school (Farrell & Bruce, 1997). Declining academic performance could be related to intrusive feelings, internalizing and externalizing disorders, and increased physiological arousal, which makes it difficult to concentrate (Jenkins & Bell, 1997).

In addition, brain development during the early years of life is particularly vulnerable and sensitive to overarousal, which affects the organization and development of specific brain areas (Perry, 1997). Thus, children exposed to trauma may experience abnormal neurological development due to overstimulation of certain brain structures. Exposure to community violence may affect children's arousal and their ability to react to stress. Perry (1997) found that children exposed to violence and early trauma have increased overall arousal, an increased startle response, sleep disturbance, and abnormalities in cardiovascular regulation (Perry & Pate, 1994). Early childhood is already marked as a very vulnerable time, and violent trauma within the first 3 years of life may cause profound or permanent brain damage (Perry, 1997; Perry, Pollard, Blakley, Baker, & Vigilante, 1995). Preschool children tend to exhibit passive reactions and regressive symptoms, such as enuresis, decreased verbal skills, and clinging behavior (Garbarino, Dubrow, Kostelny, & Pardo, 1992). School-age children who have experienced vicarious violence in the community tend to manifest more aggressive behavior, more inhibition, somatic complaints, cognitive distortions, learning disabilities and academic achievement (Garbarino et al., 1992; Osofsky, 1995), as well as anxiety and sleep disturbance (Pynoos, 1993). In adolescence, youth emerge with self-defeating behavior such as acting out, self-destructive behavior such as substance abuse and self-mutilation, delinquent behavior, and early sexual experimentation (Garbarino et al., 1992; Jenkins and Bell, 1994).

Protective Factors for Community Violence

Social and environmental risk factors that may protect children include middle to high socioeconomic status, access to health care and social services, consistent parental employment, adequate housing, family participation in a religious faith, good schools, and supportive adults outside the family who serve as role models or mentors (Family Support Network, 2002). Some recent studies have found that families with two married parents encounter more stable home environments, fewer years in poverty, and diminished material hardship (Lerman, 2002).

Protective factors that can help build resiliency and reduce overall risk for violent behavior at the environmental level include national, state, and local policies that support child- and youth-oriented programs. One of the most powerful protective factors emerging from resiliency studies is the

Table 2.3 Risk and Resiliency Factors

Risk factors	Resiliency factors
Rebelliousness	Self-control
Low self-esteem	High self-esteem
Shyness	Good communication skills
Antisocial behavior	Good team member skills
Susceptibility to negative peer pressure	Good decision-making skills, responsibility
Feelings of helplessness	Sense of contributing to something greater than oneself
Poor academic performance	Good academic performance
Lack of connection to school or neighborhood	Active and contributing participation in positive school and neighborhood activities
Lack of positive role models	Availability of positive role models
Lack of goal-setting abilities and future goals	Ability to set goals and plan for education and vocational opportunities

presence of caring, supportive relationships (U.S. Department of Health and Human Services, 2001). Thus, the commitment of resources to programs that support meaningful opportunities for adult–youth interaction will help more adults understand youth perspectives and behaviors and can contribute to a culture of caring instead of one that ignores youth or, worse, labels them as deviant or antagonistic. Communities can create opportunities for youth to participate in activities where they have choices, decision-making power, and shared responsibility. Such experiences help them to develop new skills and to increase self-confidence and self-efficacy.

Thus, some children grow up with a number of risk factors, yet do not evidence developmental or adjustment problems. Many children and adolescents who fit the profile of risk—the lower achiever, potential dropout, drug abuser, or teen parent—defy the prophecy that they will not succeed. They demonstrate the personal quality of resilience. The construct of resilience refers to individual variation in response to stress, risk, and adversity. (Some risk and resiliency factors are included in Table 2.3.)

Werner (1982, 1986, 1992) and colleagues (Werner & Smith, 1977, 1982, 1992; Werner, Bierman, & French, 1971) undertook an ambitious longitudinal study that followed a cohort of high-risk children (n = @700) born in 1955 to study resilient children—those able to overcome risks in family and environment and go on to lead healthy lives. Participants in Werner's studies experienced four or more of the following risk factors: poverty, perinatal stress, family discord, divorce, parental alcoholism, and parental mental illness. The children studied faced many of the same pressures confronting today's youth, such as erosion of the family, abuse, neglect, and alcohol dependency.

Werner (1982) identified three key qualities of resilient children:

1. A personal temperament that elicits positive responses from family members.
2. A close bond with a caregiver during the first year of life.
3. An active engagement in acts of required helpfulness in middle school and adolescence (e.g., community service learning projects).

Marton, Golombek, Stein, and Korenblum (1988) found that self-esteem, sense of self, and attachment to adult figures enhance adaptive skills. Bolig and Weddle (1988) and Jens and Gordon (1991) noted that the experience of stressful events made resilient youth stronger.

Brendtro, Brokenleg, and Van Bockern (1990) described autonomous, independent, and resilient children as coping successfully in the face of seemingly overwhelming difficult environments. These children seemed invulnerable to family problems, disadvantaged neighborhoods, and inadequate schools. Hawkins, Lishner, and Catalano (1985) and Hawkins, Lishner, Catalano, and Howard (1985) found that resilient children share a number of characteristics (or sets of conditions) that provide immunity to risk factors, including these:

1. Resilient children think for themselves and can solve problems creatively.
2. They tolerate frustration and manage emotions.
3. They avoid making other people's problems their own.
4. They show optimism and persistence in the face of failure.
5. They resist being put down and shed negative labels.
6. They have a sense of humor and can "forgive and forget."
7. They build friendships based on care and mutual support (p. 46).

Other factors that promote these critical resiliency skills in children are a sense of autonomy, an internal locus of control, and an ability to manage their lives and influence their environment (Werner, 1982). Schools, institutions, and community groups can foster these qualities by helping young people establish relationships with caring adult role models and by providing environments that recognize achievements, provide healthy expectations, nurture self-esteem, and encourage problem-solving and critical-thinking skills. Resilient children and adolescents overcome their vulnerability because of protective factors within themselves, in their families, or in critical support systems.

Individual factors that provide a buffer to stressful events include efforts toward self-improvement, good communication skills, good problem-solving skills, an internal locus of control, a personal orientation toward achievement, and good coping and self-help skills. Other longitudinal studies (Garmezy, 1981; Garmezy, Masten, & Tellegen, 1984; Rak & Patterson, 1996; Rutter, 1983, 1985; Werner & Smith, 1992) identified critical personality factors that distinguish resilient children from those who become overwhelmed by risk factors:

- An active, evocative approach toward problem solving.
- An ability to negotiate an array of emotionally debilitating experiences.
- An ability from infancy to gain positive attention from others.
- An optimistic view of experiences even in the midst of suffering.
- An ability to maintain a positive vision for a meaningful life.
- An ability to be alert and autonomous.
- A tendency to seek novel experiences.
- A proactive experience (Rak & Patterson, 1996, p. 369).

Family factors that buffer children from stressful events include ample attention by a primary caretaker during the first 5 years, adequate rule structure during adolescence, stable behavior on the part of parents during chaotic times, a self-confident mother, and a support network of caregivers. Rak and Patterson (1996) identified family conditions that buffer youth from risk:

- Age of opposite-sex parent (younger mothers for resilient boys; older fathers for resilient girls).
- Four or fewer children in the family, spaced more than 2 years apart.
- Focused nurturing during the first year of life and little prolonged separation from the primary caregiver.
- An array of alternative caregivers—grandparents, siblings, neighbors—who supervise children when parents are not consistently present.
- A network of kin of all ages who share similar values and beliefs, and to whom the child can turn for counsel and support.
- The availability of sibling caretakers in childhood or another young person to serve as a confidant.

- Structure and rules in the household during adolescence despite poverty and stress.

Environmental or external social support factors that buffer a person from stressful events include a close adult with whom to share experiences; a supportive figure who can serve as a model for a child; positive recognition for activities; and informal sources of support from peers, relatives, teachers, and clergy. Beardslee and Podorefsky (1988), Bolig and Weddle (1988), Dugan and Coles (1989), and Werner (1986) identified a number of role models outside the family as potential buffers for vulnerable youth. Resilient youth often have mentors outside their family network, including teachers, school counselors, caregivers at before- and after-school programs, coaches, social workers, mental health workers, clergy, and neighbors.

Rak and Patterson (1996) developed an informal, 25-item resiliency questionnaire for children (ages 6 to 12 years) and adolescents (Table 2.3). The questionnaire was designed to identify risk factors and protective or buffering factors in the life stories of youth. It highlights temperament, family environment, interactions and support outside the family, self-understanding, self-esteem, previous history of stress response, influences on the child that promote optimism, and a positive attitude about service to others and to the community (Rak & Patterson, 1996).

By evaluating both at-risk and resiliency factors, helping professionals can plan interventions that either protect the at-risk youth or activate his or her resiliency factors to respond to the stress or crisis. This questionnaire facilitates a thorough evaluation of the client's life space, support system, and capacity to endure and overcome stressful factors.

Intervention efforts are shifting toward enhancing resiliency with gender-specific adolescent programs (Turner, Norman, & Zunz, 1995). Some researchers have discovered that boys and girls may require different protective mechanisms, since they go through different developmental stages at different times and are subject to different social, cultural, and psychological mores at each developmental stage. Resiliency factors for girls include having been perceived as affectionate infants and toddlers, having a mother who is successful in a career and a highly educated father, experiencing few behavior problems prior to middle school, and having a caring network of significant adults. Protective factors for girls that can be nurtured include responsibility, assertiveness, problem-solving skills, and an environment that encourages positive risks and independence (Turner et al., 1995).

Protective factors for boys are difficult to influence during early development. They include being viewed as active in infancy, with few distressing habits; having an educated mother and a father present; being the first-born son; and being a high-achieving adolescent with realistic educational and career goals. Turner et al. (1995) suggested that, because of developmental differences, gender-specific strategies for enhancing self-esteem, self-efficacy, and problem-solving would have more significant outcomes in same-sex groups. They also proposed social skills training in preschool to encourage the emotional responsiveness of boys.

Developmental Assets

The growing body of research on how youth are negotiating environmental risks and challenges provides evidence of the resilience factors, both external and internal, that influence positive youth development and protect adolescents from engaging in health risk behaviors (Benard, 1999; Glantz & Johnson, 1999; Masten & Coatsworth, 1998; Resnick, Bearman, Blum, Bauman, Harris, Jones, Tabor, Beuhring & Udry, 1997; Scales & Leffert, 1999; Tolan, Guerra, & Kendall, 1995; Werner & Smith, 1992). Risk factors tend to increase the chances for problems, whereas protective factors tend to decrease dysfunctional behaviors. Some studies have further demonstrated that resilience factors, also called *protective factors* or *developmental assets*, can predict change in adolescents' health behaviors over time (Jessor, Van Den Bos, Van der ryn, Costa, & Turbin, 1995).

Researchers in youth development, family social science, school effectiveness, brain neuropsychology, community development, social work, medicine, and a growing body of other disciplines are now making significant contributions in examining the construct of resilience as a *dynamic developmental process* (Werner & Smith, 1992). This approach is based on the premise that it is adult society's responsibility to provide the developmental supports and opportunities (protective factors, also known as *external assets*) that meet the needs that concurrently promote positive developmental outcomes in youth (resiliency traits, also known *internal assets*) with the long-term goal of improving health, social, and academic outcomes. The most important protective resource for development is a strong relationship with a competent, caring, compassionate adult. The most important individual qualities are normal cognitive development, better IQ scores, good attention skills, and "street smarts." Table 2.4 and Table 2.5 outline 40 developmental assets that protect youth against risk factors.

Constantine and Benard (2001) capture the value of internal and external assets in their technical report for California Healthy Kids Survey Resilience Assessment Module, shown in Figure 2.2.

Table 2.4   External Assets

External assets: category	Name and definition
Support	1. **Family support.** Family life provides high levels of love and support.
	2. **Positive family communications.** Young person and his or her parent(s) communicate positively, and young person is willing to seek advice and counsel from parent(s).
	3. **Other adult relationships.** Young person receives support from three or more nonparent adults.
	4. **Caring neighborhood.** Young person experiences caring neighbors.
	5. **Caring school climate.** School provides a caring, encouraging environment.
	6. **Parent involvement in schooling.** Parent(s) are actively involved in helping the young person succeed in school.
Empowerment	7. **Community values youth.** Young person perceives that adults in community value youth.
	8. **Youth as resources.** Young people are given useful roles in the community.
	9. **Service to others.** Young person serves in the community one or more hours per week.
	10. **Safety.** Young person feels safe at home, at school, and in the neighborhood.
Boundaries and expectations	11. **Family boundaries.** Family has clear rules and consequences and monitors the young person's whereabouts.
	12. **School boundaries.** School provides clear rules and consequences.
	13. **Neighborhood boundaries.** Neighbors take responsibility for monitoring young people's behavior.
	14. **Adult role models.** Parent(s) and other adults model positive, responsible behavior.
	15. **Positive peer influence.** Young person's best friend models responsible behavior.
	16. **High expectations.** Both parent(s) and teachers encourage the young person to do well.

Table 2.4   External Assets

External assets: category	Name and definition
Constructive use of time	17. **Creative activities.** Young person spends three or more hours per week in lessons or practice in music, theater, or other arts.
	18. **Youth programs.** Young person spends three or more hours per week in sports, clubs, or organizations at school and or in the community.
	19. **Religious community.** Young person spends one or more hours per week in activities in a religious institution.
	20. **Time at home.** Young person is out with friends "with nothing special to do" two or fewer nights per week.

Source: From "Healthy Communities—Healthy Youth Tool Kit" by the Search Institute, 1998, Minneapolis, MN: the Search Institute, http://www. search-institute.org.

Table 2.5   Internal Assets

Internal asset category	Asset name and definition
Commitment to learning	21. **Achievement motivation.** Young person is motivated to do well in school.
	22. **School engagement.** Young person is actively engaged in learning.
	23. **Homework.** Young person reports doing at least one hour of homework every school day.
	24. **Bonding to the school.** Young person cares about his or her school.
	25. **Reading for pleasure.** Young person reads for pleasure three or four hours per week.
Positive values	26. **Caring.** Young person places high value on helping other people.
	27. **Equality and social justice.** Young person places high value on promoting equality and reducing hunger and poverty.
	28. **Integrity.** Young person acts on convictions and stands up for her or his beliefs.
	29. **Honesty.** Young person tells the truth, even when it is not easy.
	30. **Responsibility.** Young person accepts and takes responsibility.
	31. **Restraint.** Young person believes it is important not to be sexually active and not to use alcohol or other drugs.

Table 2.5   Internal Assets

Internal asset category	Asset name and definition
Social competencies	32. **Planning and decision making.** Young person knows how to plan ahead and make choices.
	33. **Interpersonal competence.** Young person has empathy, sensitivity, and friendship skills.
	34. **Cultural competence.** Young person has knowledge of and comfort with people of different cultural, racial, and ethnic backgrounds.
	35. **Resistance skills.** Young person can resist negative peer pressure and dangerous situations.
	36. **Peaceful conflict resolution.** Young person seeks to resolve conflict nonviolently.
Positive identity	37. **Personal power.** Young person feels he or she has control over "things that happen to me."
	38. **Self-esteem.** Young person reports high self-esteem.
	39. **Sense of purpose.** Young person reports that "my life has a purpose."
	40. **Positive view of personal future.** Young person is optimistic about his or her personal future.

Source: From "Healthy Communities—Healthy Youth Tool Kit" by the Search Institute, 1998, Minneapolis, MN: the Search Institute, http://www.search-institute.org.

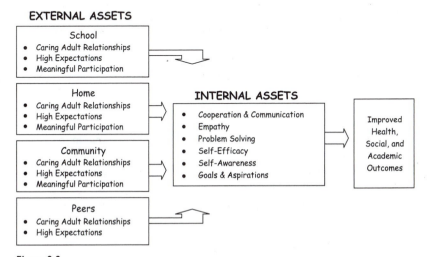

Figure 2.2

Conclusion

Counselors, teachers, helping professionals, youth leaders, the clergy, and other support staff who encourage and reinforce a child's coping efforts may promote more adaptive development in the presence of risk factors. Ideally, children and adolescents need coping strategies and behaviors to help tolerate stressors. The current developmental perspective is that children are all born with innate resilience and the capacity to develop the traits found in resilient survivors. These traits have been identified as social competence, problem solving, critical consciousness, autonomy, and a sense of purpose (Bernard, 1991). Social competence includes qualities such as responsiveness, especially the ability to elicit positive responses from others; flexibility, including the ability to move between different cultures; empathy; communication skills; and a sense of humor. Problem solving encompasses the ability to plan; to be resourceful in seeking help from others; and to think critically, creatively, and reflectively. In the development of critical consciousness, a reflective awareness of the structures of oppression (such as an alcoholic parent, insensitive school, or racist environment) and the ability to create strategies for overcoming them are critical. Autonomy is having a sense of one's own identity and an ability to act independently and exert some control over one's environment, including a sense of mastery, internal locus of control, and self-efficacy. Resilience is manifested in having a sense of purpose and a belief in a bright future, including goal direction, educational aspirations, achievement motivation, persistence, hopefulness, optimism, and spiritual connectedness.

TABLE 2.6   A Resiliency Questionnaire

1.	What is your position in the family? Oldest? Youngest? Middle? Oldest girl? Oldest boy?
2.	Do your have any memories or recollections about what your mother or father said about you as a young baby? Or anyone else?
3.	Did anyone ever tell you about how well you ate and slept as a baby?
4.	Do members of your family and friends usually seem happy to see you and to spend time with you?
5.	Do you feel like you are a helpful person to others? Does anyone in your family expect you to be helpful?
6.	Do you consider yourself a happy and hopeful (optimistic) person even when life becomes difficult?
7.	Tell me about some times when you overcame problems or stresses in your life. How do you feel about them now?
8.	Do you think of yourself as awake and alert most of the time? Do others see you that way also?
9.	Do you like to try new life experiences?

TABLE 2.6   A Resiliency Questionnaire

10.	Tell me about some plans and goals you have for yourself over the next year. Three years. Five years.
11.	When you are in a stressful, pressure-filled situation, do you feel confident that you'll work it out, or do you feel depressed and hopeless?
12.	What was the age of your mother when you were born? Your father?
13.	How many children are in your family? How many years are there between children in your family?
14.	What do you remember, if anything, about how you were cared for when you were little by Mom and others?
15.	When you were growing up, were there rules and expectations in your home? What were some of them?
16.	Did any of your brothers or sisters help raise you? What do you remember about this?
17.	When you felt upset or in trouble, to whom in your family did you turn for help? Whom outside your family?
18.	From whom did you learn about the values and beliefs of your family?
19.	Do you feel it is your responsibility to help others? Help your community?
20.	Do you feel that you understand yourself?
21.	Do you like yourself? Today? Yesterday? Last year?
22.	What skills do you rely on to cope when you are under stress?
23.	Tell me about a time when you were helpful to others.
24.	Do you see yourself as a confident person? Even when stressed?
25.	What are your feelings about this interview with me?

Source: From "Promoting resilience in at-risk children," by C. F. Rak and L. E. Patterson, 1996, *Journal of Counseling and Development, 74*(4), p. 372. Copyright 1996 American Counseling Association. Reprinted with permission. No further reproduction is authorized without written permission of the American Counseling Association.

Note: This quiz can be used to assess your own life, or you can use it in your role as a parent, educator, or counselor to help others assess and strengthen the resiliency-building conditions in their lives.

Part One

Do you have the conditions in your life that research shows help people to be resilient?

People bounce back from tragedy, trauma, risks, and stress by having the following conditions in their lives. The more times you answer yes (below), the greater the chances you can bounce back from your life's problems with more power and more smarts. And doing that is a sure way to increase self-esteem.

Answer yes or no to the following. Celebrate your yes answers and decide how you can change your no answers to yes answers.

1. Caring and Support

_____ I have several people in my life who give me unconditional love, nonjudgmental listening, and who I know are there for me.

_____ I am involved in a school, work, faith, or other group where I feel cared for and valued.

_____ I treat myself with kindness and compassion and take time to nurture myself (including eating right and getting enough sleep and exercise).

2. High Expectations for Success

_____ I have several people in my life who let me know they believe in my ability to succeed.

_____ I get the message *You can succeed* at my work or school.

_____ I believe in myself most of the time and generally give myself positive messages about my ability to accomplish my goals— even when I encounter difficulties.

3. Opportunities for Meaningful Participation

_____ My voice (opinion) and choice (what I want) are heard and valued in my close personal relationships.

_____ My opinions and ideas are listened to and respected at my work or school.

_____ I volunteer to help others or a cause in my community, faith organization, or school.

4. Positive Bonds

_____ I am involved in one or more positive after-work or after-school hobbies or activities.

_____ I participate in one or more groups (such as a club, faith community, or sports team) outside of work or school.

_____ I feel close to most people at my work or school.

5. Clear and Consistent Boundaries

_____ Most of my relationships with friends and family members have clear, healthy boundaries (which include mutual respect, personal autonomy, and each person in the relationship both giving and receiving).

_____ I experience clear, consistent expectations and rules at my work or in my school.

_____ I set and maintain healthy boundaries for myself by standing up for myself, not letting others take advantage of me, and saying no when I need to.

6. Life Skills

_____ I have (and use) good listening, honest communication, and healthy conflict resolution skills.

_____ I have the training and skills I need to do my job well or all the skills I need to do well in school.

_____ I know how to set a goal and take the steps to achieve it.

Part Two

People also successfully overcome life difficulties by drawing upon internal qualities that, research has shown, are particularly helpful when encountering a crisis, major stressor, or trauma.

The following list can be thought of as a "personal resiliency builder" menu. _No one has everything on this list._ When the going gets tough, you probably have three or four of these qualities that you use most naturally and most often.

It is helpful to know which are your primary resiliency builders, how have you used them in the past, and how can you use them to overcome the present challenges in your life.

You can also decide to add one or two of these to your resiliency-builder menu, if you think they would be useful for you.

Personal Resiliency Builders
Individual qualities that facilitate resiliency

Put a plus sign by the top three or four resiliency builders you use most often. Ask yourself how you have used these in the past or currently use them. Think of how you can best apply these resiliency builders to current life problems, crises, or stressors.

(Optional) You can then put a check mark by one or two resiliency builders you think you should add to your personal repertoire.

_____ **Relationships.** Sociability, ability to be a friend, ability to form positive relationships.

_____ **Service.** Giving of yourself to help other people, animals, organizations, or social causes.

_____ **Humor.** Having and using a good sense of humor.

_____ **Inner direction.** Basing choices and decisions on internal evaluation (internal locus of control).

_____ **Perceptiveness.** Insightful understanding of people and situations.

_____ **Independence.** "Adaptive" distancing from unhealthy people and situations; autonomy.

_____ **Positive view of personal future.** Optimism; expecting a positive future.

_____ **Flexibility.** The ability to adjust to change, to bend as necessary to positively cope with situations.

_____ **Love of learning.** Capacity for and connection to learning.

_____ **Self-motivation.** Internal initiative and positive motivation from within.

_____ **Competence.** Being "good at something"; personal competence.

_____ **Self-worth.** Feelings of self-worth and self-confidence.

_____ **Perseverance.** Keeping on despite difficulty; not giving up.

_____ **Creativity.** Expressing yourself through artistic endeavor.

You Can Best Help Yourself or Someone Else Be More Resilient By...

1. Communicating the resiliency attitude: What is right with you is more powerful than anything that is wrong with you.
2. Focusing on the person's strengths more than on problems and weaknesses, asking "How can these strengths be used to overcome problems?" One way to do this is to help yourself or another identify and best utilize top personal resiliency builders listed in The Resiliency Quiz, Part Two.
3. Providing for yourself or another the conditions listed in the Resiliency Quiz, Part One.
4. Having patience ... successfully bouncing back from a significant trauma or crisis takes time.

CHAPTER 3

Psychoeducational Groups in Schools, Communities, and Institutional Settings

Self-understanding promotes change by encouraging individuals to recognize, to integrate, and to give free expression to previously dissociated
parts of themselves. When we deny or stifle parts of ourselves, we pay a
heavy price: We feel a deep amorphous sense of restriction; we are "on
guard"; we are often troubled and puzzled by inner, yet alien, impulses
demanding expression. When we can reclaim these split-off parts, we
experience a wholeness and a deep sense of liberation (Yalom, 1985, p. 86).
Any school, community, or institutional setting is a microcosm of group
work. Formal and informal groups already exist for the purpose of fur-
thering the educational process and promoting community involvement.
These communities include task-oriented groups to complete projects,
cooperative learning groups, groups to organize and plan social events,
groups to learn new athletic skills, groups to socialize, assessment groups
to scrutinize curricula, and community projects groups.

Psychoeducational groups should be an integral component of prevention and intervention efforts in these communities. Psychoeducational
groups help members learn new, effective ways to deal with problem-
atic issues and behavior; these groups teach and encourage members to
practice and use these new behaviors with current and future problems

(Association for Specialists in Group Work [ASGW], 1990). The efficacy of psychoeducational groups in helping people change attitudes, perspectives, values, and behavior has been well documented (Dyer & Vriend, 1977; Egan, 1982; Ohlsen, 1977; Yalom, 1975).

Young people, however, need to gain a sense of trust, confidence, and ownership in the group in order to feel secure and to remain loyal. The following components are necessary for the group process to work with young people:

- **A sense of belonging.** Young people need to feel that they are sincerely welcome, that no one objects to their presence, and that they are valued for who they are rather than for what they have or where they have been.
- **Planning.** Young people need to be involved in planning the ground rules and goals of the group, suggesting group guidelines and testing boundaries.
- **Realistic expectations.** Young people need to know in some detail what is expected of them. Their role in the group, their level of involvement, and issues of confidentiality are important. This information should also be made available to parents, teachers, and administrators so that they can support the program.
- **Reachable goal.** Young people need to feel that their goals are within reach.
- **Responsibility.** Young people need to have responsibilities that are challenging and within the range of their abilities. They need to stretch for improvement and growth.
- **Progress.** Young people need to experience some successes and see some progress for what they want to achieve. Milestones should be celebrated and shared with family and peers.

Group-Focused Facilitation Skills

Many helping professionals want to be able to identify group helping behaviors to provide structure and accountability of service delivery. Gill and Barry (1982) provided one of the most comprehensive classifications of counseling skills for the group process. Such a classification system can assist helping professionals by delineating an organized, operational definition of group-focused facilitation skills. A classification of specific group-focused facilitation skills has a number of significant benefits, including clear objectives, visible procedures, competency-based accountability, and measurable outcomes. This information is an important component of the group process that needs to be shared with all those involved in prevention and intervention efforts.

Gill and Barry (1982) suggested the following selection criteria for building a system of group-focused counseling skills to change behavior:

- **Appropriate.** The behavior can be reasonably attributed to the role and function of a group counselor.
- **Definable.** The behavior can be described in terms of human performances and outcomes.
- **Observable.** Both experienced and inexperienced observers can identify the behavior when it occurs. The behavior can be repeated by different people in different settings.
- **Measurable.** Objective recording of both the frequency and quality of the behavior can occur with a high degree of agreement among observers.
- **Developmental.** The behavior can be placed within the context of a progressive relationship with other skills, all contributing to movement of the group toward its goals. The effectiveness of the behaviors at one stage in the counseling process is dependent on the effectiveness of the skills used at earlier stages.
- **Group-focused.** The target of the behavior is the group or more than one participant. The behavior is often related to an interaction between two or more participants. "The purpose of the group is to facilitate multiple interactions among participants, to encourage shared responsibility for promoting participation, or to invite cooperative problem solving and decision making" (Gill & Barry, 1982, pp. 304–305).

Further, the group setting is a pragmatic approach for adjustment concerns of children and adolescents, allowing them to share anxieties in a secure environment and to enhance their self-sufficiency.

Types of Psychoeducational Groups

Primary Prevention and Structured Intervention Groups

Counseling groups can be categorized into two types:

1. Developmental/primary prevention groups.
2. Problem-centered/structured intervention groups.

Developmental/primary prevention counseling is a proactive approach to avert dysfunctional or debilitating behavior by providing critical social, emotional, and cognitive skills to promote healthy functioning. Primary prevention refers to early programmatic strategies designed to promote cognitive, emotional, and social well-being by preventing debilitating behavior before it occurs. It focuses on strengthening and supporting existing skills. Preventive counseling exists along a continuum with remedial and developmental counseling (Albee & Ryan-Finn, 1993). Multiple strategies can be used to reduce risk factors and to promote protective factors. Some researchers contend that prevention strategies can be used to address behaviors such as self-sufficiency, social support, conflict resolution, problem solving, decision making, communication, peer-pressure resistance training, mental and emotional disorders, and disease prevention to reduce social pathogens, such as those identified in Chapter 4 through Chapter 9, and to enhance competencies (Albee, 1986; Albee, Bond, & Monsey, 1992; Albee, Gordon, & Leitenberg, 1983; Albee & Joffe, 1977; Bond & Compas, 1989; Botvin, 1985, 1986; Botvin & Tortu, 1988; Comer, 1989; Garland & Zigler, 1993; Pedro-Carroll, 1991).

Acquiring the desired competencies will help prevent potential problems. For example, for date rape a prevention might be "to be able to negotiate clearly one's wants and needs with a date." For substance abuse, a prevention might be "how to say no without losing your friends."

> Primary prevention is defined as being proactive and is aimed predominantly at high-risk groups not yet affected by the condition to be prevented. Its success is measured in a decline in the incidence of the condition. ... Only through prevention can we reduce its incidence, and it seems that it is the only feasible way to deal with the unbridgeable gap between the enormous number of individuals at risk for emotional disturbance and the limited availability of treatment resources. (Albee & Ryan-Finn, 1993, p. 115)

The purposes of developmental/primary prevention groups are to provide information and skills for more accurate decision making and to prevent critical developmental issues from becoming intervention concerns. Descriptions of developmental/primary prevention groups gleaned from the literature include, but are not limited to, the following:

- Listening skills (Merritt & Walley, 1977; Rogers, 1980).
- Dealing with feelings (Papagno, 1983; Vernon, 1989, 1990).

- Social skills and interpersonal relationships (Barrow & Hayaski, 1980; Brown & Brown, 1982; Cantor & Wilkinson, 1982; Johnson, 1990; Keat, Metzger, Raykovitz, & McDonald, 1985; Morganett, 1990; Rose, 1987; Vernon, 1989).
- Academic achievement, motivation, and school success (Ames & Archer, 1988; Blum & Jones, 1993; Campbell & Myrick, 1990; Chilcoat, 1988; Gage, 1990; Gerler, Kinney, & Anderson, 1985; Malett, 1983; Morganett, 1990; Thompson, 1987).
- Self-concept, personal identity, and self-esteem (Canfield & Wells, 1976; Morganett, 1990; Omizo & Omizo, 1987, 1988; Tesser, 1982; Vernon, 1989).
- Career awareness, exploration, and planning (McKinlay & Bloch, 1989; Rogala, Lambert, & Verhage, 1991; Super, 1980).
- Problem solving and decision making (Bergin, 1991; Vernon, 1989).
- Communication and assertiveness (Alberti & Emmons, 1974; Donald, Carlisle, & Woods, 1979; Huey, 1983; Morganett, 1990; Myrick, 1987).

Primary prevention programs promote a nurturing and caring environment for high-risk youth, reducing such maladies as the debilitating consequences of poverty by providing transition skills and employment and identifying and encouraging the development of social support groups. Further, the developmental task of youth is to achieve a sense of identity, autonomy, and differentiation from their family of origin. For youth to accomplish this life transition, they need to acquire skills, knowledge, and attitudes that may be classified into two broad categories: those involving self-development and those involving other people. Table 3.1 provides a framework of basic needs and basic skills inherent for all children, regardless of race, sex, or ethnic origin. It focuses on the continuum from deficiency to fulfillment and serves as a graphic organizer for prevention and intervention efforts. Inherent are the critical need to belong, the need to communicate and to be understood, the need to be respected, the need to be held in high esteem, the need to be assertive, and the need to resolve conflicts.

Maslow's needs hierarchy and levels of personality function (Table 3.1) illustrate the conditions of efficiency and conditions of fulfillment, providing a more detailed dimension of developmental tasks and behavior. Preventive counseling with developmental/primary prevention groups helps youth to actualize their full potential.

The developmental task may serve as a catalyst or a bridge between an individual's needs, environmental demands, and the total framework

Table 3.1 Hierarchy of Developmental Needs: Conditions of Deficiency and Fulfillment

Need hierarchy	Conditions of deficiency	Conditions of fulfillment	Illustration
Self-actualization	Alienation Defenses Absence of meaning in life Boredom Routine living Limited activities	Healthy curiosity Understanding Realization of potentials Work that is pleasurable and embodies values Creative living	Realizing what friendship really is or feeling awe at the wonder of nature
Esteem	Feeling incompetence Negativism Feeling of inferiority	Confidence Sense of mastery Positive self-regard Self-respect Self-extension	Receiving an award for an outstanding performance on some subject
Love	Self-consciousness Feeling of being unwanted Feelings of worthlessness Emptiness Loneliness Isolation Incompleteness	Free expression of emotion Sense of wholeness Sense of warmth Renewed sense of life and strength Sense of growing together	Experiencing total acceptance in a love relationship
Safety	Insecurity Yearning Sense of loss Fear Worry Rigidity	Security Comfort Balance Poise Calm Tranquility	Being secure in lifetime job or career
Physiological	Hunger, thirst Tension Fatigue Illness Lack of shelter	Relaxation Release from tension Experiences of pleasure from senses Physical well-being Comfort	Feeling satisfied after a good meal

of such tasks, providing a comprehensive network of important psychosocial learning essential for living and well-being. Further, according to Burrett and Rusnak (1993), personal growth is seen as a function of knowledge, emotion, and environment and occurs in the following developmental stages:

Ages 1 to 7. Development of a sense of hope (openness and trust), autonomy, and imagination.

Age 7 to adolescence. Development of competence (beyond simple skill and technique) in the expression of self and of harmony with one's physical and social environment.

Adolescence. Development of consistency and fidelity predicated on a combined sense of ability and commitment.

Adulthood. Development of a sense of justice, love, care, and wisdom (Burrett & Rusnak, 1993, p. 8).

Problem-Centered Intervention Groups

Problem-centered intervention groups are initiated to meet the needs of clients who are having dysfunctional or self-defeating behaviors. The stressors from a client's particular circumstances may interfere with or hinder normal functioning. The group experience allows clients to handle more serious concerns, rather than resolve typical developmental problems. Group members share anxieties in a secure environment and attempt to empower themselves to act on their decisions by providing support, feedback, and unconditional acceptance. With the assistance of the group, members try out new behaviors and develop and implement strategies to resolve their problems. These groups build on young people's inherent tendencies to turn to their peers for needed support, understanding, and advice.

A problem-centered intervention group provides young people with experiences that enhance their self-awareness and increase their problem-solving and decision-making skills so that they can better cope with real-life situations. Themes for problem-centered intervention groups range from dealing with physical or sexual abuse to coping with loss or adjustments such as parental death, separation, or divorce. Topics for problem-centered intervention groups include, but are not limited to, the following:

- Obesity, bulimia, or anorexia nervosa (Frey, 1984; Lokken, 1981).
- Physical or sexual abuse (Baker, 1990; Powell & Faherty, 1990).
- Grief and loss (McCormack, Burgess, & Hartman, 1988; Peterson & Straub, 1992; Thompson, 1993).
- Aggressive behavior (Amerikaner & Summerlin, 1982; Huey, 1987; Lane & McWhirter, 1992; Lawton, 1994; Prothrow-Stith, 1993; Reiss & Roth, 1992).

- Divorce, loss, and separation (Bonkowski, Bequette, & Boonhower, 1984; Bradford, 1992; Burke & Van de Streek, 1989; Cantrell, 1986; Gwynn & Brantley, 1987; Hammond, 1981; Omizo & Omizo, 1987).
- Drug abuse prevention (Berkowitz & Persins, 1988; Daroff, Marks, & Friedman, 1986; Sarvela, Newcomb, & Littlefield, 1988; Tweed & Ruff, 1991).
- Teen pregnancy (Blythe, Gilchrist, & Schinke, 1981; Thompson, 1987).

Group membership is targeted at youth who are currently having difficulty with a specific problem or are considered at risk. Problem-focused groups frequently use media and structured activities to stimulate discussion of issues and to present relevant information (Bergin, 1993). Role-playing, homework, contracts, and journal writing enhance problem-solving and coping skills.

The group setting provides a secure arena to share anxieties, express feelings, and identify coping strategies. Members learn that their feelings are normal and that their peers share similar experiences. Bergin (1993, p. 2) "stressed the concept of involvement, maintaining that the interactive process of the group affects members in a number of positive ways":

- The group offers acceptance and support for each member and encourages mutual trust and the sharing of individual concerns.
- The groups' orientation to reality and emphasis on conscious thoughts lead members to examine their current thoughts, feelings, and actions, and to express them in a genuine manner.
- The group's overt attempt to convey understanding to each member encourages tolerance and acceptance of individual differences in personal values and goals.
- The group's focus on personal concerns and behavior encourages members to consider alternative ways of behaving and to practice them within the context of a supportive environment.

Curative and Therapeutic Factors

Hansen, Warner, and Smith (1980), Yalom (1985), and others have stressed the curative and therapeutic factors responsible for producing change in productive groups. The 11 primary factors that are highly visible in groups with children and adolescents are listed as follows:

1. **Instillation of hope.** Group members develop the belief that their problems can be overcome or managed. By learning new skills, such as listening, paraphrasing, and expressing empathy, the child or adolescent develops a stronger sense of self and a belief in the efficacy of the helping process (i.e., that the child or adolescent has meaning and relatedness to school, community, and family).

2. **Universality.** Group members overcome the debilitating notion that their problem is unique to them. Through mutual sharing of problems in a secure environment, the members discover a commonality of fears, fantasies, hopes, needs, and so on. Problems are no longer unique to them; problems are universal and shared with others.

3. **Imparting information.** Group members receive new information, as well as advice, suggestions, and direct guidance about developmental concerns. Advice-giving and advice-seeking behavior is central to the school counselor's role. When they receive specific information, children and adolescents feel more self-sufficient and in control of their own behavior. Vicarious learning also occurs in the group setting as children and adolescents observe the coping strategies of others.

4. **Altruism.** Group members offer support, reassurance, and assistance to one another. Adolescents become other-centered rather than self-centered, often rediscovering their self-importance by learning that they are of value to others. They feel a sense of purpose and that others value their expertise. Altruism can extend from the group to the community to more global concerns, such as service learning projects to protect the environment, help the homeless, or assist the elderly.

5. **The corrective recapitulation of the primary family group.** The group environment promotes a mirror of experiences typical of one's primary family group. During the group experience, the focus is on the vitality of work in the here and now. Outside of the group experience, the adolescent may internalize behavior change and enhance more interpersonal skills.

6. **Development of social skills.** The development and rehearsal of basic social skills is a therapeutic factor that is universal to all counseling groups. Adolescents learn such skills as establishing relationships, refraining from critical judgment, listening attentively, communicating with empathy, and expressing warmth and genuineness. Once assimilated, these skills create opportunities for personal growth and more rewarding interpersonal interactions, which are transferred to daily functioning at home, in school, or on the job.

7. **Imitative behavior.** Group members learn new behaviors by observing the behavior of the leader and other members. In training, the process of modeling serves to create positive behavior that the adolescent can assimilate (e.g., body language, tone of voice, eye contact, and other important communication skills). The learner not only sees the behavior in action but also experiences the effects of it.

8. **Interpersonal learning.** Within the social microcosm of the group, members develop relationships typical of their lives outside the group. Group training facilitates self-awareness and interpersonal growth. Adolescents often come to a training program with distorted self-perceptions. These distortions can be the impetus of self-defeating behaviors, such as procrastination, unrealistic expectations, self-pity, anxiety, guilt, rigid thinking, ethnocentricity, psychological dependence, or an external locus of control. The nature and scope of the training process encourage self-assessment, risk taking, confrontation, feedback, goal setting, and decision making.

9. **Group cohesiveness.** Group membership allows participants an arena to receive unconditional positive regard, acceptance, and belonging, which enables them to fully accept themselves and to be congruent in their relationships with others. The group community creates a cohesiveness, a "we-ness," or a common vision. Once a group attains cohesiveness with established norms, members are more receptive to feedback, self-disclosure, confrontation, and appreciation, making themselves more open to one another. An effective training process facilitates this component.

10. **Emotional expression.** Learning how to express emotions reduces the need for debilitating defense mechanisms. Sharing emotions and feelings diminishes destructive fantasy building and repressed anger and sets the stage for exploring alternatives to self-defeating behaviors.

11. **Responsibility.** As group members face the fundamental issues of their lives, they learn that they are ultimately responsible for the way they live, no matter how much support they receive from others. Contributions of the adolescent are validated, issues of personal responsibility and consequences are stressed, choice and the development of his or her potential are encouraged.

When a helping professional observes the group process with children and adolescents, many of these therapeutic factors appear. The curative factors that emerge most consistently in child and adolescent groups are universality, instillation of hope, and interpersonal learning. For example, adolescents often feel that no one else has a problem as devastating as theirs. They are relieved when they realize that others share similar pain, such as feelings of abandonment or guilt regarding a parent's divorce or post-traumatic stress disorders from a recent traumatic loss. From that realization, adolescents gain a more hopeful perspective, believing that they, like their peers, can effect change, improve their conditions, or build their coping skills. This fosters personal empowerment. Rather than relying on the collective adolescent angst of blaming others or blaming the system, children and adolescents are provided with skills to enhance relationships and effect changes in themselves and others.

Therapeutic Intentions

Within the therapeutic relationship, counselors and therapists want to provide assistance effectively and efficiently. For the most part, counselors find themselves gathering information, exploring feelings, generating alternatives, or merely providing support in a secure environment. Hill (1989) and Hill and O'Grady (1985) delineated between counselor intentions and response mode when developing interventions. *Intentions* are the plans and goals the counselor develops after analyzing input data from the client (i.e., presenting problem, diagnosis, behavioral observations, personal reactions, and clinical hypotheses). Intentions guide therapeutic interventions, or response modes. Thus, "*response modes* refer to what counselors do, and intentions refer to why they do it" (Hamer, 1995, p. 261).

Research by Kivlighan (1989, 1990), Kivlighan and Angelone (1991), and Hill, Helms, Spiegel, and Tichenor (1988) suggested five distinct intention clusters:

- **Set limits.** Intention: to assess, to get information, to focus and clarify intentions.
- **Explore.** Intention: to assess cognitions, feelings, and behavioral domains.
- **Restructure.** Intention: to assess resistance, to challenge, and to offer insight.
- **Educate.** Intention: to give information.
- **Change and support.** Intention: to support and reinforce change.

Counselor intention in the therapeutic process recognizes that actions, motivation, and intention are interdependent and can affect the course of counseling and outcomes. One means that counselors and therapists might use to clarify their intended purpose and to provide a focus for interventions could revolve around Hill's and O'Grady's (1985) 18 therapeutic intentions:

1. **Setting limits**. Structure, make arrangements, establish goals and objectives of treatment, and outline methods.
2. **Getting information**. Elicit specific facts about history, client functioning, future plans, and present issues.
3. **Giving information**. Educate, give facts, correct misperceptions or misinformation, and give reasons for procedures or client behavior.
4. **Support**. Provide a warm, supportive, empathetic environment; increase trust and rapport so as to build a positive relationship; help the client feel accepted and understood.
5. **Focus**. Help the client get back on track; change subject; and channel or structure the discussion if the client is unable to begin or has been confused.
6. **Clarification**. Provide or solicit more elaboration; emphasize or specify when client or counselor has been vague, incomplete, confusing, contradictory, or inaudible.
7. **Hope**. Convey the expectation that change is possible and likely to occur; convey that the therapist will be able to help the client; restore morale and build the client's confidence to make changes.
8. **Catharsis**. Promote relief from tension or unhappy feelings; allow the client a chance to talk through feelings and problems.
9. **Cognitions**. Identify maladaptive, illogical, or irrational thoughts or attitudes (e.g., "I must perform perfectly").
10. **Behaviors**. Identify and give feedback on the client's inappropriate or maladaptive behaviors and the consequences of such; analyze behavior and point out discrepancies.
11. **Self-control**. Encourage the client to own or gain a sense of mastery or control over his or her own thoughts, feelings, behaviors, or actions; help the client become more appropriately internal in taking responsibility.
12. **Feelings**. Identify, intensify, or enable acceptance of feelings; encourage or provoke the client to become aware of deeper underlying feelings.
13. **Insight**. Encourage understanding of the underlying reasons, dynamics, assumptions, or unconscious motivations for cognitions, behaviors, attitudes, or feelings.
14. **Change**. Develop new and more adaptive skills, behaviors, or cognitions in dealing with self and others.

15. Reinforcement of change. Give positive reinforcement for behavioral, cognitive, or affective attempts to enhance the probability of change; provide an opinion or assessment of client functions.

16. Resistance. Overcome obstacles to change or progress.

17. Challenge. Jolt the client out of a present state; shake up current beliefs, patterns, or feelings; test for validity, adequacy, reality, or appropriateness.

18. Relationship. Resolve problems; build or maintain a smooth working alliance; heal ruptures; deal with dependency issues; and uncover and resolve distortions.

Structured Intervention: Collective Initiatives

Waldo (1985) differentiated the curative factor framework when planning activities in structured groups. In a six-session structured group, activities can be arranged in relation to the group's development so that group dynamics can foster curative factors. The group can be structured as follows:

Session 1. Establish goals and ground rules (installation of hope) and share perceptions about relationships (universality).

Session 2. Identify feelings about past, present, and future relationships (catharsis, family reenactment).

Session 3. Demonstrate understanding of other group members' feelings (cohesion).

Session 4. Allow feedback among group members (altruism).

Session 5. Allow confrontation and conflict resolution among group members (interpersonal learning).

Session 6. Plan ways that group members can continue to improve relations with others; create closure (existential factors).

Each session involves "lectures and reading materials (imparting information), demonstrations by the leader (interpersonal learning), and within- and between-meeting exercises (social skills and techniques"; Waldo, 1985, p. 56). This model provides a conceptual map that can be used in structured intervention groups for conflict resolution, decision making, interpersonal relations, or any intervention that teaches important life skills.

After children and adolescents have recognized that their problems are not unique but universal, they begin to feel obligations toward other people. The "I" becomes strongly submerged in the "we." When youth reach this stage of interpersonal identity, they are able to enhance their own problem solving. By observing how a member discusses his or her needs or reliance on others, the counselor can help that person realize that it is possible to change behavior and to ask for support.

Psychoeducational groups can effectively meet the needs of young people if they are conducted with these parameters in mind:

- Six to eight children or adolescents should meet for a maximum of 45 minutes at a time.
- The chronological age difference in the group should not exceed 2 years.
- The intellectual age should be controlled to prevent extremes (e.g., a gifted student and a special education student with severe handicapping conditions may not benefit from the same group experience).

The therapeutic intention is to build a caring program to support and assist youth who are experiencing problems. The group serves to provide a secure environment to share experiences, to experience and express conflicting feelings, and to share personal struggles and develop support systems.

Techniques and Strategies

This section contains a compilation of counseling techniques and strategies that can be used during the life of the group. These techniques and strategies are often experiential, to help children and adolescents process feelings and thoughts. They are not intended to be games or gimmicks but, rather, are structured activities for experiential learning. Selected techniques are useful for multimodal interventions. Selected strategies are useful for facilitating the group process. The techniques are some that I have found to work well with children and adolescents. They provide structure for further exploration for members within the group setting.

Beginnings and Universal Concerns

Each group member anonymously writes on an index card a self-defeating behavior he or she would like to change. The leader collects the completed cards and redistributes them, instructing members to take any card but his or her own. Members read their new cards aloud, and the group assigns a ranking of the presenting problem on a scale of 1 to 10 (1 = low, 10 = high). The leader tallies the scores and ranks the problems. The highest-rated problem is identified. The individual who wrote it is identified, and group work begins, focusing on the identified person's concern. One caveat is important here: The leader should assure group members that everyone's self-defeating behaviors are of equal importance. This exercise merely provides a gentle structure to begin the work of changing self-defeating behaviors that may inhibit personal growth.

Unfinished Statements

Completing unfinished statements about likes and dislikes, families and friends, or goals and wishes can help the counselor understand group members, identify problem areas, and establish rapport. Selected unfinished statements follow:

- My greatest fear is...
- The thing that creates the most difficulty for me is...
- The person in my family who helps me the most is...
- I used to be, but now I'm...
- The thing I would like people to admire me for is...
- The one thing I most want to accomplish is...

Empty Chair

Empty chair is a role-playing technique involving the client and an individual who is not present but with whom the client has a conflict. The client sits opposite an empty chair and begins a dialogue with the individual not present. Unresolved conflicts, unfinished business, and personal regrets are frequent themes.

Group Debriefing After Role-Playing

Debriefing after role-playing is an essential component of the process that often is overlooked. After role-playing, the group should join in a circle and each member, one at a time, should say, "I am not a _____; I am [the client's own name]." For example, a girl might say, "I am not an expert know-it-all; I am Jessica Thompson." The counselor can follow this exercise by having group members perform a few mathematics drills or say their addresses three times fast to make the transition from role-playing to reality.

The Three Most Important People in Your Life

Ask members, "Who were three important people in your life at age 5, age 12, age 16?" Then have them project into the future: "Who will be the most important people in your life?" This technique helps the counselor gain valuable insights into the members' worlds at various life stages, particularly in the dimension of psychological dependency, support networks, and available resources.

Writing a Letter Aloud

The leader asks a group member to write an oral letter right in the group. The recipient of the letter is an individual who is significant in the group member's life, someone with whom he or she has trouble relating or has an unresolved conflict, or someone who is deceased. The letter should contain whatever the group member would like to say that has not previously been said, the reasons for any existing bitterness, and how the relationship should change. When the letter has been completed, everyone in the group is invited to react and relate thoughts and feelings the letter elicited.

This technique is most appropriate when an individual has expressed a concern about a significant other who is troublesome, agonizing, bitter, or frustrating or when the individual has given considerable data about relationship difficulties and has expressed obvious frustration about the attitudes and abusive actions of another person (Dyer & Vriend, 1977).

Rewriting the letter is very important to demonstrate what the group member can say in a more positive and effective manner. The contrast in letters will actively demonstrate differences in effective and self-defeating thinking patterns. This is a very powerful tool (Dyer & Vriend, 1977).

I Take Responsibility for ...

The purpose of this exercise is to help clients accept personal responsibility for their own feelings. Have a client make a statement out loud describing his or her own feelings, and then add "and I take responsibility for it." For example, if the client often feels helpless, he or she might say, "I feel helpless, and I take responsibility for it." Other feelings that can be objects of this exercise are boredom, isolation, rejection, stupidity, feeling unloved, and so on.

I Have a Secret

This exercise can be used to explore fears, guilt, and catastrophic expectations. Group members are asked to think of some personal secret. They do not actually share the secret with others but imagine themselves revealing the secret. They explore the fears they have about other people knowing their secret and how they imagine others might respond.

Playing the Projection

The purpose of this exercise is to demonstrate how often we see clearly in others qualities or traits that we do not want to see or accept within ourselves. Group members make a direct statement to each person in the group and then apply that statement to themselves. For example, one member might say to another, "I think you are very manipulative." The same member would then say, "*I* am manipulative." "I don't think you really care about me" becomes "*I* don't care about me." This technique serves to create a deeper awareness of one's own projections.

Reversal Technique

This exercise is useful when a group member has attempted to deny or disown a side of his or her personality. For example, a client who often plays the role of the tough guy might be covering up a gentle side, or someone who is always excessively nice might be trying to deny or disown negative feelings toward others. Have members select one of their traits, then assume the opposite characteristic as fully as possible. Have clients process what the experience was like for them.

Here-and-Now Face

The here-and-now face is used to help group members disclose and discuss their feelings and emotions. The counselor instructs members to draw a face that represents the feelings they are experiencing at the present. Below the face, they write a verbal description of those feelings and the reasons for them. The discussion should include both what the feelings are and why they exist. For example, "I am feeling ... because ...." This exercise generates a discussion of the importance of feelings in group members' lives and brings the group into personal contact.

Life-Picture Map

Ask group members to draw an illustrated road map that represents their past, present, and future. The map should pictorially depict experiences the members have had, obstacles they have overcome, their present lives, their goals for the future, and the barriers that stand in the way of accomplishing those goals. After completing the drawings, members share their maps with the group, explaining the various illustrations; finally, the experience is processed.

Paint a Group Picture

Divide the group into smaller groups of four to eight, and supply these smaller groups with paper and markers. Ask each group to paint a picture as a team that reflects the personality of the subgroup. The picture should be creative and integrate individual efforts. Members could also decide on a group name and sign the picture with it. (This also can be used in the classroom when building cooperative learning teams; see Chapter 8 for details.)

Break In

In this exercise, members are asked to stand in a tight circle, and one person is left outside the circle. The "outsider" attempts to penetrate the group in any way that he or she can. Break in can be used as a springboard for members to explore their feelings of being rejected, isolated, or "out of the group," either with the current group or in their own lives at present. The use of territoriality to define ingroup–outgroup expectations also can be processed.

Meeting Someone Halfway

Divide the group into two sections at opposite sides of the room, facing each other. Members are instructed that, when they choose (or if they choose), they may walk out to the center of the room and wait for someone on the other side to join them. When the two meet, whatever communication they desire can take place—but all communication is to be nonverbal. Members should process their reactions to the experience and explore their relationships with the person who met them and with those who did not.

Competitive Thumb Wrestling

This exercise is useful when the leader perceives that two members may be experiencing hidden aggression or hostility toward one another. Those involved should select their preferred hand and interlace their fingers, hooking their thumbs. One person then attempts to force the thumb of the other person down for a count of three. The leader assists in processing the feelings of hostility between members.

Territoriality and Group Interaction

After the group has been in session for a time, ask the members to change seats. Process the issues of territoriality: Did they tend to arrange themselves in the same seating order? How did they feel when they saw someone else sitting in their territory? Ask members to diagram with arrows the interactions of a given period of group discussion. Discuss crosscurrents in the group. Who are isolates? Who are stars? Is there ease of communication, direct eye contact, and equal airtime?

Strength Bombardment

One group member volunteers to tell his or her personal strengths; the group responds by telling the strengths they see in that person. The member then asks, "What do you see that is preventing me from using my strengths?" The group responds again. Finally, group members construct a group fantasy in which they imagine what the focus member can be doing in 5 or more years if he or she uses his or her strengths to their full potential. The focus member reflects on this experience in the group.

I Am Becoming a Person Who...

Group members are given paper and pencils and are instructed to write their first names in large block letters on the top of their sheets. Then they are asked to complete the following sentence in as many ways as they can: "I am becoming a person who ...." They silently mill around the room reading one another's sheets, then process the group session.

Map of Life

On sheets of newsprint, members draw maps of their lives, illustrating significant events. In an insert, they draw a map of the current week, up to the here and now. Each member explains his or her map to the group.

Think–Feel

Each members is instructed to write on one side of an index card a sentence beginning with the phrase "Now I am thinking …" and on the other side a sentence beginning with "Now I am feeling …." Members are asked to process their thoughts and feelings from both sides of their cards.

Making the Rounds

In this exercise a person goes around the group and says something that is difficult to say. For example, a member might have mentioned that she doesn't trust the other group members enough to risk any self-disclosure. She may be given the opportunity to go around the group and say to each member: "I don't trust you, because …" or "If I were to trust you then …." The person making the rounds completes the sentence with a different ending for each group member. The purpose of the exercise is to give participants the experience of confronting a given fear and concretely stating that fear.

The Here-and-Now Wheel

This can be used as a closure activity to enable people to get in touch with the emotions they are feeling, to label each emotion, and to try to determine why they are feeling those emotions. Have group members draw a circle on a piece of paper and divide the circle into four quadrants. In each quadrant, group members write a word that describes a feeling they have at the moment. The leader can ask for five volunteers to share their wheels with the entire group.

Unfinished Story

This is a counseling technique in which in an unfinished story is completed through role-playing or discussion or in writing to stimulate identification, personal information, or a group member's concerns.

The What-If Technique

This technique is used to get the client to project, imagine, or explore what it would be like if he or she could attain desired wishes, feelings, or behaviors.

Strength Test

An index card for each group member is passed around the group. The leader asks each member to write a positive strength for every group member on his or her card.

Group Reentry Questions

Group reentry questions help to establish the level of group rapport that has been developed and to enhance the self-concepts of group members. Here are some examples of group reentry questions:

- What was the most exciting thing that happened to you in the last week? Over the weekend? Yesterday? What was the most exciting thing you did?
- Share with the group an experience in which you made someone happy.
- If you could be talented in something you are not talented in now, what would it be? Why? Is it something that would please you? Would it please others?

Table 3.2 Comparison of Psychoeducational and Counseling/Therapy Groups

Psychoeducational groups	Counseling/therapy groups
Emphasize didacticism and instruction	Emphasize experience and feelings
Use planned, structured activities	Little use of planned, structured activities
Goals usually defined by leader	Goals defined by group members
Leader operates as facilitator, teacher	Leader guides, intervenes, protects
Focus on prevention	Focus on self-awareness, remediation
No screening of members	Screening prior to beginning group
Cannot set limits on number in group	Can set limits on number in group
Self-disclosure accepted but not mandated	Self-disclosure expected
Confidentiality not primary concern	Privacy and confidentiality are critical
Sessions may be limited to one	Usually consists of several sessions
Task functions emphasized	Maintenance functions emphasized over task

Source: Adapted from *Psychoeducational Groups: Process and Practice* (2nd ed.), by N. Brown, 2004, New York and Hove: Brunner-Routledge. Copyright 2004 by Brunner-Routledge. Adapted with permission.

The Psychoeducational Life Skill Intervention Model to Enhance Self-Sufficiency and Promote Resiliency in Children, Adolescents, and Adults

Youth and adults across the nation are increasingly manifesting serious social, emotional, and cognitive deficits. The indicators of emotional deficits include increased incidents of violence, suicide, and homicide. Social deficits manifest themselves in poor peer relations and an inability to resolve conflicts and manage anger. Cognitive deficits place youth and adults at a disadvantage academically and reduce their career options, making these people more vulnerable to criminal influences because they do not have the marketable skills to compete in a global economy. Increasingly, children, adolescents, and adults are not receiving adequate teaching or modeling in life, and their daily functioning and interactions with others are impaired.

Yet, social, emotional, and cognitive well-being provides children and adolescents with a strong foundation to make healthy choices. *Psychoeducational groups* usually are defined as groups where the primary focus is education about a psychological concept or topic (Gladding, 1995). Psychoeducational groups help participants to develop new skills as they acquire and share information. These groups are often organized around topic areas, such as managing stress, assertion skills, or coping with depression. Support groups also often include individuals who share common problems or issues and who are seeking help as they adjust to new roles or experiences. Examples include groups to help individuals cope with parental divorce, sexual assault, bereavement, sexual orientation issues, and family substance abuse. These groups also serve to educate those facing developmental life crises and to teach coping skills to those dealing with an immediate interpersonal adjustment issue. The ultimate goal of psychoeducational groups is to "prevent an array of educational and psychological disturbances from occurring" (Gladding, 1995, p. 436).

The skill repertoire of youth and adults can be enhanced using a Psychoeducational Life Skills Remediation model. Teaching a life-skill group session follows a six-step learning model:

1. Teach an overview of the skill.
2. Model the skill for participants.
3. Discuss the skill that was modeled and how it can be used in daily life.
4. Practice the skill by role-playing.
5. Provide group feedback to participants to reinforce positive aspects of the role-play.
6. Assign "ownwork" to practice applying the skill outside of the group.

Modeling, feedback, role playing, instruction, situation logs, and ownwork assignments are used to reinforce desired behavior. The term *ownwork* is used rather than *homework* to reinforce one's own responsibility for changing behavior. The term *homework* is often associated with isolated drudgery. The Psychoeducational Life Skill Remediation model is a comprehensive and systematic approach to the remediation and enhancement of interpersonal and intrapersonal effectiveness. It is practiced in a group setting and involves a combination of cognitive and experiential components.

This comprehensive skill-delivery system emphasizes a psychoeducational life-skill remediation model, which is provided by a counselor where the child's difficulties are seen as gaps in knowledge or experience, rather than maladaptive behavior viewed through a deficit lens. An experiential group approach, rather than a didactic one-on-one approach, is the most successful way to diminish self-defeating behavior, particularly among youth. The life-skills model has also empirically demonstrated reduction of drug use, violence, and disruptive behavior.

The instructional psychoeducational intervention techniques are derived from social learning theory. Social skills are acquired primarily through learning (e.g., by observing, modeling, rehearsing, and providing feedback) and are maximized through social reinforcement (e.g., positive responses from one's social environment). Essentially, social, emotional, and cognitive skill deficits can be remedied through direct instruction and modeling. Behavioral rehearsal and coaching reinforce learning. Youth need these prerequisite skills to defeat dysfunctional behaviors and to enhance their resiliency during stressful events. This model can be used with any age group and any population.

The Psychoeducational Life-Skill Process

The psychoeducational life-skill process is a simulation of what a typical life-skill session would look like using the social skill of assertiveness. The psychoeducational group leader assumes the role of director, teacher, model, evaluator, encourager, motivator, facilitator, and protector. Role-playing within the Psychoeducational Life Skill Intervention model provides the opportunities

- to try out, rehearse, and practice new learning in a safe setting;
- to discover how comfortable new behaviors can become;
- to assess which alternative actions work best; and
- to practice and repractice new learning by reality testing.

Essentially, intellectual insight alone is not sufficient to change self-defeating behavior, nor can an isolated didactic dialogue between client and therapist serve to integrate new social, emotional, or cognitive skills into the client's behavioral repertoire. Role-playing is a fundamental force in self-development and interpersonal learning.

A Demonstration of the Six-Step Process to the Psychoeducational Life Skill Intervention Model

Steps are outlined according to what the group leader should say and do to help youth integrate social, emotional, and cognitive skills into their behavioral repertoires. Training sessions are a series of action–reaction sequences in which effective skill behaviors are first rehearsed (role-playing) and then critiqued (feedback). Groups should be small (6 to 10 members) with genders and races mixed. Groups should cover one skill in one or two sessions. Every member of the group role-plays the given skill correctly at least once. Role-playing is intended to serve as behavioral rehearsal or practice for future use of the skill. Further, a hypothetical future situation, rather than a reenactment of a past event, should be selected for role-playing.

Step 1: Present an Overview of the Social, Emotional, or Cognitive Skill
This is the instructional portion of the process. An instructional vignette (5 to 10 minutes) is presented to teach the social, emotional, or cognitive skill. Introduction to the benefits of the skill in enhancing relationships and the pitfalls of not learning the skill are also presented.

The following sections provide suggested instructional overviews for the social skill of assertiveness.

Social literacy skill: understanding your assertive rights.
You have the right

- to decide how to lead your life;
- to express thoughts, actions, and feelings;
- to have your own values, beliefs, opinions, and emotions;
- to tell others how you wish to be treated;
- to say, "I don't know; I don't understand";
- to ask for information or help;
- to have thoughts, feelings, and rights respected;
- to be listened to, heard, and taken seriously;
- to ask for what you want;
- to make mistakes;
- to ask for more information;
- to say no without feeling guilty;
- to make a decision to participate or not to participate; and
- to be assertive without regret.

Social literacy skill: components of assertiveness.
Very often, people who are aggressive do not have within their interpersonal repertoires the ability to express themselves assertively. There are essentially six attributes that are specific to assertiveness:

1. **Self-awareness.** A developed knowledge of one's goals, aspirations, interpersonal and intrapersonal behavior, and the reasons for them. Realization where changes are needed and belief in your rights.
2. **Self-acceptance.** Acknowledging one's own particular strengths and weaknesses.
3. **Honesty.** Congruency between verbal and nonverbal thoughts, feelings, actions, and intentions.
4. **Empathy.** Sensitivity and acceptance of others' feelings, behavior, and actions (i.e., to be able to walk in another person's shoes).
5. **Responsibility.** Assuming ownership of thoughts, feelings, actions, needs, goals, and expectations.

6. Equality. Accepting another person as equal with a willingness to negotiate with that person's needs, wants, or desires.

Ask a question to help the members define the skill in their own words. Use language such as in the following questions: "Who can define assertiveness?" "What does being assertive mean to you?" "How is assertiveness different from aggression?"

Make a statement about what will follow the modeling of the skill: "After we see the examples of the skill, we will talk about how you can use the skill."

Distribute skill cards and asks a member to read the behavioral steps aloud, then ask members to follow each step as the skill is modeled.

Step 2: Model the Behavior Following the Steps Listed on a Flipchart or Chalkboard
Moving into the experiential component, the leader models for the group members what he or she considers to be appropriate mastery of the skill. This enables group members to visualize the process. The model can be a live demonstration or a simulated media presentation. Identify and discuss the steps of the social literacy skill, assertiveness.

Social literacy skill: assertiveness.
Lack of assertiveness is one reason why conflicts occur in relationships. To foster understanding and cooperation rather than resentment and resistance, use these strategies:

- **Be direct.** Deliver your message directly to the person with whom you are in conflict, not to a second party (i.e., avoid the "he said, she said" trap).
- **Take ownership for your message.** Explain that your message comes from your point of view. Use personalized "I" statements such as "I don't agree with you" rather than "You're wrong."
- **State what you want, think, and feel as specifically as possible.** Preface statements with statements like these:
  - "I have a need."
  - "I want to…"
  - "Would you consider…?"
  - "I have a different opinion; I think that…"
  - "I don't want you to…"
  - "I have mixed reactions for these reasons…"

Have group members practice these four steps:

1. Concretely describe the other person's behavior.
2. Describe objectively how the other person's actions have affected you.
3. Accurately describe your feelings: "I feel…."
4. Suggest what you would like to see happen: "I prefer this instead…."

Example

Step 1. When you are late picking me up for school in the morning,

Step 2. I am always late for first bell and I always get detention.

Step 3. I feel hurt and angry with you.

Step 4. I am hoping we can make plans so that I don't have to be late anymore.

Ask for feedback to correct any misperceptions. Encourage others to be clear, direct, and specific in their feedback to you: "Am I being clear?" "How do you perceive the situation?" "What do you want to do about this?"

Step 3: Invite Discussion of the Skill That Is Modeled

Ask questions like "Did any of the situations you observed remind you of times when you had to use that skill?" Encourage a dialogue about skill usage and barriers to implementation among group members.

Step 4: Organize a Role-Play between Two Group Members

Designate one member as the behavior-rehearsing member (i.e., the individual who will be working on integrating a specific social, emotional, or cognitive skill). Go over guidelines for role-playing. Guidelines are as follows:

- Role-playing will give a perspective on your own behavior.
- It is a tool to bring a specific skill and its consequences into focus.
- By rehearsing a new skill you will be able to feel some of the same reactions that will be present when the behavior occurs outside our group in a real-life setting.
- Role-playing is intended to give you experience in practicing skills and in discussing and identifying effective and ineffective behavior.
- Practice will enhance your confidence, and you will be able to feel more comfortable in real-life settings.
- Role-playing that feels real leads to more emotional involvement, which will increase what you will learn.

- Role-playing situations make it possible for you to try ways of handling situations without suffering any serious consequences if the methods fail.

To proceed, follow these steps:

1. Ask the behavior-rehearsing member to choose a partner, someone in the group who reminds him or her of the person with whom he or she would most likely use the skill. Here are some example questions: "Which member of the group reminds you of that person in some way?" or "Which member of the group would you feel most comfortable doing the role-playing with?" If no one is identified, ask someone to volunteer to rehearse the skill with the behavior-rehearsing member.

2. Set the stage for the role-play, including setting, props, and furniture if necessary. Ask questions such as "Where will you be talking?" "What will be the time of day?" "What will you be doing?" Review with the behavior-rehearsing member what should be said and done during the role-play, such as "What will be the first step of the skill?" "What will you do if your partner does…?"

3. Provide final instructions to the behavior-rehearsing member and the partner:

   To the behavior-rehearsing member: "Try to follow the steps as best you can."

   To the partner: "Try to play the part the best that you can by concentrating on what you think you would do when the practicing member follows the steps."

4. Direct the remaining members of the group to be observers of the process. Their role is to provide feedback to the behavior-rehearsing member and the partner after the exercise.

The role-play begins. One group member can stand at chalkboard or flip chart to point out each step for the role-playing team. Coach and prompt role-players when needed.

Step 5: Elicit Feedback from Group Members and Processes after the Exercise Is Completed

Generous praise should be mixed with constructive suggestions. Avoid blame and criticism. The focus should be on how to improve. Suggestions should be achievable with practice. What follows is the social literacy skill of giving constructive feedback, which is an integrated part of every

Psychoeducational Life Skill Intervention model. The suggested dialogue for giving constructive feedback, another social literacy skill, is represented by the following steps:

1. Ask permission. Ask the person whether he or she would like some feedback. (If no, wait for a more appropriate time; if yes, proceed.)
2. Say something positive to the person before you deliver the sensitive information.
3. Describe the behavior.
4. Focus on behavior the person can change, not on the person's personality.
5. Be specific and verifiable about the behavior. (Have other people complained?)
6. Include some suggestion for improvement.
7. Go slowly. True behavior change occurs over time.

Here is an example: "Jessica, I've noticed something about your behavior at the student government meeting. Would you like to hear it? Well, at the last few meetings of the homecoming committee, whenever Ryan suggested a theme, you interrupted him and changed the subject."

The following are important considerations for the feedback process:

- The behavior-rehearsing member is instructed to wait until everyone's comments have been heard.
- The partner processes his or her role, feelings, and reactions to the behavior-rehearsing member. Observers are asked to report on how well the behavioral steps were followed, specific likes and dislikes, and comments about the roles of the behavior-rehearsing member and the partner.
- Process group comments with the behavior-rehearsing member. The behavior-rehearsing member is asked to respond to how well he or she did in following the behavioral steps of the skill, for example, "On a scale of 1 to 10, how satisfied were you about following the steps?"

Step 6: Encourage Follow-through and Transfer of Learning to Other Social, Emotional, or Cognitive Settings
This is a critical component. Participants need to transfer newly developed life skills to personally relevant life situations. The behavior-rehearsing member is assigned ownwork to practice and apply the skill in real life (Ownwork, like homework, is a task that is assigned for the behavior-rehearsing member to try out between sessions.) Group members are

assigned to look for situations relevant to the skill they might role-play during the next group meeting.

To follow through and transfer learning to future situations:

- Ask the behavior-rehearsing member how, when, and with whom he or she might attempt the behavioral steps before the next group meeting.
- Assign the Ownwork Report to get a written commitment from the practicing member to try out the new skill and report back to the group the next group meeting. Discuss how and where the skill will be used. Set a specific goal for using the skill outside the group.

Ownwork is assigned to enhance the work of the session and to keep the behavior-rehearsing member aware of the life skill he or she wishes to enhance. The ultimate goal is to practice new behaviors in a variety of natural settings. Ownwork puts the onus of responsibility for change on the behavior-rehearsing member, that is, he or she must do ownwork to resolve the problem. The following examples are appropriate ownwork assignments:

- **Experiential and behavioral assignments.** Assignments for specific actions between sessions. For example, a behavioral assignment for lack of assertiveness may be to instruct the behavior-rehearsing member to say no to unreasonable requests from others.
- **Interpersonal assignments.** Assignments to enhance perceived communication difficulties by writing down unpleasant dialogues with others. These can be reviewed during the next session to show how someone inadvertently triggers rejection, criticism, and hostility in others.
- **Thinking assignments.** Assignments such as making a list of things that are helpful to think about and practicing thinking these new thoughts throughout the day. For example, a person with low self-esteem could be instructed to spend time thinking about his or her proudest accomplishments.
- **Writing assignments.** Assignments such as writing in a journal or diary. These can help participants develop an outlet for their feelings while they are away from the sessions. An example would be keeping a daily diary that lists the frequency of new behaviors.
- **Solution-focused assignments.** Assignments that actively seek solutions to problems identified in the sessions. An example would be seeking a resolution to an interpersonal problem by negotiating or resolving a conflict with another person.

Life Skills Exercise Example for Social Literacy
Skill: Maintaining Impulse Control

Step 1: Instruction—Present an Overview of the Social, Emotional, or Cognitive Skill
Question: How would you define impulse control?
Impulse control is learning to stop and look at the consequences of your actions before you commit yourself to something. It is the ability to stop and think about who else will be affected by your actions and what the consequences will be. Is it worth it?

Simulation.
Shelly is constantly overcommitting herself by being impulsive. She has a problem saying no and working within the boundaries that are comfortable for her. When she is asked to do something, she will say yes even if she does not have the time or resources to complete the task. Shelly was looking at the course schedule book for the fall and saw a class that looked interesting, so she signed up for it. She was already taking 15 graduate hours and working 20 hours per week. She is feeling extremely stressed because of her overload of classes and is not she is not sure that she will get her assignments completed on time. How can we help?

Signs of loss of control.
- Acting impulsively consumes lots of energy and resources.
- You feel driven, impelled, and think of nothing else.
- You feel like the decision is the only possible answer, and you let it take over all rational thinking.

Control strategies.
1. Ask yourself, "Who else will be affected by this behavior?"
2. Ask yourself, "How will they be affected by what I do?"
3. Delay the action. Give yourself some time to think the decision through so that you can see the consequences and alternatives. Remember that choice is important.
4. Think back to the past and consider the situations you had to get yourself out of because of being too impulsive.

Step 2: Modeling Self-help Strategies
- Reward yourself each time you stop and think through a situation instead of acting impulsively.
- Keep a journal and record your feelings about decisions you make and whether you make those decisions impulsively.
- Write yourself a bill of rights and read it when you get ready to make a decision.

Step 3: Invite Discussion of the Skill That Will Be Practiced Reminders for Yourself
- Having a choice is critical. It allows you freedom to act or not to act. It puts you in charge of yourself.
- If you always do what you've done, you will always get what you've always gotten.

Consequences of acting impulsively.
- The consequences of acting impulsively are confusion, self-loathing, and feeling out of control.
- The results of acting impulsively are you spend a tremendous amount of time trying to resolve conflicts, mend relationships, or balance time and money.

Step 4: Organize a Role-Play Between Two Group Members

Shelly: Hey Beth, I just saw this great course in the spring catalog. I think I will take it.

Beth: Shelly, how many hours of classes are you already taking?

Shelly: Fifteen, but this course sounds interesting and I really want to take it.

Beth: Shelly, I realize you really want to take it and it sounds interesting, but is it something that you can handle right now with work and school?

Shelly: It will mean more homework and being up late at night, but I really think I can do it.

Beth: Remember how stressed you were last semester during finals. Do you want that again?

Shelly: No, but you don't understand. I really want to take this class.

Beth: Look at your "plus versus minus" ratio. How is it going to benefit you, and how is it going to affect your family?

Shelly: It's going to help me with general knowledge but not toward my degree. I hadn't thought about my family.

Beth: Do you think you could wait until tomorrow to make your decision? That way, you could talk it over with Brian and the kids and think about it more.

Shelly: I guess I could, but what if the class is full by then?

Beth: What if it is? Will you still be able to graduate? Could you take it later?

Shelly: You've got a point. I'll think about it and talk it over with Brian.

Table 3.3 Decision Balance Matrix: Personal Time Commitment for Self and Others

	Positive consequences (+)	Negative consequences (−)
Social and family relationships		
Academic responsibilities		
Job and career responsibilities		
Leisure pursuits		
Church and community obligations		

"Ownwork" Assignment

❑ Skill to be practiced: Learning to Say "No" and Establishing Healthy Boundaries

❑ "I will use this skill with..."

❑ "I will use it when..........................and where........................."

❑ The steps are as follows:
1.
2.
3.
4.
5.

On a scale from 1 to 10 (1 = lowest; 10 = highest) rate yourself on how well you felt that you did practicing this skill.

Figure 3.1

Step 5: Provide Feedback to the Role-Playing Pair
Elicit feedback from group members.

Step 6: Assign "Ownwork:" Encourage Follow-through and Transfer of Learning to other Social, Emotional, or Cognitive Settings
Assign Shelly to complete a Decision Balance matrix, shown in Table 3.3. Have Shelly look at the aspects of her life mentioned in the matrix and how her decision to take on more course work would affect her.

Assign Shelly to analyze the time commitment required for all her course commitments—how much research for each paper per class, how many readings per class, and how many special projects—and merge those commitments with family and job responsibilities. Bottom line: Are there enough hours in the week to do all she has obliged herself to do? Ownwork assignments serve to strengthen behavior rehearsal of skills between sessions.

Conclusion

Before children and adolescents can change self-defeating behaviors, they need a secure environment to share their anxieties and developmental concerns. Small-group counseling provides this opportunity. Psychoeducational and problem-centered intervention groups provide the safety, security, and confidentiality that youth need. Group process fosters positive peer pressure, encouraging youth to learn from each other; this process has proved quite effective. Support groups bring a manageable solution to the dilemma of overwhelming numbers and devastating problems.

Further, a growing body of evidence shows that life-skills training, using a psychoeducational approach, is making a significant difference in the lives of children and adults. For example, drug-using and at-risk adolescents have been studied in various ways since more investigation of this topic was proposed in a National Institute on Drug Abuse (NIDA) Research Monograph (Krasnegor, 1988). Research on how to teach children basic decision-making skills and an understanding of the relationship between behavior and consequences must be expanded (Botvin and Wills, 1985). This domain includes developing educational packages on assertiveness to be taught to at-risk children. Also needed are effective training packages to teach children how to differentiate between the immediate and long-range consequences of their behavior, particularly as such consequences affect their health. Research should be targeted at developing materials that can be used by health educators and health-care providers.

Although the focus of this exercise was on decision-making skills, the statement also includes assertiveness, which has been typically defined as a behavioral rather than a cognitive skill. A *skill* can be defined as the exact words to say, the way to say them, and the nonverbal behavior needed to convey a message. Or a skill can be defined much more broadly: to listen, for example. As a treatment approach, skills training has been proposed and evaluated as a prevention intervention for adolescent drug abuse (Schinke, Orlandi, Botvin, Gilchrist, Trimble, & Locklear, 1988). Hawkins, Lishner & Catalano and colleagues (1985) identified several factors that can lead to adolescent drug abuse, including parental influences, peer influences, beliefs and values, and involvement in certain activities. Their social development model proposed that "youths who have not become socially bonded to family and school as a result of family conflict, school failure, and aggressive behaviors will be easily influenced by drug prone peers and will find little reason to resist pressures to initiate drug use early in adolescence" (p. 36).

One recommendation is to improve interpersonal skills as a way of improving bonding with family members and conventional peers and decreasing the attractiveness of drug-using peers. Botvin and Wills (1985) also argued for the use of skills training as a prevention intervention with adolescents. Their support of skills training among adolescents to prevent drug use and abuse rests on the assumption that improved skills help to reduce or eliminate drug use. Inderbitzen-Pisaruk and Foster (1990) justified the use of skills training if related to peer acceptance and friendship. After reviewing the empirical literature related to peer acceptance and friendship, they concluded that important behaviors are anchored in specific relationships and that skills trainers need to help teens judge the qualitative aspects of a skill, rather than just the frequency of occurrence. Group approaches were recommended as most appropriate for teens, and both negative and positive behaviors were targeted so that teens could learn how to decrease their self-defeating behaviors.

Skills training has been advocated for a variety of problems, ranging from family conflict (Lewis, Piercy, Spenkle, & Trepper, 1990) to adolescent drug abuse (Hawkins, Jenson, Catalano, & Wells, 1991). The main assumption has been that improvement of skills—however defined—will lead to better personal and interpersonal functioning and to decreases in problems (e.g., drug use, criminal activity).

Skills training has also been advocated as an effective prevention strategy. In general, the term *psychoeducational skills training* has been cited extensively in the psychological literature. A general review of the psychological literature since 1986 found over 1,000 articles that mentioned skills training as a descriptive label. Even when the search was limited to adolescents, 125 articles were identified—too many to be reviewed effectively here. Other investigators have studied the efficacy of skills training for use with the mentally ill (Fine, Forth, Gilvert & Haley, 1991); (Foxx, Kyle, Faw & Bittle, 1989) physically or developmentally disabled (Duran, 1986; Gerstein, 1988; Hardoff & Chigier, 1991; Hinderscheit & Reichle, 1987; Hostler, Gressard, Hassler & Linden, 1989; Oswald Lingnugaris-Kraft & West, 1990); children diagnosed with attention deficit hyperactivity disorder (ADHD) (Abikoff Ganeles, Reiter, Blum Foley & Klein, 1988); adolescent offenders (Becker, Kaplan & Kavoussi, 1988; Guerra & Slaby, 1990; Shorts, 1989; Walker, 1989); pregnant and parenting teens (Balassone, 1988; Bennett & Morgan, 1988; Kissman, 1991; Ladner, 1987); teens and their parents (Anderson & Nuttall, 1987; Brown & Mann, 1991; Mittl & Robin, 1987; Noble, Adams & Openshaw, 1989); juvenile delinquent, troubled, behavior-disordered, conduct-disordered, or anti-social teens (Baum Clark, McCarthy, Sandler & Carpenter, 1987; Epstein & Cullinan, 1987; Hains & Herman, 1989; Sema, Schumaker, Hazel & Sheldon, 1986; Svec & Bechard, 1988; Tannehill, 1987; Tisdelle & St. Lawrence, 1988); hospitalized, inpatient, mentally ill, or cognitively impaired teens (Dryfoos, 1991; Jackson, 1987; Jamison, Lambert & McCloud, 1986; Lichstein, Wagner, Krisak & Steinberg, 1987); acquired immunodeficiency syndrome (AIDS)–risk adolescents (Boyer & Kegeles, 1991); female sexual abuse victims (Davis, 1990); Native Americans (LaFromboise & Bigfoot, 1988); and even sports-injured teens (Smith & Johnson, 1990).

Skills training has been used with parents and teens to improve communication and problem solving. The work of Lewis and colleagues (1990) involving Purdue Brief Family Therapy (PBFT) is a key study. Mittl and Robin (1987) investigated the acceptability of alternative interventions for parent–adolescent conflict and found that problem-solving communication skills training was significantly more acceptable than behavioral contracting, medication, and paradox interventions, in that order.

Several investigators have studied the effectiveness of skills training with teens who were involved with the legal system (Hudson, 1989; Tannehill, 1987). Guerra and Slaby (1990) used a cognitive mediation model of skills training to improve the thinking skills of adolescent offenders. After 12 sessions, those in the experimental group showed increased skills in solving social problems, decreased endorsement of beliefs supporting aggression, and decreased aggressive behavior. Their focus on cognitive skills was developmentally more in line with the operationalization stage for middle-year teens but was not consistent with the more behaviorally oriented skills training used with other delinquent teens (see Hawkins et al., 1991). In a combined family approach with parents and their delinquent adolescents, Sema and colleagues (1986) tested the efficacy of training both the teens and their parents in communication skills.

An extensive literature about pregnant teens exists, with many of the recommendations emphasizing education, job training, improved opportunities for jobs, peer support, inclusion of teen fathers, sex education, and family life education (Ladner, 1987). As with previously cited studies (Hawkins et al., 1991; Schinke et al., 1988), five specific treatment techniques are used to teach social skills:

- Providing information.
- Demonstrating desired behaviors by appropriate models.
- Role-playing desired behaviors by teens.

- Giving structured and supportive feedback.
- Assigning homework to practice skills in the teen's natural environment.

A total of 14 corresponding skills were included in the treatment program:

1. Speaking assertively (as opposed to passively or aggressively).
2. Listening assertively ("What I hear you saying is...").
3. Giving positive feedback (offering praise).
4. Receiving positive feedback (accepting compliments).
5. Giving negative feedback (criticizing).
6. Receiving negative feedback (handling criticism from others).
7. Engaging in social conversation with peers and adults (participating in small talk and asking questions).
8. Handling questions for information, help, or support.
9. Refusing requests to engage in high-risk behaviors (drinking alcohol, using drugs, stealing, having unprotected or unwanted sex).
10. Practicing assertive self-talk (what you say to yourself).
11. Handling uncomfortable feelings.
12. Solving problems assertively before, during, and after problems.
13. Describing and assessing one's social network.
14. Modifying one's network to increase positive support and to decrease negative support.

Each lesson focuses on a new skill and reviews previous skills that are relevant to the session topic.

An example describes the situation used to teach the skill of handling aggressive criticism from a parent:

> It is Saturday night and your parents are staying home. You ask your mother for the car so you can drive to your friend's house on the other side of town. Your mother says, "No, your friend can come here to pick you up. You think you can do just what you want when you want! You always want the car whenever you want, but never on Sunday when your father washes it! You don't take any responsibility around here for anything! You're just a lazy, selfish kid! You always want things given to you. You have never had to work for anything!" *WHAT DO YOU SAY OR DO NOW?*

In the session introduction, the teens are asked what they would normally do in this situation. In the skills-training exercise, leaders focus on the desired behaviors and specifically on the assertive components developed based on the assertion training paradigm (Alberti & Emmons, 1978) and on feedback from professionals who work with teens in a variety of settings. For this situation, the assertive components are the following:

- **Seek more information.** For example, ask a question: "Can we talk about this, Mom?"
- **Agree with speaker.** For example, defuse the anger: "You're right, Mom. I haven't done too well with taking care of the car."
- **Be self-assertive.** For example, apologize, state a positive goal for yourself, or do both: "I sure would like to figure out a way to do better, so I can use the car in the future."
- **Describe plan.** For example, propose a compromise through negotiation: "I'll change my plans for tonight and stay here with my friend, OK?"

Overall, 10 assertive components have been identified and grouped with the various problem situations presented in group sessions:

1. Agree with the speaker.
2. Seek more information.
3. Be self-assertive.
4. Describe a plan.
5. Perform self-questioning (cognitive).
6. Describe the problem.
7. Evaluate the consequences.
8. Disagree with the speaker or say no.
9. Provide a reason.
10. Cope with a mistake.

After each of the practice situations, the counselor asks the teen to rate the response using three questions:

1. How realistic was your response?
2. How many times has this, or something similar, happened to you before?
3. How satisfied were you with how you just handled this situation?

Social Skills Checklist

As a secondary measure, the teen's parent was asked to rate the teen's social skills using the social-skills checklist developed from the work of Goldstein (1989) and associates. Goldstein lists 50 social skills and groups them by level of difficulty (basic skills to advanced problem-solving skills). The parent rates the general competency of each of these 50 skills using this scale:

N = Never good at using this skill.
R = Rarely good at using this skill.
S = Sometimes good at using this skill.
O = Often good at using this skill.
A = Always good at using this skill.

A psychoeducational approach to remediating children has demonstrated empirically that this approach does improve self-sufficiency and resilience among children and adolescents. Educators, counselors, therapists, helping professionals, and community volunteers from a variety of backgrounds can be excellent group leaders and use this tool to make a significant difference in the lives of young adults. With the appropriate training in skills, such as problem solving, decision making, and conflict resolution, all those who interact within the school and the community can be involved in delivering effective services in a genuinely caring and empathetic environment. It takes an entire community to raise a healthy child. Only collective involvement can provide enduring interventions in the well-being of our youth.

PART **II**

Manifestations of Behaviors and Related Skills

CHAPTER 4

Alcohol and Other Drug Abuse

Tell the people to hear this. If they want to get rid of drugs, they better focus on the problem. Drugs just ain't the problem, man. Drugs is the crutch. Loneliness is the problem. Drugs is a way of getting away from the problem. (Baucom, 1989, p. 34)

The truth about drug use by contemporary youth is elusive. Self-reported data are sometimes of dubious validity, but nevertheless they are an important source of information on substance use and abuse. *Monitoring the Future* (1993) addressed a broad array of research objectives, including measuring and explaining changes in drug use among American young people. At present, 50,000 8th-, 10th-, and 12th-graders in more than 400 schools are surveyed annually by the University of Michigan's Institute for Social Research. Substance abuse among children and adolescents increased explosively in the 1960s and 1970s. Alcohol and drug use remain prevalent in this population group. Today, the United States has the highest incidence of alcohol and other drug abuse among adolescents of any country in the world (Anderson, Kinney, & Gerler, 1984; Substance Abuse and Mental Health Services Administration, 2003). The research data reflect a number of concerns about alcohol and other drug abuse among children and adolscents.

The National Survey on Drug Use and Health

The National Survey on Drug Use and Health (NSDUH, 2004) obtained information on nine different categories of illicit drug use: marijuana, cocaine, heroin, hallucinogens, inhalants, nonmedical use of prescription-type pain relievers, tranquilizers, stimulants, and sedatives. In these categories, hashish is included with marijuana, and crack is considered a form of cocaine. Several drugs are grouped under the hallucinogens category, including LSD, PCP, peyote, mescaline, mushrooms, and Ecstasy.

Illicit Drug Use

The following data were gleaned from the National Survey of Drug Use and Health (2004) and lend some insight to the depth and breadth of drug use in America:

- In 2003, an estimated 19.5 million Americans aged 12 or older were current illicit drug users, meaning they had used an illicit drug during the month prior to the survey interview. This estimate represents 8.2% of the population aged 12 years or older.
- There was no change in the overall rate of illicit drug use between 2002 and 2003. In 2002, there were an estimated 19.5 million illicit drug users (8.3%).
- Marijuana is the most commonly used illicit drug (14.6 million past-month users). In 2003, it was used by 75.2% of current illicit drug users. An estimated 54.6% of current illicit drug users used only marijuana, 20.6% used marijuana and another illicit drug, and the remaining 24.8% used an illicit drug (but not marijuana) in the past month.
- The number of current users of Ecstasy decreased between 2002 and 2003, from 676,000 (0.3%) to 470,000 (0.2%). Although there were no significant changes in the past-month use of other hallucinogens, there were significant declines in past-year use of LSD (from 1 million to 558,000) and in past-year overall hallucinogen use (from 4.7 million to 3.9 million) between 2002 and 2003, as well as in past year-use of Ecstasy (from 3.2 million to 2.1 million).
- Of the 8.8 million current users of illicit drugs other than marijuana in 2003, 6.3 million were current users of psychotherapeutic drugs. This represents 2.7% of the population aged 12 or older. Of those who reported current use of any psychotherapeutics, 4.7 million used pain relievers, 1.8 million used tranquilizers, 1.2 million used stimulants, and 0.3 million used sedatives. These estimates are all similar to the corresponding estimates for 2002.

- In 2002, approximately 1.1 million persons used cocaine for the first time. Incidence of cocaine use generally rose throughout the 1970s to a peak in 1980 (1.6 million new users) and subsequently declined until the early 1990s. Cocaine initiation steadily increased after 1993, averaging over a million new users per year during 2000 to 2002.
- First use of cocaine usually occurs at age 18 or later, a pattern consistent since the 1960s. Approximately 70% of cocaine initiates in 2002 were age 18 or older. During the early 1980s, when cocaine initiation reached a peak, approximately 80% of initiates were age 18 or older.
- The number of new users of stimulants generally increased during the 1990s, but there has been little change since 2000. Incidence of methamphetamine use generally rose between 1992 and 1998. Since then, there have been no statistically significant changes. There were an estimated 323,000 methamphetamine initiates in 2002.

Age of Drug Use

- Rates of drug use showed substantial variation by age. For example, 3.8% of youth aged 12 or 13 reported current illicit drug use in 2003. As in other years, illicit drug use in 2003 tended to increase with age among young persons, peaking among 18- to 20-year-olds (23.3%) and declining steadily after that point with increasing age.
- Among youth aged 12 to 17, the rate of current illicit drug use was similar for boys (11.4%) and girls (11.1%). Although boys aged 12 to 17 had a higher rate of marijuana use than girls (8.6% vs. 7.2%), rates of nonmedical use of any prescription-type psychotherapeutics were 4.2% for girls and 3.7% for boys (not a statistically significant difference).
- About half of Americans aged 12 or older reported being current drinkers of alcohol in the 2003 survey (50.1%). This translates to an estimated 119 million people, similar to the 2002 estimate of 120 million current drinkers.
- More than one fifth (22.6%) of persons aged 12 or older participated in binge drinking at least once in the 30 days prior to the survey in 2003. This translates to about 54 million people, comparable with the number reported in 2002.

Heavy Drinking and Binge Drinking

- In 2003, heavy drinking was reported by 6.8% of the population aged 12 or older, or 16.1 million people. These figures are similar to those of 2002, when 6.7% (15.9 million people) reported heavy drinking

- Rates of binge alcohol use were 0.9% at age 12, 2.2% at age 13, 7.1% at age 14, 11.7% at age 15, 18.0% at age 16, and 24.5% at age 17. The rate peaked at age 21 (47.8%) and then decreased beyond young adulthood.
- The highest prevalence of both binge and heavy drinking in 2003 was for young adults aged 18 to 25, with the peak rate of both measures occurring at age 21. The rate of binge drinking was 41.6% for young adults aged 18 to 25 and 47.8% at age 21. Heavy alcohol use was reported by 15.1% of persons aged 18 to 25 and by 18.7% of persons aged 21.
- About 10.9 million persons aged 12 to 20 reported drinking alcohol in the month prior to the survey interview in 2003 (29.0% of this age group). Nearly 7.2 million (19.2%) were binge drinkers, and 2.3 million (6.1%) were heavy drinkers. These figures were essentially the same as those obtained from the 2002 survey.
- More males than females aged 12 to 20 reported binge drinking (21.7% vs. 16.5%) and heavy drinking (7.9% vs. 4.3%) in 2003.
- Driving under the influence varied by age group in 2003. About 9.7% of 16- and 17- year-olds, 20.1% of 18- to 20-year-olds, and 28.7% of 21- to 25-year-olds reported driving under the influence of alcohol. Beyond age 25, these rates declined with increasing age.
- There were an estimated 2.6 million new marijuana users in 2002. This means that each day an average of 7,000 Americans tried marijuana for the first time. About two thirds (69%) of these new marijuana users were under age 18, and about half (53%) were female.

Attitudes about School

Youth were asked if they liked going to school, if assigned schoolwork was meaningful and important, if their courses at school during the past year were interesting, if the things learned in school during the past year would be important later in life, and if teachers in the past year let them know that they were doing a good job with schoolwork (NSDUH, 2004). Youth who had positive attitudes about school were less likely to use substances than other students. For example, in 2003, 79.1% of youth reported that they "liked [going to school] a lot" or "kind of liked" it. Among those youth, 9.1% had used an illicit drug in the past month; however, among youth who either "didn't like [going to school] very much" or "hated" going to school, 19.9% had used an illicit drug in the past month.

For each of the school characteristics listed previously, at least 75% of youth aged 12 to 17 indicated positive attitudes. Youth ratings of these school factors in 2003 were similar to the ratings from 2002, with the exception of whether youth thought teachers "always" or "sometimes" let students know that they were doing a good job with schoolwork. In this instance, the percentage increased from 75.7% in 2002 to 77.6% in 2003.

Delinquent Behavior

In 2003, youth were asked if they had engaged in the following delinquent behaviors during the past year: been involved in a serious fight at school or work, participated in a group-on-group fight, attacked someone with the intent to seriously hurt him or her, carried a handgun, sold illegal drugs, or stolen or tried to steal something worth $50 or more. Youth who had engaged in these behaviors were more likely than other youth to have used illicit drugs in the past month. For example, compared with youth who had not engaged in these behaviors, youth in 2003 were more likely to have used an illicit drug in the past month if they had been involved in a serious fight at school or work (19.6% vs. 8.6%), carried a handgun (32.5% vs. 10.4%), sold illegal drugs (67.0% vs. 9.1%), or stolen or tried to steal something worth $50 or more (39.1% vs. 9.9%).

Increase in Girls' Delinquent Behavior

- In 2003, about 2.4 million girls aged 12 to 17 reported taking part in one or more serious fights at school or work during the past year.
- From 2002 to 2003, the proportion increased of girls who had participated in serious fights at school or work during the past year (from 16.2% to 20%) and who had participated in a group-against-group fight in the past year (from 13.5% to 16.8%).
- Past-year substance use was the most prevalent delinquent behavior among girls aged 12 to 17, with 36.5% (4.5 million) reporting past-year alcohol use and 21.9% (2.7 million) reporting past-year illicit drug use.

Gender Differences

- Based on SAMHSA's 2003 National Survey on Drug Use and Health, 74.5 million (61%) females aged 12 or older and 30.0 million (70%) males aged 12 or older had used alcohol during the past year. Also, 15.2 million (12%) females and 19.8 million (17%) males had used an illicit drug during the past year. Females were less likely than males to be dependent on or abuse alcohol or an illicit drug.
- Among those aged 12 to 17, 9% of both females and males were dependent on or abusing alcohol or an illicit drug.

- Among respondents aged 18 or older, males were more likely than females to be dependent on or abusing alcohol or an illicit drug. Among those aged 18 to 25, the rate of dependence or abuse was 26.3% for males and 15.7% for females.
- Among those aged 26 or older, males were twice as likely as females to be dependent on or abusing alcohol or an illicit drug. The rate of substance dependence or abuse for those age 50 or older was 4.9% for males and 1.5% for females.
- In general, males were more likely than females to report past-month alcohol use. In 2003, 57.3% of males aged 12 or older were current drinkers compared with 43.2% of females. However, for the youngest age group (12 to 17), the rates were not significantly different (17.1% for males vs. 18.3% for females).

Runaways

- Among youth aged 12 or 13, 6% had run away and among those aged 16 or 17, 10% had run away from home in the past 12 months. Youth who had run away from home in the past 12 months were more likely to have used alcohol, marijuana, or an illicit drug other than marijuana in the past year than youth who had not run away.
- Alcohol was used in the past year by 50% of the runaway youth aged 12 to 17 and by 33% of those who had not run away from home.
- Marijuana was used in the past year by 23% of the runaways aged 12 to 18 and by 12% of those who had not run away from home.

Inhalant USE

- In 2002, more than 2.6 million youth aged 12 to 17 reported using inhalants at least once in their lifetime. Among youth, the rate of past year inhalant use was about the same for boys (4.6%) and for girls (4.1%).
- Inhalants are defined in the survey as "liquids, sprays, and gases that people sniff or inhale to get high or to make them feel good." The categories of inhalants asked about in the survey are
  - Amyl Nitrite, "poppers," locker room odorizers, or "rush";
  - correction fluid, degreaser, or cleaning fluid;
  - gasoline or lighter fluid;
  - glue, shoe polish, or toluene;
  - halothane, ether, or other anesthetics;
  - lacquer thinner or other paint solvents;
  - lighter gases, such as butane or propane;
  - nitrous oxide or "whippets";

- spray paints; and
- other aerosol sprays.
- The categories of inhalants most frequently used in the youth lifetime were glue, shoe polish, or toluene (4.5%); gasoline or lighter fluid (3.5%); and spray paints (2.5%). Over half (53%) of the youth who used an inhalant, however, had used more than one type in their lifetime.
- Youth who had used an inhalant in the past year were about three times more likely to use marijuana, four times more likely to use prescription drugs nonmedically, and seven times more likely to use hallucinogens than those who had not used inhalants in the past year.
- The number of new inhalant users was about 1 million in 2002. As in prior years, these new users were predominantly under age 18 (78%), and about half (53%) were male.

How Youth Obtain Marijuana

- Based on SAMHSA's National Survey on Drug Use and Health, in 2002, over 60% of youth aged 12 to 17 who had used marijuana in the past year had obtained their most recently used marijuana for free or had shared someone else's marijuana.
- Among youth who obtained marijuana for free or shared it, blacks (18%) were more likely than whites (9%) or Hispanics (7%) to have obtained it from a relative or family member.
- Among youth who bought their most recently used marijuana, white youth (9%) were more likely than black youth (4%) to have purchased it inside a school building.
- Males were more likely than females to have purchased their most recently used marijuana.
- In 2003, slightly more than half of youth aged 12 to 17 indicated that it would be fairly or very easy to obtain marijuana if they wanted some (53.6%). However, the ease of obtaining marijuana varied greatly by age among youth aged 12 to 17. Only 25.2% of 12 or 13 year olds indicated that it would be fairly or very easy to obtain marijuana, but 77.2% of those 16 or 17 years of age indicated that it would be fairly or very easy to obtain this substance.
- In 2003, approximately one in six youth (16.1%) reported that he or she had been approached by someone selling drugs in the past month. Those who had been approached reported a much higher rate of past-month use of an illicit drug (35.0%) than those who had not been approached (6.7%). Between 2002 and 2003, there was no significant change in the percentage of youth who were approached by someone selling drugs (16.7% in 2002).

Drug Use among Incarcerated Youth

- Based on SAMHSA's National Survey on Drug Use and Health, in 2002, almost 1.5 million youth aged 12 to 17 had been in a jail or a detention center at least once in their lifetime.
- Youth who had been detained (i.e., who had ever been in a jail or a detention center) were more likely than youth who had never been in a jail or a detention center to have used illicit drugs, alcohol, or cigarettes in the past year.
- Past-year substance abuse or dependence was almost three times higher among youth who had been in a jail or a detention center at least once in their lifetime than among youth who had never been in a jail or a detention center.
- Prescription-type drugs were used in the past year by 21.2% of youth who had been in a jail or detention center, compared with 8.4% of the youth who had never been detained.

Exposure to Prevention Messages and Programs

- In 2003, a majority of youth aged 12 to 17 (83.6%) reported having seen or heard alcohol- or drug-prevention messages outside of school in the past year. Youth who had seen or heard these messages indicated a slightly lower prevalence of past-month use of an illicit drug (10.8%) than youth who had not seen or heard this type of message (13.7%). The percentage of youth hearing these messages remained unchanged from 2002 to 2003.
- In 2003, 78.1% of youth aged 12 to 17 who were enrolled in school during the past 12 months reported having seen or heard drug- or alcohol-prevention messages in school. This was similar to the percentage reporting exposure to such messages in 2002. Of youth indicating they had seen or heard these messages, the rate of past month illicit drug use was 10.4%, compared with 14.8% for youth who had not been exposed to prevention messages in school.
- In 2003, over half of all youth aged 12 to 17 (58.9%) indicated that they had talked with at least one parent in the past year about the dangers of tobacco, alcohol, or drug use. The estimate for 2002 was similar (58.1%). Youth who had talked with a parent about the dangers of substance use were less likely to have used an illicit drug in the past month (10.0%) than youth who had not had such conversations (13.0%).
- Youth were asked if they had participated in various special programs dealing with substance use and other related problems in the past year. The specific types of programs (and the percentages of youth

participating in them) were problem-solving, communication skills, or self-esteem groups (25.0%); violence prevention programs (17.2%); alcohol, tobacco, or drug prevention programs outside of school (13.9%); pregnancy- or sexually transmitted disease (STD)–prevention programs (14.9%); and programs for dealing with alcohol or drug use (6.0%). Youth participation in all of these programs, except violence prevention programs and programs dealing with alcohol or drug use, increased between 2002 and 2003.*

Research continues to show that drug use among children is 10 times more prevalent than parents suspect. In addition, many youth know that their parents do not recognize the extent of drug use, which leads them to believe they can use drugs with impunity. Alcohol and substance abuse correlate significantly with school vandalism, absenteeism, tardiness, truancy, discipline problems, classroom disruptions, violence, declining academic achievement, dropout rates, and automobile-related deaths. Marijuana, the most frequently used illegal drug, can result in impaired psychomotor performance and impaired immediate recall. Passivity and loss of motivation also have been reported (Cohen, 1981). In addition, decreased pulmonary function, bronchitis, and sinusitis have been reported for frequent users (Millman & Botvin, 1983).

Alcohol continues to be the drug most frequently associated with violent crime. America's schools have assumed responsibility for primary prevention and intervention activities. Ironically, schools are perceived both by those who sell drugs and by those who would prevent their sale as the single most important point of access to young people. Today, the activities of both groups intrude on instruction, discipline, and school safety.

Predictors of Alcohol and Drug Use

Prevention begins with parents and families, and requires the support of schools and communities. The most important tool we have against drug use is not a badge or a gun, it is the kitchen table. Parents can prevent drug use by sitting down with their children and talking with them—honestly and openly—about the dangers of drugs to young lives and dreams.

Barry McCaffrey, Former Director,
Office of National Drug Control Policy

---

* Source: National Survey on Drug Use & Health (2004) U.S. Department of Health and Human Services Substance Abuse and Mental Health Services Administration (SAMHSA) retrieved 12.04.04 www.samhsa.gov.

TABLE 4.1   Summary of Risk Factors for Drug Use

Domain risk factor	
Cultural and social	Laws favorable to drug use
	Social norms favorable to drug use
	Availability of drugs
	Extreme economic deprivations
	Neighborhood disorganization
Interpersonal	Parent and family drug use
	Positive family attitudes toward drug use
	Poor or inconsistent family management practices
	Family conflict and disruption
	Peer rejection
Psychobehavioral	Association with drug-using peers
	Early or persistent problem behavior
	Academic failure
	Low commitment to school
	Alienation
	Rebelliousness
	Favorable attitudes toward drug use
	Early onset of drug use
Biogenetic	Inherited susceptibility to drug abuse
	Psychophysiological vulnerability to drug effects

Source: From *Identifying High-Risk Youth: Prevalence and Patterns of Adolescent Drug Abuse* by M. D. Newcomb, Rockville, MD: Division of Clinical and Services Research, National Institute on Drug Abuse. Copyright 1995 by National Institute of Drug Abuse. Reprinted with permission.

Family Factors

It is estimated that 28 million Americans have at least one addicted parent. Parental drug use is correlated with initiation of use of many substances, as is parental use of alcohol and other legal drugs. Children of alcoholics are four times more likely to become chemically dependent than the rest of the population. Research on family dynamics reveals that children of alcoholics suffer emotional damage, which may create a predisposition to alcoholism. In addition, children of chemically dependent parents have a high probability of marrying chemically dependent spouses (Berkowitz & Persins, 1988; Brook, Whiteman, & Gordon, 1983; Gravitz & Bowden, 1985).

Further, the self-esteem of children who grow up with alcoholism often is severely damaged. Children from alcoholic homes often have self-defeating expectations. For example, many criticize their accomplishments when they succeed. The enabling atmosphere in the alcoholic home can cause children to feel they must be perfect or their parents will not love them, or that what they do is never good enough. Years later, the grown child as employee experiences greater anxiety, stress, and dissatisfaction with self and performance that comes from feeling "not good enough" (Martin, 1988).

When there is a standard or a performance level to be met, children of alcoholics worry about their ability to meet that standard (as do children from any dysfunctional home environment). They reexperience their anxiety, their all-or-nothing thinking, their sense of inadequacy, their guilt, and their lack of self-esteem (Gravitz & Bowden, 1985). These are the children who have mastered the art of "looking good"—of concealing the reality of their lives by overachieving, striving for perfection—so that no one will suspect what they are really living with or without (Black, 1984).

Among the problems children of alcoholics seem to carry into adulthood are issues of control, difficulty expressing feelings and trusting others, issues related to guilt, compulsive behaviors, and an overdeveloped sense of responsibility (Gravitz & Bowden, 1985; Wilson & Blocher, 1990). From another perspective, Goodman (1987) maintained that, although there can be little argument that some people growing up in alcoholic families are negatively affected by the experience, it is unwise to assume

- that all people are affected in the same way;
- that their experiences were necessarily negative; or
- that these people, as adults, are psychologically maladjusted or in need of counseling or a recovery program.

And one does well to remember that parental inconsistencies, double-bind messages, hidden feelings, incomplete information, shame, uncertainty, mistrust, and roles that stifle development and identity can be found in nonalcoholic families, too.

Family risk factors include parental absence, inconsistent discipline, poor communication, parental conflicts, and family breakup. Factors that place youth at risk include being latchkey children or coming from an abusive family, a single-parent family, a blended family, or a family with inconsistent rules for behavior (Black, 1984; Daroff, Marks, & Friedman, 1986; Harbach & Jones, 1995). However, Newcomb and Bentler (1990) found that family disruption per se does not lead directly to drug use; rather, family problems may lead to disenchantment with traditional values and to the development of deviant attitudes, which in turn lays the foundation for substance use or other high-risk behavior.

School Factors

A range of school problems—academic failure, poor performance, truancy, placement in a special education class, early dropping out, and a lack of commitment to education—are common antecedents to initiation, use, and abuse of alcohol and other drugs (Bahr, Marcos, & Maughan, 1995; Jessor & Jessor, 1978). Early antisocial behavior also has direct implications for substance abuse. Boys who are aggressive in kindergarten through third grade are at higher risk for substance abuse. Beginning in the fourth, fifth, and sixth grades, academic failure increases the risk for both drug abuse and delinquent behavior. For the early elementary grades, it seems that social adjustment is more important than academic performance as a predictor of later delinquency and drug use. Alcohol and other drug abuse is more likely to occur in students who do not care about their education or about going to college. As drug involvement increases, academic performance decreases. However, school problems themselves may not lead to drug use; rather, social factors that lead to poor school performance may be linked to drug involvement.

Peer Factors

Association with drug-using peers is perhaps the most strongly supported predictor of adolescent substance use (Bahr et al., 1995; Hawkins, Lishner, Catalano, & Howard, 1986). Youth who associate with peers who use drugs are much more likely to use drugs themselves. This is one of the most consistent predictors researchers have identified regarding experimentation and use. Even for children from well-managed families, simply being with friends who use drugs greatly increases the risk of drug use. Newcomb and Bentler (1989) suggested that modeling drug use, providing substances, and encouraging use are the most salient components of peer influence.

Influence of the Media

The average young adolescent in this country watches television 22 hours a week; some watch as many as 60 hours. By the time they reach 18, adolescents as a group will have logged more hours in front of the television than in the classroom. During this viewing time, the average adolescent will see about 1,000 murders, rapes, or aggravated assaults each year.

The young people who have the poorest chances in life watch more television than any adolescent group (Carnegie Foundation, 1990). Passive consumption of commercial television can lead to attention deficits, nonreflective thinking, irrational decision making, confusion between external reality and packaged representation, and juvenile obesity

(Carnegie Foundation, 1990). Further, on television, perpetrators of violent acts go unpunished 73% of the time.

Alcohol and drug abusers have cited the media most frequently as their source of information (Aas, Klepp, Labert, & Aaro, 1995; Peters & Peters, 1984). Previous studies suggested that drug users learned about drugs from their friends and their own experiences (Sarvela, Newcomb, & Littlefield, 1988). Yet behaviors presented in the media can be interpreted as "the norm" by many viewers. Many movies, for example, imply that people use substances for recreation or to enable them to cope better with stress. The implications foster the belief that it is all right to use drugs (Redican, Redican, & Baffi, 1988).

Attitudes, Beliefs, and Personality Traits

Attitudes, beliefs, and personality traits closely linked with substance use include lack of attachment to parents, lack of commitment to education, and alienation from dominant societal norms and values (Bahr et al., 1995; Hawkins, Lishner, & Catalano, 1985; Hawkins, Lishner, Catalano, & Howard, 1986; Hussong & Chassin, 1994) synthesized and correlated research descriptions of the personality traits and characteristics of alcohol and other drug abusers. These traits and characteristics included the following:

- High emotional arousal, anxiety, and panic attacks.
- Low frustration tolerance.
- Inability to express anger.
- Difficulty with authority.
- Low self-esteem.
- Obsessiveness and compulsiveness.
- Feelings of loneliness and isolation.
- Dependence and possessiveness in interpersonal relationships.
- Anger and hostility.
- Rigidity and inability to adapt to change.
- Simplistic, black-and-white thinking.
- Depression.

Psychosocial factors include external locus of control, low self-esteem, high need for social approval, low self-confidence, high anxiety, lack of assertiveness, and impulsivity (Forman & Neal, 1987). Pulkinnen and Pikanen (1994) found different protective factors (variables that buffer against substance abuse) between males and females. Their research confirmed that school success and prosociality were protective factors against problem drinking for both males and females. Yet they found one factor that led to widely different results in males and females: anxiety. For females it was a risk factor for problem drinking, whereas for males anxiety protected against problem drinking (Pulkinnen & Pikanen, 1994).

A high incidence of phobic and anxiety disorders also is found in substance abusers. A large number of chemically dependent persons experience panic attacks and high levels of psychopathology and report significant levels of distress and avoidance as a result of the panic. There is evidence that these individuals may be using alcohol primarily for self-medication (Cox, Norton, Dorward, & Fergusson, 1989). Newcomb and Bentler (1990) studied substance abuse in adolescents as a response to perceived loss of control, a sense of meaninglessness, and a lack of direction in life. Teenagers may use drugs as a means of temporarily alleviating discomfort connected to life events that they perceive as being out of their control.

Finally, certain negative or perfectionist personality traits are associated with alcohol use among adolescents. Negative personality traits can be predictive of increased alcohol use (Newcomb, Bentler, & Collins, 1986). Alcohol and other drug use appears to be associated with pessimism, unhappiness, boredom, aggression, frustration, impulsiveness, distrust, cynicism, rigidity, and dissatisfaction (Kozicki, 1986). In addition, various studies have pointed out that the rates for both suicide and suicide attempts are between 5 and 20 times greater for drug abusers than for the general population (Allen, 1985; Cox, Norton, Dorward, & Fergusson, 1989; Hussong & Chassin, 1994). Substance abusers usually have long histories of abuse, extremely strong defenses against change, and relatively little ability to follow through on commitments (Schneider & Googins, 1989).

Defense Mechanisms

Defense mechanisms are cognitive processes that individuals use to distance themselves from situations that are unpleasant, threatening, or anxiety-provoking. Defense mechanisms are generated automatically and unconsciously. For the chemically dependent, defense mechanisms become embedded in the illness and are used to block reality. For example, denial becomes a defense mechanism when drug users become unable to recognize the unpleasant situations that result from their drug use. Even when adolescents face unhappy consequences of their chemical abuse, they often decide that the good feelings outweigh the consequences. They see the pain they are receiving from the drug use, feel bad momentarily, then regroup by using defense mechanisms such as making excuses, making promises, and rationalizing to continue their use (Brook, Whiteman,

& Gordon, 1983). This dysfunctional cognitive process affects both them and their relationships.

Adolescents continually struggle with boundary and identity issues. The transition from adolescence to young adulthood is fraught with difficult decisions and important changes that set the direction for one's life. The stress of this life transition may contribute to the use of alcohol to relieve discomfort and anxiety (Newcomb, Bentler, & Collins, 1986).

Research on risk and resiliency factors indicates that substance use by youth is associated with multiple factors. Programs must be comprehensive and all-inclusive. Schools and communities must identify ways to integrate the prevention message into multiple service areas—including community agencies, health services, the courts, clergy, businesses, and education—to provide comprehensive services for youth and their families. Until the alcohol and drug problem is controlled, we cannot expect other adolescent problems—teen pregnancy, suicide, violence, poor academic performance, and juvenile crime—to diminish significantly.

Concurrently, providing awareness, information, and motivation to "just say no" is not enough. The goals of early intervention with children and adolescents should include these:

- Establish a warm and caring environment.
- Help children understand and express their feelings.
- Help children understand the effects of alcoholism on their families and on themselves.
- Promote friendships and reduce isolation.
- Generate openness to formal and informal help.
- Improve coping skills and reinforce new ways of expressing emotions (National Institute on Alcohol Abuse and Alcoholism, 1990).

Substance abuse prevention programs that help youth to develop social and emotional coping skills have received empirical support. The social and emotional approach views alcohol and other drug use as a socially learned behavior—having both purpose and function—that is the result of social and emotional factors. Information, education, and skill-based training, such as training in assertiveness and decision-making skills, can help the adolescent make informed decisions about high-risk behavior such as substance abuse (McWhirter, McWhirter, & McWhirter, 1993). Dryfoos (1990) maintained that incorporating behavioral, cognitive, and affective strategies is important in prevention efforts. Drug-specific assertiveness training and peer-pressure refusal skills also seem to have a positive effect in reducing experimental drug use. Social skills training for adolescents has been associated with positive outcomes such as improved self-esteem, increased problem-solving and assertiveness skills, refusal of drugs, and refusal of sex (Thompson, Bundy, & Broncheau, 1995).

The Life Skills Training (LST) program encompasses affective, cognitive, and behavioral components, including short- and long-range consequences of use, critical-thinking skills, decision-making skills, anxiety-coping skills, and social skills to resist peer pressure (Botvin,1983; Botvin & Botvin, 1997; Botvin & Griffin, 2001; Botvin, Griffin, Paul, & Macaulay, 2003). The social inoculation model assumes that resistance to social pressures for substance abuse will be greater if the individual has been given experience with social pressures in a controlled setting.

The LTS program (Botvin 1983) teaches general life skills and skills specifically related to substance abuse and other self-defeating behaviors. The 10-week training sessions consist of five major components:

1. **Cognitive.** Presents information concerning short- and long-term consequences of substance abuse, prevalence rates, social acceptability, and the process of becoming dependent on tobacco, alcohol, and marijuana.
2. **Decision-making.** Addresses the process of critical thinking and decision making.
3. **Anxiety management.** Provides youth with cognitive and behavioral techniques, such as imagery and physical relaxation, to cope with anxiety.
4. **Social skills training.** Includes general social and communication skills and assertiveness training, which can be used to resist peer pressure.
5. **Self-improvement.** Provides youth with the principles of behavioral self-management and improving self-esteem.

LST can be conducted by counselors, peer leaders, teachers, administrators, or community agencies.

Risk and Protective Factors

Research over the past two decades has tried to determine how drug abuse begins and how it progresses. Many factors can add to a person's risk for drug abuse. Risk factors can increase a person's chances for drug abuse, whereas protective factors can reduce the risk. Please note, however, that most individuals who are at risk for drug abuse do not start using drugs or

Developmental Perspective on Adolescent Alcohol and Drug Abuse

This section provides a developmental perspective on adolescent alcohol and drug abuse. Adolescence is a critical developmental period where youth struggle with identity, differentiate from family, and learn to master their environment. Alcohol or other drug abuse affects physical maturation, cognitive growth, peer group relations, sexual relationships, differntiation from family, belief system, academic chievement and career choices.

Developmental Task: Physical Maturation

Prominent developmental issues. Physical development is erratic and sometimes traumatic. Adolescents often feel insecure, ugly, or gawky.

Alcohol and other Drug Abuse (AODA) effects on adolescent health. Vitamin depletion, AIDS, hepatitis, lung problems, over-stressed physical system, impaired hormone secretion (cocaine), loss of muscle tone due to lethargy and lack of exercise.

Developmental Task: Cognitive Growth

Prominent developmental issues. Abstract thinking and reasoning begin to emerge. Adolescents begin to generate ideas of their own, have more thoughts about the future, show flexible thinking and systematic problem-solving strategies, and process information from a variety of outside sources.

AODA effects on adolescent cognitive development. Delayed, impaired, distorted.

Developmental Task: Membership in Peer Group

Prominent developmental issues. Adolescents often turn to friends for acceptance and reassurance. The peer group provides security, gives support to challenge authority, and follows a group code and standards.

AODA effects on the peer group. Peer pressure, diminished judgment, conflicts in interpersonal interactions with families and friends, increased risk-taking behavior, proclivity to act without considering consequences.

Developmental Task: Sexual Relationships

Prominent developmental issues. Increased dating becomes the focus of social life. Adolescents experience emotions such as anxiety, curiosity, confusion, pride, embarrassment, and stress. Values may conflict or need to be clarified. Peer interactions often revolve around flirting, teasing, and approach and avoidance issues.

AODA effects on sexual relationships. Reduces impulse control; promiscuity increases; AIDS, sexually transmitted diseases, pregnancy, and suicide (because of love loss) increase under the influence of alcohol and other drugs.

Developmental Task: Autonomy and Differentiation from Family

Prominent developmental issues. Conflict may emerge as a result of discrepancies among the adolescent's need to be assertive and independent, his or her skills and resources available to achieve independence, and parental perceptions and expectations. Control issues revolve around money, curfew, rules, decisions, and consequences. Defiance, anger, frustration, criticism, and self-doubt emerge from the tension of autonomy.

AODA effects on autonomy. Diminishes potential, clouds thinking, generates stress around trust issues, impedes this developmental task.

Developmental Task: Internalized Belief and Value System

Prominent developmental issues. Adolescents begin to select standards, values, and beliefs from among many systems in their environment to internalize for themselves.

AODA effects on internalized belief and value system. Adolescent feels guilty, becomes defensive, rationalizes use, drops out, or creates distorted systems to struggle against or succumb to.

Developmental Task: Academic Achievement and Career Choice

Prominent developmental issues. Social and family pressures revolve around being part of the "in" group, achieving scholastically, staying in school, and making decisions about one's future.

AODA effects on academic achievement and career choice. Interferes with academic progress, reduces motivation, damages reputation, and alters self-image. Preoccupation with alcohol and other drugs may distort values and alter priorities.

Risk and Protective Factors Where Interventions Can Be Effective

Risk Factors	Domain	Protective Factors
Early Aggressive Behavior	Individual	Self-Control
Lack of Parental Supervision	Family	Parental Monitoring
Substance Abuse	Peer	Academic Competence
Drug Availability	School	Anti-Drug Use Policies
Poverty	Community	Strong Neighborhood Attachment

Figure 4.1   Effects of alcohol and other drug abuse (AODA) on adolescent social, emotional, and cognitive development.

become addicted. Also, a risk factor for one person may not be a risk factor for another. Research-based prevention programs focus on intervening early in a child's development to strengthen protective factors before problem behaviors develop.

Risk factors can influence drug abuse in several ways. The more risks a child is exposed to, the more likely the child will abuse drugs. Some risk factors could include peer pressure, poor relationship skills, and lack of impulse control. Protective factors could include a caring school and community and a positive relationship with parents. Other signs of risk can be seen as early as infancy or early childhood, such as aggressive behavior, lack of self-control, or a difficult temperament. As the child gets older, interactions in the family, at school, and within the community can affect that child's risk for later drug abuse. Family situations can heighten a child's risk for later drug abuse, for example, when there is a lack of attachment and nurturing by parents or caregivers, ineffective parenting, or a caregiver who abuses drugs.

Structured Interventions for High-Risk Behaviors

Therapeutic Initiatives

Enabling is camouflaging addiction by telling family, friends, employers, or neighbors that the addicted person has some malady (e.g., the flu, a migraine, a cold) to explain why that person was absent from school, work, or a social occasion;

taking upon themselves the major responsibilities of running a household or a business or an office; becoming acutely responsive to the addictive person's mood swings; rescuing the addicted person by driving when that person is incapable; cleaning up after they have become sick from drinking; bailing that person out of jail, then minimizing the situation, telling oneself "Things could be worse." (Storti, 1988, p. 13)

Therapeutic intervention can be informational, educational, or more comprehensive, depending on the climate and resources within the school, the home, and the community. Often, intervention focuses on the concept of *enabling*. Enablers are those who allow drug problems to continue or worsen by preventing the drug user from experiencing the consequences of his or her actions in order to enhance, maintain, or promote the enablers' sense of well-being.

Exemplary Programs for Drug Abuse Prevention

The programs shown in Table 4.2 have been designated by the U.S. Department of Education 2004 as exemplary programs for reducing the risk of alcohol or other drug abuse.

The solution to the disease involves education, intervention, and follow-up support. It is important to "carefront" the person, sharing concerns without lecturing, threatening, or berating the individual. Intervention often involves a team of people close to the individual who share the same concerns, who want the individual to regain control of his or her life. After treatment, it is critical that a support group become available to prevent alcohol or drug relapse.

Interventions can involve collaborative partnerships between community agencies such as the local community services board, office of youth services, and health department, and public–private partnerships with organizations that foster the well-being children and adolescents. The current climate in most cities across the nation is one of collaboration. It is important to share the responsibility when nurturing young people. The following sections present counseling treatment and session plans for structured interventions for high-risk behaviors, including a multimodal treatment plan. The chapter concludes with a section outlining primary prevention initiatives.

Treatment Plan: Stress Management

Counseling intention: To manage the situation causing the stress (problem-focused coping) and relieve or regulate the emotional responses associated with the stress (emotion-focused coping).

Table 4.2 Exemplary Programs at a Glance

Exemplary programs	Emphasis	Grade level	Duration and intensity	Costs, materials, training*
Athletes Training and Learning to Avoid Steroids (ATLAS)	Alcohol, tobacco, and other drug abuse prevention	Grades 9–12	10 sessions 45 minutes per session Total 9 classroom hours plus 100 hours team contact	$149.95 for manual and 10 athlete packs $39.95 for set of 10 athlete packs, which include a curriculum workbook, sport menu nutrition booklet, and training guide Training for teachers and coaches additional
CASASTART	Combined building social competencies; violence prevention; and alcohol, tobacco, and other drug abuse prevention	Ages 8–13	Case management structure, ongoing, neighborhood-based	For cost of CASASTART manual guide (under development) contact program: 212-841-5208\ $4.25 for CASASTART Mission and History: A Program of National Center on Addiction and Substance Abuse
Life Skills Training	Combined building social competencies; violence prevention; and alcohol, tobacco, and other drug abuse prevention	Grades 6–9	15 sessions year 1 10 booster sessions year 2 5 booster sessions year 3 45 minutes per session	$625 for middle school set (teacher manual and 30 student guides) $275 for grades 6–7 $225 for grades 7–8 $175 for grades 8–9 2-day training for up to 20 participants
OSLC Treatment Foster Care	Treatment program	Adolescents	Ongoing case management structure Average stay: 7 months	$27,755 for 7 months per student

Table 4.2 Exemplary Programs at a Glance *(continued)*

Exemplary programs	Emphasis	Grade level	Duration and intensity	Costs, materials, training*
Project ALERT	Alcohol, tobacco, and other drug abuse prevention	Grades 6–8	11 sessions for grade 6 or 7 3 booster sessions 1 year later	$125 for training per teacher, including teacher's manual, videos, posters, and handouts
Project Northland	Alcohol, tobacco, and other drug abuse prevention	Grades 6–8	6 sessions in 6 weeks (6th grade) 8 sessions in 8 weeks or 4 weeks (7th grade) 8 sessions in 4 weeks (8th grade) Approximately 45 minutes per session	$245 per grade for materials for 30 students and teacher's guide $755 for materials for all 3 grades and community component $1,750 on first day for training up to 30 teachers $1,500 for each additional day (3-day training) National training events
Project TNT: Toward No Tobacco Use	Tobacco abuse prevention	Grades 5–8	10 sessions in 2–4 weeks 45 minutes per session 2 booster sessions 1 year later	$45 for teacher's manual and student workbook $18.95 for set of 5 workbooks 2-day training is additional 3-day train the trainer is additional Videos are optional
Second Step: A Violence Prevention Curriculum	Violence prevention and building social competencies	Pre-K–Grade 9	20 sessions in 10–20 weeks per grade level 20–50 minutes per session	$259 for pre-K kit $269 for grades 1–3 kit

Program	Focus	Grades	Sessions	Costs*
The Strengthening Families Program: For Parents and Youth 10–14	Combined building social competencies; violence prevention; and alcohol, tobacco, and other drug abuse prevention	Grades 5–9	7 sessions 2 hours per session 4 booster sessions 6–12 months later	$249 for grades 4–5 kit $545 for middle school/junior high kit (all 3 levels) $475 for Family Guide kit $379 for Second Step train the trainer workshop $175 for a leader's manual (sessions 1–7) $250 for a set of 9 videos $50 for a booster session leader manual $60 for booster videos (2) $2,500 for 2-day training $3,500 for 3-day training Costs average $10 per family for other supplies; booster sessions additional

* Current costs need to be verified with the program.

Source: U.S. Department of Education (2004).

Session 1. Introductions and overview of the manifestations of stress and coping skills.

Session 2. Deep breathing, muscle relaxation, and positive imagery exercises.

Session 3. Exercise and physical fitness. Deep breathing and simple yoga exercises for muscle relaxation.

Session 4. Time management and systematic organization. Role-play assertiveness and how to say "no."

Session 5. Identifying situations that enable self-defeating behavior, setting boundaries in relationships, and discussing the difference between assertiveness and aggression.

Session 6. Handling anger through patience. Life-skill practice. Role-playing appropriate and inappropriate anger responses to various experiences.

Session 7. Dealing with feelings and expressing emotions.

Session 8. Getting social support from friends and family.

Session 9. Problem solving and decision making. Brainstorming creative strategies for coping with stressful situations.

Treatment Plan: Education Group

Counseling intention: To provide a follow-up for violations of drug policies, to determine the student's involvement with drugs, to contract with the student and parents for "no use" of drugs, to offer a structured curriculum that will provide the following:

- Information about the health risks and legal, social, and emotional effects of drug use.
- Decision-making skills.
- Communication skills.
- Support for becoming drug free.
- Peer pressure–refusal skills.

The group was structured into seven sessions, covering the following:

Session 1: Introductions. Getting acquainted; establishing group rules.

Session 2: History of alcohol or other drug use. Stages of adolescent alcohol and drug use.

Session 3: Reasons for using chemicals. Identifying relationships between feelings and chemical use.

Session 4: Defense mechanisms. Identifying defenses related to alcohol and other drugs.

Session 5: Learning about the family illness of alcohol or other drug dependency. Identifying consequences of use. Identifying youth affected by family chemical dependence. Understanding effects of chemical dependence on the family.

Session 6: Working with feelings. Dealing with anger.

Session 7: Evaluation and closure. Final personal assessment. Developing plans and goals.

Treatment Plan: Aftercare Group

Counseling intention: To provide care to children or adolescents who have finished a recovery program, to support their drug-free lifestyle, and to prevent relapse.

One of the most difficult transitions for adolescents is leaving their drug-using friends and establishing new relationships. Essentially, recovering abusers must change their "playmates and their playground" and forge new, healthy relationships.

Session 1: Introductions. Getting acquainted, establishing group goals.

Session 2: Problem solving regarding recovery issues. Staying sober and staying clean.

Session 3: Exploring a sober lifestyle. Peer pressure–refusal skills.

Session 4: Identifying symptoms of sobriety. Planning relapse prevention. Establishing a buddy system for support and understanding. Identifying warning signs of relapse (HALT = hungry, angry, lonely, tired).

Session 5: Covering the 12 steps of Alcoholics Anonymous. Feedback and self-disclosure.

Session 6: Exploring family illness. Codependency and enabling behaviors.

Session 7: Learning stress management. Relaxation techniques, establishing an exercise regimen.

Session 8: Planning for wellness. Developing action plans and support networks. Integrating new behaviors.

Session 9: Closure. Opportunities for support group meetings.

Comprehensive Interventions with Multimodal Counseling

Another trend in counseling and psychotherapy is the move toward a multidimensional, multidisciplinary, and multifaceted approach that does not attempt to fit clients into a preconceived treatment plan (Lazarus, 1977,

1981, 1989, 1992, 1992a, 1992b, 1993). In multimodal therapy, the therapist–client interaction focuses on seven modalities of human interaction, known as BASIC ID: behavior, affect, sensation, imagery, cognition, interpersonal relationships, and diet/physiology. These modalities are both interactive and interdependent as they relate to behavior change.

Multimodal intervention uses techniques from behavior modification and incorporates elements of social learning theory, general systems theory, and group communication theory. It emphasizes growth and actualization rather than pathology (Lazarus, 1981; Seligman, 1981; Thompson, 1986). Its major thrust is educational; it views counseling as a broad-based learning process, aimed at helping clients function more effectively with concrete and measurable improvement. It offers a comprehensive structure for assessing client needs and developing treatment plans. This structure also allows counselors to maximize the use of referral sources and adjunctive modes of treatment.

Several researchers and practitioners have reported distinct advantages of the multimodal approach with youth (Breunlin, 1980; Edwards, 1978; Green, 1978; Keat, 1976a, 1976b, 1979; O'Keefe & Castaldo, 1980). Gerler (1977, 1978a, 1978b, 1979, 1980, 1982, 1984), Gerler and Herndon (1993), and Gerler and Keat (1977) applied multimodal theory to educational settings such as career education programs, school counseling offices, reading programs, and elementary classrooms. Smith and Southern (1980) applied multimodal techniques to the fields of vocational development and career counseling. Edwards and Klein (1986) outlined a multimodal consultation model for the development of gifted adolescents.

Research and case studies have demonstrated the positive effects of multimodal interventions on social and emotional development (Keat, 1985), on self-concept (Durbin, 1982) and on performance of various school-related tasks (Starr & Raykovitz, 1982). Multimodal counseling groups improved school attendance (Anderson, Kinney, & Gerler, 1984; Keat, Metzger, Raykovitz, & McDonald, 1985) and achievement in mathematics and language arts (Gerler, Kinney, & Anderson, 1985), and reduced procrastination (Morse, 1987) and psychoemotional difficulties such as oppositional defiant disorder, conduct disorder, and attention deficit disorder (Martin-Causey & Hinkle, 1995). Finally, Judah (1978) found that multimodal parent training provided a framework for achieving significant changes in parental levels of acceptance and for decreasing authoritarian attitudes, with benefits to elementary school children.

Multimodal therapy assumes that one effective way to understand clients is to assess their problems across the seven modalities of functioning. It provides a systematic and comprehensive assessment and treatment approach. Debilitating behaviors among children and adolescents are represented within these seven domains in a variety of ways. Lazarus (1992) provided a brief description of the BASIC ID as follows:

1. **Behavior** refers mainly to the over responses, actions, habits, gestures, and motor reactions that are observable and manageable. Adolescents' feelings or their need to conform to others' expectations may be one of the most powerful factors in determining their behavior. Behavior can be erratic and out of control or withdrawn and self-absorbed. What remains true is that every behavior is a communication.

2. **Affect** refers to emotions, moods, and feelings. Adolescence is often characterized by emotional highs and lows. Anxiety is a common malady. Self-medication with drugs and alcohol often begins to emerge in adolescence in an effort to cope with interpersonal pain. Adolescents often feel shut off from family and friends, with delusions that no one else has had a similar experience.

3. **Sensation** covers input from each of the five senses. Issues of sensuality are rarely addressed by adults, whereas the media bombards adolescents relentlessly and has a tremendous impact on high-risk behavior such as the use of alcohol, drugs, and high-risk sexual behavior.

4. **Imagery** includes dreams, fantasies, and vivid memories; mental pictures; and the way people view themselves (self-image). Auditory images such as recurring tunes or sounds also fall into this category. Dreams of future potential are often filled with feelings of anxiety regarding failure.

5. **Cognition** refers to attitudes, values, opinions, ideas, and self-talk. (Clinically, in this modality, the main task is to identify and modify dysfunctional beliefs and replace them with views that enhance adaptive functioning.) Adolescents often have irrational beliefs about themselves in relation to others, with unrealistic expectations such as "I must be liked by everyone" or "I must be the perfect student." Thinking is often black or white; such rigidity perpetuates anxiety.

6. **Interpersonal relationships** include all significant interactions with other people (relatives, lovers, friends, colleagues, coworkers, acquaintances, etc.). The peer group and a growing circle of interpersonal relationships are an integral part of adolescence. Negative self-perceptions often lead adolescents to regard themselves as uniquely unacceptable to others. Such feelings can be very debilitating, leading to self-destructive behaviors such as suicide.

7. **Diet/physiology** includes drugs (self-medication or physician pre-scribed), nutrition, hygiene, exercise, and all basic physiological and pathological inputs. It involves the panoply of neurophysiological-biochemical factors that influence temperament and personality. Adolescents are often preoccupied with the way they look. Extreme behavioral manifestations are recognized as anorexia nervosa and bulimia. Substance abuse often emerges as an attempt to fit in with peers or to deal with stress or for the purposes of self-medication for anxiety. Physical health and well-being are often neglected, with many health advocates claiming that we are creating a genera-tion of "couch potatoes" with serum cholesterol levels that exceed recommendations.

Essentially, the multimodal treatment intervention embraces four principles:

1. Clients act and interact across the seven modalities of the BASIC ID.
2. These modalities are connected by complex chains of behavior and other psychophysiological events, and exist in a state of reciprocal transaction.
3. Accurate evaluation (diagnosis) is served by the systematic assess-ment of each modality and its interaction with every other.
4. Comprehensive therapy calls for the specific correction of signifi-cant problems across the BASIC ID (Lazarus, 1992a, p. 50).

A multimodal orientation is considerably more systematic and com-prehensive than most cognitive and cognitive–behavioral approaches (Lazarus, 1992a). Treatment and intervention have demonstrated positive outcomes (Brunell, 1990; Gumaer, 1990; Martin-Causey & Hinkle, 1995; Weed & Hernandez, 1990; Weikel, 1989, 1990). Multimodal therapy is pragmatic and didactic in approach, reflecting a technical eclecticism in constructing a modality profile for the client. The multimodal therapy model has been successful in treating such maladies as depression, alco-holism, agoraphobia, obesity, anorexia, procrastination, teen pregnancy, and assertiveness deficits. Some of the most frequently used group tech-niques or strategies are listed in the following section. The multimodal approach assumes a holistic intervention with the intent to create long-term behavioral, cognitive, and emotional changes.

Multimodal Techniques

the following sections describe multimodal techniques that can be integrated into the child's or adolescent's treatment plan.

Bibliotherapy

This technique uses recommended readings or literature to facilitate therapeutic change. Goals of bibliotherapy might include teaching positive thinking, making self-improvements, encouraging free expression concerning problems, helping others to analyze their attitudes and behaviors, and looking for alternative solutions to problems. Bibliotherapy provides the opportunity to discuss story outcomes, behavioral consequences, and alternative behaviors. Martin, Martin, and Porter (1983) and Timmerman, Martin, and Martin (1990) cited the merits of using bibliotherapy with children and adolescents.

Contingency Contracting

A *contract* is a verbal or written agreement between counselor and client that facilitates the achievement of a therapeutic goal. It provides structure, motivation, incentives for commitment, and assigned tasks for the client to carry out between counseling sessions. It also can be viewed as a consulting and teaching technique for reaching agreed-upon goals and activities.

Meditation

This technique encompasses mental and sometimes physical exercises for relaxation, improved thought processes, and insight into self and the world. It includes transcendental meditation, Zen meditation, positive affirmations, and various yoga methods.

Communication Training

This technique teaches sending and receiving skills. To improve sending skills, the client learns the importance of eye contact, voice projection, and body posture. The client also learns to use simple, concrete terms, to avoid blaming, and to make statements of empathy. Good receiving skills require active listening, verification, acknowledgment, and rewarding the sender for communicating. Role-playing and behavioral rehearsal reinforce the development of communication skills (Lazarus, 1993).

Feeling Identification

This technique centers on exploring the client's affective domain in order to identify significant feelings that might be obscured or misdirected. For example, have the client identify emotional triggers, (such as anxiety) that lead to self-defeating behaviors.

Friendship Training

Friendship is dependent on sharing, caring, empathy, concern, self-disclosure, give-and-take, and positive reinforcement. Power plays, competitiveness, and self-aggrandizement undermine friendship. In friendship training, prosocial interactions are explored and put into practice.

Social Skills and Assertiveness Training

Often, clients need to learn how to stand up for their personal rights and how to express their thoughts, feelings, and beliefs in direct, honest, and appropriate ways without violating the rights of others. Assertive behavior can be reduced to four specific response patterns:

- The ability to say no.
- The ability to ask for favors or to make requests.
- The ability to express positive and negative feelings.
- The ability to initiate, continue, and terminate conversations.

Behavioral rehearsal and modeling assertive behavior are two techniques used to train clients to develop social skills and assertive responses (Lazarus, 1993).

Stimulus Control

The presence of certain stimuli tends to increase the frequency of certain behaviors. *Stimulus control* can increase desired behaviors by arranging environmental cues to trigger them. For example, a student who wants to study more might arrange her desk so that no distracting stimuli are present and sit at her desk only while studying and not while listening to CDs or talking to friends. Thus, sitting at the desk sets the stimulus conditions for studying.

Journal Writing

Clients may use journals to record their innermost feelings and thoughts about events. Children and adolescents often respond well to a homework assignment of keeping a diary; this technique also provides a feeling of closeness to the counselor between sessions. The journal provides the counselor and client with a record of feelings, thoughts, and events to be explored. In addition, it is helpful to have group members write comments at the end of every group session. An index card entitled *Group Reflections* provides a useful format. The cards can be signed so that the leader can keep in closer touch with each member. The index cards never should be read aloud to the group or referred to in the group by the leader.

Assertiveness Training

In assertiveness training, the client learns to stand up for his or her rights *without infringing on the rights of others.* Assertive behaviors include saying no without feeling guilty and learning to ask for what one wants more directly. Activities include instruction, modeling behavior, role-playing, and homework assignments.

Brainstorming

Brainstorming is a group problem-solving technique that collects everyone's ideas without evaluation or censure to gain all possible input before a decision is reached.

Cognitive Restructuring

At-risk children and adolescents exhibit an inordinate number of self-defeating beliefs (Bradshaw, 1988; Elkind, 1988; McMullin, 1986; Whitfield, 1987). It is crucial that they be taught to correct faulty belief systems, to "unlearn" irrational beliefs (for example, "I must be liked by everyone" or "I must be perfect in everything"), and to replace them with new ones that are more rational.

Relaxation and Imagery Training (RIT)

In this technique, the client is asked simply to relax and envision the desired behavior as if it were occurring at that moment (Carey, 1986).

Systematic Desensitization

This is a behavioral technique used to reduce anxiety about a situation or event. The client is taught complete muscle relaxation techniques. An *anxiety hierarchy* is constructed, from least anxiety-provoking experience to most anxiety-provoking experience. (In the example of test anxiety, the least anxiety-provoking time is a month before the exam, and the most anxiety-provoking is the day of the test.) An anxiety-causing stimulus is then paired with positive mental images and the process of relaxation. The pairing continues up the hierarchy (from least to most) until the entire hierarchy can be imagined without anxiety.

Cognitive Aids

Cognitive aids are short inventories, exercises, strategies, or experiential activities designed to facilitate awareness, knowledge, and greater understanding of experiences, thoughts, feelings, or behaviors. For example, have the client go on a guided imagery of a conflict with another person. Ask questions such as: "What did you do?", "How did you feel?", "How satisfied were you with yourself and the way you handled the situation?"

Behavioral Rehearsal

This technique uses repetition or practice to help the client learn effective interpersonal skills; decrease social, cognitive, or emotional skill deficits; and increase appropriate behaviors. It involves techniques such as teaching the client relaxation techniques and deep breathing exercises in order to deal with anxiety provoking situations.

Guided Fantasy

Using this technique, the counselor leads a client through a guided fantasy, in which the client resolves on paper some unresolved event of the past. Reliving past events and fantasizing different outcomes can relieve feelings of guilt or unfinished business. Guided fantasy also can be used to test out newly learned behaviors and to construct future scenarios on paper before actually trying the new behavior. An event can be rewritten to include more positive outcomes.

Role-Playing

In this technique the client assumes a role or character and acts out a scene for the purpose of better understanding him- or herself and significant relationships. For example, place a chair in front of the client. The client then stands behind the chair and introduces himself as he would expect his "best friend" to introduce him. Process this projected experience.

Role Reversal

This is a role-playing technique in which the client is asked to play a role opposite to his or her own natural behavior (e.g., an assertive role vs. a submissive role). The client also may play the role of another person he or she knows or switch roles with another person in a dyadic role-playing situation within a group setting.

The ABCs of Stopping Unhappy Thoughts

Clients are directed to respond in their journals when they notice that they are upset following a situation or an event (Maultsby, 1975):

A. **Facts and events.** Record the facts about the unhappy event.
B. **Self-talk.** Record the things you told yourself about the event.
C. **Feelings.** Record how you felt.
D. **Debate.** Debate or dispute any statement in *A* that is not logical or objective.
E. **Examination of the future.** "This is how I want to feel in the future in this kind of situation."

Self-Management

The major difference between self-management and other procedures is that clients assume major responsibility for carrying out their programs, including arranging their own contingencies or reinforcements. To benefit from self-management strategies, clients must use the strategies regularly and consistently. Clients should be given the following instructions:

1. Select and define a behavior you want to increase or decrease.
2. Self-record the frequency of the behavior for a week to establish a baseline measure before you start your self-management procedures. Record the setting in which the behavior occurs, the events leading to the behavior, and the consequences resulting from the behavior.
3. Using self-monitoring, either increase or decrease the targeted behavior, depending on your goal. Do this self-monitoring for two weeks. (A contract with the client will reinforce this process.)
4. Evaluate the use of self-management on the targeted behavior at the end of the contractual period. Arrange a plan to maintain the new, more desirable behavior.

Goal Rehearsal or Coping Imagery

Goal rehearsal implies the deliberate and thorough visualization of each step in the process of assimilating a new behavior. The deliberate picturing of a new situation enhances transfer to the actual event. Clients should be encouraged to be realistic in reaching their goals and not to expect perfection. For example, a client may still experience a severe panic attack when called on to speak in public. If he or she can reduce three out of five anxiety symptoms, that should be viewed as a success.

Reframing

This is a technique that relabels behavior in a more positive framework (e.g., "When you fight, you are demonstrating that you care about the issue"). This changes the perspective of individuals involved and allows them to explore new options.

Play

Cognitive and emotional development can be enhanced through constructive play (Eheart & Leavitt, 1985; Hartley & Goldenson, 1963). Play provides the venue for children to master fundamental physical, social, emotional, and cognitive skills and to learn new skills and receive feedback in a setting that is less threatening than directly talking to the child.

Modeling

Through the process of *modeling* (Bandura, 1976) appropriate skills and behavior can be demonstrated. Videotaping the behavior that is practiced also provides an opportunity for the transfer of learning.

The Step-up Technique

Some clients are paralyzed by anxiety or panic about upcoming events, such as a public speech, a job interview, or a blind date. The *step-up technique* consists of picturing the worst thing that could possibly happen, then imagining oneself coping with the situation—surviving even the most negative outcome. Once the client successfully pictures him- or herself coping with the most unlikely catastrophes imaginable, anticipatory anxiety tends to recede. When the real situation occurs, the individual may feel less anxious. Difficult cases may require self-instruction training (Lazurus, 1977, p. 240).

Self-Instruction Training

This technique is used to break a chain of negative feelings, such as fear, anger, pain, and guilt. Michenbaum & Cameron (1974) and Ellis (1962) showed empirically that negative self-talk contributes to people's failures and anxiety. At the other end of the spectrum, the deliberate use of positive, self-creative statements can facilitate successful coping.

Lazurus (1977) cited the following sequence of self-instruction to use with a client experiencing anxiety over an upcoming event:

> I will develop a plan for what I have to do instead of worrying. I will handle the situation one step at a time. If I become anxious I will pause and take in a few deep breaths. I do not have to eliminate all fear; I can keep it manageable. I will focus on what I need to do. When I control my ideas, I control my fear. It will get easier each time I do it. (p. 238)

Collective Community Initiatives

Positive relationships that emerge in one's life are dependent on the critical life skills that children and adolescents learn during the developmental process. For example, helping professionals need to stress communication skills and effective cooperation as critical educational goals. Group dynamics, techniques, and strategies can facilitate relationship skills among members of a group. The following activities are useful for support groups for youth. With some basic training in communication skills, process skills, and the developmental needs of children and adolescents, other adults can be on the team for youth empowerment.

Table 4.3   Treatment Plan: Multimodal Profile for Substance Abuse

Counseling intention: **To provide a more comprehensive intervention for substance abuse prevention. Lazarus (1981) provided this profile.**

Modality	Problem	Proposed treatment
Behavior	Drinks excessively	Aversive imagery and other self-control procedures
	Avoids confronting most people	Assertiveness training
	Makes negative self-statements	Positive self-talk
	Always drinks to excess when home alone at night	Change in stimulus conditions by developing social outlets
Affect	Holds back anger (except with siblings)	Assertiveness training
	Has feelings of anxiety	Self-hypnosis with positive imagery
	Is depressed	Increased range of positive reinforcement
Sensation	Has butterflies in stomach	Abdominal breathing exercises
	Feels pressure at back of head	Relaxation of neck muscles
Imagery	Has vivid pictures of parents fighting	Desensitization
	Received beatings from father	Retaliation images
	Was locked in bedroom as a child	Images of escape and/or release of anger
Cognition	Engages in irrational self-talk about low self-worth	Disputation of irrational ideas
	Has numerous regrets	Elimination of categorical imperatives (remove *shoulds, musts, oughts*)
Interpersonal relationships	Has ambivalent responses to parents and siblings	Possible family therapy and specific training in the use of positive reinforcement
	Is secretive and suspicious	Discussion and training in greater self-disclosure
Drugs/biological	Engages in self-medication; uses alcohol as an antidepressant and as a tranquilizer	Possible use of antidepressants (ask M.D.)

Conclusion

Today, children and adolescents are endangered primarily by their own behavior. As children grow into adolescence, they become increasingly at risk for ever more complex problems. Among adolescents, the three major causes of death (accidents, homicide, and suicide) and the major causes of serious illness or disability (sexually transmitted disease, unintended pregnancy, depression, and nonfatal accidents) often are caused by a cluster of risk-taking behaviors, particularly the use of alcohol and other drugs. Studies demonstrate that alcohol and other drug abuse correlates significantly with school vandalism, truancy, absenteeism, tardiness, delinquency, violence, irresponsible sexual activity, teen pregnancy, running away, poor academic performance, and automobile-related deaths. This high-risk behavior emanates from such elusive variables as low self-esteem, poor family support, poor relationship skills, immaturity, low frustration tolerance, problems with communication, and problems with authority.

Both prevention and intervention programs need to be directed at enhancing social, emotional, and cognitive deficits of youth. It is important to recognize that no single strategy or technique has demonstrated long-range implications (Wallack & Corbett, 1990). Broadly based school- and community-level prevention and intervention programs must involve a wide variety of agencies and institutions, target multiple subpopulations, and provide multiple interventions aimed at reducing risk factors and enhancing resiliency factors. Comprehensive programs must be of long duration in order to realize significant change. The importance of prevention and early intervention cannot be overemphasized.

Social, Emotional, and Cognitive Skills

If we are to help today's youth develop the social, emotional, and cognitive skills they need, we must focus on significant developmental issues such as the need to belong, the need to clarify values, the need to make good decisions, and the need to resolve conflicts. What follows is a series of exercises that helping professionals can use with young people to assist them in developing the skills they need to prevent high-risk behaviors.

Social Literacy Skills

Social literacy skills, which are essential for constructive interpersonal interaction, are significantly lacking for many of today's youth. Social skills are such interpersonal skills as the ability to know one's feelings and inner experiences and the capacity for handling relationships skillfully. Social skills are those behaviors that, within a given situation, predict important social outcomes such as peer acceptance, popularity, self-efficacy, competence, and high self-esteem. Social skills fall into such categories as being kind, cooperative, and compliant to reduce defiance, aggression, and antisocial behavior; showing interest in people; and socializing successfully to reduce behavior problems associated with withdrawal, depression, and fear. Social skills include problem solving, assertiveness, thinking critically, resolving conflict, managing anger, and utilizing peer pressure refusal skills.

Skills Boxes
Permission is granted to reproduce skills boxes for individual client use.

How to Say "No" and Still Keep Your Friends

Reverse the peer pressure with statements such as these:
"Drugs are boring. I can't believe you want to do that stuff."

Excuse yourself. Let personal obligations excuse your presence: *"I can't drink; I'm in training for football"* or *"I can't go with you; I have a concert and I have to rehearse."*

Give the person the cold shoulder; act preoccupied or ignore him or her.

Avoid places where drugs or alcohol are being used. Hang out with nonusers.

If pressure seems too threatening, walk away.

Learn to say "no" repeatedly: *"Want a drink?" "No, thanks." "C'mon!" "No thanks." "Not even a sip?" "Nope."*

Allude to the unhealthy effects: *"No. Drugs are illegal and unsafe."*

Change the subject: *"No thanks. By the way, are you going to Janice's party Saturday night?"*

Return the challenge: *"What's wrong? Scared to do it by yourself?"*

Put the blame on someone else: *"No thanks. I don't want to get into trouble with my parents, [coach, stepmother, etc.]"*

Blame yourself: *"No thanks, I usually end up getting stupid." "No thanks, drinking makes me tired." "No thanks. I want to keep a clear head." "No thanks, it's just not me." "No thanks, I just don't drink."*

Peer-Pressure Refusal Skills

Children and adolescents need skills in refusing peer pressure. High-risk behaviors can include drinking, drugs, and premature sexual activity. A list of responses follows:

Invent a routine excuse: *"I have to be at work at..."*

Use delay tactics: *"I'm not ready."*

Walk away and avoid the situation.

Shift the blame and try to make the pressure group feel guilty.

Act ignorant about how to do something.

Identify other things that are more important to do at the moment.

Get away from the situation as soon as possible.

Take control of the situation: *"I don't want to get high. I want to meet my girlfriend at the movies."*

Ask the pressure group to justify why you should do what they want you to do. *"What's in it for me?"*

Resisting Peer Pressure

This program involves five steps and can be used for high-risk situations that involve alcohol, drugs, or sex.

Step 1. Ask questions regarding the proposed activity to avoid potential trouble.

Risk Proposer: *"Let's go over to my brother's apartment after school."*
Risk Resister: *"What are we going to do over there?"*
Risk Proposer: *"Well, my brother and his roommate are away."*
Risk Resister: *"So?"*
Risk Proposer: *"I thought we'd raid his fridge for beer and wine coolers."*

Step 2. Name the crime and identify the consequences.

Risk Resister: *"That's illegal; we could lose our licenses just having the stuff in our possession, even if we aren't driving in a car."*

Step 3. Suggest an alternative activity.

Risk Resister: *"Lets go rent some movies instead."* A response such as this says that the friendship is important but the high-risk activity is not.

Step 4. Walk away, but leave the door open for the risk proposer.

Risk Proposer: *"No, I don't think so. That sounds pretty lame."*
Risk Resister: *"If you change your mind, I'll be home around four. I'm going to rent...."*

This response suggests an alternative that is positive and saves face on the part of the risk resister.

Defusing Anger

1. Let the person vent, uninterrupted.
2. Relax and go with the flow. Above all, don't become defensive.
3. Paraphrase. In your own words, repeat back to the person what you understood him or her to say.
4. Try to solve it together; compromise.
5. Keep listening.
6. Keep talking.
7. Keep seeking a solution.

Formula for Attentive Listening

C - H - O - I - C - E - S

C is *concentrating*. Focus completely on the individual's concerns; listen attentively; maintain eye contact.

H is *hearing* totally and completely. Ask for feedback to check for understanding.

O is being *open*. Listen for the "unspoken" words; listen for the feelings behind the words.

I is *insisting* on listening critically. Think about the content.

C is *comparing*. Read gestures and body language; check for accuracy; ask direct, open questions.

E is *emphasizing*. Learn to provide feedback with an emphasis on feeling and on content.

S is *sensing*. Ask questions to listen actively, check for understanding, use silence diplomatically, become an expert in paraphrasing and summarizing what others say.

Sending an Effective Message

If an individual's needs are known, problems or conflicts can be confronted without making others feel defensive. Confirming expectations and feelings involves three parts:

1. Owning feelings.
2. Sending feelings.
3. Describing behavior.

Ownership of feelings focuses on *behaviors and expectations*. The communication formula for sending feeling messages looks like this:

Ownership + Feeling Word + Description of Behavior
= Feeling Message

For example: "*I* (ownership) *am nervous* (feeling word) *about fulfilling the requirements of this course* (description of behavior)." Such feeling messages promote open communication.

Behavioral descriptions provide feedback about the other person's behavior without evaluating it.

"I" messages honestly express feelings and place the responsibility on the sender. They reduce the other person's defensiveness and resistance to further communication. Behavioral descriptions also provide feedback about the other person's behavior without evaluating it.

When you want to modify another person's behavior, "I" messages let the other person know

1. how his or her behavior makes you feel, and
2. that you trust him or her to respect your needs by modifying the behavior appropriately. "You" messages tell people they are not responsible for changing their behavior, whereas "I" messages make it clear that such responsibility rests with the person who receives the message, rather than with the sender.

Using an "I" Message to Change Behavior

Identify the unacceptable behavior. Without blaming, describe what the other person says or does that you find unacceptable. (Do not make inferences about the person's motives, character, or personality.)

Explain the effects. Describe in factual, observable ways how the person's behavior is affecting you adversely.

Describe congruent feelings. Describe your feelings about the effects of the other's behavior on you. "*I want to continue car pooling, but when you are late, I am late, and that gets me into trouble with my boss. He's a stickler about being on time.*"

Responding Assertively Using the "I" Message

The use of "I" messages is especially beneficial for responding assertively and for resolving interpersonal conflicts. Alberti and Emmons (1986) developed the following three-step empathetic/ assertive response model:

1. Let the person know you understand his or her position: "*I know it's not your fault.*"
2. Let the person know your position (what the conflict is): "*But I ordered my steak well done, not medium rare.*"
3. Tell the person what you want or what you plan to do: "*I would like you to take it back and have it cooked some more.*"

The communication formula for an assertive response is this:

"*I know* (their position), *but* (your position) *and* (what you want)."

Emotional Literacy Skills

The model of emotional literacy was first proposed by Salovey and Mayer (1990). Emotional literacy skills are intrapersonal abilities such as knowing one's emotions by recognizing a feeling as it happens and monitoring it; managing emotions (i.e., shaking off anxiety, gloom, irritability, and the consequences of failure); motivating oneself to attain goals, delay gratification, stifle impulsiveness, and maintain self-control; recognizing emotions in others with empathy and perspective taking; handling the relationships among thoughts, feelings, and actions; establishing a sense of identity and acceptance of self; learning to value teamwork, collaboration, and cooperation; regulating one's mood; empathizing; and maintaining hope.

Indications of troubled youth are all too familiar: school dropouts, drug abuse, unintended pregnancy, crime, violence, and suicide. Contemporary youth are confronted indiscriminately with a number of critical issues and decisions without the practice of critical social, emotional, and cognitive skills. Solutions lie within the combined efforts of the entire community—children and families, schools and institutions, and business and industry. Collective efforts are an investment with multiple returns.

Skills Boxes

Permission is granted to reproduce skills boxes for individual client use.

Handling Stress Effectively

1. **Work it off.** Hard physical activity—sports, running, working out, karate—is a good outlet.
2. **Talk it out.** Share your feeling of being overwhelmed and stressed with others. Sometimes another person can help you get a new perspective on your problem and suggest coping strategies.
3. **Learn to accept what you cannot change.** Modify your expectations about people and situations: If you have no expectations, you won't be disappointed.
4. **Avoid self-medication, such as alcohol or over-the-counter drugs.** The ability to cope with stress comes from developing strategies that work for you.
5. **Get enough sleep and rest.** Eat the right foods and schedule "down time" to give your mind some space and distance from stressful situations.
6. **Do something for others.** Another way of getting your mind off your own problems is to help someone else.
7. **Take one thing at a time.** Don't overobligate yourself. This creates even more demands that may be out of your control. Distance yourself from stressful environments.
8. **Make yourself available.** Don't isolate yourself from others and feel sorry for yourself. You aren't the only one experiencing stress.

Carefrontation

People need to hear you care about their well-being. It must be a genuine concern if confronting is to be effective; hence, a better term is *carefronting*. State the behavior, how you feel, and then reiterate your caring and concern:

> *"The concerns I have about you are because I care about you and our relationship."*
> *"I care about you too much to let this go and not say anything about what I see happening."*

Other guidelines include these:

Maintain a sense of calm. Be simple and direct. Speak to the point. Don't become emotional. It is all right to show your feelings, but do not direct anger at the person.

Keep on the subject and be specific. Talk about the problem and specific ways it has affected the person's behavior.

Be prepared for promises, excuses, and counteraccusations, especially when confronting drinking behavior. Denial and resistance to receiving help may occur.

Ask permission.

Gently point out discrepancies in the person's thoughts, feelings, or actions.

Help identify important relationships and behavioral patterns that promote self-defeating behavior.

For example: *"Doug, can I share something about you that I'm concerned about?"* If Doug says yes, proceed. *"Every Monday you tell me that you aren't going to drink on the weekends anymore, but by Friday you have already connected with someone to buy you beer. I care about you, and I don't want you to become dependent."*

Describing Feelings and Empathizing

Describing feelings is putting your emotional state into words so that others can understand what you are experiencing.

1. **Get in touch with the feelings you are experiencing.** Identify them specifically (e.g., anger, embarrassment, helplessness, hopelessness).
2. **Acknowledge and confirm those feelings.**
3. **Make a statement that contains the emotion you feel.**
4. **Share the feeling and your reaction.** *"I felt rejected and alone when you broke your date with me."*

Empathizing is identifying what someone else is feeling, and responding to it as if the feeling were your own.

1. Listen attentively to what the person is saying and try to understand the feeling behind the words.
2. Imagine how you would feel in the same situation.
3. Respond with the appropriate feeling words to share your own sensitivity to the person's circumstance:

"I feel so stupid in Herr Bradshaw's class, everyone is passing his German vocabulary test but me."

"Yeah, I understand the feeling. I had to stay after school a couple of days last year to really catch on to what he wanted in class. I felt embarrassed."

Self-Disclosure

Self-disclosure is sharing personal thoughts, feelings, or experiences that are unknown to another person. Self-disclosure enhances interpersonal relationships if it is reciprocated. Refrain from revealing intimate self-disclosures to short-time acquaintances.

1. Determine the level of risk. On a scale of 1 to 10, how risky is the information you will disclose?
2. If appropriate, move to a deeper level of self-disclosure.
3. Continue self-disclosure only if it is reciprocated by the other person.
4. Understand that everyone shares personal information differently.

For example, while being pressured to try cocaine, Bill responds, *"You know my stepfather is not my real dad. My real dad is doing time for dealing and doing drugs. I don't want to end up like him."*

Supporting

Supporting is a communication skill to help people feel better about themselves by soothing and reducing tension.

1. Listen to the message the person is sending, for the feelings behind the words.
2. Try to empathize with the person's feeling, try to walk in their shoes.

3. Paraphrase the other person's feelings.
4. Support them by indicating your willingness to be of help if possible.

> Here's an example: *"I've been on my fifth interview and I have yet to find a job."* Or *"I can understand your disappointment; you've really worked hard. Let's practice an interview session and I'll record it. Then, we can play it back and see how you look in an interview situation."*

Expressing Anger

There is a special formula for expressing anger. It goes like this:

> *"I feel ... when this happens .... I would feel better if this would happen ...."*

For example: "I feel rejected when you read the paper while I am talking to you. It would feel better if you looked at me when I am talking to you."

Stressful Coping Statements

Upcoming stressful events can be broken down into stages: preparing, confronting, coping, and making positive self-statements. The following stress coping statements for each stage can be used, modified, or developed:

1. **Preparing:**
    I've succeeded with this before.
    I know I can do each one of these tasks.
    I'll jump in and be all right.
    Tomorrow I'll be through it.
    Don't let negative thoughts creep in.
2. **Confronting:**
    I'm ready; I'm organized.
    Take it step by step; don't rush.
    I can do this; I'm doing it now.
    I can only do my best.
    Any tension I feel is a signal to use my coping exercises.
    I can get help if I need it.
    It's okay to make mistakes.
3. **Coping:**
    Relax now; breathe deeply.

There's an end to it.
I can keep this within limits I can handle.
I've survived this and worse before.
Being active will lessen the fear.

4. **Making positive self-statements:**
   I did it right. I did it well.
   Next time, I won't have to worry as much.
   I am able to relax away anxiety.
   I've got to tell ... about this.

Reflective Listening

Reflective listening is mirroring back to another person what he or she has said. To reflect back what was heard, use phrases such as these:

"Sounds like ...."
"In other words ...."
"What I hear you saying is ...."
"Let me see if I understand this correctly ...."

When you paraphrase, try to reflect both the content and the feeling that the individual is trying to convey. The following formula is useful: *"Sounds like you feel ... because ...."*

This is a perception-checking technique that allows you to confirm or correct information that is presented, for example, *"Sounds like you feel frustrated because no one seems to understand how important it is to do this job right."*

Resent, Request, Appreciate

This is a highly structured technique that is particularly useful in cases of disagreement or conflict. The strategy consists of three steps: share resentment, request, and appreciate. First, each person responds to each area in writing.

1. **Share resentment.** Each participant states what he or she dislikes about the other and outlines specific things that have been done to cause the resentment.
2. **Request.** Each participant tells the other what can be done to solve the problem.
3. **Appreciate.** Each participant identifies a quality her or she likes or finds admirable in the other.

Here's an example: *"I resent when you come late to class. I request that you leave earlier so we can get started and finish on time. I appreciate your sense of humor and your willingness to listen."*

Diffusing Anger in Others

The ability to diffuse anger can help to prevent conflict from escalating into violence. In a potentially explosive situation, try not to overreact or take the issues personally. First, let the person verbalize and express his or her anger; don't debate, argue, interrupt, or bring up past experiences—just listen. Second, as you listen try to understand the person's perspective. Put yourself in his or her shoes. Third, paraphrase in your own words what you understood the person to say. The formula is as follows:

1. **Listen.** Let the angry person verbalize. Don't argue or interrupt.
2. **Paraphrase content and feeling.** Make sure the other person knows you understand.
3. **Problem solve and compromise.** Explore what can be done to make things better; try to compromise so that everyone's needs can be met.

Dealing with Anger

Here are some things to try when you are angry:

Say something positive, if possible.
Use appropriate internal dialogue and positive self-talk.
Express how you feel and why.
Ask to discuss how to solve the problem.
Seven Skills for Handling Conflict and Anger

There are seven skills that can be used when you are angry and in conflict. It is important to RETHINK to gain control of the situation:

1. **Recognize** when you feel angry. Recognize what makes your parents, friends, or siblings angry. Recognize when anger covers up other emotions such as fear, stress, anxiety, embarrassment, or humiliation.
2. **Empathize** with the other person. Try to see the other person's point of view; step into their shoes. Learn to use the "I" message: *"I feel ... because ...."*

3. **Think** about it. Anger comes from our perceptions of situations or events. Think about how you interpreted what the other person said. What can you tell yourself about what you feel? Can you reframe the situation to find a constructive solution?

4. **Hear** what the other person saying so you can understand where he or she is coming from. Show that you are listening by establishing eye contact and giving feedback.

5. **Integrate** love and respect when expressing your anger, for example, *"I'm angry with you, but I want us to be friends."*

6. **Notice** your body's reaction when you are angry. How can you gain control of your behavior, and how can you calm yourself?

7. **Keep** your attention in the here and now. Do not bring up the past. Bringing up the past is disrespectful.

Note. Adapted from *RETHINK* (p. 4),1995, Washington, DC: the Institute for Mental Health Initiatives. Copyright 1995 by the Institute for Mental Health Initiatives. Adapted with permission.

Using Positive Self-Statements

When the conflict is resolved or coping is successful, be sure to give yourself positive feedback:

I handled that one pretty well. It worked!
That wasn't as hard as I thought it would be.
I could have gotten more upset than it was worth.
I actually got through that without getting angry.
I guess I've been getting upset for too long when it wasn't even necessary.

Note. From "Anger control: The development and evaluation of an experimental treatment," by R. Novaco, in *Thoughts and Feelings,* edited by M. McKay, M. Davis, & P. Fanning, 1975, Oakland, CA: New Harbinger Publications, Inc. Copyright 1975 by New Harbinger Publications. Reprinted with permission.

CHAPTER 5

Unintended Pregnancy and High-Risk Sexual Activity

"It's harder than I expected it would be. Harder. I'm 18 now and pretty soon I'll be on my own ... I want to go to college. I have to find somebody to keep my kids. And plus, I have to work—with two kids."

—Lakeisha, 18, mother of a 2-year-old son and an infant daughter

"She's 99% my responsibility and not 1% his ... I assumed he would be there like every day ... I'd really like him to get a job and help out with some money."

—Rachel, 17, mother of an infant daughter

Although statistics on sexual behavior do not summarize adolescent sexuality, they do confirm that many adolescents initiate sexual activity during a developmental stage characterized by risk-taking behavior and a propensity to act without a full sense of the potential consequence of their actions. The United States continues to have an alarmingly high rate of teenage pregnancies and a concurrent increase in youth infected by human immu-nodeficiency virus (HIV). In 1991, the pregnancy rate for females ages 15 to 19 was nearly twice that of Great Britain, which had the second-highest rate (Lawton, 1995). Each year in the United States, 800,000 to 900,000 adolescents aged 19 years or younger become pregnant. Adolescent pregnancy and childbearing have been associated with adverse health and social consequences for young women and their children. The CDC (2001) presents estimated national and state-specific pregnancy rates for adolescents aged 19 years or younger from 1995 to 1997. The findings indicate a decline in national and state-specific adolescent pregnancy rates during 1985 to 1987 and a continuing downward trend beginning in the early 1990s (Centers for Disease Control and Prevention [CDC], 2001).

Teen Pregnancy and High-Risk Sexual Activity in the 21st Century

Teen pregnancy remains a serious problem in the United States. Although the nation's teen pregnancy and birth rates are declining, there is still plenty of room for improvement. According to the most recent data available from the Centers for Disease Control and Prevention (CDC, 2001), 46% of high school students have had sexual intercourse, 14% of high school students have had four or more sex partners during their lifetime, and 42% of sexually active high school students did not use a condom the last time they had sex (CDC, August, 2003). As a result, approximately 860,000 teenagers become pregnant each year in the United States, and approximately three million cases of sexually transmitted diseases (STDs) occur in this age group (CDC, August 2003). These rates surpass those of all other industrialized nations (Panchaud, Singh, Feivelson, & Darroch, 2000; Singh & Darroch, 2000). Moreover, every year nearly one quarter of all new HIV infections in the United States occur among teenagers (CDC, June 2003).

There also is growing evidence that adolescent problem behaviors (e.g., sexual irresponsibility, alcohol and other drug abuse, delinquency, and school dropouts) are interrelated. Having an unintended pregnancy during adolescence can be viewed as a major developmental crisis. Potential negative outcomes include forgoing education, becoming dependent on welfare, and the dilemma of trying to deal with the developmental issues of adolescence while simultaneously trying to meet the needs of an infant. The following statistics further illustrate the issue:

- Since 1991, U.S. teenage pregnancy, abortion, and birth rates have declined steadily in every age and racial or ethnic group (Elam-Evans, Jones, Darroch, & Henshaw, 2002; Ventura et al., 2001).

Teenage birth rates declined in every state as well as in the District of Columbia and the Virgin Islands (Ventura, 2001). Research indicates that sexually active teens are becoming more knowledgeable and less reluctant to use contraceptives. More adolescents are also choosing to remain abstinent during early and middle adolescence (Darroch & Singh, 1999). Nonetheless, the United States continues to have higher rates of teen pregnancy, birth, and abortion than other industrialized nations (Darroch, Singh, & Frost, 2001; UNICEF, 2001). Adolescents ages 18 and 19 account for as much as 66% of U.S. teen births (Martin & Hamilton, 2002). Most teenage mothers come from socially or economically disadvantaged backgrounds; adolescent motherhood often compounds this disadvantage (Alan Guttmacher Institute, 1994, 1998; Kaufmann, Spitz, Strauss, Morris, Santelli, Koonin, & Marks, 1998).

- Teen pregnancy rates have reached historic lows, dropping 25% from 1990 to 1999. The birth rate dropped 19% and the abortion rate was down 39% in this age group. More recent data indicate the teen birth rate has continued to drop through 2002, which is a decrease of 28% (CDC, 1998).
- Pregnancy rates for women in their 30s and over have been increasing modestly since the mid-1990s (CDC, 1998).

Race and Ethnicity

- The 1999 pregnancy rates for black and Hispanic teenagers were more than twice the rate of non-Hispanic white teens. These differences narrowed for women in their 20s and disappeared by age 35 (CDC, 1998).
- Black women had an average of 4.5 pregnancies during their lifetimes, compared with 4.1 pregnancies for Hispanic women and 2.7 for non-Hispanic white women. The lifetime pregnancy rate is calculated by projecting pregnancy rates by age over the course of a woman's childbearing years (CDC, 1998).

Sexual Behavior

Unprotected sexual intercourse and multiple sex partners place young people at risk for HIV infection, other STDs, and pregnancy. Each year, there are approximately 15 million new STD cases in the United States, and about one fourth of these are among teenagers (Kaufmann et al., 1990). Nearly 900,000 adolescents under the age of 19 become pregnant (CDC, 1998). In 2003, 47% of high school students had had sexual intercourse, 14% of high school students had had four or more sex partners during their lifetime, and 37% of sexually active high school students did not use a condom at last sexual intercourse (The Alan Guttmacher Institute, 1999).

Many Births Occurred to Teens Living in Poverty and to Unmarried Teens

- Compared to teens from higher-income families, poor and low-income teens are somewhat more likely to be sexually active and somewhat less likely to use contraceptives or to use contraception successfully. Poor and low-income adolescents make up 38% of all women ages 15 to 19, yet they account for 73% of all pregnancies in that age group (Alan Guttmacher Institute, 1998).
- Nearly 60% of teens who become mothers are living in poverty at the time of the birth (Alan Guttmacher Institute, 1998).
- Teenage mothers are much less likely than older women to receive timely prenatal care and are more likely to smoke during pregnancy. Because of these and other factors, babies born to teenagers are more likely to be preterm and of low birth weight and are at greater risk of serious and long-term illness, of developmental delays, and of dying in the first year of life, compared to infants of older mothers (Ventura et al., 2001).
- Adolescent mothers are less likely to complete their education and are more likely to face limited career and economic opportunities than women whose first children are born after age 20 (Spitz, Velebil, & Koonin, 1996). They are more likely to live in poverty and to rely on welfare (Annie E. Casey Foundation, 1998).
- Both adult and teen women today are less likely to marry in response to a pregnancy than were earlier generations, and they are less likely to choose abortion (Ventura et al., 2001). In 2002, about one fourth of all nonmarital births occurred among teenagers (Martin, Hamilton, Sutton, Menacker, & Park, 2003). Nonmarital birth rates were highest among women ages 20 to 24 and 25 to 29, followed by 18- to 19-year-old and 30- to 34-year-old women (71, 62, 59, and 41 per 1,000 women in the given age group, respectively). Teens ages 15 to 19 and 15 to 17 had lower nonmarital birth rates (35 and 21, respectively) (Martin et al., 2003).

Delaying First Sexual Experience

When it comes to delaying first sex among teens, progress is clearly possible. The percentage of high school teens who report ever having had sexual intercourse declined from 54.1% in 1991 to 46.7 % in 2003 (CDC, 2003). Still, almost half of those in grades 9 through 12 are sexually experienced, and approximately 6 in 10 have had sex by the time they graduate

(CDC, 2002, 2003). Moreover, one in five teens reports having had sexual intercourse before age 15 (National Campaign to Prevent Teen Pregnancy, 2003). Research points to several reasons why it is beneficial for teens to delay first sex:

- **Teens who begin having sexual intercourse at younger ages are more likely to express regret about their first sexual experience than are older teens.** A recent national survey found that two thirds of sexually experienced teens said they wished they had waited longer to have sex (National Campaign to Prevent Teen Pregnancy, 2003). The percentage was higher among younger teens, aged 12 to 14 (83%), than those aged 15 to 19 (60%).
- **Teens who have sex in their early teens have more sexual partners, are less likely to use contraception, and are more likely to get pregnant.** Adolescents who first have sex in their early teens have more lifetime sexual partners than teens who wait until they are older (Finer, Darroch, & Singh, 1999; Shrier, Emans, Woods, & DuRant, 1996). Younger sexually active teens also are less likely than older teens to use contraception (Manning, Longmore, & Giordano, 2000; Mauldon & Luker, 1996; Santelli, Lowry, Brener, & Robin, 2000) and are more likely to get pregnant and to give birth during their teen years (Manlove, Terry, Gitelson, Papillo, & Russell, 2000; Thornberry, Smith, & Howard, 1997). Note, however, that age alone may not fully explain observed differences. These increased risks may also reflect other aspects of these young teens that are not measured in the studies.
- **Teens who first have sex at an early age are more likely to have older partners.** This is troublesome because teens (both males and females) with older sexual partners are less likely to use contraception and are more likely to become pregnant or to cause a pregnancy than those with a partner who is close in age (Abma, Driscoll, & Moore, 1998; Darroch, Landry, & Oslak, 1999; Manlove, Ryan, & Franzetta, 2003; Zavodny, 2001). In addition, many girls who have sex at a young age report that their first sexual experience was coercive. Fully 24% of teen girls who had sexual intercourse before age 14 report that their first sexual experience was nonvoluntary, defined as having sex against one's will (Abma et al., 1998). Another study found that about half of nonvoluntary intercourse among females (aged 18 to 22) occurred when they were age 13 or younger (Moore, Nord, & Peterson, 1989). Nonvoluntary intercourse may also increase the risk of multiple partners, contraceptive failure, and adolescent pregnancy (Boyer & Fine, 1992; Laumann, 1996; Roosa, Tein, Reinholtz, & Angelini, 1997; Stock, Bell, Boyer, & Connell, 1997).

- **Teens in families with higher education and income levels are more likely to postpone sexual intercourse.** Having a two-parent family, parents with higher levels of education and income, or both is also associated with teens delaying first sex (Santelli, Lowry, Brener, & Robin, 2000). Youth whose mothers were teen mothers and those with sexually experienced or pregnant siblings also are more likely to have sex at an earlier age (Manning, Longmore, & Giordano, 2000; Miller, 1998; Mott, Fondell, Hu, Kowaleski-Jones, & Menaghan, 1996).

- **Higher quality parent–teen relationships help delay sexual initiation.** Teens who feel they have a high-quality relationship with their parents and whose parents communicate their strong disapproval of sexual activity are more likely to delay sex (Jaccard, Dittus, & Gordon, 1996; Miller, 1998; Widmer, 1997). So are teens whose parents closely monitor their behavior through supervision and rules about dating and outside activities (Hogan & Kitagawa, 1985; Miller, 1998). However, excessive parental control can be associated with *more* problem behaviors (Miller, 1998).

- **Attitudes about sex and peer norms affect timing of first sex.** Adolescents who personally feel that they should and will delay sex and whose peers also feel that they should avoid sex are more likely to do so (Carvajal, Parcel, Basen-Engquist, Banspach, Coyle, Kirby, & Chan, 1999; Santelli, Kaiser, Hirsch, Radosh, Simkin, & Middlestadt, 2004). Conversely, teens who believe having sex will increase others' respect for them or those who perceive that their peers are sexually active are more likely to have sex (Kinsman, Romer, Fustenberg, & Schwarz, 1998; Miller, 1998). In addition, taking a virginity pledge is associated with first having sex at an older age for those teens attending schools where less than half of their peers have taken such a pledge (Bearman & Brückner, 2001).

- **Other factors influence timing of first sex.** Teens who do well in school (Resnick, Bearman, Blum, Bauman, Harris, Jones, Tabor, Beringer, & Udry, 1997) and attend religious services (Halpern, Joyner, Udry, & Suchindran, 2000; Resnick et al., 1997) are more likely to delay sexual initiation. Girls who participate in sports also delay first sex longer than those who do not (Miller, Sabo, Farrell, Barnes, & Melnick, 1998). In addition, teens whose friends have high educational aspirations, who avoid such risky behavior as drinking or using drugs, and who perform well in school are less likely to have sex at an early age than teens whose friends do not (Bearman & Brückner, 2001). Teens who report they have been sexually abused (), who are already involved in other risky behavior such as alcohol and drug use (Kowaleski-Jones & Mott, 1998; National Center on Addiction and Substance Abuse, 1999), or who perceive that their peers use alcohol and drugs are more likely to have first sex earlier (Blum, Beuhring, Shew, Bearinger, Sieving, & Resnick, 2000; Costa, Jessor, Donovan, & Fortenberry, 1995; Kowaleski-Jones & Mott, 1998).

Other Complications That Result from Unintended Pregnancy

- Teenage girls with poor basic academic skills are five times as likely to become mothers before the age of 16; adolescent males with poor basic academic skills are three times as likely to be fathers as are those with average basic skills (U.S. Congress, 1986). Disadvantaged youth are three to four times more likely to give birth out of wedlock than are more advantaged teens (Robinson, 1988). Pregnancy is the most common reason that females leave school (Robinson, 1988).
- In actual numbers, more white than minority teenagers become pregnant, but disadvantaged minority youth account for a disproportionate number of teen pregnancies and births in the United States. Although 27% of the teenage population is composed of minorities, they account for 40% of adolescent pregnancies and births (Edelman, 1988).
- The social costs of unintended teenage pregnancy are enormous. Teenage pregnancy poses a substantial financial burden to society, estimated at $7 billion annually in lost tax revenues, public assistance, child health care, and involvement with the criminal justice system (Annie E. Casey Foundation, 1998).
- A strong relationship exists among teen pregnancy, poverty, and crime (Brookman, 1993). Census Bureau data showed child poverty in 1993 rose to its highest level in three decades, affecting 15.7 million children. Adolescent pregnancy and parenthood evolve from a complex and interrelated combination of factors such as culture, economy, family education, environment, and sexual development (Brewster, Billy, & Grady, 1993; Hofferth, 1991; Kiselica & Sturmer, 1993).
- Persons under the age of 20 account for one in four cases of gonorrhea, chlamydia, and genital herpes, and one in seven cases of syphilis (Brookman, 1993).

As of 1993, 300,000 cases of AIDS had been reported in the United States (Brookman, 1993). Of these, more than one fifth involved persons 29 years of age and younger. AIDS is the sixth leading cause of death among 15- to 24-year-olds. Despite growing public awareness of HIV and AIDS, the rates of premarital intercourse among female teenagers between 1985 and 1988 grew from 44% to 52%, an increase not seen since the early 1970s (CDC, 1991). Newly released data, however, indicate that there may have been a decline in teenage sexual activity. According to the 1995 National Survey of Family Growth, the proportion of sexually active females ages 15 to 19 fell 8% between 1988 and 1995 (Abma, Chandra, Mosher, Peterson, & Piccinino, 1997). The 1995 National Survey of Adolescent Males also found an 8% decline in sexual activity among teenage males since 1988 (Sonenstein & Ku, 1997).

According to the Alan Guttmacher Institute (1989, 1999), the United States now has higher teenage pregnancy, birth, and abortion rates than most developed countries in the world. The adolescent unintended pregnancy rate is 9.8% in the United States, whereas most European countries have shown an average of approximately 3.5% (Olson, 1989). Caught between peer values, parent values, and the image of sex portrayed in the media, adolescents frequently act impulsively, without thought to the consequences of their actions. The gross annual cost to society of adolescent childbearing—and the entire web of social problems that confront adolescent mothers and ultimately lead to the poorer and sometimes devastating outcomes for these children—is calculated to be $29 billion (Maynard, 1996).

Predictors of High-Risk Sexual Behaviors

A number of variables seem to predispose adolescents to risk-taking behavior. These factors have direct implications for school and community prevention and intervention initiatives.

Attitude and Expectations for the Future

Adolescents who see opportunities in their futures are more likely to delay pregnancy and childbirth than those who lack hope. Adolescent mothers often have a feeling of hopelessness about the future resulting from transgenerational poverty and economic deprivation. Codega (1990) found that some pregnant or parenting adolescents use indirect or avoidance-type responses more frequently as a means of coping with stress. Life skills in coping, problem solving, decision making, and conflict resolution could enhance feelings of self-worth and self-sufficiency in adolescents.

Poor Academic Achievement

There is a strong association between poor school achievement and pregnancy. Poor academic ability may influence the onset of sexual activity and early parenthood (Children's Defense Fund, 1986). A study conducted by

Northeastern University revealed that females 16 years of age or older with poor basic skills are 2.5 times more likely to be mothers than their peers with average basic skills. Males with poor academic skills who were 16 years and older were three times more likely to be fathers than their peers with average academic skills. More than one fifth of all girls who drop out of school do so because they are pregnant. No more than 50% of teenage parents eventually graduate from high school. In addition, teen parents are more likely to have difficulties getting employment. Finally, more than one half of the money invested in Aid to Families with Dependent Children goes to families with mothers who first gave birth when they were teenagers (Black & DeBlasse, 1985).

False Assumptions about Reproduction

Misunderstandings, false assumptions, and ignorance surrounding reproduction play a large role in teenage unintended pregnancy. The belief that pregnancy will not occur as the result of first-time intercourse is particularly widespread. Further, adolescents often do not have the future orientation needed to understand their personal vulnerability to sexually transmitted diseases. They may engage in risk-taking behaviors, such as sexual intercourse, without the cognitive ability or abstract reasoning to see the consequences of their actions (Hofferth & Kahn, 1987).

Higher educational aspirations, better-than-average grades, internal locus of control, and high socioeconomic status are positively related to contraceptive use. Variables associated with responsible sexual behavior include older age of initiation of sexual activity; stability of relationship with partner; knowledge of sexuality, reproduction, and contraception; higher academic aspirations; a realistic attitude toward personal risks; and the presence of parental supervision and support.

Family Influences

Girls who get pregnant often have mothers who gave birth in their teens. Parents of teen mothers and fathers often are considered by their own children to have "permissive attitudes" regarding premarital sexual activity and pregnancy (Robinson, 1988). There also are cultural differences in the value placed on having children. For example, striking differences were found in a rigorous fieldwork study designed to compare values related to parenthood of white, middle-class and black, low-income adolescents. Gabriel and McAnarney (1983) found that, although teenage pregnancy was seen as detrimental and threatening to the goals of achieving adult status in the middle-class, white subculture, low-income African-American teenage girls saw motherhood and its concomitant responsibilities as a pathway to womanhood. In a study of 300 adolescents, Thompson (1980) found that African-Americans expressed stronger beliefs than whites that children promote greater personal security, marital success, and approval of others.

Young girls also become pregnant as an expression of rage against early deprivation or out of a need to find someone to belong to, either of which leads to a potentially precarious attachment relationship (Bolton & Bolton, 1987). Within this context, for an adolescent who lives in poverty, a child represents the only tangible possession she truly owns. Finally, children who do not have open, supportive relationships with their parents are at higher risk for unintended pregnancies. Fundamental problems in parent–child communication about sexual behavior include lack of knowledge, embarrassment, unclear values, fear that discussion will encourage sexual activity, and inability to initiate and sustain conversations related to sex. Parents' education and religious orientation also affect their communication with their child about sex.

Child Abuse and Social Disorganization

A number of studies in the area of child abuse have linked youthfulness of the mother with child maltreatment (DeAnda, 1983). Adolescent mothers frequently have been described as emotionally deprived or rejected by their families. The term *affect hunger* has been used to describe the early impoverishment of the overprotective mother who tries to create a new childhood for herself through her child.

In an analysis of child abuse and neglect reports, DeAnda (1983) concluded that, although there is an association between teenage parenting and child maltreatment, child abuse may be a correlate of high levels of social disorganization in the family history rather than an outcome of youthful pregnancy. Further, Furstenberg, Brooks-Gunn, and Morgan (1987) found that teenage mothers have more than their share of out-of-wedlock births and marital upheavals, and their children are at increased risk for school and social failure.

Health Risks

Girls under the age of 16 are five times more likely to die during or immediately after pregnancy than women aged 20 to 24. Their infants have a higher incidence of toxemia, anemia, nutritional deficiencies, low birth weight, and retardation than infants of older women (Black & DeBlasse, 1985). A premature baby of a teenage mother can cost $158,000 in health care costs (U.S. Congress, 1986). In addition, approximately 400,000 children are born annually to mothers who used crack or cocaine during pregnancy; many of these drug-using mothers are also teenagers (Yazigi, Odem, & Polakoski, 1991). Chasnoff, Landress, and Barrett (1990) reported that about 14% of pregnant women use drugs or alcohol, which can cause permanent physical damage to a child during pregnancy. Add to this poor nutrition and low birth weight (variables that often affect teenage mothers and their children), and infant survival and future potential are significantly diminished.

Extensive medical research has documented actual changes in the fetal central nervous system in response to alcohol, crack, and cocaine (Chasnoff, Burns, & Schnoll, 1985; Chasnoff, Burns, Burns, & Schnoll, 1986; Chasnoff, Griffith, MacGregor, Dirkes, & Burns, 1989; Chasnoff, Landress, & Barrett, 1990; Lewis, Bennett, & Schmeder, 1989; Rodning, Beckwith, & Howard, 1989; Ryan, Ehrlich, & Finnegan, 1987). This has tremendous importance for schools, both academically and socially.

Teachers report that cocaine-affected school-aged children are impulsive and often violent. They are hyperactive, disruptive, unresponsive to discipline, and manifest learning and memory problems. Middle-school teachers have reported that the cumulative and sequential nature of mathematics poses a substantial problem to cocaine-affected teens. Further, social skills of cocaine-affected school-aged children are impeded by their inability to set limits or to recognize appropriate limits for speech and behavior (Waller, 1992). Cocaine-affected children are unable to catch nonverbal cues, and their efforts to establish relationships with others suffer because they do not understand what another's smile or frown means in terms of their own behavior. Other behavioral characteristics commonly seen in these cocaine-affected children include heightened response to internal and external stimuli, irritability, agitation, tremors, hyperactivity, speech and language delays, poor task organization, processing difficulties, problems related to attachment and separation, poor social and play skills, and motor development delays (Lumsden, 1990).

Waller (1992) maintained that social skills must be taught both verbally and by appropriate modeling. Direct instruction in sharing, greeting, and thanking are essential, and these are primary lessons children learn from play. However, play has no intrinsic value to crack-cocaine children because they are disorganized and gain little reward from their interactions and experiences with others. Play and games must be taught by direct instruction, through guided play, and under direct supervision. Without intervention, the impulsivity and inability to internalize rules of appropriate behavior will result in violence, early sexual activity, and drug and alcohol use (Waller, 1992, p. 60).

Adolescent Fathers

> Intercourse is not a problem for males .... Pregnancy is defined
> by society as the problem. Males can have as much intercourse
> as they like ... a problem occurs only when intercourse results in
> a pregnancy. However, what transcends this issue is responsible
> behavior, responsible sex. (Elster & Panzarine, 1983, p. 700)

Teen fathers are underrepresented in the research literature. Far less
is known about young, unwed fathers than about young, unwed mothers. Data from available studies indicate that young unwed fathers are
demographically a heterogeneous group: They come from all regions of
the country and all income and racial groups. Harvey and Spigner (1995)
found that males who were sexually experienced reported more frequent
use of alcohol and higher levels of stress, and were more likely to engage
in physical abuse.

African-American youth who father children outside of marriage are
not very different in other respects from their peers who have not become
fathers. However, Smollar and Ooms (1987) found that white unwed fathers
are more likely than their counterparts to have histories of socially deviant behavior (e.g., alcohol and other drug use and juvenile delinquency).
Pirog-Good (1995) found teen fathers more likely to come from poor and
unstable families and to have family members who are less educated. Of
infants born to teenage girls, 53% have fathers who are 20 years of age or
younger (Sonenstein, 1986).

Research shows that young men in their early 20s who have earnings
high enough to support a family of three above the poverty level are three
to four times more likely to be married than are young men with below-
poverty wages (Sullivan, 1988). As the educational requirements for entry
into the labor market increase and the remuneration for entry-level jobs
declines, the close relationship between fatherhood and providing support threatens to exempt increasing numbers of disadvantaged young men
from being responsible parents and providers for the families they help to
create.

Hendricks (1988), Hendricks and Montgomery (1983), and Hendricks
and Solomon (1987) examined the concerns expressed by Caucasian, African-American, and Hispanic-American teen fathers and found that adolescent fathers desired the following: relationship counseling with their
partners, their partners' families, and their families of origin; assistance
with career counseling, employment, job training, and education; health
care; instruction in childcare and financial planning; and emotional support. At this juncture, it is clear that the needs of teenage fathers are left out
of the dialogue on adolescent unintended pregnancy.

An early pregnancy that is unplanned (as most are for adolescents) generally is a crisis not only for the young woman but also for her family and for the baby's father, and should be treated as such by helping professionals (Maracek, 1987). Brazzell and Acock (1988) found that a pregnant adolescent's choices about pregnancy resolution are influenced in part by her own attitudes toward abortion, by her perceptions of the attitudes of parents and friends, by her parents' and her own aspirations, and by how close she is to her boyfriend. This suggests that the process of resolving an unplanned pregnancy should include significant individuals in the adolescent's life whenever possible.

Activities promoting high self-esteem may help deter young males from fathering children in order to enhance their own self-image. Teen fathers have a more external locus of control and could benefit from being taught responsibility for their actions and for their children's welfare (Pirog-Good, 1995, p. 15).

Risk and Protective Factors

It is important to recognize that sexual expression is a critical component of a teenager's development. Concurrently, it is important to guarantee that adolescents have appropriate access to accurate educational programs and services that empower them to express their sexuality in safe and healthy ways. Abstinence should also be promoted. Lower teenage pregnancy rates will follow as a natural outcome of these services. Table 5.1 shows the risk and protective factors that service providers need to understand in order to serve the needs of all adolescents.

A shift in attitudes toward teenage sexuality must occur in the United States to promote the development of appropriate policies and programs to reduce teenage pregnancy and high-risk behaviors. Currently sexual activity, rather than the pregnancies that can result from it, should be viewed as the problem requiring intervention.

Structured Interventions for High-Risk Behaviors

Therapeutic Initiatives

> In the broadest sense, efforts to help American teens develop responsible sexual attitudes and behavior are hampered by society's ambivalence about sexuality. This ambivalence is shown in the odd contradiction between glamorization of sex in the national media (where sex is usually shown as bliss without consequences) and the unwillingness of many national television networks to advertise contraception. "We are castigating our teenagers for what we ourselves are unwilling to discuss." (Elster & Panzarine, 1983, p. 703)

Table 5.1 Important Risk and Protective Factors That May Affect Adolescent Sexual Behavior, Use of Condoms and Contraception, STDs, and Pregnancy

Risk Factor	Protective Factor
High unemployment rate	High level of education
High crime rate	High income level
Changes in parental marital status	Two (vs. one) parents
Mother's early age at first sex and first birth	High level of parents' education
Single mother's dating and cohabitation behaviors	High parental income level
Older sibling's early sexual behavior and age of first birth	Parental support and family connectedness
Peers' substance use and delinquent and non-normative behavior	Sufficient parental supervision and monitoring
Sexually active peers (or perception thereof)	Conservative parental attitudes toward premaritalsex or teen sex
Older age and greater physical maturity	Positive parental attitudes about contraception
Higher hormone levels	High grades among friends
Alcohol or drug use	Positive peer norms or support for condom orcontraceptive use
Problem behaviors or delinquency	Partner support for condom and contraceptive use
Peers' substance use and delinquent and non-normative behavior	Good school performance; high grades among friends
Sexually active peers (or perception thereof)	Educational aspirations and plans for the future
Early and frequent dating	Conservative attitudes toward premarital sex
Going steady, having a close relationship	Greater perceived susceptibility to pregnancy,STD, HIV
Greater number of romantic partners	Importance of avoiding pregnancy, childbearing,and STD
Having a partner 3 or more years older	Greater knowledge about condoms andcontraception
History of prior sexual coercion or abuse	Positive attitudes about condoms and contraception
Higher perceived costs and barriers to using condoms	Greater perceived self-efficacy in using condoms or contraception

Source: From *Preventing Teen Pregnancy: Youth Development and After-School Programs,* by D. Kirby, N. Lezin, R. A. Afriye, and G. Gallucci, 2003, Scotts Valley, CA: ETR Associates and New York, NY: YWCA of the U.S.A. Copyright 2003 by ETR Associates. Reprinted with permission.

Today, high-quality family life education programs are offered in many schools. The literature suggests that successful programs focus on teaching the skills necessary for responsible and informed decision-making and include the following aspects:

- They expose youth to good *decision-making models* and give them opportunities to make decisions in real or simulated situations.
- They encourage youth to *explore their values and behavior* and to confront discrepancies between the two.
- They give *accurate information* about acquiring and using contraceptives.
- They provide opportunities to explore *alternatives to sexual activity.*
- They expose youth to the *realities of teenage marriage and parenting,* about which youth often have idealistic concepts.
- They teach that sexual thoughts, feelings, and emotions are normal, but *behavior must be monitored* for its appropriateness.
- They teach *effective communication skills* and provide opportunities to practice them.
- They teach new skills to *improve the students' sense of worth* and to help them understand their feelings and impulses.

Adolescents need structured experiences in building self-esteem, developing life management skills, and understanding long-term consequences of high-risk behavior. They also need education on the consequences of sexual experimentation and potential long-term consequences. Other skills youth need are analytical reasoning, interpersonal communication skills, and skills in recognizing and avoiding high-risk behaviors.

Research indicates that youth who participate in life-skill intervention programs have better problem-solving, negotiating, and communication skills; greater comprehension of reproduction and contraception; and more favorable attitudes toward family planning (Hofferth, 1991). Further, these youth place a higher value on sexual activity, pregnancy, and parenthood. When discussing sexual activity and parenthood, the message to teens is not simply "don't do it," but a more subtle "wait until you are better prepared." This message makes sense to teens whose futures hold promise, but for teens with poor academic skills, no high school diploma, and few job prospects, this message translates into an unacceptable "don't ever have children" (Sullivan, 1988).

The school's role is not to stereotype single parents but to build on the resiliency the child and parent bring to the school. Single parents often experience increased stress linked to finding childcare, solving childbearing problems, and meeting basic economic needs. Offering comprehensive social and health services on school grounds can ease the burden for both educators and families. Schools and communities need to improve the social, educational, and wellness prospects of all youth.

Treatment Plan: Teen Parenthood Support Group

Counseling intention: To provide youth with a place to speak freely about their parenting concerns, to educate students in childcare and development, to aid youth in locating community services of benefit to them as parents, to promote good prenatal care, to impress upon youth the importance of staying in school for themselves and for their children's welfare.

Students who have children may be referred to the group by teachers, counselors, concerned others, parents, or self-referral.

- **Session 1: Family planning and adolescent sexuality.** A local family planning agency provides a comprehensive workshop with discussion and pertinent literature for group recipients.
- **Session 2: Enhancing self-esteem.** This session focuses on participants' strengths. Positive reinforcement from other members is encouraged.
- **Session 3: Finding social support.** Local community agencies present available resources, such as social services, childcare organizations, and parenting groups.
- **Session 4: Problem-solving skills.** Members are guided through the problem-solving process, with repeated rehearsals and role-playing. The focus is on gaining control of life situations, to enhance the student's sense that he or she has the power to make things happen.
- **Session 5: Developing an informal support network.** Students are encouraged to develop a support network among themselves, to educate themselves in child development and child discipline.
- **Session 6: Addressing concerns.** Specific concerns of group members are addressed. The session focuses on enhancing coping skills and finding alternative solutions.
- **Session 7: Strengthening self-sufficiency.** Students are encouraged to build their self-sufficiency skills as parents and prospective employees, with a focus on responsibility, consistency, and encouragement.

Barnes and Harrod (1993) also developed a contemporary life issues clinic to work with teenage mothers. The program outlined these seven objectives:

1. "To increase the decision-making skills of youth.
2. To encourage responsibility for one's actions.
3. To encourage the development of coping skills.
4. To foster emotional growth and maturation.
5. To cultivate forward-looking, success-oriented attitudes.
6. To provide information in areas of health-related, sexual issues (e.g., pregnancy prevention, sexually transmitted diseases, HIV/AIDS prevention).
7. To provide information regarding the financial and legal implications of parenthood" (p. 138).

Successful programs also

- focus on specific behavioral goals;
- are based on theoretical approaches;
- deliver clear messages about sexual activity and contraceptive use;
- provide basic information about risks associated with teen sexual activity and methods to avoid pregnancy and STDs;
- address social pressures toward having sex;
- provide activities to practice communication and refusal skills;
- incorporate multiple teaching methods and personalize information to individual needs;
- are tailored to participants' age level, culture, and level of sexual experience;
- are long enough to cover all information and activities; and
- provide appropriate training for teachers or peer leaders who are committed to the program (Kirby, 2001).

To enhance initiative and motivation, Barnes and Harrod (1993) used a drop-in curriculum so that youth were free to choose the sessions that appealed to their interests and concerns. Topics included fitting in with the crowd, handling peer pressure, stress management, and self-esteem and date abuse.

Collective Community Initiatives

Developmental needs of adolescent mothers are to be assertive, to make good decisions, and to understand the consequences of high-risk behavior. Effective prevention programs must target multiple services and agencies to meet the needs of this high-risk population. The school, health department, social services, and court services should coordinate a systematic delivery of services.

Table 5.2 Treatment Plan: Multimodal Group for Adolescent Mothers

Modality	Problem assessment	Potential intervention
Behavior	Poor academic performance and school attendance problems	Self-contracting; recording and self-monitoring
	Negative self-statements	Positive self-talk
	Discipline of children by yelling or hitting	Teaching of training principles in child management
Affect	Feelings of little self-worth	Increased range of positive reinforcement
	Anger toward significant others	Exercises in anger expression
	Conflict with others	Behavior rehearsal / Role reversal
Sensation	Anxiety and depression over present circumstances and future goals	Anxiety-management training goal rehearsal or coping imagery
Imagery	Unproductive fantasies	Positive imagery
	Image of self as incapable	Goal rehearsal
Cognition	Poor study habits	Study skills training
	Assertiveness training	
	Lack of educational or occupational information	Career counseling; assessment and information
	Sexual misinformation	Sex education; bibliotherapy
	Expectations of failure	Positive self-talk
Interpersonal relations	Poor relationships with peers	Social skills and assertiveness training
Drugs (biological functioning)	Poor dietary habits	Involvement in weight reduction program; nutrition and dietary information

A multifaceted counseling approach that focuses on strengthening the adolescent through this difficult developmental crisis should be paramount. Resources should include individual counseling, small-group counseling, and collaboration and consultation with family members. Intervention programs should raise awareness of the risk of unprotected sex and enhance skills related to sexual negotiations.

Intervention also should consider the adolescent's belief structures regarding alcohol use and accountability for high-risk behavior under its influence (Harvey & Spigner, 1995). For both males and females, the strongest predictor of sexual activity is alcohol consumption. Gender-specific strategies should be considered in more comprehensive intervention efforts. Finally, comprehensive family life education that encourages abstinence, teaches youth how to say no, and provides contraceptive information has the potential to delay the onset of sexual activity.

Conclusion

Children and adolescents need to realize the emotional consequences of high-risk sexual behavior: emotional distress, guilt, anxiety, victimization, and sexual and physical abuse. They need to be aware of the physical consequences as well: sexually transmitted infections, HIV/AIDS infection, and cervical or genital cancers. Children and adolescents need life-skills training in such areas as problem solving, assertiveness, impulse control, critical thinking, and peer pressure resistance. Through a variety of experiential exercises, simulations, bibliotherapy sessions, and structured discussions, adolescents can learn skills critical to developing a healthy, positive sense of self.

The goal is to prevent problems before they happen and to provide a framework of information to deal more effectively with challenges that arise throughout the life span. Several programmatic approaches to pregnancy prevention exist. The approaches cited most often in the literature include encouragement for use of birth control, school-based clinics, condom distribution, HIV and AIDS education, family life education, enhancing life options, and encouraging abstinence.

Effective Teenage Prevention Programs
Based on the Principles of Best Practices

In prevention, there is a growing body of literature highlighting what works in prevention in various domains (e.g., individual, family, peer, school, community). Incorporating evidence-based programming is a major step toward demonstrating accountability. This is what is considered following the principles of best practices. One type of best practice is the use of evidence-based programs, which are often synonymous with science-based or research-based programs. The term *evidence-based* refers to a process that is based on scientific methodology. To determine whether a program is truly evidence based, clearly defined, objective criteria have been established for rating program effectiveness. Several examples of these criteria are

- the degree to which the program is based on a well-defined theory or model,
- the degree to which the target population received sufficient intervention (i.e., dosage),
- the quality and appropriateness of data collection and data analysis procedures, and
- the degree to which there is strong evidence of a cause-and-effect relationship (i.e., a high likelihood that the program caused or strongly contributed to the desired outcomes).

Ten programs that prevent pregnancy or high-risk behavior such as AIDS are provided in the sections that follow.

*Skills-Based Sexuality Education**

Be Proud, Be Responsible
This 5-hour session is designed to reduce AIDS risk behaviors in youth aged 13 through 18. It includes information about how sexually transmitted diseases (particularly AIDS) are contracted and how to prevent them; practice of skills needed to refuse sex, negotiate use of a condom, and use condoms; and examination of attitudes that may contribute to risky sexual behavior. Role-plays, games, exercises, demonstrations, and videotapes are all used to increase active participation and enhance learning. Educators already knowledgeable about AIDS and adolescent sexuality receive 16 hours of training in the delivery of this program; others receive 24 hours of training.

The results: In comparison with a control group, program participants reported that, over the 3 months since receiving the intervention, they

- had sex less often,
- used condoms more often,
- had fewer sexual partners, and
- engaged in anal intercourse less often.

Behavioral Skills Training †

This program takes place over eight group meetings, each lasting 1½ to 2 hours. Groups of 5 to 15 participants are led by trained project staff. The

---

* From "Reductions in HIV Risk-Associated Sexual Behaviors among Black Male Adolescents: Effects of an AIDS Prevention Intervention," by J. Jemmott, L. Jemmott, and G. Fong, 1992, *American Journal of Public Health, 83*(3), pp. 372–377. Copyright 1992 by American Journal of Public Health. Reprinted with permission.

† From "Cognitive-behavioral intervention to reduce African American adolescents' risk for HIV infection," by J. S. St. Lawrence, T. L. Brasfield, K. W. Jefferson, E. Alleyne, R. E. Bannon, and A. Shirley, 1995, *Journal of Consulting and Clinical Psychology, 63*(2), pp. 221–237. Copyright 1995 by American Journal of Public Health. Reprinted with permission.

curriculum includes education about how AIDS is transmitted and how to minimize or prevent the risk of transmission (including abstinence as a strategy). Other components include discussion and video about sexual decisions and values; practice using condoms and discussion of why adolescents might not use them; and role-plays using communication and assertiveness skills to help participants resist pressure to have sex, initiate discussion about using condoms with a sexual partner, and discuss HIV risk reduction information with peers. The curriculum also seeks to build accurate perceptions of risk for HIV, problem-solving skills in preparation for future high-risk situations, and social support from the group.

The results: One year after the program, young women who received the behavioral skills training were using condoms significantly more often than girls in an education-only comparison group. Only 12% of participants who were abstinent at the beginning of the program had initiated sexual intercourse one year after the program, compared to 31% of youths in the comparison group.

*Get Real About AIDS**

This school-based sexuality education program is delivered over 14 class periods and includes the following topics: teens' perception of their vulnerability to HIV; knowledge about HIV and other sexually transmitted diseases, including how they are transmitted and prevented; how to use condoms, if engaging in sex; skills needed to identify, avoid, and resist situations that may lead to risky sexual behavior; and beliefs and norms about sex and AIDS. Teachers use entertaining activities as learning tools, including discussions, role-plays, and videos. For the demonstration from which results are reported here, teachers attended a 5-day training session (a minimum of 3 days' training is recommended), and the impact of the intervention was further strengthened by posters displayed in schools and by student distribution of wallet-sized HIV information cards to fellow students.

The results: At a follow-up 6 months after the intervention, sexually active program participants reported that in the past 2 months, they

- used condoms more frequently than students in comparison schools and
- had fewer sexual partners than students in comparison schools.

---

* From "Preventing HIV Infection among Adolescents: Evaluation of a School-Based Education Program," by D. S. Main, D. C. Iverson, J. McGloin, S. Banspach, J. Collins, D. Rugg, and L. Kolbe, 1994, *Preventive Medicine, 23,* 409-417. Copyright 1994 by Preventive Medicine. Reprinted with permission.

Reducing the Risk: Building Skills for Pregnancy Prevention*

This is a skill-building curriculum delivered to 10th graders by high school teachers over 15 sessions of approximately 50 minutes each. The curriculum includes sessions on abstinence and contraception and gives students the skills to delay initiation of, or resist pressure to engage in, sexual intercourse, as well as skills necessary to obtain and use contraceptives for those who are already sexually active. Role-plays are used extensively, becoming more challenging as the curriculum builds upon skills learned earlier in the program. Examples of other exercises are visits to family planning clinics and homework assignments to interview parents about their opinions on love, sex, abstinence, and contraception.

The results: At a six-month follow-up, participants reported using contraceptives significantly more often than members of a control group who received traditional sex education. This effect was particularly strong for those who initiated sexual intercourse subsequent to their participation in the program.

Abstinence-Based Sexuality Education †

Girls Incorporated: Preventing Adolescent Pregnancy Project

The program, tested on a population of girls aged 12 to 14 who had never engaged in sexual intercourse, consists of two components: Will Power/Won't Power and Growing Together. Will Power/Won't Power is a curriculum held over six sessions of 2 hours each meeting that includes discussion, exercises, activities, and films. The goals are

1. to help participants recognize how social and peer pressure push young people to engage in sexual activity,
2. to review reasons to abstain from sexual intercourse, and
3. to explore the consequences of early sexual involvement.

Exercises and role-playing are also used to practice assertiveness skills for resisting pressure to have sexual intercourse.

Growing Together is an additional component designed to promote communication between parents and their daughters, presented over five 2-hour sessions, the first of which is attended by parents only. The focus is on giving parents and

---

* From *Reducing the Risk: Building Skills to Prevent Pregnancy* by R. P. Barth, 1989, Santa Cruz, CA: Network Publications and from "Preventing Adolescent Pregnancy with Social and Cognitive Skills," by R. P. Barth, J. V. Fetro, N. Leland,and K. Volkan, 1992, *Journal of Adolescent Research*, 7(2), 208–232.

† From "Effectiveness in Delaying the Initiation of Sexual Intercourse of girls Aged 12–14: Two Components of the Girls Incorporated Preventing Adolescent Pregnancy Program," by L. T. Postrado and H. J. Nicholson, 1992, *Youth & Society*, 23(3), 356–379. Copyright 1992 by Youth and Society. Reprinted with permission.

their daughters practice in discussing difficult topics, such as myths and facts about sexuality and pregnancy, values around sexuality, and dating rules.

The results: Among girls with 10 to 12 hours of participation in Will Power/Won't Power, 7% initiated sexual intercourse during the year in which the program was evaluated, compared to 14% among nonparticipants and 16% among participants with only 1 to 9 hours of participation. Participants in Growing Together were 2½ times less likely to initiate sexual intercourse than nonparticipants.

School-Linked Health Clinics*

A health clinic situated adjacent to one school and a couple of blocks from another provided contraceptive and other health services to students at the two schools. Students were African-American and came primarily from poor neighborhoods. A social worker and a nurse practitioner or nurse midwife from the clinic were placed in each school to assist in classroom presentations, lead small group discussions, counsel students, and schedule appointments at the clinic. Contraception was among the services provided at the clinic, which was open only after school hours.

The results: There was a 30% decrease in the pregnancy rate for a subgroup of students who had access to the clinic for the maximum length of time (2½ years), compared to a 58% increase in pregnancy rates among students at comparison schools. Students at the program schools delayed initiation of sexual intercourse an average of 7 months longer than students at the comparison schools.

Teen Outreach Program (TOP)†

Through TOP, at-risk students aged 11 through 19 participate in volunteer activities in their communities for a minimum of one-half hour each week. Volunteer activities vary widely, including participation in walkathons, working as aides in nursing homes or hospitals, and volunteer work at school. Groups of program participants meet for curriculum-based discussions at least once a week for 1 hour throughout the school year. Topics covered in these discussions include understanding yourself and your values, communication skills, dealing with family stress, human growth and development (including sexu

---

* From "Evaluation of a Pregnancy Prevention Program for Urban Teenagers," by L. S. Zabin, M. B. Hirsch, E. A. Smith, R. Streett, and J. B. Hardy, 1986, *Family Planning Perspectives, 18,* pp. 119–126. Copyright 1986 by Family Planning Perspectives. Reprinted with permission.

† From "Life Options and Community Service: Teen Outreach Programs," by S. Philliber, S. and J. P. Allen, in B. C. Miller, J. J. Card, R. L. Paikoff, and J. L. Peterson (Eds.), *Preventing Adolescent Pregnancy: Model Programs and Evaluations* (pp. 139–155), 1992, Newbury Park, CA: Sage. Copyright 1992 by Sage Publications. Reprinted with permission.

ality and sex education), and parenting issues. The general program emphasis is on making "good decisions about important life options"; prevention of teen pregnancy is one of these "life options" behaviors. These group meetings also provide a forum for discussion of the volunteer activities in which students participate as part of their experience in TOP.

The results: Students participating in TOP across several different sites became pregnant or caused pregnancy significantly less often than comparison students over each of the 5 years of this evaluation.

High/Scope Perry Preschool Project, Ypsilanti, Michigan*

The overall objective for this program was to prepare 3- and 4-year-old children for success in school. The children included in this evaluation were African-American and of low socioeconomic status. They received 2½ hours of intensive, high-quality early childhood education 5 days a week for 1 or 2 years (depending on their age), coupled with weekly home visits. The program was designed to promote cognitive, social, behavioral, and language development and to broaden each child's information base and experience. The program involved a high degree of interaction between children and adults. Teaching strategies incorporated active learning opportunities with a problem-solving curriculum. For example, the children set goals for themselves that they planned to accomplish each day. The families of participating children received home visits lasting 90 minutes each week, with the goal of promoting parental interest in their child's learning. Children receiving these services, along with a comparison group of children who did not receive these services, were followed for 16 years.

The results: By the time the children in this program reached adulthood, the children who participated in the preschool program had experienced fewer pregnancies during their teenage years than children who did not receive these services (68 vs. 117 pregnancies per 1,000 girls).

School–Community Program for Sexual Risk Reduction among Teens †

This was an intensive adolescent pregnancy prevention initiative implemented in Denmark, South Carolina. The approach included several components. Teachers were offered graduate-level courses in sexuality education, which promoted an integrated curriculum approach to sexuality education. Workshops for parents,

---

* From "The High/Scope/Perry Preschool Program," by L. J. Schweinhart and D. P. Weikart, in R. H. Price (Eds.), *14 Ounces of Prevention: A Casebook for Practitioners*, 1989, Washington, DC: American Psychological Association.
† From "Reducing Adolescent Pregnancy through a School- and Community-Based Intervention: Denmark, South Carolina, Revisited," by H. Koo, G. Dunteman, C. George, Y. Green, and M. Vincent, 1994, *Family Planning Perspectives, 26*(5), pp. 206–217.

clergy, and community leaders were designed to improve their skills as parents and role models. Students were trained to serve as peer counselors. Additionally, a school nurse provided contraceptive counseling, condoms to male students who requested them, and transportation to a family planning clinic for female students. Local media reinforced the message of avoiding unintended pregnancy and highlighted special events associated with the initiative.

The results: The teen pregnancy rate in this community was compared to that of other communities before, immediately after, and several years after the active phase of this intervention. Pregnancy rates declined from 77 per 1,000 women before the intervention to 37 per 1,000 immediately after the initiative was implemented. During the same period, the pregnancy rates of comparison communities also declined, though only slightly. Four years after the observed decrease, the pregnancy rate in the targeted community climbed again to 66 per 1,000 women, a rate similar to that of the comparison communities. Researchers concluded that this was due to the cessation of contraceptive counseling in the school, combined with the program's loss of momentum.

Researchers noted that communities attempting to replicate this program need to ensure that it not lose any of its important components to sustain reduction in teen pregnancy rates.

Abstinence-Based Sexuality Education Postponing Sexual Involvement*

This is a sexuality education curriculum for young teens, led by slightly older peer educators. It focuses on providing teens aged 13 and 14 with the skills to resist social and peer pressure to engage in sexual activity. Although information about contraception and basic reproductive health is included, a pro-abstinence message is emphasized.

The results: Fewer program participants reported being sexually active at 12 and 18 months following participation than did youth in a comparison group. Program participants who were sexually active reported using contraception more often than members of the comparison group.

Social, Emotional, and Cognitive Skills

In addition to exemplary programs based on best practices, the following social, emotional, and cognitive skills provide additional resources to integrate into exemplary programs that have empirically demonstrated a reduction in the incidence of unintended teenage pregnancy.

---

* From Preventing Teen Pregnancy: Effective Programs and Their Impact on Adolescents' Risk for Pregnancy, HIV & STIs, by U.S. Department of Health and Human Services, 1996, Washington, D.C.: Author.

Table 5.3 Best Practices in Pregnancy Prevention

Programs	Behavioral outcomes						Health impacts	
	Delayed initiation of sex	Reduced frequency of sex	Reduced number of sex partners	Reduced incidence of unprotected sex	Increased use of condoms	Increased use of contraception	Decreased incidence of STIs	Decreased number or rate of teen pregnancies/births
Reducing the Risk	◆					◆		
Postponing Sexual Involvement (augmenting a five-session human sexuality curriculum)	◆	◆		◆		◆		
Postponing Sexual Involvement (human sexuality and health screening)	◆					◆		
Safer Choices	◆	◆			◆	◆		
Reach for Health Community Youth Service					◆	◆		
AIDS Prevention for Adolescents in School			◆		◆		◆	

	Get Real about AIDS	School–Community Program for Sexual Risk Reduction among Teens	Self Center (school-linked reproductive health center)	California's Adolescent Sibling Pregnancy Prevention Project	Adolescents Living Safely: AIDS Awareness, Attitudes, and Actions	Becoming a Responsible Teen	Children's Aid Society—Carrera Program
		♦	♦	♦			♦
			♦	♦			♦
	♦	♦			♦	♦	♦
			♦			♦	
	♦				♦		
					♦	♦	
		♦	♦	♦		♦	♦

Table 5.3   Best Practices in Pregnancy Prevention

Programs	Behavioral outcomes						Health impacts	
	Delayed initiation of sex	Reduced frequency of sex	Reduced number of sex partners	Reduced incidence of unprotected sex	Increased use of condoms	Increased use of contraception	Decreased incidence of STIs	Decreased number or rate of teen pregnancies/births
Be Proud! Be Responsible! A Safer Sex Curriculum	◆	◆	◆		◆			
Making Proud Choices!	◆	◆		◆	◆			
Poder Latino: A Community AIDS Prevention Program for Inner-City Latino Youth			◆					
Seattle Social Development Project	◆		◆		◆			◆
Abecedarian Project								◆
Teen Outreach Program								◆

Note: Blank boxes indicate either: 1) The program did not measure or aim at this particular outcome/impact; or 2) the program did not achieve a significant positive outcome in regard to the particular behavior or impact.

Social Literacy Skills

Social literacy skills are interpersonal skills essential for meaningful interaction with others. Social skills are those behaviors that, within a given situation, predict important social outcomes such as peer acceptance, popularity, self-efficacy, competence, and high self-esteem. Social skills fall into such categories as being kind, cooperative, and compliant to reduce defiance, aggression, conflict, and antisocial behavior; showing interest in people; and socializing successfully to reduce behavior problems associated with withdrawal, depression, and fear. Social skills include problem solving, assertiveness, thinking critically, resolving conflict, managing anger, and utilizing peer pressure refusal skills.

Skills Boxes
Permission is granted to reproduce skills boxes for individual client use.

Being ASSERTive*

A. **"A" stands for "attention."** Before you can solve your problem, you have to get the other person to listen to you. Find a time, place, or method that helps them to focus their attention on you.

S. **The first "S" stands for "soon, simple, and short."** When possible, speak up as soon as you realize your rights have been violated. ("Soon" may be a matter of seconds, hours, or days.) Look the person in the eye, and keep your comments to the point.

S. **The second "S" stands for "specific behavior."** Focus on the behavior the person used, not on the person's personality. Otherwise, he or she will feel attacked. Tell the person exactly which behavior disturbed you.

E. **"E" stands for "effect on me."** Share the feelings you experienced as a result of the person's behavior: *"I get angry when ..."* or *"I get frustrated when ...."*

R. **"R" stands for "response."** Describe your preferred outcome, what you would like to see happen, and ask for some feedback on it.

---

* Note. From *A Leader's Guide to Fighting Invisible Tigers: 12 Sessions on Stress Management and Lifeskills Development*, by C. C. Schmitz with E. Hipp, 1995, Minneapolis, MN: Free Spirit Publishing. Copyright 1995 by Free Spirit Publishing, Inc. Reprinted with permission. All rights reserved.

T. "T" stands for "terms." If all goes well, you may be able to make an agreement with the other person about how to handle the situation in the future. Or you may "agree to disagree" (respectfully), or simply come to an impasse.

Even if no agreement has been reached, you have accomplished your goal of asserting yourself with dignity.

Assertiveness 1

Here are some ways to change someone else's undesirable behavior:

Identify your needs, wants, rights, and feelings about the situation. Establish a goal for what it is you wish to accomplish.

Arrange a meeting time that is convenient for you and the other person where a dialogue can take place.

Define the problem clearly to the other person.

Describe your feelings using "I" messages. "I" messages enable us to take responsibility for our feelings: *"I feel ..." "I need ...."*

Express yourself in an assertive manner using a couple of clear sentences.

Reinforce your statement by saying what the positive consequences will be when the other person makes the appropriate changes in the behavior.

Assertiveness 2

Assertiveness is the ability to state your position boldly and confidently, and to state clearly how you think and feel about a situation or position.

1. Identify how you think and feel about a situation.
2. Analyze the source of those feelings.
3. Choose the appropriate skills necessary to communicate feelings, such as "I" messages (Thompson, 1996, p. 149) or a DESC (describe, express, specify, consequences) Script (Thompson, 1996).
4. Communicate your thoughts or feelings to the source.

Here is an example: *"I have never been charged a service fee before. Has there been a change in your bank's policy?"*

Rules for Assertive Requests*

Assertive requests should be as clear, direct, and uncritical as possible. To make your request successfully, follow these basic rules:

1. Select a convenient time and place for your dialogue.
2. Make your request simple and manageable, limiting it to one or two specific actions.
3. Don't blame or attack the other person or bring up past experiences. Use "I" messages and stick to the facts.
4. Be specific. Describe the behavior, not the attitude, that you want to change. Do not make requests that are unreasonable or that have attached conditions.
5. Communicate assertively, both verbally and nonverbally. Keep your tone of voice moderate, clear, and firm. Maintain eye contact, an erect posture, and a close proximity to the other person.
6. Keep the dialogue upbeat and positive by mentioning the positive consequences of giving you what you want.

---

* *Note.* Adapted from *Self-Esteem: A Proven Program of Cognitive Techniques for Assessing, Improving, and Maintaining Your Self-Esteem,* by M. McKay and P. Fanning, 1987, Oakland, CA: New Harbinger Publications. Copyright 1987 by New Harbinger Publications, Inc. Adapted with permission.

Managing Anger

---

1. Recognize angry feelings.
   Identify how your body feels.
   Identify what you are saying to yourself.
2. Calm down.
   Pause and take three deep breaths.
   Count backward slowly from 10 to 0.
   Tell yourself to stay calm and maintain control.
3. Talk aloud to solve the problem.
   Express what you need and what you want.
   See if you both can get what you want.
4. Think about it later.
   What exactly made you angry?
   Did you maintain control over the situation?
   Were you pleased with the outcome?
   Could you have done things differently?
   Did you do the best that you were capable of doing?

Speaking for Yourself

When you speak for yourself, you express your intentions and clearly indicate that you are the owner of your thoughts and actions. The phrases *I think ...*, *I feel ...*, and *I want ...* identify you as the owner. When you speak for yourself, you use *I, me, my,* and *mine.*

Statements such as these are good examples:

"It's important to me."
"I want more time to think about it."
"My perspective is different."
"I'm really pleased about our project."

These statements indicate that you recognize your feelings, intentions, and actions and that you are the owner of your perceptions, thoughts, feelings and wants. They also add to the accuracy and quality of communication.

Emotional Literacy Skills

Emotional literacy skills are intrapersonal abilities such as knowing one's emotions by recognizing a feeling as it happens and monitoring it; managing emotions (i.e., shaking off anxiety, gloom, irritability, and the consequences of failure); motivating oneself to attain goals, delay gratification, stifle impulsiveness, and maintain self-control; recognizing emotions in others with empathy and perspective taking; and handling interpersonal relationships effectively. Emotional skills fall into such categories as knowing the relationship between thoughts, feelings, and actions; establishing a sense of identity and acceptance of self; learning to value teamwork, collaboration, and cooperation; regulating one's mood; empathizing; and maintaining hope.

Skills Boxes
Permission is granted to reproduce skills boxes for individual client use.

Validating Experiences with Sense Statements

Validating with sense statements means documenting what you perceive (i.e., see, hear, touch, taste, and smell). It clarifies sensations and intuition and serves as a perception check. It provides feedback and helps you avoid the pitfalls of making global statements, generalizations, or stereotyping. Validating with sense statements makes the dialogue of "yes, you are" and "no, I'm not" harder to start and more difficult to continue. To validate sense statements:

1. Be specific about time, location, action, or behavior.
2. Document the behavior or action; do not stereotype or make a character assassination.
3. Engage in a perception check with the other person.
4. Avoid making global statements or generalizations.

Here is an example of how you might document time and behavior: *"This morning when you began to respond to my question, I saw you pause and look away, and then I heard you say ..."*

Here is an example of *a perception check* and an opportunity to clarify the message:

Ryan: I don't think you like my new shirt.
Jessica: That's bogus! What makes you say that?

Ryan (documenting): When I tried it on for you, you were very quiet and you were grinning.

Jessica: Wait a second! I was quiet because I was thinking about how nice you looked. I guess I was grinning because it looked so cool on you.

Finally, here is an example of global judgments and overgeneralizing (i.e., what *not* to do), followed by an example of documenting (i.e., how to do it better):

Global judgment, generalization: *"I get frustrated that you are so careless with our money."*

Documenting: *"I got frustrated this morning when I noticed that you hadn't recorded the checks you had written over the weekend."*

Making Interpretative Statements

Interpretative statements express what you think, believe, or assume about a situation or experience. Identify your thoughts as your own, and avoid talking for others. Here are some examples:

"I think it's time to stop."
"It's my impression that you would be interested in going."
"I think that's the wrong way to go about it."
"I'm wondering if you're feeling what I'm feeling."

Atonement*

Atonement is making up for what you have done. Four guidelines to help you choose an appropriate atonement:

1. **It is important to acknowledge that what you did was wrong.** This makes it clear that you accept responsibility for your behavior.
2. **You should atone *directly to the person you have wronged.*** Donating money to charity, becoming a Big Brother or Big Sister, or joining the Peace Corps will atone less effectively than directly helping the one you hurt.
3. **The atonement should be real, rather than symbolic.** Lighting candles or writing a poem will not rid you of guilt or responsibility. What you do to atone has to cost you something in time, money, or effort. It also has to be tangible enough so that it has an impact on your relationship with the person who is hurt.
4. **Your atonement should be commensurate with the wrong done.** If your offense was a moment of irritability, then a brief apology should be sufficient. However, if you have been noncommunicative and cold toward someone for the past few weeks, then you will have to do a little better than saying, "I'm sorry."

---

* *Note.* Adapted from *Self-Esteem: A Proven Program of Cognitive Techniques for Assessing, Improving, and Maintaining Your Self-Esteem,* by M. McKay and P. Fanning, 1987, Oakland, CA: New Harbinger Publications. Copyright 1987 by New Harbinger Publications, Inc. Adapted with permission.

Acknowledgment*

Acknowledgment means agreeing with a critic. Acknowledgment allows you to stop criticism immediately. When someone criticizes you and the criticism is accurate, the following steps of acknowledgment may be helpful:

1. Say, "You're right," and let it go.
2. Paraphrase the criticism so that the critic is sure you heard him or her correctly.
3. Thank the critic for the observation, if appropriate.
4. Explain yourself, if appropriate. (Note that an explanation is not an apology.)

---

* Note. Adapted from *Self-Esteem: A Proven Program of Cognitive Techniques for Assessing, Improving, and Maintaining Your Self-Esteem*, by M. McKay and P. Fanning, 1987, Oakland, CA: New Harbinger Publications. Copyright 1987 by New Harbinger Publications, Inc. Adapted with permission.

The Compassionate Response*

The compassionate response begins with three questions you should ask yourself to promote an understanding of a problem or behavior:

1. What need was (he, she, I) trying to meet with that behavior?
2. What beliefs or perceptions influenced the behavior?
3. What pain, hurt, or other feelings influenced the behavior?

Next are three statements to remind yourself that you can accept a person without blame or judgment, no matter how unfortunate his or her choices have been:

4. I wish … had not happened, but it was merely an attempt to meet (his, her, my) needs.
5. I accept (him, her, myself) without judgment or feeling of wrongness for that attempt.

---

* Note. From *Self-Esteem: A Proven Program of Cognitive Techniques for Assessing, Improving, and Maintaining Your Self-Esteem*, by M. McKay and P. Fanning, 1987, Oakland, CA: New Harbinger Publications. Copyright 1987 by New Harbinger Publications, Inc. Reprinted with permission.

6. No matter how unfortunate (his, her, my) decision, I accept the person who did it as someone who is, like all of us, trying to survive.

Finally, there are two statements to remind you that it is time to forgive and let go:

7. It's over, I can let go of it.
8. Nothing is owed for this mistake.

Make a commitment to use the compassionate response whenever you notice that you are judging yourself or others. The basic thrust of the compassionate response is *understanding, acceptance,* and *forgiveness.*

Conveying the Whole Message*

Often, people need to better understand your perspective on a problem or situation. It may be helpful for them to know your feelings—how the situation or problem has affected you emotionally. The *whole message* means conveying your *thoughts* (how you perceived the situation), your *feelings*, and your *wants* as an assertive statement.

The formula is very simple:

"*I think* ... (my understanding, perceiving, and interpretations)."

"*I feel* ... ('I' messages only)."

"*I want* ... (an assertive request)."

Here is an example: "*When you tease me in front of my friends, you make me sound pretty stupid. I am getting the feeling that that is what you really think of me. I feel embarrassed and angry. I'd really appreciate it if you would lighten up and not tease me or anyone else in our group.*"

* Note. From *Self-Esteem: A Proven Program of Cognitive Techniques for Assessing, Improving, and Maintaining Your Self-Esteem,* by M. McKay and P. Fanning, 1987, Oakland, CA: New Harbinger Publications. Copyright 1987 by New Harbinger Publications, Inc. Reprinted with permission.

"I Want" Statements

"I want" statements clarify to others what you want and how you want to fulfill your wants. They reduce the anxiety of being afraid to ask and of worrying whether the other person will know what you want. Many relationships have failed because needs and wants were unspoken.

For example, *"I want to know what I did to make you so angry, but I don't want you to call me names."*

"I want" statements can be framed as follows:

1. Say what you want: *"Instead of going to the theater, I want to stay home and rent a video."*
2. Rate your want on a scale of 1 to 10: *"I want to go to the movie theater, it's a strong preference—about an 8."*
3. State what your "I want" statement means and what it does not mean: *"I want to go to the movie theater sometime in the next two weeks. That's just for information; no pressure if you can't make it this weekend."*

Estimating Consequences

Look at a situation by evaluating the consequences logically. First, do not become emotional; be emotionally neutral. Second, when appropriate, use the following formula: *"When you ... (description of behavior), then... (statement of consequences). You will have another opportunity to ... (statement of when this can occur)."*

Here is an example: *"When you continue to leave your car unlocked, you run the risk your stereo will get stolen. If it's stolen, you can get another stereo when you have saved enough money, because our insurance will not cover it."*

CHAPTER **6**

Loss, Depression, Suicide, and Self-Injury

People often assume that adolescence is an exciting and carefree time of life, yet the stress of establishing self-identity, self-sufficiency, and autonomy is exceptionally difficult. The escalating rate of emotional disorders in our society can be attributed to several precipitating variables. For example, many teenagers from dysfunctional families live with alcoholism, violence, incest, and abuse. Add to these risk variables rapid social change, cultural pluralism, occupational diversity, poor interpersonal skills, and disintegration of the traditional family—and a teenager's hopelessness and disillusionment with planning for the future are understandable.

The overall rate of suicide among youth has declined slowly since 1992 (Lubell, Swahn, Crosby, & Kegler, 2004). However, rates remain unacceptably high. Adolescents and young adults often experience stress, confusion, and depression from situations occurring within their families, schools, and communities. Such feelings can overwhelm young people and lead them to consider suicide as a "solution." Few schools and communities have suicide prevention plans that include screening, referral, and crisis intervention programs for youth.

Recent statistics related to youth suicide include the following data:

- Suicide is the third leading cause of death among young people ages 15 to 24. In 2001, 3,971 suicides were reported in this group (Anderson & Smith, 2003).
- Of the total number of suicides among ages 15 to 24 in 2001, 86% (n = 3,409) were male and 14% (n = 562) were female (Anderson & Smith, 2003).
- American Indian and Alaskan natives have the highest rate of suicide in the 15-to-24 age group (CDC, 2004b).
- In 2001, firearms were used in 54% of youth suicides (Anderson & Smith, 2003).

Adolescent Suicide

- Each year, 1 in 5 teens in the United States seriously considers suicide. A total of 5% to 8% of adolescents attempt suicide, representing approximately 1 million teenagers, of whom nearly 700,000 receive medical attention for their attempt (Grunbaum, Kann, Kinchen, Ross, Hawkins, Lowry, Harris, McManus, Chyen, & Collins, 2003; Grunbaum, Kann, Kinchen, Ross, Lowry, & Harris, 2004). Approximately 1,600 teens die by suicide each year (Anderson & Smith, 2003).
- According to the U.S. Centers for Disease Control and Prevention (CDC, 2004c), suicide is the third leading cause of death for young people aged 15 to 24.
- During the period of 1991 to 2001, significant decreases occurred in the percentage of students who seriously considered suicide. (CDC, 2004c).

Predictors or Precipitating Events That Make Youth Vulnerable to Suicide

Depression

Increasingly, researchers and the public alike are acknowledging that depression is a serious disorder of children and adolescents and perhaps the most common impetus to suicide. Some researchers have estimated that depression affects nearly 30% of the adolescent population (Lewinsohn, Hops, Roberts, Seeley, & Andrew, 1993). According to Brookman (1993), 7 million to 9 million American children have mental health problems requiring treatment—and 70% to 80% receive inadequate or no service. Brookman also estimates that 20% of teenagers have significant emotional disorders. This is further confirmed by the First Surgeon General's Report on Adolescent Mental Health (1999).

Recent clinical and research data on depression indicate an occurrence rate of 20% among school-aged children (Bauer, 1987; Worchel, Nolan, & Wilson, 1987), with a rate of 51% to 59% among children in psychiatric settings (McConville & Bruce, 1985). Inherently, the pattern of a teenager's life, and how that teenager feels about it, affects all of his or her attitudes and actions.

Typically, major depression is diagnosed if a child or adolescent describes depressed moods or irritability or a loss of interest in normal activities for at least 2 weeks, accompanied by other symptoms such as weight loss, inability to concentrate, chronic pain, or insomnia that is not part of some other disorder such as schizophrenia (Forrest, 1990). When applied to adolescents, depression describes behavior ranging from common mood swings or short-lived situational episodes to chronic, recurring feelings of worthlessness, helplessness, and hopelessness (Garrison, Schuchter, Schoenbach, & Kaplan, 1989). Depression often is characterized by withdrawal from normal social interactions, sleep disturbances, poor concentration, feelings of inferiority, and self-blame. Bartell and Reynolds (1986) suggested that depression can be considered primarily

- **affective** (characterized by worry and anxiety),
- **cognitive** (characterized by self-deprecation),
- **motivational** (indicating withdrawal or decreased performance), or
- a combination of these.

McConville and Bruce (1985) further delineated depression as follows:

- **The affective type.** Characterized by prominent sadness and helplessness.
- **The self-esteem type.** Characterized by prominent discouragement and negative self-esteem.
- **The guilt type.** Characterized by prominent guilt and self-destructive ideation or behavior.

The first two types typically are receptive to support from school, the community, teachers, or counselors; the third type usually requires referral for clinical treatment.

Mental Illness and Substance Abuse

One of the most telling risk factors for adolescents is mental illness or emotional disorders. Mental or addictive disorders are associated with 90% of suicides (Poland & Lieberman, 2003). One in ten youth suffers from mental illness serious enough to be impaired, yet fewer than 20% receive treatment (Thomerson, 2002). In fact, 60% of those who complete suicide suffer from depression (Poland & Lieberman, 2003). Alcohol and drug use, which clouds judgment, lowers inhibitions, and exacerbates depression, is associated with 50% to 67% of suicides. The high rates of substance use may be due to the combination of the increasing accessibility to these substances and the young age at which youth are now able to acquire them (Dying Young, 2002).

Aggression and Fighting

Recent research has identified a connection between interpersonal violence and suicide. Based on a nationally representative survey of youth in grades 9 through 12, students who reported attempting suicide in the past 12 months were nearly 4 times as likely to report involvement in physical fights. Further, 1 in 20 high school students reported both suicide attempts and involvement in physical fights in the past year. As many as 61.5% of students who attempted suicide also reported engaging in physical fights, compared with only 30.3% of students who did not attempt suicide. Suicide is associated with fighting for both males and females, across all ethnic groups, and for youth living in urban, suburban, and rural areas. Researchers hope that efforts to reduce violence can also reduce suicides (CDC, 2004b).

Hopelessness and Helplessness

The severity of the depression often profiles this equation:

$$\text{Severity} = \text{Distress} \times \text{Uncontrollability} \times \text{Frequency (or FID: Frequency, Intensity, and Duration)}$$

Depression, hopelessness, and anxiety appear to be the important factors in both suicidal ideation and suicidal behavior in adolescents (Bernstein, Garfinkel, & Hoberman, 1989; Kazdin, French, Unis, Esveldt-Dawson, & Sherick, 1983). Research data also show that adults often do not recognize the signs of depression and suicidal ideation in adolescents. If significant adult figures in the adolescent's life do not perceive the child's despairing emotional state, they are not able to respond to it.

Family Dysfunction and Interpersonal Loss

Teenagers whose lives are disrupted by frequent changes in residence, schools, or parental figures show an increased risk for suicide (Davidson,

Franklin, Mercy, Rosenburg, & Simmons, 1989). Perrone (1987) found that suicidal children and adolescents often have experienced more dysfunction in their families and loss of significant others, witnessed repeated traumas (e.g., family violence, chemical abuse), and were themselves subjected to abuse and neglect. Gibbs (1985) found significant relationships between depression and three independent variables: parental occupation, number of household moves, and number of self-reported problems.

Compared to healthy youth, depressed youth reported more stressors and fewer social resources in the areas of family, extended family, school, friends, and support networks (Daniels & Moos, 1990; Feldman, Rubenstein, & Rubin, 1988). Most suicide victims experienced family disruption, and nearly half were functioning poorly in school (Allen, 1985). Functioning poorly in school should be recognized as a significant loss for many children and adolescents. Failure can be devastating. A history of mental illness and suicide among immediate family members places youth at greater risk for suicide (Poland & Lieberman, 2003). Exacerbating these circumstances are changes in family structure such as death, divorce, remarriage; moving to a new city; and financial instability (Shaffer & Pfeffer, 2001). Within the home, a lack of cohesion, high levels of violence and conflict (Poland & Lieberman, 2003), a lack of parental support, alienation from and within the family (Portes, Sandhu, & Longwell-Grice, 2002), a lack of communication, and a failure to meet parental expectations are all risk factors for suicide (Butler, Novy, Kagan, & Gates, 1994). Any number of these factors can create a hostile environment that does not meet the needs of adolescents or serve as a much-needed support system. Moreover, this type of family atmosphere can result in youth having low self-esteem, depression, and behavior problems (Butler et al., 1994).

Loss of Status

Hawton (1986) found that predominant problems immediately preceding adolescent suicide included school failure, a loss of status among family or friends, the feeling of letting others down, being publicly reprimanded or humiliated, and a significant love loss. Cohen-Sandler, Berman, and King (1982), Gill-Wigal (1988), and Pfeiffer (1982, 1986) suggested that suicidal children and adolescents have experienced higher levels of stress than "normal" adolescents. Youth found most at risk for completed suicides are males who have an affective disorder, who abuse alcohol or other drugs, and who have experienced an acute proximal stressor that involves either a social loss or a blow to self-image (Crumley, 1990). Suicidal thoughts occur most frequently between the seventh and ninth grades (Perrone, 1987).

Community Environment

Adolescents with high levels of exposure to community violence are at serious risk for self-destructive behavior (Vermeiren, Ruchkin, Leckman, Deboutte, & Schwab-Stone, 2002). This can occur when an adolescent models his or her own behavior after what is experienced in the community. Additionally, more youth are growing up without making meaningful connections with adults; therefore, these youth are not getting the guidance they need to help them cope with their daily lives (Thomerson, 2002).

Cultural Factors

Changes in gender roles and expectations, issues of conformity and assimilation, and feelings of isolation and victimization can all increase the stress levels and vulnerability of individuals (Lazear, Roggenbaum, & Blase, 2003). Additionally, in some cultures (particularly Asian and Pacific cultures) suicide may be seen as a rational response to shame (Lester, 1997; Lewin, 1986; Sachdev, 1990). Minority youth who expressed more feelings of alienation, cultural and societal conflict, academic anxiety, and feelings of victimization are also a high-risk group for suicide (Institute of Medicine, 2002). In the general population, whites and Native Americans have the highest suicide rates (Institute of Medicine, 2002). Native American males have the highest suicide rate among minority youth (Poland & Lieberman, 2003), though young Native American females have suicide rates more than twice that of females in the general population (Institute of Medicine, 2002). The high suicide rates for this population have been attributed to factors including the stress of acculturation, cultural conflict, loss of ethnic identity, and a lack of cultural and spiritual identity (Lazear et al., 2003). In the most recent National Youth Behavior Surveillance Survey (which did not have enough data on Native Americans to report population statistics for them), data showed that the prevalence of having attempted suicide was higher among Hispanic (10.6%) than white (6.9%) and black (8.4%) students; higher among Hispanic female (15.0%) than white female (10.3%) and black female (9.0%) students; and higher among black male (7.7%) and Hispanic male (6.1%) than white male (3.7%) students (CDC, 2004a).

Lesbian, Gay, Bisexual, and Transgendered Youth

Sexual minority youth, that is, gay, lesbian, bisexual, transgendered, and questioning (GLBTQ), are considered to be at high risk for suicidal behavior because they are the targets of a great deal of victimization. Feelings of not being safe in their schools were reported by 41.7% of GLBTQ youth.

More than two thirds reported experiencing some form of verbal, physical, or sexual harassment or violence (Hetrick-Martin Institute, 2002). GLBTQ youth also suffer from high rates of depression (Committee on Adolescence, 2000), a risk factor for youth suicide, perhaps due to factors such as the abuse they receive, the confusion they feel about their sexuality, or the difficulty in "coming out" to family and friends. Nevertheless, despite a widespread perception that GLBTQ youth are at higher risk for suicide than their peers, some data do not uphold this perception (Rutter & Soucar, 2002). However, for *completed* youth suicides, the sexual orientation of the youth is often unknown to others before the tragic event.

School Environment

Youth who are struggling with classes, who perceive their teachers as not understanding or caring about them, or who have poor relationships with their peers have increased vulnerability to suicide (Shaffer & Pfeffer, 2001).

Firearms

Guns are the most common method of suicide for both males and females, accounting for approximately 60% of youth suicides (Poland & Lieberman, 2003). Homes with guns are 4.8 times more likely to experience a suicide of a resident than homes without guns (Roggenbaum & Lazear, 2003). Removing firearms from the homes of suicidal youth is a great step in preventing suicide, as more than 90% of suicides involving firearms are fatal due to the minimal chance for rescue (Committee on Adolescence, 2000).

Suffocation

Among youth aged 10 to 14, suffocation (mostly hangings) has replaced firearms as the most common method of suicide. In 2001, suffocation suicides in this age group occurred nearly twice as often as firearms suicides (CDC, 2004c).

Situational Crises

Approximately 40% of youth suicides are associated with an identifiable precipitating event, such as the death of a loved one or the loss of a valued relationship.

Isolation and Alienation

The adolescent suicide attempter often feels alienated from his or her family. Edwards and Lowe (1988) found some common issues that may trigger suicidal gestures in adolescents:

- Failure to manage problems or stressors successfully.
- Failure to live up to expectations of self or others.
- A wish to retaliate against adults or peers by making them feel guilty.
- Desire to join a deceased loved one.
- Desire to rid oneself of unacceptable feelings of guilt, failure, and despair.
- Feelings of hopelessness.
- Feelings of being emotionally overwhelmed.
- Feelings of low self-esteem.
- Desire to commit the ultimate act of self-destruction and abandonment.

Adolescents who feel little control over their environment often experience their families and social institutions (such as the schools) as unavailable, rejecting, or overprotective. Sometimes in order to reach out for help, an adolescent may have to expose family secrets such as alcoholism, violence, or sexual victimization. This poses the additional stress of possible retaliation or at least of further rejection from other family members (Gibbs, 1985).

All-or-Nothing Thinking

Suicide usually is the final act in a sequence of maladaptive behaviors. Central themes in assessing risk are the attraction death holds for the youth, the degree of isolation or alienation he or she feels in the family, his or her social status with peers, and his or her ability to express emotions and cope with problems. Escalating problems lead to an increasing sense of helplessness and impotence, eventually ending in a suicidal mindset.

Garland and Zigler (1993) studied cognitive and coping-style factors—generalized feelings of hopelessness and poor interpersonal problem-solving skills—as risk factors for adolescent suicide.

Capuzzi (1988) maintained that suicidal adolescents often distort their thinking patterns in conjunction with avoidance, control, and communication functions, so that suicide becomes the best or only problem-solving option. All-or-nothing thinking emerges in which no options for coping with or overcoming problems seem possible. Suicidal adolescents often have trouble developing solutions to troublesome situations or uncomfortable relationships. Expressing emotions is critical, because depressed adolescents generally suppress negative emotions at home, in school, and among peers. In addition, adolescents who abuse psychoactive substances—particularly those with any type of depressive disorder—appear to be at higher risk for suicidal behavior.

Previous Attempts

Youth who have attempted suicide are at risk to do it again. In fact, they are 8 times more likely to make another suicide attempt than adolescents who have never attempted suicide are to make an attempt (King, 1999).

Changes in Self

These can include changes in behavior, appearance, thoughts, or feelings (Poland & Lieberman, 2003). For example, an adolescent may withdraw from friends and family, display changes in patterns of eating and sleeping, and show a loss of interest in pleasurable activities and things that he or she used to care about (Doan, Lazear, & Roggenbaum, 2003).

Preoccupation with Death

Excessive interest in death, including reading, writing, and talking about the subject should cause alarm. Anyone who hints of suicide or a suicide plan is at great risk, and immediate action should be taken (Poland & Lieberman, 2003).

Making Final Arrangements

Actions in this category might include giving away possessions or putting personal affairs in order (Doan et al., 2003; Poland & Lieberman, 2003).

Medical Symptoms

Especially in cases of depression, an adolescent may seek treatment for recurrent or persistent complaints, including abdominal or chest pains, headaches, lethargy, weight loss, and dizziness (Committee on Adolescence, 2000).

Behavior Problems

Actions that may be manifestations of depression include running away, truancy, vandalism, self-destructive behavior, drug or alcohol abuse, and sexual deviance (Committee on Adolescence, 2000; Doan et al., 2003).

Verbal Statements

Both direct and indirect statements may be heard from youth. It is important to take immediate action if such statements are ever spoken (Doan et al., 2003).

- **Direct statements.** "I want to die"; "Life sucks and I want to get out."
- **Indirect statements.** "I want to go to sleep and never wake up"; "Soon the pain will be over"; "They'll be sorry when I'm gone."

TABLE 6.1   Risk Factors for Adolescent Suicide

Personal factors

Sexual and physical abuse
Alcohol and drug use and abuse
Homosexuality
Previous suicide attempt
Chronic illness

Psychological factors

Depression
Conduct disorder
Bipolar disorder
Psychosis
Schizophrenia

Family factors

Low income
History of substance abuse
Suicide in first-degree relative
History of domestic violence
Family conflict
Firearm in home

Antecedent event factors

Recent death of family or friend
Romantic conflict or breakup
Divorce or remarriage of parent
School failure

Source: From "Fatal Injuries in Adolescents," by G. McIntosh and M. Moreno, 2000, *Wisconsin Medical Journal 99*, p. 9. Copyright 2000 by Wisconsin Medical Journal. Reprinted with permission.

Table 6.2 Risk and Protective Factors for Suicide Prevention

Risk factors

- Previous suicide attempt(s)
- History of mental disorders, particularly depression
- History of alcohol and substance abuse
- Family history of suicide
- Family history of child maltreatment
- Feelings of hopelessness
- Impulsive or aggressive tendencies
- Barriers to accessing mental health treatment
- Loss (relational, social, work, or financial)
- Physical illness
- Easy access to lethal methods
- Unwillingness to seek help because of the stigma attached to mental health and substance abuse disorders or suicidal thoughts
- Cultural and religious beliefs—for instance, the belief that suicide is a noble resolution of a personal dilemma
- Local epidemics of suicide

Protective factors

- Protective factors buffer people from the risks associated with suicide. A number of protective factors have been identified (Department of Health and Human Services, 1999).
- Effective clinical care for mental, physical, and substance abuse disorders
- Easy access to a variety of clinical interventions and support for help seeking
- Family and community support
- Support from ongoing medical and mental health care relationships
- Skills in problem solving, conflict resolution, and nonviolent handling of disputes
- Cultural and religious beliefs that discourage suicide and support self-preservation instincts
- Isolation, a feeling of being cut off from other people

Note. From Department of Health and Human Services, Office of Surgeon General (1999). First Surgeon General's report on adolescent mental health. Washington, D.C. Substance Abuse and Mental Health Services Administration.

Risk and Protective Factors

The first step in preventing suicide is to identify and understand the risk factors. A risk factor is anything that increases the likelihood that a person will harm him- or herself. However, risk factors are not necessarily causes. Research has identified the risk factors for suicide listed in Table 6.2 (U.S. Department of Health and Human Services, 1999).

Table 6.3   Principles of Suicide Prevention Effectiveness

- Prevention programs should be designed to enhance protective factors. They should also work toward reversing or reducing known risk factors. Risk factors for negative health outcomes can be reduced or eliminated for some or all of a population.
- Prevention programs should be long term, with repeat interventions to reinforce the original prevention goals.
- Family-focused prevention efforts may have a greater impact than strategies that focus only on individuals.
- Community programs that include media campaigns and policy changes are more effective when individual and family interventions accompany them.
- Community programs need to strengthen norms that support help-seeking behavior in all settings, including family, work, school, and community.
- Prevention programming should be adapted to address the specific nature of the problem in the local community or population group.
- The higher the level of risk of the target population, the more intensive the prevention effort must be and the earlier it must begin.
- Prevention programs should be age specific, developmentally appropriate, and culturally sensitive.
- Prevention programs should be implemented with no or minimal differences from how they were designed and tested.

Source: From *Suicide Prevention: Prevention Effectiveness and Evaluation* by SPAN USA, 2001.

Self-Mutilation or Self-Injury

Self-mutilation or self-injury behaviors include head banging, cutting, burning, biting, and digging at wounds (Nichols, 2000). These behaviors are becoming increasingly common among adolescents, especially adolescent girls (Ross & Heath, 2002). Although self-injury typically signals the occurrence of broader problems, the reason for this behavior can vary from peer-group pressure to severe emotional disturbance. Other motives for this behavior can include relief of intolerable stress, poor coping skills, inadequate problem-solving skills, inability to express feelings in words, beliefs that are irrational and untrue, and suicidal ideation (Nichols, 2000). Self-injury is a complex issue that has recently emerged among today's youth with the overwhelming message that self-injury is a means of self-protection and not self-destruction. Self-injury is a coping mechanism. It may be called self-inflicted violence, self-injury, self-harm, parasuicide, delicate cutting, self-abuse, self-mutilation, self-injurious behavior (SIB), or self-inflicted violence (SIV).

Various life factors and research correlates are related to self-injurious behaviors. Self-injury is most often associated with childhood sexual abuse and subsequent posttraumatic stress disorder reactions. A history of sexual abuse is one of the best predictors of self-injury (Darche, 1990; Favazza & Rosenthal, 1993; Ghaziuddin, Tsai, Naylor, & Ghaziuddin, 1992;

Table 6.4 Key Components of a Comprehensive Suicide-Prevention System

Intervention opportunity	Service-oriented programs	Service settings
Provide outreach to individuals at risk of committing suicide	Screening, assessment and referral programs	Primary-care settings Schools
	Peer support programs	Schools
Educate those in gatekeeper positions to recognize individuals exhibiting suicidal behaviors	Gatekeeper training (gatekeeper programs are educational programs designed to help community members recognize those contemplating suicide and refer them to appropriate caregivers)	Schools Community Health care system
Respond effectively to those in a suicide crisis and those who have made a previous suicide attempt	Crisis treatment Telephone crisis hotline	Mental health setting
Provide professional services to suicide survivors	Mental health treatment Community support group	Mental health setting
Offer support to the families and loved ones of suicide victims	Suicide support programs	Medical care/ mental health Community support group
Educate the community about the suicide problem and prevention strategies	Community education Restrict access to lethal means	Community-wide

Source: From *Suicide in Colorado* (p. 38), by K. Gallager, 2002, Denver, CO: The Colorado Trust. Copyright 2002 by The Colorado Trust. Reprinted with permission.

Langbehn & Pfohl, 1993). Life conditions that are related to self-injury include loss of a parent, childhood illness including surgical procedures, depression, physical abuse, parental alcoholism or depression, domestic violence, a significant loss, peer conflict and intimacy problems, impulse control problems, and familial self-injury (Briere & Gil, 1998; Favazza, 1996; Walsh & Rosen, 1988). In addition to these factors, an inability to tolerate or express feelings and emotions, sexual assault or rape, perfectionism, eating disorders, and a negative body image have been linked to self-injury (Cross, 1993; Greenspan & Samuel, 1989; Strong, 1998).

An individual harms his or her physical self to deal with emotional pain or to break feelings of numbness by arousing sensation. It is also not a distinct syndrome and is often associated with syndromes such as personality disorders, anxiety disorders, compulsive disorders, posttraumatic stress disorder, dissociative disorder, eating disorders, impulse control disorders, and forms of depression. Although self-injury may be a way of coping, it also is indicative of profound emotional distress. There is a strong link between low self-esteem and self-injury.

Individuals use several different methods such as cutting (usually with razors, knives, or broken glass), burning, hitting walls, using alcohol or drugs, jumping from high places, and self-strangulation. Some even report blood letting, chopping off their hair, letting themselves be hurt by others, and solvent abuse. The average age at which those under 25 said they first starting injuring themselves was 13, with the most common period of starting to self-injure was between 12 and 14 (Favazza, 1998; Favazza & Rosenthal, 1993; Suyemoto & MacDonald, 1995).

The following types of SIB seen in the study and the frequency of their occurrence are listed next:

- Cutting: 90%.
- Scratching: 70%.
- Hitting: 60%.
- Interfering with wounds, hair pulling, biting: 50%.
- Head banging, nail biting/injuries, burning: 40%.
- Piercing body parts, using needles, trying to break bones: 30%.

An earlier age of onset, higher frequency of SIB, and greater number of addictive features were noted in a subgroup of more severe repetitive self-injurers (Owens, Horrocks, & House, 2002).

Babiker & Arnold (1997) distinguished between *self-injury* and *self-harm*, maintaining that self-injury implies no suicidal intent, whereas self-harm means suicide and attempted suicide. A self-injuring girl named Kirsty explained:

> When I self-harm I don't want to die, because basically, if when I self-harmed I wanted to die, I'd cut underneath, rather than the top of my forearms. I'd cut where my veins were, obviously…If I wanted to die when I self-harmed, then I wouldn't be here, because I'd have made sure. (Bywaters & Rolfe, 2002, p. 22)

Fundamentally, self-injury and self-harm were much more commonly seen by the participants as ways of coping with depression and emotional distress and a means of preventing suicide.

Most self-injurers linked the first time they harmed themselves to things that were happening in their lives, such as an unwanted pregnancy, being bullied at school, not getting along with parents, divorce, physical abuse, bereavement, and foster care. A key reason for repeating self-injury, in particular, was often the relief of pent-up emotions, the release of tension and distress. The text below illustrates the range of factors and distress experienced by individuals who self-injure.

Reasons for Self-Injury*
Self-hatred. It was different. Taking control. Bad things that happened in the past. Anger. Release, calm. Turning mental pain into physical pain. A way of coping. Deserving it. Negative feelings about self. Childhood trauma. Severe stress. Purification. Going into institutional care. At lowest ebb. No one caring. Suicidal intent. Difficulty coping. Getting feelings out to the surface. Taking anger out on self rather than others. Visual sign of feelings. Social exclusion. Discrimination. Being bullied. Trying to live up to others' expectations and conform. Being raped. Not being listened to. Self-punishment. Childhood sexual abuse. Physical abuse. To get high. It's fun. Testing people out. Only way of getting attention and care. Severe guilt. An addiction. Rebellion. A way to keep living. People breathing down your neck. Seeing a counselor. Insomnia. Depression. Emotional hurt. Wanting help.

Source: P. Bywaters & Rolfe, A. (2002b). *Look beyond the Scars: Understanding and Responding to Self-injury and Self-harm*. National Children's Home, London, England. Reprinted with permission.

Problems with Neurotransmitters in the Brain May Play a Role in Self-Injury

Serotonin plays a major role in the implication of depression in children and adolescents. Researchers have speculated that problems in the serotonin system may predispose some people to self-injury by predisposing them to be more aggressive and impulsive than their peers. This predisposition toward impulsive aggression, in combination with a belief that one's feelings are wrong or reprehensible, can lead to the aggression being turned on oneself. With this perspective, the person may learn that self-injury reduces his or her level of distress, and the cycle begins. Simeon, Stanley, Frances, Mann, Winchel, and Stanley (1992) found that self-injurers have fewer platelet imipramine binding sites, a level of serotonin activity that may reflect central serotonergic dysfunction with reduced presynaptic serotonin release (i.e., serotonin dysfunction may facilitate self-mutilation). In addition, serotonin has as many as seven receptor types, and one of those has five subtypes. These receptors are involved in regulating mood, impulsivity, aggression, digestion, smooth muscle relaxation, and sexual behavior. Fundamentally the brain does not have enough serotonin available for use (Simeon et al., 1992).

Coping with Past or Present Events

Some precipitating or present factors relating to coping with events influence the feelings and emotional responses and can lead to self-harm. These include the following:

- Past life events (trauma and abuse) can influence self-injurers. Many self-injurers experienced sexual, physical, or emotional abuse, leading them to self-harm.
- Stress resulting from current life events often leads to self-injury, which is used as a coping mechanism.
- Coping with emotions leads many self-injurers to use the behavior to release emotional distress.
- The act of self-harm provides a form of relief and a sense of escape.
- Self-punishment is used as a means of releasing feelings of self-hatred and feelings of inadequacy. It can also serve as a form of punishment in and of itself, with some individuals feeling they deserved this level of punishment.
- Self-injurers create a visual sign as a form of communication. Some people self-harm in order to convert unbearable emotional pain into physical pain, which is easier to manage. It also serves to express how bad they were feeling through a means other than words.
- Many self-injurers want to be heard and use self-injury as an attempt to communicate, trying to get others to listen and to understand the degree of distress they are experiencing.
- Some individuals indulge in self-injury for the good feelings that it brings. They feel better when they self-harm, gaining a certain rush or high from the act. They comment about how warm and soothing the blood felt against their skin.
- Issues of control are central to some who self-harm themselves. Self-harming is something over which they have control.
- Many feel self-harm started for specific reasons or for particular benefits and had become habitual and similar to addiction.

Therapeutic Factors That Seemed to Help Those Who Self-Harm

A multidimensional, nonstigmatizing approach seems to be preferred by this high-risk population. Ideal services recipients would prefer included these:

- A nonclinical setting such as a drop-in center.
- A nonclinical setting staffed by people who are approachable, non-judgmental, and understanding, including those with personal experience in self-injury.
- A relaxed atmosphere where service users can have fun and participate in activities as well as receive support.
- Nurses who are available to treat cuts and other injuries without the stigma of going to the hospital (Bywaters & Rolfe, 2002).

Therapeutic Interventions to Help Youth Prevent Self-Injury

There are a number of techniques or strategies self-injurers can use to prevent their self-defeating behavior. For example, Alderman (1997) suggests a checklist of support statements to stop self-injury:

- I have a solid emotional support system of friends, family, and/or professionals that I can use if I feel like hurting myself.
- There are at least two people in my life whom I can call if I want to hurt myself.
- I have at list of at least 10 things I can do instead of hurting myself.
- I have a place to go if I need to leave my house so as not to hurt myself.
- I feel confident that I could get rid of all the things that I might be likely to use to hurt myself.
- I have told at least two other people that I am going to stop hurting myself.
- I am willing to feel uncomfortable, scared, and frustrated.
- I feel confident that I can endure thinking about hurting myself without having to actually do so.
- I want to stop hurting myself (Alderman, 1997).

Concrete strategies to prevent the tendency to self-injure could also include the following:

- Hit a punching bag.
- Use a pillow to hit a wall, pillow-fight style.
- Rip up an old newspaper or phone book.
- On a sketch or photo of yourself, mark in red ink what you want to do. Cut and tear the picture.
- Make a Play-Doh or clay model and cut or smash it.
- Throw ice into the bathtub or against a brick wall hard enough to shatter the ice.

- Break sticks.
- Turn up the music and dance.
- Clean a room or a whole house.
- Go for a walk, jog, or run.
- Stomp around in heavy shoes.
- Play racket ball or tennis.
- Do something slow or soothing like a hot bath.
- Squeeze ice very hard.
- Put ice on a spot you want to burn, which creates a strong painful sensation and leaves a mark but does not harm.
- Bite into a hot pepper or chew a piece of ginger root.
- Snap your wrist with a rubber band.
- Do deep breathing exercises.
- Do a task that requires focus and concentration.
- Choose a random object, like a paper clip, and try to list 30 different uses for it.
- Pick a subject and research it on the Web.
- Try the 15-minute game. Wait 15 minutes before harming yourself. When the time is up, see if you can do it again (Alderman, 1997, p. 134).

Bradley (2003) offers additional ways for people who self-injure to work through the overwhelming urge to hurt themselves. The following are some alternative behaviors and thinking strategies for the person who self-injures:

- Work to increase the adolescent's ability to tolerate emotional distress. Many people find that strengthening their spiritual practices helps them accept their situation and often find a sense of peace.
- Help the adolescent use techniques to stay focused in the present, taking the spotlight off the past or the future. Meditation, yoga, tai chi, and other activities help to gain control over the mind, reducing the frequency and severity of the intense mood states that trigger the urge to self-injure.
- Develop ways to self-soothe. Help the adolescent try many different experiences to identify things that feel good. Experiment with the senses. Take a warm bath, prepare and eat healthy foods, wrap up in a warm blanket, watch a favorite movie, and listen to relaxing music.
- Teach the adolescent who has the urge to self-injure to distract him- or herself. Some people find that frequently telling themselves "no!" or "stop!" can be helpful. Others can benefit from an action plan that

lists activities that a person can do to distract him- or herself, as well as people to call for help.

- Have the adolescent carry a "safe" object such as a squish ball, crystal, small book, Beanie Baby—anything that provides comfort and relieves stress.
- Use art for self-expression. Try painting, sculpture, pottery, or dance. Use finger paints. Have the adolescent experiment with different ways to express him- or herself such as creating a collage to symbolize the self. Collages are beneficial in a number of ways: they keep hands busy; they provide an attractive finished product; and they often provide insight, as well.
- "Help the adolescent track their "triggers" (i.e., those thoughts, feelings, memories, or events that trigger the urge to self-injure). Pay attention to feelings, memories, or events that trigger the urge to self-injure. Experiment with new ways to create the same feeling without doing damage. Actively work on altering habitual responses" (p. 5).

Conterio, Lader, and Bloom (1998) recommend that clients keep "impulse control logs" to track every time they feel an impulse to injure. The goal is to recognize that self-injury is a clue to some kind of feeling they don't want to experience. Rather than trying to self-medicate it with self-injury, to the adolescent must figure out at that moment why they have the impulse, understand what they are feeling, label their feelings, and challenge those irrational thoughts.

Kehrberg (1997) suggested using writing assignments that emphasize the expression of feelings to help students identify, tolerate, and manage their feelings instead of self-injuring. Similarly, verbal expression and management of feelings can be facilitated by having students document when they have impulses to self-injure, what precipitated the urge, and what the outcome would have been had they self-injured or not self-injured (Conterio et al., 1998).

Structured Interventions for High-Risk Behaviors

Therapeutic Initiatives

Children and adolescents with depression can be treated successfully if better programs are developed for awareness, education, primary prevention, and intervention. Downing (1988) provided a multidimensional intervention system based on a learning-theory approach for countering depression. Learning life skills to change debilitating behavior also

Table 6.5   Risk and Protective Factors for Child and Adolescent Self-Injury Behaviors

Risk factors

Individual

Attention deficits/hyperactivity
Antisocial beliefs and attitudes
History of early aggressive behavior
Involvement with drugs, alcohol, or tobacco
Early involvement in general offenses
Low IQ
Poor behavioral control
Social cognitive or information-processing deficits

Family

Authoritarian child-rearing attitudes
Exposure to violence and family conflict
Harsh, lax, or inconsistent disciplinary practices
Lack of involvement in the child's life
Low emotional attachment to parents or caregivers
Low parental education and income
Parental substance abuse and criminality
Poor family functioning
Poor monitoring and supervision of children

Protective factors

Individual

Intolerant attitude toward deviance
High IQ
Positive social orientation

Peer/school

Commitment to school
Involvement in social activities

is productive. In collaboration with therapist, parents, and counselor, children and adolescents can learn depression-coping and control techniques, such as recognizing depressive feelings and learning to increase their activity level, to relax, and to engage in positive self-talk.

Coping and control techniques lead to improved levels of functioning in all aspects of a child's or adolescent's life. Children learn these techniques best through a multifaceted support system involving the home, the school, and the child. Inherent in the intervention should be consistent, frequent, and regular monitoring of the process. Primary prevention and early intervention initiatives should be supported, since some research shows that children and adolescents seem to respond better than adults to techniques that prevent depression (de Shazer, 1982, 1988, 1991).

Helping professionals should concentrate on teaching adolescents specific skills to improve targeted symptom behaviors. These skills include positive self-talk, talk, cognitive awareness strategies, study skills, time management, coping skills, assertiveness, guided imagery, relaxation techniques, and increased physical activity. Downing (1988) also outlined several intervention strategies to counter depression in children and adolescents. These strategies are outlined as follows:

Ensuring success experiences. According to Downing (1988), "to reverse the depression sequence, significant adults can systematically manipulate success and positive feedback for the child" (p. 235). Schaefer, Briesmeister, and Fitton (1984) reported similar findings, maintaining that one of the most important intervention strategies for children with self-defeating or self-destructive behaviors is ensuring daily successes in the child's life. It is critical that the child experience some feeling of control, however small, if he or she is to make a behavior change. Intervention team members should ensure successes by establishing small, attainable goals. As coach, the counselor can help the youth break down the goal into steps that can be made in small, success-assured increments. The child or adolescent, depending on his or her developmental readiness, should be actively involved in this process.

Improving social skills and interactions. When subjected to environmental stress and situational pressures, children with poor social skills are more likely to succumb to depression. McLean (1976) illustrated this with the following equation: *Poor social skills yield marginal social interaction, resulting in less social recognition, which produces lower self-esteem and increased vulnerability to depression.* Techniques in assertiveness and self-confidence training can be used to improve social interactions skills.

Increasing activity levels. Supervised exercise with a partner or at a gym has been shown to produce positive changes in brain chemistry. Confidence and success in gaining control over one's physical well-being can be enhanced by jogging, aerobics, walking, or working out with free weights. Cantwell and Carlson (1983) found that increasing a client's activity level helps control depression. Again, involving the client in selecting and planning the activities improves the likelihood of success. Enjoyable activities enhance the probability of a positive response. School attendance, however, should be a priority, and parents should insist that the child do chores and participate in family activities, as well (Downing, 1988). The more commitments or obligations the child meets, the more he or she maintains a self-perception of normalcy, confidence, and control of feelings. The counselor also can encourage clients to develop a "pleasant events schedule by having them make a list of daily events, rank them according to enjoyment, and keep track of how often they do each one" (Forrest, 1990, p. 6).

- **Creating positive team support.** Consistency, continuity, and commitment of all team members are critical to the success of any intervention. Everyone involved should be regularly reminded of their value and appreciated for their contributions of time and energy.
- **Limiting inappropriate attention.** Sometimes family relationships become codependent—with individuals taking responsibility for another person's behavior and consequences. Members of the intervention team should not continually ask how the child is feeling. Response efforts should be focused on behaviors that gain attention in positive ways.
- **Teaching coping and change skills.** Children and adolescents can be taught to be aware of depressive feelings and thoughts when they occur and can learn ways to avoid feelings or ideas that provoke depression. It might help to use Matthews's stress management formula (Matthews, 1986) to teach this skill:

$$\text{Awareness} + \text{Benefits} + \text{Change} + \text{Dependency} = \text{Relaxation}$$
$$(A + B + C + D = R)$$

Essentially, the formula suggests that the awareness of stress plus the benefits of coping techniques lead to a changed response to stress. The child should also develop a repertoire of activities that he or she can implement when feeling depressed. This repertoire might include the following:

- Increasing activity level.
- Redirecting thoughts to pleasant experiences.
- Using deliberate internal affirmations.
- Using productive fantasies or imagery.
- Using biofeedback to increase or decrease the pulse rate.

All these approaches have one thing in common: They empower the youth with strategies that put him or her in control of making the change.

Using Classroom-Focused Strategies

Schloss (1983) identified several classroom-based strategies that can counteract a depressed youth's passivity and sense of helplessness by providing opportunities for success and experiences of control. These strategies include the following:

- Help the student avoid a sense of constant failure by providing work tasks in small, incremental steps that give him or her a sense of mastery and success.
- Neutralize helplessness by providing opportunities for choice and power (for example, in selecting work assignments or self-rewards).
- Provide increased verbal feedback and explanations for the depressed student, who may lack the ability to see cause and effect.
- Encourage depressed students to identify behaviors and outcomes themselves to encourage self-sufficiency.
- Encourage positive self-talk. Cognitive therapists consider depression a result of the influence of negative, irrational beliefs. Clarizio (1985) recommended cognitive restructuring activities within the school or community, in which teachers or helping professionals incorporate into lessons instruction on the relationship between feelings and thoughts. Also useful are role-playing activities that focus on specific problems relevant to childhood depression, such as peer rejection, failure, and guilt.
- Teach thought substitution. Negative emotional reactions and behaviors can be changed by teaching children a thought-substitution process: First they learn to become aware of negative thoughts, then they learn to talk to themselves positively. So, instead of saying to themselves, "Everyone thinks I'm a nerd," they might say, "Chemistry comes easily to me, I really know my stuff. I can help others in the class by being on their study team."
- Teach communication skills. Lack of communication skills and limited positive interpersonal feedback often precipitate depression. Intervention should emphasize increasing the quality, quantity, and breadth of the student's interpersonal communications. Counselor-prescribed contacts—such as making a personal phone call, writing a letter, or walking home with someone and talking to them—develop "internal competition" with the negative self-talk going on inside (Forrest, 1990, p. 7).
- Teach decision-making and problem-solving strategies. Making clear decisions and coping with the sources of stress that precipitate

depression are vital skills. The counselor can teach problem-solving skills by having the depressed client follow these basic steps:

- "Clearly specify the problem.
- Entertain and list several alternative solutions.
- Evaluate the possible and likely outcomes of each solution in terms of time and money spent and short- and long-term effects.
- Think through time constraints, workload, resources, support networks, and coping skills to prevent stress as the client carries out the plan" (Forrest, 1990, p. 7).
- Help the client assume responsibility for choices and actions. To help students assume ownership of their own problems, direct them to think of an incident that made them angry or resentful and that they still have strong feelings about. Have them write about the incident, describing it as if others were completely responsible for causing it. In this exercise, the students are to blame others, making the problem clearly someone else's fault. Then, ask them to rewrite the incident as if *they* were solely responsible for starting, developing, and getting stuck with the problem. Insist that they take full account of what they could have done to change or avoid the situation. Process with them the issues of blame, responsibility, and victimization.

Other important strategies and techniques for classroom initiatives include The Family Safety Watch and Posttraumatic Loss Debriefing. Treatment plans for a loss group and a divorce group also follow.

Treatment Plan: the Family Safety Watch

Counseling intention: Crisis intervention; to provide a collaborative intervention strategy for eliminating or decreasing self-destructive behavior or ideation.

The Family Safety Watch (Landau-Stanton & Stanton, 1985) is an intensive intervention strategy to prevent threatened self-destructive behavior. The safety watch also can be applied to such problems as self-mutilation, anorexia, bulimia, and alcohol or other drug abuse. The procedure is as follows:

1. Family members conduct the watch. They select people to be involved from their nuclear family, extended family, and network of family friends.
2. An around-the-clock schedule is established to determine what the adolescent is to do with his or her time over a 24-hour period: when he or she is to sleep, eat, attend class, do homework, play games, view a movie, and so on.

3. The intervention team leader (a counselor, parent, teacher, or principal) consults with the family to accomplish the following:
   - Determine family resources and support systems.
   - Find ways of involving these support systems in the effort, for example, "How much time do you think Uncle Harry can give to watching your child?"
   - Design a detailed plan for the safety watch.
   - Determine schedules and shifts so that someone is with the at-risk child 24 hours a day.
4. A back-up system is established so that the person on watch can get support from others if needed. A cardinal rule is that the child be within view of someone at all times, even while in the bathroom or when sleeping. The family is warned that the at-risk youth may try to manipulate situations to be alone—for example, by pretending to be fine—and that the first week will be the hardest.
5. The family makes a contractual agreement stating that, if the watch is inadvertently slackened or compromised and the at-risk youth makes a suicide attempt or challenges the program in some way, the regime will be tightened. This is a therapeutic move that reduces the family's feeling of failure should a relapse occur during the year.

The primary goal of the watch is to mobilize the family members to take care of their own and to help them feel competent in doing so (Landau-Stanton & Stanton, 1985). The family, adolescent, and helping professionals collaborate in determining what the adolescent must do in order to relax and ultimately terminate the watch. Task issues should focus on personal responsibility, age-appropriate behavior, and handling of family and social relationships, such as these:

- Rising in the morning without prompting.
- Completing chores on time.
- Substituting courteous and friendly behavior for grumbling and sulking.
- Talking to parents and siblings more openly.
- Watching less TV and spending more time conversing with family, friends, and support networks.

The family and therapeutic team jointly decide to terminate the watch. It is contingent upon the absence of self-destructive behavior and the achievement of an acceptable level of improvement in the other behavioral tasks assigned to the adolescent. If any member of the team believes there is still a risk, full supervision with the safety watch is continued.

This approach appeals to families because it makes them feel empowered and useful and lessens the need for (and so the expense of) an extended hospitalization. It also reestablishes intergenerational boundaries, opens communication within the family, reconnects the nuclear and extended families, and makes the adolescent feel cared for and safe. In addition, it functions as a "compression" move, pushing the youth and family members closer together and holding them there until the rebound or disengagement that almost inevitably follows. This rebound is a necessary step in bringing about appropriate distance within enmeshed subsystems, opening the way for a more viable family structure—a structure that does not require a member to exhibit suicidal or self-destructive behavior in order to communicate a need for attention.

After-care transition and support procedures for The Family Watch include the following:

- Ascertaining the posttreatment plan for the youth and providing support at school.
- Providing feedback to staff.
- Monitoring student behavior.
- Providing feedback to parent or guardian regarding adjustment concerns.

Treatment Plan: Posttraumatic Loss Debriefing

Counseling intention: To help participants process loss and grief after the death of a loved one; to teach them about typical stress response reactions and their implications.

Each of the six stages of the debriefing takes 2 to 6 hours to complete, depending on need and available coping skills. Follow-up debriefing may be performed with the entire group, a portion of it, or an individual. More than one session may be necessary to process the collection of painful physical, emotional, and cognitive reactions. Once survivors come to terms with stress reactions, they can return to their precrisis equilibrium (Thompson, 1990, 1993).

1. Introductory Stage
Briefly introduce the debriefing process and establish rules for the process.

- Define the nature, limits, roles, and goals of the process.
- Clarify time limits, number of sessions, confidentiality rules, possibilities, and expectations to reduce unknowns and anxiety.

2. Fact Stage

This is the warm-up and information-gathering stage, when participants are asked to re-create the event for the leader. The focus of this stage is facts, not feelings.

- Group members are asked to make brief statements about their role, relationship with the deceased, how they heard about the death, and circumstances surrounding the event.
- Members take turns adding details to make the incident come to life again.
- Members engage in a moderate level of self-disclosure. Questions such as "Could you tell me what that was like for you?" encourage this process.

The counselor needs to be aware of members' choices of topics regarding the death to gain insight into their priorities for the moment. To curtail self-blaming, the counselor should help members see the many factors contributing to the death.

This low-level initial interaction is a nonthreatening warm-up and naturally leads into a discussion of feelings in the next stage. It also provides a safe climate for sharing the details of the death.

3. Feeling Stage

At this stage, survivors should have the opportunity to share the feelings they are experiencing in a nonjudgmental, supportive, and understanding environment. Survivors must be permitted to talk about themselves, to identify and express feelings, to identify their own reactions, and to relate to the immediate present. Thoughtful clarification or reflection of feelings can lead to growth and change, rather than to self-deprecation and self-pity.

At this stage, it is critical that no one gets left out of the discussion and that no one dominates the discussion at the expense of others.

Members often will discuss their fears, anxieties, concerns, guilt, frustration, anger, and ambivalence. All of these feelings—positive or negative, big or small—are important and need to be expressed and heard. Most important, this process allows members to see that subtle changes are occurring between what happened *then* and what is happening *now*—that things do get better, however small the changes may be.

4. Reaction Stage

At this stage, the counselor explores the physical and cognitive reactions to the traumatic event. There are two important steps to follow during this stage:

- Ask such questions as "What reactions did you experience at the time of the incident or when you were informed of the death? ... What are you experiencing now?"
- Encourage members to discuss what is going on with them in their peer, school, work, and family relationships.

5. Learning Stage

This stage is designed to teach members new coping skills to deal with their grief. It is also therapeutic to help survivors realize that others are having similar feelings and experiences:

- Teach the group something about their typical stress response reactions.
- Describe how typical and natural it is for people to experience a wide variety of feelings, emotions, and physical reactions to any traumatic event. It is not unique but a universal, shared reaction.

It is critical in this stage to be alert to danger signals in order to prevent negative outcomes and to help survivors return to their precrisis equilibrium and interpersonal stability.

6. Closure

In this stage, the counselor provides final reassurances and follow-up, wrapping up loose ends and answering outstanding questions. Specifically, the counselor determines that initial stress symptoms have been reduced or eliminated, assesses survivors' increased coping abilities, and determines whether participants need further intervention. The counselor also makes arrangements for follow-up contact once the sessions have been completed.

The group may close by planning a group activity—for example, going to a movie or concert or on a similar outing—to promote a sense of purpose and unity.

Treatment Plan: Loss Group for Adolescents

Counseling intention: To assist members who have suffered the loss of a parent or other caregiver; to help them understand the stages of grief; to clarify and accept their feelings; to provide a supportive place to share their experiences with death.

Session 1: Getting-to-know-you exercise. This session focuses on helping students discover they are not alone in their loss and on getting acquainted with group members. The counselor should lead the group in a low-risk, get-acquainted exercise that emphasizes similarities among group members.

Session 2: Explore the causes of death. Members identify the many ways people die: for example, accidents, murder, old age, illness, or suicide. The counselor leads the group in a discussion of how some causes of death are easier to accept than others. Each member shares his or her experience with the group.

Session 3: Stages of grief. The counselor explains the stages of grief— denial, anger, bargaining, depression, and acceptance—and discusses the progression to each stage. The group identifies which stages take longer to move through. Members determine what stages they are in now.

Session 4: Concerns and acceptance. The counselor helps determine concerns members have about death that interfere with their acceptance. Members draw pictures illustrating dreams they have had about their parent or caregiver since that person's death. Older students may prefer to describe their dreams. The counselor should look for similarities in themes such as fear, loneliness, wishing for the parent to return, or other unfinished business. The counselor also emphasizes the importance of talking about their concerns with someone they trust.

Session 5: Special personal achievement. Members are asked to write a letter to their late parent or caregiver, sharing something they are especially proud of and wish they could tell the person about. It is important to leave the group on a positive note. The counselor should briefly summarize the issues discussed and ask whether the group would like to continue meeting as a support group.

Treatment Plan: Divorce Group for Children or Adolescents

Counseling intention: To clarify members' feelings toward divorce; to help members understand that others have similar feelings and concerns; to help them gain a realistic awareness of the situation; to teach them to cope with their feelings.

Wilkinson and Bleck (1977) outlined the following activities for a divorce group for children or adolescents:

Session 1: Introductions. Explain roles, expectations, and membership rules.

Session 2: Nondivorce-related self-disclosure. Pleasant and unpleasant feeling words are introduced so that the members can feel more comfortable about disclosing and discussing feelings.

Session 3: Bibliography on divorce and discussion. The counselor reads a story about parents getting divorced. Members discuss their reactions to the characters' feelings and behaviors.

Session 4: Divorce-related self-disclosure. A sheet of paper is divided into four quadrants. Members are asked to draw a picture of a good time they had with their families, an unpleasant time, why they think their parents got divorced, and what they would like to see happen to their families during the coming year. Members share their papers with the group (Omizo & Omizo, 1988).

Session 5: Role-playing the problems of divorce. Members brainstorm the problems of divorce, then pair off and select one problem to role-play for 3 to 5 minutes.

Session 6: Continued role-playing. Members role-play other problems. The counselor then leads an in-depth discussion.

Session 7: Positive aspects of divorce. The group discusses positive aspects of divorce (for example, parents no longer fighting). Each member completes a personal collage that reflects these positive attributes and shares it with the group.

Session 8: Building self-esteem. The counselor provides a checklist of positive adjectives; members select positive attributes of others to share in the group.

Sessions 9 and 10: Coping with parental divorce. The counselor introduces coping skills and techniques such as time management, stress management, communication skills, positive self-talk, and conflict resolution.

Session 11: Closure. The counselor solicits feedback on group learning and follow-up concerns.

Several group approaches are applicable to children and adolescents:

Situational and transition groups offer information, emotional support, shared feelings, and experiences within a group context, emphasizing the universality of experiences and feelings.

Structured groups teach children and adolescents how to deal with crisis situations through group discussions, role-playing, experiential activities, and expressive techniques such as art therapy.

Saturday workshops (for youth ages 10 to 17) focus on various themes regarding divorce, such as assertiveness training, learning to express feelings, boundary issues, communication skills, and joint custody issues.

The counselor's role is to provide a stable environment to discuss anxieties and concerns; to maintain consistent expectations and routines; to engage in a supportive, therapeutic alliance to encourage communication; and to inform parents about their child's progress or difficulties.

The counselor also provides instruction in specific social, emotional, and cognitive skills to improve targeted symptom behaviors, such as positive self-talk, cognitive awareness strategies, study skills, coping skills, assertiveness, opportunities to discharge emotions through increased physical activity, and biofeedback techniques to aid in relaxation or mood states (Downing, 1988; Hart, 1991).

Collective Community Initiatives

Young people need to develop coping skills and support networks and to be held in high esteem. A developmentally appropriate prevention model proposed by McWhirter, McWhirter, McWhirter, and McWhirter (1993) suggested that counselors follow these three steps:

1. Use generic skills-training and prevention programs for children in early elementary grades (e.g., programs on identifying feelings, dealing with conflict, and managing emotions).
2. Focus on topic-specific prevention and intervention efforts for youth during preadolescence.
3. Use more topic-specific preventions and interventions for adolescents (e.g., on dealing with loss, stages of grief, and seasonal affective disorders).

Conclusion

Suicide and self-injury do not typically have a sudden onset. A number of stresses can contribute to a youth's anxiety and unhappiness, increasing the possibility of a suicide attempt. Suicide is preventable, and education is the key. The causes of childhood and adolescent depression are multidimensional and probably differ from case to case. Adolescent depression may have its own distinct causes. Many researchers maintain that childhood and adolescent depressions often manifest themselves in other behaviors or symptoms, such as irritability, hyperactivity, aggressiveness, delinquency, somatic complaints, hypochondria, anorexia nervosa, substance abuse, obesity, poor school performance, school phobia,

Table 6.6   Treatment Plan: Multimodal Treatment for Depression

Counseling intention: To provide a comprehensive intervention for behavior change.

Modality and referral problems	Related interventions
Behavior Reduced work performance Diminished activity Statements of self-denigration	• Implement a "pleasant event schedule" (ascertain behaviors, sensations, images, ideas, and people the student used to find rewarding) to ensure a daily sampling of pleasing activities.
Affect Sadness, guilt, "heavy-heartedness" Intermittent anxiety and anger	• Use standard anxiety-reduction methods (e. g., relaxation, meditation, calming self-statements combined with assertiveness training; a repertoire of self-assertive and uninhibited responses).
Sensation Less pleasure from food Diminished enthusiasm for life Easily fatigued	• Add a specific list of pleasant visual, auditory, tactile, olfactory, and gustatory stimuli to the "pleasant events schedule" to create a "sensate-focus" of enjoyable events.
Imagery Visions of loneliness and failure Visions of himself or herself being rejected by important people in life	• Recall past successes. • Picture small but successful outcomes. • Apply coping imagery, the use of "time projection" (i.e., the client pictures him- or herself venturing step by step into a future characterized by positive affect and pleasurable activities).
Cognition Negative self-appraisal Exaggerates real or imagined shortcomings: "I'm not good at anything"; "Things will always be bad for me."	• Employ Ellis's (1989) methods of cognitive disputation, challenge categorical imperatives ("shoulds and oughts") and irrational beliefs. • Identify worthwhile qualities and recite them every day.
Interpersonal Decreased social participation	• Teach clients four skills: saying "no!" to unreasonable requests; asking for favors by expressing positive feelings; volunteering criticism; and "disputing with style" (the client learns to ask for what he or she wants, resists unwelcome requests or exploitation from others, initiates conversations, and develops more interpersonal relationships). • If appropriate, recommend family therapy to teach family members how to avoid reinforcing depressive behavior and how to encourage the client to engage in pleasurable activities.
Drugs/Biology Appetite unimpaired but has intermittent insomnia	• Address issues pertaining to increased exercise, relaxation, appropriate sleep patterns, and overall physical fitness. • If appropriate, recommend biological intervention, such as antidepressants in the case of bipolar disorders.

loss of initiative, social withdrawal, sleep disturbances, and attention deficit disorder (Angold, 1988; Carlson, 1981; Carlson & Cantwell, 1980; Carlson & Garber, 1986; Husain & Vandiver, 1984; Strober, McCracken, & Hanna, 1989).

The negative effects of divorce also are linked to depression and to excessive anger, aggression, self-destructive behaviors, decreased academic achievement, juvenile delinquency, thoughts of suicide, and sexual promiscuity (Benedek & Benedek, 1979; Bundy & Gumar, 1984; Farber, Primavera, & Felner, 1983). Kelly and Wallerstein (1976) found that children of divorce often experience feelings similar to those associated with death: shock, disbelief, and denial. Children of divorce also suffer from low self-esteem and feelings of abandonment, guilt, helplessness, and inadequacy. Omizo and Omizo (1988) found that being aware of their feelings, being able to express them, giving and receiving positive feedback, and knowing that others experience similar feelings had a positive impact on adolescents in group counseling.

Depression is positively correlated to suicidal behavior, so recognizing the symptoms of depression is extremely important in preventing teen suicide. Adolescents in particular are likely to have little verbal communication with parents, turning instead to peers or other concerned individuals whom they trust. Therefore, a workable referral system that uses resources within the schools (counselors, social workers, and psychologists) and within the community (mental health professionals, private professionals, and treatment agencies) is crucial.

Social, Emotional, and Cognitive Skills

Social Literacy Skills

Social literacy skills are interpersonal skills essential for meaningful interaction with others. Social skills are those behaviors that, within a given situation, predict such important social outcomes as peer acceptance, popularity, self-efficacy, competence, and high self-esteem. Social skills fall into such categories as being kind, cooperative, and compliant to reduce defiance, aggression, conflict, and antisocial behavior; and showing interest in people and socializing successfully to reduce behavior problems associated with withdrawal, depression, and fear. Social skills include problem solving, assertiveness, thinking critically, resolving conflict, managing anger, and utilizing peer-pressure refusal skills.

Skills Boxes
Permission is granted to reproduce skills boxes for individual client use.

Giving Constructive Criticism

A formula for giving someone constructive criticism involves six steps:

1. Give the person two compliments. Be honest, sincere, and specific.
2. Address the person by name.
3. In a pleasant tone of voice, state your criticism in one or two short, clear sentences.
4. Tell the person what you would like him or her to do. Keep it simple. Set a time limit, if it's appropriate to do so.
5. Offer your help, encouragement, and support.
6. Thank the person for his or her time and for listening.

Helpful Feedback

Helpful feedback tells someone how his or her actions are affecting others. It is important to give feedback in a way that will not be threatening or lead to defensiveness. Some characteristics of helpful feedback are listed here:

- Focus your feedback on the person's behavior, not on personality.
- Focus your feedback on descriptions, not on judgments.
- Focus your feedback on a specific situation, not on abstract generalizations.
- Focus your feedback on the here-and-now, not on the there-and-then.
- Focus your feedback on sharing your perceptions and feelings, not on giving advice.
- Focus your feedback on actions the person can change.

Giving Constructive Feedback

To give constructive feedback, it is important to follow these guidelines:

1. **Ask permission.** Ask the person if he or she would like some feedback on behavior. (If no, wait for a more appropriate time; if yes, proceed.)
2. **Say something positive** to the person before you deliver sensitive information.
3. **Describe the behavior.** Be specific and verifiable. (Have other people complained?) Consider only behavior that can be changed.
4. **Focus on only one behavior at a time.** Include some suggestion for improvement.

Here is an example: "Jessica, I've notice something about your behavior at our meetings. Would you like to hear it? ... At the last two meetings of the homecoming committee, whenever Ryan suggested a theme, you interrupted him and changed the subject. It would be helpful if you would listen to him."

Asking for What You Want*

Asking for what you want involves making an assertive request. It is important to make clear statements so that others understand what you want. Here are the facts you need to include:

From ... Write down the name of the person who can give you what you want.

I want ... Be specific about what you want the other person to do. Specify exact behavior, for example, "I want to have an equal vote on where we go on Friday night" or "I want the real reason why you don't include John in our plans anymore."

---

* *Note.* From *Self-Esteem: A Proven Program of Cognitive Techniques for Assessing, Improving, and Maintaining Your Self-Esteem,* by M. McKay and P. Fanning, 1987, Oakland, CA: New Harbinger Publications. Copyright 1987 by New Harbinger Publications, Inc. Reprinted with permission.

When ... State the deadline for getting what you want, the exact time of day, or the frequency with which you want something. For example, you may want extra help with chemistry. Be specific: "Every Thursday night after dinner."

Where ... Write down the place where you want something, the location that will serve to define precisely what you want. If you want to be left alone when you are in your room, specify that place as your special place to be alone.

With... Specify any other people who have to do with your request. For example, if you want your brother to stop teasing you about your braces in front of his friends, spell out all the friends' names.

Here is an example:

From: Ryan

I want: No more jokes or remarks about my clothes, my braces, or my friends. I want to be treated with respect.

When: When your friends come over.

Where: At home, at the mall, or at the burger place.

With: John, Ralph, and Bobby.

Emotional Literacy Skills

Emotional literacy skills are intrapersonal abilities such as knowing one's emotions by recognizing a feeling as it happens and monitoring it; managing emotions (e.g., shaking off anxiety, gloom, irritability, and the consequences of failure); motivating oneself to attain goals, delay gratification, stifle impulsiveness, and maintain self-control; recognizing emotions in others with empathy and perspective taking; and handling interpersonal relationships effectively. Emotional skills fall into categories such as knowing the relationship among thoughts, feelings, and actions; establishing a sense of identity and acceptance of self; learning to value teamwork, collaboration, and cooperation; regulating one's mood; empathizing; and maintaining hope.

Positive Affirmations

Many people are limited by their negative thinking. They may be judgmental, opinionated, or highly critical of themselves. Positive affirmations can soften self-imposed demands or criticisms. Guidelines for positive affirmations follow:

- Begin with the words, "*I am.*"
- Include your name in the affirmation.
- Choose positive words.
- Phrase it in the present tense.
- Keep statements short.
- Incorporate your strengths.
- Once you have constructed an affirmation, close your eyes, repeat the affirmation several times (at least three), and notice what inner picture it creates. If the picture it creates matches your desired outcome, your affirmation is a good one.

Here is an example: "I, Jessica, am capable, conscientious, and intelligent. I will be successful in what I attempt to do."

Paraphrasing

To convey to other people that you understand the meaning of what they said, paraphrase what you heard them say in your own words. Follow these guidelines:

- Listen attentively.
- Pause to determine what the message means to *you.*
- Restate the meaning you got from the message, using your own words.
- Obtain a confirmation from the other person that the meaning you conveyed was correct.
- Here is an example:
  "My history teacher just assigned three more chapters for the test tomorrow and I am scheduled to work tonight."
  Jessica replies, "You must feel stressed and overwhelmed about what you need to do."

Dealing with Perfectionism

Some people are driven to perfectionism, so much so that the anxiety interferes with their performance. Panic attacks, self-doubt, and negative self-talk are common. Below are some thoughts to counteract the need to be perfect:

- I would like to do my best, but I do not have to be perfect.
- Making a mistake doesn't mean I have failed.
- I can do something well and appreciate it without it being perfect.
- I will be happier and perform better if I try to work at a realistic level rather than demanding perfection of myself.
- It is impossible to function perfectly every time.
- It is important to stop and smell the roses.

Expressing Intentions

Expressing intention lets others know more about your immediate or long-range expectations. Expressing intentions is a way of being direct about what you would or would not like to do. Intention statements begin with words like these:

"I want ..."
"I'd like ..."
"I intend ..."

Here are some examples:

"I want to be with you today, but I don't want to spend all our time shopping."
"I'd like to do my studying in the afternoon, then catch the game this evening."
"I'd like to be with you, but I want to be with my family tonight too, because it's my brother's birthday."

Perception Checking

Perception checking is a verbal statement that reflects your own understanding of the meaning of another person's nonverbal cues. The process for perception checking is as follows:

1. Pause and observe the behavior.
2. Describe the behavior mentally.
3. Ask yourself, "What does the behavior mean to me?"
4. Put your interpretation of the nonverbal behavior into words to check whether your perception of the situation is accurate.

For example, Ryan, speaking in an abrupt tone of voice, gives Jessica the assignment she missed in class.

Jessica (using a perception check) says, "From the sound of your voice, Ryan, I get the impression you're upset with me. What's going on?"

CHAPTER 7

Violence, Delinquency, Gangs, and Bullying Behavior

Violence

Violence is perhaps one of the most pervasive and serious threat to the mental health and well-being of youth in the United States. Young people are disproportionately represented as both victims and perpetrators of violence. National school-based data indicate that violence, especially bullying behavior, is prevalent in many schools. The 2003 Youth Risk Behavior Surveillance Survey indicates that 42% of adolescents were in a physical fight during the 12 months preceding the survey and 22% carried a weapon during the 30 days preceding the survey. Another study found that 50% of boys and 25% of girls reported being physically attacked by someone at school (Centers for Disease Control and Prevention [CDC], 1992). The CDC also reported 105 violent deaths in school in the 2-year period from 1992 to 1994. The National Center for Education Statistics (NCES) (1998) found that more than half of public schools experienced some crime during the 1996–1997 school year, and 1 in 10 schools reported at least one serious violent crime during that year (NCES, 1998).

The homicide rate for men ages 15 to 24 in this country has increased at an alarming rate in the past 2 decades (Prothrow-Stith, 1991, 1993) with more than half of all serious crimes (murders, rapes, assaults, and robberies) committed by youth ages 10 to 17 (Winbush, 1988). However, after years of relative stability in the number of juvenile Violent Crime Index arrests, the increase in these arrests between 1988 and 1994 focused national attention on the problem of juvenile violence. After peaking in 1994, these arrests dropped each year from 1995 through 2002, then held constant for 2003. For all Violent Crime Index offenses combined, the number of juvenile arrests in 2003 was the lowest since 1987. The number of juvenile aggravated assault arrests in 2003 was lower than in any year since 1989. The number of juvenile arrests in 2003 for murder and for forcible rape were both lower than in any year since at least 1980. Finally, even with the marginal 3% increase in the number of juvenile arrests for robbery between 2002 and 2003, the counts for these years were still lower than in any year since at least 1980. In 2003, for the ninth consecutive year, the rate of juvenile arrests for Violent Crime Index offenses—murder, forcible rape, robbery, and aggravated assault—declined (Snyder, 2005). Media images, violent films and music (e.g., "gangster rap" and "death metal"), and video games such as *Grand Theft Auto* often glorify interpersonal violence. Violence has become a crisis of epidemic proportions for children in urban centers in the United States (Pynoos & Nader, 1988).

Violence is most prevalent among the poor, regardless of race. And the victims and perpetrators of the carnage are getting younger and more violent. Socioeconomic inequity fosters a sense of relative deprivation among the poor, and the lack of opportunities to improve their life circumstances manifests itself in higher rates of violence and a lack of hope about the future.

The increase in juvenile violent crime over the last decade should serve as a wake-up call to the nation that current policies have not worked to diminish violence among young people. The corridors of juvenile courts are increasingly populated by parents who are still children themselves, children who have no parent but the state, and baby-faced teenagers charged with crimes worthy of the most hardened criminals.

Today, it is painfully clear that children are committing more serious crimes at ever younger ages. The most common crimes committed by adolescents are vandalism, motor vehicle theft, burglary, larceny, robbery, and stolen property. Vandalism and theft often correlate with drug and alcohol use; children steal in order to pay for a drug habit.

Statistics paint an alarming picture:

- In 2002, more than 877,700 young people ages 10 to 24 were injured from violent acts. Approximately 1 in 13 required hospitalization (CDC, 2004).
- Homicide is the second leading cause of death among young people aged 10 to 24. In this age group, it is the leading cause of death for African-Americans; the second leading cause of death for Hispanics; and the third leading cause of death for American Indians, Alaskan Natives, and Asian Pacific Islanders (Anderson & Smith, 2003).
- In 2001, 5,486 young people aged 10 to 24 were murdered—an average of 15 each day (CDC, 2004).
- In 2001, 79% of homicide victims aged 10 to 24 were killed with firearms (CDC, 2004).
- Between 1994 and 1999, 172 students aged 5 to 18 were killed on or near school grounds or at school-related activities (Anderson & Smith, 2003).
- More than 50% of all school-associated violent deaths occur at the beginning or end of the school day or during lunch (Anderson & Smith, 2003).
- In a nationwide survey, 17% of students reported carrying a weapon (e.g., gun, knife, or club) on one or more days in the 30 days preceding the survey (Grunbaum, Kann, Kinchen, Ross, Lowry, & Harris, 2004).
- Among students nationwide, 33% reported being in a physical fight 1 or more times in the 12 months preceding the survey (Grunbaum et al., 2004).
- Data from a study of eighth and ninth grade students showed 25% had been victims of nonsexual dating violence and 8% had been victims of sexual dating violence (Foshee, Linder, Bauman, Langwick, Arriaga, Heath, McMahon, & Bangdiwala, 1996).
- Nationwide, 9% of students reported being hit, slapped, or physically hurt on purpose by their boyfriend or girlfriend in the 12 months prior to being surveyed (Grunbaum et al., 2004).
- The child homicide rate in the United States (2.6 per 100,000 for children younger than 15 years) is 5 times higher than the rate of 25 other industrialized countries combined (CDC, 2001).
- The 2001 National Household Survey on Drug Abuse (NHSDA) report found that 28% of the nation's youth have participated in a serious fight either at school or at work, have taken part in a group-against-group fight, or have attacked others with the intent of seriously hurting them (U.S. Department of Health and Human Services,

Substance Abuse and Mental Health Services Administration Office of Applied Studies, 2002).

- The U.S. Department of Justice (2000) reported that juveniles are twice as likely as adults to be victims of serious violent crime and 3 times as likely to be victims of assault.
- In a comprehensive study by the U.S. Department of Justice, Office of Delinquency Prevention (2000) reported that 8.8 million youth indicated that they had seen someone else being shot, stabbed, sexually assaulted, physically assaulted, or threatened with a weapon.

Special Groups at Risk

- Among 10- to 24-year-olds, homicide is the leading cause of death for African-Americans; the second leading cause of death for Hispanics; and the third leading cause of death for American Indians, Alaskan Natives, and Asian Pacific Islanders (Anderson & Smith, 2003).
- Of the 5,486 homicides reported in the 10-to-24 age group in 2001, 85% (4,659) were males and 15% (827) were females (CDC, 2004).
- A nationwide survey found male students (41%) more likely to have been involved in a physical fight than female students (25%) in the 12 months preceding the survey (Grunbaum et al., 2004).
- A nationwide survey found female students (12%) more likely than male students (6%) to have been forced to have sexual intercourse (Grunbaum et al., 2004).

School Shootings

School shootings are a rare but significant component of school violence in America. It is clear that other kinds of problems are far more common than the targeted attacks that have taken place in schools across this country. However, each school-based attack has had a tremendous and lasting effect on the school in which it occurred, the surrounding community, and the nation as a whole.

To put the problem of targeted school-based attacks in context, from 1993 to 1997 the odds that a child in grades 9 through 12 would be threatened or injured with a weapon in school were 7% to 8%, or 1 in 13 or 14; the odds of getting into a physical fight at school were 15%, or 1 in 7 (Vossekuil, Fein, Reddy, Borum & Modzeleski, 2002). In contrast, the odds that a child would die in school—by homicide or suicide—are, fortunately, no greater than 1 in 1 million (Vossekuil et al., 2002). In 1998, students in grades 9 through 12 were the victims of 1.6 million thefts and 1.2 million nonfatal violent crimes; in this same period 60 school-associated violent deaths were reported for this student population (Vossekuil et al., 2002). Support for these suggestions is found in 10 key findings of the Safe School Initiative study (Vossekuil et al., 2002). These findings are as follows:

1. Incidents of targeted violence at school rarely were sudden, impulsive acts.
2. Prior to most incidents, other people knew about the attacker's idea or plan to attack.
3. Most attackers did not threaten their targets directly prior to advancing the attack.
4. There is no accurate or useful "profile" of students who engaged in targeted school violence, although many felt bullied, picked on, isolated, and were depressed.
5. Many attackers felt bullied, persecuted, or injured by others prior to the attack.
6. Most attackers engaged in some behavior prior to the incident that caused others concern or indicated a need for help.
7. Most attackers had difficulty coping with significant losses or personal failures.
8. Moreover, many had considered or attempted suicide.
9. Most attackers had access to and had used weapons prior to the attack.

In many cases, other students were involved in some capacity. Despite prompt law enforcement responses, most shooting incidents were stopped by means other than law enforcement intervention. Most incidents of targeted school violence were thought out and planned in advance. The attackers' behavior suggested that they were planning or preparing for an attack. Prior to most incidents, the attackers' peers knew that the attack was to occur. And most attackers were not "invisible" but already were of concern to people in their lives.

The solution from current research, the use of a threat-assessment approach, may be a promising strategy for preventing a school-based attack. Educators, law enforcement officials, and others with public-safety responsibilities may be able to prevent some incidents of targeted school violence if they know what information to look for and what to do with such information when it is found. In sum, these officials may benefit from focusing their efforts on formulating strategies for preventing these attacks in two principal areas:

Table 7.1 Personality Traits and Behaviors That May Be Warning Signs of Potential Violence, Divided into Preliminary Clusters

Cluster	Personality traits/behaviors
Coping/anger management	Low tolerance for frustration
	Poor coping skills
	Lack of resiliency
	Failed love relationship
	Injustice collector
	Anger management problems
Behavior signs	Leakage
	Change of behavior
	Behavior relevant to threat
Depression	Alienation
	Signs of depression
	Mask for low self-esteem
Narcissism	Narcissism
	Dehumanization of others
	Lack of empathy
	Exaggerated sense of entitlement
	Attitude of superiority
	Exaggerated or pathological need for attention
	Externalizes blame
Fascination with violence and violent people	Inappropriate humor
	Unusual interest in sensational violence
	Fascination with violent entertainment
	Negative role models
Rigidity	Intolerance
	Manipulation of others
	Lack of trust
	Closed social group
	Rigid and opinionated

Source: From *The School Shooter: A Threat Assessment Perspective* by M. E. O'Toole, 2002, Quantico, VA: Federal Bureau of Investigation. Copyright 2002 by Federal Bureau of Investigation. Reprinted with permission.

1. Developing the capacity to pick up on and evaluate available or knowable information that might indicate that there is a risk of a targeted school attack.
2. Employing the results of these risk evaluations, or "threat assessments," in developing strategies to prevent potential school attacks from occurring.

Table 7.2 Family, School, and Social Dynamics That May Be Warning Signs of Potential Violence

System	Dynamics
Family dynamics	Turbulent parent–child relationship
	Acceptance of pathological behavior
	Access to weapons
	Lack of intimacy
	Student rules the roost
	No limits on or monitoring of TV and Internet
School dynamics	Student's detachment from school
	Tolerance for disrespectful behavior
	Inequitable discipline
	Inflexible culture
	Pecking order among students
	Code of silence
	Unsupervised computer access
Social dynamics	Peer groups
	Drugs and alcohol
	Outside interests
	The copycat effect

Source: From *The School Shooter: A Threat Assessment Perspective* by M. E. O'Toole, 2002, Quantico, VA: Federal Bureau of Investigation. Copyright 2002 by Federal Bureau of Investigation. Reprinted with permission.

The threat-assessment model outlined by the Federal Bureau of Investigation (O'Toole, 2000) delineated four prongs of influence in the outcome of potential violence among youth:

1. Personality traits and behavior.
2. Family dynamics.
3. School dynamics.
4. Social dynamics.

Each prong was further developed to include categories of warning signs linked to potential violence (see Table 7.1 and Table 7.2). These prongs were used to determine the frequency with which student were able to identify different categories of behavior in themselves and others as warning signs of potential violence (Schaefer-Schiumo & Ginsberg, 2003). Although these are still preliminary data, the implications are that violence prevention programs must be implemented long term and must address not only student behavior and personality traits, but family, school, and social components, as well (Moffitt, 1997; Pallone & Hennessy, 1996).

Finally, in a poignant report on lethal violence in schools, Gaughan, Cerio, and Myers (2001) maintained:

> If we want to address this agonizing problem, perhaps we should pay some attention to what the children are telling us. We need "kinder, gentler" schools. We cannot continue to allow bullying and abuse as normal milestones of child development. We need to communicate the value of caring, and demonstrate that care. We need to provide alternatives to violence for problem solving to encourage more frequent, open, and genuine communication between students and the adults who care for them at home, at school, and in the community. (p. 38)

Truly, every behavior is a communication, and today's youth are demonstrating by their behavior that they do not feel connected to school and that the system often reflects a school-as-institution rather than a school-as-community atmosphere. School culture and an atmosphere of tolerance and acceptance are necessary for students to feel they belong, that they are cared for, and that they have a sense of trust and well-being.

Bullying Behavior

Bullying behavior has emerged as a serious problem in schools today, marked by intimidation or by repeated physical, verbal, sexual, or psychological attacks. There are typically three parties involved in the process: the victim, the bully, and the bystander. Many of the school shooters were victims of taunting, bullying, and deprecating behavior by their peers. In general, a student is being bullied or victimized when he or she is exposed, repeatedly and over time, to negative actions on the part of one or more other students (Olweus, 2003). Some experts believe that bullying should be considered a special form of child abuse, that is, "peer abuse," the cruelty of children to one another (Fried & Fried, 2003).

Youth who are bullied have higher rates of suicide, depression, posttraumatic stress disorder, and substance abuse (U.S. Department of Health and Human Services, Center for Mental Health Services, 2003). Hostile kids who mistrust or do not bond with peers are much more likely than their peers to develop physical symptoms linked to diabetes, heart disease, and hypertension in the future (Raikkonen, Matthews, & Solomon, 2003). Finally, according to the most recent Secret Service Safe Schools Research Initiative (2000), almost 75% of students who used violent weapons at school (e.g., guns, knives or other weapons) to attack educators or peers felt persecuted, bullied, threatened, taunted, attacked, ridiculed, or injured by others prior to the violent event (Nansel, Overpack, Pilla, Ruan,

Simons-Morton, & Scheidt, 2001). Children and adolescents exposed to violence, either domestically or publicly, often suffer long-term problems such as anxiety, depression, posttraumatic stress, low self-esteem, anger, and self-destructive behavior (Flannery & Singer, 1999).

Essentially, bullying in schools has become a serious threat to the well-being and productiveness of many children and adolescents that cannot be ignored, as these statistics show:

- Law-enforcement agencies made 129,600 juvenile arrests for violent crimes in 1992, a 55% increase from 1983, when there were 83,400 arrests (Portner, 1995).

- Today, homicide is the third leading cause of death for all children between the ages of 5 and 14; the second leading cause of death for all young people between the ages of 10 and 24; and the leading cause of death among African-Americans of both sexes between the ages of 15 and 34. Teenagers are more than twice as likely to be victims of violent crime than those over the age of 20 (Sautter, 1995).

- Juvenile arrests for violent crimes increased by 50% between 1983 and 1992—double the adult increase. Juvenile arrests for murder rose 85%—four times the increase for adults. Today, 3 of every 10 juvenile murder arrests involve a victim under the age of 18. National surveys repeatedly show that people under the age of 20 account for a disproportionate percentage of violent-crime victims and that teenage victimization is most likely to occur at school (Gallup International Institute, 1995).

- Juvenile arrests for murders, forcible rapes, robberies, and other violent crimes have reached an all-time high, accounting for 17% of all arrests for such crimes. One in 20 persons arrested for a violent crime today is under the age of 15 (Brookman, 1993).

- Researchers contend that the increase in the murder rate of young men is linked, in part, to the recruitment of youth into drug markets, where guns are used to settle disputes (Lawton, 1994). In 1991, 88% of all homicides among 15- to 19-year-olds were firearm related (Portner, 1995).

- In larger, more urban communities, 20% of all males belong to gangs (Brookman, 1993).

- Homicide is the leading cause of death among African-American youth (Lawton, 1994).

- In 1994, there were more than 1 million people in federal prisons and an additional 500,000 in local jails. The annual cost of incarcerating federal prisoners has been estimated at $70,000–100,000 per inmate (Snyder & Sickmund, 1999).

- As the crime rate rose during the 1980s, so did the number of children living in poverty. In 1992, 14.6 million juveniles lived below the poverty level, a 42% increase from 1976 (Portner, 1995).

Violence also has a psychological impact. Posttraumatic stress experienced by victims of and witnesses to violence "includes intrusive imagery, emotional constriction or avoidance, fears of recurrence, sleep disturbance, disinterest in significant activities, and concentration difficulties" (APA, 1993 p. 16; Thompson, 1990, 1993). Violence and posttraumatic stress interfere with normal development, with learning in school, and with a child's inherent right to a happy childhood. All fall victim to the fear, the anger, the guilt, and the helplessness that follow an act of violence.

Strategies to Counter Bullying in Schools

Successful antibullying programs suggest that a comprehensive approach in schools can change student behaviors and attitudes and increase adults' willingness to intervene. Efforts to prevent bullying successfully must address individual, familial, and community risk factors, as well as promote an understanding of the severity and long-range implications of the problem. Research supports a schoolwide approach requiring interventions at the school, class, and individual levels. A comprehensive approach includes the following factors:

- Establishing a schoolwide policy that addresses indirect bullying (e.g., rumor spreading, isolation, social exclusion), which is more hidden, as well as direct bullying (e.g., physical aggression).
- Providing guidelines for teachers, support staff, and students (including bystanders) on specific actions to take if bullying occurs.
- Educating and involving parents so they understand the problem, recognize its signs, and intervene appropriately.
- Adopting specific strategies to deal with individual bullies and victims, including meeting with their parents.
- Encouraging students to be helpful to classmates who may be bullied.
- Developing tailored strategies to counter bullying in specific school hot spots, using environmental redesign, increased supervision (e.g., by teachers, other staff members, parents, volunteers), or electronic surveillance equipment.

- Conducting postintervention surveys to assess the strategies' impact on school bullying (Sampson, 2004, pp. 19–20).

Bullying can be direct or indirect and can be accomplished through physical, verbal, or other means. Although bullying among children and adolescents can occur in any setting, it typically occurs at school or on the way to or from school. The racial composition and setting of the school are not predictive of bullying. Boys tend to use physical and verbal bullying, whereas girls use more subtle and psychological manipulative behaviors, such as alienation, ostracism, and character defamation.

Predictors of Violent Behavior

The American Psychological Association (APA, 1993) found that "the strongest developmental predictor of a child's involvement in violence is a history of previous violence" (p. 4). Being a victim of abuse also is a factor. About 70% of men involved in the criminal justice system were abused or neglected as children. The long-range implications and overt ramifications of abuse are documented in violent crimes. The criminal profiles that follow illustrate how dysfunctional and abusive relationships in childhood can play out tragically in adulthood:

> "My future is small, my past an insult to any human being. My mother must have thought I was a canoe, she paddled me so much" (Arthur Bremer, who, on May 15, 1972, attempted to assassinate Governor George Wallace of Alabama).

> Sirhan Sirhan, the man who assassinated Robert Kennedy, was beaten by his father with sticks and fists, and had a hot iron held to his heel because he was disobedient.

> James Earl Ray lived under chaotic conditions as a child, drifting from foster home to foster home after having been abused by an alcoholic father. He allegedly shot and killed Dr. Martin Luther King, Jr.

> Lee Harvey Oswald was a troubled child, brought up by a single mother who physically abused him. He spent much of his youth in a children's training institution for deprived children. On November 22, 1963, he assassinated the President of the United States, John F. Kennedy (Fontana, 1985, p. 22).

Checklist of Characteristics of Youth Who Have
Caused School-Associated Violent Deaths*

1. Has a history of tantrums and uncontrollable angry outbursts.
2. Characteristically resorts to name calling, cursing, or abusive language.
3. Habitually makes violent threats when angry.
4. Has previously brought a weapon to school.
5. Has a background of serious disciplinary problems at school and in the community.
6. Has a background of drug, alcohol, or other substance abuse or dependency.
7. Is on the fringe of his or her peer group with few or no close friends.
8. Is preoccupied with weapons, explosives, or other incendiary devices.
9. Has previously been truant, suspended, or expelled from school.
10. Displays cruelty to animals.
11. Has little or no supervision or support from parents or a caring adult.
12. Has witnessed or been a victim of abuse or neglect in the home.
13. Has been bullied and/or bullies or intimidates peers or younger children.
14. Tends to blame others for difficulties and problems he or she causes him- or herself.
15. Consistently prefers TV shows, movies, or music expressing violent themes and acts.
16. Prefers reading materials dealing with violent themes, rituals, and abuse.
17. Reflects anger, frustration, and the dark side of life in school essays or writing projects.
18. Is involved with a gang or an antisocial group on the fringe of peer acceptance.
19. Is often depressed or has significant mood swings.
20. Has threatened or attempted suicide.

---

* *Note.* From "Checklist of Characteristics of Youth Who Have Caused School-Associated Violent Deaths," by the National School Safety Center, 1998, in *School Associated Violent Deaths Report*, Westlake Village, CA: Author. Copyright 1998 by National School Safety Center. Reprinted with permission.

The APA (1993) also found that "children who show a fearless, impulsive temperament very early in life may have a predisposition for aggression and violent behavior" (p. 4). The single strongest predictor of violence in adolescence and adulthood, however, is antisocial behavior (aggression, stealing, lying, or dishonesty) during late childhood and early adolescence. Having an antisocial parent is the next best predictor of adult antisocial behavior. "The association between parental criminality and delinquency is especially strong when the parent is a repeat offender and when parental criminal activity occurred during the child-rearing period" (Charles Stewart Mott Foundation 1994, p. 16). The impetus for violence is born of distorted emotions and depraved values—unbridled anger, unyielding vengeance, cold-hearted retribution, misplaced loyalty, false bravado—skewed motivations that continue to perplex educators, counselors, social workers, probation officers, police officers, law makers, juvenile courts, judges, and others as they try to devise strategies to arrest the momentum of youth violence.

Child advocates and social workers also warn that relentless poverty, inequitable educational opportunities, latchkey homes, child abuse, domestic violence, and family disintegration, as well as the general abandonment of children to a constant barrage of televised chaos, will result in escalating real-world violence (Edelman, 1994; Sautter, 1995). The typical adolescent of any ethnic or economic group witnesses on television more than 8,000 murders and more than 100,000 other violent acts by the time he or she enters seventh grade (Charles Stewart Mott Foundation, 1994; Sautter, 1995). Without the opportunity to process random acts of violence in the media, youth become desensitized and begin to have destructive social expectations and a proclivity for aggressive behavior.

Well-established antecedents of serious, violent, and chronic juvenile crime, then, are neglect, weak family attachments, a lack of consistent discipline, poor school performance, delinquent peer groups, physical or sexual abuse, residence in high-crime neighborhoods, economic inequity coupled with lack of opportunity, media influences, and emotional and cognitive deficits (APA, 1993).

Finally, violence may also have a chemical factor. Recent studies of the brain suggest that fluctuations in the availability of the neurotransmitter serotonin can play an important role in regulating our self-esteem and our propensity for violence. Researchers have associated high serotonin levels with high self-esteem and social status, and low serotonin levels with low self-esteem and low social status. Behaviorally, high serotonin levels are associated with calm assurance. Low levels are associated with irritability that leads to impulsive, reckless, aggressive, violent, or suicidal behaviors that often are directed at inappropriate targets (Sylwester, 1995).

Gangs

Youth at Risk for Gang Membership

Youth gangs are groups of adolescents and young adults who interact frequently with one another; are frequently and deliberately involved in illegal activities; share a common collective identity that is usually, but not always, expressed through a gang name; and typically express that identity by adopting certain symbols and claiming control over certain turf (Goldstein & Huff, 1993, p. 4). Spergel (1989) suggested the following working definition for a gang: "juvenile and young adults associating together for serious, especially violent, criminal behavior with special concerns for 'turf.' Turf can signify the control of a physical territory, a criminal enterprise, or both" (p. 24). These bondless men, women, and children see those around them as objects, targets, stepping stones. Most lie, steal, and cheat without a concern about the consequences to others. They have no conscience and they feel no remorse for their actions. If the suppressed rage ever surfaces, they are capable of much more than a con. The sickest commit the senseless murders so prevalent in the newspapers today. And they do it just for kicks (Magid & McKelvey, 1987, p. 26).

> The homeboys call him Frog.... He rakes in $200 a week selling crack, known as "rock" in East Los Angeles. He proudly advertises his fledgling membership in an ultra-violent street gang: the Crips. And he brags that he used his drug money to rent a Nissan Z on weekends. He has not yet learned how to use a stick shift, however, and at 4 ft. 10 in., he has trouble seeing over the dashboard. Frog is 13 years old (Lamar, 1988, p.37).

Conflicted youth are likely candidates for gang membership. Marginally adjusted in school, they may be perceived as withdrawn and passive or as sullen and intense. They often show problems with anger and are sensitive to humiliation or teasing. A family history of abuse or mistreatment—with the residual outcomes of low self-esteem, resentment, and substance abuse—often is present. Rejected by family, school, and peers, conflicted youth repeatedly experience failure, stress, depression, hopelessness, and alienation. Conflicted youth often join gangs because they do not find caring and mutual support in the home environment. They might join out of a need for family, to gain acceptance from someone else, or to get peer approval. A gang also fulfills status and esteem needs, as well as providing material wealth from the drug trade.

Many immigrant children—those dealing with the transition from one culture to another—are also vulnerable to the attractions of gangs of youth in similar situations. Young men from single-parent families and from female-dominated homes often are attracted to gangs, because the gang provides male-bonding experiences. There are varying debates about why youth join gangs, but the predominant factors include these:

- A lack of caring and mutual support in the home (family) environment, feeling neglected by parents, a need for a family.
- A need for acceptance, a need to gain approval from peers, a need for status or self-esteem.
- A need for money available through the drug trade or other illegal methods.

The National School Safety Center (1998) reported these findings:

- Once a boy or girl is in a gang, the odds are overwhelmingly against him or her leaving it.
- Gang membership, while dangerous, often provides the best protection available to inner-city youth.
- Most violent crimes are committed by youth in "packs" of three or more.

To help identify young people most at risk, several publications have included lists of behaviors that, when seen in definite patterns, are strong indicators of possible gang involvement (National School Safety Center, 1998). The warning signs include these:

- Rumors or reliable information that a youth has not been home for several nights.
- Evidence of increased substance abuse; abrupt changes in behavior and personality.
- Newly acquired and unexplained "wealth," often showered on or shared with peers (from sharing bags of candy with younger children to a flurry of extravagant spending by older youth).
- Requests to borrow money.
- "Hanging around," but being unable to discuss problems.
- Evidence of mental or physical child abuse.

- A dress code that applies to a few: wearing a color, a style, an item of clothing, a particular hairstyle, or symbols of identification (National School Safety Center, 1998, p. 10).

Gangs and Criminal Behavior

For several years crack cocaine has been the principal commodity for large-scale gang drug trafficking. Youth participation in such activity has changed the character of many gangs. Youth gangs have become increasingly involved with controlling drug markets, often far beyond their original territories. In this context, several reasons for the crushing wave of youth violence emerge: the escalation of drug wars and the engagement of young "soldiers" to conduct the street battles, society's desensitization toward violence, the deterioration of family bonds, and the lack of cohesiveness in communities nationwide.

Keeping Youth out of Gangs

Some states are beginning to crack down on teenage law-breakers with new parent-liability laws. In Arkansas, California, and Florida, for example, parents can be fined or jailed for their child's offenses. However, many leaders in the field of child and adolescent development believe that stable parent–child relationships, not stronger juvenile laws, are the best way to prevent teens from breaking the law. They believe parents should encourage their children's participation in community organizations, such as the YMCA, sports, music, and other activities, so that the children develop self-esteem and a sense of responsibility to their community.

In their study *Violence & Youth: Psychology's Response*, the APA maintained that early childhood intervention to prevent future violence is critical. Children who show signs of antisocial behavior need to be targeted early for school and family intervention, not only to teach them alternatives for resolving conflicts but also to ensure that their aggressive tendencies do not interfere with reaching their full academic potential (APA, 1993).

Risk and Protective Factors

> Kids can walk around trouble if there is some place to walk to and someone to walk with.
>
> **Tito, ex-gang member (McLaughlin, Irby, & Langman, 1994)**

In the past decade, experts in the field of prevention have begun to design programs that increase protective processes and decrease risk

Table 7.3   Correlation between Risk Factors and Adolescent Problem Behaviors

Community

Availability of drugs
Availability of firearms
Community laws and norms favorable toward drug use, firearms, and crime
Media portrayals of violence
Transitions and mobility
Low neighborhood attachment and community disorganization
Extreme economic deprivation

Family

Family history of the problem behavior
Family management problems
Family conflict
Favorable parental attitudes toward and involvement in the problem behavior

School

Early and persistent antisocial behavior
Academic failure beginning in late elementary school
Lack of commitment to school

Individual/peer

Alienation and rebelliousness
Friends who engage in the problem behavior
Favorable attitudes toward the problem behavior
Early initiation of the problem behavior

Source: From *Youth Violence: A Report of the Surgeon General*, U.S. Department of Health and Human Services, 2001, 106, 107, 114. Copyright 2001 by U.S. Department of Health and Human Services. Reprinted with permission.

factors for delinquency and other adolescent problem behaviors. There is a large literature available documenting the risk factors in youth. In reviewing more than 30 years of research across a variety of disciplines, Hawkins and Catalano (1992) identified 19 risk factors, shown in Table 7.3, that are reliable predictors of adolescent delinquency and violence.

Protective Factors   Research on resilience has added much to our knowledge of protective factors and processes. In the words of noted resilience researcher Dr. Emmy Werner (1996, p. 18), "Protective buffers...appear to make a more profound impact on the life course of individuals who grow up and overcome adversity than do specific risk factors" (1996). According to Hawkins and Catalano (1992), "Protective factors hold the key to understanding how to reduce those risks and how to encourage positive behavior and social development" (p. 84). Hawkins and Catalano provide the protective factors discussed in the sections that follow.

Individual characteristics   Some children are born with characteristics that help to protect them against problems as they grow older and are exposed to risk. These include the following:

- **Gender.** Given equal exposure to risk, girls are less likely than boys to develop health and behavior problems in adolescence.
- **Resilient temperament.** Children who adjust to change or recover from disruption easily are more protected from risk.
- **Outgoing personality.** Children who are outgoing, enjoy being with people, and engage easily with others are more protected.
- **Intelligence.** Bright children appear to be more protected from risk than less intelligent children.

Healthy beliefs and clear standards   Parents, teachers, and community members who hold clearly stated expectations regarding the behavior of young children and adolescents help to protect them from risk. When family rules and expectations are consistent with, and supported by, other key influences on children and adolescents (e.g., school, peers, media, and the larger community), the young person is buffered from risk even more.

Bonding   One of the most effective ways to reduce children's risk of developing problem behaviors is to strengthen their bonds with family members, teachers, and other socially responsible adults. Children living in high-risk environments can be protected from behavior problems by a strong, affectionate relationship with an adult who cares about, and is committed to, the children's healthy development. The most critical aspect of this relationship is that the young person has a long-term investment in the relationship and that he or she believes that the relationship is worth protecting. Hawkins and Catalano (1992) have identified three protective processes that build strong bonds between young people and the significant adults in their lives:

1. **Opportunities for involvement.** Strong bonds are built when young people have opportunities to be involved in their families, schools, and communities—to make a real contribution and feel valued for it.
2. **Skills for successful involvement.** In order for young people to take advantage of the opportunities provided in their families, schools, and communities, they must have the skills to be successful in that involvement. These skills may be social, academic, or behavioral skills.

3. **Recognition for involvement**. If we want young people to continue to contribute in meaningful ways, they must be recognized and valued for their involvement.

School community initiatives to prevent violence Communication and reinforcement of clear, consistent norms about behavior through rules, reinforcement of positive behavior, and schoolwide initiatives (such as antibullying campaigns) to reduce crime, delinquency, and substance abuse have been successful. Curricula such as social competency skills curricula (which teach, over a long period of time, such skills as stress management, problem solving, self-control, and impulse control) reduce delinquency, substance abuse, and conduct problems. Other strategies include the following:

- Design community-based interventions *based on a scientific analysis of the problem* to reduce or eliminate risk factors and enhance or introduce protective factors.
- Evaluate and monitor interventions to establish and improve their effectiveness.
- Share information about the problem and effective and ineffective interventions through public education (Elliott, Hamburg, & Williams, 1998).
- Focus on academic achievement.
- Involve families in school and community programs.
- Develop links to the community.
- Emphasize positive relationships among students and staff.
- Discuss safety issues openly.
- Treat students with equal respect.
- Create ways for students to share their concerns.
- Help children feel safe expressing their feelings.
- Have a system in place for referring children suspected of being abused or neglected.
- Offer extended day care programs for children.
- Promote good citizenship and character.
- Identify problems and assess progress toward solutions.
- Support students in making the transition to adult life and the workplace (pp. 20–42).

Best practices are practices that incorporate the best objective information currently available regarding effectiveness and acceptability of

Table 7.4 Best Practices of Youth Violence Prevention: A Sourcebook for Community Action (2004)

	Curriculum scope for different age groups		
	Preschool/early elementary (K–2) school	Elementary/ intermediate	Middle school	High school
		Personal		
Behavior	• Learning self-management (e.g., when waiting one's turn, when entering and leaving classrooms at the start and end of the day and other transition times, when working on something in a group or alone) • Learning social norms about appearance (e.g., washing face or hair, brushing teeth) • Recognizing dangers to health and safety (e.g., crossing the street, electrical sockets, pills that look like candy) • Being physically healthy (e.g., adequate nutrition; screenings to identify visual, hearing, language problems)	• Understanding safety issues such as interviewing people at the door when home alone; saying no to strangers on the phone or in person • Managing time • Showing respect for others • Asking for, giving, and receiving help • Negotiating disputes, deescalating conflicts • Admitting mistakes, apologizing when appropriate	• Initiating own activities • Emerging leadership skills	

Integration	• Integrating feeling and thinking with language; replacing or complementing that which can be expressed only in action, image, or affectivity • Differentiating the emotions, needs, and feelings of different people in different contexts—if not spontaneously, then in response to adult prompting and assistance • Recognizing and resisting inappropriate touching, sexual behaviors	• Ability to calm self down when upset and to verbalize what happened and how one is feeling differently • Encouraging perspective taking and empathetic identification with others • Learning strategies for coping with, communicating about, and managing strong feelings	• Being aware of sexual factors, recognizing and accepting body changes, recognizing and resisting inappropriate sexual behaviors • Developing skills for analyzing stressful social situations, identifying feelings and goals, carrying out requests and refusal skills
Key concepts	• Honesty, fairness, trust, hope, confidence, keeping promises, empathy	• Initiative, purpose, goals, justice, fairness, friendship, equity, dependability, pride, creativity	• Democracy, pioneering, importance of the environment (Spaceship Earth, Earth as habitat, ecological environment, global interdependence, ecosystems), perfection and imperfection, prejudice, freedom, citizenship, liberty, home, industriousness, continuity, competence	• Relationships, healthy relationships, intimacy, love, responsibility, commitment, respect, love and loss, caring, knowledge, growth, human commonalities, work and the workplace, emotional intelligence, spirituality, ideas, inventions, identity, self-awareness

— *(continued)*

Table 7.4 *(continued)* Best Practices of Youth Violence Prevention: A Sourcebook for Community Action (2004)

	Curriculum scope for different age groups			
	Preschool/early elementary (K–2) school	**Elementary/ intermediate**	**Middle school**	**High school**
Peer/social	• Being a member of a group: sharing, listening, taking turns, cooperating, negotiating disputes, being considerate and helpful • Initiating interactions • Resolving conflict without fighting; compromising • Understanding justifiable self-defense • Empathy toward peers: showing emotional distress when others are suffering; developing a sense of helping rather than hurting or neglecting; respecting rather than belittling, and supporting and protecting rather than dominating others; awareness of the thoughts, feelings, and experiences of others (perspective taking)	• Listening carefully • Conducting a reciprocal conversation • Using tone of voice, eye contact, posture, and language appropriate to peers (and adults) • Skills for making friends, entering peer groups—can judge peers' feelings, thoughts, plans, actions • Learning to include and exclude others • Expanding peer groups • Friendships based on mutual trust and assistance • Showing altruistic behavior among friends • Becoming assertive, self-calming, cooperative • Learning to cope with peer pressure to conform (e.g., dress) • Learning to set boundaries, to deal with secrets • Dealing positively with rejection	• Choosing friends thoughtfully but being aware of group norms and popular trends • Developing peer leadership skills • Dealing with conflict among friends • Recognizing and accepting alternatives to aggression and violence • Recognizing belonging as very important	• Behaving effectively in peer groups • Peer leadership or responsible membership • Using request and refusal skills • Initiating and maintaining cross-gender friends and romantic relationships • Understanding responsible behavior at social events • Dealing with drinking and driving

Family			
• Being a family member: being considerate and helpful, expressing caring, and developing capacity for intimacy • Making contributions at home: chores, responsibilities • Relating to siblings: sharing, taking turns, initiating interactions, negotiating disputes, helping, caring • Internalizing values modeled in family • Being self-confident and trusting: knowing what to expect from adults; belief in one's own importance; belief that one's own needs and wishes matter; belief that one can succeed; trust in their caregivers; belief that adults can be helpful • Being intellectually inquisitive: enjoying exploration of the home and the world • Homes (and communities) free from violence • Home life includes consistent, stimulating contact with caring adults	• Understanding different family forms and structures • Cooperating around household tasks • Acknowledging compliments • Valuing one's own uniqueness as an individual and as a family contributor • Sustaining positive interactions with parents and other adult relatives, friends • Showing affection, negative feelings appropriately • Being close, establishing intimacy and boundaries • Accepting failure or difficulty, and continuing effort	• Recognizing conflict between parents' and peers' values (e.g., dress, importance of achievement) • Learning about stages in adults' and parents' lives • Valuing of rituals	• Becoming independent • Talking with parents about daily activities, learning self-disclosure skills • Preparing for parenting, family responsibilities

— (continued)

Table 7.4 *(continued)* Best Practices of Youth Violence Prevention: A Sourcebook for Community Action (2004)

	Curriculum scope for different age groups			
	Preschool/early elementary (K–2) school	Elementary/ intermediate	Middle school	High school
		School-related		
Reasonable expectations	• Paying attention to teachers • Understanding similarities and differences (e.g., skin color, physical disabilities) • Working to the best of one's ability • Using words effectively, especially for feelings • Cooperating • Responding positively to approval • Thinking out loud, asking questions • Expressing self in art, music games, dramatic play • More enjoyment in starting than in finishing • Deriving security in repetition, routines	• Setting academic goals, planning study time, completing assignments • Being self-confident and trusting: knowing what to expect from adults in the school; belief in one's own importance; belief that one can succeed; belief that adults in school are trustworthy; belief that adults in school can be helpful • Learning to work on teams • Accepting similarities and differences (e.g., appearance, ability levels) • Cooperating, helping—especially younger children • Bouncing back from mistakes	• Most accepting of modified roles • Enjoying novelty over repetition • Ability to learn planning and management skill to complete school requirements	• Making a realistic academic plan, recognizing personal strengths, persisting to achieve goals in spite of setbacks • Planning a career or post–high school pathways • Group effectiveness: interpersonal skills, negotiation, teamwork • Organizational effectiveness and leadership—making a contribution to classroom and school

- Articulating likes and dislikes, clear sense of strengths, areas of mastery (and the ability to articulate these), and opportunities to engage in these
- Exploring the environment

- Ability to work hard on projects
- Beginning, carrying through on, and completing tasks
- Good problem solving
- Forgiving after anger
- Generally telling the truth
- Showing pride in accomplishments
- Ability to calm down after being upset, losing one's temper, or crying
- Ability to follow directions for school tasks, routines
- Carrying out commitments to classmates, teachers
- Showing appropriate helpfulness
- Knowing how to ask for help
- Refusing negative peer pressure

Appropriate environment

- Clear classroom, school rules
- Opportunities to comfort peer or classmate in distress, help new person feel accepted or included

- Minimizing lecture-mode of instruction

- Guidance and structure for goal setting, future planning, post-school transition

— (continued)

Table 7.4 (*continued*) Best Practices of Youth Violence Prevention: A Sourcebook for Community Action (2004)

	Curriculum scope for different age groups			
	Preschool/early elementary (K–2) school	Elementary/intermediate	Middle school	High school
	• Opportunities for responsibility in the classroom • Authority clear, fair, deserving of respect • Frequent teacher redirection • Classrooms and school-related locations free from violence and threat • School life includes consistent, stimulating contact with caring adults	• Being in groups, group activities • Making or using effective group rules • Participating in story-based learning • Opportunities to negotiate • Time for laughter, occasional silliness	• Varying types of student products (deemphasizing written reports) • Opportunities to participate in setting policy • Clear expectations about truancy, substance use, violent behavior • Opportunities for setting and reviewing personal norms and standards • Group, academic, and extracurricular memberships	• Opportunities for participating in school service and other nonacademic involvement • Being a role model for younger students
Community	• Curiosity about how and why things happen • Recognizing a pluralistic society (e.g., awareness of holidays, customs, cultural groups) • Accepting responsibility for the environment • Participating in community events (e.g., religious observances, recycling)	• Joining outside the school • Learning about and accepting cultural community differences • Helping people in need	• Understanding and accepting differences in one's community • Identifying and resisting negative group influences • Developing involvements in community projects • Apprenticing or training for leadership roles	• Contributing to community service or environmental projects • Accepting responsibility for the environment • Understanding the elements of employment • Understanding issues of government

| Events triggering preventive services | • Coping with divorce
• Dealing with a death in the family
• Becoming a big brother or sister
• Dealing with family moves | • Coping with divorce
• Dealing with a death in the family
• Becoming a big brother or sister
• Dealing with family moves | • Coping with divorce
• Dealing with a death in the family
• Dealing with a classmate's drug use or delinquent behavior | • Coping with divorce
• Dealing with a death in the family
• Dealing with a classmate's drug use or delinquent behavior, injury or death due |

Source: From National Center for Injury Prevention and Control, Atlanta, GA accessed 12/31/04

Note: Table from Chapter Two, Social Cognitive Strategy (pp. 153–160) prevention and intervention programs. They generally demonstrate that they empirically reduce the effects of dysfunctional behavior.

Fundamentally, programs that endorse proactive skill development should begin in early childhood. School programs should include coping skills for loss, impulse control, anger management, problem solving, conflict resolution, emotional liability, and depression management. In addition, they should promote developmental assets and resiliency.

Structured Interventions for High-Risk Behaviors

Therapeutic Initiatives

To help conflicted youth resist the temptations of gang membership, Goldstein, Glick, Irwin, Pask-McCartney, and Rubama (1989) advocate aggression-replacement training that focuses on interpersonal skills, anger control, and moral education. Interpersonal skill training would center on such social skill deficits as these:

- Listening and maintaining a conversation.
- Asking for help and giving instructions.
- Apologizing and expressing feelings.
- Dealing with someone's anger, negotiating, using self-control.
- Assertiveness and keeping out of fights.
- Responding to persuasion and to failure.
- Dealing with an accusation and group pressure.

Components of an anger-control training curriculum might include keeping a "hassle log" to record angry situations, identifying more effective coping skills, receiving training in self-awareness of anger, and learning relaxation techniques. Group discussions of moral dilemmas and role-playing alternatives also are important components. In addition, the APA (1993) found that school programs that promote social and cognitive skills seem to have the greatest impact on attitudes about violent behavior among children and adolescents. Such skills include "perspective taking, alternative solution generation, self-esteem enhancement, peer negotiation skills, problem-solving training, anger management, and the cognitive skill of thinking things through" (APA, 1993, p. 34.) One such curriculum was developed by the National Institute on Alcohol Abuse and Alcoholism (1990) to teach a think-first model, in which students go through four steps:

1. **Keep cool.** Violent offenders often are "hot reactors" (i.e., quick to anger); this step teaches the difference between being cool-headed and being hot-headed.
2. **Size up the situation.** Violent offenders define a problem in a hostile way and automatically treat other people as adversaries. This step seeks to show alternative ways of viewing problems. The way an individual defines a problem influences the solution he or she chooses.
3. **Think it through.** Violent offenders simply do not think things through; they are concrete in their thinking and cannot see consequences. The emphasis of this step is on thinking of alternative solutions and thinking about the consequences of actions.
4. **Do the right thing.** Students are taught to pick the response that is most likely to succeed and be effective in solving the problem and preventing violence.

Violence is a learned behavior—one that can be unlearned or prevented altogether. Children and adolescents need to be taught how to think of alternatives clearly and how to prevent violence. These are cognitive skills that can be taught by the classroom teacher and reinforced in the classroom setting. Johnson and Johnson (1991, 1995) promoted integrating social and cognitive skill training in the classroom, maintaining that cooperative learning, in addition to contributing to academic improvement, teaches social and mediation skills that enable young people to interact with others more positively.

Further, children and adolescents should be given the strategies and information to integrate various conflict resolution styles. Helping them to differentiate among conflict resolution approaches also is helpful. Most conflicts can be defined as issues resulting from circumstances that affect both parties. Conflict is perceived as a challenge to personal beliefs, opinions, actions, and authority.

The key to making conflict work in a positive way is to remember that conflict, like other problems, is solvable. This assumption tends to bring about solutions. Collectively, there are at least 12 conflict resolution, mediation, or management styles:

1. **Mediation** is a structured process in which a neutral third party facilitates an agreement between two or more parties. The disputing parties have responsibility for making recommendations, determining final decisions, and finding mutually agreeable solutions (Girard, Rifkin, & Townley, 1985).

2. **Conciliation** refers to an informal voluntary negotiation process in which a third party brings the disputing parties together and facilitates communication by lowering tensions, carrying information between parties, and creating a safe environment to share issues. Conciliation may be a prerequisite to formal mediation (Messing, 1993).

3. **"Alternative dispute resolution (ADR)** is intended to facilitate settlement of civil cases before they go to trial by encouraging voluntary agreements as a result of informal sessions with magistrates or judges" (Messing, 1993, p. 67).

4. **Arbitration** is submission of a dispute to a neutral third party, who presents a decision after hearing arguments and evaluating evidence. In binding arbitration, the parties agree to an assigned arbitrator and are legally bound by the decision (Girard, Rifkin, & Townley, 1985; Messing, 1993).

5. **Confrontation** is a direct conflict of issues or persons. Power strategies include the use of physical force, bribery, extortion, or punishment. Gang behavior would be an example of this approach. The intention is to provide a win–lose situation, in which one person wins and the other person loses something of value. The limitation of this approach is that it produces feelings of hostility, anxiety, or physical damage to self, others, or personal property (Johnson & Johnson, 1991).

6. **Competition** can be viewed as self-serving or assertive about a conviction. It is self-serving when an individual is pursuing personal concerns or goals at another person's expense. In this form it is uncooperative, unyielding, and power-oriented. Selling poor merchandise to unsuspecting consumers would be an example of this type of behavior. It is assertive when it is portrayed as standing up for a conviction or defending a position a person believes is right. Being patriotic about one's country during war is an example of this approach. The user's intention often is to secure immediate resources or to stand up for beliefs. The limitation of this approach is that it often intimidates other people.

7. **Collaboration** involves attempting to work with the other person to find some solution to the dilemma, negotiating the best fit between individuals or groups by exploring disagreements and generating alternatives. The user's intentions are to learn from another person's perspective and to identify all issues or concerns to a dilemma. The limitations are that it is time-consuming and not applicable to crisis situations (Johnson & Johnson, 1991).

8. **Compromising** is assertive and cooperative when parties seek a middle ground. The goal is to find some expedient, mutually acceptable solution that partially satisfies both parties. The user's intention is to reach expedient decisions on minor disagreements. The limitation is that everyone's ultimate goal may not be reached. Revision, revaluation, and reinvention may be the next step.

9. **Accommodation** is unassertive but cooperative. The individual or group yields to another point of view. It means obeying another person's order when one's preference would be otherwise. The user's intention usually is a self-check on his or her perspective by yielding that he or she may be wrong. Critical personal concerns that may be neglected or tabled for the time being are the main limitations.

10. **Diffusion** is an approach that delays immediate action or confrontation. The individual or group uses strategies to try to cool off the situation or to keep the issues so unclear that attempts at confrontation are inhibited. The intention often is to delay a discussion of a major problem or to postpone a confrontation until a more auspicious time. The limitation is that it avoids clarification of the salient issues underlying a conflict, typically resulting in dissatisfaction, anxiety about the future, and concerns about self or others.

11. **Avoidance** is withdrawing from the situation or not addressing it, attempting to avoid conflict situations altogether or to avoid certain types of conflict situations. The user's intention may be to avoid situations in which confronting is dangerous, to afford an opportunity to cool down, or to provide more time to prepare for the situation. Individuals repress emotional reactions or escape conflicting situations with this approach and often are left without much satisfaction.

12. **Negotiation** attempts to promote an encounter in which both parties win. The aim of negotiation is to resolve the conflict with a solution that is mutually satisfying to both parties. Negotiation provides the most positive and least negative consequences of all conflict resolution strategies. Negotiation skills include a clear identification of the conflict, effectiveness at initiating a "carefronting" solution, an ability to hear the other person's point of view, and the ability to use problem-solving processes to bring about a consensus decision. This resolution style is a component of most peer-mediation programs today.

Nattive, Render, Lemire, and Render (1990) defined conflict resolution as a complex skill built on the practice and mastery of simpler communication skills that promote positive interaction. The ability to interact requires several things:

- Awareness of others.
- Awareness of the distinction between self and others.
- Skills in listening and hearing.
- Awareness of one's feelings and thoughts.
- An ability to respond to the feelings and thoughts of others.

Social and emotional skills necessary for conflict resolution include active listening, empathy, critical thinking, problem solving, and communicating with "I" messages. Effective and continued communication is vitally important in conflict resolution. It is quite common, however, for the individuals in a conflict to refuse to communicate with one another. Only when communication is aimed at an agreement fair to all parties involved is it helpful in resolving conflict. It is important to help others realign their attitudes toward conflict so they can view it constructively.

Mediation characteristics that align with counseling include confidentiality, acceptance, active listening, development of rapport and empathy, role-playing, clarification, and emphasis on the here-and-now (Kelly, 1983; Messing, 1993). Other useful counseling techniques include the following:

- **Ivey's (1988) five-stage interview process**, which includes defining the problem, defining a goal, exploring alternatives, confronting incongruity, and generalizing to daily life.
- **Verbal reframing**, in which clients rephrase negative descriptions in positive ways. Reframing is an influencing skill that offers another way of seeing how a situation or event happened (Cormier & Cormier, 1985; Ivey, 1988; Messing, 1993).
- **Selective reinforcement** to develop desired cooperative behaviors and problem-solving strategies like brainstorming.
- **Mediation contracts** to reinforce expectations for compliance by each party, to attest the belief was fair, and that external consequences related to the failure of a negotiated agreement serve as the motivation to maintain the agreement (Egan, 1982; Messing, 1993).

Treatment Plan: Conflict Resolution and Anger Management

Counseling intention: To teach a framework for resolving conflict in a systematic way; to provide conflict resolution skills for adolescent and adults. Johnson and Johnson (1991) outlined the following steps in negotiating resolutions to conflicts. This process is most appropriate with adolescents and adults who possess a mature cognitive reasoning ability. Participants need to follow these steps:

1. Agree on a definition of the conflict.
   Describe the other person's actions.
   Define the conflict as a mutual problem to be solved, not as a win–lose struggle.
   Define the conflict in the smallest and most specific way possible.
   Describe your feelings about, and your reactions to, the other person's actions.
   Describe your actions (what you are doing and neglecting to do) that help create and continue the conflict.
2. Exchange proposals and feelings.
   Present your proposed agreements and feelings.
   Listen to the other person's proposals and feelings.
   Clarify, evaluate, and refute one another's proposals.
   Stay flexible, changing your position and feelings when persuaded to do so.
   Focus on needs and goals.
   Find out about the differences between your underlying needs and goals and those of the other person.
   Communicate cooperative intentions.
   Clarify your motivation and the motivation of the other person to resolve the conflict.
3. Understand the other person's perspective.
   Do not second-guess the other person's intentions.
   Do not blame the other person for your problem. It is counterproductive and will make the other person defensive and closed-minded.
   Discuss one another's perceptions.
   Look for opportunities to act inconsistently with the other person's negative perceptions.
   Give the other person a stake in the outcome by making sure he or she participates in the process.
4. Invent options for mutual gain.
   Focus on needs and goals, not on positions.
   Clarify differences before seeking similarities.

Empower the other person by staying flexible and giving choices.

Avoid obstacles to creative thinking.

Avoid judging prematurely.

5. Reach a wise agreement.
6. Keep trying, over and over again.

Younger children can be empowered with mediation training to serve as peer mediators. It is important to start prevention programs in the early elementary grades in order to circumvent gang influence.

Treatment Plan: Mediation Training

Counseling intention: To teach mediation skills to preadolescents and early adolescents; to empower them to handle their own conflicts; to provide the necessary skills so that peers can resolve their own conflicts in a systematic way. Teaching children mediation skills empowers them to have control over their own behavior. The following guidelines can be posted in the classroom, the team room, or the clubroom and are most appropriate for preadolescents:

1. **Introduction.** Disputants are welcomed and people introduce themselves. The mediation process is explained. Mediators explain the ground rules:
   Do not interrupt when someone is talking.
   Do not call anyone names.
   Disputants must tell the truth.
   Disputants must try to solve the problem.
2. **Help disputants define the problem.** Ask the first party to define the problem briefly, as he or she sees it, and to express feelings about it. Then ask the second party to define the problem and express feelings about it. Ask questions after each person speaks to help them focus on the issues and identify feelings. Finally, summarize the problem as each person stated it.
3. **Help parties understand each other.** Ask each person to summarize the other's feelings and concerns about the problem. Ask if there is a way they could have handled the problem differently.
4. **Help parties find a solution to the problem.**
   Ask the first party what he or she likes or dislikes about the solution.
   Ask the second party what he or she likes or dislikes about the solution.
   Ask the second party what would be a fair solution.

Ask the first party to respond.

Help disputants find a solution to which they can both agree.

Summarize the solution and check with disputants for accuracy.

5. **Write up agreement.** Read the agreement out loud. Make changes if necessary. When both parties are satisfied, have them sign the agreement. Congratulate them for coming to the agreement.

Treatment Plan: Anger-Reduction Technique

Counseling intention: To channel angry feelings into socially acceptable directions; to foster an environment in which the norm is cooperation, respect, and nonviolence instead of aggression and exploitation. Anger from another, if responded to skillfully, can broaden interpersonal learning and strengthen a relationship. The following steps (RACN) are important:

1. **Recognize** and affirm the other person's feelings. Acknowledge that you hear him or her and that you are willing to respond. Not recognizing feelings intensifies the situation.
2. **Accept** your own defensiveness.
3. **Clarify** and request specific feedback. Distinguish between what you want and what you need. When needs and wants are clarified, the resolution of the conflict becomes more probable. Give and receive specific feedback.
4. **Negotiate** or renegotiate the relationship. Plan together how you both will deal with similar situations in the future. Acknowledge regret and exchange apologies. Establish a verbal or written contract about practicing new behavior.

Throughout the resolution process, it is important to be open, to be willing to generate alternatives, to search for a solution, and to commit to the solution after extensive dialogue. Maintaining anger and discord, refusing to listen, and being defensive do not help resolve conflicts or improve relationships. The following treatment plans could be useful for working with angry or conflicted youth.

Treatment Plan: the Win–Win Support Group

Counseling intention: To teach the separation of people from the problems they are having; to help youth learn to respond instead of merely reacting; to offer an opportunity to practice the skills taught; to teach positive human interaction skills. Youth participating in this support group have the opportunity to learn how to achieve a win–win situation, to improve relationship skills, to increase self-esteem, and to reduce intensity and frequency of conflict in their lives. Dysinger (1993, p. 307) outlined the following conflict resolution strategies to use with adolescents:

Session 1: Conflict and people. Introduce the technique of separating people from problems so that, in negotiating conflicts, people understand the differences between personal interest, individual wants, and human rights and responsibilities. List examples of situations such as ganging up, forming alliances, or being left out. Encourage youth to watch for these situations in the coming week and to jot down how they felt and reacted.

Session 2: Conflicts, feelings, and reactions. Ask for reports on feelings or reactions noted in the previous week. Listen for inclinations to report reactions erroneously. Discuss how conflict resolution requires acceptance of the equal value of each person, and how individuals *must* resolve problems differently because their feelings, wishes, wants, and reactions are different. Point out the value of considering options instead of reacting. Encourage youth to be aware of problems, feelings, reactions, and consequences in the coming week.

Session 3. Discussing a problem. Introduce several roadblocks to communication, such as labeling another person, listening to hearsay, or magnifying a situation. Encourage a discussion of a designated problem, describing feelings, thoughts, and opinions on it.

Session 4. Responding versus reacting. Introduce specific responses useful in conflict situations, such as using "I" messages.

Session 5. Making choices. Have youth practice learning from criticism, and ask them to separate the harmful messages from possible truths.

Session 6. Considering options. Ask youth the following questions: *"Have you noticed any changes in the frequency or intensity of conflict in your life? ... If so, what do you believe you did to bring about those changes? ... If not, what do you believe you need to do to cause positive changes?"* Distribute bookmarks listing these truisms:

Problems can be defined and thought about carefully.

Problems are different for people, and people's problems are different.

Roadblocks of communication and problem solving can be removed.

Specific skills can help resolve conflict: "I" messages, using helpful criticism, changing chain reactions, and choosing the best option are four of them.

Friendliness helps reduce conflict.

Session 7. Friendship. Describe levels of friendship. Brainstorm relationship skills, such as complimenting sincerely, inviting, listening and responding, telling the truth, considering feelings, allowing differences, understanding mistakes, and supporting someone in need.

Session 8. Conclusion. Plan a reunion in 4 to 6 weeks to check on members' progress.

Treatment Plan: Self-Disclosing and Expressing Anger

Counseling intention: To identify feelings associated with anger.

Each member completes the following open-ended sentences on index cards (one per card). Members are to write down the few responses that occur to them without censoring or modifying the responses.

- I feel angry when others ….
- When others express anger toward me, I feel ….
- I express my anger by ….

Members pin their responses to their shirts. Process the experience by focusing on the personal impact of sharing their feelings about anger with the group. Provide feedback on the extent to which each individual's responses to anger seem congruent or incongruent. The processing phase may be followed by a practice session on expressing anger.

Johnson and Wilborn (1991) provide the following treatment plan for managing anger:

Session 1: Ask members to describe an experience when they were angry and to focus on the feeling connected with the anger. Have them recall how their parents expressed anger and decide which parent they most resemble in their experience and expression of anger. For homework, ask them to be aware of their own anger and that of others during the following week.

Session 2: Begin the group with members sharing their anger experiences of past week and their observations of other people's expression of anger. Explain Ellis's Rational Emotive ABC theory (Walen, DiGuiseppe, & Wessler, 1980). Talk about how many people have trouble with C (their emotion) because of underlying beliefs about the emotion. Explain that all emotions are justified simply because they exist. Help group members distinguish between thoughts and feelings.

Session 3: Relate an anger-provoking incident and ask members to respond to it in terms of the degree of anger experienced and how they would feel and react in such a situation. Introduce the "push-button technique" (Mosak, 1984), in which group members are asked to close their eyes and see themselves in a pleasant experience. Ask them to remember how they felt, and to feel the same feeling in their bodies. Then ask them to change and remember an unpleasant experience, to remember how they felt, who was there, and so on. Then have them remember the pleasant experience again. This helps participants experience the changing of feelings and their power to create the feeling they choose. Members are led to see the control they have over events and experiences in their lives.

Session 4: Ask members to recall how anger was expressed in their families of origin and to discuss the differences between the male and female experience and expression of anger. Introduce reflective listening and "I" messages as tools for dealing with anger. During the week ask them to observe anger expressions by men and women with whom they associate and as portrayed on television to compare observations at the next meeting.

Session 5: Ask members what advice they would give their parents about helping their children deal with anger, and what general advice they would give to today's teenagers about expressing anger. Ask them to discuss the most stressful events in their lives and how they dealt with those events.

Session 6: Introduce the concept of anger experienced as a task and problem-solving technique (Novaco, 1975). Summarize the content of the group discussion and provide an opportunity for follow-up.

Table 7.5 Individual Multimodal Treatment Plan for Conflicted Youth

Counseling intention: To provide a comprehensive intervention for behavior change

Modality	Problem assessment	Potential intervention
Behavior	Poor academic performance and attendance problems	Self-contracting; recording and self-monitoring
	Negative self-statements	Positive self-talk

	Aggressive acting out	Aggression replacement training
Affect	Feelings of little self-worth Anger toward significant others Conflict with others	Increase range of positive reinforcement Exercises in anger expression Behavior rehearsal Role reversal
Sensation	Anxiety and depression over present circumstances and future goals	Anxiety-management training goal rehearsal or coping imagery
Imagery	Unproductive fantasies Image of self as incapable	Positive imagery Goal rehearsal
Cognition	Poor study habits Lack of educational or occupational information Sexual misinformation Expectations of failure	Study-skills training Assertiveness training Career counseling; assessment and information Sex education; bibliotherapy Positive self-talk
Interpersonal relations	Poor relationships with peers	Social skills and assertiveness training
Drugs (biological functioning)	Poor dietary habits; substance abuse	Nutrition and dietary information; alternative "highs"

Collective Community Initiatives

Young people need to know how to communicate effectively, how to resolve conflicts, and how to manage anger. It also is critical to teach our young people interpersonal communication, leadership, problem solving, and assertiveness to enhance self-esteem. Slovacek (1993) suggested that comprehensive prevention or early intervention programs must include the following areas:

- Drug, gun, and gang policy awareness.
- Drug and gang prevention education.
- Racial and cultural sensitivity development.
- Before- and after-school alternative programs for structured supervision with recreation, remediation, and enrichment opportunities.
- Mentoring role models and partnerships.
- Community service opportunities.
- Career and education awareness.
- Early intervention counseling.

- Childcare and parent education.

Moreover, the media, community leaders, and high-profile role models must join forces with educators and helping professionals to promote non-violence. Concurrently, the flight of businesses and employment opportunities from the urban core has created a climate of hopelessness, loss of discipline, and diminished self-confidence, undermining the moral structure of those neighborhoods. People tend to be more aggressive when they are deprived of basic needs. Poverty, deprivation, and adverse conditions affect a growing proportion of American children and adolescents. These pervasive conditions provide fertile ground for aggressive conduct and subversive activities. Until these trends are reversed through collective intervention, it unlikely that violence among youth will decline.

The ramifications of youth violence are not limited to urban communities. Domestic violence, hate crimes, sexual violence, and violence among peers have jeopardized the safety and well-being of children and adolescents in every community.

Conclusion

Conflict can serve many purposes: to escalate already tense situations, to motivate another person to action, or to inhibit new ideas. Conflict often is

---

Dealing with Conflict without Violence

Here is a list of things to try when you are faced with a conflict situation:

Share or take turns.

Ignore what someone says or does.

Ask for help from someone else.

Use assertive behavior and say no.

Negotiate and work out a mutual plan.

Compromise; give up something.

Apologize, explain, and try to understand.

Postpone and get some distance from the situation; sleep on it.

Change the subject or suggest doing something else to avoid a conflict.

Find humor in the situation.

Anger Management

Here is a checklist of steps for dealing with anger:
Stay in control.
Stay calm and cool.
Stand in the other person's shoes; try to see his or her perspective.
Give the other person a way out.
Lighten up and relax.
Apologize or excuse yourself.

Rules of Conflict Resolution

Here is a list of rules to follow when you are engaged in conflict resolution:
I agree to work to solve the problem.
I will not call the other person names, use put downs, or "dis" the other person.
I will not interrupt when the other person is talking.
I will be honest and follow through on resolving the problem.

The Peer Mediation Process

Here is a process for mediating conflicts:

1. **Introduction and ground rules:**
   Introduce yourselves.
   Ask if the parties want to solve the problem with you.
   Explain that what is said will be kept confidential.
   Get agreement to the four rules:
   Do not interrupt.
   No name calling or put-downs.
   Be as honest as you can.
   Work hard to solve the problem.
2. **Defining the problem:**
   Decide who will talk first.
   Ask person #1 what happened. *Restate.* Ask person #1 how he or she feels and why. *Restate feeling.*
   Ask person #2 what happened. *Restate.* Ask person #2 how he or she feels and why. *Restate feeling.*

Ask both persons if they have anything to add.

3. **Finding solutions:**

Ask person #1 what he or she can do to solve the problem.

Ask person #2 if he or she can agree to the solution. If he or she cannot, ask person #2 if he or she has a solution to the problem.

Ask person #1 if he or she can agree to this solution. Go back and forth until agreement is reached.

4. **Final agreement:**

Restate the final solution to make sure both parties agree to the same thing and hear all the parts.

Ask each what he or she can do to keep the problem from happening again.

Ask the disputants if they feel the problem is solved.

Ask the disputants to tell their friends that the conflict has been solved to prevent rumors from spreading.

Congratulate the students for their hard work.

Fill out the mediation agreement form.

Have the disputants sign the agreement form.

Note. From "A Peer Mediation Model: Conflict Resolution for Elementary and Middle School Children," by P. S. Lane & J. J. McWhirter, 1992, *Elementary School Guidance and Counseling, 27,* p. 124–127. Copyright 1992 by the American School Counselor Association (ASCA). Reprinted with permission.

Negotiating

Negotiating is an important skill for managing conflict when both people feel strongly about their position or circumstance.

1. Determine whether activities in conflict can both be accomplished in time (i.e., can you create a win–win situation?).
2. Are negotiable elements of equal importance?
3. Are words or phrases used that indicate or imply that one position or circumstance is superior to the other?
4. If so, reframe the position or circumstance in a more equitable banner.
5. Suggest a compromise or another plan of action. For example, if one person's idea is followed first, the second activity will fulfill the other person's needs.

Here is an example: "You need a ride to your choral concert, and I need someone to type my paper for English class. I'll give you a ride and help you set up if you will type my paper in the morning."

a struggle for power. It can be intimidating. It can create ideas or estrange previous relationships. Within multicultural and diverse settings, conflicts can expand exponentially. Our typical response to conflict is to compete, collaborate, compromise, accommodate, or avoid. The ability to resolve conflicts successfully is one of the most important social and emotional skills an individual can possess.

Social, Emotional, and Cognitive Skills

Social Literacy Skills

Social literacy skills are *interpersonal skills* essential for meaningful interaction with others. Social skills are those behaviors that, within a given situation, predict such important social outcomes as peer acceptance, popularity, self-efficacy, competence, and high self-esteem. Social skills fall

---

How to Let Someone Know He or She Is Bothering You

Here are some steps to follow for letting someone know his or her behavior is bothering you:

1. Keep a serious facial expression and maintain eye contact. In a serious tone of voice, ask if you could talk to the person for a moment.
2. Say something positive: "*I like …*"
3. Tell the person what's bothering you using an "I" message: "*When you … (specify behavior), I feel … because I … (consequences).*"
4. Listen attentively—let the other person know you heard what he or she said.
5. Paraphrase. Repeat what the other person said in your own words.
6. Check for understanding: "*Do you mean …?*"
7. Reflect feelings. Say how you think the other person feels: "*You really seem angry.*"
8. Ask for more information (*how, what, when, where*).
9. Problem solve. Give the person suggestions for changing. Be specific. Ask for a small behavior change. Work toward a compromise.
10. Discuss positive and negative consequences, and give the person a reason for changing.
11. Thank the person for listening.

into such categories as being kind, cooperative, and compliant to reduce defiance, aggression, conflict, and antisocial behavior; and showing interest in people and socializing successfully to reduce behavior problems associated with withdrawal, depression, and fearful. Social skills include problem solving, assertiveness, thinking critically, resolving conflict, managing anger, and utilizing peer-pressure refusal skills.

Skills Boxes
Permission is granted to reproduce skills boxes for individual client use.

Emotional Literacy Skills

The model of emotional literacy was first proposed by Salovey & Mayer (1990). Emotional literacy skills are intrapersonal abilities such as knowing one's emotions by recognizing a feeling as it happens and monitoring it; managing emotions (e.g., shaking off anxiety, gloom, irritability, and the consequences of failure); motivating oneself to attain goals, delay gratification, stifle impulsiveness, and maintain self-control; recognizing emotions in others with empathy and perspective taking; and handling interpersonal relationships effectively. Emotional skills fall into categories such as knowing the relationship between thoughts, feelings, and actions; establishing a sense of identity and acceptance of self; learning to value teamwork, collaboration, and cooperation; regulating one's mood, empathizing; and maintaining hope.

Handling Peer Pressure

1. Listen to what someone wants you to do and give it a name (e.g., underage drinking, stealing, cutting class, using a false I.D.).
2. Think about what would happen if you were caught; what would be the consequences (e.g., suspension from school, committing a felony, getting a DUI)?
3. Think about what you want or need to do (e.g., walk away, suggest an alternative, or ignore it).
4. Examine possible consequences and rate them 1 to 10.
5. Decide what to do to maintain your best interest.
6. Explain to others your needs and wants (e.g., I need to stay straight; I want to avoid trouble).

CHAPTER 8

Alienation, Underachievement, and Dropping Out

> If education ever gets to the place where there are no dropouts, we can feel secure that we're getting the job done in our schools. People rarely drop out when they experience a sense of purpose, success, and growth. What will it take for us to realize that the dropout issue is a symptom of unwellness in our schools? It will not require long-term studies and extensive funding to eliminate the dropout problem. It will take making sure that our young people experience success instead of failure in our schools. (Wright, 1989, p. 47)

Statistical manipulations often have the effect of trivializing a significant social and educational problem. For example, dropout rates in nearly all large U.S. cities are tabulated annually, rather than according to how many high school freshmen actually receive diplomas 4 years later. One reliable estimation is provided by the U.S. General Accounting Office (GAO, 2002). To count dropouts, the GAO uses the all-inclusive definition adopted by the Current Population Survey (CPS), which polls a national sample of households representative of the working-age civilian population. The CPS defines dropouts as "persons neither enrolled in schools nor high school graduates." This definition does not exclude such categories as "pregnant teenagers" or "needed at home." It simply assumes if you are not in school and you have not graduated, you are a dropout.

The most common reason for leaving school is poor academic performance. The National Center for Educational Statistics (1995) found "didn't like school" and "couldn't get along with teachers" as significant social and emotional variables. Being older than average for one's grade level also is a strong predictor of dropping out. The ramifications are extensive:

- Nearly 700,000 youth drop out of school each year in the United States.
- Dropouts will earn $237 billion less during their lifetimes than high school graduates; state and local governments will collect $71 billion less in taxes.
- Welfare, unemployment, and crime prevention costs for dropouts will total $6 billion.
- In some areas, 30% of inner-city students never complete the eighth grade.
- Dropouts are more likely to engage in other high-risk behaviors, such as premature sexual activity, unintended pregnancies, crime and delinquency, alcohol and other drug use, and attempts at suicide (Asche, 1993).

McKinlay and Bloch (1989) listed these factors as contributing to dropping out:

- **Socioeconomic factors**, such as cultural isolation, ethnicity, and a language other than English.
- **Home and family factors**, such as poor family relationships or lack of parental encouragement.
- **Psychosocial development factors**, such as substance abuse, lack of goals or career decisions, lack of motivation, and poor self-concept.
- **Academic development factors**, such as lack of basic academic skills, alienation from school, and academic failure.
- **Institutional factors**, such as inadequate programs, youth "falling between the cracks, and lack of counseling services" (p. 8).

Fundamentally, however, over the past 50 years the value of a high school education has changed dramatically. During the 1950s, a high school degree was considered a valued asset in the labor market, and through the 1970s, a high school diploma continued to open doors to many promising career opportunities. In recent years, however, advances in technology have fueled the demand for a highly skilled labor force, transforming a high school education into a minimum requirement for entry into the labor market.

Because high school completion has become a requirement for accessing additional education, training, or the labor force, the economic consequences of leaving high school without a diploma are severe. On average, dropouts are more likely to be unemployed than high school graduates and to earn less money when they eventually secure work. High school dropouts are also more likely to receive public assistance than high school graduates who do not go on to college. This increased reliance on public assistance is likely due, at least in part, to the fact that young women who drop out of school are more likely to have children at younger ages and are more likely to be single parents than high school graduates. The individual stresses and frustrations associated with dropping out have social implications as well: dropouts make up a disproportionate percentage of the nation's prison and death row inmates.

Secondary schools in today's society are faced with the challenge of increasing curricular rigor to strengthen the knowledge base of high school graduates while increasing the proportion of all students who successfully complete a high school program. Monitoring high school dropout and completion rates provides one measure of progress toward meeting these goals (U.S. Department of Education, National Center for Educational Statistics, 1999).

Dropouts in General

- Over the last decade, between 347,000 and 544,000 tenth- through twelfth-grade students dropped out of school each year without successfully completing a high school program (U.S. GAO, 2002).
- In October 2000, about 11% of 16- through 24-year-olds who were not enrolled in a high school program had neither a high school diploma nor an equivalent credential (U.S. GAO, 2002).
- The last significant federal funding for a dropout prevention program ended in 1995 (U.S. GAO, 2002).
- In 2000, the national status dropout rate was 10.9% of 16- through 24-year-olds (U.S. GAO, 2002).
- In 2000, the national Hispanic status dropout rate was 27.8% of 16- through 24-year-olds, compared to 6.9% for White students and 13.1% for Black students (U.S. GAO, 2002).
- Over 3.9 million of 16- through 24-year-olds in the United States (11.8%) were not enrolled and had not completed high school in October 1998 (National Center for Education Statistics, 1999).

- High school completion rates remained roughly the same overall from 1988 to 1998, fluctuating between 84.5% and 86.5%. However, the method is changing sharply with alternative testing, such as the GED, rising steadily from 4.2% in 1988 to 10.1% in 1998. High school completers receiving diplomas have decreased from 80.3% in 1988 to 74.7% in 1998 (NCES, 1999).
- Although dropout rates were highest among students age 19 or older, about two thirds (69%) of the current-year dropouts were ages 15 through 18; moreover, about one third (34%) of the 1998 dropouts were ages 15 through 17 (NCES, 1999).
- Students who drop out of high school differ significantly from their graduating peers in behavior, grades, retentions, and achievement scores by the third grade (Finn, 1989).
- On the average, dropouts are more likely to be unemployed than high school graduates and to earn less money when they eventually secure work (U.S. Department of Education, National Center for Education Statistics, The Condition of Education, 1999).
- High school dropouts are more likely to receive public assistance than high school graduates who do not go on to college (U.S. Department of Education, National Center for Education Statistics, The Condition of Education 1998).
- Two thirds of inmates in the Texas prison system are high school dropouts (Texas Department of Criminal Justice, 1998).
- The percentage of young adults dropping out of school each year has stayed relatively unchanged since 1987 (U.S. Department of Education, National Center of Education Statistics, Dropout Rates in the United States 1999).
- Historically, the General Educational Development (GED) credential was established as a means of offering a high school credential to World War II veterans who might have interrupted their schooling to go to war (U.S. Department of Education, National Center of Education Statistics, Dropout Rates in the United States, 1999).
- Over the last quarter of a century, approximately 30% to 40% of GED test-takers have been ages 16 through 19 (U.S. Department of Education, National Center of Education Statistics, Digest of Education Statistics, 1999).

Income Implications and Socioeconomic Status

- The overall proportion of 15- through 24-year-olds in low-income homes was 14.4% in 1998, but those students accounted for 38.5% of all dropouts. Middle-income students accounted for 56.8% of the

15- through 24-year-old population and 44.9% of dropouts, whereas high-income students were 28.8% of the population and 16.6% of dropouts (U.S. Department of Education, National Center of Educational Statistics, 1999).

- High school graduates earn an average of $6,415 more per year than those who drop out of high school (National Dropout Prevention Network, 2000).

Socioeconomic Status

The overall proportion of 15- through 24-year-olds in low-income homes was 14.4% in 1998, but those students accounted for 38.5% of all dropouts. Middle-income students accounted for 56.8% of the 15- through 24-year-old population and 44.9% of dropouts, whereas high income students were 28.8% of the population and 16.6% of dropouts (National Center of Educational Statistics, 1999).

Race and Ethnicity

- Overall, 29.5% of Hispanic 16- through 24-year-olds were not enrolled and had not completed high school, in contrast to 13.8% of non-Hispanic Blacks and non-Hispanic Whites. Despite comprising 15.1% of the young adult population, Hispanics accounted for 37.7% of all dropouts (National Center of Educational Statistics, 1999).
- Asian/Pacific Islanders had the highest rate of high school completion (94.2%), whereas Hispanics had the lowest (62.8%). Non-Hispanic Whites completed high school at a rate of 90.2%, and 81.4% of non-Hispanic Blacks completed high school.

Age

Of the 17-year-old population in the United States, 6.7% were dropouts. That number increases to 13.2% for the 18-year-old population, 14.7% for the 19-year-old population, and 13.9% for people ages 20 to 24 (National Center of Educational Statistics, 1999).

Gender

In 1998, 56.8% of all status dropouts were male, and 43.2% were female. Females had an overall high school completion rate of 87%, whereas 82.6% of males completed high school (National Center of Educational Statistics, 1999).

Implications of Dropping Out

The cumulative effect of hundreds of thousands of youths leaving school each year short of finishing a high school program translates into several million young people who are out of school yet lack a high school credential. In 2000, there were 3.8 million 16- through 24-year-olds who, although not enrolled in school, had not yet completed a high school program. Overall, 10.9% of the 34.6 million 16- through 24-year-olds in the United States were dropouts. Although there have been year-to-year fluctuations in this rate, over the past 29 years dropout rates have gradually decreased in a pattern with an average annual decline of 0.1 percentage points per year.

Low regard for self seems to be present in all studies on underachievement, no matter what else is involved. Several special populations should be specifically targeted for dropout prevention:

- Pregnant and parenting youth
- Substance abusers
- Disruptive students
- Truants
- Students who lack motivation

The profile that often emerges from the data is not an unconcerned, unmotivated, disruptive youth, but one with high levels of stress-related anxiety who lacks adaptive ways to reduce that stress and methods to increase self-management skills.

Gage (1990) maintained that "reducing the national dropout rate would verify our dedication to social justice and to an enlightened and humane national self-interest" (p. 280). Intervention and prevention, however, require change in social organizations on a grand scale: families; schools; communities; business and industry; and local, state, and federal governments. Any dropout prevention program should plan for the success of *all* youth. The fact is that the further a child moves from competing with his or her peers academically, the greater his or her chance of competing with peers in less constructive ways, such as joining gangs, doing drugs, or dropping out of school.

Skills for the 21st Century

An adolescent's decision to drop out of school often is the end result of a long series of negative school experiences: academic failure, grade retention, and frequent suspensions. Yet today's dropouts will be at an even greater disadvantage tomorrow than ever before. Today, information seems to multiply exponentially. Communication, mathematics, science, and computer literacy skills have been identified as the basic academic skills required of high school graduates. In addition, changes in the U.S. economy now require youth to have a substantial knowledge base and higher-order thinking skills. These skills include the ability to solve complex problems, to function in an uncertain environment, to think and reason abstractly, and to apply this knowledge in creative and imaginative ways.

New performance standards and advanced technologies have changed the workforce's educational requirements. International competition and new technologies dictate the need for a well-educated workforce. Participatory management, sophisticated quality control, decentralized production services, and increased use of information-based technology are common in both large and small businesses. These new workforce skills are categorized as follows:

- **Academic skills.** Reading, writing, computing.
- **Adaptability skills.** Learning to learn, creative thinking, problem solving.
- **Self-management skills.** Self-esteem, goal setting, motivation, employability, and career development.
- **Social skills.** Intra- and interpersonal skills, negotiation, and team work.
- **Communication skills.** Listening and communicating well.
- **Influencing skills.** Organizational effectiveness and leadership.

Advanced technology also has changed the organization of the workplace from pyramidal to more participatory structures, increasing the need for skills in conflict resolution, interpersonal facilitation, problem solving, and cooperative learning. Employability skills for the 21st century include these:

- **Individual competence.** Communication skills, comprehension, computation, and tolerance of diversity.
- **Personal reliability skills.** Personal management, ethics, and vocational maturity.
- **Group and organizational effectiveness skills.** Interpersonal skills; organization skills; and skills in negotiation, creativity, and leadership.

The vast changes in the workplace have increased the autonomy, responsibilities, and value of personnel at all organizational levels. These changes, in turn, call for workers with higher levels of academic competencies and broader technical knowledge. Prerequisite social skills for the potential worker may include working as a team, being a leader in building consensus, being able to see things from the perspective of others, and being able to persuade and promote cooperation while avoiding conflicts. Prerequisite emotional skills for the potential leader may include taking initiative, managing and coordinating the efforts of a network of people, being self-motivated to take on responsibilities above and beyond one's stated job, and self-management in regulating time and work commitments. High scores on measures of intelligence may secure enrollment into a prestigious university and a comparative career; however, doing well in the corporate culture may be more dependent on social or emotional intelligences not yet measured quantitatively.

Structured Interventions for High-Risk Behaviors

The emphasis on higher-order thinking and not just basic skills is a key concern in addressing the education of at-risk youth. Keeping lesser-achieving youth only in the realm of the basic may mean they will be dependent thinkers all their lives. Given the experience of thinking skills programs, teaching metacognition behavior may be one of the most important goals to pursue in the education of at-risk youth. These children and adolescents are episodic in their learning, fail to make connections that others may see more spontaneously, and too often they miss the central meaning that is the key to learning. Educators and helping professionals of at-risk youth should be "mindful of the emphasis on metacognition in teaching thinking and learning" (Presseisen, 1988, p. 48).

Therapeutic Initiatives

Intelligence is not a simple thing but a compound of influences. The circumstances can be summarized with the following equation:

Intelligence = power + tactics + content (Perkins, 1986, p. 5)

Research has increased our knowledge of how children learn and retain information (Armstrong, 1994). Because problems in academic performance relate to study skills deficits and to emotional and personal problems, the complex needs of a child with academic difficulties are best served by an interactive learning system consisting of primary strategies (study skills) and support strategies (counseling). Successful study skills programs that enhance cognitive deficits incorporate a dual approach by including the following components:

- Study skills instruction combined with counseling.
- Group rather than individual counseling.
- High levels of warmth, empathy, genuineness, and acceptance.
- Skills instruction related to content material (i.e., different approaches to studying different subjects).
- Structured rather than unstructured formats.
- Programs of 10 hours or more.

Specific skill development can be integrated and reinforced at all educational level around specific themes such as these:

- **Locating information and reference materials** such as reader's guides, tables of content, catalogues, and computerized information.
- **Organizing information** such as note-taking, summarizing, listening, and recognizing patterns.
- **Understanding graphic aids** such as tables, charts, or graphic organizers.
- **Following both oral and written directions.**
- **Reading strategies** such as rapid reading for the main idea and techniques to improve comprehension.
- **Remembering information** with use of mnemonic devices, peg words, and memorization strategies.
- **Studying effectively** and efficiently, and managing time.

In addition, direct thinking skills instruction—that is, instruction that introduces a skill, then provides guided practice and reinforcement in using the skill in a variety of settings with a variety of media—helps with retention of information. Direct instruction uses a five-step process as an introduction to a thinking skill (Beyer, 1987):

1. The instructor introduces the skill by describing an example of it in action or by having the student actually do it.
2. Referring to the examples, the instructor explains the specific steps and rules for the skill.
3. The instructor demonstrates how the skill works with the content being studied.
4. Working in pairs, under the instructor's supervision, youth apply the skill procedures and rules to similar data.

5. Restating and explaining the basic components of the skill as it has been used thus far with follow-up experiences reinforces learning.

Thinking skills instruction should be direct and frequent, introduced in small pieces, and adequately reinforced. It also should be developmental in approach, increasingly more complex as children progress. Providing systematic, developmental instruction in thinking skills builds on the cognitive development of youth. Further motivation studies (Alderman, 1990; Alderman & Cohen, 1985; Ames & Ames, 1989; Dweck, 1986) and cognitive learning studies (Gardner, 1983, 1991, 1993; Pressley & Levin, 1987; Weinstein & Mayer, 1986) offer counselors and educators an abundant repertoire of strategies to foster success and enhance self-worth. To acquire a high degree of motivation, one must know how one personally contributes to one's own success. There must be a link between what the student does and the outcome that follows. Drawing from research on motivation and learning strategies, Alderman (1990) developed the *links-to-success model* for helping the helpless student become successful and, in turn, developing an increased sense of self-worth:

Link 1: Proximal goals. The first link to success is setting goals for performance. Goal setting provides the mechanism for self-assessment and promotes self-monitoring. To be effective, the goal setting should be specific rather than general, attainable, and short-term. Preintervention assessments (such as study skills inventories and feedback forms from teachers on student performance) should set a baseline of performance and list deficits in study and social skills in the classroom that inhibit academic achievement.

Link 2: Learning strategies. Low-achieving youth are often "inefficient learners" (Pressley & Levin, 1987) because they fail to apply a learning strategy that could enhance their performance. The goal here is for youth to identify the learning strategies that will help them to accomplish their goals. Examples of learning strategies are basic and complex rehearsal strategies; comprehensive monitoring strategies (Weinstein & Mayer, 1986); task-limited and across-domains strategies, with meta-cognitive knowledge about when to use them; and various reading comprehension strategies, such as summarization, clarification, prediction, and asking the right questions.

Link 3: Successful experience. A learning goal rather than a performance goal ensures greater success. Dweck (1986) maintained that focusing on the learning goal in relation to performance improvement and goal attainment produces more lasting effects.

Link 4: Attribution for success. Youth should be encouraged to attribute success to their personal efforts or abilities. Abilities are skills that have been learned (e.g., reading comprehension skills, time-managed study, or composition writing). Increased self-efficacy leads to increased confidence about goal accomplishment. Failure should be reframed within the context of not using the proper strategy. Within this context, students are more likely to try again (Alderman, 1990).

This four-link approach helps youth take responsibility for their learning, which enhances motivation and performance. Low-achieving youth need to know exactly what they are expected to do and be given criteria for measuring their success. This link-to-success model provides a framework for beginning the cycle of progress that fosters self-responsibility for learning and self-efficacy in achievement.

Cooperative Learning: Enhancing Cognitive Skills and Promoting Teamwork

To compete in the 21st century, children and adolescents need good interpersonal skills. Cooperative learning fosters these skills. The variety of cooperative learning models provide a repertoire of strategies educators can use to accommodate wide-ranging differences in skill and achievement levels in mixed-ability classrooms, including classrooms in which special education and general education students are integrated. Research indicates that these approaches have many possible advantages over traditional instructional models, and may have especially important benefits for more culturally diverse classroom environments. Documented cognitive and affective benefits include the following:

- Higher achievement for all youth, especially for the most vulnerable.
- Greater use of higher-level reasoning.
- More on-task behavior and increased motivation and persistence in completing a task.
- Greater peer interaction, teamwork, and development of collaborative skills; better rapport between students.
- Better attitudes toward school, peers, and educators.
- Higher personal and academic self-esteem.
- More positive relationships among youth of various races and ethnic backgrounds and between handicapped students and their nonhandicapped peers.

- A lessening of the importance of intergroup distinctions, less stereo-typing, less grouping, and more complex perceptions of members of other groups.

Children and adolescents mature intellectually in reciprocal relationships with other people. Vygotsky (1978) maintained that higher functions actually originate in interactions with others. Every integration of cultural development appears twice: first on the social level and later on the individual level. This is applicable to voluntary attention, to logical memory, and to the formation of concepts. All higher functions originate as actual relationships between individuals (Vygotsky, 1978). Cooperative learning promotes the skills needed to collaborate. It is important to determine which interpersonal skills youth need. What follows is a list of some of the most important:

- **Forming skills.** Moving into groups quickly and quietly; sitting face-to-face; talking in quiet voices; using names and making eye contact when speaking to each other.
- **Functioning skills.** Carrying out assigned tasks; staying on task; being sure everyone understands the task
- **Communication skills.** Paraphrasing what another team member said; asking for explanations.
- **Brainstorming skills.** Asking questions; generating alternative answers; giving evidence for conclusions.
- **Trust-building skills.** Praising others; encouraging participation; showing respect for others' ideas; avoiding put-downs.
- **Conflict-management skills.** Clarifying disagreements within the group; asking questions to help understand another's point of view.

Cooperative learning helps young people feel successful at every academic level: low-achieving youth can make contributions to a group and experience success, and all students can increase their understanding of ideas by explaining them to others. Cooperative learning also has been shown to improve relationships among youth from different ethnic backgrounds (Slavin, 1987). A variety of social and communication skills are involved in cooperative work groups. These skills can transfer to the classroom and later to the workplace. Students working in groups perform better and achieve more if they receive training in group process skills. These skills can be grouped in five different categories, such as the following:

1. Be a team player:
   - Follow directions.
   - Use each other's names.

- When you are working together, don't work ahead of the others.
- When you are unsure, ask for help or say you don't understand.
- Participate: Share an idea, take your turn answering, suggest ways the group could solve a problem or complete an assignment.

2. Be an attentive listener:

- Look at the person who is talking.
- Politely tell someone when you agree or disagree: "I respect your opinion, but I disagree."
- Let others finish. Wait to see if their idea is wrong or just different.
- Listen for the other group members' points of view.
- Check to make sure you understand what someone said or how it relates to the assignment: "Do you mean ...?" or "Are you saying ...?" A *T-chart* can teach this interpersonal skill:
- Identify the interpersonal skill that will be emphasized in the cooperative learning activity.
- Create a T-chart by asking what this skill "looks like." (See the T-chart in Table 8.1 for attentive listening.) List responses and add others if necessary.
- Ask what this skill "sounds like." List their responses and add others if necessary. Hang the chart in a place where all groups can see it during the activity.

3. Be a team supervisor:

- Check to make sure everyone can see, has the materials needed, has space to work, and is working and making progress.
- Make sure everyone understands: Ask each member for an answer; ask someone to demonstrate how to find an answer; call for an "answer check," in which everyone individually works a problem and shows his or her answer; ask someone to summarize what was said or what the problem is.

Table 8.1   Attentive Listening

Sounds like	Looks like
Say "uh-huh" as speaker talks	Nod
Use open-ended questions to keep the speaker talking	Make eye contact
Paraphrase what the speaker says	Lean forward
Use encouragement to keep the speaker talking	Smile
Accept what the speaker says rather than giving your opinion	Relaxed posture
Summarize the speaker's comments	Hands unclenched, arms not crossed

- Check back with other group members on ideas and points that were discussed earlier in the period or week. Do not have a group member learning something new without checking to see that he or she remembers it.

4. Be a cooperative teacher:
  - Explain how you found an answer or worked a problem.
  - Show how to do the same type of problem using different numbers. Do not be satisfied with correct answers; think of new problems that relate to the lesson.
  - Help to concentrate the group's efforts by watching the time.
  - Make up a similar problem or an easier problem to help students who are having trouble understanding. Do not stop when they finally do a problem right. Have them do three or four more to help them remember.
  - Help your group get the main idea by having group members say it in their own words, summarize the main idea, or give an example.

5. Be a group manager:
  - If members of your group are off-task, tell them what they should be doing.
  - Encourage the group to solve problems on their own rather than asking the teacher for help.
  - Help the group stay on task by saying, "We are supposed to be doing …" or "We'd better get back to work."
  - Summarize what the group has decided at the end of a discussion.
  - Set goals and challenge the group to do its best: "Can the group do better than last time?" or "Can we finish problems 1 through 5 by 10:15?"

Building relationships in the classroom is perhaps the most advantageous way to empower students. Cooperative learning teaches critical social skills that can be experienced, observed, and integrated. With cooperative learning strategies, one educator has the power to significantly change the relationship skills of thousands of youth during his or her career.

Treatment Plan: Study Improvement Program

Counseling intention: To improve study skills, organizational skills, time management, goal setting, and decision making.

This study improvement program was adapted from Malett (1983) and consists of 11 half-hour group sessions. Seven sessions are technique oriented, directed primarily to teaching behavioral self-control as a study technique; three sessions are semistructured discussions of personal factors affecting academic performance.

Session 1: Introductions and self-control techniques. Behavior modification techniques are used to teach youth to control their own behavior and to change undesirable habits. Self-observation and self-monitoring are used to chart current study behaviors to establish a baseline for evaluating change.

Session 2: Time management. Universal components of time management instruction include record keeping procedures (daily schedules or diaries to identify self-defeating habits), schedule planning, life support activities, leisure time, study time blocked out to allow a commitment for each course, realistic goals for each study session, study breaks coordinated with individual energy periods, and planned use of short study intervals (distributive vs. mass practice).

Session 3: Textbook reading efficiency skills. Underlining, outlining, highlighting, and the use of graphic organizers are standard methods for focusing attention and increasing understanding of written texts. *SQ3R* and *REAP* methods are useful for processing and retaining information. The SQ3R technique for reading and studying textbooks involves five steps:

Survey. Glance at chapter headings, read summaries, review questions, and determine organization.

Question. Formulate questions about each section.

Read. While reading, actively search for answers to formulated questions.

Recite. Answer questions without reference to the text.

Review. List major points under each heading.

The REAP reading and study method has four basic steps:

Read to discover the message.

Encode the message in one's own words.

Annotate by writing the message notes.

Ponder the message by processing it through thinking and discussion.

Session 4: Discussion of the importance of grades. Show the relationship between grades, achievement scores, aptitude, and interests. Identify strengths and weaknesses.

Session 5: Stimulus control. This technique involves changing the environment. Finding a new, less distracting place to study is an example of environmental change. Identify optimal study environments at school, home, and the library.

Session 6: Test taking and anxiety management. Instruction counseling in this component should consist of the following steps:

Test preparation. Frequent, scheduled, and organized study void of distractions.

Test strategies. Strategies for taking objective and essay tests.

Test wiseness. Following instructions, scanning, pacing, making educated guesses, eliminating the obvious wrong answer, reviewing.

Managing test anxiety. Replacing negative self-statements with positive self-statements, deep breathing techniques, progressive relaxation, and systematic desensitization for test anxiety.

Session 7: Discussion of academic and nonacademic pressures. Discuss life balance between academic and leisure activities, along with part-time work schedules; the need to be with peers; and the need to succeed academically for oneself, for family, and for the future.

Session 8: Taking lecture notes. Note-taking often is an individual study style. However, one strategy for keeping notes, developed at the Cornell Study Center, incorporates the basic process of effective reading in a "5R process":

Record. Pick out main ideas.

Reduce. Summarize, note key terms.

Recite. Repeat key ideas to oneself.

Reflect. Think about content.

Review. Recall and commit information to memory.

Session 9: Discussion of values. Exercises from Chapter 11 are helpful here, according to group needs and developmental stages.

Session 10: Writing papers. Enlist the help of colleagues in the English department and use style books.

Session 11: Problem solving. Graphic organizers for problem solving are included in this chapter, as well as in Chapter 11.

Treatment Plan: Succeeding in School

Counseling intention: To improve study skills, to encourage help-seeking behavior and cooperation with peers and adults.

This exercise involves 10 50-minute sessions and was developed by Gerler and Herndon (1993).

Session 1: Successful people. The first meeting consists of the following elements:

Purpose of the group and discussion of ground rules.

Discussion of common traits of successful people; what it takes to be successful.

Sharing of successes in and out of school.

Exploration of successes members expect to experience in the future.

Session 2: Being comfortable in school. Group leaders present material on relaxation methods, with practice exercises. Members discuss times they felt comfortable and relaxed in school.

Session 3: Being responsible in school. Leaders review how to feel relaxed and comfortable at school. Members discuss the meaning and importance of behaving responsibly, define *responsibly*, and give examples of how they have behaved responsibly in and out of school.

Session 4: Listening in school. Leaders review how to be responsible in school, giving examples of responsible behavior. Members discuss how listening to others may influence behaving responsibly and define a good listener. Members role-play to sharpen their listening skills.

Session 5: Asking for help in school. Leaders introduce exercises to improve listening skills. Members discuss the importance of asking appropriate questions and list situations when listening and asking for help from teachers had positive outcomes.

Session 6: How to improve at school. Leaders review listening skills. Members identify school subjects that needed improving and brainstorm strategies that will lead to improvements. The session closes with members identifying improvements already made in school.

Session 7: Cooperating with peers at school. Leaders review reactions from the previous session. Members discuss the importance of getting along and cooperating with peers, role-play cooperative behaviors, and discuss personal experiences of cooperating with peers.

Session 8: Cooperating with teachers. Leaders review the importance of cooperating with peers and teachers. Members complete the following sentences:

"If I were teacher for a day, I'd ...."

"I wish my teachers would ...."

"I would like to talk with a teacher about ...."

Blank cards are distributed, and members are asked to finish the statement: *"I would like to get along better with my teacher, but my problem is ...."* The session concludes with members sharing how they have cooperated with their teachers.

Session 9: The bright side of school. Leaders review the value of cooperating with others and encourage members to consider how cooperation might improve the atmosphere at school. Members identify some things about school they dislike and consider what might be positive about those things. The session ends with members describing some positive aspects of being in the classroom and at school.

Session 10: The bright side of me. Leaders review some of the highlights of the previous sessions. Members share what they have learned about themselves and their strengths. The session concludes with the opportunity for members to receive positive feedback.

Another format for delivering necessary study and time management skills was highlighted in *The Study Improvement Program* (Malett, 1983) offered to college freshmen at the University of New York. Training consisted of 3-hour seminars held once a week in basic counseling skills, study skills, and self-control techniques. The seminars offered didactic presentations, modeling, practice, and videotape feedback, with the goal of teaching attending, paraphrasing, questioning, reflection of feelings, interviewing, and related small-group discussion techniques. The session topics are as follows:

1. Introduction; self-control techniques.
2. Time management.
3. Textbook reading efficiency skills.
4. Discussion of the importance of grades.
5. Stimulus control.
6. Test taking and anxiety management.
7. Discussion of academic and nonacademic pressures.
8. Lecture note-taking.
9. Discussion of values.
10. Writing papers.
11. Problem solving.

Proponents of multimodal counseling and psychotherapy maintain that cognition and learning are affected by what happens in other domains of individual functioning as well. Young people who manifest behavior problems such as emotional disturbances, attention deficits, or interpersonal difficulties also are likely to experience learning problems. To promote cognitive development and academic success, educators and helping professionals have infused regular classroom instruction with innovative approaches, such as creative physical fitness programs (Carlson, 1990), social skills programs (Stickel, 1990), and computer interventions (Crosbie-Burnett & Pulvino, 1990).

In addition, helping professionals can positively influence learning through the use of encouragement (Rathvon, 1990), video-assisted study skills training (Heldenbrand & Hixon, 1991), interpersonal communication training (Asbury, 1984), and stress-reduction and relaxation methods (Danielson, 1984; Omizo, 1981).

Treatment Plan: Multimodal Counseling for Children

Counseling intention: Keat (1990), changing the acronym *BASIC ID* (Lazarus, 1992) to HELPING to meet the developmental needs of children, offers a pragmatic and technically eclectic way of helping children learn skills to help themselves.

In this program, the developmental needs and problems of children are presented from a multimodal point of view as shown in Table 8.2.

Treatment Plan: Multimodal Treatment Plan
for Students with Deadline Disorder

Counseling intention: To empower students who procrastinate with essential cognitive skills.

Students who procrastinate usually have not learned the strategies to approach and complete a task or an assignment in an organized way. Incomplete assignments or frantic last-minute efforts often leave a student with feelings of frustration, anxiety, failure, and low self-esteem. Morse (1987) provided the multimodal profile for procrastinators shown in Table 8.3.

Strategy: Partnerships to Assist Academically Resistant Youth

Counseling intention: To provide a more comprehensive solution focused intervention for specific classroom behaviors.

Teaching problem solving, goal setting, and time management is helpful, but a more comprehensive intervention that addresses the fears and negative feelings procrastinators often experience may have more long-term benefits. Focusing on the structured modalities of emotions, learning, interpersonal relationships, interests, and guidance of actions in a group setting may be the pivotal link to behavior change. It is often overwhelming to attend to all the behaviors that may emerge in a typical classroom or group setting. Fundamentally, every behavior is a communication about needs, expectations, goals, and aspirations. Table 8.2 provides a brief

Table 8.2 *HELPING* Children Change

Mode	Rank	Concern number	Concern	Intervention
Health	5	H1	Pain	Avoidance/relief
		H2	Sickness	Wellness
Emotions	2	E1	Anxiety	Stress management
		E2	Anger	Madness management
		E3	Feeling	Fun training
Learning	5	L1	Deficiencies	Life skills
		L2	Failing	Study skills
		L3	Sensory shallowness	Music
Personal relationships	1	P1	Getting along (adults)	Relationship enhancement (RE)
		P2	Lack of friends	Friendship training
Imagery	4	I1	Low self-worth	IALAC
		I2	Lack of coping skills	Heroes (cartoons)
Need to know	7	N1	Despair	Hope cognitive restructuring
		N2	Mistaken ideas	Bibliotherapy
		N3	Lack of information	Bibliotherapy
Guidance of actions, behaviors, and consequences	3	G1	Behavior deficits	Modeling
		G2	Motivation	Contracts

Table 8.3 Multimodal Group Intervention for Deadline Disorder

Mode	Group activities	Procrastinator characteristics
Health	Participate in relaxation exercises	Locus of control
Emotions	Brainstorm and discuss feeling words	Fear of failure
		Fear of success
	Share common fears	Fear of failure
		Fear of success
	Discuss and share feelings of frustration	Perfection
	Discuss power and the power one feels	Locus of control

Table 8.3 Multimodal Group Intervention for Deadline Disorder (continued)

Mode	Group activities	Procrastinator characteristics
Learning/school	Share feelings about school, favorite subjects, performance levels	Self-concept
	Discuss problems in completing assignments	Rebellion against authority, fear of failure, fear of success
	Complete worksheet "Getting Work Done Survey"	Perfection, fear of failure
People/ personal relationships	Share feelings about family and friends	Rebellion against authority
	Discuss relationships with classmates and the ability to function in the classroom group	Rebellion against authority, locus of control
Imagery/interests	Discuss strengths and weaknesses	Fear of failure, self-concept
	Share likes and dislikes	Self-concept
	Discuss putdowns by others	Self-concept
	Discuss putdowns by self	Fear of failure, self-concept
	Participate in guided imagery to develop positive self-image	Self-concept
Need to know	Discuss differences between thoughts and feelings	Self-concept, rebellion against authority
	Identify thoughts and feelings under positive or negative categories	Self-concept, rebellion against authority
	Practice positive self-talk	Self-concept
	Role-play positive and negative aspects of putdowns	Self-concept
Need to know	Discuss how choices are made	Lack of skill Locus of control
	List choices students make during their day	Locus of control
Guidance of actions	Identify "putting-off" behaviors	Perfection, fear of failure, fear of success
	Discuss ways time is wasted and saved	Lack of skill
	List activities to be done in a day and time required to accomplish them	Lack of skill
	Set priorities for completing tasks	Lack of skill
	Write short-term goals and implementation strategies	Lack of skill
	Record progress toward goals	Lack of skill
	Write long-term goals (1-, 5-, and 10-year) and implementation strategies	Lack of skill

glimpse of behaviors that may interfere with the progress of any group (i.e., the classroom), paired with suggested interventions.

Collective Community Initiatives

Young people have a fundamental need to achieve, solve problems, and establish long-range goals. Educators, helping professionals, and community agencies can use a variety of methods to encourage youth to stay in school. Successful programs often separate youth from the mainstream, accelerated curriculum, and provide counseling and supportive services. Many programs emphasize flexibility and a curriculum tailored to the learning needs of the individual and integrate vocational education or GED preparation. Successful programs also involve a broad range of special services for at-risk youth that focus on enhancing self-esteem, tutoring, childcare services, medical care, substance abuse prevention, bilingual instruction, and employment training in collaboration with community agencies, such as juvenile and family services, the courts, the health department, social services, and the community services board.

Breaking Ranks, the latest report on the restructuring of high schools from the National Association of Secondary School Principals, in partnership with the Carnegie Foundation for the Advancement of Teaching, found that young people on the brink of adulthood must contend with a whirlwind of destabilizing forces that undermine their scholastic potential (Maeroff, 1996). The report recommended that high schools restructure to reduce in size and personalize the educational experiences for youth to promote identification and connectedness.

Each adolescent also should have a "personal adult advocate," an adult in the school or community who meets with the youth individually on a regular basis to serve as a liaison between the youth and others in and out of school. The report also called for every adolescent in high school to have a "personal learning plan" to identify and accommodate individual learning styles and to encourage adolescents to achieve. Table 8.4 and Table 8.5 outline risk and protective factors for youth and effective dropout intervention strategies for schools and communities.

Conclusion

Nationally, over 25% of high school students drop out before graduation, including a disproportionate number of males and minorities. Once a child is behind one grade level at grade 4, two grade levels by grade 7, and does not pass grade 9, his or her chances of graduating are significantly diminished. Trends in the evolution of the information age make primary

Table 8.4 Risk and Protective Factors for Dropout Interventions

Risk factors	Protective factors
Inappropriate expression of anger	Positive and support school climate
Deviant peer relationships	High self-esteem
Conduct disorder	Parental support and involvement
Anxiety disorder	Academic success
Arrests for assaults	Social-skills training
Posttraumatic stress	Cognitive-skills training
Truancy/absenteeism	Emotional-skills training
Aggressive/disruptive classroom behavior	Problem-solving skills
Lack of social, emotional, and cognitive skills	High expectations
Low social competence	Goals for the future
Learning disability	Positive school climate
Lack of bonding to school	Many opportunities to succeed
Poor school performance	
Lack of engagement in school activities	
Severe lag between chronological age and school age	
Immigrant youth	
Gang involvement	

Table 8.5 Effective Dropout Intervention Strategies

Tutoring and peer tutoring	Early identification
Attendance monitoring	Early intervention
Counseling	Linking home with school
Mentoring	Modeling strategies for parents
Service learning	Alternative schooling
Out-of-school enhancement	Early childhood education
Reading and writing programs	Professional development
Differentiating instruction	Individual instruction
Career education and workforce readiness	Conflict resolution and violence prevention

prevention and intervention strategies imperative. Successful programs often separate underachieving students from other students, accelerate the curriculum, relate work to education, and provide counseling and supportive services. Effective programs include a broad range of special supportive services, such as remediation programs, tutoring, childcare, medical care, substance abuse awareness programs, bilingual instruction, and employment training.

Social, Emotional, and Cognitive Skills

Cognitive Literacy Skills

Educators no longer can conceptualize the process of learning as the result of rote memory and mnemonic strategies that merely link meaningless bits of information to one another (Anderson, 1980; Armstrong, 1994; Gardner, 1991, 1993; Resnick, 1984). The productive workers of the next millennium must think for a living. Youth with poor cognitive literacy will not have the skills to function in a society that increasingly demands higher-order thinking skills such as inference, analysis, interpretation, problem solving, decision making, critical and creative thinking, and time and stress management. It is paramount that we teach students to construct meaning from reading; solve problems; develop effective reading, thinking, and learning strategies; and transfer skills and concepts to new situations.

Cognitive skills fall into categories such as knowing how to solve problems, describe, associate, conceptualize, classify, evaluate, and think critically. Cognitive psychologists advocate teaching at-risk youth a repertoire of cognitive and metacognitive strategies using graphic organizers, organizational patterns, monitoring, self-questioning, verbal self-instruction, self-regulation, and study skills. Inherently, social, emotional, and cognitive skills can be taught and cultivated, giving youth advantages in their interpersonal adjustment and their academic or vocational success, as well as enhancing their resiliency through life's ultimate challenges.

Skills Boxes

Permission is granted to reproduce skills boxes for individual client use.

Higher-Order Thinking Using Analysis

Analysis involves breaking down an issue, problem, or situation into its component parts. Identifying characteristics and components; recognizing attributes and factors; comparing and contrasting; and ranking, prioritizing, and sequencing are all skills that promote analysis. Examples of these skills include the following:

Compared to ..., these attributes are similar.
On the positive/negative side ..., these attributes are present.
A logical sequence would be ...
What are the parts of ...?
Classify ... according to ... .
How does ... compare with ...?
What evidence can you list for ...?

Compare/Contrast Frame		
	Name 1	Name 2
Trait 1		
Trait 2		
Trait 3		

Higher-Order Thinking Using Synthesis

Synthesis is the combination of ideas, facts, or principles to form a new perspective. For example:

What would you predict if ... happened?

How would you design a new ...?

What might happen if you combined ... with ...?

What solutions would you propose for ...?

I.N.F.E.R.

Identify literal, face-value interpretation, facts.

Note indicators of further meaning; verbal and nonverbal clues.

Feeling nuances: Analyze nuances and indicators, subtle shades of meaning, feelings.

Extend original interpretation based on inferences made from "hidden clues."

Restate revised interpretation.

Higher-Order Thinking Using Evaluation

Evaluation is developing opinions, judgments, or decisions after careful study. Here are some examples:

What did the study reveal about ...?

What are the points of view about ...?

What is the best and worst about ...?

One point of view is ....

Affective Processing of a Lesson

PMI = Talk about the pluses and minuses about a particular lesson

What I liked (+)   P _____

What I didn't like (-)   M _____

Questions or thoughts I found interesting I _____

Higher-Order Thinking Using Application

Application is the use of facts, rules, or principles to a issue, concept, or situation. Here are some examples:
How is ... related to ...?
What can ... also apply to?
I think this applies to ....
A connecting idea is ....
A situation like this reminds me of ... because ....

Goal:

What to look for:	Evidence or Examples of	Connections (+) (-)
1.		
2.		
3.		
4.		
5.		

Other Possible Clues/Criteria Found:

6.

7.

Higher-Order Thinking Using Critical Thinking Skills

Using *critical thinking skills* involves identifying point of view, determining the accuracy of presented information, judging the credibility of a source, and determining warranted and unwarranted claims. Here are some examples:
This is reality .... This is fallacy ....
This is a warranted claim backed by empirical evidence. This is an unwarranted claim backed by hearsay.
These are the benefits ... and these are the drawbacks ....
This is essential evidence ... and this is incidental evidence ....
This ... is a value judgment.
This ... is a point of view.

Graphic Organizer for Analyzing

Graphic Organizer: Fact/Opinion Chart

Statement(s)	Fact(s)	Opinion(s)	Evidence

Analysis for Bias

Analysis for bias involves reading, listening, and acting as a critical thinker when viewing advertising, political candidates, and other perspectives for possible misrepresentation. To analyze for BIAS, follow these steps:

- **Be aware** of point-of-view.
- **Indicate** examples of bias clues (EOIOC):
- **Exaggeration** *("never," "always").*
- **Overgeneralization.**
- **Imbalance** (one-sided story).
- **Opinion** as fact *("They say ...").*
- **Charged** words *("You don't have to be a rocket scientist to know").*
- **Account** for possible bias by citing proofs.
- **State** opinion based on "reasoned judgment."

Note. From *Catch Them Thinking*, by J. Bellanca and R. Fogarty, 1986, Palatine, IL: IRI/Skylight Training and Publishing, Inc. Copyright 1986 by IRI/Skylight Training and Publishing, Inc. Reprinted with permission.

Analyzing for Assumptions

An *assumption* is an unproven claim, a broad assertion without proof, or a generalization that lacks specific backup. For example, "Choosy people choose ..." or "Nine out of ten doctors recommend ...."

Assume assertions are present.

Search deliberately for the hidden message.

Sense gaps in logic.

Use linking statements to check validity.

Make revisions to clarify.

Express revised statement.

Note. From *Catch Them Thinking,* by J. Bellanca and R. Fogarty, 1986, Palatine, IL: IRI/Skylight Training and Publishing, Inc. Copyright 1986 by IRI/Skylight Training and Publishing, Inc. Reprinted with permission.

Analyzing for Personification

Analyzing for personification means separating text into its parts (articles or stories into paragraphs, sentences, clauses, and phrases) to distinguish the figures of speech and personification.

Here are some rules for using this skill:

1. Keep the purpose for analysis clearly in mind.
2. Identify "parts" to look for, clues helpful to your analysis, and questions to guide your analysis before you begin.
3. Examine each sentence or clause by asking the following clue questions:

- What is the sentence or clause talking about?
- Is that subject an object or thing?
- Is that subject behaving as if it were a person?

1. **What if the clues prove inadequate?** Consult reference books for definition, examples, and so on. Rewrite clue questions.
2. **What if I don't find evidence of the author's use of personification?** Reevaluate the purpose and redesign the clues. Lack of evidence may be as important as evidence in supporting an opinion.

In order to analyze for personification, you need to know two things:

1. Sentence structure and personification.
2. Classifying and generalizing skills.

Steps involved include these:

1. Divide the article into paragraphs, sentences, and clauses.
2. Run a sentence or clause through the gamut of clue questions; record results; repeat.
3. Draw inferences and make generalizations to satisfy your goal. Did the author use personifications in his or her writing? Does this use (or disuse) support an opinion of the writing?

Note. From "One District's Approach to Implementing Comprehensive K-12 Thinking Skills Program," by D. E. Arredondo and R. J. Marzano, 1986, *Educational Leadership, 43*(8), pp. 28–32. Copyright 1986 by ASCD. Reprinted with permission. All rights reserved.

Teaching for Thinking

A code of silence regarding classroom conduct seems to permeate the halls of today's high schools. Irrational fears of being wrong or ridiculed often inhibit active student involvement. Bellanca and Fogarty (1992) developed a number of strategies to promote positive behavior. They maintained that the DOVE guidelines are helpful:

Do accept other's ideas. (Avoid criticism and put-downs.)

Originality is okay. (We need to examine lots of ideas. The way each individual looks at an idea will vary. Share your view.)

Variety and vastness of ideas provide a start. (After we explore many ideas, we can become critical thinkers. Put your brain to work.)

Energy and enthusiasm are signs of intelligent and skillful thinkers. (Put your brain to work.)

Note. From *Catch Them Thinking*, by J. Bellanca and R. Fogarty, 1986, Palatine, IL: IRI/Skylight Training and Publishing, Inc. Copyright 1986 by IRI/Skylight Training and Publishing, Inc. Reprinted with permission.

Drawing Conclusions from Evidence

Drawing conclusions from evidence can only be done with sufficient proof. This means differentiating between soft data and hard data. Soft data include opinions, bias, and personal views. Hard data are reliable facts that can be observed and measured. In order to debate or support an argument, it is helpful to follow the five PROVE rules:

1. **Pick** as much data as you can for evidence.
2. **Review** the facts to make sure they logically support the argument.
3. **Organize** the data to show the pattern.
4. **Validate** the data by checking for accuracy.
5. **Evaluate** the reliability of the data source.

To make generalizations from the data, use the RULE acronym:

Round up specific data.

Uncover the patterns.

Label the patterns.

Evaluate the validity of the generalizations with the 80–20 rule:

Do at least 80% of the randomly selected samples fit the pattern?

Note. From *Catch Them Thinking*, by J. Bellanca and R. Fogarty, 1986, Palatine, IL: IRI/Skylight Training and Publishing, Inc. Copyright 1986 by IRI/Skylight Training and Publishing, Inc. Reprinted with permission.

Dealing with Deadline Disorder

What is deadline disorder? When you inappropriately put off doing something that you could do now, should do now, and would do now if you just knew how to begin, you are exhibiting deadline disorder. Some strategies to prevent procrastination include these:

Divide and conquer. Divide the big task into manageable parts.

Start with a believable part. Start with the part you think you can complete.

Make a game of doing it. See if there are any new ways to approach the project.

Make it ridiculous. Use your imagination. Make it amusing. Pretend it is something greater than it actually is.

Reward yourself. Choose a part of the task that you have been putting off. Do it. Give yourself a big reward.

Put it on automatic. Just do it. Don't question it; don't judge it. Just do it, and get over it.

Academic Growth Group and Mentoring Program
Study Habits Survey

Name_____ Date _____

My improvement goal for this quarter is:_____

I can and want to improve these study habits:

Attend school every day that I am not sick.

Be more attentive in class.

Have paper and pencil, books, and other necessary supplies in class.

Ask questions when I don't understand.

Turn in my daily work.

Complete all homework.

Organize my notebook with sections for each subject, clean paper, and everything fastened in place.

Stay after school with my teacher for extra help.

Review all notes before a test.

Have the following supplies with me in all classes and at home for my study:

- Three-ring loose-leaf notebook.
- Loose-leaf notebook paper.
- Index sheets or dividers.
- Sharpened pencils.
- Eraser.
- Ballpoint pens.

Note. From "Academic Growth Group and Mentoring Program for Potential Dropouts" by D. J. Blum and L. A. Jones, 1993, *The School Counselor, 40*, p. 3. Copyright 1993 by the American School Counselor Association (ASCA). Reprinted with permission.

Note-Taking

The Cornell University Note-Taking Method is a systematized method for recording and remembering notes. The major steps involve the five Rs, as listed below.

Make a vertical line on a piece of paper 2½ inches from the left edge. Use the right side for taking notes in class. Loose-leaf paper works best for this procedure.

1. **Record.** Write down the main ideas presented by the teacher. Write on one side of the page only.

2. **Reduce** the notes you have taken into fewer words. This should be a summary of the ideas on the right side of your page.

3. **Recite.** Cover the Record column with a piece of paper and attempt to recite an explanation of the words in the Reduce column. In this stage you will be expanding to yourself what you reduced. If you have any difficulty during this step, refer to the Record column for help. Reciting in this manner will help you learn and remember the material. You are actually testing yourself on a regular basis.

4. **Reflect.** After you test yourself, you should reflect on the material. How does it relate to what you already know and understand?

5. **Review.** This should be done on a regular basis. The more often you review, the easier it will be to prepare for tests. Regular short reviews will strengthen your memory and improve your test performance.

Here is an example:

Reduce	**Record**
Organization	Good organ, is cent. to learning, & mem.
	To learn w/eff, we need to be organ.

The SQ3R Method for Reading

1. **Survey.** Before you start to read, take a minute or two to read the chapter title and the section headings. Also, be sure to read the summary paragraph and any review questions at the end of the chapter.

    Your survey takes only a minute, but it will give you a good idea about what your reading is going to be.

2. **Question.** Now go back to the beginning of your assignment and turn the first heading into a question. You can do this by asking how, what, why, or who about it.

    If you turn the heading into a question, you'll know what you're trying to find out when you start reading.

3. **Read.** Now read the section to find the answer to your question.

4. **Recite.** First, ask yourself the question about the section that you've just read; then, tell yourself the answer you've learned from your reading.

    Reciting is the step that most helps you learn what you've read. The best way to recite is to take brief notes in an outline form. Why?

    • Writing something down on paper helps you to remember it better than simply saying it to yourself.

    • Writing down the SQ3R questions and answers takes only a few minutes and gives you a record of what you've read that you can use later.

Below is an example of a good way to organize these notes:

1. Question.   1. Main idea of section
    A. Detail
    B. Detail
    C. Detail

    Write your question on the left side of your paper, your notes on the right side. Taking notes in this way will help you later, when you want to review.

    When you have finished taking notes for the first section, go on to the next section and follow the same steps.

5. **Review:** When you've finished the question, read, and recite steps for all the sections in your assignment, it's time to review. Cover up the right-hand side of your notes. Ask yourself the questions on the left-hand side, and see if you can tell yourself the answers.

Emotional and Social Literacy Skills

Initial school success is more dependent on emotional and social factors than a child's precocious ability to read. A child's readiness for school is more dependent on the following emotional and social measures: being self-assured and interested; knowing what kind of behavior is expected and how to rein in the impulse to misbehave; being able to wait, to follow directions, and to turn to teachers for help; expressing needs while getting along with other children; a sense of control, mastery, and competence over one's world; and the ability to exchange ideas, feelings, and concepts verbally with others (Brazelton, 1992).

Emotional literacy skills are *intrapersonal* abilities such as knowing one's emotions by recognizing a feeling as it happens and monitoring it; managing emotions (e.g., shaking off anxiety, gloom, irritability, and the consequences of failure; motivating oneself to attain goals, delay gratification, stifle impulsiveness, and maintain self-control; recognizing emotions in others with empathy and perspective taking; and handling interpersonal relationships effectively. Emotional skills fall into categories such as knowing the relationship between thoughts, feelings, and actions; establishing a sense of identity and acceptance of self; learning to value teamwork, collaboration, and cooperation; regulating one's mood; empathizing; and maintaining hope.

Social literacy skills are *interpersonal* skills essential for meaningful interaction with others. Social skills are those behaviors that, within a given situation, predict such important social outcomes as peer acceptance, popularity, self-efficacy, competence, and high self-esteem. Social skills fall into such categories as being kind, cooperative, and compliant to reduce defiance, aggression, conflict, and antisocial behavior; and showing interest in people and socializing successfully to reduce behavior problems associated with withdrawal, depression, and fear. Social skills include problem solving, assertiveness, thinking critically, resolving conflict, managing anger, and utilizing peer pressure refusal skills.

Skills Boxes
Permission is granted to reproduce skills boxes for individual client use.

Turning Negative Thoughts about Studying into Positive Thoughts

Brainstorm with students all the possible negative thoughts they might tell themselves about studying. Turn the negative thoughts around or replace them with positive thoughts.

There are three steps to this process:
1. Identify your goals.
2. Try to figure out the negative messages you are giving yourself.
3. Rephrase the message in positive terms.

For example, here are some negative thoughts:
- The work is too hard.
- I'm dumber than everyone else.
- I don't know how to begin.
- I'm tired.
- This is boring.
- I can't stand the teacher.
- My teacher doesn't like me.

Here are some affirmations:
- I am bright and capable.
- My teacher and friends like me.
- I know how to ask questions and get started.
- I am ready for action.
- Ask for volunteers to share their goals, and go through the process with them, following these steps:
  1. Have each student practice writing affirmations.
  2. Lead a "go around" so that all students can practice saying their affirmations aloud.
  3. Have the students pick the affirmation they like best.
  4. Tell them to write it 10 times and say it to themselves as they write it.
  5. Have them practice it every night and at the beginning of every class.

Note. From "Group Guidance for Academically Undermotivated Children," by C. A. Campbell, 1991, *Elementary School Guidance and Counseling, 25*(1). Copyright 1991 by [Name of Copyright Holder]. Reprinted with permission.

Overcoming Public Speaking Anxiety

There are five steps to follow in overcoming the fear of speaking in public:

1. **Identification.** Identify exactly what you are most afraid of. For example, is it getting up in front of class to give a report or leading a discussion?

2. **Self-talk.** Verbalize your "fearful self-talk" aloud. Write it down. Here is an example: "I could stutter. I could faint. I might get laughed at for sounding stupid."

3. **Action plan.** Write down a plan of action for your greatest fear. For example, read a self-help book on effective presentations, join the debate team, practice a talk in front of the mirror, or tape a talk and play it back.

4. **Rehearse.** Rehearse doing what you fear in your mind; visualize it. Practice and prepare your talk. Use a tape recorder to record your voice and play it back. Ask a friend to listen to a practice session. Practice your talk in front of the mirror. Become comfortable with your public self.

5. **Positive self-talk.** Tell yourself to relax. Tell yourself that no one else has prepared as well as you did. Tell yourself that your presentation will be your best.

Academic Growth Group and Mentoring Program
Evaluation to Be Completed by Teachers

To the teachers of …

This student will participate in group counseling to improve his or her academic work and grades. It would be helpful if you would complete this questionnaire before the student begins the group sessions and again after he or she has completed eight group sessions. I will send you another copy of this form after the group sessions. Please keep me informed of this student's academic progress as we work together to help him or her improve his or her written work and performance in class. Thank you.

Directions: Please indicate by circling A if you agree and D if you disagree.

This student:

1.	Is self-confident.	A	D
2.	Is aware of his or her strengths.	A	D
3.	Is aware of his or her assignments.	A	D
4.	Completes his or her assignments.	A	D
5.	Does satisfactory work in class.	A	D
6.	Uses good study skills.	A	D
7.	Gets along well with other students.	A	D
8.	Gets along well with me and other adults.	A	D

Note. From "Academic Growth Group and Mentoring Program for Potential Dropouts," by D. J. Blum and L. A. Jones, 1993, *The School Counselor, 40*, p. 3. Copyright 1993 by the American School Counselor Association (ASCA). Reprinted with permission.

Table 8.6 Partnership to Assist Academically Resistant Youth

Behavior manifestations	Suggested interventions
1. Truancy/absenteeism	Weekly contingency contracting for attendance; focus on the benefits of attending school (e.g., increased income and worth); visualize the future and describe what it would be like without an education; establish an attendance card and weekly reward schedule; reframe the perception about school through cognitive restructuring.
2. Impulsiveness	Teach ways to delay responding (e.g., count to 10 or 1-minute pause for *think time*); model slow and careful problem solving and decision making; instruct how to scan alternatives and use different problem-solving methods; encourage verbalization to solve the problem (e.g., "I need to take time to look at all possible answers not just the first one that comes along"); limit overstimulation and distractors (listening to music, however, often may enhance attention, concentration, and memory, providing a sense of predictability and consistency); contract for the completion of short assignments.

3. Inattention	Use a cue or signal that means it is time to pay attention; structure seating arrangements based on sociometric ratings with team leaders chosen to be the most influential peer of least attentive youth; train to self-monitor; teach self-questioning strategies (e.g., "What am I doing? How is that going to affect others?"). Develop mechanisms to enhance control and integrate successful strategies for paying attention: strategies such as stopping to define a problem, considering and evaluating various solutions (critical thinking) before acting on one, checking for accuracy, persisting in using every strategy to solve the problem, and congratulating for a job well done. "Stop, listen, think, do." The following three sentence stems are often helpful ("I-message"): "(Name of child), when you _____, I feel _____, because _____." "I feel this way when this happens: _____; I would feel better if this would happen: _____." "I resent your inattention when I _____; what I need from you is _____; what I appreciate in you is _____."
4. Poor academic performance	Instruct in goal setting; instruct in self-recording of study intervals and rates; establish accountability logs; instruct in time management; write down all assignments to take home; involve parents in checking assignments; cooperatively develop a learning plan.
5. Low self-esteem	Share personal success experiences; keep a personal journal of successes during the week; start each day with positive affirmations; create a climate that stresses strengths rather than weakness; teach assertiveness skills; structure opportunities for success; change self-dialogue from "I can't" to "I will try"; enhance social skills such as conversation skills, making and responding to comments or questions.
6. Inability to follow-up or follow through on assignments	Instruct in goal setting and problem solving; show how to break large jobs into achievable parts; establish dates and timelines for work completion; provide examples and specific steps to accomplish each part. Assist student in setting long-range goals; break the goal into realistic parts. Use a questioning strategy: "What do you need to be able to do this?" Keep asking that question until the child has reached an obtainable goal. Have the child set clear timelines (i.e., what he or she needs to do to accomplish each step (monitor student's progress frequently).

7. Attention-seeking behavior	Model how to gain others' attention appropriately. Highlight others who are behaving appropriately; move the attention seeker out of the spotlight; distract the attention-seeker with a question about the current topic; attend to the attention-seeker only when he or she is on task.
8. Prioritization of most-to-least important tasks	Provide a model hierarchy to demonstrate least-to-most important tasks that can be generalized to other situations; post the model around the room and refer to it often.
9. Inability to maintain effort and accuracy consistently	Reduce assignment length; increase the frequency of positive reinforcements; teach specific methods of self-monitoring such as double-checking written work; encourage proofreading.
10. Inability to complete assignments on time	List, post, and repeat all steps necessary to complete each assignment; develop a checklist and timeline for completing components of an assignment; reduce the assignment into manageable sections; make frequent checks for work/assignment completion; implement a "study buddy" program where students team up to maintain academic responsibilities.
11. Power-seeking behavior	Ignore the behavior in the moment and elicit feedback from the power seeker during a less confrontational time; ask how he or she might handle a similar situation; express your feelings regarding the behavior (e.g., "I feel this way when this happens ...; I would feel better if this would happen... .").
	Place the power-seeker in a leadership role; discuss roles and responsibilities of a good leader; contract with the power-seeker regarding expectations; evaluate follow-through of desired behavior; reinforce the positive leadership.
12. Difficulty with taking tests	Teach test-taking skills and strategies; allow extra time for testing; use clear, readable, and uncluttered test forms; use the test format with which the student is most comfortable.
13. Revenge-driven behavior	Clearly define acceptable and unacceptable behavior; form a positive relationship through cooperative trust-building strategies (e.g., think-pair-share) and creative problem-solving activities; find ways to encourage group members to show that they care for the member; improve self-esteem and base group activities that encourage the processing of feelings such as "*Today, I felt _____ in the group*"; set up a "graffiti board" in the room for writing out feelings or recording positive things people have done or said.

14. Poor reading comprehension skills (e.g.), difficulty finding main idea in a paragraph)	Provide student with copy of reading material with main ideas underlined or highlighted; outline important points from reading. Teach outlining, main-idea concepts. Provide audio tape of the text.
15. Inability to follow oral instructions or directions	Accompany oral directions with written directions; give one direction at a time; repeat directions and check for understanding; strategically place general methods of operation and expectations on charts around the room; provide a copy of presentation notes; allow peers to share carbon-copy notes from presentations (have student compare own notes with copy of peer's notes); provide framed outlines of presentations (introducing visual and auditory cues to important information); encourage use of tape recorder; teach and emphasize key words (*the following, the most important point is*, etc.).
16. Withdrawal or shyness	Lower the student's anxiety about mistakes; build the student's confidence by breaking the group task into smaller chunks; remind the student of past successes; ask what the student could do to ensure a repeat of that success; use self-concept strategies ("me bag" or "me collage") with the help of the group; give *extra* recognition for individual contributions to the group; arrange for a study buddy.
17. Sloppiness and carelessness	Teach organizational skills. Introduce the importance of daily, weekly, or monthly assignment sheets; list materials needed daily; require consistent format for papers; have a consistent way for students to turn in and receive back papers; reduce distractions. Give reward points for notebook checks and proper paper format. Provide clear copies of handouts and consistent format for worksheets; establish a daily routine; provide models for what you want the student to do. Arrange for a peer who will help the student with organization. Assist student in keeping materials in a specific place (e.g., pencils and pens in pouch). Repeat expectations.
18. Poorly developed study skills	Teach study skills specific to the subject area: organization (e.g., assignment calendar), textbook reading, note taking (e.g., finding main idea/ supporting detail, mapping, outlining), skimming, summarizing.
19. Poor self-monitoring	Teach specific methods of self-monitoring (e.g., stop-look-listen).

	Proofread finished work after some time has elapsed.
20. Difficulty maintaining effort to complete tasks or assignments	Allow for an alternative method for completing assignment (e.g., oral presentation, taped report, visual presentation, graphs, maps, pictures, etc., with reduced written requirements).
	Allow for alternative method of writing (e.g., typewriter, computer, cursive, or printing).
21. Disruptive class participation; inappropriate attention seeking; interference with the progress of the group	Seat student in close proximity to the teacher. Reward appropriate behavior. Use study carrel if appropriate.
22. Frequent excessive talking	Provide hand signals to indicate when and when not to talk; reinforce listening.
23. Difficulty making transitions from activity to activity; tendency to give up; refusal to leave previous task; appearance of agitation during change	Program for transitions (e.g., give advance warning of when a transition is going to take place ["Now we are completing the worksheet; next we will... ."] and the expectations for the transition [e.g., "... and you will need... ."]); list steps necessary to complete each assignment; arrange for an organized helper [i.e., peer]).
24. Inappropriate responses in class often blurted out; answers given to questions before they have been completed	Seat individual in close proximity to teacher to monitor behavior visually and physical; state the appropriate behavior desired.
25. Tense, anxious, or panicked when pressured to perform athletically or academically	Teach techniques of desensitization, relaxation, cognitive restructuring, anxiety management, assertiveness, disputing irrational beliefs, gradual step-by-step role-playing, meditation (counted breathing); increase actual exposure to anxiety-producing situation.
	Use yoga to reduce tension, relieve stress, improve vitality, increase calmness, and enhance a sense of well-being; bibliotherapy; cognitive restructuring; classical music to reduce test anxiety.
	Lessen the pressure to compete and excel; teach deep-breathing exercise to promote relaxation and control; establish a learning contract that is realistic and manageable; stress effort and enjoyment for self rather than competition with others; minimize timed activities.
26. Inappropriate behaviors in a team or group setting (e.g., difficulty waiting turns in group situations, unable to give members "equal air time")	Assign a responsible job or leadership role (e.g., team captain, care and distribution of the materials); put in close proximity to teacher or group leader.

27. Poor interactions with adults or authority figures	Provide positive attention; outline appropriate versus inappropriate behavior, (e.g., "What you are doing is …; a better way of getting what you need or want is to… .").
28. Difficulty using unstructured time: recess, hallways, lunchroom, locker room, library, assembly, etc.	Define the purpose of unstructured activities (e.g., "The purpose of doing _____ is to get _____"); encourage group games, participation, and team building.
29. Tendency to lose things necessary for task or activities at school or at home (e.g., pencils; books; assignments before, during, and after completion of a given task)	Teach organization skills; frequently monitor organizational habits with "A place for everything and everything in its place"; provide positive reinforcement for good organization.
30. Poor use of time (e.g., daydreaming, staring off into space, not working on task at hand)	Establish periodic eye contact; teach designated reminder cues (e.g., a gentle touch on the shoulder); outline expectations of what paying attention looks like (e.g., "You look like you are paying attention when _____."); give a time limit for a small unit of work with positive reinforcement for accurate completion; tape an index card on the desk and place a check mark to reward on-task behavior; use a contract or timer for self-monitoring.
31. Depression and anxiety	Teach depression-coping and control techniques, such as recognizing depressive feelings, ways to increase activity level, positive self-talk, and redirecting thoughts to pleasant experiences. Use cognitive restructuring techniques to enhance coping skills; teach how to dispute irrational thoughts about expectations; keep a journal of success experiences in highly anxious situations; learn biofeedback techniques and anger management strategies.

CHAPTER 9

Isolation, Victimization, and Abuse of Children and Adolescents

Miranda did suffer repeated childhood beatings at the hands of both parents, especially her father. But Miranda also remembers his frequent neglect, and somehow that was even worse. "I now see that I did a lot of things to get my father's attention," she admits. "If I was good, daddy ignored me. So I stayed out late, stole from stores, and didn't go to school; that got his attention." And a beating. Miranda learned that the kind of attention she "deserved" was violent. When she later became involved with abusive lovers, she believed she had caused—deserved—those beatings too. The fact that men hit her convinced Miranda that they cared about her. (Baker, 1983, p. 313)

Innumerable scientific studies have demonstrated the link between the abuse and neglect of children and a wide range of medical, social, emotional, psychological, and behavioral disorders. Subsequently, abused and neglected children are more likely to suffer from depression, alcoholism, drug abuse, and severe obesity. They are also most likely to require special education services in school and to become juvenile delinquents and adult criminals.

The National Child Abuse and Neglect Data System (NCANDS, 2004) reported an estimated 1,400 child fatalities in 2002. This translates to a rate of 1.98 children per 100,000 children in the general population. NCANDS defines "child fatality" as the death of a child caused by an injury resulting from abuse or neglect, or where abuse or neglect were contributing factors. Many researchers and practitioners believe child fatalities due to abuse and neglect are underreported. States' definitions of key terms such as *child homicide, abuse,* and *neglect* vary (therefore, so do the numbers and types of child fatalities they report). In addition, some deaths officially labeled as accidents, child homicides, or Sudden Infant Death Syndrome (SIDS) might be attributed to child abuse or neglect if more comprehensive investigations were conducted or if there was more consensus in the coding of abuse on death certificates.

Recent studies in Colorado and North Carolina have estimated as many as 50% to 60% of deaths resulting from abuse or neglect are not recorded (Crume, DiGuiseppi, Byers, Sirotnak, & Garrett, 2002; Herman-Giddens, Brown, Verbiest, Carlson, Hooten, & Butts, 1999). These studies indicate that neglect is the most underrecorded form of fatal maltreatment.

This increase demonstrates that too many families see violence against children as an option (Prevention Update, 1997). Compared to other industrialized countries, the United States lags far behind in the development of human resources to address this crisis. Further, in 2000, nearly 2 million reports of alleged child abuse or neglect were investigated by child protective services agencies, representing more than 2.7 million children who were alleged victims of maltreatment and who referred to investigation (U.S. Department of Health and Human Services, 2004). Of these children, approximately 879,000 were found to be victims of maltreatment, meaning that sufficient evidence was found to substantiate or vindicate the report of child maltreatment (U.S. Department of Health and Human Services, 2004). The rate of child abuse and neglect fatalities reported by NCANDS has increased slightly over the last several years from 1.84 per 100,000 children in 2000 to 1.96 per 100,000 children in 2001 and 1.98 per 100,000 children in 2002. However, experts do not agree whether this represents an actual increase in child abuse and neglect fatalities, or whether it may be attributed to improvements in reporting procedures. For example, statistics on approximately 20% of fatalities were from health departments and fatality review boards for 2002, compared to 11.4% for 2001, an indication of greater coordination of data collection among agencies.

A number of issues affecting the accuracy and consistency of child fatality data from year to year have been identified, including the following:

- Variation among reporting requirements and definitions of child abuse and neglect.
- Variation in state child fatality review processes.
- The amount of time (as long as a year, in some cases) it may take a fatality review team to declare abuse or neglect as the cause of death.
- Miscoding of death certificates.

The selected data that follow give an idea of the magnitude and nuances of the problem:

- In 2000, an estimated 1,356 children died as a result of child abuse and neglect, nearly four children every day (U.S. Department of Health and Human Services, 1999).
- In 2000, the estimated rate of deaths per 100,000 U.S. children in the population was 1.84 (U.S. Department of Health and Human Services, 1999).
- In 2000, nearly 2 million reports of alleged child abuse and neglect were investigated by child protective services agencies, representing more than 2.7 million children who were alleged victims of maltreatment and who were referred for investigation (U.S. Department of Health and Human Services, 2004). Of these children, approximately 879,000 were found to be victims of maltreatment, meaning that sufficient evidence was found to substantiate or indicate the report of child maltreatment.
- Children under 5 years old account for four out of five of all fatalities reported, rivaling congenital anomalies as the second lead cause of death of children 1 to 4 years of age in the United States (U.S. Department of Health and Human Services, 1999).
- Children under 1 year old account for two out of five of all fatalities reported (U.S. Department of Health and Human Services, 1999).
- In the United States, one out of three girls, and at least one out of five boys, will be sexually abused before they are 18 (Buel, 1993).
- A million adolescents run away from home every year. Most are victims of abuse, and a majority of them become prostitutes or delinquents (U.S. Department of Health and Human Services, 2004).
- Statistics show that one out of eight women in the U.S. have been raped (Martin, 1992), and that 29% of rape victims are younger than 11; another 32% are between 11 and 17. This means that, in 61% of all rapes in this country, the victim is 17 years old and younger (Martin, 1992).

- Domestic violence is even more prevalent: Researchers estimate that 21% to 34% of women in this country are physically assaulted by an intimate partner at some time in their lives—an astonishing 3 to 4 million every year (Biden, 1993).
- Some 350,000 newborns each year are exposed prenatally to drugs, including alcohol.
- The incidence of pediatric HIV infection has risen dramatically in recent years, affecting some 15,000 to 30,000 infants (Burgess & Streissguth, 1992).

Because of the vast range of maltreatment behavior, this phenomenon is perhaps more readily understood if classified into categories presenting both acts of commission (e.g., physical abuse) and acts of omission (e.g., emotional neglect). Acts of commission include these:

- **Physical abuse.** Infliction of physical injury (e.g., burns, bites) on a child.
- **Sexual abuse.** Subjection of a child to sexual acts by an adult.
- **Physical neglect.** Failure to provide a child with a nurturing home environment that supplies the basic necessities of life (i.e., food, clothing, shelter, supervision, and protection from harm).
- **Medical neglect.** Failure of a caretaker to provide medical treatment in cases of suspected or diagnosed physical ailments.

Acts of omission include these:

- **Emotional abuse.** Speech and actions by a caretaker that inhibit the healthy personal and social development of a child.
- **Emotional neglect.** Failure of a caretaker to show concern for a child or his or her activities.
- **Educational neglect.** Failure of a caretaker to ensure that a child is provided with the opportunity to learn.
- **Abandonment.** Failure of a caretaker to make provisions for the continued sustenance of a child.
- **Multiple maltreatment.** A severe and complex combination of several types of abuse and neglect.

It is estimated that 60% of domestic violence victims and 80% of batterers come from families with a history of violence (Buel, 1993). Low self-esteem and feelings of inadequacy can result in problems ranging from low productivity on the job to delinquency, character disorders, and mental illness (Dean, 1979). Furthermore, the problems are often self-propagating in that they may be passed on from one generation to the next (Schrut, 1984). Children who have been psychologically abused throughout their lives often act out once they become adolescents. For example, Foreman and Seligman (1983) stated:

> In the courts, the abused adolescent is once again the loser; he or she may be punished as an offender rather than treated as a victim. Such responses from legal or social authorities tend to reinforce adolescents' own negative self-images and encourage them to view themselves as offenders and provokers, to be blamed for their own abuse. (p. 19)

There are also concerns that as many as 50% to 60% of deaths resulting from abuse and neglect are not recorded (Crume, DiGuiseppi, Byers, Sirotnak, Garrett, 2002; Herman-Giddens, Brown, Verbiest, Carlson, Hooten, Howell, & Butts, 1999).

Sexual Abuse in the Family

In an extensive study, Alter-Reid (1992) found that the majority of child abuse victims had been sexually abused by a family member, including natural parents (19%); surrogate parents, such as stepfathers or live-in boyfriends (21%); and other relatives (22%). Only 3% were victimized by strangers. Alter-Reid (1992) also found that children at the highest risk of incest are those with stepfathers. A stepfather is 6 times more likely than a biological father to sexually abuse a daughter. Children under the age of 9 are abused more frequently by relatives and acquaintances than are older children (those from 9 to 16). Therefore, sexual abuse prevention programs should not be limited to stranger abduction.

That the effects of abuse are long-lasting is not news. Children report postabuse fear, poor self-esteem, guilt, and a sense of being "damaged goods." As adults, they report depression, fear, and problems in sexual relationships. The impact of physical and sexual abuse is not easily quantifiable, but it is clearly seen in school and clinical settings and supported by the clinical experience of counselors and others. Some effects include these:

- Loss of trust, security, and the innocence of childhood.
- Ambivalence and conflict of feelings: love and hate, rage and guilt, stoicism and fear.
- The creation of defenses: walls of denial, repression, and dissociation; the armors of anorgasmia, anorexia, and obesity; the weapons of the

fist, the tongue, and the belt; the retreat to the bottle, the pill, and depression; escape from family, society, and reality.
- "Death—frequently invisible, unnoticed, unmourned—by overt or covert suicide" (Alter-Reid, 1992, p. 16).
- Several studies have suggested that child sexual abuse victims may internalize their victimization to such a degree that they *expect* further abuse, resulting in a choice of partners who continue to abuse them, their children, or both (Gillman & Whitlock, 1989).

Indicators of Abuse

In terms of impact, there is little difference between physical, sexual, and emotional abuse. All that ultimately distinguishes one from another is the abuser's choice of weapons against the victim. What emerges from such a punitive relationship is pervasive sadness, a severely damaged self-concept, difficulty with other relationships, and a lifelong quest to gain the approval of others. This quest for approval often is eclipsed by the notion that one does not really deserve it. Self-defeating, self-destructive behaviors often manifest themselves in obesity, drug addiction, anorexia, bulimia, alcoholism, domestic violence, child abuse, attempted suicide, and depression.

Most counselors and practitioners are aware of the physical indicators of abuse, including these:

- **Physical abuse.** Unexplained bruises, burns, bites, fractures, lacerations, or abrasions
- **Physical neglect.** Abandonment, unattended medical needs, lack of supervision, hunger, poor hygiene.
- **Sexual abuse.** Torn, stained underclothing; vaginal pain or itching; venereal disease.
- **Emotional abuse.** Speech disorders, delayed physical development, substance abuse, ulcers, asthma, severe allergies.

Many, however, may not recognize behavioral indicators. Table 9.1 provides behavioral indicators of abuse for educators, counselors, and other helping professionals.

Children from violent homes are likely to show several emotional reactions, according to their coping skills and developmental age:

- **Feeling responsible for the abuse.** "If only I had been a good girl, Daddy would not have hit Mommy."

Table 9.1 Types of Abuse

Physical abuse	
☐ Is self-destructive	☐ Chronically runs away
☐ Arrives at school early or stays late	☐ Is uncomfortable with physical contact
☐ Is withdrawn and aggressive	☐ Wears clothing inappropriate for age

Physical neglect	
☐ Regularly displays fatigue	☐ Falls asleep in class
☐ Reports no caretaker at home	☐ Is frequently absent or tardy
☐ Is self-destructive	☐ Steals food, begs from classmates

Sexual abuse	
☐ Is withdrawn, experiences chronic depression	☐ Displays excessive seductiveness
☐ Shows lack of confidence	☐ Shows hysteria, lack of emotional control
☐ Has peer problems	☐ Engages in promiscuity
☐ Encounters sudden school difficulties	☐ Has poor self-esteem
☐ Is threatened by physical contact	

Emotional maltreatment	
☐ Has habit disorders (sucking, rocking)	☐ Is antisocial, destructive
☐ Has sleep disorders	☐ Is passive aggressive
☐ Is developmentally delayed	☐ Displays delinquent behavior

Source: Adapted from "Supporting victims of abuse," by T. Bear, S. Schenk, and L. Buckner, 1993, *Educational Leadership, 50*(4), p. 44. Copyright 1993 by ASCD. Reprinted with permission. All rights reserved.

- **Anxiety and guilt.** Anxiety about the next violent situation and guilt about good feelings the child may have toward the abuser.
- **Fear of abandonment or abduction.** When children are removed from one parent because of violent acts, they often have fears that the other parent will abandon them or that the abuser will abduct them or retaliate.
- **Shame, embarrassment, and uncertainty about the future.** Sensitivity to the stigma of abuse may result in shame, uncertainty in interpersonal relationships, and anxiety over future planning.

Reactions also vary according to the type of abuse a child experiences and whether the child internalizes or externalizes blame for the abuse:

- The results of sexual abuse include self-blame, confusion about sexuality, and distorted negative views of self and others.
- Pynoos and Eth (1985) maintained that children who witness extreme acts of violence are at "significant risk of developing anxiety, depression, phobic conduct, and post-traumatic stress disorder" (p. 19).
- Children and adolescents who internalize blame for abusive situations may manifest the following symptoms: self-destructiveness, depression, suicidal thoughts, passivity, withdrawal, shyness, constricted communication, nervous habits, nightmares, and somatic complaints (Blume, 1990).
- Children and adolescents who tend to externalize blame manifest a different set of symptoms: anxiety, aggression, hostile behavior, overactivity, impulsivity, readiness to strike back, and fearful responses.

Researchers, practitioners, and policy stakeholders are now increasing promoting protective factors within children and families that can reduce risk and, build family potential, and foster resilience. Resilience in maltreated children was found to be related to personal characteristics that included a child's ability to recognize danger and adapt, distance him- or herself from intense feelings, create relationships that are crucial for support, and project him- or herself into a time and place in the future in which the perpetrator is no longer present (Mrazek & Mrazek, 1987). Table 9.2 lists additional risk and protective factors.

Long-Term Effects of Abuse and Neglect on Children and Adolescents

The long-term effects of chronic long-term neglect are especially significant for later social and emotional functioning of children and adolescents. Abuse and neglect manifest themselves in poor school performance. Neglect during early childhood has negative consequences for later social relationships, problem solving, and the ability to cope adequately with new or stressful situations. Children experiencing abuse or neglect are also at risk for delinquency, violence, and other self-destructive behaviors, such as alcohol and other drug abuse as a means to self-medicate and forget painful experiences. Emotionally, abused and neglected children are at risk for post-traumatic stress disorder, major depressive disorder, anxiety disorders and other diagnostic conditions (National Research Council, 1993). Maltreatment can have devastating immediate and long-term physical, psychological, and behavioral effects on children.

Table 9.2   Risk and Protective Factors for Child Abuse and Neglect

Risk factors	Protective factors
Child risk factors	**Child protective factors**
Premature birth, birth anomalies, low birth weight	Good health, history of adequate development
Exposure to toxins *in utero*	Above-average intelligence
Temperament: difficult or slow to warm up	Hobbies and interests
Physical, cognitive, or emotional disability	Good peer relationships
Chronic or serious illness	Personality factors:
Childhood trauma	Easy temperament
Antisocial peer group	Positive disposition
Age	Active coping style
Child aggression, behavior problems, attention deficits	Positive self-esteem
	Good social skills
	Internal locus of control
	Balance between help-seeking and autonomy
Parental/family risk factors	**Parental/family protective factors**
Personality factors:	Secure attachment; positive parent–child relationship
External locus of control	Supportive family environment
Poor impulse control	Household rules and structure; parental monitoring
Depression or anxiety	Extended family support, involvement, and caregiving
Low tolerance for frustration	Stable relationship with parents
Feelings of insecurity	Parents model competence, have good coping skills
Lack of trust	Family expectations of prosocial behavior
Insecure attachment with own parents	High parental education
Childhood history of abuse	
High parental conflict, domestic violence	
Family structure (single parent with lack of support combined with high number of children in household)	
Social isolation, lack of support	
Parental psychopathology	
Substance abuse	
Separation or divorce, especially high conflict divorce	
Age	

Table 9.2   Risk and Protective Factors for Child Abuse and Neglect (continued)

Risk factors	Protective factors
High general stress level	
Poor parent–child interaction; negative attitudes and attributions about child's behavior	
Inaccurate knowledge and expectations about child development	

Social/environmental risk factors	**Social/environmental protective factors**
Low social economic status (SES)	Middle to high SES
Stressful life events	Access to health care and social services
Lack of medical care, health insurance	Consistent parental employment
Lack of adequate child care and social services	Adequate housing
Parental unemployment; homelessness	Family religious faith participation
Social isolation or lack of social support	Good schools
Poor schools	Supportive adults outside the family who serve as role models and mentors to child
Exposure to environmental toxins	
Dangerous or violent neighborhood	
Community violence	

Note. From U.S. Department of Health and Human Services (2004). Child Maltreatment, 2002. Washington, D.C., U.S. Printing Office, Washington, D.C.

Characteristics of Adults Who Abuse or Mistreat Children and Adolescents

Inherently, many factors can contribute to the tendency to abuse, rather than nurture, children. Maladaptive parenting can evolve from a number of variables. A parent's behavioral repertoire or characteristics such as excessive anger, anxiety, impulsivity, depression, history of childhood abuse, or poor coping skills can be factors that influence the tendency to maltreat children. Environmental factors can include marital conflict, social isolation, unemployment, lack of community support, and violence in the community. Further, several studies have found that abusive parents are more psychologically disturbed than nonabusive parents (English, 1995). Fortunately, some researchers have identified protective factors that seem to break the cycle of abuse. Parents with reported histories of abuse who do not abuse their own children are more likely to have

1. a better current social support system, including a supportive spouse;
2. a positive relationship with a significant adult in childhood or a positive experience with therapy as an adolescent or adult;
3. an ability to provide a clear account of their childhood abuse, with anger appropriately directed at the perpetrator, rather than at themselves (National Research Council, 1993).

Child Abuse Prevention Efforts

Efforts to prevent child abuse and neglect include a wide range of activities with goal of helping families and children receive the necessary support and education (Cohn Donnelly & Shaw, 2001; Harding, 2002). To be effective, prevention efforts require a thorough understanding of the dynamics, types, and causes of maltreatment and fatalities. Effective prevention and intervention efforts must address the risk factors for maltreatment as well as strengthen families and communities to create a healthier environment for raising children. Prevention promotes the actions, thoughts, and interactions that lead to familial well-being and the healthy, optimal development of children (Britton, 2001). The most common prevention services across the nation are home-visiting programs such as Healthy Families America (HFA), a neonatal home visiting program for families. Other prevention services include school- and home-based services for youth and domestic violence prevention programs (Peddke, Wang, Diaz, & Reid, 2002).

Rape

Rape has been declared a social disease of epidemic proportions. McCann, Sakheim, and Abrahamson (1988) estimated that 46% of women in the United States will be raped at least once in their lives. Other researchers place the figure at 22% (Koss, Gidycz, & Wisniewski, 1987; Koss & Oros, 1982; Russell, 1984). Rape victims constitute the largest single group of posttraumatic stress disorder (PTSD) sufferers (Steketee & Foa, 1987). Rape-related symptoms that are consistent with PTSD include intrusive and unpleasant imagery, nightmares, exaggerated startle responses, disturbance in sleep pattern, guilt, impairment in concentration or memory, and fear and avoidance of rape-related situations (Steketee & Foa, 1987). The aftermath of sexual trauma is a major mental health problem with both short- and long-term effects (Roth & Lebowitz, 1988). In recent years, researchers and the media have raised new awareness of a kind of rape that has gone unreported for years: date rape. Victims of date rape often have serious concerns about their self-perceptions and view themselves as weak, helpless, and out of control.

Armsworth and Holaday (1993) "examined the cognitive, affective, behavioral, and somatic–physiological effects of sexual assault on children and adolescents." Cognitive effects of trauma in children and adolescents that meet the criteria of PTSD include these:

- Time distortion regarding the event.
- Inability to recall details of the event in sequence.
- Intrusive imagery and thoughts with conscious suppression and avoidance.
- A foreshortened sense of the future.
- No goals or altered goals.
- Hypervigilance.
- Alertness to reminders.
- Guardedness against attack.

Affective effects of trauma in children and adolescents include these:

- Labile affect, including anxiety, panic, and irritability.
- Fears, including excessive worry, generalized phobias, and fears of retraumatization.
- Tension.
- Constricted emotions.
- Inability to express or fear of expressing feelings.
- Distress at reminders of objects, situations, or people.
- Traumatic dreams.
- Avoidance of pleasurable activities.
- Reexperiencing the event emotionally.

Several behavioral effects meet the criteria for PTSD, including these:

- Posttraumatic play.
- Regressive behaviors.
- Loss of previously learned skills (academic and social).
- Reenactment of the events.
- Retelling the event without affect.
- Poor concentration, inattentiveness, hyperactivity, and impulsivity.
- No regard for consequence of actions.
- Alteration of behavior to avoid activities, people, situations, and objects that are reminders of the events.

- Alteration of behavior that results from feeling alone, estranged, left out, or different (Armsworth & Holaday).

Physiological and somatic effects of trauma noted in the literature that meet the criteria of PTSD include these:

- Autonomic response to traumatic reminders.
- Hyperarousal.
- Low tolerance for stress.
- Startle response to reminder stimuli alternating with numbing.
- Sleep disorders.
- Fatigue.

If child sexual abuse is not effectively treated, long-term symptoms may persist into adulthood. These may include the following:

- PTSD or anxiety.
- Depression and thoughts of suicide.
- Sexual anxiety and disorders.
- Poor body image and low self-esteem.
- The use of unhealthy behaviors, such as alcohol abuse, drug abuse, self-mutilation, or bingeing and purging, to help mask painful emotions related to the abuse (Cohen, 1998).

Young children may report more generalized fears such as stranger or separation anxiety, avoidance of situations that may or may not be related to the trauma, sleep disturbances, and a preoccupation with words or symbols that may or may not be related to the trauma. These children may also display posttraumatic play in which they repeat themes of the trauma (Cohen, 1998). Elementary school–aged children experience time skew and omen formation. *Time skew* refers to a child mis-sequencing trauma related events when recalling the memory (Cohen, 1998). *Omen formation* is a belief that there were warning signs that predicted the trauma. As a result, children often believe that if they are alert enough, they will recognize warning signs and avoid future traumas. School-aged children also reportedly exhibit posttraumatic play or reenactment of the trauma in play, drawings, or verbalizations.

Posttraumatic play is different from reenactment in that posttraumatic play is a literal representation of the trauma, involves compulsively repeating some aspect of the trauma, and does not tend to relieve anxiety. An example of posttraumatic play is an increase in shooting games after exposure to a school shooting. Posttraumatic reenactment, on the other hand, is more flexible and involves behaviorally recreating aspects of the trauma (e.g., carrying a weapon after exposure to violence). PTSD in adolescents may begin to more closely resemble PTSD in adults. Sexually abused children often have problems with fear, anxiety, depression, anger and hostility, aggression, sexually inappropriate behavior, self-destructive behavior, feelings of isolation and stigma, poor self-esteem, difficulty in trusting others, and substance abuse.

Runaways and Homeless Youth

Without a systematic, centralized system for collecting information about runaways, the number of young people who run away is difficult to determine with certainty. Estimates range from 700,000 to almost 1 million each year, and one study indicated that 12% of all American youth have run away at least once before the age of 18 (Jones, 1988). The significant fact is that many of these young people are refugees from unbearable situations or circumstances.

Furthermore, current research shows a trend toward long-term homelessness for runaway youth. This is caused by such factors as family breakdown, rejection, physical, homosexuality and sexual abuse (Jones, 1988; McCormack, Burgess, & Hartman, 1988). Kufeldt and Nimmo (1987) found that as many as 30% of long-term runaways no longer even knew where their parents lived and that 6% of sporadic runaways had lost track of their parents. These researchers also noted that the tendency to assume a pattern of street life is associated with the length of time away from the family and the distance from the home.

Runaway behavior seems to reflect a multidimensional problem. The reasons for running away are multiple and complex, as the following list indicates:

- Negative psychological or social adjustment (Ferran & Sabatini, 1985; Kammer & Schmidt, 1987).
- An attempt to find a value system that the runaway can accept (Adams & Munro, 1979; Loeb, Burke, & Boglarsky, 1986).
- An attempt to "find" oneself or gain control over one's life (Adams & Munro, 1979).
- Poor self-image and low self-confidence (Englander, 1984; Miller, 1981).
- Family disturbance, including poor communication, alcoholism or drug abuse, and parent–child conflict (Ferran & Sabatini, 1985; Kammer & Schmidt, 1987; Kogan, 1980; Morgan, 1982; Stiffman, 1989).

- Parental rejection or expulsion (Adams, Gullotta, & Clancy, 1985; Levine, Metzendorf, & Van Boskirk, 1986).
- A rational and appropriate reaction to detrimental circumstances (Aptekar, 1989).
- Economic stress, including a lack of adequate resources to sustain a stable pattern of life (Aptekar, 1989; Ferran & Sabatini, 1985).
- Sexual and physical abuse (Daly & Wilson, 1985; McCormack, Burgess, & Hartman, 1988). Female runaways report having experienced some form of sexual abuse (Stiffman, 1989.)
- Engaging in confrontations in school (Zieman & Benson, 1980).
- Difficulty with school authorities (Nielsen & Gerber, 1979; Zieman & Benson, 1980).
- Lack of academic success (Levine, Metzendorf, & Van Boskirk, 1986; Miller, 1981).

Compared to nonrunaways, runaways have lower self-esteem, less self-confidence, and more difficulty with interpersonal relationships, including a lack of social poise. Generally, runaways feel less control of their environments, which perhaps accounts for research findings that they are more likely to be anxious, to be defensive, and to exhibit suicidal tendencies. In a study by Roberts (1982), the runaway population sample also manifested inadequate problem-solving methods. They attempted to deal with stressful situations by sleeping, crying, turning to drugs or alcohol, forgetting about major elements in their lives, or attempting suicide. All these coping strategies involve removing oneself from the situation rather than confronting it. This pattern of destructive thinking has been labeled *cognitive confusion* by Janus, Burgess, and McCormack (1987).

Structured Interventions for High-Risk Behaviors

Therapeutic Initiatives

Eliminating victimization and abuse takes a school–community multidisciplinary approach to helping children and adolescents. Networks and resource centers can operate in a wide variety of local settings: hospitals, schools, community mental health centers, recreation centers, libraries, community colleges, civic centers, daycare centers, social service agencies, and churches. Network members should be drawn from the medical, educational, law enforcement, and social work disciplines and include key leaders from business, political, and volunteer segments of the community. Committees of network members should concentrate on such areas as these:

- **Mental health services for sexually abused children.** Interviewing techniques that provide potential cues through toys, materials, and photographs can elicit much more information than verbal questioning alone.
- **Family life education programs.** These programs teach adolescents about the social aspects of sexuality, including the importance of sexual consent. Such programs also should teach parenting skills and address such areas as self-esteem, coping skills, decision making, communication, developmental issues, and parental control.
- **Systematic teacher education.** Because of their daily contact with children, teachers often are the first finders of child abuse. They need to learn to recognize the warning signs of child abuse, including aggression, withdrawal, poor personal hygiene, low self-esteem, and reluctance to dress for physical education activities.
- **Self-help groups.** These groups may be at churches or community centers.
- **Volunteer teachers.** Teachers act as facilitators of school-based sexual abuse prevention programs.
- **Helping families.** Families need help in searching for solutions to problems such as parental conflict, divorce, alcoholism, legal problems, and sexual or emotional abuse.

Helping Abused Children in the Classroom

Children who have been abused usually attempt to keep the abuse a secret and to control the emotional turmoil they feel inside. When they do confide the abuse, it often is to a teacher. In addition to reporting the abuse, classroom teachers have a unique opportunity to identify abused children and to start the healing process that will restore safety to their lives. Bear, Schenk, and Buckner (1993) outlined the following suggestions for helping:

1. "**Expectations.** Set reasonable goals and provide the support needed for the child to feel confident in his or her abilities. School can be a place where children rebuild their self-esteem, assert themselves, and see themselves as successful.
2. **Structure.** To help the child feel a sense of control in a positive manner, give accurate information and build trust. Allow expression of

feelings when appropriate through art, music, drama, or creative writing to help the child release pent-up emotion.

3. **Identity.** Point out the child's strengths: "You are a hard worker." "You are a good team leader." Ask questions that help the child formulate a position on issues. Administer interest inventories and teach decision-making and problem-solving skills to enhance interpersonal relationships and self-understanding.

4. **Self-esteem.** Help children learn they are valued, accepted, and capable by fostering an environment that honors each child's uniqueness. Valuing their differences enables children to begin seeing themselves as having something to contribute that others appreciate.

5. **Sense of belonging.** To facilitate a sense of belonging, provide designated places for possessions, display work in the classroom, and make a conscious attempt to include abused children in classroom activities. Teach social skills individually, in small-group settings, and through cooperative learning to help children gain experience in interacting with others in a nonthreatening atmosphere.

6. **Social skills.** A classroom environment that fosters caring, appreciation of differences, consistent rules and boundaries, and recognition for small successes will nurture a child who has experienced family deprecation.

7. **Consistency.** Teachers, counselors and other helping professionals can support a child's need for structure by maintaining a consistent daily schedule; by having clear expectations for performance academically, behaviorally, and affectively; and by allowing the child to provide structure in his or her own way" (pp. 46–47).

A teacher's or counselor's natural concern and caring for students also will promote the process of healing. Teachers, counselors, and other helping professionals have the opportunity to give an abused child the hope of a childhood, the joy of learning, the delight of play, and the sense of belonging by being cared for and valued by others. Further, teachers, counselors and helping professionals can use age-appropriate discussions with children and adolescents to help them understand and avoid abuse:

18 months to 3 years: Teach children the proper names for body parts.

3 to 5 years: Teach children about private parts of the body and how to say "no" to sexual advances. Give straightforward, frank information about sex.

5 to 8 years: Discuss safety away from home and the difference between a good touch and a bad touch. Encourage honest discussion of experiences.

9 to 12 years: Stress personal safety. Discuss appropriate sexual conduct.

13 to 18 years: Stress personal safety. Discuss rape, date rape, unintended pregnancy, and sexually transmitted diseases.

Treatment Plan: Prevention of Sexual Assault

Counseling intention: To identify and distinguish between comfortable and uncomfortable kinds of touches; to identify specific ways of saying "no" to adults and other children; to help students understand that they can tell if they encounter a difficult situation; to know what to say to a caring person.

Finklehor (1986) provided the treatment plan for children described in the next section.

You Can Say "No"

Session 1: Identifying uncomfortable feelings. For the first few minutes, the children and the counselor think of words that describe feelings. The counselor helps the children place these words into a list of comfortable feelings and another list of uncomfortable feelings. A third list may be added for confusing feelings, either comfortable or uncomfortable, depending on the maturity of the children.

Next, the counselor asks the children to describe situations in which uncomfortable feelings might occur. Children tend to focus on peer-pressure situations and threats of kidnapping by strangers. Thus, it might be necessary to explain sexual assault as an uncomfortable touch on the part of the body covered by a bathing suit. Counselors working with kindergartners sometimes explain the private area as "where you go to the bathroom." Because children focus on assault by strangers, counselors need to explain that persons whom children know might want to touch the children's private parts or want the children to touch theirs.

Session 2: Why it's hard to say "no." Often children realize that they need to say "no" but find it difficult to do so. This lesson emphasizes the reasons for that difficulty. The counselor begins by asking children why it is hard to say "no." Children typically describe bribes, threats of harm, withdrawal of affection, secrecy, and peer pressure, but counselors need to be prepared to add to these ideas. The lesson also recognizes that children often are expected to obey without question. Fears about saying "no" because of lost status with peers or punishment by an adult need to be recognized and taken seriously.

To reinforce the session, pictures are used depicting situations in which children might want to say "no." The children explain what they think is happening in the picture and are asked what they could do if something like this happened to them, emphasizing that they can say "no."

Session 3: How to say "no." When they have an understanding of uncomfortable feelings and of the difficulty in saying "no," children are ready to learn techniques for saying "no," including these:

1. **Broken record:** "No, I don't want to! No, I don't want to!"

2. **Delaying:** "Not now."

3. **Explanation:** "I don't feel that it would be right for me."

4. **Leaving.**

5. **Avoiding the situation:** "No, my mom wants me home now."

6. **Changing the subject:** "No, I don't want to. Did you see the movie last night?"

7. **Taking personal credit:** "No, I don't want to be your friend if I have to do that."

Because the last three techniques are more complicated, counselors need to determine the appropriateness of the techniques for the children's age level. For each technique, children practice different ways of saying "no" and are encouraged to develop their own responses. Generally, this is accomplished by having children role-play in pairs, with the counselor and other children supplying encouragement and feedback.

Session 4: Role-playing saying "no." The fourth session is a continuation of the previous one and may be combined easily with the third, depending on the children's maturity and time constraints. The counselor shows children pictures of situations in which they might want to say "no." Children then act out situations in which there is peer pressure, and the counselor cautiously assumes the role of perpetrator in sexual assault situations. This procedure avoids putting the children in awkward situations and allows them to practice saying "no" to an adult.

Session 5: I can tell a caring person. This session helps children identify appropriate helping persons, structures what the child should say, and identifies appropriate times for talking. Occasionally, children will find adults who will not believe them, so suggestions are provided on how to find someone who will believe them.

Session 6: Telling a caring person. In this final session, three situations are described in which a child is approached sexually, once by a stranger and twice by a known adult. Children gain additional experience in saying "no" and in reporting to a caring adult. Because the adult is known, children have the opportunity to discuss their fears about "tattling" on the person. Again, discussions sometimes flow more smoothly if the counselor takes the part of the abuser and openly acknowledges the difficulties of saying "no."

Treatment Plan: Guided Exercise for Telling the Story of Sexual Abuse

Counseling intention: To provide structure for a trauma-focused sexual abuse treatment group; to engage the support of peers.

De Young and Corbin (1994) provided the following treatment plan for adolescents. The young person is provided with the following guided exercise for telling his or her story.

Remember, you are in charge of how much or how little you tell. Telling what happened to you can lift shame off your shoulders. The shame belongs to those who have sexually abused you and told you lies.

1. *Today* I feel _____ about the possibility of telling others my story.
2. The *worst* thing that can happen while telling my story is
   _____ I won't remember telling it.
   _____ someone may laugh.
   _____ someone may not believe me.
   _____ I will feel pain.
   _____ I will explode with emotion.
   _____ I will be embarrassed.
   _____ I may cry.
   _____ someone may think I'm weird.
   _____ or something else, like _____.
3. I *need* the group to
   _____ be understanding.
   _____ not laugh or talk while I'm talking.
   _____ be patient with me.
   _____ ask me questions in a caring way.
   _____ tell me what they think and feel about what I just said.
4. The *person* (or persons) who sexually abused me *was* (include)
   _____ my mother.
   _____ my father.

_____ my stepfather.

_____ my mother's boyfriend.

_____ my brother.

_____ my sister.

_____ my uncle.

_____ my grandfather.

_____ a family friend.

_____ a stranger.

_____ another person, like _____.

5. This *happened* to me

_____ one or two times.

_____ many times.

_____ more times than I can count.

6. The sexual abuse *felt*

_____ good sometimes.

_____ gross.

_____ scary.

_____ painful.

_____ weird/confusing.

_____ I can't remember.

_____ I'm too scared to remember.

_____ other feelings, like _____.

7. *After* the sexual abuse happened, I thought

_____ I did something wrong.

_____ this happens to all girls (boys).

_____ there might be something wrong with my body.

_____ I might be pregnant.

_____ I might have AIDS or some other disease.

_____ that if I told, something terrible would happen.

_____ that I could have stopped it, but I'm not sure how.

_____ that people could tell I was abused by just looking at me.

8. The person or persons who sexually abused me *told me*

_____ never to tell.

_____ nothing.

_____ they would hurt me or someone I love if I told.

_____ nobody would believe me if I told.

_____ they were in love with me.

_____ confusing things about my mom.

_____ that I was a slut or whore.

_____ that they were doing nothing wrong.

_____ that they would give me money or special favors if I kept doing it.

_____ other things, like _____.

9. My *mother* (or parent)

_____ blamed me.

_____ didn't believe me.

_____ seems not to care how I feel.

_____ knew it was happening and didn't protect me.

_____ was helpful and supportive.

_____ did something else, like _____.

10. The *person* who touched me wrong

_____ admitted to some of the things, but not everything.

_____ admitted it, but still said it wasn't wrong.

_____ told the police about the sexual abuse.

_____ admitted it to me, but to no one else.

_____ did or said other things, like _____.

_____ didn't admit to anything.

11. The *person* who sexually abused me

_____ went to prison or jail.

_____ had to leave our house.

_____ I don't know where he or she is.

_____ something else happened to that person, like _____.

12. If the sexual abuse had *never happened* maybe

_____ I would be able to sleep through the night.

_____ I would make friends more easily.

_____ I wouldn't cry all the time.

_____ I wouldn't feel like hurting myself so often.

_____ I wouldn't feel like people are staring at me.

_____ or something else, like _____.

13. In the *future*, I would like to be able to

_____ tell my mom or dad how I feel.

_____ be more friendly.

_____ stop putting myself down.

_____ walk tall and proud without shame.

_____ or something else, like _____.

14. I *wish*

_____ I could go back home.

_____ my family would believe me.

_____ I could feel safe.

_____ I could stop having bad dreams.

_____ some other wish, like _____.

I must always remember: *I deserve* to be treated with respect and to be safe. Nothing that I did caused these bad things to happen to me.

Treatment Plan: Preventing Sexual Assault

Counseling intention: To provide adolescents with strategies to prevent date rape or acquaintance rape.

Martin (1992) provided the following exercises for preventing sexual assault (the exercises have been modified for this book).

> **Describe first impressions.** After meeting someone for the first time, take a few minutes to write down your thoughts about him or her. List some concrete questions about the person:
> Where does this person work?
> What is he or she studying?
> Where does he or she live?
> How does he or she look?
> Next list your **intuitive feelings:**
> Do you feel safe with this person?
> Does he or she seem sensitive to your feelings?
> Does he or she seem overpowering?
> Could he or she have an uncontrollable temper?
> **Listen to your inner thoughts and feelings about this individual.**
> **Find a safe place and an escape route.** Find a place where you feel physically safe: This could be your home, the library, a museum, the school, or inside a shopping mall. Then draw an escape route on paper, the route to take you to safety if you were attacked. Try to think of as many alternatives as possible and rate them as to how successful you think they would be.
> **Pay attention to detail.** Police will tell you that the most useful clues in identifying someone are characteristics that make that person stand out from the rest. Birthmarks, tattoos, unusual facial or hair features are all good characteristics to report. Pick someone you recently saw (a parent, teacher, friend). Describe what they were wearing when you saw them, special characteristics, weight, height, information about how they walk or talk. You may be surprised at how little you remember about someone you are close to. Sharpen your awareness skills and practice recalling details.

Strategy: Increasing Self-Esteem

Intervention intention: To help children with some of their developmental deficits and emotional issues.

Have the child or adolescent develop a scrapbook about him- or herself. Include photos, pictures from magazines, clever saying by the child, affirmations, accomplishments, and memorabilia. Help the child or adolescent develop a list of all the good things he or she has ever done and put them in the scrapbook. The counselor or human services professional can work with teachers and caregivers to reward the child or adolescent for accomplishments of small steps when undertaking new tasks. Have the child or adolescent also keep a record of all the compliments he or she has received and include them in the scrapbook.

Strategy: Life-Sized Silhouette

Intervention intention: To get in touch with the positive side of one's whole self.

Have the child or adolescent stand in front of a full length piece of paper and trace his or her silhouette. The child then gets to draw in and decorate the life-sized drawing with positive aspects of him- or herself.

Treatment Plan: Multimodal Treatment Plan for Victimization

Counseling intention: To provide a comprehensive intervention for victimization.

Table 9.3   Multimodal Treatment Plan for Victimization

Modality and referral problems	Related interventions
Behavior Reduced work performance Diminished activity Statements of self-denigration	Implement a "pleasant event schedule" to ensure a daily sampling of personally pleasing activities
Affect Sadness, guilt, "heavy heartedness" Intermittent anxiety and anger	Use standard anxiety reduction methods (e.g., relaxation, meditation, calming self-statements) combined with assertiveness training; develop a repertoire of self-assertive and uninhibited responses
Sensation Less pleasure from food Easily fatigues	Add a specific list of pleasant visual, auditory, tactile, olfactory, and gustatory stimuli to the "pleasant events schedule" to create a "sensate-focus" of enjoyable events

Table 9.3 *(continued)* Multimodal Treatment Plan for Victimization

Modality and referral problems	Related interventions
Imagery	
Visions of loneliness and failure	Recall past successes
Pictures him- or herself being rejected by important people in his life	Picture small but successful outcomes
	Apply coping imagery, using "time projection" (i.e., client pictures him- or herself venturing step-by-step into a future characterized by positive affect and pleasurable activities)
Cognition	
Negative self-appraisal	Employ Ellis's (1989) methods of
Exaggeration of real or imagined shortcomings. "I'm not good at anything." "Things will always be bad for me."	cognitive disputation; challenge categorical imperatives, "should and oughts," and irrational beliefs
	Identify worthwhile qualities and recite them every day
Interpersonal	
Decreased social participation	Teach clients to say, "No!" to unreasonable requests; to ask for favors by expressing positive feelings; to volunteer criticism; and to "dispute with style"
	If appropriate, recommend family therapy to teach family members how to avoid reinforcing depressive behavior and how to encourage the client to engage in pleasurable activities
Drugs/Biology Modality	
Appetite unimpaired but has intermittent insomnia	Address issues pertaining to increased exercise, relaxation, appropriate sleep patterns, and overall physical fitness
	If appropriate, recommend biological intervention, such as antidepressants in the case of bipolar disorders

Treatment Plan: Confronting Shyness

Counseling intention: To assist the client in becoming more assertive.

The following guidelines should be considered when framing or defining assertive behavior:

- The best way to get what you want is to ask for it.
- The best way not to get what you do not want is to say "no" to it.

- The best way to get someone to stop doing something you do not want them to do is to tell them how their actions make you feel.
- Assertiveness implies a special type of self-disclosure.
- Do not avoid expressing "negative" feelings. Negative feelings are just as important as positive ones.
- Focus on first-person "I" language to signify that the statement you are making is an indication of your own feelings (Wassmer, 1978).

Treatment Plan: Cost and Benefits

Counseling intention: To assess missed opportunities for growth.

Has being shy cost you anything? Have you missed opportunities and passed by unique experiences because you were shy? Make an itemized cost. See Table 9.4: Cost versus benefits of being shy.

Technique: Shyness Journal

Counseling intention: To evaluate dimensions of shyness.

Keep a journal of the times you feel shy. White down the time, what happened, your reaction, and the consequences for you.

Table 9.4 Confronting Shyness: Cost versus Benefits

Time of your life	Valued event, opportunity that was delayed or diminished	Personal consequence to you
1.		
2.		
3.		
4.		

Table 9.5 Keeping a Shyness Journal

Time	Situation or setting	Physical symptoms	Mental notation reactions	Consequences (+) (−)
Third bell	U.S. Government class discussion of daily current events	Heart pounding, feeling nervous, looking down, avoiding eye contact	"I can't remember anything I read this morning. I'm going to fail this class. I'll have to go to summer school."	"I've lost another opportunity for my grade. Time is running out." Panic

Treatment Plan: Write Yourself a Letter

Counseling intention: To identify and validate personal attributes that are positive.

Write yourself a letter focusing on your positive attributes or record a message about your successes, hopes, and possibilities; play the recording back.

Treatment Plan: First-Time Talking

Counseling intention: To focus on critical social skills.

If you find that you have a hard time talking to "anyone," try some of these less threatening experiences.

- Call information and ask for the telephone numbers of people you want to call. Thank the operator and note his or her reaction.
- Call a department store and check on the price of something advertised in the paper.
- Call a radio talk show, compliment the format, then ask a question.
- Call a local movie theater and ask for the discounted show times.
- Call the library and ask the reference librarian a question about the population in your town or the United States.
- Call a restaurant and make reservations for four, then call back within the hour and cancel them. Thank the person at the reservation desk and note his or her reaction.

Treatment Plan: Saying Hello

Counseling intention: To begin a experiential hierarchy of anxiety-provoking situation.

On the campus or in the workplace, smile and say hello to people you don't know.

Treatment Plan: Beginning a Dialogue with a Stranger

Counseling intention: To continue structured interpersonal experiences.

An ideal way to practice initial conversational skills is to initiate safe conversations with strangers in public places, like grocery store lines, theater lines, the post office, a doctor's waiting room, the bank, the library, or the lunch room.

Start a conversation about a common experience, such as, "It looks like mystery meat for lunch again," "I hope this will be my lucky lotto ticket," or "Who do you hope will win the Super Bowl?"

Treatment Plan: Giving and Accepting Compliments

Counseling intention: To provide an opportunity to integrate social skills into interpersonal relationships.

Giving and accepting compliments is an easy way to start a conversation and make the other person feel good. Yet offering a compliment is probably the most overlooked ice breaker between people. Here are some examples:

- Comment on what a person is wearing: "That's a cool jacket."
- Comment on how a person looks: "I like your haircut."
- Note a skill: "You sure know how to catch those waves."
- Compliment a personality trait: "I love your laugh."
- Note a possession: "That car is awesome!"

To get further into the conversations, simply ask a question: "What an awesome car. How long have you had it?"

Treatment Plan: Starting a Conversation

Counseling intention: To identify comfort levels in interacting with others.

There are a number of ways to start a conversation. Choose the one that is the most appropriate and comfortable for you.

Introduce yourself. "Hello, my name is …." (Practice this in a mirror at home.) This is a good approach at gatherings where everyone is a stranger.

Give a compliment, and then follow it up with a question. "That's a terrific suit. Where did you get it?"

Request help. Make it obvious you need help and be sure the other person can provide it. "Last time I came to this library, I used the card catalogue. How can I find the works of Carl Rogers with this computer terminal?"

Try honesty and self-disclosure. When you make an obviously personal statement, it will create a positive, sympathetic response. Be honest and say, "I'm not sure what I'm doing here. I'm really quite shy."

Cultivate your normal social graces: "Looks like you need a refill; let me get it for you; I'm headed that way" or "Here, let me help you with those groceries."

Once you have initiated a conversation, there are several techniques you can use to keep it going:

- Ask a question that is either factual ("Can you believe how bad the Redskins look this year?") or personal ("How do you feel about the new school rules?").
- Offer one of your own personal stories or opinions.
- Read about political or cultural issues and become knowledgeable about them (e.g., the national deficit or violence in society).
- Come up with a few interesting things that have happened to you recently and turn them into brief, interesting stories. For example, you could talk about registering for classes, incidents on the job, a new video game, learning to surf or skate, teachers, parents, brothers, and sisters. When you meet people, be ready with several stories to tell or interesting comments to make. Practice ahead of time in the mirror or on a tape recorder.
- Get the other person to talk about him- or herself: interests, hobbies, work, and education.
- Express interest in the other person's expertise: "How were you able to land a job like that?" "How did you make it through Gaskin's class?"
- Above all, share your reactions to what is taking place at that moment. Relate your thoughts or feelings about what the other person has said or done (Zimbardo, 1977, p. 180).

Treatment Plan: Becoming More Outgoing

Counseling intention: To increase the client's repertoire of interpersonal experiences.

Start with the easiest reaching-out exercise and progress to those that are more difficult. Record your reactions to each of these opportunities.

- Introduce yourself to a new person in one of your classes.
- Invite someone who is going your way to walk with you.
- Ask someone you don't know if you can borrow a quarter for a phone call. Arrange to pay him or her back.
- Find someone of the opposite sex in your class. Call him or her on the phone and ask about the latest class assignment.
- Stand in line at a grocery store. Start a conversation about the line with whomever is near you.
- Ask three people for directions.

- Go to the beach, swimming pool, or sports stadium and converse with two or three strangers you meet.
- Notice someone who needs help in school or class. Offer to help.
- Invite someone to eat with you.
- Say "hi" to five new people during the week. Try to provoke a smile and a return "hi" from them.

Treatment Plan: Making a Date with Someone of the Opposite Sex

Counseling intention: To decrease irrational fears of rejection.

Dating is a social contact that is anxiety-provoking for many. Shy daters feel more vulnerable to irrational thoughts of rejection. Here are some guidelines for overcoming fears:

- Make your date by telephone initially. Be prepared ahead of time and have two specific activities in mind.
- When you contact the person by phone, identify yourself by name and explain when you met (if applicable). "This is Jim Thompson. I met you at the yearbook signing party."
- Be sure you are recognized.
- Pay the person a compliment related to your last meeting, one that recognizes his or her talent, values, or position on an issue. "You really did a great job designing the cover of the yearbook."
- Be assertive in requesting a date: "I was wondering if you'd like to come to a movie with me this Saturday?" Be specific in your request; state the activity in mind and the time it will take place.
- If the other person's answer is "yes," decide together on the movie and the time. End the conversation smoothly, politely, and quickly.
- If the other person's answer is "no," suggest an alternative, such as a more informal get together: "How about meeting me at McDonald's after school on Monday—my treat?"
- If the answer is still "no," politely end the conversation. Refusal is not necessarily rejection. There may be previous commitments such as school, work, or family.

Treatment Plan: Speaking in Public

Counseling intention: To alleviate performance anxiety and stage fright.

The following strategies are useful for combating stage fright:

Rehearse. Practice listening to your voice. Use a tape recorder and a mirror to detect distracting verbal and visual mannerisms. Time your presentation. Focus on making the phraseology comfortable and conversational. Also consider enunciation (nervousness can make you slur or clip the ending of words), organization (speakers cannot rely on punctuation marks and headings), and speed (inexperienced speakers tend to rush).

Declare your anxiety. If you start speaking and you hear your voice tightening and feel your mouth getting dry, your anxiety will also begin to rise. The worse you sound, the more upset you will feel. To break this destructive cycle, tell your audience at the beginning how you feel. If the audience knows you are anxious, you know you will not need to hide your discomfort.

Prepare an out. Anxiety can be so acute that you feel trapped. Once your name is called, you are "it" until you finish. Rehearse a graceful exit, such as, "I'm sorry, but I don't feel comfortable enough to present today; I'll do it another time" (Wassmer, 1978).

Treatment Plan: Expressing Anger

Counseling intention: To study styles of expressing anger in a group setting; to study effects of anger in a group setting; to identify behaviors that elicit anger in others; to explore ways of coping with anger.

For this exercise you will need felt-tipped markers, four 3″ × 8″ strips of paper for each participant, and masking tape.

Distribute four strips of paper, a felt-tipped marker, and strip of masking tape to each participant. Tell participants they will be given four sentences to complete, one at a time, and that they are to write down the few responses that occur to them, without censoring or modifying the response. They are to print their responses clearly on the newsprint so that others will be able to read them.

Read the following four sentences, one at a time, allowing each participant to complete his or her response. After each sentence is read and the responses have been made, ask each participant to tape the strip of paper to his or her chest.

1. I feel angry when others ….
2. I feel my anger is ….
3. When others express anger toward me, I feel ….
4. I feel that the anger of others is ….

As a variation, participants can tape their strips to a wall behind them or to the backs of their chairs.

The processing phase can be followed by a practice session on expressing anger. Dyads may be formed to role-play various situations from the group's history. Members should be urged to explore how they may cope with anger more effectively within the group session.

The same design can be used with other emotions, such as fright, tenderness, or boredom. Several rounds can be experienced.

Subgroups can be formed of participants who have similar (or highly dissimilar) responses to the four items. Participants can share critical incidents in which they have been involved in which anger was present. Alternative coping behaviors are then discussed.

Collective Community Initiatives

Young people who are isolated, who have been victimized, or who have been abused need to learn how to be assertive and how to manage anxiety and posttraumatic stress. Empowerment also is critical. Rencken (1989) outlined the sequence of empowerment as follows:

- Reinforcement of the report.
- Rebonding with the nonabusing adult.
- Assertiveness and self-protection.
- Redefining the relationship with the abuser.
- Resumption of age-appropriate roles.
- Positive control and attitudes regarding violence (physical abuse) or sexuality (sexual abuse).
- The right to safety, to saying "no" to inappropriate touches, and assertiveness in reporting abuse.

Empowerment includes the concept of positive, assertive control and mutual support during confrontation of inappropriate behavior. Being victimized, homeless, or isolated from the mainstream affects physical, psychological, social, emotional, and cognitive well-being. Collaborative efforts between various institutions and community agencies are paramount in providing essential services, resources, prevention, and intervention.

Conclusion

Helping professionals are active in professional growth and educational renewal in most school or community agencies and institutional or counseling settings. All helping professionals working with children and adolescents can create a heightened awareness among colleagues regarding the epidemic of child abuse and neglect in this country, and assist through referral or treatment opportunities. Helping professionals concerned with violence can help by clarifying attitudes toward rape, developing an awareness of the epidemic proportions, and creating an understanding that the legal definition of rape includes date rape.

It is imperative that counselors and mental health professionals respond to the developmental challenges that follow victimization and abuse by providing more than traditional clinical services. When issues are not addressed, children and adolescents are at significant risk for developing anxiety, depression, phobias, and posttraumatic stress disorder.

Social, Emotional, and Cognitive Skills

Social Literacy Skills

Social literacy skills are interpersonal skills essential for meaningful interaction with others. Social skills are those behaviors that, within a given situation, predict such important social outcomes as peer acceptance, popularity, self-efficacy, competence, and high self-esteem. Social skills fall into such categories such as being kind, cooperative, and compliant to reduce defiance, aggression, conflict, and antisocial behavior; and showing interest in people and socializing successfully to reduce behavior problems associated with withdrawal, depression, and fear. Social skills include problem solving, assertiveness, thinking critically, resolving conflict, managing anger, and utilizing peer pressure refusal skills.

Skills Boxes

Permission is granted to reproduce skills boxes for individual client use.

Problem Solving

A convenient acronym for the five steps of problem solving is SOLVE:

State your problem.

Outline your response.

List your alternatives.

View the consequences.

Evaluate your results.

Note. From *Thoughts and Feelings,* by M. McKay, M. Davis, and P. Fanning, 1981, Oakland, CA: New Harbinger Publications, Inc. Copyright 1981 by New Harbinger Publications, Inc. Reprinted with permission.

Assertive Responses

Step 1. *"When ..."* (describe the other individual's behavior).

Step 2. *"The effects are ..."* (describe how the other person's actions have affected you).

Step 3. *"I feel ..."* (describe your feelings).

Step 4. *"I prefer ..."* (describe what you would like to happen).

Being Socially Responsible

Being socially responsible means analyzing and responding to the needs of others. Analyze the needs of others by considering the following:

Openness and acceptance of diversity: Our differences enhance our relationships.

Togetherness: We can do things together that can't be done alone.

Helping: Be ready to lend a hand.

Empathy: Refine your sensitivity to others' needs.

Respect: Show respect for others' ideas.

Sowing good deeds: What you sow, you reap.

Note. Adapted from *The Big R: Responsibility* (p. 107), by G. Bedley, 1985, Irvine, CA: People-Wise Publications. Copyright 1985 by People-Wise Publications. Adapted with permission.

DESCA Inspirations

DESCA inspirations are comments designed to stir appreciation of the inherent dignity of all students; appropriate personal energy; intelligent self-management; healthful community of relationships; and searching, open awareness. Their purpose is to inspire new growth in dignity, energy, self-management, community, and awareness (DESCA). Here are some "I appreciate" messages that promote DESCA:

Dignity:
   I really appreciate the way that you spoke up for yourself.
   I recognize the confidence you are showing.
   I like how you said it like you mean it.

Energy:
   I like the way that you are persisting at this task.
   I appreciate your brain power.
   I like how you go one more step rather than giving up.

Self-management:
   I like how you organize your papers.
   I'm impressed with your time-management plan.
   I like it when you can think it through on your own.

Community:
   I appreciate that you respect the rights of others.
   I like it when you pitch in and help without being asked.
   Your ability to listen to the opinions of others is highly valued.

Awareness:
   Thank you for being so perceptive and aware.
   Thank you for noticing that someone needed help.
   Thank you for ignoring the distraction outside.

Note. Adapted from *Inspiring Active Learning: A Handbook for Teachers*, by M. Harmin (1994), Alexandria, VA: Association for Supervision and Curriculum Development (ASCD). Copyright 1994 by M. Harmin. Printed with permission.

Steps in Negotiating a Conflict of Interest

Even when people are striving for the same goals, sometimes there are conflicts of interest. Cooperators resolve conflicts as partners, not as adversaries. Below are six steps in negotiating a conflict of interests:

1. Describe what each person wants.
2. Describe how each person feels.
3. Exchange reasons for positions.
4. Understand each other's perspective.
5. Invent options for mutual benefit.
6. Reach a wise agreement.

Note. Adapted from *Reducing School Violence Through Conflict Resolution* (p. 52), by D. W. Johnson and R. T. Johnson, 1995, Alexandria, VA: Association for Supervision and Curriculum Development. Copyright 1995 by ASCD. Adapted with permission.

Conventional Arbitration

Mediation is an extension of negotiation in which the mediator assists disputants in negotiating a constructive resolution. By contrast, in *arbitration*, an outside person makes a judgment. The arbitrator does not assist the disputants in improving their conflict. Disputants leave the decision to the arbitrator, who hears both sides and then makes a decision. The process goes as follows:

1. **Both persons agree to abide by the arbitrator's decision.** Agreement is based on the assumption that after disputants have presented their sides of the conflict, the arbitrator will be able to make a fair decision. The arbitrator should be familiar with the subject matter of the case and have access to all available documents and evidence.

2. **Each person defines the problem.** Each has the opportunity to tell his or her side of the conflict.

3. **Each person presents his or her case, with documented evidence to support it.** No interruptions are allowed.

4. **Each person has an opportunity to refute the other's contentions.** After one person has presented his or her case, the other may attempt to refute the person's contentions. Both have a turn to show the arbitrator a different perspective on the issues.

> **5. The arbitrator makes a decision.** After each person has pre-sented his or her case, refuted the other person's case, and given a closing statement, the arbitrator decides what to do. Usually, the decision is a win–lose situation. Winning or losing is secondary to having had the fair opportunity to be heard.
>
> *Note.* Adapted from *Reducing School Violence Through Conflict Resolution* (pp. 96–97), by E. W. Johnson and R. T. Johnson, 1995, Alexandria, VA: Association for Super-vision and Curriculum Development. Copyright 1995 by ASCD. Adapted with permission.

Emotional Literacy Skills

Emotional literacy skills are intrapersonal abilities such as knowing one's emotions by recognizing a feeling as it happens and monitoring it; manag-ing emotions (e.g., shaking off anxiety, gloom, irritability, and the conse-quences of failure); motivating oneself to attain goals, delay gratification, stifle impulsiveness, and maintain self-control; recognizing emotions in others with empathy and perspective taking; and handling interpersonal relationships effectively. Emotional skills fall into categories such as know-ing the relationship between thoughts, feelings, and actions; establishing a sense of identity and acceptance of self; learning to value teamwork, col-laboration, and cooperation; regulating one's mood; empathizing; and maintaining hope.

Skills Boxes
Permission is granted to reproduce skills boxes for individual client use.

> ### "I" Language Assertion
>
> Language assertion is helpful when expressing difficult feelings. "I" language assertion can be broken down into four steps:
> 1. Objectively describe the behavior that is creating negative feelings.
> 2. Describe how the behavior affects you, such as costing you money, time, or effort.
> 3. Describe your own feelings.
> 4. Describe what you want the other person to do.
>
> Here is an example: *When you cancel a meeting with just a few hours' notice* (describe the behavior), *I don't have enough time to make other arrangements and I'm left with empty down time* (describe how it affects you). *I feel irritated and unproductive* (describe how you feel). *We need to make other arrangements about changing meetings at the last minute* (describe what you want the other person to do)."

Assertive Empathy

Assertive empathy can be used to express sensitivity toward a person's circumstances.

First, make a statement that expresses sensitivity to the person's circumstances, situation, or needs. Then, describe your circumstances, situation, or needs.

Here is an example: "I can understand you are upset with me and probably not in the mood to discuss it right now. I would very much like to talk it over when you're ready."

Note. From *The Assertive Option: Your Rights and Responsibilities* (p. 162), by J. Jakubowski and A. J. Lange, 1978, Champaign, IL: Research Press. Copyright 1978 by J. Jakubowski and A. J. Lange. Adapted with permission.

Confrontive Assertion

A confrontive assertion can be used when someone has neglected to follow through on a previous agreement. It is most appropriate when someone's actions contradict their words. A confrontive assertion has three steps:

1. Describe what the other person said would be done.
2. Describe what the person actually did (i.e., the discrepancy between what they said and what they did).
3. Reiterate your need and express what you want.

Here is an example: "I was supposed to review the article before it was sent to the typesetter, but I see the typesetter is working on it as we speak. Before he finishes it, I want to review the article and make the corrections I think are needed. In the future, I want to the opportunity to review the article before it goes to the typesetter."

Note. From *The Assertive Option: Your Rights and Responsibilities* (p. 162), by J. Jakubowski and A. J. Lange, 1978, Champaign, IL: Research Press. Copyright 1978 by J. Jakubowski and A. J. Lange. Adapted with permission.

Checking Your Perception

Perception checking can help avoid actions you may later regret, actions based on false assumptions. Our impressions are often biased by our own fears, expectations, and feelings.

Before you respond to someone's feelings, it is important to make sure you know what the person actually feels. A perception check communicates the message, "I want to understand your feeling. Is this the way you feel?" It shows you care enough about the person to want to understand how he or she feels. Here are the steps to follow in a perception check:

1. Describe what you think the other person's feelings are.
2. Ask whether your perception is accurate.
3. Refrain from expressing approval or disapproval of the feelings.

Here is an example: *"You seem confused about the roles and responsibilities. Are you?"*

Note. Adapted from *Reducing School Violence through Conflict Resolution* (p. 63), by D. W. Johnson and R. T. Johnson, 1995, Alexandria, VA: Association for Supervision and Curriculum Development. Copyright 1995 by ASCD. Adapted with permission.

Avoiding Conflict by Paraphrasing

Paraphrasing in conflict mediation helps you clarify a person's views of the problem and their feelings about it. It is important to listen attentively and summarize accurately using the following techniques:

Restate the facts and summarize the events. Follow these paraphrasing rules:

- Put yourself in the other person's shoes.
- State the other person's ideas and feelings in your own words.
- Use "you" to begin your statements (e.g., "You want," "You feel," or "You think").
- Show understanding and acceptance by nonverbal behaviors, such as tone of voice, facial expressions, gestures, eye contact, and posture.

Reflect feelings. Pay attention to the emotional element in each person's position. Use the statement, *"You feel ... (name the feeling) because ... (explain why)."*

- Offer alternatives.
- Reach a compromise.
- Agree on a solution.

Note. Adapted from *Reducing School Violence through Conflict Resolution* (p. 81), by D. W. Johnson and R. T. Johnson, 1995, Alexandria, VA: Association for Supervision and Curriculum Development. Copyright 1995 by ASCD. Adapted with permission.

Reframing a Conflict

Reframing means thinking of the conflict and the other person's actions from another angle. There are a number of ways to reframe perceptions:

- View the conflict as a mutual problem to be jointly solved rather than as a win–lose situation.
- Change perspectives.
- Distinguish between the intent of an action and the actual result of the action.
- Continue to differentiate between one's interest and one's reasoning. Seeking information about the other person's reasoning will result in a new "frame."
- Explore the multiple meanings of any one behavior. Ask, "What else might that behavior mean?"

Note. Adapted from *Reducing School Violence through Conflict Resolution* (p. 84), by D. W. Johnson and R. T. Johnson, 1995, Alexandria, VA: Association for Supervision and Curriculum Development. Copyright 1995 by ASCD. Adapted with permission.

CHAPTER **10**

Sexual Minority Youth (formerly Gay, Lesbian, Bisexual, and Transgendered Youth [GLBT])

If we are to achieve a richer culture, rich in contrasting values, we must recognize the whole gamut of human potentialities, and so we weave a less arbitrary social fabric, one in which each diverse gift will find a fitting place.

Margaret Mead

The American Psychiatric Association reclassified homosexuality as a sexual orientation/expression rather than as a mental disorder (American Psychiatric Association, 1987). The etiology of homosexuality remains unclear, but the current literature and vast majority of research scholars in this field maintain that one's sexual orientation is not a choice; in other words, individuals no more choose to be homosexual than to be heterosexual (Savin-Williams,1988; Rowlett, Patel, & Greydanus, 1992). The American Academy of Pediatrics issued its first statement on homosexuality and adolescence in 1983 (American Academy of Pediatrics, 1983), with a revision in 1993 (American Academy of Pediatrics, 1993). Finally, the Delegate Assembly of the National Association of School Psychologists adopted a position statement that gay, lesbian, and bisexual youth should be identified as "sexual minority youth" (Position statemement on Sexual Minority Youth, National Association of School Psychologists, July 18, 2004).

Homosexuality is the persistent sexual and emotional attraction to members of one's own gender and is part of a continuum of sexual expression. Many gay and lesbian youth first become aware of and experience their sexuality during adolescence. Concurrently, according to a November 1993 *Newsweek* article entitled "Tune In, Come Out," "... more students seem to be coming out [about their homosexuality], and they're coming out younger. A climate of greater tolerance is making it possible for teens to explore more openly what they've historically sampled in secret" (Gelman, 1993, p. 70). Educators across the country are attending sensitivity training sessions to learn about homosexuality and bisexuality. In 1993, Massachusetts passed a historic gay- and lesbian-rights law that led the way for state-funded school programs on homosexuality. In addition, thousands of American teens are banding together to form gay and lesbian youth alliances to explore and celebrate their sexual identities.

Sexual Minority Youth, formally (GLBT) refer to sexual orientation, that is, whom one is attracted to sexually, emotionally, and spiritually (Savin-Williams, 1990; Remafedi, 1990; Thompson, 1994). *Gay* most often refers to men who are attracted to men, *lesbian* to women who are attracted to other women, and *bisexual* to people who are attracted to both sexes. *Bisexual* refers to men or women who are attracted to both sexes. *Transgendered* (the *T* in GLBT) pertains more to gender identity than to sexual orientation. Gender identity refers to one's self-identity as a man or a woman (i.e., one's physical or genetic sex does not correspond to one's gender identity as a man or a woman). Transgendered individuals often choose sexual reassignment surgery. However, for congruency in exploring the research and implications for youth, this chapter will focus on gay, lesbian, bisexual, and transgendered youth as sexual minority youth.

Sexual self-concept is an individual's evaluation of his or her own sexual feelings and actions. Developing a sexual self-concept is a key developmental task of adolescence. During adolescence, young people tend to experience their first adult erotic or romantic feelings, experiment with sexual behaviors, develop a strong sense of their own gender identity, and claim their sexual orientation. *Gender identity* includes understanding that a person is male or female, as well as understanding the roles, values, and responsibilities of being a man or a woman.

A national survey of 1,752 college students found

- 48% of self-identified gay and bisexual college students became aware of their sexual preference in high school, whereas 26% found their true sexuality in college;
- 20% of self-identified gay and bisexual men knew that they were gay or bisexual in junior high school, and 17% said they knew in grade school; and
- 6% of self-identified gay or bisexual women knew that they were gay or bisexual in junior high school, and 11% knew in grade school (Elliott & Brantley, 1997).

Precise data among gay, lesbian, bisexual, and transgendered youth present a challenge for researchers to collect and analyze; many gay, lesbian, bisexual, and transgendered youth are reluctant to report their sexual orientation to service providers and other helping professionals. Estimates of the number of lesbian, gay, and bisexual youth in the United States vary, but most researchers believe that between 5% and 6% of youth fit into one of these categories. Based on the 2003 U.S. census, 51.6 million students were projected to be enrolled in elementary and high schools (grades K through 12) in the fall of 2004, which means that 2.5 million school-aged children in the United States are dealing with issues related to their sexual orientation.

A 1996 study of youth found that homosexual girls become aware of an attraction to other girls at age 10 and have their first same-sex experience at age 15. Homosexual boys have their first awareness of same-sex attraction at age 9 and their first same-sex experience at age 13. Girls and boys both begin to identify themselves as lesbian or gay at age 16 (Herdt & Boxer, 1996). The statistics and their sources presented in the sections that follow are not a definitive compilation but a collection of the most current scientific surveys, studies, and research available to the public.

Suicide

Suicide was the third leading cause of death for young people aged 10 to 19 years old in 2000 (Centers for Disease Control and Prevention [CDC], 2002). More teenagers die from suicide than from cancer, heart disease, AIDS, birth defects, stroke, pneumonia and influenza, and chronic lung disease combined (U.S. Public Health Service, 1999). In 2000, 1,921 young people aged 10 to 19 died by suicide in the United States (CDC, 2002). Survey data from 2001 indicate that 19% of high school students had seriously considered attempting suicide, almost 15% had made plans to attempt suicide, and almost 9% had made a suicide attempt during the year preceding the survey (CDC, 2002).

Several state and national studies have found that gay, lesbian, and bisexual teens are more likely to seriously consider or attempt suicide than heterosexual teens (Faulkner & Cranston, 1998; Remafedi, French, Story, Resnick, & Blum, 1998; Russell & Joyner, 2001). Because public dialogue regarding the well-being of sexual minority youth is relatively new, data are not sufficient to determine whether rates of death by suicide are similarly elevated.

Why are sexual minority youth more likely to attempt suicide? The reasons are not entirely clear. Research suggests that discrimination due to the social stigmatization of homosexuality in our culture may have important mental health consequences (Mays & Cochran, 2001). Sexual minority youth are more likely than their peers to report past victimization and problems with substance abuse and depression, all of which are risk factors for suicide in adolescents (Garofalo, Wolf, Kessel, Palfrey, & DuRant, 1998; Gonsiorek, 1988; Russell & Joyner, 2001). According to Fleischer and Fillman (1995), a 1989 Department of Health report on youth suicide found that sexual minority youth are up to five times more likely to attempt suicide. The increased risk among these youth stems from isolation, rejection, confusion, and shame due to the stigmatization of homosexuality, which can result in depression, suicide, and low self-esteem.

Presently, there are no published studies of suicide prevention or intervention programs that target gay, lesbian, and bisexual youth (Russell, 2003). Past research has shown that gay, lesbian, and bisexual youth are at greater risk for suicide. Perhaps future research needs to address the risk and protective factors to develop possible prevention and intervention strategies. Suicide completions and attempts by adolescents, however, decrease with age (Hetrick & Martin, 1987). This decrease is thought to be related to the increased freedom of movement and attendant diminished sense of isolation that occurs for older teens.

School Dropout

In a national study, 28% of sexual minority high school students were seen to have dropped out of school because of harassment resulting from their sexual orientation (Remafedi, 1987). Sexual minority youth in U.S. schools are often subjected to such intense bullying that they are unable to receive an adequate education (Chase, 2001). These teens are often embarrassed or ashamed of being targeted and may not report the abuse. Sexual minority students are more apt to skip school due to the fear, threats, and property vandalism directed at them (Garofalo et al., 1998).

One survey revealed that 22% of sexual minority respondents had skipped school in the past month because they felt unsafe there (Chase,

2001). Twenty-eight percent of sexual minority students will drop out of school; this is more than three times the national average for heterosexual students (Bart, 1998). Many gay students are forced to switch schools, get their GED, or drop out of school altogether.

Isolation

Eighty percent of sexual minority youth report severe isolation problems. They experience social isolation, emotional isolation, and cognitive isolation. A 1988 national survey of heterosexual male youth 15 to 19 years of age found that only 12% felt that they could have a gay person as a friend (Marsiglio, 1993). In a 14-city survey, nearly three fourths of sexual minority youth first disclosed their sexual identity to friends. Forty-six percent lost a friend after coming out to him or her (Ryan & Futterman, 1997). In a study of sexual minority adolescents 14 to 21 years of age, less than one in five of the surveyed sexual minority adolescent students could identify someone who was very supportive of them (Telljohann & Price, 1993).

Violence

Forty-five percent of gay males and 20% of lesbians report having experienced verbal harassment, physical violence, or both during high school as a result of their sexual orientation (National Gay and Lesbian Task Force, 1984). Two out of five youth (41.7%) did not feel safe in their school because they are sexual minority youth (n = 191), and 86.7% of sexual minority youth who felt safe in their schools still reported sometimes or frequently hearing homophobic remarks. Despite reporting feeling safe, 46% of sexual minority youth reported verbal harassment, 36.4% reported sexual harassment, 12.1% reported physical harassment, and 6.1% reported physical assault in their school. In addition, 91.4% of sexual minority youth reported that they sometimes or frequently hear homophobic remarks in their school (words such as "faggot," "dyke," or "queer"). Sexual minority youth are nearly three times as likely as their heterosexual peers to have been assaulted or involved in at least one physical fight in school and are three times as likely to have skipped school because they felt unsafe (Massachusetts High School Students and Sexual Orientation Youth Risk Behavior Survey, 1999).

Depression

Sexual minority youth spend a tremendous amount of energy coping with society's negativity and discrimination. Many conclude that they have no hope of ever becoming happy and productive (Cook, 1998). Verbal and physical abuse is common in the lives of lesbian, gay, and bisexual youth and is a source of stress that is detrimental to their mental health (Savin-Williams, 1994). Many youth described experiencing sleeplessness, excessive sleep, loss of appetite, feelings of hopelessness, and other classic signs of depression. Many students who are subjected to sexual harassment report symptoms of depression, which may include loss of appetite, loss of interest in their usual activities, nightmares or disturbed sleep, feelings of isolation from friends and family, and feelings of sadness or anger. They also may have difficulties at school, such as missing school days, not performing as well in school, skipping or dropping classes, or being late to class (Fineran, 2001, Trigg & Wittenstrom, 1996).

Alcohol and Drug Abuse

Sexual minority youth may turn to alcohol and other drugs as a means to self-medicate, to deal with feelings of isolation and the stigma of their sexual orientation. DuRant, Krowchuk, and Sinal (1998) found that youth who identified themselves as lesbian, gay, or bisexual had higher lifetime rates of marijuana use (70% compared to 49% of all youth), cocaine use (29% compared to 9%), methamphetamine use (30% compared to 7%), and injected drug use (18% compared to 2%). The connection between victimization and alcohol and other drug abuse was revealed by Jordan (2000).

Risky Sexual Behavior

Sexual minority youth may engage in unprotected sex and other risky sexual behaviors. This increased risk extends to HIV infection and other sexually transmitted diseases. Further, the pervasiveness of AIDS within the gay community has resulted in feelings of futility among many gay males; they may believe that HIV infection is inevitable and thus that prevention is futile (Ryan & Futterman, 1997). Gay and bisexual adolescents and young men are the greatest risk for sexually transmitted diseases, including HIV. A study of gay and bisexual adolescents in San Francisco and Berkeley, California, found that 33% had engaged in unprotected sex within the past 6 months. In New York city, according to another study, 28% of young gay and bisexual males reported having unprotected sex in the last year (Lemp, Hirozawa, & Givertz, 1994). Approximately 20% of all persons with AIDS are 20 to 29 years old; accounting for the long latency period between infection and the onset of the disease, many were probably infected as teenagers (Lehman, 1993).

Homeless, Runaway, and Throwaway Youth

A disproportionate number of sexual minority youth who are subjected to harassment and violence may also end up homeless and resort to living on the street. Many have been forced out of their homes or out of the foster-care system because their sexual orientation was discovered. Many were thrown out of their homes when their parents discovered their sexual orientation; others fled because family members subjected them to repeated physical violence (Mallon, 1998). Large urban areas with prominent gay communities have larger proportions of street youth who identify themselves as sexual minority youth (Kruks, 1991). In Houston, Texas; Los Angeles, California; and New York City, studies of homeless youth have found that between 16% and 38% identified themselves as lesbian, gay, or bisexual (Busen & Beech, 1998). Once confined to the streets, these youth are more vulnerable for risk of HIV infection and other sexually transmitted diseases because significant numbers engage in "survival sex" (i.e., trading sex for food and shelter).

Student Attitudes

Ninety-seven percent of students in public high schools report routinely and persistently hearing homophobic remarks from their peers (Report of Massachusetts Governor's Commission on Gay and Lesbian Youth, 1999). For some sexual minority youth, the burden of coping each day with the endless harassment is too much. They drop out of school. Some commit suicide. Others just barely survive as they navigate within a school community that fosters open hostility of peers and deliberate indifference of school officials. Although some lesbian, gay, bisexual, and transgendered students in the United States experience a positive, welcoming environment at school, the vast majority are not so fortunate. sexual minority youth are nearly three times as likely as their heterosexual peers to have been assaulted or involved in at least one physical fight in school, three times as likely to have been threatened or injured with a weapon at school, and nearly four times as likely to skip school because they felt unsafe, according to the (Massachusetts High School Students and Sexual Orientation Youth Risk Behavior Survey, 1999).

Staff Attitudes

Fifty-three percent of students reported hearing homophobic comments made by school staff (Massachusetts Governor's Commission on Gay and Lesbian Youth, 1993). In a random sample of high school health teachers, one in five surveyed said that students in their classes often used abusive language when describing homosexuals (Telljohann, Price, Poureslami, & Easton, 1995). A national study of secondary school counselors' perceptions of adolescent homosexuals found that 25% perceived that teachers exhibited significant prejudice toward homosexual students and that 41% believed that schools were not doing enough to help sexual minority students adjust to their school environments (Price & Telljohann, 1991). In a study of gay and lesbian adolescents 14 to 21 years of age, 23% of females and 25% of males reported that they were able to talk with their school counselors about their sexual orientation (Telljohann et al., 1995). Unfortunately, teachers, administrators, and other staff often fail to protect lesbian, gay, and transgendered youth from harassment.

Verbal harassment that goes unchecked may quickly escalate into physical violence, including sexual assaults. Concurrently, when teachers and administrators fail to act to prevent harassment and violence, they send a message that it is permissible for students to engage in harassment, and they allow the formation of a climate in which students may feel entitled to escalate their harassment of gay youth to acts of physical and sexual violence. Harassment also comes via other methods, such as whisper campaigns, obscene phone calls, written notes, cyber-bullying, obscene or suggestive cartoons, graffiti scrawled on walls or lockers, and pornography.

Some school officials have blamed the students being abused of provoking the attacks because they have paraded their identity to peers and staff. Other school officials justify their inaction by arguing that students who "insist" on being gay must "get used to it." Regretfully, some school officials have even encouraged or participated in the abuse by publicly taunting or condemning the students for not being "normal." Many sexual minority youth who have survived the school culture have done so by carefully concealing their sexual orientation or gender identity. They have learned that they will be protected only if they deny who they are. This kind of harassment and abuse often leads to self-hatred, a fractured sense of identity, and low self-esteem.

Attitudes of Parents

A recent national survey of 1,000 American parents found

- 76% of parents nationwide would be comfortable talking to their child about issues related to homosexuality or gay and lesbian people;
- 67% of parents nationwide favor teaching children that gay people are just like other people;

- 62% of parents nationwide would be comfortable talking to their child's teacher about issues related to homosexuality or gay and lesbian people;
- 61% of parents nationwide said that homosexuality is "something I would discuss with my children if they asked me questions, but not something I would raise with them on my own";
- 56% of parents nationwide favor allowing groups or clubs on school campuses to promote tolerance and prevent discrimination against gay and lesbian students; and
- 55% of parents nationwide would be comfortable if their child's teacher were gay or lesbian (Horizons Foundation, 2001).

However, sexual minority adolescents often feel forced by parents to pass as heterosexually "normal" because of their own feelings of denial regarding their child's sexual orientation. As a result, sexual minority adolescents hide their sexual orientation and feelings, especially from their parents. This is due in part to American society's strictly delineated roles for male and female genders. Conformity is highly valued. Many parents force gender conformity in elementary children and even preschool children when children display nonconformist gender roles. Going against conformity, especially concerning gender, is viewed in many cases with disgrace and contempt. If their child's sexual orientation does not meet their expectations, parents may go through the stages of

1. denial,
2. avoidance,
3. anger,
4. guilt, and
5. rejection.

Further, adolescents whose families demonstrated more traditional values often found it harder to come out than those whose families lived by less traditional values (Savin-Williams, 1989). Children of families who supported their adolescent regardless of their sexual preference had higher self-esteem and an easier transition through adolescence. Reciprocally, those with no family support or acceptance had a more difficult transition through this identity formation. Most families, however, have chosen not to be open about their child's sexual orientation, presenting themselves instead as heterosexually parented families and limiting channels of communication when incidents occurred.

Legal Responsibilities of Schools

The increasing awareness of sexual minority youth issues has sparked a public debate that is ruminating in school boards, courtrooms, and state assembly houses across the nation. A small but increasing number of states (e.g., California, Connecticut, Massachusetts, Vermont, and Wisconsin) have explicitly prohibited harassment and discrimination in public schools. In a 1999 landmark decision for educational policy, the U.S. Supreme Court declared that school officials who ignored student-on-student sexual harassment can be held liable for violating the federal civil rights law under Title IX of the Education Amendments of 1972 (Davis v. Monroe County Board of Education, 1999). In another case, Jamie Nabozny sued his Ashland, Wisconsin, school district, two principals, and one assistant principal for failing to protect him from peer abuse. He endured physical attacks that required two surgeries and attempted suicide three times (Nabozny v. Podlesny, 1996). He was denied equal protection of the law under the 14th Amendment to the U.S. Constitution, based on his gender and sexual orientation. In 1997, the Office of Civil Rights (OCR) released new Title IX guidelines (U.S. Department of Education, 1997). Title IX is a federal statute that prohibits sex discrimination, and for the first time the guidelines made explicit references to gay and lesbian students as being protected from sexual harassment and prohibiting actions that create a sexually hostile environment. More recently, Colin v. Orange Unified School District (2003) proved victorious for Anthony Colin, a 16-year-old high school student from Orange County California, and several of his peers, who formed a gay–straight alliance (GSA) in their high school. The school board voted unanimously to prohibit the GSA from meeting on school property. Sullivan, Sommer & Moff (2001) found that the school board "violated the federal Equal Access Act... [and] the students' rights to free speech, association, and equal protection under the U.S. Constitution."

Finally, in Henkle v. Gregory (2003), Lambda Legal Defense and Education Fund assisted Derek Henkle in a suit filed against Washoe County School District in Reno, Nevada. Henkle suffered verbal and physical abuse almost daily from classmates. His principal told him, "Stop acting like a fag." Two school guards stood by and watched as Henkle was beaten until bloody by other students. School officials had him take classes at a local community college to obtain a GED. In an August 2002 settlement, the school district agreed to pay Henkle $450,000 and make 18 policy changes because the school failed to create a safe educational environment in their own school.

Essentially, every youth deserves to be treated with respect and to be protected from violations of his or her human rights; every youth deserves to be free from discrimination, harassment, and violence and to be encouraged to learn and to grow intellectually and emotionally without being asked to deny an essential component of his or her identity.

Gender and Harassment

Our society is predicated on rigid rules regarding sexual stereotypes and how males and females should relate to one another. Males and females must adhere to rigid rules of conduct, dress, and appearance based on their sex. Males are expected to be strong, athletic, sexist, and hide their emotions. By contrast, females are expected to be attentive, accept subordinate status, and be flirtatious with males.

Youth with conflicted sexual orientation or gender identity who violate these cultural norms are often relentlessly punished by both peers and adults. For example, it is an unforgivable transgression for females to compete with other males for the attention of other girls. Thus lesbians—and particularly lesbians who are perceived as being "butch"—are punished for violating gender norms and because of their sexual orientation (Fineran, 2001). Gay men get more physical threats, whereas female students are more likely to get sexually harassed and be threatened with sexual violence (Fineran, 2001). In a 2000 study of students in western Massachusetts, Fineran (2001) found that young lesbian and bisexual girls experienced more sexual harassment than heterosexual girls. For example, 72% of lesbian and bisexual girls reported that they were "called sexually offensive names" by their peers, compared with 63% of heterosexual girls. Lesbians and bisexual girls were significantly more likely than heterosexual girls to be "touched, brushed up against, or cornered in a sexual way" (63% of lesbian and bisexual girls compared to 52% of heterosexual girls) and to be "grabbed or have their clothing pulled in a sexual way" (50% of lesbian and bisexual girls compared to 44% of heterosexual girls). Further, 23% of young lesbians and bisexual girls reported that their peers had "attempted to hurt them in a sexual way (attempted rape or rape)," whereas only 6 % of the heterosexual girls surveyed had experienced sexual violence of this nature. As with gay males, young lesbians may appear to be successful students who are doing well in school even as they struggle internally with self-hatred, depression, isolation, and thoughts of suicide.

Lesbian and Gay Parents

There are approximately 163,879 self-reported households headed by lesbian or gay parents in the United States. In the dominant heterosexual culture, however, three major biases about lesbian and gay parents are commonly perpetuated:

1. That lesbians and gays are mentally ill.
2. That lesbians are less maternal than heterosexual women.
3. That lesbians' and gays' relationships with their sexual partners leave little time for their relationships with their children (Patterson, Fulcher, & Wainright, 2002).

Current research however, has failed to provide a basis for these cultural biases (Patterson, 2000, 2000a; Perrin, 2002; Tasker, 1999):

1. There is no reliable evidence that homosexual orientation impaired psychological functions, although exposure to isolation, harassment, prejudice, and discrimination based on sexual orientation may cause acute distress (Mays & Cochran, 2001; Meyer, 2003).
2. Attitudes that lesbian and gay adults are not fit parents have no empirical foundation (Patterson, 2000a, 2000b; Perrin, 2002). Members of gay and lesbian couples with children have been found to divide the work involved in childcare evenly and to be satisfied with their relationships with their parents (Patterson, 2000a, 2000b). The results of some studies revealed that lesbian mothers' and gay fathers' parenting skills may be superior to those of matched heterosexual parents. (Patterson, 1995).
3. There is no scientific basis for concluding that lesbian mothers or gay fathers are unfit parents on the basis of their sexual orientation (Armesto, 2002; Patterson, 2000; Tasker & Golombok, 1997).

Research has suggested that lesbian and gay parents are as likely as heterosexual parents to provide a supportive, nurturing, and healthy environment for their children. Research also has suggested that sexual identities (including gender identity, gender-role behavior, and sexual role orientation) have developed in much the same way among children of lesbian mothers as they have among children of heterosexual parents (Patterson, 2000a). Research studies of other aspects of personal development (including personality, self-concept, and conduct) similarly revealed few differences among children of lesbian mothers and children of heterosexual parents (Perrin, 2002; Stacey & Biblarz, 2001; Tasker, 1999). Recent evidence also revealed that children of lesbian and gay parents have normal social relationships with peers and adults (Patterson, 2000, 2000a; Perrin, 2002; Stacey & Biblarz, 2001; Tasker, 1999). From this finding, it becomes imperative that helping professionals understand that the development, adjustment, and well-being of children with gay and lesbian parents do not differ significantly from those of children with heterosexual parents. Yet even though the children of gay or lesbian parents are no more likely than any other youth to be lesbian, gay, bisexual, or transgendered, these children are often targeted for harassment and violence because of their parents' sexual orientation or because their peers believe they share their parents' sexual orientation (Patterson, 1995). This population of youth often suffers many of the same repercussions that sexual minority youth suffer—and in much higher numbers (Casper & Schultz, 1999).

Stages of Sexual Minority Youth Identity Formation

> Most youth are raised in heterosexual families, associate in heterosexual peer groups, and are educated in heterosexual institutions. Youth who are not heterosexual often feel they have little option except to pass as "heterosexually normal." The fact that they must hide their sexual orientation makes it assume a global significance to them considerably beyond necessary proportions. (Savin-Williams, 1990, p. 1)

The overall goal in caring for youth who are or think they might be sexual minority remains the same as for all youth: to promote normal adolescent development, social and emotional well-being, and physical health. The social environment of these youth is a critical venue for their emerging sexual orientation. Yet, these adolescents may experience profound isolation and fear of discovery, which interferes with achieving developmental tasks of adolescence related to self-esteem, identity, and intimacy (Kreiss & Patterson, 1997; Remafedi, 1987).

Several models of the development of homosexual identity have been proposed (Cass, 1979; Coleman, 1982; Scrivner, 1984; Sophie, 1986; Troiden, 1989, 1993). Homosexual identity formation is largely a cognitive process. Although these stages have been outlined and formulated, this does not mean that each individual must go through every stage or in the exact order stated. In fact, an individual can be in more than one stage at a time or regress to a previous stage. These theories of homosexual identity development are merely a generalization of the process of identifying as a homosexual.

Cass (1979) developed the first model of homosexual identity formation that was nonpathologizing. Cass proposed a six-stage process:

1. **Identity awareness.** The individual is conscious of being different.
2. **Identity comparison.** The individual believes that he or she may be homosexual but tries to act heterosexually.
3. **Identity tolerance.** The individual realizes that he or she is homosexual.
4. **Identity acceptance.** The individual begins to explore the gay community.
5. **Identity pride.** The individual becomes active in the gay community.
6. **Synthesis.** The individual fully accepts him- or herself and others.

Cass's (1979) model assumes that sexual identity is acquired rather than inborn. It suggests that questioning youth are either in the stage of identity confusion (identity and experiences are disruptive in that they are not heterosexual) or identity comparison (behaviors are compared to feedback from others or to gay people in general). Cass's model allows that, given changes in social attitudes, labeling the young person as gay or lesbian may be inaccurate.

Coleman (1981) described a five-stage model:

1. **Pre–coming out.** Similar to Troiden's first stage or early awareness.
2. **Coming out.** Admitting the experience of homosexual feelings.
3. **Exploration.** The beginning of sexual experimentation.
4. **First relationships.**
5. **Identity integration.** The process of integrating the homosexual self with other aspects of one's personality.

Scrivner (1984) also described a five-stage model:

1. Identity tolerance.
2. Identity acceptance.
3. First relationships.
4. Identity commitment and pride.
5. Identity synthesis.

Sophie (1986) also outlined a four-stage coming out process for lesbian identity development:

1. First awareness.
2. Testing and exploration.
3. Identity acceptance.
4. Commitment.

Finally, Troiden (1989) postulated a four-stage, age-graded model of homosexuality identity development:

1. **Sensitization.** The early feelings of being different.
2. **Identity confusion.** Teenage recognition.
3. **Identity assumption.** The early process of acceptance that takes place in late adolescence.
4. **Commitment.** The acceptance of being gay and coming out to others.

In Troiden's model, it is in the last stage that true intimacy can begin. Because Troiden's is the most recent model it will be outlined in more detail in this chapter. Troiden's model presumes that questioning youth are moving from the stage of sensitization into identity confusion. At this period, they are experiencing both heterosexual and homosexual feelings and behaviors but are confused by the dissonance between their new insight and their previously held images of what it means to be gay or lesbian. The social condemnation of homosexuality and general misinformation regarding sexuality and sexual orientation may lead them to defer the assumption of a homosexual identity.

A Caveat Regarding Literature on Sexual Identity Development

The literature on sexual identity development has assumed a stable, core sexual orientation in gay men and lesbians. Bisexual identity development has been underexamined. It has been suggested that bisexuals have a similar trajectory as lesbians and gay men, except that the last stage involves a "continued uncertainty" (although perhaps "flexibility" might be a better term). Models of transgender identity development are still in their early stages. Further, developmental models of sexual identity have come under some scrutiny regarding their crosscultural applicability. These models are probably best understood as illustrative of modern gay and lesbian identities within contemporary Western culture, so caution should be used regarding generalizations regarding sexual minority youth. Additional work in sexual minority psychological development is also needed, particularly work that goes beyond identity formation and explores other significant stages in the experience of sexual minority youth. Areas needing greater study include how parenting, family formation, peer relations, societal values, environmental and systemic influence of socialization on thinking processes and interpersonal relationships affect psychological development.

Table 10.1   Troiden's Four-Stage Age-Graded Model of Homosexuality

Sensitization	The feeling of differentness as a prepubertal child or adolescent. The first recognition of attraction to members of the same gender before or during puberty.
Sexual identity confusion	Confusion and turmoil stemming from self-awareness of same-gender attractions. Often this first occurs during adolescence. This confusion usually is not so much due to a questioning of one's feelings as it is to an attempt to reconcile feelings with negative societal stereotypes. The lack of accurate knowledge about homosexuality, the scarcity of positive gay or lesbian role models, and the absence of an opportunity for open discussion and socialization as a gay or lesbian person contribute to this confusion. During this stage the adolescent develops a coping strategy to deal with social stigma.
Sexual identity assumption	The process of acknowledgment and social and sexual exploration of one's own gay or lesbian identity and consideration of homosexuality as a lifestyle option. This stage typically persists for several years during and after late adolescence.
Integration and commitment	The stage at which a gay or lesbian person incorporates his or her homosexual identity into a positive self-acceptance. This gay and lesbian identity is then increasingly and confidently shared with selected others. Many gays and lesbians may never reach this stage; those who do are typically in adulthood when this acceptance occurs.

Note. From "Homosexual Identity Development," by R. R. Troiden, 1989, *Journal of Adolescent Health Care, 9,* p. 105. Copyright 1989 by *Journal of Adolescent Health Care.* Reprinted with permission.

Coming out Strategies for Adolescents

Coming out to parents is a decision filled with turmoil and approach–avoidance decision making. Many youth choose to come out for their own self-respect and self-esteem and to close the barriers between themselves and their families The stages typically experienced by adolescents are

1. shock,
2. denial,
3. guilt,

4. expressing the full range of emotions,

5. making decisions for the future, and

6. genuine acceptance of sexual orientation.

For adolescents, telling the truth about themselves helps to build their sense of self-esteem, integrity, character, and self-respect. Honesty can also contribute to a more meaningful and respectful relationship with parents, providing that parents are open and receptive to their child's sexual orientation. For adolescents, coming out to parents is filled with fear and anxiety ("Will they reject me?" "What will they say?" "Will they throw me out of their house?"). For parents, hearing a son's or daughter's admission that he or she is a sexual minority can create fear, anxiety, denial, and loss. Fears usually concern their child's health and well-being (e.g., the fear of HIV/AIDS) and loss (e.g., the parents will never have grandchildren). Helping professionals and trusted educators who work with youth should prepare adolescents for their decision to come out by exploring the following issues:

- Affirm that they are certain that they are a sexual minority. They may wish to seek a support group or gay alliance to affirm their beliefs.
- Explore their support systems in the event that their parents reject them at their initial revelation that they are a sexual minority.
- Confirm the appropriateness of the timing. Make sure the adolescent is not coming out as the result of anger or a turbulent time in the family. Or do they really want to unburden themselves about hiding their sexuality and deceiving their parents?
- Most adolescents are financially dependent on their parents. Would coming out to parents interfere with college plans or force them out of the house? If so, they may need to delay the decision.
- Ascertain if they are knowledgeable about being a sexual minority. Do they have resources? Can they provide books and other literature to provide their parents to assist them in their adjustment?
- Patience is also critical. Parents may take 6 months to 2 years to deal with this new, often unexpected information.
- Develop a plan to personalize and rehearse their message to their parent, for example: "I have something very important I need to tell you, something I have been meaning to tell you for a long time" or "I don't want this to hurt our relationship, because no matter what I will always love you."

It is important to share with the adolescent the stages that their parents may go through when they learn that their child is a sexual minority. Explain that different people go through the stages at different rates and may regress, and that in most circumstances the adolescent will not receive immediate acceptance. Families respond to coming out in different ways. For many parents, the knowledge that their child is a sexual minority will be a traumatic discovery. With understanding and patience within the family, relationships can be restored. In fact, in most cases it improves because it is based on mutual honesty. The stages described in the sections that follow have been gleaned from the organization Parents, Families, & Friends of Lesbians & Gays (PFLAG).

Stage 1: Shock

An initial state of shock can be anticipated if parents had no idea that their child was a sexual minority. Shock is a universal reaction to avoid acute distress and unpleasantness when a situation is unexpected.

Stage 2: Denial

Denial helps to shield one from a threatening or painful message. Denial responses take many forms:

- Hostility. "No son/daughter of mine is going to be gay/lesbian."
- Preaching morality. "Homosexuality is a sin, you will go to hell."
- Avoidance. "If you choose that lifestyle, I don't want to hear about it."
- Dismissal. "It's just a phase; you'll get over it."
- Rejection. "If you choose that lifestyle, you won't live under this roof!"

The following sentences are examples of phrases can hurt instead of help:

- I can't believe it. This is so unlike you.
- This is just a phase you're going through.
- Think of what this is going to do to your family and classmates.
- You'll never be happy. You'll rob yourself of normal love and children.
- Just try to be straight. I know this nice boy/girl you could date.
- If you just let me pray over you, this will go away.

Stage 3: Guilt

When first learning of their son's or daughter's homosexuality, some parents initially perceive of it as a problem for which there must be a cause. It is not uncommon for parents to think that they are to blame, that something they did or did not do is responsible for their child's being "different."

Stage 4: Expressing the Full Range of Emotions

As the feelings of guilt and self-incrimination that many parents initially experience subside, parents become ready to acknowledge some of what they are feeling, to ask questions and to be receptive to their child's answers. Even though anger and hurt may be the predominant feelings expressed, it is more therapeutic to experience the full range of emotions, even the existence of some of the more distressing emotions (e.g., isolation, fear of rejection, hurt, confusion, fear of the future, etc.).

Stage 5: Making Decisions for the Future

When the initial emotional trauma subsides, parents will be increasingly able to deal rationally with the issue and consider the options for the future. The eventual stance that each parent makes is a reflection of the attitudes that he or she is ready to adopt in dealing with the child's sexual orientation. Four typical perspectives are assimilated into the family system:

- **A supportive perspective.** Parents accept the reality of their child's homosexuality and become aware of and supportive of the child's needs.
- **Restrictive boundaries.** Parents make it clear that their child's sexual orientation is an issue that they no longer want to discuss. This does not necessarily reflect a negative attitude but does establish a boundary of acceptance.
- **Constant conflict.** Parents take the negative position that their son's or daughter's homosexuality is a "problem," which then becomes a constant source of disagreements, criticism, and conflict.
- **Regression.** Parents may regress to previous stages. Accepting new information and changing personal attitudes is not uncommon. When parents are dealing with understanding their child's homosexuality, it is not at all unusual for them to feel the need to revisit previous stages of understanding that were seemingly already resolved. This is a natural course of events that is often required for change and resolution to come about eventually.

Stage 6: True Acceptance of Sexual Orientation

Many, but not all, parents reach this stage. Some parents even become ardent advocates on behalf of raising community awareness about gay issues and speak out against societal oppression so that others can live a happy and fulfilling life without having to deal with the threat of rejection or fear. Many reach the point where they can celebrate their child's uniqueness. These fortunate ones view homosexuality as a legitimate expression of human sexuality. Information, education, and support are vital. These can come from self-study, from other parents of sexual minority youth, or both (Warwick, Oliver, & Aggleton, 2000).

Protective Factors

Not all gay, lesbian, bisexual, transgendered, or questioning youth will be depressed or suicidal. Strong support systems and efforts to help sexual minority youth maintain confidence, mastery, and self-esteem help to offset the risks identified previously. More research is needed, however, to identify additional protective factors.

Supporting GLBTQ Youth in Schools

Because most adolescents with sexual identity concerns will remain concealed throughout their school careers, systems advocacy on their behalf is critical. In this regard, helping professionals and educators, in collaboration with policy makers, need to implement school policies that provide safety from physical and verbal threats and abuse and that acknowledge the existence and legitimacy of individuals with sexual minority orientation. Although such initiatives often provoke controversy, the alternative is to perpetuate an environment that places sexual minority youth at risk of mental health problems and dropping out of school. The following are initiatives that support sexual minority youth in schools:

- Develop and enforce school policy to support and protect sexual minority youth from verbal and physical harassment (Morrison & L'Heureux, 2001).
- Help with the discussion of when and how factual materials about sexual orientation should be included in school curricula and in school and community libraries (Perrin, 1996; Perrin, 2002).
- Educate school staff on issues related to sexuality.
- Provide appropriate referrals for sexual minority youth with mental health problems.
- Develop support groups for sexual minority youth (Warwick et al., 2000).
- Help raise awareness among school and community leaders of issues relevant to nonheterosexual youth (Perrin, 1996; Perrin, 2002).
- Support the development and maintenance of school- and community-based support groups for nonheterosexual students, their friends, and their parents.

- Support HIV and AIDS prevention and education efforts.
- Develop or request continuing education opportunities for health-care professionals related to issues of sexual orientation, nonheterosexual youth, and their families.

Classroom or Group Interventions

As emphasized in this chapter, sexual minority youth need intervention in social, emotional, and cognitive domains. Table 10.2 provides a succinct outline of these needs.

The National Association of School Psychologists (2004) supports equal access to education and mental health services for sexual minority youth within public and private schools. This can be accomplished through

- education of students and staff;
- direct counseling of students who are questioning or adjusting to their own sexual identity or who are experiencing difficulties with others due to actual or perceived minority sexual orientation;
- advocacy for such youth within the school and the community settings;
- support and dissemination of research and effective interventions and programs designed to address the needs of gay, lesbian, bisexual, transgendered, and questioning youth in schools; and
- support of health programs, including those for HIV prevention directed at sexual minority youth.

TABLE 10.2 Isolation Experienced by Lesbian and Gay Youth

Social	Feels alone in social situations (with family, peers, or in school or religious settings). Feels he or she has no one to talk to. Fearful of discovery.
Emotional	Feels he or she must be vigilant at all times, increasing emotional distance. Feels separated affectionally and emotionally from others, especially family. Fears that friendships will be misunderstood by same-sex friends, who may give away his or her secret.
Cognitive	Lacks accurate information about homosexuality, including appropriate role models. Bases information of other lesbians and gay males on crude stereotypes.

Note. Adapted from "Designing an AIDS Risk Reduction Program for Gay Teenagers: Problems and Proposed Solutions" by A. D. Martin and E. S. Hetrick, in *Biobehavioral Control of AIDS,* ed. D. Ostrow, 1987, New York: Irvington Publishers. Copyright 1987 by Irvington Publishers. Adapted with permission.

Strategy: Abusive and Harassing Name Calling in the Classroom
Intervention intention: To sensitize students about the effects of harassment and humiliation.

Insults that are racial, ethnic, and sexual are abusive. Most educators and helping professionals would not allow a racist slur to occur unchecked; however, the same standards often are neglected when insults are directed at sexual minority youth—such insults may even become socially acceptable. Many young people use terms such as "lezzie," "faggot," or "queer" when referring to gay and lesbian people or to people whom they do not like or respect. This behavior attacks the self-esteem of sexual minority youth and teaches all young people that hatred of homosexuals is condoned by adults and the school community.

Educators, administrators, and counselors must create a cooperative learning environment where all students are safe to express themselves and where diversity is respected. It is also the responsibility of educators to teach students that diversity is something to be celebrated rather than ridiculed.

A simple exercise for establishing an inclusive classroom follows:

1. Have students brainstorm names they have heard people call others.
2. Write all of these words on the board.
3. Assign categories: racial, ethnic, sexual, or religious bias.
4. Discuss each category.
5. Make students aware that all name calling involves prejudice and disempowerment and is harmful to the person being oppressed.
6. State that none of the listed names is acceptable in your classroom.
7. Make it clear that you will not tolerate any form of name calling.
8. Help class participants to establish classroom rules and to brainstorm and agree upon the social consequences of breaking this rule.

To process the exercise, discuss these statements: Disrespectful behavior should be confronted in the classroom. Everyone needs to feel safe and respected in the classroom in order to learn.

Note: From Uribe, V. (1984). Fairfax High School, Los Angeles Unified School District, Founder and Director of PROJECT 10.

Strategy: Identifying Historical People from Many Different Backgrounds
Counseling intervention: To understand that many famous people had different sexual orientations.

It is important that young people learn of different historical people with diverse backgrounds. Multicultural issues and diversity are increasingly becoming poignant issues for discussion. This exercise gives young people an opportunity to participate actively in an activity that involves writing down names of famous people. Gay and lesbian people can be naturally included as one diverse topic.

1. Place blank poster boards around the room with titles such as Jewish American, African-American, Gays and Lesbians, Native American, Hispanic, and so on.
2. Provide a marker next to each poster board.
3. Have students walk around the room and write names of famous people under the particular subtopics.
4. When they are done, include a time to discuss the people on the posters.
5. Look also at the context of the responses to this exercise. For example, are fewer people identified on one or two posters? What associations (positive or negative) do students have with the named people? How many students knew more about one category of people than another? What do the students think about homophobia or invisibility after having done this exercise?

Here is a list of famous sexual minority people:

Melissa Etheridge	Greg Louganis	Oscar Wilde
Audre Lorde	James Baldwin	Martina Navratilova
Michelangelo	Truman Capote	John Maynard Keynes
Barney Frank	Leonardo da Vinci	Rita Mae Brown
Elton John	Ellen DeGeneres	Adrienne Rich
Tchaikovsky	RuPaul	Gore Vidal
Sandra Bernhard	George Gershwin	Tennessee Williams
Virginia Woolf	Frieda Kahlo	David Geffen

Strategy: Sexual Orientation Timeline
Intervention intention: To help students understand the concepts of the development of sexual orientation.

The purpose of this timeline activity is to think about how and when sexual orientation develops. Sexual orientation is something that is not chosen. Homosexuality, however, is often viewed as chosen and something that can be changed. Review the concepts for this activity and explain that sexual minority people struggle with "coming out" to friends and family. Cultural and societal factors may cause lesbian and gay people to self-identify at a much older age. This activity encourages discussion about when sexuality is formed. Student responses should be kept confidential.

Explain to students that heterosexuality is assumed until expressed otherwise. Review these developmental concepts:

- Sexual orientation is established by age 4 or 5.
- Sexual orientation is realized during puberty.
- People self-identify as sexual minority at many different ages.

To do the timeline activity, follow these steps:

1. Have students draw a timeline.
2. Ask students to write their date of birth at the beginning of the timeline.
3. Students should write their present age at the end of the timeline.
4. Have students draw a circle around the age when they think sexual orientation is established.
5. Ask them to draw a star around the age when people have a first crush or first love (attraction).
6. Students should then underline the age when people know or realize they are gay, lesbian, straight, or bisexual.
7. Have students draw a cloud around the age when people tell others about their orientation (self-identify).

Strategy: Assessing Losses
Intervention intention: To understand the many losses sexual minority youth go through when coming out to family and friends.

Although gay, lesbian, and bisexual young people have different coming-out experiences, many go through losses described in this exercise:

1. Have students take out a piece of paper and number from 1 to 5.
2. Ask them to write down the name of their best friend after number 1.
3. Ask them to write down where they like to hang out after number 2.
4. Have students write down the name of their closest family member after number 3.
5. Have them write down their favorite possession after number 4.
6. Finally, have the students write down their dream for the future after number 5.

Read the following storyline to students:

You are at your locker and your best friend comes up to you and confronts you with the rumors that you are gay. You feel uncomfortable, but you don't want to lie, so you tell your best friend that the rumors are true. Your best friend tells you that he or she doesn't want to hang out with you anymore. He or she tells everybody at school that you are gay. Nobody at school wants anything to do with you.

At this point you have just lost your best friend. Please rip off your best friend from the list and crumple up the paper.

You decide to go to your favorite hangout spot and you find all your friends. They tell you that you are no longer welcome to hang out there and you need to leave.

At this point you have just lost your favorite hangout spot. Please rip off and crumple up the paper.

You go home very upset, and your favorite family member is there. You tell your favorite family member why you are upset, while coming out to him or her. When your closest family member has heard you, he or she tells you that he or she wants nothing to do with you and that you are crazy. He or she then tells your entire family about you being gay. Your parents tell you that you must move out.

At this point you have lost your closest family member, and you've lost a place to live. Please rip off and crumple up the paper.

As you are moving out of the house, you realize you can't take your favorite possession with you because you don't even know where you are going.

At this point you have just lost your favorite possession. Please rip off and crumple up the paper.

You are now realizing that your dreams are being destroyed. Since you have no money or financial support, you now know that you won't be able to attend the school that you've always dreamed of attending.

You have just lost all of your hopes and dreams for the future. Please rip off and crumple up the paper.

To process, the exercise, ask students questions such as these: How did it feel to do this exercise? How did it feel to lose the things you did? Were some things more difficult to lose than others?

Strategy: Hanging out with the Barnyard Animals
Intervention intention: To experience what it is like to be in a minority group.
This exercise is intended to have students experience what it is like to be in a minority group. Have the students stand in a circle, then follow these steps:

1. Explain to the students that you are going to whisper the name of an animal in their ear.
2. Randomly whisper "cow" in most students' ears, whisper "pig" in fewer than most, whisper "cat" in only a few ears, and whisper "bird" in only one student's ear.
3. Ask the class to close their eyes and make the sounds of their animal. Then ask them to walk around and try to find and link arms with other like animals.

Allow them to do this for a few minutes, or until you notice that all like animals are together.

To process this exercise, ask students to discuss their experience being their particular animal. Start with the largest group. What was it like when you found out there were a lot of cows? How did you feel when you found your first cow? How did you feel when you found your first pig? How did you feel when you found your first cat? What was it like when you realized there were only a few other cats? When you realized you were the only bird, how did it make you feel? Explain to the students that being the bird or a cat can be somewhat representative of being a sexual minority student. They sometimes are tempted to join the majority in order to feel less alone (isolated) and more accepted.

Interventions for Individual Sexual Minority Students

Adolescence is a period that is often characterized by storm and stress, as well as the developmental task of identity formation. Because this is a very self-conscious period for many teenagers, some teenagers may manifest the following irrational beliefs identified by Walters (1981):

- "It would be awful if peers didn't like me. It would be awful to be a social loser.
- I shouldn't make mistakes, especially social mistakes.
- It's my parents' fault I'm so miserable.
- I can't help it, that's just the way I am and I guess I'll always be that way.
- The world should be fair and just.
- It's awful when things do not go my way.
- It's better to avoid challenges than to risk failure.
- I must conform to my peers.
- I can't stand to be criticized.
- Others should always be responsible." (p. 6)

Rational emotive behavior therapy is a helpful therapeutic approach to use with sexual minority youth because it differentiates itself from other schools of therapy in three areas:

1. It de-emphasizes early childhood experience.
2. It applies scientific thinking to irrational thinking and attempts to shift the youth's point of view.
3. It uses homework to reinforce what was learned in the therapeutic setting.

The classic model for examining the relationships among thoughts, feelings, and behavior was developed by Ellis (1989): the A-B-C model. Point A is the activating event; point C is feelings about the event. The critical component between points A and C is point B, one's self-talk. Our self-talk influences our feelings and behavior. Self-talk can be rational or irrational, functional or dysfunctional. Self-statements can become habitual responses to stress or conflict. By cognitively restructuring his or her thinking, the adolescent can learn specific "coping skills" to restructure thoughts, reduce stress, and increase positive or reduce negative feelings.

Strategy: Ellis's A-B-C-D-E Paradigm
Counseling intention: To correct distorted thinking or self-defeating belief systems.

Albert Ellis maintained that people upset themselves via their own belief systems. Individuals are taught how they falsely attribute their own upsets to outside or activating events. When feeling upset, individuals are directed to examine their *B*s (beliefs) instead of blaming the *A*s (activating events).

Individuals are shown that activating events (*As*) do not result automatically in emotional and behavioral consequences (*Cs*), but that it is mainly the beliefs about *A* (i.e., *Bs*) that are responsible for the impact at point *C*. By disputing (*D*) the irrational beliefs at point *B*, the effect (*E*) is the elimination of negative consequences (*Cs*).

Adolescents may be provided with a homework exercise to begin identifying self-defeating feelings such as anger. An example follows:

> **A = Activating event.** Describe a situation about which you became angry.
>
> **B = Beliefs.** What do you tell yourself about the situation?
>
> **C = Consequences (behavioral or emotional).** Describe the upset feeling. Describe what you did because of being angry.
>
> **D = Dispute.** Question your angry thoughts, expectations, disappointments. Is there a different way of looking at the situation?
>
> **E = Effect.** What would you like to see happen? What can you change and what should you accept?

Strategy: Charting Irrational Beliefs (Ellis, 1988)
Counseling intention: To correct distorted thinking or self-defeating belief systems.

The chart shown in Table 10.3 is helpful in charting irrational beliefs.

Strategy: Identifying Unpleasant Emotions
Counseling intention: To identify antecedents with subsequent feelings.

Identify the last time you felt a strong, unpleasant emotion. Write the emotion under *C*. Under *A*, write in the event before the emotion occurred. Under *B*, identify what you were thinking between the event and the emotion.

> **A = Activating event.** "My friends won't accept me if I tell them my true identity."
>
> **B = My thinking.** "Maybe they will reject me." "Maybe I'm really a loser." "She really doesn't know all the best attributes about me."

Counseling intention: To identify antecedents to subsequent feelings. Identify the last time you were feeling a strong, unpleasant emotion. Write the emotion under "C." Under "A," write in the event before the emotion occurred. Under "B" identify what you were thinking between the event and the emotion.

TABLE 10.3   Identifying Unpleasant Emotions

(A) Activating events: Thoughts or feelings that happened just before I felt emotionally disturbed or acted as if I were defeated.		
(B) Beliefs: Self-defeating talk about the experience or situation.		
(C) Consequence or conditions: Disturbed feelings or self-defeating behavior that I produce and would like to change.		

(B) **Beliefs: Irrational beliefs** (IB) leading to my consequences (emotional disturbance or self-defeating behavior). Circle all that apply to these activating events (A).	(D) **Disputes** for each circled IB. *Examples: "Why 'must' I do very well?" "Where is it written that I am a bad person?" "Where is the evidence that I 'must' be approved and accepted?"*	(E) **Effective rational beliefs** (RBs) to replace my IBs *Examples: "I'd 'prefer' to do very well, but I don't 'have to.'" "I am a person who acted badly, not a bad person." "There is no evidence that I 'have' to be approved, though I would like to be."*
1. I must do well or very well!		
2. I am a bad or worthless person when I act weakly or stupidly.		
3. I must be approved or accepted by people I find important.		
4. I am a bad, unlovable person if I get rejected.		
5. People must treat me fairly and give me what I need.		
6. People who act immorally are undeserving, rotten people.		
7. People must live up to my expectations or it is terrible.		
8. My life must have few major hassles or troubles.		
9. I can't stand really bad things or very difficult people.		

(B) **Beliefs: Irrational beliefs** (IB) leading to my consequences (emotional disturbance or self-defeating behavior). Circle all that apply to these activating events (A).	(D) **Disputes** for each circled IB. *Examples: "Why 'must' I do very well?" "Where is it written that I am a bad person?" "Where is the evidence that I 'must' be approved and accepted?"*	(E) **Effective rational beliefs** (RBs) to replace my IBs *Examples: "I'd 'prefer' to do very well, but I don't 'have to.'" "I am a person who acted badly, not a bad person." "There is no evidence that I 'have' to be approved, though I would like to be."*
10. It's awful or horrible when major things don't go my way.		
11. I can't stand it when life is really unfair.		
12. I need to be loved by someone who matters to me a lot!		
13. I need a good deal of immediate gratification and have to feel miserable when I don't get it!		
14. I should be promoted; I have worked hard.		
15. Everyone I meet should like me 100%.		
16. Life should be fair, because I am in control.		
17. Other people should live up to my expectations.		

C = **My feelings and behavior.** Self-doubt about acceptance; anger about friend's lack of openness.

Next, analyze the accuracy of the facts and events written in *A*. This can be accomplished through rational self-analysis (e.g., "Where is the evidence that what you believe is true?"). In addition, one can differentiate between rational and irrational beliefs by answering the following questions:

- Do the adolescent's beliefs reflect an objective reality? Would a second party perceive the situation in the same way? Are the beliefs exaggerated and personalized?

- Are the beliefs helpful to the adolescent? (Self-destructive thoughts are usually irrational.)
- Are the beliefs helpful in reducing conflicts with others or do they foster an "us versus them" mentality?
- Do the beliefs help or get in the way of short- or long-term goals?
- Do the beliefs reduce or exacerbate emotional conflict?

Write the objective version of the facts and events at *D*. Only the event that can be reproduced by camera, video camera, or tape recorder is a fact. If the event cannot be recorded, it is probably an opinion, a feeling, or an evaluation. This strategy should help sexual minority youth see how misperceptions of situations can alter one's self-talk or inner dialogue that in turn affects one's emotional response. Irrational thoughts lead to negative emotional feelings. Negative emotional feelings ultimately lead to depression.

Next, help the youth decide how he or she would like to feel in the situation described in *D*, and enter the feeling under *F*. Is it realistic to have a positive emotional response to a stressful situation, or is it more appropriate to accept a neutral feeling?

Finally, have the client attend to the *E* section and develop more rational alternatives to the irrational thoughts at *B*. The rational alternatives should be acceptable to the youth and meet at least three of the five criteria for rational thinking. This exercise merely outlines some strategies for developing a rational plan of action and changing unwanted feelings and behaviors. Irrational beliefs could be reframed in the following manner:

D = **Objective event.** "My friends may not accept me."

E = **My rational thinking.** "They will get over it and eventually come around."

F = **Desired feeling or behavior.** "I'm relaxed with the idea of coming out to friends."

Strategy: Direct Questioning (Waters, 1981)
Counseling technique: To understand different cognitions that may be influencing emotions.

General prompts to use with the adolescent include these:

- "What were you thinking when _____ happened?"
- "What sorts of things were you saying to yourself?"
- "What name did you call your friend when he _____?"
- "Tell me the first thing that comes into your mind when you think _____."

- "Picture yourself back in class; what did you think when _____?"

Strategy: Conceptual Shift (McMullin, 1986)
Counseling intention: To diminish damaging pattern of thinking about him- or herself.
Have the youth list all the thoughts connected to a targeted negative emotion:

1. "Collapse the thoughts into one major, negative core belief or theme.
2. List the situations (past and present) that are connected to the core theme.
3. Develop a list of alternative, more positive beliefs for each negative thought.
4. Summarize and concisely outline the positive beliefs into one core theme.
5. Help the youth reinterpret the past and present situations in terms of the new perspective. Go through each individual thought and situation and demonstrate how the youth misinterprets situations.
6. Have the client practice reviewing more situations and reinterpreting them in terms of the new themes" (p. 85–86).

Strategy: Rational Self-Analysis (RSA)
Counseling intention: To provide a systematic way to change unpleasant emotions and to follow up on inappropriate behavior (Sabatino & Smith, 1990).
Record (write or tape record) just what happened—not what you think about it, just a description of the event. Address the following issues:

- **Self-talk or opinion.** Record what you said to yourself about the event.
- **Emotions and actions.** Record the emotions and actions that you experienced.
- **Rational challenges.** Take each statement you made and substitute a rational statement based on what you know to be fact. Ask why you tell yourself each of these things.
- **New ways of thinking and feeling.** Record new feelings and the thinking that might lead to solving the problem.

Strategy: Changing Inner Beliefs
Counseling intention: To enhance positive inner beliefs.

Have the youth decide what behavior he or she would like to change. Think positively by creating a positive inner belief:

- Write down a negative inner belief and change it to positive. State the belief in the present tense: "I believe this about myself...."
- Repeat your positive inner belief at least 10 times a day. Write your positive inner belief on a card that you can see frequently.
- Visualize your positive inner belief as if it were already happening. See and feel what it would be like to let go of your negative inner beliefs. Picture yourself being successful.
- Act as if the positive inner belief is already true.

Strategy: Writing a Learning History of Angry Reactions

Counseling intention: To assess the extent of angry reactions.

Over a period of 2 weeks, the client carefully and systematically records anger-causing thoughts to become aware of the common but subtle triggers for his or her emotional reactions and to learn how to avoid future conflict. A learning history of the behavior or angry reactions should include the following:

- Record the specific situations that triggered the reaction.
- Record the nature and intensity of your anger.
- Note your thoughts and feelings of the situation immediately before and during the anger.
- List the self-control methods you used and how well they worked.
- Record the consequences and how others responded following your emotional reaction.
- Evaluate the payoffs you get from your anger, clarify to yourself the purpose of your aggression, and give up some of your unhealthy payoffs.

Technique: Stress Inoculation

Counseling intention: To reduce the effects of stress and anxiety.

For some, stress inoculation is basically learning to "talk yourself down": facing stress and finding ways to handle it. For others, stress inoculation training is a complex therapy process. Stress inoculation is a major part of cognitive behavior therapy and involves

1. helping youth become a better observer and a more accurate interpreter of incoming information;
2. teaching stress management skills, such as social interaction, problem solving, and how to use self-instructions for relaxation, self-control, and praise; and
3. helping youth to apply the various self-help skills in life.

There are many strategies youth can use to manage stress:

- **Use "nervous energy."** Channel the anxiety created by stress into constructive, beneficial activities, such as taking a course, preparing for a promotion, or helping others. Good stress keeps us motivated and enthusiastic about life.
- **Develop psychological toughness.** Physical demands must be made on the body to develop strength. For example, we must be exposed to bacteria and diseases to develop an immunity to them, and humans may need to be exposed to stresses and emotions before we develop coping mechanisms and toughness. Clients can develop toughness by being repeatedly exposed to demanding situations while having the skills, power, courage, and confidence to deal with the challenges. A client can increase toughness by being committed to work, having a sense of control over what happens in his or her life, embracing challenges, feeling that he or she will learn from the experience, solving problems to reduce stress, and focusing on self-improvement.
- **Skills training.** Reduce stress by acquiring helpful skills such as problem-solving ability, decision-making skills, social skills, assertiveness skills, empathy-responding skills, and time-management skills. Change self-talk and thinking by substituting constructive, positive self-statements for self-defeating statements to reduce fears.
- **Correct faulty perceptions.** Change automatic assumptions from "I will fail" to "I can handle it." Validating or having our perceptions confirmed by others can be a critical step. Learn to recognize tendencies to distort, such as exaggerating one's importance, denying one's own responsibility, expecting the worst, being overly optimistic, blaming oneself, and distrusting others. Be aware of perceptual biases, and constantly check impressions or views in that area with others. Replace the catastrophic thinking with rational, reassuring thoughts: "I can prevent this panic attack." "My heart is beating fast, but that is okay."

Strategy: Accessing Social Support

Intervention intention: To identify support networks available to GLBTQ youth.

Draw a circle in the center of a piece of paper and surround the circle with boxes.

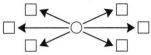

Have the GLBTQ youth write his or her name in the circle. In the boxes extending from circle write the names of people who provide emotional, mental, financial, academic, social, and spiritual support to him or her. If necessary, add more boxes. Then have the client rate each individual according to how much her or she depends on that individual for support. Use the following rating scale:

1 = I rely on the person rarely.
2 = I rely on the person sometimes.
3 = I rely on the person often.
4 = I rely on the person almost always.
5 = I rely on the person on a daily basis.

Note: From *The Therapist's Notebook for Lesbian, Gay, and Bisexual Clients: Homework, Handouts, and Activities for Use in Psychotherapy*, by J. S. Whitman and C. J. Boyd and Associates, 2003, Binghamton, NY: Haworth Press.

Conclusion

In our society, heterosexism can affect sexual minority youth by causing internalized homophobia, shame, a negative self-concept, or fragmented identity. Some sexual minority youth may resort to risky or dysfunctional coping behaviors as a means to alleviate negative feelings. These dysfunctional choices may result from the effects of prejudice and discrimination and are not a consequence of one's sexuality. It is not uncommon to find that many sexual minority youth report feeling isolated, fearful, depressed, anxious, or angry and having difficulty developing meaningful relationships and trust in others.

The stigma, tensions, and stressors of being a member of a marginalized community make sexual minority youth more vulnerable to using mind-altering substances and engaging in other high-risk behaviors. Prevention programs call for educational workshops, sensitive counseling, and access to nonjudgmental information, as well as support groups to improve self-esteem and provide affirmation for students struggling with stigmatization based on their sexual orientation. Schools and caring communities need to have a central location for resources on sexual minority issues, ongoing workshops for district staff, an on-site team to which students can turn for information, library collections of books on gay and lesbian subjects, development and enforcement of nondiscrimination and harassment policies, advocacy for sexual minority rights, and networking with community agencies.

Social, Emotional, and Cognitive Skills

Social Literacy Skills

Social literacy skills are interpersonal skills essential for meaningful interaction with others. Social skills are those behaviors that, within a given situation, predict such important social outcomes as peer acceptance, popularity, self-efficacy, competence, and high self-esteem. Social skills fall into such categories as being kind, cooperative, and compliant to reduce defiance, aggression, conflict, and antisocial behavior; showing interest in people; and socializing successfully to reduce behavior problems associated with withdrawal, depression, and fear. Social skills include problem solving, assertiveness, thinking critically, resolving conflict, managing anger, and utilizing peer-pressure refusal skills.

Your Assertive Rights

Assertive rights reflect basic democratic rights. Everyone has the right to
- express thoughts, actions, and feelings;
- have thoughts, feelings, and rights;
- be listened to, heard, and taken seriously;
- ask for what is wanted;
- make mistakes;
- ask for more information;
- say "no" without feeling guilty;
- make a decision to participate or not to participate; and
- be assertive without regrets.

Coping with Anger in Public

Anger is a strong human emotion that often signals that one or more of your basic needs are not met, such as belonging, power, freedom, happiness, safety, or self-esteem. Try using some of these statements the next time you feel yourself getting angry in a public situation:

- Stay calm. I don't need to prove myself to anyone.
- There's no point in getting mad.
- As long as I keep my cool, I'm in control.
- It's really a shame that she has to act like this.
- He's probably really unhappy if he's acting this way.
- She'd probably like me to fly off the handle. I am not going to give her that satisfaction.
- I'm not going to let this get to me.
- I maintained control. I handled this successfully

How to Apologize

Identify how you may have hurt or offended someone by word, deed, or action.

Identify ways that you could make amends (e.g., send a card, apologize in writing, make a phone call, send flowers, wait until both parties have had time to deal with their anger or disappointment).

Choose the best way to apologize for the current situation.

Select a time and place to apologize. Apologize honestly, sincerely, and thank the person for listening.

Emotional Literacy Skills

Emotional literacy skills are intrapersonal abilities such as knowing one's emotions by recognizing a feeling as it happens and monitoring it; managing emotions (e.g., shaking off anxiety, gloom, irritability, and the consequences of failure); motivating oneself to attain goals, delay gratification, stifle impulsiveness, and maintain self-control; recognizing emotions in others with empathy and perspective taking; and handling interpersonal relationships effectively. Emotional skills fall into categories such as knowing the relationship among thoughts, feelings, and actions; establishing a sense of identity and acceptance of self; learning to value teamwork, collaboration, and cooperation; regulating one's mood; empathizing; and maintaining hope.

Working toward a Happier Mental Outlook

The first acronym, **I SAW IT AS A CURSE!**, consists of two parts: I SAW tells the youth what to do; IT AS A CURSE shows the emotional literacy skills.

Inspire yourself to work on your attitude by remembering that many people have become more involved in life, happier, and more productive by using (Rational Emotive Behavior Therapy) REBT principles and that many people have used other common sense, nonperfectionist, noncondemning philosophies to enjoy life more.

Set rational and reasonable goals. Be happy with progress.

Accept behavior in the moment. Work calmly to become more relaxed. Change behavior to gain more of what is wanted.

Write or record some thoughts and progress of growth and self-help.

Challenge the following:

Insufficient allocation of priorities, time, energy, and money; learn to live more happily.

Too hard, too intense trying can be self-defeating.

Absolute, perfectionist standards only lead to grief.

Childish catastrophizing. Even though a client often says, "I can't stand this," he or she has not yet died of it.

Useless urgency. It will take as long as it takes to get to where the client wants to go! Set priorities, allocate time for relaxation, and "stop and smell the roses."

Ridiculous rating of self. We are all alive, including those who have a tendency to falter—and all of us do! We have so many characteristics and deeds and misdeeds that we cannot be globally rated.

Silly performance shame.

Expecting failure. Just because the client has not succeeded in the past does not mean he or she will not succeed in the future.

DEFUSE spelled D PHEWES

The following acronym is helpful in overcoming a client's irrational *shoulds, musts,* and *oughts*:

Don't place demands on self, others, or the world. Demands in self-talk are expressed by terms as "*I must*" or "*he should*."

Prioritize, plan, subdivide in achievable goals. And then do them (one at a time).

Humor yourself and others; take life less seriously.

Exude relaxed calmness using REBT techniques and calmly accept one unpleasant reality every day of your life.

Work on bad moods, challenging irrationalities, and tasks at hand.

Establish a routine to tackle problems.

Shun the use of the words *should, must,* and *have to* when these are used in the sense of being a demand. REBT is a semantic therapy, and even though it is quite correct to say, "From all the signs it should rain tomorrow," it is quite illegitimate to say, "You should be able to get the highest score on this test." A better way is to be more accurate, for example, "If I study harder than anybody else and know more than they do, I will probably receive a high score on the exam. If nobody else is either extraordinarily lucky or a genius, I may even get the highest score."

The ACT Formula: Accept, Choose, Take Action

If an adolescent is experiencing painful, overwhelming anxiety, introduce the ACT formula:

Accept your current reality.

Choose to create your own vision, that is, your picture of what you want in life.

Take action to create it.

Disputing Irrational Beliefs with A-FROG

A-FROG is 5-step thought process to think and behave more rationally. Use the acronym A-FROG to decide if you are thinking rationally:

A—Does it keep me **alive?**
F—Do I **feel** better as a result?
R—Is it based on **reality?**
O—Does it help me get along with **others?**
G—Does it get me to my **goals?** (Beck & Emery, 1985)

Positive Affirmations

Many people are limited by their negative thinking: "I can't…" "I don't deserve…." Such negative beliefs block positive action. Sometimes you must work consciously to maintain good feelings about yourself.

Here are some guidelines for positive affirmations:
Begin with the words, "I am…."
Include your name in the affirmation.
Choose positive words.
Phrase in the present tense.
Keep statements short.
Incorporate your strengths within your affirmations.
Choose action words.
Include positive feeling words such as *enthusiastic, awesome, tremendous.*
Include a feeling word to motivate action: "I am happy when I receive compliments."

After you have constructed an affirmation, close your eyes, repeat the affirmation several times (at least three), and notice the inner picture it creates. If the picture it creates matches your desired outcome, your affirmation is a good one.

Preparing for a Difficult Conversation

1. Prepare what you are going to say. Write it down. Read it and revise it for tone and content.
2. Think about how you will feel during the conversation (e.g., tense, nervous, afraid).
3. Plan your self-talk (your inner dialogue): What will you say to yourself to keep yourself calm and composed?
4. Think about how the other person will feel (e.g., angry, cold, aloof, inattentive).
5. Practice what you want to say.
6. Think about what the other person might say back to you.
7. Think about other issues that may come up during the course of the conversation.
8. Choose your best approach and do it.

Dealing with Rumors or False Accusations

- Acknowledge the rumor: Is it accurate or is it false?
- Is the rumor intended to hurt you or help you? Was the motivation constructive or destructive?
- Maintain your composure. Evaluate whether the rumor was started by someone else. Is it a true or a false accusation?
- Think about the ways to answer the person's accusation without being defensive or angry. Use these strategies:
  - Deny it and walk away.
  - Express your side of the rumor and explain your own behavior.
  - Correct the other person's perceptions.
  - Assert yourself.
  - Apologize for what has occurred.
  - Express your regrets and offer to make up for what happened.
- Review your options, choose the best one for the situation, and do it.

Increasing Your Frustration Tolerance

Use the DESC model to deal with frustration:

Describe. Give a concrete description of what leads to the feelings of frustration.

Express. Express to others how the situation makes you feel.

Specify. Visualize an alternative behavior for an aggressive impulse.

Choose. Choose the better way.

Maintaining Your Personal Power

It is not easy to maintain your personal power when you are being taunted by peers. Learn to identify your personal anger response components by answering the following questions:

- What are they doing that is getting to me? (This identifies environmental triggers.)
- How am I feeling inside? (This describes physiological feelings of anger.)
- What am I saying to myself? ("Stay cool; let them be the fool.")
- What am I going to do? (This suggests behavioral responses, for example, keep your distance but maintain eye contact, to appear composed but not provoking.)

Will this make a difference next week?

Mutual Problem Solving

To change unwanted behavior, it is important to do the following:

- Express empathy sincerely.
- Provide realistic explanations.
- Outline both positive and negative consequences.
- Restate the importance of the relationship.
- Invest in mutual problem solving.

Here is an example:

Expression of empathy. "I think I understand where you are coming from …"

Description of behavior. "But when you do this…"

Expression of feeling. "I feel…"

Explanation of consequences of impact. "Because it…."

Desired behavior, requested specifically. "I would prefer that you…"

Consequences. "If you do this, we will gain…" (positive consequences). "If you do not, we will lose…" (negative consequences).

Affirmation of the relationship's value. "The reason I am concerned is…"

Investment in mutual problem solving. "How can we work this out together?"

PART III

Creating Positive Relationships through Engagement of All Stakeholders

CHAPTER 11

Empowering Youth, Families, Schools, and Communities

Too often we underestimate the power of a touch, a smile, a kind word, a listening ear, an honest compliment, or the smallest act of caring, all of which have a potential to turn a life around. It's overwhelming to consider the continuous opportunities there are to make our love felt.

Leo Buscaglia

We must not, in trying to think about how we can make a big difference, ignore the small daily differences we can make which, over time, add up to big differences that we often cannot foresee.

Marian Wright-Edelman

Schools, Neighborhoods, and Communities

Collectively, schools, neighborhoods, and communities develop distinctive norms that draw youth and families toward or away from particular activities and domains of development (social, emotional, and cognitive). These norms often have profound and long-term effects on self-esteem, values, wellness, and coping skills. Personalities interact within the social system productively or unproductively, with subtle influences on achievement, motivation, employment readiness, and interpersonal relationships. And there is no "escape to the suburbs." Many "exclusive" schools, neighborhoods, and communities manifest a superficial sophistication, in which the primary goals are finding "the right friends, the right drugs, the right clothes, and the right kind of car." The goals reflect a "depressive core in the school/community." Without goals or traditions to unite energies, hostility is directed inward and divisions intensify across racial, class, and ethnic lines. Major cliques or gangs within these divisions also create highly stratified cultures that exaggerate differences. The brains, the jocks, the hicks, the metal heads, the skaters and surfers, the skinheads, the grunge rockers, the crips, and the bloods are examples of subgroups that emerge in oppressive environments.

The emphasis on community in most cities is not particularly strong, as reflected by the presence of youth subcultures and the lack of tolerance for different values, preferences, and cultures manifested in hate crimes and gang membership. Indeed, many young people come to school alienated and depersonalized and find little to help them cope with this alienation. Many schools, neighborhoods, and communities are repressive and punitive places where youth feel little power to change things. Lawton (1995) asserted that "families, schools, youth-serving organizations, healthcare agencies, and the media have fallen behind in their vital functions" (p. 7) and must now join together to create a mutually reinforcing system of support for children.

Perhaps the most fundamental and critical intervention for youth and families is to develop trust. Margolis and Brannigan (1986) captured this notion when they wrote this:

> To build trust you need to (a) cultivate a cooperative rather than a competitive or dominating mind set; (b) make your involvement with parents understanding and concerned; (c) be open about your objectives; (d) subtly demonstrate expertise without being oppressive or signaling superiority. Building trust cannot be rushed. It is an interactive process, involving the sharing of information, ideas, and feelings. The operative word in trust building is reciprocity. It is important to share rather than conceal your feelings. Thoughts, however, should be expressed in ways parents can understand and appreciate. Estimate the parents' level of sophistication regarding

each topic on the agenda so that you do not patronize or overwhelm them with information they cannot comprehend. (p. 71)

Educators and Helping Professionals as Partners

Educators and helping professionals frequently reflect on how to motivate youth more effectively. And they come, again and again, to the same conclusion: *Encouragement* increases motivation among recipients and lessens feelings of inadequacy. It communicates trust, respect, competence, and ability. Dinkmeyer and Dreikurs (1963) maintained that the proper use of encouragement involves several facets:

- **Value individuals as they are,** not as their reputations indicate or as one hopes they will be. Believing individuals are good and worthwhile facilitates acting positively toward them.
- **Have faith in the abilities of others.** This enables the helper to win confidence while building the self-respect of the other person.
- **Use a group to help the person develop.** For social beings, the need to belong is basic; integrate the group so that the individual can discover his or her place and begin working positively from that point.
- **Plan for success** and assist in the development of skills that are sequentially and psychologically paced.
- **Identify and focus on strengths and assets** rather than on mistakes.
- **Give recognition** for effort and for a job well done.

Educators and helping professionals possess a unique characteristic called *sigfluence*: a positive, significant, long-term interpersonal influence over others. It requires an average of 2 years for youth to appreciate and understand the extent of a positive influence over their lives. The optimal influence occurs between 14 to 19 years of age. Adults with sigfluence can affect a young person's academic, social, and emotional achievement, influencing career choice and generating positive changes in self-image. Adults can nurture a positive self-concept by making all youth feel safe, accepted, wanted, appreciated, and successful. Achievement must be planned, structured, designed, implemented, and reinforced.

Vernon (1989) suggested that educators and helping professionals implement an emotional education curriculum containing a self-acceptance component. Developmentally sequenced topics could be introduced and reinforced at the appropriate grade levels. Specific topics for children could include these:

- Recognizing uniqueness.
- Learning that people have many different qualities and characteristics.
- Learning that people have both strengths and weaknesses.
- Learning that making mistakes is natural and does not make people bad or stupid.
- Distinguishing between what people say about you and who you are.
- Topics for adolescents could include these:
- Recognizing the relationship among self-acceptance, behavior, and feelings.
- Identifying the physical, intellectual, spiritual, emotional, and social aspects of self.
- Learning the importance of self-acceptance despite the risk of others' disapproval.
- Recognizing one's degree of personal control over events.
- Differentiating criticism of *what one does* from criticism of *who one is.*
- Learning to accept compliments.
- Developing goal-setting techniques to overcome failure.
- Using positive affirmations to increase a sense of self-worth.

The task of raising competent children is becoming increasingly difficult. Dramatic changes in family structures and lifestyles and growing societal pressures for children to possess specific knowledge and skills at an early age are just two of the challenges facing contemporary parents.

Solution-Focused Encouragement

The single most important factor in motivating youth is encouragement. The feeling of inferiority that young people experience in one form or another must be overcome if they are to function well. Even small gains demonstrate growth and should be applauded. If any progress is noted, there is less chance of discouragement. It is discouragement that educators fear. Discouraged youth tend to become discourage adults. Genuine competency comes from self-sufficiency. Youth need to feel competent and autonomous. Failure and defeat will not encourage a deeply discouraged child who has lost all hope of succeeding.

Competition usually does not encourage youth. Those who see hope of winning may put forth extra effort, but the stress is on winning rather than on cooperation, contribution, or competency. Preoccupation with the obligation to succeed—to win—is intimidating, and the resulting fear and anxiety often contribute to failure. Focusing on one's contributions and cooperation promotes success.

Necessary Collaboration

Complex problems require comprehensive services. To ensure enduring interventions, a number of processes must evolve. Initially, demographics must be collected and shared with key officials and stakeholders. Agencies and institutions should be assessed regarding categorical drift (i.e., agencies, institutions, organizations working on issues in isolation rather than together with a common vision and shared goals). We must encourage information sharing, joint partnerships, and collective community initiatives; develop action plans, timelines, and outcome accountability; and be willing to commit time, energy, and long-term participation.

Barth (1996), Davies (1989), Krasnow (1990), and Ziegler (1987) listed several approaches for overcoming institutional and community obstacles, including these:

- Approach at-risk programs with the premise that no single race, religion, culture, or ethnic group holds a monopoly on at-risk youth.
- Recognize that all families have strengths. Successful programs reinforce these strengths. Focusing on deficits or failures is counterproductive.
- Start with the assumption that most parents care deeply about their children, yet may not know how to help.
- Teach parents to overcome obstacles and to learn new techniques, such as helping with homework, teaching children to be more responsible, and developing boundaries and family rules.
- Ask parents what they are interested in doing, focusing on their agenda first.

Educational Alternatives

The challenges of educating today's children are unprecedented: Educators face classrooms of young people who are tired, hungry, and abused; who have no permanent homes; and who seldom have the kind of interaction with supportive adults necessary for mental, emotional, and moral development in their growing years. More and more children—from all classes, all racial and ethnic backgrounds, and all income levels—are at risk not only of failing in school but also for their personal safety and well-being. We must do all we can to increase our children's chances of success.

Currently, academic and social missions are mixed indiscriminately in our public schools. Driver's education, English as a second language, diversity, violence, health services, special education programs, high-stakes testing, and closing the achievement gap are only a few of the social missions our schools are currently fulfilling. Schools in this country are being asked to take on more responsibilities with smaller staff and fewer resources. In addition, schools are asked to pick up where others have failed and to accept the blame for falling short of our collective unrealistic expectations. No institution or public entity could accommodate the burden of expectations under which the American school now labors.

As an alternative, Banner (1992) proposed a new social institution: *the parallel school*. The parallel school works in tandem with the academic school but serves entirely separate ends. The mission of the parallel school would be to provide for the diverse and critical *nonacademic needs* of young people today (p. 486). The parallel school would be service-directed and offer largely elective programs. It would be home to extracurricular activities, athletic teams, band, chorus, recreation, and service learning projects. It also would provide tutorials and instruction in English as a second language. Early intervention and life skills instruction would be a viable part of the parallel school. Child care, health services, extended library hours, and quiet rooms for study would be available. In addition, extensions of community services and agencies could be housed within high-risk schools such as the Boys and Girls club, the YMCA, Boys Scouts, Girl Scouts, 4-H, and other youth-serving programs and services. Bringing critical services to schools in need fosters positive youth development.

Dryfoos (1996) proposed the evolution of *the full-service school*, one that provides both education and comprehensive social services under the same roof. To serve youth and their families better, some schools have formed *partnerships with outside agencies*, including mental health, social services, health, probation, police, housing, drug, and alcohol agencies, as well as nonprofit health and service agencies. Others have integrated *family resource centers* on campus, which provide a wide range of activities along with interagency case management teams to connect families with needed services. The list that follows outlines some of the parameters of the full-service school.

- Quality education provided by schools includes these:
  - High standards for all students
  - Accountability of students and teachers
  - Collaboration between schools and families
  - Effective basic skills
  - Individualized instruction
  - Team teaching
  - Cooperative learning
  - School-based management
  - Healthy school climate

- Alternatives to tracking
- Parent involvement
- Effective discipline
- Integrated curriculum
- Outcome accountability
- Technology in instructional use and communication among teachers, students, and parents
- Comprehensive health education
- Health promotion
- Social, emotional, and cognitive skills training
- Preparation for the world of work
- Psychoeducational groups

- Quality support services provided by community agencies include these:
  - Primary health services
  - Health screening
  - Immunizations
  - Dental services
  - Family planning
  - Individual counseling
  - Group counseling
  - Substance abuse treatment
  - Mental health services
  - Nutrition and weight management
  - Referral with follow-up
  - Basic services: housing, food, clothes
  - Recreation, sports, culture
  - Mentoring
  - Family welfare services
  - Parent education and literacy
  - Child care
  - Employment training and jobs
  - Case management
  - Crisis intervention
  - Community policing
  - Legal aid

- On-site community services in the schools such as Boy Scouts/Girl Scouts, Boys and Girls Clubs, YMCA, and other United Way Agencies

Dryfoos (1996) maintained that combining prevention and intervention with school restructuring will create stronger institutions—schools as neighborhood hubs, where children's well-being is paramount and where families will want to go. Further, in full-service schools with health clinics, clients have demonstrated lower substance use, better school attendance, and lower dropout rates. Graduation rates are significantly higher, property destruction and graffiti have diminished, and neighborhood violence has decreased (Dryfoos, 1996, p. 20). Full-service schools have the potential to integrate critical services and to enhance the well-being of schools and communities, children, and families.

Collective Initiatives for At-Risk Youth

An Action-Planning Paradigm

Action planning is an important part of the program implementation experience. Write a plan of action for projects in your community. At first, this task may seem tedious, but your planning time and action plan will make your projects much easier to pull together. In addition, as your team becomes familiar with the planning process, you can more easily plan other projects as opportunities develop or if barriers make it difficult to carry out your current plans.

There are four steps to the action planning process:

1. Needs assessment.
2. Program design.
3. Implementation.
4. Evaluation.

The process is ongoing. Your evaluation becomes information you can use in your next phase of needs assessment. The plan you write is important, but the continuing process of planning and developing activities is even more important.

Needs Assessment

Needs assessment is the first phase of the action-planning process. It involves three steps:

1. Gather information about your community, the extent of at-risk behavior, resources available, and potential barriers (people or things that could get in the way of completing projects).

2. Put this information in the form of a problem statement that simply states what the problem is, not how to solve it. An example of a problem statement would be this: "Youth in Community, USA, do not have enough recreational activities."

3. Prioritize or order the problems so that you will know which ones are realistically solvable and important to work on.

Program Design

Program design is the actual process of writing goals, objectives, and tasks.

Goals are the opposite of problem statements. Goals are solution statements that are not specific or detailed but that state the general direction of what you want to accomplish.

A goal might be "To increase the number of recreational activities for youth who live in Community, USA." Another goal might be "To increase community support for recreational activities." One to three goals should be enough for your team to work on during a school year.

Objectives are measurable activity statements. They are very specific. Each objective has four parts, so you can tell when you are finished with the objective and whether you actually did what you said you were going to do in that objective. The four parts are listed here:

- What? (the activity)
- Who? (the target group)
- How many? (the number of people)
- When? (the completion date)

An example of an objective would be this: "To organize a recreational club for all interested students who attend School, USA, by May 30, 20XX."

This example answers the four questions:

- What? A recreational club.
- Who? Targeted youth who live in Community, USA.
- How many? All interested youth.
- When? May 30, 20XX.

Always start an objective with the word *to*. Try not to use the word *and*. If you use *and*, you have written two objectives. Be realistic in the number of people with whom you will work. Start small and work your way up to bigger things. You can always write more objectives. Remember, planning is cyclical or ongoing.

Tasks are the specific activities necessary to complete the objective. Tasks should be written in the order in which they will be accomplished. Tasks include all the logistical details you can think of. Often one missed detail can make it difficult to complete the objective. Some of these details might include obtaining permission, finding a meeting room, creating flyers to announce an event, and sending out mailings. Each objective may have as many as 15 different tasks.

Implementation

Implementation involves doing your project, monitoring your progress, and modifying your project as necessary. If you assess your needs, plan well, and write good, easy-to-achieve objectives, this step will be relatively easy.

Evaluation

Evaluation involves collecting information about whether or not you achieved your objectives or did what you said you were going to do. It also involves reporting this information to other individuals or organizations that were involved in planning or funding your program, and using the information to plan other programs. Your evaluation becomes information you can use in your next cycle of needs assessment. Learn from your failures and successes and work up to dealing with more difficult problems.

Remember, these are the steps and substeps in the action-planning paradigm:

- Needs assessment:
  - Collect information
  - Write problem statements
- Program design:
  - Identify goals
  - List objectives
  - Identify tasks
- Implementation:
  - Do it
  - Monitor it
  - Change it
- Evaluation:
  - Measure it
  - Report it

- Use it for more needs assessment
- And the cycle continues.

Your team already may have completed the needs assessment phase of the action planning process. When you return to your community, it is up to your team to put your plans to work. (See Table 11.1, Table 11.2, and Table 11.3 for further guidance.) Good luck!

Team Action Plan

TEAM NAME

Community, USA

GOAL # 1 # OF OBJECTIVES 2

Community, USA youth do not have enough recreational activities.

OBJECTIVES _____

Organize a recreational club. _____

Team Action Plan

TEAM NAME

Community, USA

GOAL # 1 # OF OBJECTIVES 1

To increase the number of recreational activities for youth who live in Community, USA.

OBJECTIVE: To organize a recreational club for all interested students by May 30, 20___.

Team Action Plan

TEAM NAME

GOAL # __ # OF OBJECTIVES ___

OBJECTIVES _____

With this second edition of this book, prevention researchers have developed a system to evaluate best practices in your risk prevention. Intervention programs have been rated based on scientific principles that empirically demonstrate that the program reduces drugs, violence, or disruptive behavior. The next section describes the most recent findings (Greenberg, 2004) for best practices.

Quick Reference to Best Practices in Table 11.4

The best-practice programs information in this section was compiled by the Development Services Group(DSG) (http://www.dsgonline.com). DSG is committed to conducting science in the service of people, to improving the lives of youth and families, and to strengthening communities. They fulfill this commitment by dedicating their state-of-the-art subject matter expertise and extensive operational experience to support the operations of government and nongovernmental agencies and by emphasizing the development of community solutions balanced with effective use of federal, state, and private-sector resources and expertise.

Through large, multiyear projects as well as smaller, targeted initiatives, DSG addresses a wide range of concerns in the health, social services, and justice arenas. Health areas have included minority health; community- and school-based prevention programs targeting multiple risk behaviors; substance-abuse prevention for youth, substance abuse in the workplace, and substance abuse–related violence; HIV/AIDS; mental health; research on health risk behaviors, health care access, and health care utilization; and international development. Social services areas have included at-risk youth; runaway youth; alternatives to suspension and expulsion; youth employment; teen pregnancy; child abuse intervention, prevention, and treatment; child welfare; and domestic violence. Justice areas have included juvenile justice, criminal justice, juvenile delinquency, youth gangs, violence prevention, diversion programs, status offenders, juvenile courts, management information systems, graduated sanctions, cultural competency, gender-specific programming, aftercare and reentry programs, and corrections.

The demonstrated effectiveness rating of each program listed below is based on two criteria: quality of design and the scientific evidence suggesting a deterrent effect. The brief description of the rating is outlined as follows:

- **Exemplary.** These programs have been scientifically demonstrated to prevent delinquency or to reduce risk factors or enhance protective factors for dysfunctional behavior in special social contexts using an evaluation of the highest quality (i.e., experimental design with a randomized sample of people).

Effective. These programs have been scientifically demonstrated to prevent delinquency or to reduce risk factors or enhance protective factors for dysfunctional behavior in specific social contexts using either an experimental or a quasi-experimental design. The evidence

TABLE 11.1 Example of a Poor Team Action Plan

Tasks	Time line									Person(s) responsible	Resources, blocks, and barriers
	20__				20__						
	S	O	N	D	J	F	M	A	M	J		
Ask permission.					O							
Put up announcements.							O					
Hold a meeting.									O			
BAD EXAMPLE!												

TABLE 11.2 Example of a Positive Team Action Plan

Tasks	Time Line 20__				Time Line 20__						Person(s) responsible	Resources, blocks, and barriers
	S	O	N	D	J	F	M	A	M	J		
1. Obtain permission to organize a club from the Community Services Board.	O										Steve	The Community Services Board is very supportive.
2. Make plans to have a recreational club interest meeting.	O										All (school team)	
3. Create flyers to announce the interest meeting.	O										All	Our sponsor will provide materials to make the flyers.
4. Put up flyers around the community.		O									All	
5. Make announcements about the meeting.		O									Joan	The secretary may forget to make the announcement.
6. Hold the meeting.		O									All	
7. Sign up members.		O									Bill	Youth may not attend because of other activities.
8. Set date for next meeting.		O									All	

GOOD EXAMPLE!

Table 11.3   Template for a Team Action Plan

Tasks	Time line											Person(s) responsible	Resources, blocks, and barriers
	20__				20__								
	S	O	N	D	J	F	M	A	M	J			

Table 11.4 Exemplary Effective Promising

	Exemplary	Effective	Promising
Academic skills enhancement			
Schools and Families Education Children, ages 4 to 6	☒	☐	☐
Boys and Girls Club, ages 0 to 99	☐	☒	☐
Child Development Project, ages 5 to 12	☐	☒	☐
Communities in Schools, Inc., ages 12 to 18	☐	☐	☒
After school/recreation			
LA's Best, ages 7 to 11	☐	☒	☐
Quantum Opportunities Program, ages 9 to 12	☐	☒	☐
Extended-Services Schools Initiative, ages 6 to 14	☐	☐	☒
Police Athletic League, ages 7 to 17	☐	☐	☒
Behavior management			
Bicultural Competence Skills Approach, ages 12 to 18	☒	☐	☐
Anger Coping Program, ages 9 to 12	☐	☒	☐
Bry's Behavioral Monitoring and Reinforcement, ages 12 to 15	☐	☒	☐
FAST Track, ages 5 to 10	☐	☒	☐
Positive Adolescent Choices Training, ages 10 to 18	☐	☒	☐
PARITY (Promising Academic Retention for Indian Trial Youth), ages 11 to 18	☐	☐	☒
Project Aids Community Health Initiative En route to a Vaccine Effort (ACHIEVE), ages 3 to 14	☐	☐	☒
Community and problem-oriented policing			
Chicago Alternative Policing Strategy, ages 0 to 99			
Kansas City Gun Experiment, ages 0 to 99	☐	☒	☐
Operation Ceasefire, ages 0 to 99	☐	☐	☒
Family therapy			
Brief Strategic Family Therapy, ages 8 to 18	☒	☐	☐
Creating Lasting Family Connections, ages 7 to 17	☒	☐	☐
Families and Schools Together (FAST), ages 5 to 12	☒	☐	☐
Functional Family Therapy, ages 11 to 18	☒	☐	☐
Multidimensional Family Therapy, ages 11 to 18	☒	☐	☐
Multidimensional Treatment Foster Care, ages 11 to 18			
Multisystemic Therapy, ages 12 to 17	☒	☐	☐
Strengthening Families Program, ages 6 to 12	☒	☐	☐
Family Effectiveness Training, ages 6 to 12	☐	☒	☐
Nurturing Parenting Program, ages 1 to 18	☐	☒	☐
Raising a Thinking Child: I Can Problem Solve, ages 4 to 7	☐	☒	☐
Homebuilders, ages 0 to 18	☐	☐	☒

Table 11.4   Exemplary Effective Promising

	Exemplary	Effective	Promising
Gang prevention			
Comprehensive Gang Strategy, ages 17 to 25	☐	☒	☐
Gang Resistance Education, ages 13 to 14	☐	☒	☐
Boys and Girls Club Gang Prevention Through Targeted Outreach, ages 6 to 18	☐	☐	☒
Leadership and youth development			
All Stars, ages 11 to 15	☐	☒	☐
Early Risers' Skills for Success Program, ages 6 to 10	☐	☒	☐
Friendly PEERsuasion, ages 11 to 14	☐	☐	☒
Girl Power, ages 10 to 15	☐	☐	☒
Leadership and Resiliency Program, ages 7 to 17	☐	☐	☒
Learn and Serve America, ages 12 to 18	☐	☐	☒
Practical and Cultural Education (PACE) Center for Girls, ages 12 to 18	☐	☐	☒
Peer Assistance and Leadership, ages 14 to 18	☐	☐	☒
Project Venture, ages 9 to 13	☐	☐	☒
Mentoring			
Across Ages, ages 10 to 13	☒	☐	☐
Big Brothers/Big Sisters, ages 10 to 16	☒	☐	☐
Other community approaches			
Communities Mobilizing for a Change on Alcohol, ages 18 to 24	☒	☐	☐
Oakland Beat Health Program, ages 0 to 99	☒	☐	☐
Project Northland, ages 10 to 14	☒	☐	☐
Midwestern Prevention Project, ages 10 to 12			
Parenting training			
Adolescent Transitions Program, ages 11 to 18	☒	☐	☐
Guiding Good Choices, ages 9 to 14	☒	☐	☐
Helping the Noncompliant Child, ages 3 to 7	☒	☐	☐
Parenting Wisely, ages 6 to 18	☒	☐	☐
Parents as Teachers, ages 0 to 5	☒	☐	☐
Parents Who Care, ages 12 to 17	☒	☐	☐
Strengthening Families Program: For Parents and Youth, ages 10 to 14	☒	☐	☐
The Incredible Years, ages 2 to 10	☒	☐	☐
DARE to Be You, ages 2 to 5	☐	☒	☐
Effective Black Parenting, ages 2 to 18	☐	☒	☐
Focus on Families, ages 0 to 99	☐	☒	☐
Healthy Families America, ages 0 to 5	☐	☒	☐
Parent–Child Development Center, ages 0 to 3	☐	☒	☐

Table 11.4 Exemplary Effective Promising

	Exemplary	Effective	Promising
Preventive Treatment Program, ages 7 to 9	☐	☒	☐
Syracuse Family Development Research Program, ages 5 to 10	☐	☒	☐
NICASA (Northern Illinois Council on Alcoholism and Substance Abuse) Parent Project, ages 0 to 18	☐	☐	☒
Parenting Partnership, ages 0 to 18	☐	☐	☒
Parents Anonymous, ages 0 to 18	☐	☐	☒
Project Seek, ages 0 to 11	☐	☐	☒
Peer mediation			
Skills to Managing Anger and Resolution Together (SMART) Team, ages 11 to 15	R	☐	☐
Peers Making Peace, ages 5 to 22	☐	☒	☐
Prevention curricula			
Keep a Clear Mind, ages 8 to 12	☒	☐	☐
Life Skills Training, ages 10 to 14	☒	☐	☐
Positive Action, ages 5 to 18	☒	☐	☐
Promoting Alternative Thinking Strategies (PATHS), ages 5 to 12	☒	☐	☐
Responding in Peaceful and Positive Ways, ages 10 to 14	☒	☐	☐
Second Step: A Violence Prevention Curriculum, ages 4 to 14	☒	☐	☐
Too Good for Drugs, ages 5 to 18	☒	☐	☐
I Can Problem Solve, ages 3 to 12	☐	☒	☐
Linking the Interests of Families and Teachers (LIFT), ages 5 to 10	☐	☒	☐
Native American Prevention Project Against AIDS and Substance Abuse, ages 13 to 15	☐	☒	☐
Bullying Prevention Program, ages 6 to 14	☐	☐	☒
Social Competence Promotion Program for Young Adolescents, ages 11 to 15	☐	☐	☒
Think First, ages 10 to 18	☐	☐	☒
Violence Prevention Curriculum for Adolescents, ages 11 to 15	☐	☐	☒
Prevention services			
Cognitive Behavioral Therapy for Child and Adolescent Traumatic Stress, ages 3 to 8	☒	☐	☐
Nurse–Family Partnership (NFP), ages 12 to 18	☒	☐	☐
Perry Preschool Project, ages 3 to 4	☒	☐	☐
Project SUCCESS, ages 14 to 18	☒	☐	☐
STARS for Families (Start Taking Alcohol Risks Seriously), ages 11 to 14	☒	☐	☐
CASASART, ages 8 to 13	☐	☒	☐

Table 11.4 Exemplary Effective Promising

	Exemplary	Effective	Promising
Infant Health and Development, ages 0 to 3	☐	☐	☒
Project Link, ages 15 to 21	☐	☐	R
Project PACE, ages 9 to 10	☐	☐	R
SISTERS, ages 15 to 20	☐	☐	R
Starting Early Starting Smart, ages 0 to 7	☐	☐	R
School/classroom environment			
Project ALERT, ages 11 to 14	☒	☐	☐
Seattle Social Development Project, ages 6 to 14	☒	☐	☐
Consistency Management & Cooperative Discipline, ages 3 to 18	☐	☒	☐
Good Behavior Game, ages 6 to 10	☐	☒	☐
Project BASIS, ages 10 to 14	☐	☒	☐
Project PATHE (Positive Action Through Holistic Education), ages 11 to 18	☐	☒	☐
Reconnecting Youth, ages 14 to 18	☐	☒	☐
STEP (School Transitional Environment Program), ages 12 to 18	☐	☒	☐
PeaceBuilders, ages 5 to 18	☐	☐	R
Truancy prevention			
Operation Save Kids, ages 3 to 18	☐	☐	R
THRIVE (Truancy Habits Reduced, Increasing Valuable Education initiative), ages 3 to 18	☐	☐	☒
Vocational/job training			
Job Corps, ages 16 to 24	☒	☐	☐
Jobs for America's Graduates, Inc., ages 13 to 21	☐	☐	☒

Governmental entities that support these programs are:
U.S. Department of Education: Safe and Drug-Free Schools
U.S. Department of Health and Human Services: Surgeon General's Youth Violence Report
National Institute on Drug Abuse (NIDA): Preventing Drug Use
National Institute of Justice (NIJ): What Works
Office of Juvenile Justice and Delinquency Prevention (OJJDP): Blueprints
Office of Juvenile Justice and Delinquency Prevention/Center for Substance Abuse Prevention (OJJDP/CSAP): Strengthening Families
Substance Abuse and Mental Health Services Administration (SAMHSA): Model Programs

Note. From The OJJDP Model Programs Guide, by Development Services Group, Inc. Retrieved June 30, 2004, from http://www.dsgonline.com.

suggests program effectiveness, but the evidence is not as strong as for the exemplary programs.

- **Promising.** These programs display a strong theoretical base and have been demonstrated to prevent dysfunctional behavior or to reduce risk factors or enhance protective factors in specific social contexts using limited research or nonexperimental designs.

Finally, every program that is implemented in a school, community, or family setting should be evaluated in terms of effectiveness along six steps:

1. Engagement of stakeholders.
2. Description of the program initiatives.
3. Focus on the program design.
4. Collection of credible evidence.
5. Justification of conclusion of results.
6. Sharing lessons learned from the intervention.

A summary of these six steps is shown in Table 11.5.

Conclusion

Many of the successes and failures people experience in life are closely related to the ways they have learned to view themselves in relation to others. In the past, parents routinely sought the advice and counsel of relatives, friends, and extended family. Traditional sources of help and support are less available and less nurturing than at any time in history. Over the years, policy makers and educators have joined forces to battle a series of social and behavioral problems, waging war on drugs, abuse, unwanted pregnancy, AIDS, suicide, violence, and dropouts. Shriver and Weissberg (1996) maintained that schools and communities should also proactively build comprehensive programs that help children develop socially, emotionally, and cognitively.

Comprehensive social and emotional development programs are based on the understanding that many different kinds of problem behaviors are caused by the same risk factors, and that the best learning emerges from supportive and challenging relationships. Preventing problems such as violence, drug abuse, or dropping out is most effective when multiyear, integrated efforts develop children's social and emotional abilities through engaging classroom instruction; prosocial learning activities outside the classroom; and broad parent and community participation in program planning, implementation, and evaluation. Destructive behaviors develop in part from a complex web of familial, economic, and cultural circumstances.

TABLE 11.5 Summary of the Six Steps to Program Evaluation

1. Engage stakeholders
• Identify the information that stakeholders will need to drive the evaluation.

2. Describe the program
• Provide a statement of need: Why was the program needed? (Gather statistics, e.g., number of dropouts, truancy, unintended pregnancies, poverty, free-and-reduced lunch recipients, etc.)

- Expected effects of the program: How will the program address the needs?
- Activities: What did the program do (e.g., what programs, services, or activities could occur because of this intervention)?
- Resources: What existing resources does the program have that will enable its activities (e.g., community leaders, compassionate teachers, volunteers, etc.)?
- Stage of development: How far along is the program in addressing the need(s)?
- Context: What is the environment of the program?
- Logic model: What is the planned sequence and design of the program?

3. Focus of the evaluation design
- Purpose: What are the objectives of the evaluation?
- Users: Who is consuming the evaluation output?
- Uses: What are the users' information needs?
- Questions: What information will address users' needs?
- Methods: How will the information be collected, analyzed, and reported?
- Agreements: Who is going to what and when?

4. Gather credible evidence
- Indicators: What information will address questions?
- Sources: Where will the information come from?
- Quality: How good is the information?
- Quantity: How much information is needed?
- Logistics: What are the systems for collecting and managing information?

5. Justifying conclusions
- Standards: What is evaluation information compared to with regard to previous behavior?
- Analysis and synthesis: How is gathered intervention information summarized and organized?
- Interpretation: How is information communicated to stakeholders?
- Judgment: How is information from interventions compared to the original standards?
- Recommendations: What should be done with the findings?

6. Ensure and share lessons learned
- Design: Think through the entire evaluation.
- Preparation: Plan for evaluation and dissemination of the intervention plan.
- Feedback: Communicate results with users and others.
- Follow-up: Help users and stakeholders interpret findings and recommendations.
- Dissemination: Share the results with stakeholders, participants, parents, teachers, counselors, helping professionals, and faith community.

Note. Adapted from *Suicide Prevention: Prevention Effectiveness and Evaluation*, by SPAN USA, 2001, Washington, DwC: SPAN USA. Copyright 2001 by SPAN USA. Adapted with permission.

Youth-serving professionals need to provide children and families with information and support. Partnerships have become increasingly critical. The content of parent programs has broadened to include significant attention to the social context of parenthood. This shift in emphasis reflects an interest in the interconnectedness of child, family, school, and community. Shriver and Weissberg (1996) suggested implementing a kinder-garten-through-twelfth-grade program for all students, focusing on the promotion of social and emotional development. The impetus in such a program revolves around six basic principles:

1. Social development services should simultaneously and seamlessly address students' mental, emotional, and social well-being rather than focusing on one categorical outcome. Ultimately, comprehensive and integrated programs targeting multiple social and health problem behaviors have greater potential than short-term interventions targeting the prevention of a single problem behavior.

2. Social development services should be based on developmentally appropriate, sequential, preschool-to-high-school classroom instruction. Programming should start before youth are pressured to experiment with risky behaviors and should continue through adolescence.

3. Social development services must address youth's cognitive, social, and emotional skills; their attitudes and values about themselves and others; their perceptions of social norms; and their understanding of information about targeted social and health domains. Currently, there are too many ineffective prevention programs that stress knowledge about specific problems and fail to concentrate on the skills and values necessary to help children engage in health-protective behaviors.

4. Social development services should revolve around effective instruction and teaching methods that ensure active engagement, emphasize positive behavior, and change the ways in which children and adults communicate about problem situations. Innovative teaching techniques such as cooperative learning, modeling, role-playing, performance feedback, and positive reinforcement are critical.

5. Social development services should support multilevel interventions. Children grow and develop at home and in the school and community. Combining environmental support and reinforcement from peers, family members, school personnel, helping professionals, religious leaders, and the media increases the likelihood that youth will adopt healthier lifestyles.

6. System-level policies and practices to support program implementation and institutionalization must be developed. It is critical, for example, for teachers to be trained before the program is implemented and to be supported and coached for extended periods of practice. Support and information provide buffers against stressful life experiences and precarious transitions. Our youth are in crisis;

our families, schools, and communities are overwhelmed. In determining sound intervention strategies for schools and communities, policy makers, helping professionals, and parents must proceed beyond the rhetoric surrounding the maladies of American youth and begin implementing strategies that provide outcomes that can be implemented, integrated, measured, and evaluated.

Epilogue

Generation Next: They Are Your Kids and Mine.

They balance precariously on skateboards, cruise the strip in mud-sprayed four-wheel-drive vehicles, surf hurricane swells without the slightest trepidation, and spend hours molding their locks into the latest color-streaked or cut-and-buzz craze. They spill from buses, bikes, and customized VW bugs protesting the brevity of their break from academic rigor with an occasional notebook to disclose their destination.

Who are they? They are your kids. And mine. They look like us. They share our names. They carry "our hopes" and "their dreams" on shoulders more than a boy's, less than a man's; more than a girl's, less than a woman's. They are candidates put on a waiting list for adulthood, and for some they are drafted all too quickly.

They conform to profiles of surfer, preppy, and hip-hopper, hailing their styles as "baaad," wicked," "nasty," or "awesome." They can bully, and brag, and be cruel—chastising weaker peers with labels such as "geek," "dweeb," or "dork." They can cry over a rumor, laugh uncontrollably over nothing, smile to cover their hurt, and amaze us at how quickly they can move from one emotion to another.

They can find a contact lens within a radius of a thousand feet and not be able to avoid that one wet spot in an empty hallway. They can remember to get to Thursday's sale at the mall but forget their homework all too often.

They are slow to settle down after a classroom interruption but can sit absolutely silent in a crowded gym when one of their peers attempts a long shot on the basketball court. They can cook, sew, run a household, publish a newspaper, put together a yearbook, handle dangerous tools, understand computer programming, make the honor roll, hold a part-time job, come to school grief-stricken, and spend time in a detention home.

They experience many "firsts" as adolescents—their first time behind the wheel, their first love, their first grief, their first loss of a peer, their first failure, their first arrest, or their first child. This will also be the last time that adolescents will be assembled collectively with their own unique generation sharing the same interests and values among a caring community of significant adults, whom many will choose to emulate. They will spend their 4 years in high school shedding a variety of impostor-selves who change constantly, from academic term to academic term, searching for their real selves. Some of our kids are surviving against all odds, with lives filled with turmoil, stress, and clashes with adult authority.

They get tired and hurt, and they need a word of encouragement, a concerned look, or a pat on the back more often than we think. They will walk for any charity, sell everything from raffle tickets to flower bulbs in order to support their extracurricular activities, work for weeks on a homecoming float, party until they drop, and then come to physical education class with a medical excuse. They can memorize and understand the lyrics from the latest rap song but protest because of lack of understanding a parallel assignment of Shakespeare or Frost.

They can maintain their energy level on a diet of a pizza and french fries for lunch, topped off by a snack cake and three cartons of chocolate milk. They revel in snowball fights on the front lawn, skateboarding down the sidewalk, and rotating soccer balls from head to toe. They never, never smoke but always hold a lit cigarette for a friend; never cut anything but study hall or the substitute's class; are sometimes truant from school; may lie, cheat, forge notes, or misrepresent their parent on the phone; and use language fit to curl the ears of the commander of the U.S.S. Saratoga.

They play for our athletic teams in rain and snow, wallow in mud and sweat, and break bones—all in front of a very few people. They compete academically without hesitation or intimidation. They sing and play music with a talent beyond their years. They fit everything in among doctors' appointments, part-time jobs, private lessons, after-school practice, volunteer work, church activities, field trips, measles, mumps, mono, family discord, family celebrations, and homework.

They are not made of steel. They have serious illnesses, spend time in the hospital, and suffer from perhaps the most devastating experience for an adolescent—a broken heart. They experience family violence and dysfunction, family illness, and death. They find comfort in a friend; support from peers; and—we hope—love, direction, and understanding from us.

Who are they? They are your kids. And mine. They look like us. They share our names. And they will spend most of their lives away from our direct influence. But our indirect influence, in the form of directions charted and concern given, will remain with them to strengthen and guide them in the challenges ahead. The greatest sign of a successful counselor, teacher, or parent is not what the child did while in the classroom or in the home, but what he or she does with his or her life when we are a memory or a phone call away. May that memory never be too faint or our phone too busy.

ROSEMARY A. THOMPSON

References

Aas, H., Klepp, K. I., Laberg, J. C., Aaro, L. E. (1995). Predicting adolescents' intention to drink alcohol: Outcome expectancies and self-efficacy. *Journal of Studies on Alcohol, 56*, 293–299.

Abikoff, H., Ganeles, D., Reiter, G., Blum, C., Foley, D., & Klein, R. G. (1988). Cognitive training in academically deficient ADHD boys receiving stimulant medication. *Journal of Abnormal Child Psychology 16*(4), 411–432.

Abma, J.C., Chandra, A., Mosher, W., Peterson, L., & Piccinino, L. (1997).Fertility, Family Planning, and Women's Health: New Data from the 1995 National Survey of Family Growth, *National Center for Health Statistics Vital Health Statistics, 23,19, 14–21.*

Abma, J., Driscoll, A., & Moore, K. (1998). Young women's degree of control over first intercourse: An exploratory analysis. *Family Planning Perspectives, 30*(1), 12–18.

Acredolo, C., Adams, A., & Schmid, J. (1984). On the understanding of the relationships between speed, duration, and distance. *Child Development, 55,* 2151–2159.

Adams, G. R., & Munro, G. (1979). Portrait of the North American runaway: A critical review. *Journal of Youth and Adolescence, 8*(3), 359–373.

Adams, G. R., Gullotta, T., & Clancy, M. A. (1985). Homeless adolescents: A descriptive study of similarities and differences between runaways and throwaways. *Adolescence, 20*(79), 715–724.

Adelson, J., & Doehrman, M. (1980). The psychodynamic approach to adolescence. In J. Adelson (Ed.), *The handbook of adolescent psychology.*(pp. 97–117). New York: John Wiley.

Ainsworth, M. D. S. (1989). Attachments beyond infancy. *American Psychologist, 44,* 709–716.

Alan Guttmacher Institute. (1989). U.S. and cross-national trends in teenage sexual and fertility behavior. New York: Author.

Alan Guttmacher Institute. (1994). *Sex and America's teenagers.* New York: Author

Alan Guttmacher Institute. (1998). *Teenage pregnancy and the welfare reform debate: Issues in brief.* New York: Author.

Alan Guttmacher Institute. (1999). *Teenage pregnancy: Overall trends and state-by-state information.* New York: Author.

Albee, G. W. (1982). Preventing psychopathology and promoting human potential. *American Psychologist, 37,* 1043–1050.

Albee, G. W., & Ryan-Finn, K. D. (1993). An overview of primary prevention. *Journal of Counseling and Development, 7, 2,* 115–123.

Alberti, R., & Emmons, M. (1974). *Your perfect right.* San Luis Obispo, CA.: Impact Publishers.

Alberti, R. E., & Emmons, M. L. (1978). *Your perfect right: A guide to assertive behavior.* San Luis Obispo, CA: Impact Publishers.

Alderman, M. K. (1990). Motivation for at-risk students. *Educational Leadership, 48*(1), 27–30.

Alderman, M. K., & Cohen, M. W. (1985). *Motivational theory and practice for preservice teachers* [Monograph #4]. Washington, DC: Eric Clearinghouse on Teacher Education.

Alderman, T. (1997). *The scarred soul: Understanding and ending self-inflicted violence.* Oakland, CA: New Harbinger.

Alexander, K. L., & Entwisle, D. R. (1988). Achievement in the first two years of school: Patterns and processes. *Monographs of the Society for Research in Child Development, 53*(2, Serial No. 218).

Allen, P. B. (1985). Suicide adolescents: Factors in evaluation. *Adolescence, 20,* 754–762.

Allen, J. P., Weissberg, R. P., & Hawkins, J. (1989). The relation between values and social competence in early adolescence. *Developmental Psychology, 25,* 458–464.

Alpern, L., & Lyons-Ruth, K. (1993). Preschool children at risk: Chronicity and timing of maternal depressive symptoms and child behavior problems at school and at home. *Development and Psychopathology, 5,* 371–387.

Alter-Reid, K. (1992). Sexual abuse of children: A review of the empirical findings. *Clinical Psychology Review, 6,* 249–266.

Amato, P. R. (2000). The consequences of divorce for adults and children. *Journal of Marriage and Family, 62,* 1269–1287.

Amato, P. R. (2001). The consequences of divorce for adults and children. In R. M. Milardo (Ed.), *Understanding families into the new millennium: A decade in review* (pp. 448–506). Minneapolis, MN: National Council on Family Relations.

Amato, P. R., & Keith, B. (1991). Parental divorce and the well-being of children: A meta-analysis. *Psychological Bulletin, 110,* 26–46.

American Academy of Pediatrics (1983). Committee on Adolescence. Homosexuality and adolescence. *Pediatrics, 72,* 249–250.

American Academy of Pediatrics. (1993). Committee on Adolescence. Homosexuality and adolescence. *Pediatrics, 92,* 631–634.

American Psychiatric Association. (1987). *Diagnostic and statistical manual of mental disorders* (3rd ed., revised). Washington, DC: Author.

American Psychiatric Association. (1993). *Violence and youth: Psychology's response* (Vol. 1). Washington, DC: Author.

Amerikaner, M., & Summerlin, M. (1982). Group counseling with learning disabled children: Effects of social skills and relaxation training on self-concept and classroom behavior. *Journal of Learning Disabilities, 15*(6), 340–343.

Ames, C., & Ames, R. (1989). *Research on motivation in education goals and cognition* (Vol. 3). San Diego, CA: Academic Press.

Ames, C., & Archer, J. (1988). Achievement goals in the classroom: Students learning strategies and motivational processes. *Journal of Educational Psychology, 80*, 260–267.

Ames, L., Ilg, F., & Baker, S. (1988). *Your ten-to-fourteen-year-old.* New York: Delacrote Press.

Anderson, R. F., Kinney, J., & Gerler, E. R. (1984). The effects of divorce groups on children's classroom behavior and attitudes toward divorce. *Elementary School Guidance and Counseling, 17*, 4.

Anderson R. N., & Smith B. L. (2003). Deaths: Leading causes for 2001. *National Vital Statistics Report 52*(9):1–86.

Anderson, S. A., & Nuttall, P. E. (1987). Parent communications ranging across three stages of childrearing. *Family Relations 36*, 40–44.

Anderson, T. H. (1980). Study strategies and adjunct aids. In R. J. Spiro, B. C. Bruce, & W. F. Brewer (Eds.), *Theoretical issues in reading comprehension.* 163–182 Hillsdale, NJ: Erlbaum.

Angold, A. (1988). Childhood and adolescent depression II: Research in clinical populations. *British Journal of Psychiatry, 153*, 476–492.

Annie E. Casey Foundation. (1988). *When teens have sex: Issues and trends.* Baltimore: Author.

Annie E. Casey Foundation. (1999). *Kids count data books: State profile of child well-being.* Baltimore: Author.

Anthony, E. J. (1987). Risk, vulnerability, and resilience: An overview: In E. J. Anthony & B. J. Cohler (Eds.), *The invulnerable child* (pp. 3–48). New York: Guilford Press.

Aptekar, L. (1989). The psychology of Colombian street children. *International Journal of Health Services, 19*(2), 295–310.

Armesto, J. C. (2002). Developmental and contextual forms that influence gay fathers' parental competence: A review of the literature. *Psychology of Men and Masculinity, 3*, 67–78.

Armstrong, S. W., & McPherson, A. (1991). Homework as a critical component in social skills instruction. *Teaching Exceptional Children, 34*(6), 46.

Armstrong, T. (1994). *Multiple intelligences in the classroom.* Alexandria, VA: Association for Supervision and Curriculum Development.

Armsworth, M. W., & Holaday, M. (1993). The effects of psychological trauma on children and adolescents. *Journal of Counseling & Development, 72*(1), 49–56.

Asarnow, J. R., & Callan, J. W. (1985). Boys with social adjustment problems: Social cognitive processes. *Journal of Consulting and Clinical Psychology, 53*, 80–87.

Asbury, F. R. (1984). The empathy treatment. *Elementary School Guidance and Counseling, 18*, 181–187.

Asche, J. A. (1993). *Finish for the future: America's communities respond.* Alexandria, VA: National Association of Partners in Education.

Ashcroft, L. (1987). Defusing "empowering": The what and the why. *Language Arts, 64*(2), 142–156.

Asher, S. R., Hymel, S., & Renshaw, P. D. (1984). Loneliness in children. *Child Development, 55*, 1456–1464.

Association for Specialists in Group Work. (1990). *Professional standards for the training of group counselors.* Alexandria, VA: Author.

Atkinson, J. W., & Birch, D. (1978). *Introduction to motivation* (2nd ed.). New York: Van Nostrand.

Babiker, G., & Arnold, L. (1997). *The language of self-injury: Comprehending self-mutilation.* London: BPS Books.

Bahr, S. J., Marcos, A. C., & Maughan, S. L. (1995). Family, educational, and peer influences on the alcohol us of female and male adolescents. *Journal of Studies on Alcohol, 56*, 457–469.

Baker, N. (1983, August). Why women stay with men who beat them. *Glamour,* 312–313, 365–367.

Baker, C. (1990). Development of an outreach group for children ages five through thirteen who have witnessed domestic violence. Fort Lauderdale, FL: Nova University.

Balassone, M. L. (1988). Multiple pregnancies among adolescents: Incidents and correlates. *Health Social Work 13*(4), 266–276.

Bandura, A. (1976). Effecting change through participant modeling. In J. D. Krumboltz & C. E. Thorensen (Eds.), *Counseling methods.* New York: Holt, Rinehart, Winston.

Bandura, A. (1982). Self-efficacy mechanism in human agency. *American Psychologist, 37*, 122–147.

Bandura, A., & Schunck, D. H. (1981). Cultivating competence, self-efficacy, and intrinsic interest through proximal self-motivation. *Journal of Personality and Social Psychology, 41*, 586–598.

Banner, J. M. (1992). The parallel school. *Phi Delta Kappan, 73*(6), 486–488.

Barnes, G. M., & Welte, J. W. (1986). Patterns and predictors of alcohol use among 7–12th grade students in New York state. *Journal of Studies on Alcohol, 47*, 53–60.

Barnes, N. D., & Harrod, S. E. (1993). Teen pregnancy prevention: A model using school and community collaboration. *The School Counselor, 41*(2), 137–140.

Bart, M. (1998, September). Creating a safer school for students. *Counseling Today.*

Bartell, N. P., & Reynolds, W. (1986). Depression and self-esteem in academically gifted and nongifted children: A comparison study. *Journal of School Psychology, 24*, 55–61.

Barth, R. (1996). A personal vision of a good school. *Phi Delta Kappan, 71*(7), 512–515.

Barth, R. P. (1989). *Reducing the risk: Building skills to prevent pregnancy.* Santa Cruz, CA: Network Publications.

Barth, R. P., Fetro, J. V., Leland, N., & Volkan, K. (1992). Preventing adolescent pregnancy with social and cognitive skills. *Journal of Adolescent Research, 7*(2), 208–232.

Bauer, A. M. (1987). A teacher's introduction to childhood depression. *Clearing House, 61,* 81–84.

Baum, J. G., Clark, H. B., McCarthy, W., Sandler, J., & Carpenter, R. (1987). An analysis of the acquisition and generalization of social skills in troubled youths: Combining social skills training, cognitive self-talk, and relaxation procedures. *Child Family Behavior Therapy 8*(4), 1–27.

Baumrind, D. (1982). Are androgynous individuals more effective persons and parents? *Child Development, 53,* 44–75.

Bear, T., Schenk, S., & Buckner, L. (1993). Supporting victims of child abuse. *Educational Leadership, 50*(4), 42–47.

Beardslee, M. D., & Podorefsky, M. A. (1988). Resilient adolescents whose parents have serious affective and other psychiatric disorders: Importance of self-understanding and relationships. *American Journal of Psychiatry, 145,* 63–69.

Bearman, P. S., & Brückner, H. (2001). Promising the future: Virginity pledges and first intercourse. *American Journal of Sociology, 106*(4), 859–912.

Becker, J. V., Kaplan, M. S., & Kavoussi, R. (1988). Measuring the effectiveness of treatment for the aggressive adolescent sexual offender. *Annual New York Academy of Science, 528,* 215–222.

Bell, A. P., Weinberg, M. S., & Hammersmith, S. K. (1981). *Sexual preference: Its development in men and women.* Bloomington, IN: Indiana University Press.

Bellanca, J., & Fogarty, R. (1992). *Catch them thinking: A handbook of classroom strategies.* Palatine, IL: Skylight Publishing.

Belle, D. 1990. Poverty and women's mental health. *American Psychologist, 45,* 385–389.

Bem, S. L. (1981). Gender schema theory: A cognitive account of sex-typing. *Psychological Bulletin, 88,* 354–364.

Benard, B. (1999). Applications of resilience: possibilities and promise. In M. D. Glantz, & J. Johnson (Eds.), *Resiliency and development: Positive life adaptations* (pp. 156–186). New York: Plenum Press.

Benedek, R. S., & Benedek, M. Z. (1979). Children of divorce: Can we meet their needs? *Journal of Social Issues, 35,* 155–169.

Bennett, T., & Morgan, R. L. (1988). Teaching interaction skills to adolescent mothers. *Social Work Education 10*(3), 143–151.

Bergin, J. J. (1991). *Escape from pirate island.* Doyleston, PA: MarCo Products.

Bergin, J. J. (1993). Group counseling with children and adolescents. *Counseling and Human Development, 25*(9), 1–20.

Berkowitz, A., & Persins, H. W. (1988). Personality characteristics of children of alcoholics. *Journal of Consulting and Clinical Psychology, 56,* 2.

Berlin, R., & Davis, R. B. (1989). Children from alcoholic families: Vulnerability and resilience. In T. F. Dugan & R. Coles (Eds.), *The child of our times* (pp. 107–123). New York: Brunner/Mazel.

Berndt, T. J. (1981). Relations between social cognition, nonsocial cognition and social behavior: The case of friendship. In J. H. Flavell & L. D. Ross (Eds.), *Social cognitive development* (pp. 249–256). Cambridge, UK: Cambridge University Press.

Berndt, T. J. (1982). The features and effects of friendship in early adolescence. *Child Development, 53,* 1447–1460.

Berndt, T. J., & Savin-Williams, R. C. (1993). Peer relations and friendships. In P. H. Tolan & B. Cohler (Eds.), *Handbook of clinical research and practice with adolescents* (pp. 203–219). New York: John Wiley & Sons.

Bernstein, G. A., Garfinkel, B. D., & Hoberman, H. M. (1989). Self-reported anxiety in adolescents. *American Journal of Psychiatry, 146,* 384–386.

Beyer, B. K. (1987). Practical strategies for teaching of thinking. Boston: Allyn and Bacon.

Biden, J. (1993). Violence against women: The congressional response. *American Psychologist, 48,* 1059–1061.

Big Brothers Big Sisters program. *Evaluation Review, 22,* 403–426.

Black, C. (1984). COA: Teaching, talking, touching. *Alcoholism, 26,* 28.

Black, C., & DeBlassè R. (1985). Adolescent pregnancy: Contributing factors, consequences, treatment, and plausible solutions. *Adolescence, 20,* 281–289.

Black, M. M., & Krishnakumar, A. (1998). Children in low-income, urban settings: Interventions to promote mental health and well-being. *American Psychologist, 53*(6), 635–646.

Blum, R. W., Beuhring, T., Shew, M. L., Bearinger, L. H., Sieving, R. E., & Resnick, M. D. (2000). The effects of race/ethnicity, income, and family structure on adolescent risk behaviors. *American Journal of Public Health, 90*(12), 1879–1884.

Blum, D. J., & Jones, L. A. (1993). Academic growth group and mentoring program for potential dropouts. *The School Counselor, 40*(3), 25–29.

Blume, E. (1990). *Secret survivors.* New York: Free Press.

Blyth, D. A., Bulcroft, R., & Simmons, R. G. (1981). *The impact of puberty on adolescents: A longitudinal study.* Paper presented at the annual meeting of the American Psychological Association, Los Angeles.

Blythe, B., Gilchrist, L., & Schinke, S. (1981). Pregnancy prevention groups for adolescents. *Social Work, 26*(6), 503–504.

Bogenschneider, K., Small, S., & Riley, D. (1993). *An ecological, risk-focused approach for addressing youth-at-risk.* Chevy Chase, MD: National 4-H Center.

Bolger, K. E., & Patterson, C. J. (2001a). Developmental pathways from child maltreatment to peer rejection. *Child Development, 72*(2), 549–568.

Bolger, K. E., & Patterson, C. J. (2001b). Pathways from child maltreatment to internalizing problems: Perceptions of control as mediators and moderators. *Development and Psychopathology, 13,* 913–940.

Bolger, K. E., Patterson, C. J., Thompson, W. W., & Kupersmidt,J. B. correct as is (1995). Psychosocial adjustment among children experiencing persistent and intermittent family economic hardship. *Child Development, 66,* 1107–1129.

Bolig, R., & Weddle, K. (1988). Resiliency and hospitalization of children. *Children's Health Care, 16*(4), 255–260.

Bolton, F. G., & Bolton, S. R. (1987). Working with violent families: A guide for clinical and legal practitioners. Newbury Park, CA: Sage.

Bonkowski, S. E., Bequette, S. O., & Boonhower, S. (1984). A group design to help children adjust to parental divorce. *Social Casework: Journal of Contemporary Social Work, 65,* 131–137.

Botvin, G. J., & Botvin, E. M. (1997). School-based programs. In J. H. Lowinson, P. Ruiz, R. B. Millman, & J. G. Langrod (Eds.), *Substance abuse: A comprehensive textbook* (3rd ed.) (pp. 764–775). Baltimore, MD: Williams and Wilkins.

Botvin, G. J., & Griffin, K. W. (2001). Life skills training: theory, methods, and effectiveness of a drug abuse prevention approach. In E. F. Wagner & H. B. Waldron (Eds.), *Innovations in adolescent substance abuse interventions* (pp. 31–50). Amsterdam: Pergamon Press.

Botvin, G. J., Griffin, K. W., Paul, E., & Macaulay, A. P. (2003). Preventing tobacco and alcohol use among elementary school students through life skills training. *Journal of Child and Adolescent Substance Abuse 12*(4), 1–17.

Botvin, G. J., & Wills, T. A. (1985). Personal and social skills training: Cognitive-behavioral approaches to substance abuse prevention. In C. Ball & R. Battjes (Eds.), *Prevention research: Deterring drug abuse among children and adolescents.* National Institute on Drug Abuse Research Monograph No. 63. DHHS Pub. No. (ADM) 87-1334. Washington, DC: U.S. Government Printing Office.

Boyer, C. B., & Kegeles, S. M. (1991). AIDS risk and prevention among adolescents. *Social Science Medicine 33*(1), 11–23.

Boyer, D., & Fine, D. (1992). Sexual abuse as a factor in adolescent pregnancy and child maltreatment. *Family Planning Perspectives, 24,* 4–11.

Bradford, A. (1992). *Parting: A counselor's guide for children of separated parents.* Columbia: South Carolina State Department of Education.

Bradley, J. A. (2003). Self-injurious behavior: How to intervene before it's too late. *Healing, 8,* 1, 4–5.

Bradshaw, J. (1988). *Bradshaw on the family: A revolutionary way of self-discovery.* Deerfield Beach, FL: Health Communications.

Bray, J. H. (1999). From marriage to remarriage and beyond: Findings from the Developmental Issues in Stepfamilies Research Project. In E. M. Hetherington (Ed.), *Coping with divorce, single parenting and remarriage: A risk and resiliency perspective* (pp. 253–271). Mahwah, NJ: Erlbaum.

Brazelton, T. B. (1992). *Heart Start: The emotional foundation of school readiness.* Arlington, VA: National Center for Clinical Infant Programs.

Brazzell, J. F., & Acock, A. C. (1988). Influence of attitudes, significant others, and aspirations on how adolescents intend to resolve a premarital pregnancy. *Journal of Marriage and Family, 50*(2), 413–415.

Brendtro, L. K., Brokenleg, M., & Van Bockern, S. (1990). Reclaiming youth at risk: Our hope for the future. Bloomington, IN: National Education Service.

Breunlin, D. C. (1980). Multimodal behavior treatment of a child's eliminative disturbance. *Psychotherapy: Theory, Research, and Practice, 17*, 17–23.

Brewster, K., Billy, J., & Grady, W. (1993). Social context and adolescent behavior: The impact of community on the transition to sexual activity. *Social Forces, 71*(3), 713–740.

Briere, J., & Gil, E. (1998). Self-mutilation in clinical and general population samples: Prevalence, correlates and functions. *American Journal of Orthopsychiatry, 68*, 609–620.

Britton, J. (2001). *Federal funding for child abuse and neglect prevention.* Chicago, IL: Prevent Child Abuse America.

Brook, J. S., Whiteman, M., & Gordon, A. S. (1983). Stages of drug use in adolescence: Personality, peer, and family correlates. *Developmental Psychology, 19*(271), 184–199.

Brookman, R. (1993). *Making a difference in your community: A planning guide for community prevention of youth suicide and other youth problems.* Richmond, VA: Virginia Health Council.

Brooks, R. B. (1994). Children at risk: Fostering resilience and hope. *American Journal of Orthopsychiatry, 64*, 4, 545–553.

Brooks-Gunn, J. (1995). Children in families and communities: Risk and intervention in the Bronfenbrenner tradition. In P. Moen, G. H. Elder, & K. Luscher (Eds.), *Examining lives in context* (pp.467–451). Washington, DC: American Psychological Association.

Brooks-Gunn, J., Duncan, G. J., & Maritato, N. (1997). Poor families, poor outcomes: The well-being of children and youth. In G. J. Duncan & J. Brooks-Gunn (Eds.), *Consequences of growing up poor* (pp. 1–17). New York: Russell Sage Foundation.

Brooks-Gunn, J., & Furstenberg, F. F. (1989). Adolescent sexual behavior. *American Psychologist, 44*(2), 249–257.

Brown, I., Jr., & Inouye, D. K. (1978). Learned helplessness through modeling: The role of perceived similarity in competence. *Journal of Personality and Social Psychology, 36*, 900–908.

Brown, J. E., & Mann, L. (1991). Decision-making, competence and self esteem: A comparison of parents and adolescents. *Journal of Adolescents, 14*, 363–371.

Brunell, L. F. (1990). Multimodal treatment of depression: A strategy to break through the "strenuous lethargy" of depression. *Psychotherapy in Private Practice, 8*(3), 13–23.

Brustad, R. J. (1988). Affective outcomes in competitive youth sport: The influence of intrapersonal and socialization factors. *Journal of Sport and Exercise Psychology, 10*, 307–321.

Buel, S. (1993). Presentation to the first meeting of the Virginia Domestic Violence Coordinating Council. Richmond, Virginia.

Bundy, M. L., & Gumaer, J. (1984). Families in transition. *Elementary School Guidance and Counseling, 19*, 4–8.

Burgess, D. M., & Streissguth, A. P. (1992). Fetal alcohol syndrome and fetal alcohol effects: Principles for educators. *Phi Delta Kappan, 74*(1), 24–30.

Burke, D., & Van de Streek, L. (1989). Children of divorce: An application of Hammond's group counseling for children. *Elementary School Guidance and Counseling, 24*(2), 112–118.

Burrett, K., & Rusnak, T. (1993). *Integrated character education.* Bloomington, IN: Phi Delta Kappa Education Foundation.

Busen, N. H., & Beech, B. (1998). A collaborative model for community-based health care screening of homeless adolescents. *Journal of Professional Nursing, 13,* 316.

Bussell, D. A. (1995). A pilot study of African American children's cognitive and emotional reactions to parental separation. *Journal of Divorce and Remarriage, 25,* 3–15.

Butler, J. W., Novv, D., Kagan, N., & Gates, G. (1994). An investigation of differences in attitudes between suicidal and nonsuicidal student ideators. *Adolescence, 29,* 623–638.

Butler, R. (1989). Mastery versus ability appraisal: A developmental study of children's observations of peers' work. *Child Development, 60,* 1350–1361.

Butterfield, E. C., Nelson, T. O., & Peck, V. (1988). Developmental aspects of the feeling of knowing. *Developmental Psychology, 24,* 654–663.

Bywaters, P., & Rolfe, A. (2002a). Self-help or self-harm? *Mental Health Today,* 20–23.

Bywaters, P., & Rolfe, A. (2002b). *Look beyond the scars: Understanding and responding to self-injury and self-harm.* London: National Children's Home.

Caldera, Y. M., Huston, A. C., & O'Brien, M. (1989). Social interactions and play patterns of parents and toddlers with feminine, masculine, and neutral toys. *Child Development, 60,* 70–76.

Calhoun, G., Jr., & Morse, W. C. (1977). Self-concept and self-esteem: Another perspective. *Psychology in the Schools, 14,* 318–322.

Campos, J.J., Barrett, K.C.., Lamb, M.E., Goldsmith, H.H. & Stenberg, C. (1983). Socioemotional development. In P.H. Mussen (Series Ed.) & M.M.Haith & J.J. Campos (Vol Eds.) *Handbook of child psychology.* Vol. 2. *Infancy and developmental psychology.* New York: Wiley.

Campos, J. J., Bertenthal, B., & Kermoian, R. (1992). Early experience and emotional development: The emergence of wariness of heights. *Psychological Science, 3,* 61–64.

Cantrell, R. (1986). Adjustment to divorce. *Elementary School Guidance and Counseling, 20*(3), 163–173.

Cantwell, D. P., & Carlson, G. A. (1983). *Affective disorders in childhood and adolescence.* New York: Spectrum.

Capuzzi, D. (1988). *Counseling and intervention strategies for adolescent suicide prevention* (Contract No. 400–86–0014). Ann Arbor, MI: ERIC Clearinghouse.

Carey, A. R. (1986). Imagery: Painting in the mind. *Elementary School Guidance and Counseling, 21,* 150–154.

Carlson, G. A. (1981). The phenomenology of adolescent depression. *Adolescent Psychiatry, 19,* 411–421.

Carlson, G. A., & Cantwell, D. P. (1980). Unmasking masked depression in children and adolescents. *American Journal of Psychiatry, 137*(4), 445–449.

Carlson, G. A., & Garber, J. (1986). Developmental issues in the classification of depression in children. In M. Rutter, C. E. Izard, & P. B. Read (Eds.), *Depression in young people* (pp. 299–343). New York: Guilford.

Carlson, J. (1990). Counseling through physical fitness and exercise. *Elementary School Guidance and Counseling, 24,* 298–302.

Carnegie Foundation (1990). *Turning points: Preparing American youth for the 21st century.* New York: Carnegie Corporation.

Carr, M., Kurtz, B. E., Schneider, W., Turner, L. A., & Brokowski, J. G. (1989). Strategy acquisition and transfer among American and German children: Environmental influences on metacognitive development. *Developmental Psychology, 25,* 765–771.

Carroll, J. L., & Rest, J. R. (1982). Moral development. In B. B. Wolman (Ed.), *Handbook of developmental psychology* (pp. 434–451). Englewood Cliffs, NJ: Prentice-Hall.

Carvajal, S. C., Parcel, G. S., Basen-Engquist, K., Banspach, S. W., Coyle, K. K., Kirby, D., & Chan, W. (1999). Psychosocial predictors of delay of first sexual intercourse by adolescents. *Health Psychology, 18*(5), 443–452.

Casas, M. (1990). Respondent. In D. Brown (Ed.), *Work in America: Report of the Gallup survey. 168–184* Scottsdale, AZ: National Career Development Association.

Casper, V., & Schultz, S. B. (1999). *Gay parents/straight schools: Building communication and trust.* New York: Teachers College Press.

Caspi, A., Moffitt, T. E., Newman, D. L., & Silva, E. A.(1996). Behavioral observations at age 3 years predict adult psychiatric disorders: Longitudinal evidence from a birth cohort. *Archives of General Psychiatry, 53,* 1033–1039.

Cass, V. C. (1979). Homosexual identity formation: A theoretical model. *Journal of Homosexuality, 4,* 219–235.

Cawelti, G. (1989). Designing high schools for the future. *Educational Leadership, 47,* 30–35.

Centers for Disease Control. (1991, January). Premarital sexual experience among adolescent women. *Morbidity and Mortality Weekly Report,* 4.

Centers for Disease Control and Prevention. (1992). *Proceedings of the Third National Injury Control Conference.* Atlanta, GA: Author.

Centers for Disease Control and Prevention. (1998). State-specific pregnancy rates among adolescents—United States, 1992–1995. *MMWR, 47,* 497–504.

Centers for Disease Control and Prevention. (2000). Youth risk behavior surveillance—United States, 1999. *Morbidity and Mortality Weekly Report, 49*(SS-5), 1–96.

Centers for Disease Control and Prevention. (2001). School health guidelines to prevent unintentional injuries and violence. *Morbidity and Mortality Weekly Report, 50*(RR-22).

Centers for Disease Control and Prevention. (2002). *Adolescent and school health programs that work. health topics overview. health topics—sexual behaviors.* Retrieved September 2, 2004, at http://www.cdc.gov/nccdphp/ dash/ sexualbehaviors/index.htm.

Centers for Disease Control and Prevention. (2002a). Trends in sexual risk behaviors among high school students—United States, 1991–2001. *MMWR, 51*(38), 856–859.

Centers for Disease Control and Prevention. (2002b). Youth risk behavior surveillance—United States, 2001. *MMWR, 51*(SS-4), 6. 2000, 2000a, 2000b as cited by CDC

Centers for Disease Control and Prevention. (2003). *Trends in the prevalence of sexual behaviors [fact sheet]. Youth risk behavior surveillance system.* Retrieved December 2, 2003, from http://www.cdc.gov/nccdphp/ dash/yrbs/factsheets.htm.

Centers for Disease Control and Prevention, National Center for Injury Prevention and Control (producer). (2004). *Web-based injury statistics query and reporting system (WISQARS).* Retrieved June 21, 2004, from http://www.cdc. gov/ncipc/wisquars.

Centers for Disease Control and Prevention. (2004a, May). *Morbidity and Mortality Weekly Report, 53* (SS-2).

Centers for Disease Control and Prevention. (2004b, June). Suicide attempts and physical fighting among high school students, United States, 2001. *Morbidity and Mortality Weekly Report, 53*, 474–476.

Centers for Disease Control and Prevention. (2004c, June). Methods of suicide among persons aged 10 to 19 years, United States, 2001. *Morbidity and Mortality Weekly Report, 53*(SS-2), 2.

Chalmers, J. B., & Townsend, M. A. R. (1990). The effects of training in social perspective taking on socially maladjusted girls. *Child Development, 61*, 178–190.

Chapman, M. (1988). *Constructive evolution: Origins and development of Piaget's thought.* New York: Cambridge University Press.

Charles Stewart Mott Foundation. (1994). *A fine line: Losing American youth to violence.* Flint, MI: Author.

Chase, A. (2001, July). Violent reaction: What do teen killers have in common? *In These Times, 3.*

Chasnoff, I. J., Burns, K. A., Burns, W. J., & Schnoll, S. H. (1986). Prenatal drug exposure: Effects on neonatal and infant growth and development. *Neurobehavioral toxicology and teratology, 8*, 357–362.

Chasnoff, I. J., Burns, W. J., & Schnoll, S. H. (1985). Cocaine use in pregnancy. *The New England Journal of Medicine, 313*(11), 666–669.

Chasnoff, I. J., Griffith, D. R., MacGregor, S., Dirkes, K., & Burns, K. A. (1989). Temporal patterns of cocaine use in pregnancy: Perinatal outcome. *Journal of the American Medical Association, 261*(12), 1741–1744.

Chasnoff, I. J., Landress, H. J., & Barrett, M. E. (1990). The prevalence of illicit-drug or alcohol use during pregnancy and discrepancies in mandatory reporting in Pinellas County, Florida. *The New England Journal of Medicine, 322*(17), 1202–1206.

Chassin, L. (1994). Studying individual-level factors for adolescent alcohol problems: The example of adolescent temperament. In R. A. Zucker, G. Boyd, & J. Howard (Eds.), *The development of alcohol problems: Exploring the biopsychosocial matrix of risk* (NIH Publication No. 94-3742, pp. 109–121). Bethesda, MD: National Institute of Alcohol Abuse and Alcoholism.

Chilcoat, G. W. (1988). Developing student achievement with verbal feedback. *NASSP Bulletin, 72,* 507.

Children's Defense Fund. (1986). *Preventing adolescent pregnancy: What schools can do.* Washington, DC: Author.

Cicchetti D., & Lynch M. (1995). Failures in the expectable environment and their impact on individual development: The case of child maltreatment. In D. Cicchetti & D. J. Cohen (Eds.), *Developmental Psychopathology, Vol. 2: Risk, Disorder, and Adaptation* (pp. 32–71). New York: John Wiley & Sons.

Cicchetti, D., Lynch, M., Shonk, S., & Manly, J. T. (1992). An organizational perspective on peer relations in maltreated children. In R. D. Parke & G. W. Ladd (Eds.), *Family-peer relationships: Modes of linkage* (pp. 345–383). Hillsdale, NJ: Erlbaum.

Cicchetti, D., Rappaport, J., Sandler, I., & Weissberg, R. P. (Eds.). (2000). *The promotion of wellness in children and adolescents.* Washington, DC: Child Welfare League of America Press.

Cicchetti, D., & Rogosch, F. A. (1997). The role of self-organization in the promotion of resilience in maltreated children. *Development and Psychopathology, 9,* 797–815.

Cicchetti, D., Rogosch, F. A., Lynch, M., & Holt, K. (1993). Resilience in maltreated children: Processes leading to adaptive outcome. *Development and Psychopathology, 5,* 629–647.

Cicchetti, D., Toth, S. L., & Rogosch, F. A. (1999). The effectiveness of toddler-parent psychotherapy to increase attachment security in offspring of depressed mothers. *Attachment and Human Development, 1,* 34–66.

Clarizio, H. F. (1985). Cognitive-behavioral treatment of childhood depression. *Psychology in the Schools, 22,* 308–322.

Clark, M. L., & Ayers, M. (1988). The role of reciprocity and proximity in junior high friendships. *Journal of Youth and Adolescence, 17,* 403–411.

Clausen, J. A. (1975). The social meaning of differential physical and sexual maturation. In S. E. Dragastin & G. H. Elder (Eds.), *Adolescence in the life cycle: Psychological change and social context.* Washington, DC; Hemisphere.

Codega, S. A. (1990). Coping behaviors of adolescent mothers: An exploratory study and comparison of Mexican-Americans and Anglos. *Journal of Adolescent Research, 5,* 1.

Cohen, J. A. (1998). Summary of the practice parameters for the assessment and treatment of children and adolescents with post-traumatic stress disorder. *Journal of the American Academy of Child and Adolescent Psychiatry, 37,* 997–1001.

Cohen, P., & Hesselbart, C. (1993). Demographic factors in the use of children's mental health services. *American Journal of Public Health, 83,* 49–52.

Cohen, S. (1981). *The substance abuse program.* New York: Haworth Press

Cohen-Sandler, R., Berman, A. L., & King, R. A. (1982). Life stress and symptomatology: Determinants of suicidal behavior in children. *Journal of the American Academy of Child Psychiatry, 21,* 178–186.

Cohler, B. J. (Ed.), *Handbook of clinical research and practice with adolescents* (pp. 203–219). New York: John Wiley.

Cohn Donnelly, A. & Shaw, K. (2001). *National call to action: An effort to end child maltreatment.* Washington, DC: The Department of Health and Human Services.

Coie, J. D., & Kupershmidt, J. (1983). A behavioral analysis of emerging social status of boys. *Child Development, 54,* 1400–1416.

Coleman, E. (1981). Developmental stages of the coming out process. *Journal of Homosexuality 7,* 31–43.

Colins v. Orange Unified School District, 83. F. Supp. 2d 1135. (2003).December 8. 1999

Commission for the Prevention of Youth Violence. (2000). *Youth and violence: Medicine, nursing, and public health: Connecting the dots to prevent violence.* Retrieved March 15,2005 from http://www.ama-assn.org/violence.

Committee on Adolescence. (2000). Suicide and suicide attempts in adolescents. *Pediatrics, 105,* 871–874.

Conrad, M., & Hammen, C. (1993). Protective and resilience factors in high and low risk children: A comparison of children of unipolar, bipolar, medically ill, and normal mothers. *Development and Psychopathology, 5,* 593–607.

Consortium on the School-Based Promotion of Social Competence. (1994). The school-based promotion of social competency: Theory, research, practice, and policy. In R. Haggerty, L. Sherrod, N. Garmezy, & M. Rutter (Eds.), *Stress, risk, and resilience in children and adolescence* (pp. 268–309). Cambridge, UK: Cambridge University Press.

Constantine, N. A., & Benard, B. (2001). *California Healthy Kids Survey resilience assessment module: technical report.* Berkeley, CA: Public Health Institute.

Conterio, K., Lader, W., & Bloom, J. K. (1998). *Bodily harm: The breakthrough treatment program for self-injurers.* New York: Hyperion Press.

Cook, A. T. (1998). *Who is killing whom?* (Issue Paper 1). Washington, DC: Respect All Youth Project, PFLAG.

Cooley-Quille, M., Boyd, R. C., Frantz, E., & Walsh, J. (2001). Emotional and behavioral impact of exposure to community violence in inner-city adolescents. *Journal of Clinical Child Psychology, 30,* 199–206.

Cormier, W. H., & Cormier, L. S. (1985). *Interviewing strategies for helpers* (2nd ed.). Monterey, CA: Brooks/Cole.

Costa, F. M., Jessor, R., Donovan, J. E., & Fortenberry, J. D. (1995). Early initiation of sexual intercourse: The influence of psychosocial unconventionality. *Journal of Research on Adolescence, 5*(1), 93–121.

Costello, E. J. (1990). *Child psychiatric epidemiology: Implications for clinical child psychology* (Vol. 13, pp. 53–90). New York: Plenum.

Costello, E. J., Farmer, M. Z., Arnold, A., Burns, B. J., & Erkanli, A. (1997). Psychiatric disorders among American Indian and White youth in Appalachia: The Great Smoky Mountain Study. *American Journal of Public Health, 87,* 827–832.

Cowen, E. L. (2000). Psychological wellness: Some hopes for the future. In D. Cicchetti, J. Rappaport, I. Sandler, & R. P. Weissberg (Eds.), *The promotion of wellness in children and adolescents* (pp. 477–503). Washington, DC: Child Welfare League of America Press.

Cowan, E. L., Wyman, P. A., Work, W. C., & Parker, G. R. (1990). The Rochester Child Resilience Project: Overview and summary of first year findings. *Development and Psychopathology, 2*, 193–212.

Cox, B. J., Norton, G. R., Dorward, J., & Fergusson, P. A. (1989). The relationship between panic attacks and chemical dependency. *Addictive Behaviors: An International Journal, 14*, 1.

Crooks, T. J. (1988). The impact of classroom evaluation practices on students. *Review of Educational Research, 58*, 438–481.

Crosbie-Burnett, M., & Pulvino, C. J. (1990). Pro-tech: A multimodal group intervention for children with reluctance to use computers. *Elementary School Guidance & Counseling, 24*, 272–280.

Cross, D. R. & Paris, S. G. (1988). Developmental and instructional analysis of children's metacognition and reading comprehension. *Journal of Educational Psychology, 80*, 131–142.

Cross, L. W. (1993). Body and self in feminine development: Implications for eating disorders and delicate self-mutilation. *Bulletin of the Menninger Clinic, 57*, 41–67.

Crume, T., DiGuiseppi, C., Byers, T., Sirotnak, A., & Garrett, C. (2002). Underascertainment of child maltreatment fatalities by death certificates, 1990–1998. *Pediatrics, 110*, 2.

Crumley, F. E. (1990). Substance abuse and adolescent suicidal behavior. *The Journal of the American Medical Association, 263*, 222.

Daly, M., & Wilson, M. (1985). Child abuse and other risks of not living with both parents. *Ethnology and Sociobiology, 6*(4), 97–210.

Damon, W. (1980). Patterns of change in children's social reasoning: A two-year longitudinal study. *Child Development, 52*, 1010–1017.

Damon, W., & Eisenberg, N. (Eds.). (1998). *Handbook of child psychology, Vol.3: Social, emotional and personality development* (5th ed.). New York: Wiley.

Daniels, D., & Moos, R. H. (1990). Assessing life stressors and social resources among adolescents: Applications to depressed youth. *Journal of Adolescent Research, 5*, 3.

Daniels, J., Arredondo, P., & D'Andrea (1999, June). Expanding counselors' thinking about the problem of violence. *Counseling Today, 41*, 12, 17.

Danielson, H. A. (1984). The quieting reflex and success imagery. *Elementary School Guidance & Counseling, 19*, 152–155.

Darche, M. A. (1990). Psychological factors differentiating self-mutilating and non-self-mutilating adolescent inpatient females. *Psychiatric Hospital, 21*, 1, 31–35.

Daroff, L. H., Masks, S. J., & Friedman, A. S. (1986). Adolescent drug abuse: The parent's predicament, *Counseling and Human Development, 24*(13), 215–219

Darroch, J. E., Landry, D. J. & Oslak, S. (1999). Age differences between sexual partners in the United States, *Family Planning Perspectives, 31*(4), 160–167.

Darroch J. E., & Singh S. (1999). *Why is teenage pregnancy declining? The roles of abstinence, sexual activity, and contraceptive use* (Occasional Report, No. 1). New York: The Alan Guttmacher Institute.

Darroch J. E., Singh, S., & Frost, J. J. (2001). Differences in teenage pregnancy rates among five developed countries: the roles of sexual activity and contraceptive use. *Family Planning Perspectives, 33.*

Das Eiden, R., Cavez, F., & Leonard, K. E. (1999). Parent–infant interactions among families with alcoholic fathers. *Developmental and Psychopathology, 11,* 745–762.

Davidson, L., Franklin, J., Mercy, J., Rosenburg, M. L., & Simmons, J. (1989). An epidemiological study of risk factors in two teenage suicide clusters. *The Journal of the American Medical Association, 262*(8), 36–42.

Davies, D. (1989). *Poor parents, teachers, and the schools: Comments about practice, policy, and research* (ED308 574). Paper presented at the annual meeting of the American Educational Research Association, San Francisco, CA.

Davis v. Monroe County Board of Education, 526 U.S. 629. (1999).

Davis, N. J. (1999). *Resiliency: Status of the research and research-based programs.* Washington, DC: Substance Abuse and Mental Health Services Administration, Center for Mental Health Services.

Davis, S. (1990). Helping young girls come to terms with sexual abuse. *British Journal of Occupational Therapy 53*(3), 109–111.

de Shazer, S. (1991). *Putting difference to work.* New York: Norton.

de Shazer, S. (1982). *Patterns of brief family therapy.* New York: Guilford.

de Shazer, S. (1988). *Investigating solutions in brief psychotherapy.* New York: Norton.

de Young, M., & Corbin, B. A. (1994). Helping early adolescents tell: A guided exercise for trauma-focused sexual abuse treatment groups. *Child Welfare League of America, 75*(2), 141–151.

Dean, D. (1979). Emotional abuse of children. *Children Today, 8,* 18–20.

DeAnda, D. (1983). Pregnancy in early and late adolescence. *Journal of Youth and Adolescence, 12,* 33–42.

Demetrious, A., & Efklides, A. (1985). Structure and sequence of formal and post-formal thought: General patterns and individual differences. *Child Development, 56,* 1062–1091.

Dinkmeyer, D. (1971). Top priority: Understanding self and others. *Elementary School Journal, 72,* 62–71.

Dinkmeyer, D., & Dreikurs, R. (1963). *Encouraging children to learn: The encouragement process.* Englewood Cliffs, NJ: Prentice-Hall.

Dishion, T. J., & Loeber, R. (1985). Adolescent marijuana and alcohol use: The role of parents and friends revisited. *American Journal of Alcohol Abuse, 11,* 11–25.

Doan, J., Lazear, K., & Roggenbaum, S. (2003). *Youth suicide prevention school-based guide* (FMHI Series Publication #218). Tampa, FL: University of South Florida.

Dodge, K. A. (1983). Behavioral antecedents of peer social status. *Child Development, 54,* 1386–1399.

Dodge, K. A., Bates, J. E., & Pettit, G. S. (1990). Mechanisms in the cycle of violence. *Science, 250,* 1678–1683.

Dodge, K. A., & Feldman, E. (1990). Issues in social-cognition and sociometric status. In S. R. Asher & J. D. Cie (Eds.), *Peer rejection in childhood.* New York: Cambridge University Press.

Dodge, K. A., Murphy, R. R., & Buschsbaum, K. (1984). The assessment of intention-cue detection skills in children: Implications for developmental psychopathology. *Child Development, 55,* 163–173.

Dodge, K. A., Petit, G. S., McClaskey, C. L., & Brown, M. M. (1986). Social competence in children. *Monographs of the Society for Research in Child Development, 51* (2, Serial No. 213).

Donald, K., Carlisle, J. S., & Woods, E. (1979). *Before assertiveness: A group approach for building self-confidence.* Santa Barbara: University of California.

Downey, G., & Walker, E. (1989). Social cognition and adjustment in children at risk for psychopathology. *Developmental Psychology, 25,* 835–845.

Downing, J. (1988). Counseling interventions with depressed children. *Elementary School Guidance and Counseling, 22,* 231–240.

Dryfoos, J. G. (1990). *Adolescents at risk.* New York: Oxford University Press

Dryfoos, J. G. (1991). Adolescents at risk: A summation of work in the field programs and policies. *Journal of Adolescent Health, 12,* 630–637.

Dryfoos, J. G. (1996). Full-service schools. *Educational Leadership, 53,* 7, 18–23.

Dryfoos, J. G. (1998). *Safe passage: Making it through adolescence in a risky society.* New York: Oxford University Press.

Dubow, E. F. & Ippolito, M. F. (1994). Effects of poverty and quality of the home environment on changes in the academic and behavioral adjustment of elementary school-age children. *Journal of Clinical Child Psychology, 23,* 401–412.

Duckworth, L. (2000). Richest nations rank in child poverty. N.Y., N.Y.: *The Independent.*June 13.

Dugan, T., & Coles, R. (Eds.). (1989). *The child in our times: Studies in the development of resiliency.* New York: Brunner/Mazel.

Dumont, M., & Provost, M. A. (1999). Resilience in adolescents: Protective role of social support, coping strategies, self-esteem, and social activities on experience of stress and depression. *Journal of Youth and Adolescence, 28*(3), 343–363.

Duran, E. (1986). Developing social skills in autistic adolescents with severe handicaps and limited English competencies. *Education, 107*(2), 203–207.

DuRant, R. H., Krowchuk, D. P., & Sinal, S. H. (1998). Victimization, use of violence, and drug use among males adolescents who engage in same-sex sexual behavior. *Journal of Pediatrics, 133,* 113.

Durbin, D. M. (1982). Multimodal group sessions to enhance self-concept. *Elementary School Guidance and Counseling, 16,* 288–295.

Dweck, C. (1986). Motivational processes affecting learning. *American Psychologist, 4*(10), 1040–1048.

Dweck, C. S., & Elliot, E. S. (1983). Achievement motivation. In P. H. Mussen (Ed.), *Handbook of child psychology* (4th ed., Vol. 4). New York: Wiley.

Dyer, W. W., & Vriend, J. (1977). *Counseling techniques that work.* New York: Funk & Wagnall.

Dying young. (2002, March 13). *The Christian Century, 119,* 5. Retrieved May 13, 2004, from Questia database, http://www.questia.com.

Dysinger, B. J. (1993). Conflict resolution for intermediate children. *The School Counselor, 40*(4), 29–35.

Each day in America among all children. (2004). Washington, DC: Children's Defense Fund.

Edelman, M. W. (1988). Preventing adolescent pregnancy: A role for social work services. *Urban Education, 22,* 496–509.

Edelman, M. W. (1994). *State of America's children yearbook 1994.* Washington, DC: Children's Defense Fund.

Edwards, S. S. (1978). Multimodal therapy with children: A case analysis of insect phobia. *Elementary School Guidance and Counseling, 13,* 23–29.

Edwards, S. S., & Klein, P. A. (1986). Multimodal consultation: A model for working with gifted adolescents. *Journal of Counseling and Development, 64*(9), 214–219.

Edwards, P. A., & Lowe, J. L. (1988). Young adult books dealing with the crisis of teenage suicide. *The High School Journal, 72,* 1.

Egan, G. (1982). *The skilled helper: A model for systematic helping.* Monterey, CA: Brooks Cole.

Egeland, B., & Abery, B. (1991). A longitudinal study of high-risk children: Educational outcomes. *International Journal of Disability, Development and Education, 38*(3), 271–287.

Egeland, B., Carlson, E., & Stroufe, L. A. (1993). Resilience as process. *Development and Psychopathology, 5,* 517–528.

Egeland, B., Jacobvitz, D., & Stroufe, L. A. (1988). Breaking the cycle of abuse. *Child Development, 59*(4), 1080–1088.

Egeland, B., Pianta, R. C., & O'Brien, M. A. (1993). Material intrusiveness in infancy and child maladaptation in early school years. *Development and Psychopathology, 5*(3), 359–370.

Egeland, B., Stroufe, L. A., & Erickson, M. F. (1983). Developmental consequences of different patterns of maltreatment. *Child Abuse and Neglect, 7,* 459–469.

Egeland, B., Weinfield, N. S., Bosquet, M., & Cheng, V. K. (2000). Remembering, repeating and working through: Lessons from attachment-based interventions. In J. D. Osofsky & H. E. Fitzgerald (Eds.), *Infant mental health in group at high risk. WAIMH handbook of infant mental health* (Vol. 4, pp.35–89). New York: Wiley.

Eheart, B. K., & Leavitt, R. L. (1985). Supporting toddler play. *Young Children, 35*(2), 18–22.

Eisenberg, N., & Fabes, R. A. (1992). *New directions for child development: Developmental perspectives on self-regulation and emotion.* San Francisco: Jossey-Bass.

Eisenberg, N., Guthrie, I. K., Fabes, R. A., Reiser, M., Murphy, B. C., Holgren, R., Maszk, P., & Losoya, S. (1997). The relations of regulation and emotionality to resiliency and competent social functioning in elementary school children. *Child Development, 68*(2), 259–311.

Elam-Evans L. D., Jones, R. K., Darroch, J. E., & Henshaw, S. K. (2002). Abortion surveillance—United States, 1999, Morbidity and Mortality Weekly Report, part of the title Patterns in the socioeconomic characteristics of women obtaining abortions in 2000–2001, *Perspectives on Sexual and Reproductive Health, 34*(5), 226–235.

Elias, M. J. (1989). Schools: A source of stress to children: An analysis of causal and ameliorative influences. *Journal of School Psychology, 27,* 393–407.

Elias, M. J., Beier, J. J. & Gara, M. A. (1989). Children's responses to interpersonal obstacles as a predictor of social competence. *Journal of Youth and Adolescence, 18,* 451–465.

Elkind, D. (1988). *The hurried child: Growing up too fast too soon.* New York: Addison-Wesley.

Elliott, D. S. (1994). *Youth violence: An overview.* Boulder, Colorado: University of Colorado, Center for the Study and Prevention of Violence.

Elliott, D. S., Hamburg, B. A., & Williams, K. R. (1998). *Violence in American schools: A new perspective.* Cambridge, UK: Cambridge University Press.

Elliott, L., & Brantley, C. (1997). *Sex on campus: The naked truth about the real sex lives of college students.* New York: Random House.

Ellis, A. (1962), *Reason and emotion in psychotherapy*, New York: Stuart.

Ellis, A. (1988). *How to stubbornly refuse to make yourself miserable about anything—yes, anything.* New York: Kensington.

Ellis, A. (1989). Comments on my critics. In M. E. Bernard & R. DiGiuseppe (Eds.), *Inside rational-emotive therapy: A critical appraisal of the theory and therapy of Albert Ellis* (pp. 199–260). San Diego, CA.: Academic Press.

Elster, A. B., & Panzarine, S. (1983). Teenage fathers: Stresses during gestation and early parenthood. *Clinical Pediatrics, 22,* 700–703.

Embry, D. D., & Flannery, D. J. (1999). Two sides of the coin: Multilevel prevention and intervention to reduce youth violent behavior. In D. J. Flannery & C. R. Huff (Eds.), *Youth violence: Prevention, intervention, and social policy* (pp. 47–72). Washington, DC: American Psychiatric Press.

Emery, R. E. (1999). *Marriage, divorce, and children's adjustment* (2nd ed.). Thousand Oaks, CA: Sage.

Englander, S. E. (1984). Some self-reported correlates of runaway behavior in adolescent females. *Journal of Consulting and Clinical Psychology, 53*(3), 484–485.

English, D. (1995). *The Navy risk assessment model on child maltreatment and domestic violence: A review of the research literature.* Washington, DC: Bureau of Naval Personnel, Family Advocacy Program.

Englund, M., Levy, A., Hyson, D., & Stroufe, L. A. (2000). Adolescent social competence: Effectiveness in a group setting. *Child Development, 71,* 1049–1060.

Entwisle, D. R., Alexander, K. L., Pallas, A. M., & Cadigan, D. (1987). The emergent academic self-image of first graders: Its response to social structure. *Child Development, 58,* 1190–1206.

Epstein, M. H., & Cullinan, D. (1987). Effective social skills curricula for behaviorally disordered students. *Pointer 31*(2):21–24.

Erikson, E. H. (1963). *Childhood and society* (2nd ed.). New York: Norton.

Fabes, R. A., Eisenberg, N., McCormick, S. E., & Wilson, M. S. (1988). Preschoolers' attributions of the situational determinants of others' naturally occurring emotions. *Development Psychology, 24,* 376–385.

Family Support Network. (2002). *Child abuse and neglect.* Retrieved March 15, 2005 from http://www.familysupport.org/Abuse.cfm.

Fantuzzo, J., Sutton-Smith, B., Atkins, M., Stevenson, H., Coolahan, K., Weiss, A., & Manz, P. (1996). Community-based resilient peer treatment of withdrawn maltreated preschool children. *Journal of Consulting and Counseling Psychology, 64,* 1377–1386.

Farber, S. S., Primavera, J., & Felner, R. D. (1983). Older adolescents and parental divorce: Adjustment problems and mediators of coping. *Journal of Divorce, 7,* 59–75.

Farrell, A. D., & Bruce, S. E. (1997). Impact of exposure to community violence on violent behavior and emotional distress among urban adolescents. *Journal of Clinical Child Psychology, 26,* 2–14.

Faulkner, A., & Cranston, K. (1998). Correlates of same-sex sexual behavior in a random sample of Massachusetts high school students. *American Journal of Public Health, 88,* 262–266.

Favazza, A. (1998). The coming of age of self-mutilation. *Journal of Nervous and Mental Disease, 186,* 259–268.

Favazza, A. R. (1996). *Bodies under siege: Self-mutilation and body modification in culture and psychiatry* (2nd ed.). Baltimore: The Johns Hopkins University Press.

Favazza, A. R., & Conterio, K. (1989). Female habitual self-mutilation. *Acta Psychiatrica Scandinoviea, 79,* 233–289.

Favazza, A. R., & Rosenthal, R. J. (1993). Diagnostic issues in self-mutilation. *Hospital and Community Psychiatry, 44*(2), 134–140.

Feldman, S., Rubenstein, J., & Rubin, C. (1988). Depressive affect and restraint in early adolescence: Relationships with family process and friendship support. *Journal of Early Adolescence, 14*(1), 218–223.

Ferran, E., & Sabatini, A. (1985). Homeless youth: The New York experience. *International Journal of Family Psychiatry, 6*(2), 117–128.

Fine, S., Forth, A., Gilbert, M., & Haley, G. (1991). Group therapy for adolescent depressive disorder: A comparison of social skills and therapeutic support. *Journal of American Academy Child and Adolescent Psychiatry, 30*(1), 79–85.

Finer, L., Darroch, J. E., & Singh, S. (1999). Sexual partnership patterns as a behavioral risk factor for sexually transmitted diseases. *Family Planning Perspectives, 31*(5):228–236.

Fineran, S. (2001). Sexual minority students and peer sexual harassment in high school. *Journal of Social Work, 11*(3), 22.

Finn, J. D. (1989). Withdrawing from school. *Review of Educational Research, 59,* 117–142.

Fisher, P. A., Gunnar, M. R., Chamberlain, P., & Reid, J. B. (2000). Preventive intervention for maltreated preschool children: Impact on children's behavior, neuroendocrine activity, and foster parent functioning. *Journal of the American Academy of Child and Adolescent Psychiatry, 39,* 1356–1364.

Fitzgerald, H. E., Sullivan, L. A., Ham, H. P., Zucker, R. A., Bruckel, S., & Schneider, A. M. (1993). Predictors of behavioral problems in three-year-old sons of alcoholics: Early evidence for onset of risk. *Child Development, 64,* 110–123.

Flach F. (1988). *Resilience: Discovering a new strength at times of stress.* New York:

Fawcett Columbine.

Flannery, D. J., & Singer, M. I. (1999). Exposure to violence and victimization at school. *CHOICES Briefs, 4,* 2–4.

Flavel, J. H. (1963). *The developmental psychology of Jean Piaget.* Princeton, NJ: Van Nostrand.

Fleischer, J., & Fillman, J. (1995). Lesbian and gay youth: Treatment issues. *The Counselor, 13*(1), 2, 27–28.

Fonagy, P., Steele, M., Steele, H., Higgitt, A., & Target, M. (1994). The Emmanuel Memorial Lecture 1992: The theory and practice of resilience. *Journal of Child Psychology and Psychiatry, 34*(2), 231–257.

Fontana, V. (1985). *Report* to the Conference on Child Abuse and Neglect. Richmond, Virginia.

Foreman, S., & Seligman, L. (1983). Adolescent abuse. *School Counselor, 31*(1), 17–25.

Forman, S. G., & Neal, J. A. (1987). School-based substance abuse prevention programs. *Special Services in the Schools, 3,* 3–4.

Forrest, D. V. (1990). Understanding adolescent depression: Implications for practitioners. *Counseling and Human Development, 23*(1), 221–227.

Foshee, V. A., Linder, G. F., Bauman, K. E., Langwick, S. A., Arriaga, X. B., Heath, J. L., McMahon, P. M., & Bangdiwala, S. (1996). The safe dates project: Theoretical basis, evaluation design, and selected baseline findings. *American Journal of Preventive Medicine, 12*(Suppl.), 39–47.

Foxx, R. M., Kyle, M. S., Faw, G. D., & Bittle, R. G. (1989). Teaching a problem solving strategy to inpatient adolescents: Social validation, maintenance, and generalization. *Child Family Behavior Therapy, 11*(3–4), 71–88.

Freeman, M. (1993). *The kindness of strangers.* San Francisco: Jossey-Bass.

French, D. C. (1984). Children's knowledge of the social functions of younger, older, and same-age peers. *Child Development, 55,* 1429–1433.

Frey, D. (1984). The counselor's role in the treatment of anorexia nervosa and bulimia. *Journal of Counseling and Development, 63*(4), 248–249.

Frey, K. S., & Ruble, D. N. (1987). What children say about classroom performance: Sex and grade differences in perceived confidence. *Child Development, 58,* 1066–1078.

Fried, S., & Fried, P. (2003). *Bullies, targets, and witnesses: Helping children break the pain chain.* New York: M. Evans and Company.

Furstenberg, F. F., Brooks-Gunn, J., & Morgan, P. (1987). *Adolescent mothers in later life.* New York: Cambridge University Press.

Gabriel, A., & McAnarney, E. R. (1983). Parenthood in two subcultures: White middle-class couples and black low-income adolescents in Rochester, New York. *Adolescence, 71,* 679–694.

Gage, N. L. (1990). Dealing with the dropout problem. *Phi Delta Kappan, 72*(4), 280–285.

Gallup International Institute. (1994). Many teenagers feel fear at school, survey shows. *Education Week, 13*(11), 6.

Garbarino, J., Dubrow, N., Kostelny, K., & Pardo, C. (1992). *Children in anger.* San Francisco: Jossey-Bass.

Gardner, H. (1983). *Frames of mind: The theory of multiple intelligences.* New York: Harper & Row.

Gardner, H. (1991). *The unschooled mind.* New York: Basic Books.

Gardner, H. (1993). *Multiple intelligences: The theory in practice.* New York: Basic Books.

Garland, A., & Zigler, E. (1993). Adolescent suicide prevention: Current research and social policy implications. *American Psychologist, 48,* 169–182.

Garmezy, N. (1981). Children under stress: Perspectives on anecdotes and correlates of vulnerability and resistance to psychopathology. In A. I. Rabin, A. M. Barclay, & R. A. Zucker (Eds.), *Further explorations in personality* (pp. 196–270). New York: Wiley.

Garmezy, N. (1985), Stress-resistant children: The search for protective factors. In J. E. Stevenson (Ed.), *Recent research in developmental psychopathology* (pp. 213–233). Journal of Child Psychology and Psychiatry Book Supplement No. 4. Oxford, UK: Pergamon.

Garmezy, N. (1991). Resiliency and vulnerability to adverse developmental outcomes associated with poverty. *American Behavioral Scientist, 34*(4), 416–430.

Garmezy, N. (1993). Children in poverty: Resiliency despite risk. In E. M. Cummings, A. L. Greene, & K. H. Karraker (Eds.), *Life-span development psychology: Perspectives on stress and coping* (pp. 151–174). NJ: Lawrence Erlbaum Publishers.

Garmezy, N., & Masten, A. S. (1994). Chronic adversities. In M. Rutter, L. Herzov, & E. Taylor (Eds.), *Child and adolescent psychiatry* (pp. 191–208). Oxford, UK: Blackwell Scientific.

Garmezy, N., Masten, A. S., & Tellegen, A. (1984). The study of stress and competence in children: A building block for developmental psychopathology. *Child Development, 55,* 97–111.

Garofalo, R., Wolf, R. C., Kessel, S., & Palfrey, J., & DuRant, R. H. (1998). The association between health risk behaviors and sexual orientation among school-based sample of adolescents. *Pediatrics, 101*(5), 895–902.

Garrison, C. Z., Schoenback, V. J., & Kaplan, B. H. (1984). Depressive symptoms in early adolescence: Depression in multidisciplinary perspective. New York: Brunner/Mazel.

Garrison, C. Z., Schuchter, M. D., Schoenbach, V. J., & Kaplan, B. K. (1989). Epidemiology of depressive symptoms in young adolescents. *Journal of American Academy of Child and Adolescent Psychiatry, 28,* 343–351.

Gates, M. (1988, August 22). The changing fortunes of U.S. families: A University of Michigan study provides a surprising view of the dynamics of poverty and offers insights for upcoming welfare reform. *The Ann Arbor News,* p. B1.

Gaughan, E., J. Cerio, and R. Myers (2001) *Lethal Violence in Schools: A National Study*. New York: Alfred University.www.alfred.edu/teenviolence/.

Gavin, L. A., & Furman, W. (1989). Age differences in adolescents' perceptions of their peer groups. *Developmental Psychology, 25,* 827–834.

Gelfand, D. M., & Teti, D. M. (1990). The effects of maternal depression on children. *Clinical Psychological Review, 10*(3), 329–353.

Gelman, D. (November 11, 1993). Tune In, Come Out, *Newsweek, 122, 19, 70–72.*

Gerler, E. R. (1977). The BASIC ID in career education. *The Vocational Guidance Quarterly, 25,* 238–244.

Gerler, E. R. (1978a). The school counselor and multimodal education. *The School Counselor, 13,* 166–171.

Gerler, E. R. (1978b). Counselor-teacher collaboration in a multimodal reading program. *Elementary School Guidance and Counseling, 13,* 64–67.

Gerler, E. R. (1979). Preventing the delusion of uniqueness: Multimodal education in mainstream classrooms. *The Elementary School Journal, 14,* 35–40.

Gerler, E. R. (1980). A longitudinal study of multimodal approaches to small group psychological education. *The School Counselor, 27,* 184–190.

Gerler, E. R. (1982). *Counseling the young learner.* Englewood Cliffs, NJ: Prentice-Hall.

Gerler, E. R. (1984). The imagery in BASIC ID: A factor in education. *Journal of Humanistic Education and Development, 22,* 115–122.

Gerler, E. R., & Herndon, E. Y. (1993). Learning how to succeed academically in middle school. *Elementary School Guidance & Counseling, 27*(3), 186–197.

Gerler, E. R., & Keat, D. B. (1977). Multimodal education: Treating the BASIC ID of the elementary classroom. *The Humanist Educator, 15,* 148–154.

Gerler, E. R., Kinney, J., & Anderson, R. (1985). The effects of counseling on classroom performance. *Journal of Humanistic Education and Development, 23*(4), 155–165.

Gerstein, A. I. (1988). A psychiatric program for deaf patients. *Psychiatric Hospital 19*(3), 125–128.

Ghaziuddin, M., Tsai, L., Naylor, M., & Ghaziuddin, N. (1992). Mood disorders in group of self-cutting adolescents. *Acta Paedopsychiatrica, 55,* 103–105.

Gibbs, J. (1985). Psychological factors associated with depression in urban adolescent females: Implications of assessment. *Journal of Youth and Adolescence, 14*(1), 316–320.

Gibbs, J. C. (1979). Kohlberg's moral stage theory: A Piagetian revision. *Human Development, 22,* 89–112.

Gill, S. J., & Barry, R. A. (1982). Group-focused counseling: Classifying the essential skills. *The Personnel and Guidance Journal, 60*(5), 66–71.

Gillman, R., & Whitlock, K. (1989). Sexuality: A neglected component of child sexual abuse education and training. *Child Welfare, 68*(3), 110–115.

Gill-Wigal, J. (1988). Societal trends and the world of the adolescent. In D. Capuzzi & L. Golden (Eds.), *Preventing adolescent suicide* (pp. 140–152). Muncie, IN: Accelerated Development.

Girard, K., Rifkin, J., & Townley, A. (1985). *Peaceful persuasion: A guide to creating mediation dispute resolution programs on college campuses.* Amherst, MA: University of Massachusetts Mediation Project.

Gladding, S. (1995). *Group work: A counseling specialty* (3rd ed.). Englewood Cliffs, NJ: Prentice-Hall.

Glantz, M. D., & Johnson, J. L. (Eds.). (1999). *Resilience and development: positive life adaptations.* New York: Kluwe/Plenum.

Gold, M., & Yanof, D. S. (1985). Mothers, daughters, and girlfriends. *Journal of Personality and Social Psychology, 49,* 654–659.

Goldstein, A., & Eckstein, R. (2003). *More than 2,900 children and teens died from guns in 2001.* Washington, DC: Children's Defense Fund.

Goldstein, A., & Eckstein, R. (2005, January). *A moral outrage: One American child or teen killed by gunfire nearly every three hours.* Washington, DC: Children's Defense Fund.

Goldstein, A. P., Glick, B., Irwin, M. J., Pask-McCartney, C., & Rubama, I. (1989). *Reducing delinquency: Intervention in the community.* New York: Pergamon Press.

Goldstein, A. P., & Huff, C. R. (1993). *Gangs in the United States.* Champaign, IL: Research Press.

Goldstein, A. P., & McGinnis, E. (1997). *Skillstreaming the adolescent: New strategies and perspectives for teaching prosocial skills.* Champaign, IL: Research Press.

Goldstein, A. P., Sprafkin, R. P., Gershaw, N. J., & Klein, P. (1982). *Skillstreaming the adolescent: A structured learning approach to teaching prosocial skills.* Champaign, IL: Research Press.

Goleman, D. (1994). *Emotional literacy: A field report.* Kalamazoo, MI: Fetzer Institute.

Goleman, D. (1995). *Emotional intelligence.* New York: Bantam Books.

Gonsiorek, I. C. (1988). Mental health issues of gay and lesbian adolescents. *Journal of Adolescent Health Care, 9,* 114–122.

Goodenow, C. (2000). *Massachusetts Department of Education 1999 Massachusetts youth risk survey.* Boston: Massachusetts Department of Education.

Goodman, R. W. (1987). Point of view: Adult children of alcoholics. *Journal of Counseling and Development, 66,* 162–163.

Goodman, S. H., & Gotlib, I. (1999). Risk for psychopathology in the children of depressed mothers: A developmental model for understanding mechanisms of transmission. *Psychological Review, 106,* 458–490.

Gorman-Smith, D., & Tolan, P. H. (1998). The role of exposure to community violence and developmental problems among inner-city youth. *Development and Psychopathology, 10,* 101–116.

Gravitz, H. L., & Bowden, J. D. (1985). *Recovery: A guide for adult children of alcoholics.* New York: Simon & Schuster.

Green, B. J. (1978). HELPING children of divorce: A multimodal approach. *Elementary School Guidance and Counseling, 13,* 31–45.

Greenberger, E., & Steinberg, L. (1987). *The work of growing up.* New York: Basic Books.

472 • Nurturing Future Generations

Greenspan, G. S., & Samuel, S. E. (1989). Self-cutting after rape. *American Journal of Psychiatry, 146,* 789–790.

Gregg, S. (1996). *Preventing antisocial behavior in disabled and at-risk students.* AEL Policy Briefs. Charleston, WV: Appalachia Educational Laboratory.

Gresham, F. M. (1981). Validity of social skills measures for assessing the social competence in low-status children: A multivariate investigation. *Developmental Psychology, 17,* 390–398.

Gresham, F. M. (2000). Assessment of social skills in students with emotional and behavioral disorders. *Assessment for Effective Intervention, 26*(I), 51–58.

Gresham, F. M., & Elliot, S. N. (1984), Assessment and classifications of children's social skills: A review of methods and issues. *School Psychology Review, 13,* 292–301.

Grossman, J. B., & Tierney, J. P. (1998). Does mentoring work? An impact study of the Big Brothers Big Sisters program. *Evaluation Review, 22,* 403–426.

Growald, K. (1994). Meeting the challenge of at-risk students. *The American School Board Journal, 181*(12), 2–6.

Grunbaum, J. A., Kann, L., Kinchen, S., Ross, J. G., Hawkins, J., Lowry, R., Harris, W. A., McManus, T., Chyen, D., Collins, J. (2004). Youth risk behavior surveillance—United States, 2003. *MMWR, 5358.*(SS-2).

Grunbaum, J. A., Kann, L., Kinchen, S., Ross, J. G., Lowry, R., & Harris, W. A. (2004). Youth risk behavior surveillance—United States, 2004. *MMWR, 53*(SS-2), 1–100. Available from www.cdc.gov/mmwr/preview/mmwrhtml/ss5302a1.htm.

Guerra, N. G., & Slaby, R. G. (1990). Cognitive mediators of aggression in adolescent offenders: 2. Intervention. *Deveopmental Psychology, 26*(2), 269–277.

Gumaer, J. (1990). Multimodal counseling of childhood encopresis: A case example. *The School Counselor, 38,* 58–64.

Guo, G. (1998). The timing of the influences of cumulative poverty on children's cognitive ability and achievement. *Social Forces, 77*(1), 257–287.

Gwynn, C., & Brantley, H. (1987). Effects of a divorce group intervention with elementary school children. *Psychology in the Schools, 24,* 161–164.

Hacker, D. J. (1994). The existential view of adolescence. *Journal of Early Adolescence, 14,* 300–327.

Haggerty, R. J., Sherrod, L. R., Garmazy, N., & Rutter, M. (1994). Measuring developmental changes in exposure to adversity: A life chart and rating scale approach. *Development and Psychopathology, 11,* 171–192.

Hains, A. A., & Herman, L. P. (1989). Social cognitive skills and behavioral adjustment of delinquent adolescents in treatment. *Journal of Adolescence, 12,* 323–328.

Hallinan, M. (1979). Structural effects on children's friendships and cliques. *Social Psychology Quarterly, 42,* 43–54.

Halpern, C. T., Joyner, K., Udry, R. J., & Suchindran, C. (2000). Smart teens don't have sex (or kiss much either). *Journal of Adolescent Health, 26,* 213–225.

Halpern, R. (1993). Poverty and infant development. In C. H. Zeanah (Ed.), *Handbook of infant mental health* (pp. 73–86). New York: Guilford Press.

Hamer, R. J. (1995). Counselor intentions: A critical review of the literature. *Journal of Counseling and Development, 73*(3), 259–270.

Hammen, C. (1991). Maternal communication: predictors of outcome at follow-up in a sample of children at high and low risk for depression. *Journal of Abnormal Psychology, 100*(2), 174–180.

Hammen, C. (2003). Risk and protective factors for children of depressed parents. In Luthar, S. S. (Ed.), *Resiliency and vulnerability: Adaptation in the context of childhood adversities*. New York: Cambridge University Press.

Hammen, C., Burge, D., Burney, E., & Adrian, G. (1990). Longitudinal study of diagnosis in children of women with unipolar and bipolar affective disorder. *Archives of General Psychiatry, 47,* 1112–1117.

Hammen, C., Shih, J., Altman, M. A. & Brennan, P. A. (2003). Interpersonal impairment and the predictors of depressive symptoms in adolescent children of depressed and nondepressed mothers. *Journal of the American Academy of Child and Adolescent Psychiatry,45*(5), 571–577.

Hammond, J. (1981). *Group counseling for children of divorce: A guide for the elementary school*. Flint, MI: Cranbrook Publishing.

Hansen, J. C., Warner, R. W., & Smith, E. J. (1980). *Group counseling: Theory and practice* (2nd ed.). Chicago: Rand McNally.

Hanson, S. L., Myers, D. E., & Ginsburg, A. L. (1987). The role of responsibility and knowledge in reducing teenage out-of-wedlock childbearing. *Journal of Marriage and the Family, 49,* 241–256.

Harding, K. A. (2002). Prevention efforts: National. In E. R. Giardino (Ed.), *Recognition of child abuse for the mandated reporter* (3rd ed., pp. 393–406). St. Louis, MO: G. W. Medical Publishing, Inc.

Hardoff, D., & Chigier, E. (1991). Developing community-based services for youth with disabilities. *Pediatrician 18*(2), 157–162.

Harrell, E. (June 2005). *Violence of Gang Member, 1993-2003. Crime Data Brief.* Washington, D.C.: U.S. Department of Justice, Office of Justice Programs, Bureau of Justice Statistics.

Harris, M. J., & Rosenthal, R. (1985). Mediation of interpersonal expectancy effects: 31 meta-analyses. *Psychological Bulletin, 97,* 363–386.

Hart, S. L. (1991). Childhood depression: Implications and options for school counselors. *Elementary School Guidance and Counseling, 25,* 277–289.

Harter, S. (1982). The perceived competence scale for children. *Child Development, 53,* 87–97.

Hartley, R., & Goldenson, R. (1963). *The complete book of children's play*. New York: Cromwell.

Hartrup, W. W., & Stevens, N. (1999). Friendships and adaptation across the lifespan. *Current Directions in Psychological Science, 8,* 76–79.

Harvey, S. M., & Spigner, R. (1995). Factors associated with sexual behavior among adolescents: A multivariate analysis. *Adolescence, 30,* 253–264.

Hawkins, J. D., & Catalano, R. F. (1992). *Communities that care: Action for drug abuse prevention*. San Francisco: Jossey-Bass.

Hawkins, J. D., Catalano, R. F., & Miller, J. Y. (1992). Risk and protective factors for alcohol and other drug problems in adolescence and early adulthood:

Implications for substance abuse prevention. *Psychological Bulletin, 112*, 64–105.

Hawkins, J. D., Jenson, J. M., Catalano, R. F., & Wells, E. A. (1991). Effects of a skills training intervention with juvenile delinquents. *Research of Social Work Practice 1*(2), 107–121.

Hawkins, J. D., Lishner, D. M., & Catalano, R. F. (1985). Childhood predictors and the prevention of adolescent substance abuse. In C. L. Jones & T. L. Battjes (Eds.), *Etiology of drug abuse: Implications for Prevention.* Washington, DC: Government Printing Office.

Hawkins, J. D., Lishner, D. M., Catalano, R. F., & Howard, M. O. (1985). Childhood predictors of adolescent substance abuse: Toward an empirically grounded theory. In C. L. Jones & R. J. Battjes (Eds.), *Etiology of drug abuse: Implications for prevention* (pp. 75–126). Washington, DC: U.S. Government Printing Office.

Hawkins, J. D., Lishner, D. M., Catalano, R. F., & Howard, M. O. (1986). Childhood predictors of adolescent substance abuse: Towards an empirically grounded theory. *Journal of Children and Contemporary Society, 8*, 11–47.

Hawton, K. (1986). *Suicide and attempted suicide among children and adolescents.* Beverly Hills, CA: Sage.

Heldenbrand, L., & Hixon, J. E. (1991). Video-assisted training of study skills. *Elementary School Guidance & Counseling, 26*, 121–129.

Henderson, N. (2002). *Resiliency in Action, Inc.* R March 15, 2004 retrieved from http://www.resiliency.com.

Hendricks, L. E. (1988). Outreach with teenage fathers: A preliminary report on three ethnic groups. *Adolescence, 23*(91), 711–720.

Hendricks, L. E., & Montgomery, T. (1983). A limited population of unmarried Black adolescent fathers: A preliminary report of their views on fatherhood and the relationship with the mother of their children. *Adolescence, 18*(69), 201–210.

Hendricks, L. E., & Solomon, A. M. (1987). Reaching Black adolescent parents through nontraditional techniques. *Child and Youth Services, 9*(1), 111–124.

Henkle v. Gregory, 150 F. Supp. 2d 1067.December 1, 2003Henry, B., Feehan, M., McGee, R., Stanton, W., Moffitt, T. E., & Silva, P. (1993). The importance of conduct problems and depressive symptoms in predicting adolescent substance abuse. *Journal of Abnormal Child Psychology, 21*, 469–480.

Herdt, G., & Boxer, A. (1996). *Children on the horizons: How gay and lesbian teens are leading a new way out.* Boston: Beacon Press.

Herman-Giddens, M., Brown, G., Verbiest, S., Carlson, P., Hooten, E., & Butts, J. (1999). Underascertainment of child abuse mortality in the United States. *Journal of the American Medical Association, 282*(5), 463–467.

Herrenkohl, R. C., Egolf, B. P., & Herrenkohl, E. C. (1997). Preschool antecedents of adolescent assaultive behavior: A longitudinal study. *American Journal of Psychiatry, 67*, 422–432.

Herring, R. (1990). Suicide in the middle school: Who said kids will not? *Elementary School Guidance and Counseling, 25*, 129–137.

Hess, R. D. (1981). Approaches to the measurement and interpretation of parent-child interaction. In R. W. Henderson (Ed.), *Parent–child interaction*. New York: Academic Press.

Hetherington. E. M. (1967). The effects of familial variables on sex typing, on parent-child similarity, and on imitation in children. In J. P. Hill (Ed.), *Minnesota Symposium on Child Psychology* (Vol. 1, pp. 88–107). Minneapolis, MN: University of Minnesota Press.

Hetherington, E. M. (1993). An overview of the Virginia Longitudinal Study of Divorce and Remarriage with a focus on early adolescence. *Journal of Family Psychology, 7,* 39–56.

Hetherington, E. M. (1999). Should we stay together for the sake of our children? In E. M. Hetherington (Ed.), *Coping with divorce, single parenting and remarriage: A risk and resiliency perspective* (pp. 93–116). Mahwah, NJ: Erlbaum.

Hetherington, E. M., Bridges, M., & Insabella, G. M. (1998). What matters? What does not? Five perspectives on the association between marital transitions and children's adjustment. *American Psychologist, 53,* 167–184.

Hetherington, E. M., & Clingempeel, W. G. (1992). Coping with marital transitions: A family systems perspectives. *Monographs of the Society for Child Development 57* (2–3, Serial No. 227).

Hetherington, E. M. & Elmore, A. M. (2003). Risk and resiliency in children coping with their parents' divorce and remarriage. In S. S. Luthar (Ed.), *Resilience and vulnerability: Adaptation in the context of childhood adversities.*93–128 New York: Cambridge University Press.

Hetherington, E. M., & Jodl, K. M. (1994). Stepfamilies as settings for child development. In A. Booth & J. Dunn (Eds.). *Stepfamilies: Who benefits? Who does not?* (pp. 55–79). Hillsdale, NJ: Erlbaum.

Hetherington, E. M., & Kelly, J. (2002). *For better or worse: Divorce reconsidered.* New York: Norton.

Hetrick, E. S., & Martin, A. D. (1987). Developmental issues and their resolution for gay and lesbian adolescents. *Journal of Homosexuality, 14,* 25–44.

Hetrick–Martin Institute. (2002). *LGBTQ youth statistics.* Retrieved April 2, 2004, from http://www.hmi.org/Community/LGBTQYouthStatistics/default.aspx.

Hill, C. E. (1989). *Therapist techniques and client outcome: Eight cases of brief psychotherapy.* Newbury Park, CA: Sage.

Hill, C. E., & O'Grady, K. E. (1985). List of therapist intentions illustrated in a case study with therapists of varying theoretical orientations. *Journal of Counseling Psychology, 32*(5), 3–12.

Hinderscheit, L. R., & Reichle, J. (1987). Teaching direct select color encoding to an adolescent with multiple handicaps. *Augmentative Alternative Communication 3*(3), 137–142.

Hipwell, A. E., Goosens, E. C., Melhuish, E. C., & Kuman, R. (2000). Severe maternal psychopathology and infant–mother attachment. *Development and Psychopathology, 12,* 157–175.

Hofferth, S. (1991). Programs for high risk adolescents: What works? *Evaluation and Program Planning, 14,* 3–16.

Hofferth, S. L., & Kahn, B. W. (1987). Premarital sexual activity among U.S. teenage women over the past three decades. *Pediatrics Journal, 83*(3), 11–17.

Hoffner, C., & Badzinski, D. M. (1989). Children's integration of facial and situation cues to emotion. *Child Development, 60,* 411–422.

Hogan, D. P., & Kitagawa, E. M. (1985). The impact of social status, family structure, and neighborhood on the fertility of Black adolescents. *American Journal of Sociology, 90*(4), 825–855.

Holland, A., & Andre, T. (1987). Participation in extracurricular activities in secondary school: What is known, what needs to be known? *Review of Educational Research, 57,* 437–466.

Horizons Foundation national survey of 1000 parents. (2001). San Francisco, CA: Horizons Foundation.

Hostler, S. L., Gressard, R. P., Hassler, C. R., & Linden, P. G. (1989). Adolescent Autonomy Project: Transition skills for adolescents with physical disabilities. *Child Health Care* 18(1), 12–18.

Howell, J. C. (Ed.). (1995a). *Guide for implementing the comprehensive strategy for serious, violent, and chronic juvenile offenders.* Washington, DC: Office of Juvenile Justice and Delinquency Prevention, U.S. Department of Justice.

Howell, J. C. (Ed.). (1995b). *Guide for implementing the comprehensive strategy for serious, violent, and chronic juvenile offenders.* Washington, DC: Office of Juvenile Justice and Delinquency Prevention, U.S. Department of Justice.

Huba, G. J., & Bentler, P. M. (1980). The role of peer and adult models for drug taking at different stages of adolescence. *Journal of Youth and Adolescence, 9,* 449–465.

Hudson, B. L. Social skills training in the probation service. *Issues in Criminal and Legal Psychology 14,* 58–68.

Huey, W. (1983). Reducing adolescent aggression through group assertiveness training. *The School Counselor, 30*(3), 193–203.

Huey, W. (1987). Counseling teenage fathers: The maximizing a life experience (MALE) group. *The School Counselor, 35*(1), 40–47.

Hunter, F. T. (1985). Adolescents' perceptions of discussions with parents and friends. *Developmental Psychology, 21,* 433–440.

Husain, S., & Vandiver, T. (1984). *Suicide in children and adolescents.* New York: Medical and Scientific Books.

Hussong, A. M. & Chassin, L. (1994). The stress-negative affect model of adolescent alcohol use: Disaggregating negative affect. *Journal of Studies of Alcohol, 55,* 707–718.

Inderbitzen-Pisaruk, H., & Foster, S. L. (1990). Adolescent friendships and peer acceptance: Implications for social skills training. *Clinical Psychology Revue, 10,* 425–439.

Inhelder, B., & Piaget, J. (1958). The growth of logical thinking from childhood to adolescence. New York: Basic Books.

Institute of Medicine. (2002). *Reducing suicide.* Washington, DC: The National Academies Press.

Ivey, A. E. (1988). *Intentional interviewing and counseling* (2nd ed.). Pacific Grove, CA: Brooks/Cole.

Jaccard, J., Dittus, P. J., & Gordon, V. V. (1996). Maternal correlates of adolescent sexual. The National Campaign to Prevent Teen Pregnancy: Child trends and contraceptive behavior. *Family Planning Perspectives, 28*(4), 159–165, 185.

James-Traore, T., Magnani, R., Murray, N., Senderowitz, J., Speizer, I., & Stewart, L. (2001). Advancing young adult reproductive health: Actions for the next decade (FOCUS on Young Adults end of program report). Washington, DC: FOCUS on Young Adults.

Jamison, R. N., Lambert, E. W., & McCloud, D. J. (1986). Social skills training with hospitalized adolescents: An evaluative experiment. *Adolescence 21*(81), 55–65.

Jansen, R., Fitzgerald, H. E., Ham, H. P., & Zucker, R. A. (1995). Pathways into risk: Temperament and behavior problems in 3–5 year old sons of alcoholics. *Alcoholism: Clinical and Experimental Research, 19,* 501–509.

Janus, M. D., Burgess, A. W., & McCormack, A. (1987). *Adolescent runaways: Causes and consequences.* Lexington, MA: Lexington Books.

Jemmott, J., Jemmott, L., & Fong, G. (1992). Reductions in HIV risk-associated sexual behaviors among black male adolescents: Effects of an AIDS prevention intervention. *American Journal of Public Health, 83*(3), 372–377.

Jenkins, E. J., & Bell, C. C. (1994). Violence exposure, psychological distress, and high risk behavior among inner-city high school students. In S. Friedman (Ed.), *Anxiety disorders in African-Americans* (pp. 76–88). New York: Springer.

Jens, K. G., & Gordon, B. N. (1991). Understanding risk: Implications for tracking high-risk infants and making early service delivery decisions. *International Journal of Disability, Development and Education, 38*(3), 211–224.

Jessor, R., & Jessor, S. L. (1977). *Problem behavior and psychosocial development: A longitudinal study of youth.* New York: Academic Press.

Jessor, R., VanDenBos, J., Vanderryn, J., Costa, F. M., & Turbin, M. S. (1995). Protective factors in adolescent problem behavior: Moderator effects and developmental changes. *Developmental Psychology 31*(6), 923–933.

Jimerson, S., Carlson, E. A., Rotert, M., Egeland, B., & Sroufe, L. A. (1997). A prospective, longitudinal study of the correlates and consequences of early grade retention. *Journal of School Psychology, 35,* 1, 3–25.

Jimerson, S., Egeland, B., Sroufe, L. A., & Carlson, E. A. (2000). A prospective, longitudinal study of high-school dropouts: Examining multiple predictors across development. *Journal of School Psychology, 38,* 6, 525–549.

Johnson, D. W., & Johnson, F. P. (1991). *Joining together: Group theory and group skills.* Englewood Cliffs, NJ: Prentice-Hall.

Johnson, D. W., & Johnson, R. T. (1995). *Reducing school violence through conflict resolution.* Alexandria, VA: Association for Supervision and Curriculum Development.

Johnson, W. Y., & Wilborn, B. (1991). Group counseling as an intervention in anger expression and depression in older adults. *The Journal of Specialists in Group Work, 16,* 3.

Jones, L. P. (1988). A typology of adolescent runaways. *Child and Adolescent Social Work Journal, 5*(1), 16–29.

Jordan, K. M. (2000). Substance abuse among gay, lesbian, bisexual, transgender, and questioning adolescents. *School Psychology Review, 29*, 201.

Judah, R. D. (1978). Multimodal parent training. *Elementary School Guidance and Counseling, 13*, 46–54.

Kagan, J., & Gall. S. B. (1998). *The Gale encyclopedia of childhood & adolescence.* Detroit, Gale Research.

Kammer, P., & Schmidt, D. (1987). Counseling runaway adolescents. *The School Counselor, 35*(2), 149–154.

Kandel, D. B. (1975). Stages in adolescent involvement in drug use. *Science, 190*, 912–914.

Kann, L., Kinchen, S. A., Williams, B. I., Ross, J. G., Lowry, R., Hill, C. V., Grunbaum, J. A., Blumson, P. S., Collins, I. L., & Kolbe, L. J. (1995.) Youth risk behavior surveillance—United States, 1993. *MMWR, 44*(SS-1), 1–56.

Kashani, J. H., & Simonds, J. F. (1979). The incidence of depression in children. *American Journal of Psychiatry, 136*, 1203–1205.

Kaufman, P., Alt, M. N., & Chapman, C. D. (2000). *Dropout rates in the United States: Statistical analysis report* (Publication no. NCES 2002-114). Washington, DC: U.S. Department of Education, Office of Educational Research and Improvement.

Kaufmann, R. B., Spitz, A. M., Strauss, L. T., Morris, L., Santelli, J. S., Koonin, L. M., & Marks, J. S. (1998). The decline in US teen pregnancy rates, 1990–1995. *Pediatrics, 102*(8), 1141–1147.

Kazdin, A. E., French, N. H., Unis, A. S., Esveldt-Dawson, K., & Sherick, R. B. (1983). Hopelessness, depression and suicidal intent among psychiatrically disturbed inpatient children. *Journal of Consulting and Clinical Psychology, 51*, 504–510.

Keat, D. B. (1976a). Multimodal counseling with children: Treating the BASIC ID. *Pennsylvania Personnel and Guidance Journal, 4*, 21–25.

Keat, D. B. (1976b). Multimodal therapy with children: Two case histories, In A. A. Lazarus (Ed.), *Multimodal behavior therapy* (pp. 22–39). New York: Springer.

Keat, D. B. (1979). *Multimodal therapy with children.* New York: Pergamon Press.

Keat, D. B. (1985). Child-adolescent multimodal therapy: Bud the boss. *Journal of Humanistic Education and Development, 23*, 183–192.

Keat, D. B. (1990). Change in child multimodal counseling. *Elementary School Guidance and Counseling, 24*, 4.

Keat, D. B., Metzgar, K. L., Raykovitz, D., & McDonald, J. (1985). Multimodal counseling: Motivating children to attend school through friendship groups. *Journal of Humanistic Education and Development, 23*, 166–175.

Kehrberg, C. (1997). Self-mutilating behavior. *Journal of Child and Adolescent Psychiatric Nursing, 10*(3), 35–40.

Kelly, J. B. (1983). Mediation and psychotherapy: Distinguishing the differences. In J. A. Lemmon (Ed.), *Dimensions and practice of divorce mediation* (pp. 33–44). San Francisco: Jossey-Bass.

Kelly, J. B., & Wallerstein, J. S. (1976). The effects of parental divorce: Experiences of the child in early latency. *American Journal of Orthopsychiatry, 46,* 20–31.

Kendler, K. S., Gardner, C. O., & Prescott, C. A. (1999). A population-based twin study of lifetime major depression in men and women. *Archives of General Psychiatry, 49,* 257–266.

Kim, L., Sandler, I. N., & Jenn-Yun, T. (1997). Locus of control as stress moderator and mediator in children of divorce. *Journal of Abnormal Child Psychology, 25,* 145–155.

King, K. A. (1999). Fifteen prevalent myths about adolescent suicide. *Journal of School Health, 69,* 159–161.

Kinsman, S. B., Romer, D., Fustenberg, F., & Jackson, M. A. (1987). The LD adolescent at risk: Developmental tasks, social competence, and communication effectiveness. *Journal of Reading Writing and Learning Disabilities International 3*(3), 241–257.

Kinsman, S. B., Romer, D., Fustenberg, F. F., Jr., & Schwarz, D. F. (1998). Early sexual initiation: The role of peer norms. *Pediatrics, 102*(5), 1185–1192.

Kirby, D. (2001). *Emerging answers: Research findings on programs to reduce teen pregnancy.* Washington, DC: National Campaign to Prevent Teen Pregnancy.

Kirby, D., Lezin, N., Afriye, R. A., & Gallucci, G. (2003). *Preventing teen pregnancy: youth development and after-school programs.* Scotts Valley, CA: ETR Associates and New York: YWCA of the USA.

Kiselica, M. S., & Sturmer, P. (1993). Is society giving teenage fathers a mixed message? *Youth & Society, 24,* 4.

Kissman, K. (1991). Parent skills training: Expanding school-based services for adolescent mothers. *Research in Social Work Practice 2*(2), 161–171.

Kivlighan, D. M. (1989). Changes in the counselor intentions and response modes and in client reactions and session evaluations after training. *Journal of Counseling Psychology, 36,* 471–76.

Kivlighan, D. M. (1990). Relation between counselors' use of intentions and clients' perception of working alliance. *Journal of Counseling Psychology, 37,* 27–32.

Kivlighan, D. M., & Angelone, E. O. (1991). Helpee introversion, novice counselor intention use, and helpee-rated session impact. *Journal of Counseling Psychology, 38,* 25–29.

Kliewer, W., Leport, S. J., Oskin, D., & Johnson, P. D. (1998). The role of social and cognitive processes in children's adjustment to community violence. *Journal of Consulting Clinical Psychology, 66,* 199–209.

Klint, K. A., & Weiss, M. R. (1987). Perceived competence and motives for participating in youth sports: A test of Harter's competence motivation theory. *Journal of Sports Psychology, 9,* 55–65.

Kogan, L. (1980). A family systems perspective on status offenders. *Juvenile and Family Court Journal, 31*(2), 49–53.

Kolbe, L. J., Kann, L., & Collins, J. L. (1993). Overview of the youth risk behavior surveillance system. *Public Health Reports, 108,* 2–10.

Kolberg, L. (1976). Moral stages and moralization: The cognitive-developmental approach. In T. Lickona (Ed.), *Moral development and behavior.* New York: Holt, Rinehart & Winston.

Kominski, R., Jamieson, A., & Martinez, G. (2001). *At-risk conditions of U.S. school age children.* Washington, DC: U.S. Bureau of the Census.

Koo, H., Dunteman, G., George, C., Green, Y., & Vincent, M. (1994). Reducing adolescent pregnancy through a school- and community-based intervention: Denmark, South Carolina, revisited. *Family Planning Perspectives, 26*(5), 206–217.

Koss, M. P., Gidycz, C. J., & Wisniewski, N. (1987). The scope of rape: Incidence and prevalence of sexual aggression and victimization in a national sample of higher education students. *Journal of Consulting & Clinical Psychology, 55,* 162–170.

Koss, M. P., & Oros, C. J. (1982). The sexual experiences survey: A research instrument investigating sexual aggression and victimization. *Journal of Consulting & Clinical Psychology, 50,* 455–457.

Kowaleski-Jones, L., & Mott, F. L. (1998). Sex, contraception and child-bearing among high-risk youth: Do different factors influence males and females? *Family Planning Perspectives, 30*(4), 163–169.

Kozicki, Z. A. (1986). Why do adolescents use substances: Drugs/alcohol. *Journal of Alcohol and Drug Education, 32*(1), 34–42.

Krasnegor, N. A. (1988). Adolescent drug use: Suggestions for future research. In E. R. Rahdert & J. Grabowski, (Eds.), *Adolescent drug abuse: Analyses of treatment research.* NIDA Research Monograph Series 77. Rockville, MD.: National Institute on Drug Abuse.

Krasnow, J. (1990). *Building parent teacher partnerships: Prospects from the perspective of the schools reaching out project.* Boston: Institute for Responsive Education.

Kreiss, J. L., & Patterson, D. L. (1997). Psychosocial issues in primary care of lesbian, gay, bisexual, and transgender youth. *Journal of Pediatric Health Care, 11,* 266–274.

Kruks, G. (1991). Gay and lesbian homeless/street youth: Special issues and concerns. *Journal of Adolescent Health, 12,* 516.

Kufeldt, K., & Nimmo, M. (1987). Youth on the street: Abuse and neglect in the 1980s. *Journal of Child Abuse and Neglect, 11*(4), 531–543.

L'Abate, L., & Milan, M. A. (Eds.). (1985). *Handbook of social skills training research.* New York: Wiley.

Ladd, C., Huot, R., Thrivikraman, K. V., Nemeroff, C. B., Meaney, M., & Plotsky, P. (2000). Long-term behavioral and neuroendocrine adaptations to adverse early experience. In E. A. Mayer & C. B. Saper (Eds.), *Progress in brain research* (Vol. 122, pp. 81–103). New York: Elsevier Science.

Ladner, J. A.(1987). Black teenage pregnancy: A challenge for educators. *Journal of Negro Education 56*(1), 53–63.

LaFromboise, T. D., & Bigfoot, D. S. (1988). Cultural and cognitive considerations in prevention of American Indian adolescent suicide. *Journal of Adolescence 11*(2), 139–153.

Lamar, J. V. (1988, May). Kids who sell crack. *Time, 9,* 20–33.

Landau-Stanton, J., & Stanton, M. D. (1985). Treating suicidal adolescents and their families. In M. P. Mirkin & S. L. Koman (Eds.), *Handbook of adolescent and family therapy* (pp. 309–328). New York: Gardner.

Lane, P. S., & McWhirter, J. J. (1992). A peer mediation model: Conflict resolution for elementary and middle school children. *Elementary School Guidance and Counseling, 27*(1), 24–36.

Langbehn, D. R., & Pfohl, B. (1993). Clinical correlates of self-mutilation among psychiatric inpatients. *Annuals of Clinical Psychiatry, 5,* 45–51.

Larson, D. (1984). *Teaching psychological skills: Models for giving psychology away.* Monterey, CA: Brooks/Cole.

Larson, R., & Lampman-Petraitis, C. (1989). Daily emotional states as reported by child and adolescents. *Child Development, 60,* 1250–1260.

Laumann, E. O. (1996). *Early sexual experiences: How voluntary? How violent?* Menlo Park, CA: The Henry J. Kaiser Family Foundation.

Lawton, M. (1994, November 9). Violence prevention curricula: What works best. *Education Week, 14,* 10.

Lawton, M. (1995, October 18). Broad attack urged to meet adolescents' basic needs. *Education Week, 15,* 7.

Lazarus, A. A. (1977). *In the mind's eye: The power of imagery for personal enrichment.* New York: Rawson.

Lazarus, A. A. (1981). *The practice of multimodal therapy.* New York: McGraw-Hill.

Lazarus, A. A. (1989). *The practice of multimodal therapy.* Baltimore, MD: Johns Hopkins University Press.

Lazarus, A. A. (1992a). Multimodal therapy: Technical eclecticism with minimal integration. In J. C. Norcross & M. R. Goldfried (Eds.), *Handbook of psychotherapy integration* (pp. 231–263). New York: Basic.

Lazarus, A. A. (1992b). The multimodal approach to the treatment of minor depression. *American Journal of Psychotherapy, 46,* 50–57.

Lazarus, A. A. (1993). *The practice of multimodal therapy.* Baltimore, MD: Johns Hopkins University Press.

Lazear, K., Roggenbaum, S., & Blase, K. (2003). *Youth suicide prevention school-based Guide—overview* (FMHI Series Publication #218-0). Tampa, FL: University of South Florida.

LeCroy, C. W. (Ed.). (1983). *Social skills training for children and youth.* New York: Haworth Press.

Lehman, M. (1993). HIV/AIDS Surveillance Report, Rockville, MD; Prevention Bulletin 5(1).p 4–6

Lemp, G. F., Hirozawa, A. M., & Givertz, D. (1994). Seroprevalence of HIV and risk behaviors among homosexual and bisexual men: San Francisco/Berkeley young men's survey. *Journal of the American Medical Association, 272,* 449.

Lerman, R. (2002). Wedding bells ring in stability and economic gains for mothers and children. *Child and Youth Services Review, 2*(9–10), 755–780.

Lester, D. (1997). The role of shame in suicide. *Suicide and Life-Threatening Behavior, 27,* 352–361.

Levine, R. S., Metzendorf, D., & Van Boskirk, K. (1986). Runaway and throwaway youth: A case for early intervention with truants. *Social Work in Education,* 8(2), 93–106.

Lewin, P. (1986). The Japanese life-plan and some of its discontents. *Hiroshima Forum for Psychology,* 11, 39–56.

Lewinsohn, P. M., Hops, H., Roberts, R., Seeley, J. R., & Andrew, J. (1993). Adolescent psychopathology: I. Prevalence and incidence of depression and other DSM-III-R disorders of high school students. *Journal of Abnormal Psychology,* 102(4), 183–204.

Lewis, K. D., Bennett, B., & Schmeder, N. H. (1989). The care of infants menaced by cocaine abuse. *American Journal of Maternal Child Nursing,* 14, 324–329.

Lewis, R. A., Piercy, F. P., Spenkle, D. H., & Trepper, T. S. (1990). Family-based interventions for helping drug-abusing adolescents. *Journal of Adolescent Research* 5(1):82–95.

Lewitt, E.M., Baker, L.S., Corman, H., Shiono, P.H. (1995). The direct cost of low birth weight.*Future Child,* 5, 35–56.

Lichstein, K. L., Wagner, M. T., Krisak, J., & Steinberg, F. (1987). Stress management for acting-out, inpatient adolescents. *Journal of Child and Adolescent Psychotherapy* 4(1):19–31.

Lieberman, A. F., Weston, D. R., & Paul, J. H. (1991). Preventive intervention and outcome with anxiously attached dyads. *Child Development,* 62, 199–209.

Linn, M. C., Clement, C., Pulos, S., & Sullivan, P. (1989). Scientific reasoning in adolescence: The influence of instruction in science knowledge and reasoning strategies. *Journal of Research in Science Teaching,* 26(2), 171–187.

Loeb, R. C., Burke, T. A., & Boglarsky, C. (1986). A large-scale comparison of perspectives on parenting between teenage runaways and nonrunaways. *Adolescence,* 21, 84, 921–930.

Losel, F., Bliesener, T., & Koferl, P. (1989). On the concept of invulnerability: Evaluation and first results of the Bielefeld Project. In M. Brambring, F. Lasel, & H. Skowronek (Eds.), *Children and risk: Assessment, longitudinal research, and intervention* (pp. 186–219). New York: Walter de Gruyter.

Lubell K.M., Swahn M.H., Crosby A.E., Kegler S.R. (2004). *Methods of suicide among persons aged 10 to 19 years—United States, 1992-2001.* MMWR, (53)471-473. Available online from: URL: http://www.cdc.gov/mmwr/PDF/wk/mm5322.pdf.

Lumsden, L. S. (1990). *Meeting the needs of drug-affected children* (ERIC Digest Series EA 53). Ann Arbor, MI: ERIC Clearinghouse on Educational Management.

Luthar, S. S. (1991). Vulnerability and resilience: A study of high-risk adolescents. *Child Development,* 62, 600–616.

Luthar, S. S. (Ed.). (2003). *Resilience and vulnerablility: Adaptation in the context of childhood adversities.* New York: Cambridge University Press.

Luthar, S. S., Burack, J. A., Cicchetti, D., & Weisz, J. R. (Eds.). (1997). *Developmental psychopathology: Perspective on adjustment, risk, and disorder.* New York: Cambridge University Press.

Luthar, S. S., & Cicchetti, D. (2000). The construct of resilience: Implications for intervention and social policy. *Development and Psychopathology, 12,* 555–598.

Luthar, S. S., Cicchetti, D., & Becker, B. (2000). The construct of resilience: A critical evaluation and guidelines for future work. Child Development, 71, 543–562.

Luthar, S. S., & Suchman, N. E. (2000). Relationship psychotherapy mothers' group: A developmentally informed intervention for at-risk mothers. *Development and Psychopathology, 12,* 235–253.

Luthar, S. S., & Zigler, E. (1991). Vulnerability and competence: A review of research on resilience in childhood. *American Journal of Orthopsychiatry, 6,* 6–22.

Lynch, M., & Cicchetti, D. (1998). Trauma, mental representation, and the organization of memory for mother-referent material. *Development and Psychopathology, 10,* 739–759.

Lyons, M. J., Eisen, S. A., Goldberg, J., True, W., Lin, N., Meyer, J. M., Toomey, R., Faraone, S. V., Merla-Ramos, M., & Tsuang, M. T. (1998). A registry-based twin study of depression in men. *Archives of General Psychiatry, 55,* 468–472.

Lyons-Ruth, K., Connell, D. B., Grunebaum, H. U., & Botein, L. (1990). Infants at social risk: Maternal depression and family support services as mediators of infant developments and security of attachment. *Child Development, 61,* 85–98.

Maccoby, E. E. (1988). Gender as a social category. *Development Psychology, 24,* 755–765.

Maccoby, E. E., & Jacklin, C. N. (1987). Gender segregation in childhood. In E. H. Reese (Ed.), *Advances in child development and behavior* (Vol. 20, pp. 239–287). New York: Academic Press.

MacGillivray, I. K. (2004). *Sexual orientation and school policy: A practical guide for teachers, administrators, and community activists.* New York: Bowman & Littlefield.

Madge, N., & Tizard, J. (1981). Intelligence. In M. Rutter (Ed.), *Developmental psychiatry* (pp. 245–265). Baltimore: University Park.

Maeroff, G. I. (1996, March 6). Apathy and anonymity: Combating the twin scourges of modern post-adolescence. *Education Week, 15,* 24.

Magg, J. W., Rutherford, R. B., Jr., & Parks, B. T. (1988). Secondary school professionals' ability to identify depression in adolescents. *Adolescence, 23,* 73–82.

Magid, K., & McKelvey, C. A. (1987). *High risk: Children without a conscience.* New York: Bantam Books.

Main, D. S., Iverson, D. C., McGloin, J., Banspach, S., Collins, J., Rugg, D., & Kolbe, L. (1994). Preventing HIV infection among adolescents: Evaluation of a school-based education program. *Preventive Medicine, 23,* 409–417.

Malett, S. D. (1983). Description and subject evaluation of an objectively successful study improvement program. *The Personnel and Guidance Journal, 61*(16), 341–345.

Mallon, G. P. (1998). *We don't exactly get the welcome wagon: The experiences of gay and lesbian adolescents in child welfare systems.* New York: Columbia University Press.

Manlove, J., Ryan, S., & Franzetta, K. (2003). Contraceptive use patterns within teens' first sexual relationships. *Perspectives on Sexual and Reproductive Health, 35,* 246–255.

Manlove, J., Terry, E., Gitelson, L., Papillo, A. R., & Russell, S. (2000). Explaining demographic trends in teenage fertility, 1980–1995. *Family Planning Perspectives, 32*(4), 166–175.

Manning, W. D., Longmore, M. A., & Giordano, P. C. (2000). The relationship context of contraceptive use at first intercourse. *Family Planning Perspectives, 32*(3), 104–110.

Maracek, J. (1987). Counseling adolescents with problem pregnancies. *American Psychologist, 42*(1), 89–93.

Margolis, H., & Brannigan, G. G. (1986). Building trust with parents. *Academic Therapy, 22,* 71–74.

Marsiglio, W. (1993). Attitudes toward homosexual activity and gays as friends: National survey of heterosexual 15-to-19-year-old males, *Journal of Sex Research, 30*(1), 12–17.

Martin, A. D., & Hetrick, E. S. (1987). Designing an AIDS risk reduction program for gay teenagers: Problems and proposed solutions. In D. Ostrow (Ed.), *Biobehavioral control of AIDS.* New York: Irvington Publishers.

Martin, C. L. (1989). Children's use of gender-related information in making social judgments. *Developmental Psychology, 25,* 80–88.

Martin, J. A., & Hamilton, B. E. (2002). Births: final data for 2001. *National Vital Statistics Reports, 51*(2), 1–102.

Martin, J. A., Hamilton, B. E., Ventura, S. J., Menacker, F., & Park, M. M. (2003). Births: final data for 2002. *National Vital Statistics Reports, 52*(10): 1–113.

Martin, L. C. (1992). *A life without fear: A guide to preventing sexual assault.* Nashville, TN: Rutledge Hill.

Martin, M., Martin, D., & Porter, J. (1983). Bibliotherapy: Children of divorce. *The School Counselor, 30,* 312–314.

Martin, S. H. (1988). *Healing for adult children of alcoholics.*, Nashville, TN: Broadman Press.

Martin-Causey, T., & Hinkle, J. S., (1995). Multimodal therapy with an aggressive adolescent: A demonstration of effectiveness and accountability. *Journal of Counseling & Development, 73*(3), 305–310.

Marton, P., Golombek, H., Stein, B., & Korenblum, M. (1988). The relation of personality functions and adaptive skills to self-esteem in early adolescence. *Journal of Youth and Adolescence. 17,* 393–401.

Massachusetts Governor's Commission on Gay and Lesbian Youth. (1993). *Making schools safe for gay and lesbian youth: Report of the Massachusetts Governor's Commission on Gay and Lesbian Youth.* Author.

Massachusetts Governor's Commission on Gay and Lesbian Youth. (1999). *Massachusetts High School Students and Sexual Orientation Youth Risk Behavior Survey.* Retrieved from http://www.state.ma.us/gcgly.

Masten, A. S. (1994). Resilience in individual development: Successful adaptation despite risk and adversity. In M. Wang & E. Gordon (Eds.), *Risk and resilience in inner city America: Challenges and prospects* (pp. 3–25). Hillsdale, NJ: Erlbaum.

Masten, A. S. (2001). Ordinary magic: Resilience processes in development. *American Psychologist, 56,* 227–238.

Masten, A. S., Best, K. M., & Garmezy, N. (1990). Resilience and development: Contributions form the study of children who overcome adversity. *Development and Psychopathology, 2,* 425–444.

Masten, A. S., & Coatsworth, J. D. (1993). Competence, resilience, and psychopathology. In D. Cicchetti & D. Cohen (Eds.), *Developmental psychopathology* (Vol. 2: Risk disorder and adaptation, pp. 715–752). New York: Wiley.

Masten, A. S., & Coatsworth, J. D. (1998). The development of competence in favorable and unfavorable environments: Lessons from research on successful children. *American Psychologist, 53,* 205–220.

Masten, A. S., & Curtis, W. J. (2000). Integrating competence and psychopathology: Pathways toward a comprehensive science of adaptation in development. *Development and Psychopathology, 12,* 529–550.

Masten, A. S., Garmezy, N., Tellegen, A., Pellegrini, D. S., Larkin, K., & Larsen, A. (1988). Competence and stress in school children: The moderating effects of individual and family qualities. *Journal of Child Psychology and Psychiatry, 29*(6), 745–764.

Masten, A. S., Hubbard, J. J., Gest, S. D., Tellegen, A., Garmezy, N., & Ramirez, M. (1999). Competence in the context of adversity: Pathways to resilience and maladaptation from childhood to late adolescence. *Development and Psychopathology, 11,* 143–169.

Masten, A. S., & Wright, M. O. (1997). Cumulative risk and protection models of child maltreatment. In B. B. R. Rossman & M. S. Rosenberg (Eds.), *Multiple victimization of children: Conceptual development, research and treatment issues.* Binghamton, NY: Haworth Press.

Matthews, D. B. (1986). *A comparison of relaxation strategies* (ERIC Document Reproduction Service No. ED 283 095). Orangeburg, SC: South Carolina State College.

Mauldon, J., & Luker, K. (1996). The effects of contraceptive education on method use at first intercourse. *Family Planning Perspectives, 28*(1), 19–24.

Maynard, R. A. (Ed.). (1996). *Kids having kids. A Robin Hood Foundation special report on the cost of adolescent childbearing.* New York: Robin Hood Foundation.

Maynard, R. A. (Ed). (1997). *Kids having kids: Economic costs and social consequences of teen pregnancy.* Washington, DC: Urban Institute.

Mays, V. M., & Cochran, S. D. (2001). Mental health correlates of perceived discrimination among lesbian, gay, and bisexual adults in the United States. *American Journal of Public Health, 91,* 1869–1876.

McAuley, E., Duncan, T. E., & McElroy, M. (1989). Self-efficacy cognitions and causal attributions for children's motor performance: An exploratory investigation. *Journal of Genetic Psychology, 150,* 65–73.

McCann, I. L., Sakheim, D. K., & Abrahamson, D. J. (1988). Trauma and victimization: A model of psychological adaptation. *The Counseling Psychologist, 16*, 531–595.

McConville, B. J., & Bruce, R. T. (1985). Depressive illnesses in children and adolescents: A review of current concepts. *Canadian Journal of Psychiatry, 30*, 119–129.

McCormack, A., Burgess, A. W., & Hartman, C. (1988). Familial abuse & posttraumatic stress disorder. *Journal of Traumatic Stress, 1*(2), 231–242.

McGee, R. A., Wolfe, D. A., & Wilson, S. K. (1997). Multiple maltreatment experiences and adolescent behavior problems: Adolescents' perspectives. *Development and Psychopathology, 9*, 131–149.

McGuffin, P., Katz, R., Watkins, S., & Rutherford, J. (1996). A hospital-based twin register of the heritability of DSM-IV unipolar depression. *Archives of General Psychiatry, 53*(2), 169–179.

McGuffin, P., Katz, R., Watkins, S., & Rutherford, J. (1996). A hospital-based twin register of the heritability of DSM-IV unipolar depression. *Archives of General Psychiatry, 53*, 129–136.

McIntosh, G., & Moreno, M. (2000). Fatal injuries in adolescents. *Wisconsin Medical Journal 99*, 9.

McKinlay, B., & Bloch, D. P. (1989). Career information motivates at risk youth. *Oregon School Study Council, 31*(5).

McLanahan, S. (1999). Father absence and the welfare of children. In E. M. Hetherington (Ed.), *Coping with divorce, single parenting and remarriage: A risk and resiliency perspective* (pp. 117–146). Mahwah, NJ: Erlbaum.

McLaughlin, M., Irby, M., & Langman, J. (1994). *Urban sanctuaries: Neighborhood organizations in the lives and futures of inner-city youth.* San Francisco: Jossey-Bass.

McLean, P. D. (1976). Depression as a specific response to stress. In C. D. Spielberger & I. Sarason (Eds.), *Stress and anxiety in modern life* (Vol. 3). New York: Wiley.

McLeod, J. D., & Shanahan, M. J. (1993). Poverty, parenting, and children's mental health. *American Sociological Review, 58*, 351–366.

McLoyd, V. C. (1990). The impact of economic hardship on black families and children: Psychological distress, parenting and socioeconomic development. *Child Development, 61*, 311–346.

McLoyd, V. C. (1998). Socioeconomic disadvantage and child development. *American Psychologist, 53*(2), 185–204.

McMullin, R. (1986). *Handbook of cognitive therapy techniques.* New York: Norton Press.

McWhirter, J. J., McWhirter, B. T., McWhirter, A. M., & McWhirter, E. H. (1994). High- and low-risk characteristics of youth: The five Cs of competency. *Elementary School Guidance and Counseling, 28*(3), 188–196.

McWhirter, J. J., McWhirter, B. T., McWhirter, E. H., & McWhirter, R. J. (2004). *At-risk youth: A comprehensive response* (3rd ed.). Pacific Grove, CA: Brooks/Cole.

Merritt, R., & Walley, F. (1977). *The group leader's handbook: Resources, techniques, and survival skills.* Champaign, IL: Research Press.

Messing, J. K. (1993). Mediation: An intervention strategy for counselors. *Journal of Counseling & Development, 72*(1), 67–72.

Meyer, I. H. (2003). Prejudice, social stress, and mental health in lesbian, gay and bisexual population: Conceptual issues and research evidence. *Psychological Bulletin, 129*(5), 674–697.

Meichenbaum, D., & Cameron, R. (1974). The clinical potential of modifying what clients say about themselves. In M. J. Mahoney & C. E. Thompson (Eds.), *Self-control: Power to the person.* Monterey, CA: Brooks/Cole.

Miller, B. C. (1998). *Families matter: A research synthesis of family influences on adolescent pregnancy.* Washington, DC: The National Campaign to Prevent Teenage Pregnancy.

Miller, K. E., Sabo, D. F., Farrell, M., Barnes, G., & Melnick, M. (1998). Athletic participation and sexual behavior in adolescents: The different worlds of boys and girls. *Journal of Health & Social Behavior 39*(2), 108–123.

Miller, L. S., Wasserman, G. A., Neugebauer, R., Gorman-Smith, D., & Kamboukos, D. (1999). Witnessed community violence and anti-social behavior in high-risk-urban boys. *Journal of Clinical Psychology, 28,* 2–11.

Miller, S. A. (1981). *Identifying characteristics of truant students.* Unpublished doctoral dissertation, Lehigh University, Bethlehem, PA.

Millman, R. B., & Botvin, G. J. (1983). Substance use, abuse and dependence. In M. D. Levin, W. B. Carey, A. C. Crocker, & R. T. Gross (Eds.), *Developmental behavioral pediatrics* (pp. 683–708). Philadelphia: W. B. Saunders.

Mischel, W., Shoda, Y., & Rodriguez, M. L. (1989). Delay of gratification in children. *Science, 244,* 933–938.

Mittl, V. F., & Robin, A. (1987). Acceptability of alternative interventions for parent-adolescent conflict. *Behavior Assessment 9,* 417–428.

Moffitt, T. E. (1997). Adolescent-limited and life-course-persistent offending: A complementary pair of developmental theories. In T. Thornberry (Ed.), *Developmental theories of crime and delinquency* (pp. 11–55). New Brunswick, NJ: Transaction.

Moments in America for children. (2004, August). Washington, DC: Children's Defense Fund.

Moore, K. A, Nord, C. W., & Peterson, J. L. (1989). Nonvoluntary sexual activity among adolescents. *Family Planning Perspectives, 21*(3), 110–114.

Morgan, O. J. (1982). *Runaways: Jurisdiction, dynamics, and treatment. Journal of Marital and Family Therapy, 8*(1), 121–127.

Morrison, L. L. & L'Heureux, J. (2001). Suicide and gay/lesbian/bisexual youth: Implications for clinicians. *Journal of Adolescence, 24,* 34–49.

Morse, L. A. (1987). Working with young procrastinators: Elementary school students who do not complete school assignments. *Elementary School Guidance & Counseling, 21,* 221–228.

Mosak, H. H. (1984). Adlerian psychotherapy. In R. Corsini (Ed.), *Current psychotherapies.* Itasca, IL: F. E. Peacock Publishers.

Mott, F. L., Fondell, M. M., Hu, P. N., Kowaleski-Jones, L., & Menaghan, E. G. (1996). The determinants of first sex by age 14 in a high-risk adolescent population. *Family Planning Perspectives, 28*(1), 13–18.

Mrazek, P., & Mrazek, D. (1987). Resilience in child maltreatment victims: A conceptual exploration. *Child Abuse and Neglect, 11,* 357–366.

Murray, L., Fioru-Cowley, A., Hooper, R., & Cooper, P. (1996). The impact of postnatal depression and associated adversity on early mother-infant interactions and later outcomes. *Child Development, 67,* 2512–2526.

Murray, L., Hipwell, A., Hooper, R., & Stein, A. (1996). The cognitive development of 5-year-old children of postnatally depressed mothers. *Journal of Child Psychology and Psychiatry and Allied Disciplines, 37,* 927–935.

Myrick, R. (1987). *Developmental guidance and counseling: A practical approach.* Minneapolis: Educational Media Corporation.

Nabozny v. Podlesny, July 31, 1996, 92 F.3d4666 (W.D.Wisc).

Nansel, T. R., Overpeck, M., Pilla, R. S., Ruan, W. J., Simons-Morton, B., & Scheidt, P. (2001). Bullying behaviors among U.S. youth: Prevalence and association with psychosocial adjustment. *Journal of the American Medical Association, 285*(16), 2094–2100.

National Association of School Psychologists (2004). Position statement on sexually minority youth (formerly gay, lesbian and bisexual youth). Bethesda, MD: Author. Retrieved from http://www.nasponline.org/information/pospaper_glb.html

National Campaign to Prevent Teen Pregnancy. (2003). *Where and when teens have sex.* Washington, DC: Author. Retrieved from http://www.teenpregnancy.org/works.

National Center for Education Statistics (NCES). (1995). *Two years later: Cognitive gains and school transitions of NELS: 88 Jeighth graders.* Washington, DC: Author.

National Center for Education Statistics (NCES). (1998). *Violence and discipline problems in U.S. public schools: 1996–97.* Washington, DC: U.S. Department of Education.

National Center for Education Statistics (NCES). (1999, November). *Dropout rates in the United States: 1998.* Washington, DC: U.S. Department of Education, Office of Educational Research and Improvement.

National Center on Addiction and Substance Abuse at Columbia University. (1999). *Back to school—National survey of American attitudes on substance abuse V: Teens and their parents.* New York: Author.

National Child Abuse and Neglect Data System (NCANDS). (2004). *Child maltreatment 2002.* Washington, DC: U.S. Government Printing Office.

National Dropout Prevention Network. (2000). *Dropout statistics,* Internet posting. Washington, DC: National Dropout Prevention Network. National Institute on Drug Abuse (1988). Research Monograph No. 77. NIH Pub. No. 94-37 12. Washington, DC: Superintendent of Documents, U.S. Government. Printing Office.

National Education Association, Educational Policies Commission. (1938). *The purpose of education in American democracy.* Washington, DC: Author.

National Education Association, Educational Policies Commission. (1952). *The for all American youth: A further look.* Washington, DC: Author.

National Gay and Lesbian Task Force (1984). National anti-gay/lesbian victimization report.

National Governors Association Center for Best Practices. *Best practices.* Washington, DC: Author.

National Institute on Alcohol Abuse and Alcoholism. (1990). *Eighth special report to the U.S. Congress on alcohol and health.* Washington, DC: U.S. Government Printing Office.

National Research Council Panel on Research on Child Abuse and Neglect (1993). *Understanding child abuse and neglect.* Washington, DC: National Academy.

National School Safety Center. (1998). Checklist of characteristics of youth who have caused school-associated violent deaths. In *School-associated violent deaths report.* Westlake Village, CA: Author.

National Threat Assessment Center, U.S. Secret Service. (2000). *Secret Service Safe Schools Research Initiative.* Washington, DC: Author.

Nattiv, A., Render, G., Lemire, D., & Render, K. (1990). Conflict resolution and interpersonal skill building through the use of cooperative learning. In E. Gerler, C. Hogan, & K. O'Rourke (Eds.), *The challenge of counseling in the middle school.* Ann Arbor, MI: ERIC.

Neimark, E. D. (1975). Longitudinal development of formal operational thought. *Genetic Psychology Monographs, 91,* 171–225.

Neimark, E. D. (1982). Adolescent thought: Transition to formal operations. In B. B. Wolman (Ed.), *Handbook of development psychology* (pp. 486–499). Englewood Cliffs, NJ: Prentice-Hall.

Nelson, R., & Crawford, B. (1990). Suicide among elementary school-aged children. *Elementary School Guidance and Counseling, 25,* 123–128.

Newcomb, M. D., & Bentler, P. M. (1989). *Substance use and abuse among children and teenagers.* Washington, DC: American Psychological Association.

Newcomb, M. D., & Bentler, P. M. (1990). Consequences of adolescent drug use: Impact on the lives of young adults. *Journal of Substance Abuse Treatment, 7*(2), 134–135.

Newcomb, M. D., Bentler, P. M., & Collins, C. (1986). Alcohol use and dissatisfaction with self and life: A longitudinal analysis of young adults. *The Journal of Drug Issues, 16,* 4.

Newcomb, M. D., & Felix-Ortiz, M. (1992). Multiple protective and risk factors for drug use and abuse: Cross-sectional and prospective findings. *Journal of Personality and Social Psychology, 63,* 280–296.

Newcomber, S., & Udry, J. R. (1987). Parental marital status effects on adolescent sexual behavior. *Journal of Marriage and Family, 49,* 235–240.

Nichols, P. (2000). Bad body fever and deliberate self-injury. *Reclaiming Children and Youth, 9,* 151.

Nielsen, A., & Gerber, D. (1979). Psychological aspects of truancy in early adolescence. *Adolescence, 14*(54), 313–326.

Noble, P. S., Adams, G. R., & Openshaw, D. K. (1989). Interpersonal communication in parent-adolescent dyads: A brief report on the effects of a social skills training program. *Journal of Family Psychology 2*(4), 483–494.

Novaco, R. W. (1975). *Anger control: The development and evaluation of an experimental treatment.* Lexington, MA: Lexington Books.

O'Neil, J. (1991, January). Civic education. *ASCD Curriculum Update, 21*, 18–24.

O'Toole, M. E. (2000). *The school shooter: A threat assessment perspective.* Quantico, VA: Federal Bureau of Investigation.

Oden, S. (1987). Alternative perspectives in children's peer relationships, In T. D. Yawkey & J. E. Johnson (Eds.), *Integrative processes and socialization: Early to middle childhood* (pp.112–213). Elmford, NJ: Erlbaum.

Ohlsen, M. M. (1977). *Group counseling.* New York: Holt, Rinehart, Winston

O'Keefe, E. J., & Castaldo, C. (1980). A multimodal approach to treatment in a child care agency. *Psychological Reports, 4*, 250.

Olds, D. L., Eckenrode, J., Henderson, C. R., Kitzman, H., Powers, J., Cole, R., Sidora, K., Morris, P., Pettitt, L. M., & Luckey, D. (1997). Long-term effects of home visitation on maternal life course and child abuse and neglect: Fifteen-year follow-up of a randomized trial. *Journal of the American Medical Association, 278*(8), 637–743.

Olds, D. L., & Kizman, H. (1993). Review of research on home visiting for pregnant women and parents of young children. *The Future of Children, 3*, 53–92.

Olson, L. (1989, February 22). Governors say investment in children can curb long-term costs for states. *Education Week, 10*, 130.

Olweus, D. (2003). A profile of bullying at school. *Educational Leadership, 60, 6*, 12–17.

Omizo, M. M. (1981). Relaxation training and biofeedback with hyperactive elementary school children. *Elementary School Guidance & Counseling, 15*, 329–332.

Omizo, M. M., & Omizo, S. A. (1988). The effects of participation in group counseling sessions on self-esteem an locus of control among adolescents from divorced families. *The School Counselor, 36*(1), 54–58.

Orr, M. T. (1987). *Keeping kids in school: A guide to effective dropout prevention programs and services.* San Francisco: Jossey-Bass.

Osofsky, J. D. (1995). The effects of exposure to violence on young children. *American Psychologist, 50*, 782–788.

Osofsky, J. D., & Thompson, M. D. (2000). Adaptive and maladaptive parenting: Perspectives on risk and protective factors. In J. P. Shonkoff & S. J. Meisals (Eds.), *Handbook of early childhood intervention* (pp. 54–75). Cambridge: Cambridge University Press

Ostrov, E., Offer, D., & Howard, K. I. (1989). Gender differences in adolescent symptomatology: A normative study. *Journal of the American Academy of Child and Adolescent Psychiatry, 28*, 394–398.

Oswald, L. K., Lingnugaris-Kraft, B., & West, R. (1990). The effects of incidental teaching on the generalized use of social amenities at school by a mildly handicapped adolescent. *Educational Treatment of Children, 13*(2), 142–152.

Owens, D., Horrocks, J., House, A. (2002). Fatal and non-fatal repetition of self-harm: Systematic review. *British Journal of Psychiatry, 181,* 193–199.

Pallone, N. J., & Hennessy, J. J. (1996). *Tinder-box criminal aggression: Neuropsychology, demography, and phenomenology.* New Brunswick, NJ: Transaction.

Panchaud, C., Singh, S., Feivelson, D., & Darroch, J. E. (2000). Sexually transmitted diseases among adolescents in developed countries. *Family Planning Perspectives, 32,1,24–32.*

Papagno, N. (1983). *A single model counseling group across all special needs children.* Paper presented at the American Psychological Association Annual Meeting, Anaheim, CA.

Parker, J. G., & Asher, S. R. (1993). Friendship and friendship quality in middle childhood: Links with peer group acceptance and feelings of loneliness and social dissatisfaction. *Developmental Psychology, 29,* 611–621.

Parsons, J. E., Ruble, D. N., Hodges, K. L., & Small, A. W. (1976). Cognitive–developmental factors in emerging sex differences in achievement-related expectancies. *Journal of Social Issues, 32,* 47–61.

Patterson, C. J. (1995). Lesbian mothers, gay fathers, and their children. In A. R. D'Augelli & C. J. Patterson (Eds.), *Lesbian, gay and bisexual identities over the lifespan: Psychological perspectives* (pp. 262–267). New York: Oxford University Press.

Patterson, C. J. (2000a). Family relationships of lesbian and gay men. *Journal of Marriage and Family, 62,* 1052–1069.

Patterson, C. J. (2000b). Lesbian and gay parents and their children: Summary of research findings. In *Lesbian and gay parenting: A resource for psychologists 176–199.* Washington, DC: American Psychological Association.

Patterson, C. J., Fulcher, M., & Wainwright, J. (2002). Children of lesbian and gay parents: Research, law, and policy. In B. L. Bottoms, M. B. Kovera, & B. D. McAuliff (Eds.), *Children, social science and the law* (pp. 176–199). New York: Cambridge University Press.

Patterson, G. R. (1982). *Coercive family processes.* Eugene, OR: Castalia.

Patterson, J. M., McCubbin, H., & Neede, R. H. (1983). *A-cope: Adolescent-coping orientation for problem experiences.* Madison, WI: University of Wisconsin.

Peddke, N., Wang, C. T., Diaz, J., & Reid, R. (2002). *Current trends in child abuse prevention and fatalities: The 2000 fifty-state survey.* Chicago, IL: National Center on Child Abuse Prevention Research.

Pedro-Carroll, J. (1991). *Children of divorce intervention program.* Annual Lela Rowland Award in Prevention, National Mental Health Association, Alexandria, VA.

Pellegrini, D. S. (1984). Social cognition and competence in middle childhood. *Child Development, 56,* 253–264.

Pellegrini, D. S., Masten, A. S., Garmezy, N., & Ferrarese, M. J. (1987). Correlates of social and academic competence in middle childhood. *Journal of Child Psychology and Psychiatry and Allied Disciplines, 23*(5), 699–714.

Pepitone, E. A., Loeb, H. W., & Murdock, E. M. (1977). *Social comparison and similarity of children's performance in competitive situations.* Paper presented at the annual convention of the American Psychological Association, San Francisco.

Perkins, D. N. (1986). *Knowledge by design*. Hillsdale, NJ: Erlbaum.

Perrin, E. C. (1996). Pediatricians and gay and lesbian youth. *Pediatric Review, 17*, 311–318.

Perrin, E. C. (2002). *Sexual orientation in child and adolescent health care*. New York: Kluwer Academic/Plenum Publishers.

Perrin, E. C., & The Committee on Psychosocial Aspects of Child and Family Health. (2002). Technical reports: Coparent or second-parent adoption by same-sex parents. *Pediatrics, 109*, 341–344.

Perrone, P. A. (1987). Counselor response to adolescent suicide. *The School Counselor, 35*(1), 12–16.

Perry, B. D. (1997). Incubated in terror: Neurodevelopmental factors in the "cycle of violence." In J. D. Osofsky (Ed.), *Children in a violent society* (pp. 124–149). New York: Guilford Press.

Perry, B. D., & Pate, J. E. (1994). Neurodevelopment and psychological roots of post-traumatic stress disorders. In L. F. Koziol & C. E. Stout (Eds.), *The neuropsychology of mental illness: A practical guide* (pp.129–147). Springfield, IL: Charles C. Thomas.

Perry, B. D., Pollard, R., Blakley, T., Baker, W., & Vigilante, D. (1995). Childhood trauma, the neurobiology of adaptation and "use-dependent" development of the brain: How "states" become "traits." *Infant Mental Health Journal, 16*, 271–291.

Peters, D., & Peters, S. (1984). *Why knock rock?* Minneapolis, MI: Bethany House Publishers.

Peterson, A. C., Schulenberg, J. E., Abramowitz, R. H., Offer, D., & Jarcho, H. D. (1984). A self-image questionnaire for young adolescents (SEQYA): Reliability and validity studies. *Journal of Youth and Adolescence, 13*, 93–111.

Peterson, S., & Straub, R. (1992). *School crisis survival guide*. West Nyack, NY: Center for Applied Research in Education.

Pfeiffer, C. R. (1982). Interventions for suicidal children and their parents. *Suicide and Life Threatening Behavior, 12*, 240–248.

Pfeiffer, C. R. (1986). *The suicidal child*. New York: Guilford.

Philliber, S., & Allen, J. P. (1992). Life options and community service: Teen Outreach Program. In B. C. Miller, J. J. Card, R. L. Paikoff, & J. L. Peterson (Eds.), *Preventing adolescent pregnancy: Model programs and evaluations* (pp.139–155). Newbury Park, CA: Sage.

Piaget, J. (1932). *The moral judgment of the child*. Glencoe, IL: Free Press.

Piaget, J. (1948). *The moral judgment of the child*. Glencoe, IL: Free Press.

Piaget, J. (1970). Piaget's theory. In P. H. Mussen (Ed.), *Carmichaels's manual of child psychology* (3rd ed., Vol.1, pp. 345–365). New York: Wiley.

Piaget, J. (1972). Intellectual evolution from adolescence to adulthood. *Human Development, 15*, 1–12.

Piaget, J., & Inhelder, B. (1969). *The psychology of the child*. New York: Basic Books.

Pietropinto, A. (1985). Runaway children. *Medical Aspects of Human Sexuality, 19*, 8, 175–189.

Pirog-Good, M. A. (1995). The family background and attitudes of teen fathers. *Youth and Society, 26*, 351–376.

Plotsky, P. M., Owens, M. J., & Nemeroff, C. B. (1998). Psychoneuroendocrinology of depression. *Psychoneuroendocrinology, 21,* 293–307.

Poland, S., & Lieberman, R. (2003). Questions and answers: Suicide intervention in the schools. *National Association of School Psychologists Communiqué, 31,* 7.

Pollitt, E. (1994). Poverty and child development: Relevance of research in developing countries to the United States. *Child Development, 65,* 2, 283–295.

Portes, P. R., Sandhu, D. S., & Longwell-Grice, R. (2002). Understanding adolescent suicide: A psychosocial interpretation of developmental and contextual factors. *Adolescence, 37,* 805–814.

Portner, J. (1995, September 20). Report on juvenile crime brings calls for new policies. *Education Week, 15,* 3.

Positive Youth Development in the United States: Research Findings on Evaluations of Positive Youth Development Programs. (1999). Seattle, WA: University of Washington.

Postrado, L. T., & Nicholson, H. J. (1992). Effectiveness in delaying the initiation of sexual intercourse of girls aged 12–14: Two components of the Girls Incorporated Preventing Adolescent Pregnancy Program. *Youth & Society, 23*(3), 356–379.

Powell, L., & Faherty, S. (1990). Treating sexually abused latency aged girls. *The Arts in Psychotherapy, 17,* 35–47.

Presseisen, B. Z. (Ed.). (1988). *At-risk students and thinking: Perspectives from research.* Washington, DC: National Education Association and Philadelphia, PA: Research for Better Schools.

Pressley, M., & Levin, J. (1987). Elaborating learning strategies for the inefficient learner. In S. J. Ceci (Ed.), *Handbook of cognitive, social and neuropsychological aspects of learning disabilities* (pp. 36–52). Hillsdale, NJ: Erlbaum.

Prevention Update. (1997, April). Prevention update. *A newsletter of child abuse prevention services for St. Mary's Infant Home, Norfolk, VA, 1*(1).

Price, J. H. & Telljohann, S. K. (1991). School counselors' perceptions of adolescent homosexuals. *Journal of School Health, 61*(10) 433–438.

Prothrow-Stith, D. (1991). *Deadly consequences.* New York: HarperCollins.

Prothrow-Stith, D. (1993). *Violence prevention: A curriculum for adolescents.* Newton, MA: Education Development Center.

Pulkinnen, L., & Pitkanen, T. (1994). A prospective study of the precursors to problem drinking in young adults. *Journal of Studies on Alcohol, 55,* 578–587.

Putallaz, M. (1983). Predicting children's sociometric status from their behavior. *Child Development, 54,* 1417–1426.

Pynoos, R., & Eth, S. (1985). Children traumatized by witnessing acts of personal violence: Homicide, rape, or suicide behavior. In S. Eth & R. Pynoos (Eds.), *Post-traumatic stress disorder in children* (pp. 17–43). Washington, DC: American Psychiatric Press.

Pynoos, R., & Nader, K. (1988). Psychological first aid and treatment approaches to children exposed to community violence: Research implications. *Journal of Traumatic Stress, 1,* 445–473.

Pynoos, R. S. (1993). Traumatic stress and developmental psychopathology in children and adolescents. In J. M. Oldham, M. B. Riba, & A. Tasman (Eds.), *Review of psychiatry, 12* (pp. 205–237). Washington, DC: American Psychiatric Press.

Rae-Grant, N., Thomas, H., Offord, D., & Boyle, J. (1989). Risk, protective factors, and the prevalence of behavioral and emotional disorders in children and adolescents. *American Academy of Children and Adolescents, 18,* 262–268.

Raffaelli, M., & Duckett, E. (1989). We were just talking…Conversations in early adolescence. *Journal of Youth and Adolescence, 18,* 567–582.

Raikkonen, K., Matthews, K. A., & Salomon, K. (2003). Hostility predicts metabolic syndrome risk factors in children and adolescents. *Health Psychology, 22*(3), 279–286.

Rak, C. F., & Patterson, L. E. (1996). Promoting resilience in at-risk children. *Journal of Counseling & Development, 74*(4), 368–373.

Raspberry, W. (1994, February 19). Editorial. *The Virginian-Pilot & Ledger-Star,* C24.

Rathvon, N. W. (1990). The effects of encouragement on off-task behaviors and academic productivity. *Elementary School Guidance & Counseling, 24,* 189–199.

Redican, K. J., Redican, B. L., & Baffi, C. R. (1988). Drug use, misuse, and abuse as presented in movies. *Health Education, 19,* 6.

Reiss, A., & Roth, J. (Eds.). (1993). *Understanding and preventing violence.* Washington, DC: National Academy Press.

Remafedi, G. (1987a). Adolescent homosexuality: Psychosocial and medical implications. *Pediatrics 79,* 331–337.

Remafedi, G. (1987b). Male homosexuality: The adolescent's perspective. *Pediatrics, 79,* 326–330.

Remafedi, G. (1990). Fundamental issues in the care of homosexual youth. *Medical Clinics of North America, 74,* 5 1169–1179.

Remafedi, G., French, S., Story, M., Resnick, M. D., & Blum, R. (1998). The relationship between suicide risk and sexual orientation: Results of a population-based study. *American Journal of Public Health, 88,* 57–60.

Rencken, R. H. (1989). *Intervention strategies for sexual abuse.* Alexandria, VA: American Association for Counseling and Development.

Renshaw, P. D., & Asher, S. R. (1982). Social competence and peer status: The distinction between goals and strategies. In K. H. Rubin & H. S. Ross (Eds.), *Peer relationships and social skills in childhood* (pp. 348–358). New York: Springer-Verlag.

Resnick, L. B. (1984). Cognitive sciences as educational research: Why we need it now. *Improving Education: Perspectives on educational research, 10*(1), 1–6.

Resnick, M. D., Bearman, P. S., Blum. R. W., Bauman, K. E., Harris, K. M., Jones, J., Tabor, J., Beuhring, T., Sieving, R.E., Shew, M., Ireland, M., Beringer, L. H., & Udry, J. R. (1997). Protecting adolescents from harm: Findings from the National Longitudinal Study on Adolescent Health. *Journal of the American Medical Association 278*(10): 823–832.

Ringel, J., & Strum, P. (2001). National estimates of mental health utilization and expenditures for children in 1998. *Journal of Behavioral Health Services and Research, 28*(3), 319–332.

Roberts, A. R. (1982). Stress and coping patterns among adolescent runaways. *Journal of Social Service Research, 5,* 1–2.

Robertson, J. F., & Simons, R. L. (1989). Family factors, self-esteem and adolescent depression. *Journal of Marriage and Family, 51,* 125–138.

Robinowitz, M. (1988). On teaching cognitive strategies: The influence of accessibility of conceptual knowledge. *Contemporary Educational Psychology, 13,* 229–235.

Robinson, B. E. (1988). *Teenage fathers.* Lexington, MA: Lexington Books.

Rodning, C. L., Beckwith, J., & Howard, J. (1989). Prenatal exposure to drugs: Behavioral distortions reflecting CNS impairment? *Neurotoxicology, 10,* 629–634.

Rogala, J., Lambert, R., & Verhage, K. (1991). *Developmental guidance classroom activities for use with the national career development guidelines.* Madison: University of Wisconsin, Vocational Studies Center.

Rogers, C. R. (1980). *A way of being.* Boston: Houghton Mifflin.

Roggenbaum, S., & Lazear, K. (2003). *Youth suicide prevention school-based guide: Information dissemination in schools—The facts about adolescent suicide* (FMHI Series Publication #219-1t). Tampa, FL: University of South Florida.

Rolf, J., & Johnson, J. (1990). Protected or vulnerable: The challenges of AIDS to developmental psychopathology. In J. Rolf, A. Masten, D. Cicchetti, K. Nuechterlein, & S. Weintraub (Eds.), *Risk and protective factors in the development of psychopathology* (pp. 384–404). Cambridge, UK: Cambridge University Press.

Rolf, J., Masten, A. S., Cicchetti, D., Nuechterlein, K., & Weintraub, S. (Eds.). (1990). *Risk and protective factors in the development of psychopathology.* New York: Cambridge University Press.

Rolf, J. E., & Johnson, J. L. (1999). Opening doors to resilience intervention for prevention research. In M. D. Glantz & J. L. Johnson (Eds.), *Resilience and development: Positive life adaptations* (pp. 229–249). New York: Kluwer Academic/Plenum.

Roosa, M. W., Tein, J. Y., Reinholtz, C., & Angelini, P. J. (1997). The relationship of childhood sexual abuse to teenage pregnancy. *Journal of Marriage and the Family, 59,* 119–130.

Rose, S. (1987). Social skills training in middle school. *Journal for Specialists in Group Work, 12*(4), 144–149.

Rosenberg, M. (1979). *Conceiving self.* New York: Basic Books.

Ross, R. D., & Ross, B. (Eds.). (1995). *Thinking straight: The reasoning and rehabilitation program for delinquency prevention and offender rehabilitation.* Ottawa: AIR.

Ross, R. R., & Ross, B. (1989). Delinquency prevention through cognitive training. *Educational Horizons, 15,* 2.

Ross, S., & Heath, N. (2002). A study of the frequency of self-mutilation in a high school community sample. *Journal of Youth and Adolescence, 31,* 67–77.

Roth, S., & Lebowitz, L. (1988). The experience of sexual trauma. *Journal of Traumatic Stress, 1,* 79–107.

Rowlett, J., Patel, D. R., & Greydanus, D. E. (1992). Homosexuality. In D. E. Greydanus & M. Wolraich (Eds.), *Behavioral pediatrics* (pp. 37–54). New York: Springer-Verlag

Rubin, K. H., Coplan, R. J., Fox, N. A., & Calkins, S. D. (1995). Emotionality, emotion regulation and preschoolers' social adaptation. *Development and Psychopathology, 7,* 49–62.

Russell, D. E. H. (1984). *Sexual exploitation: Rape, child sexual abuse, and workplace harassment.* Beverly Hills, CA: Sage.

Russell, M. (1990). Prevalence of alcoholism among children of alcoholics. In M. Windle (Ed.), *Children of alcoholics: Critical perspectives.* New York: Guilford Press.

Russell, S. T. (2003). Sexual minority youth and suicide risk. *American Behavioral Scientist, 46,* 1241–1257.

Russell, S. T., & Joyner, K. (2001). Adolescent sexual orientation and suicide risk: Evidence from a national study. *American Journal of Public Health, 91*(8), 1276–1281.

Rutter, M. (1983). Stress, coping, and development. Some issues and some questions. In N. Garmezy & M. Rutter (Eds.), *Stress, coping, and development in children* (pp. 1–42). New York: McGraw-Hill.

Rutter, M. (1985). Resilience in the face of adversity: Protective factors and resistance to psychiatric disorders. *British Journal of Psychiatry, 147,* 598–611.

Rutter, M. (1987). Psychosocial resilience and protective mechanisms. *American Journal of Orthopsychiatry, 57,* 316–331.

Rutter, M. (1990). Psychosocial resilience and protective mechanisms. In J. Rolf, A. Masten, D. Cicchetti, K. Nuechterlein, & S. Weintraub (Eds.), *Risk and protective factors in the development of psychopathology* (pp. 181–214). Cambridge, UK: Cambridge University Press.

Rutter, P. A., & Soucar, E. (2002). Youth suicide risk and sexual orientation. *Adolescence, 37,* 289–299.

Ryan, C., & Futterman, D. (1997). Lesbian and gay youth: Care and counseling. *Adolescent medicine, State of the Art Reviews, 8*(2), 221.

Ryan, L. S., Ehrlich, S., & Finnegan, L. (1987). Cocaine abuse in pregnancy: Effects on the fetus and newborn. *Neurotoxicology and Teratology, 9,* 296–299.

Sabatino, J. A., & Smith, L. K. (1990). Rational self-analysis. *Journal of Counseling & Development, 69,* 167–172.

Sachdev, P. S. (1990). Whakama: Culturally determined behaviour in the New Zealand Maori. *Psychological Medicine, 20,* 433–444.

Salovey, P., & Mayer, J. D. (1990). Emotional intelligence. *Imagination, Cognition, and Personality, 9,* 185–211.

Salzinger, S., Feldman, R. S., Hammer, M., & Rosario, M. (1993). The effects of physical abuse on children's social relationships. *Child Development, 64,* 169–187.

Sameroff, A. J. (2000). Dialectical processes in developmental psychopathology. In A. J. Sameroff, M. Lewis, & S. Miller (Eds.), *Handbook of developmental psychopathology* (2nd ed., pp. 23–40). New York: Kluwer Academic/Plenum.

Sameroff, A. J., Lewis, M., & Miller, S. (Eds.). (2000). *Handbook of developmental psychopathology.* New York: Plenum.

Sameroff, A. J., & Seifer, R. (1983). Familial risk and child competence. *Child Development, 54,* 1254–1268.

Sampson, R. (2004). *Bullying in schools: Problem-oriented guides for police series* (Guide No.12 #99-CK-WX-K004). Office of Community Oriented Policing Services, U.S. Department of Justice. Washington, D.C.

Sampson, R. J., & Lamb, J. H. (1994). Urban poverty and the family context of delinquency: A new look at structure and process in a classic study. *Child Development, 65,* 523–540.

Sandler, R., & Ramsay, S. (1980). Stressors in children and adolescents. Champaign, IL.: Research Press.

Santelli, J. S., Kaiser, J., Hirsch, L., Radosh, A., Simkin, L., & Middlestadt, S. (2004). Initiation of sexual intercourse among middle school adolescents: The influence of psychosocial factors. *Journal of Adolescent Health, 34,* 200–208.

Santelli, J. S., Lowry, R., Brener, N. D., & Robin, L. (2000). The association of sexual behaviors with socioeconomic status, family structure, and race/ethnicity among U.S. adolescents. *American Journal of Public Health, 90*(10), 1582–1588.

Sarvela, P. D., Newcomb, P. R., & Littlefield, E. R. (1988). Sources of drug and alcohol information among rural youth. *Health Education, 19*(3), 27–31.

Sautter, R. C. (1995). Standing up to violence: Kappan special report. *Phi Delta Kappan, 13,* K1–K12.

Savin-Williams, R. C. (1988). Theoretical perspectives accounting for adolescent homosexuality. *Journal of Adolescent Health Care,. 9,* 95–104.

Savin-Williams, R. C. (1989). Coming out to parents and self-esteem among gay and lesbian youths. *Journal of Homosexuality, 18,* 1–35.

Savin-Williams, R. C. (1990). *Gay and lesbian youth: Expressions of identity.* Washington, DC: Hemisphere.

Savin-Williams, R. C. (1994). Verbal and physical abuse as stressors in the lives of lesbian, gay male, and bisexual youths: Association with school problems. *Journal of Consulting and Clinical Psychology, 62,* 262.

Scales, P. C., & Leffert, N. (1999). *Developmental assets: A synthesis of the scientific research on adolescent development.* Minneapolis, MN: Search Institute.

Scarr, S. (1992). Developmental theories for the 1990s: Development and individual differences. *Child Development, 63,* 1–19.

Schaefer, C. E., Briesmeister, J. M., & Fitton, M. E. (1984). *Family therapy techniques for problem behavior of children and teenagers.* San Francisco: Jossey-Bass.

Schaefer-Schiumo, K., & Ginsberg, A. P. (2003). The effectiveness of the warning signs program in educating youth about violence prevention: A study with urban high school students. *Professional School Counseling, 7*(1), 1–8.

Schinke, S. P., Orlandi, M. A., Botvin, G. J., Gilchrist, L. D., Trimble, J. E., and Locklear, V. S. (1988). Preventing substance abuse among American-Indian adolescents: A bicultural competence skills approach. *Journal of Counseling Psychology, 35*(1), 87–90.

Schloss, P. J. (1983). Classroom-based interventions for students exhibiting depressive reactions. *Behavioral Disorders, 8,* 231–236.

Schneider, R., & Googins, B. (1989). Alcoholism day treatment: Rationale, research, and resistance. *Journal of Drug Issues, 19*(4), 437–449.

Schrut, A. (1984). System theory and parenting. *International Journal of Family Psychiatry, 5*(3), 249–257.

Schweinhart, L. J., & Weikart, D. P. (1989). The High/Scope/Perry preschool program. In Price, R. H, Cowen, E.L., Lorion, E.L. & Ramos-McKay, J. (Eds.), *14 ounces of prevention: A casebook for practitioners.* Washington, DC: American Psychological Association.

Scrivner, R. W. (1984). *A model for the development of lesbian and gay identities.* Paper presented at the 42nd Annual Conference of the AAMFT. San Francisco, CA.

Search Institute. (1996). *Search Institute profiles of student life attitudes and behaviors assessment.* Minneapolis, MN: Author.

Search Institute. (1998). *Healthy Communities: Healthy Youth Tool Kit.* (1998). Retrieved from http://www.search-institute.org. (2/11/2006).

Segal, J., & Segal, Z. (1986, Summer). The powerful world of peer relationships. *American Educator,* 14–45.

Seifer, R. (2003). Young children and mentally ill parents In S. S. Luthar (Ed.), *Resiliency and vulnerability: Adaptation in the context of childhood adversities* (pp. 29–49). New York: Cambridge University Press.

Seligman, L. (1981). Multimodal behavior therapy: Case study of a high school student. *The School Counselor, 58,* 249–256.

Seltzer, J. A. (1994). Consequences of marital dissolution for children. *Annual Review of Sociology, 20,* 235–266.

Sema, L. A., Schumaker, J. B., Hazel, J. S., & Sheldon, J. B. (1986). Teaching reciprocal social skills to parents and their delinquent adolescents. *Journal of Clinical and Child Psychology 15*(1), 64–77.

Shaffer, D., & Pfeffer, C. R. (2001). Work Group on Quality Issues: Practice parameter for the assessment and treatment of children and adolescents with suicidal behavior. *Journal of the American Academy of Child and Adolescent Psychiatry, 40*(Suppl.), 24–51.

Shaw, D. S., & Vondra, J. I. (1993). Chronic family adversity and infant attachment security. *Journal of Child Psychology and Psychiatry, 34,* 1205–1215.

Shaw, D. S., & Vonda, J. I. (1995). Infant attachment security and maternal predictors of early behavior problems: A longitudinal study of low income families. *Journal of Abnormal Child Psychology and Psychiatry, 34,* 1205–1215.

Sher, K. J. (1991). *Children of alcoholics: A critical appraisal of theory and research.* Chicago: University of Chicago Press.

Shifrin, F., & Solis, M. (1992). Chemical dependency in gay and lesbian youth. *Journal of Chemical Dependency Treatment, 5,* 67.

Shorts, I. D. (1989). Community-based training programmes for young offenders: Perceptions of programme impact. *Irish Journal of Psychological Medicine, 6*(1), 26–29.

Shrier, L. A., Emans, S. J., Woods, E. R., & DuRant, R. H. (1996). The association of sexual risk behaviors and problem drug behaviors in high school students. *Journal of Adolescent Health, 20*(5), 337–383.

Shriver, T. P., & Weissberg, R. P. (1996, September 4). No new wars! Prevention should be a comprehensive strategy, not a fad. *Education Week, 15*(34) p.47.

Sidora, K., Morris, P., Pettitt, L. M., & Luckey, D. (1997). Long-term effects of home visitation on maternal life course and child abuse and neglect: Fifteen-year follow-up of a randomized trial. *Journal of the American Medical Association, 278*(8), 637–743.

Siegler, R. S., Liebert, D. E., & Liebert, R. M. (1973). Inhelder's and Piaget's pendulum problem: Teaching pre-adolescents to be scientists. *Developmental Psychology, 9*, 97–101.

Simeon, D., Stanley, B., Frances, A., Mann, J. J., Winchel, R., & Stanley, M. (1992). Self-mutilation in personality disorders: Psychological and biological correlates. *American Journal of Psychiatry, 149*(2), 221–226.

Simons, R. L.,Whitbeck, L.B., Beamon, J. & Conger, R.D.(Eds.). (1996). *Understanding differences between divorced and intact families: Stress, interaction, and child outcome.* Thousand Oaks, CA: Sage.

Singh, S., & Darroch, J. E. (2000). Adolescent pregnancy and childbearing: Levels and trends in developed countries. *Family Planning Perspectives, 32*(1), 14–23.

Skaalvik, E. M., & Hagtvet, K. A. (1990). Academic achievement and self-concept: An analysis of causal predominance in a developmental perspective. *Journal of Personality and Social Psychology, 58*, 292–307.

Slaby, R. G., Roedell, W. C., Arezzo, D., & Kendrix, K. (1995). *Early violence prevention: Tools for teachers of young children* (ED 382 384). Washington, DC: National Association for the Education of Young Children.

Slavin, R. (1987). Cooperative learning: Can students help students learn? *Instructor, 3*(1), 74–78.

Slovacek, S. P. (1993). *Project support evaluation* (Report No. 1). Los Angeles: Los Angeles Unified School District.

Smith, R. E., & Johnson, J. (1990). An organizational empowerment approach to consultation in professional baseball. *Sport Psychology 4*(4), 347–357.

Smith, R. L., & Southern, S. (1980). Multimodal career counseling: An application of the BASIC ID. *Vocational Guidance Quarterly, 29*, 56–64.

Smollar, J., & Ooms, T. (1987). *Young unwed fathers: Research review, policy dilemmas, and options.* Washington, DC: U.S. Department of Health and Human Services.

Snyder, C. R. (1989). Reality negotiation: From excuses to hope and beyond. *Journal of Social and Clinical Psychology, 8*, 130–157.

Snyder, C. R. (1994). *The psychology of hope: You can get there from here.* New York: Free Press.

Snyder, C. R. (1995). Conceptualizing, measuring, and nurturing hope. *Journal of Counseling & Development, 73*(3), 355–360.

Snyder, H.N. (2005), *Juvenile arrests 2003. Juvenile Justice Bulletin.*Washington, D.C.: Office of Juvenile Justice & Delinquency Prevention, U.S. Department of Justice,

Snyder, H. N., & Sickmund, M. (1999). *Juvenile offenders and victims: 1999 national report.* Washington, DC: Office of Juvenile Justice & Delinquency Prevention, U.S. Department of Justice.

Soderberg, L. J. (1988). Educators' knowledge of the characteristics of high school dropouts. *The High School Journal, 77,* 108–115.

Sonenstein, F. L. (1986). Risking paternity: Sex and contraception among adolescent males. In A. B. Elster & M. Lamb (Eds.), *Adolescent fatherhood.* 32–54 Hillsdale, NJ: Erlbaum.

Sonenstein, F. & Ku, L. (1997).*Fact Sheet: New Data on Sexual Behaviors of Teenage Males.*Washington, D.C.: Urban Institute, May 1.

Sophie, J. (1985/1986) A critical examination of stage theories of lesbian identity development. *Journal of Homosexuality, 12*(2), 39–51.

SPAN USA (2001). *Suicide prevention: Prevention effectiveness and evaluation.* Washington, DC: Author.

Spence, J. T. (1982). Comments on Baumrind's "Are androgynous individuals more effect persons and parents?" *Child Development, 53,* 76–80.

Spencer, M. B. (1982). Personal and group identity of black children: An alternative syntheses. *Genetic Psychology Monographs, 103,* 59–84.

Spencer, M. B. (1988). Self-concept development. In D. T. Slaughter (Ed.), *Black children in poverty: Developmental perspectives* (pp. 59–72). San Francisco: Jossey-Bass.

Spergel, I. A. (1989). *Youth gangs: Problem and response. A review of the literature.* Chicago: University of Chicago School of Social Service Administration.

Spitz, A. M., Velebil, P., Koonin, L. M. (1996). Pregnancy, abortion and birth rates among U.S. adolescents: 1980, 1985, and 1990. *Journal of American Medical Association, 275,* 989–994.

Spitz, A. M., Velebil, P., Koonin, L. M., Goodman, K. A., Wingo, P., Wilson, J. B., Morris, L., & Marks, J. S. (1996). Pregnancy, abortion and birth rates among U.S. adolescents, 1980, 1985, and 1990. *Journal of the American Medical Association, 13,* 989–994.

St. Lawrence, J. S., Brasfield, T. L., Jefferson, K. W., Alleyne, E., Bannon, R. E., & Shirley, A. (1995). Cognitive-behavioral intervention to reduce African American adolescents' risk for HIV infection. *Journal of Consulting and Clinical Psychology, 63*(2), 221–237.

Stacey, J., & Biblarz, T. J. (2001). Does sexual orientation of parents matter? *American Sociological Review, 65,* 159–183.

Stapley, J. C., & Haviland, J. M. (1989). Beyond depression: Gender differences in normal adolescents' emotional experiences. *Sex Roles, 20,* 295–308.

Starr, J., & Raykovitz, J. (1982). A multimodal approach to interviewing children. *Elementary School Guidance & Counseling, 16,* 267–277.

Stein, A. H., & Bailey, M. M. (1973). The socialization of achievement orientation in females. *Psychological Bulletin, 80,* 345–365.

Steketee, G., & Foa, E. B. (1987). Rape victims: Post-traumatic stress responses and their treatment. *Journal of Anxiety Disorders, 1,* 69–86.

Stellas, E. (1992). No more victims, no more victimizers violence prevention education: Social skills for risk reduction. In R. C. Morris (Ed.), *Solving the problems of youth at risk: Involving parents and community resources.* Lancaster, PA: Technomic Publishing.

Stickel, S. A. (1990). Using multimodal social-skills groups with kindergarten children. *Elementary School Guidance & Counseling, 24,* 281–288.

Stiffman, A. R. (1989). Physical and sexual abuse in runaway youths. *Child Abuse and Neglect, 13,* 417.

Stigler, J. W., Smith, S., & Mao, L. (1985). The self perception of competence by Chinese children. *Child Development, 56,* 1259–1270.

Stock, J. L., Bell, M. A., Boyer, D. K., & Connell, E A. (1997). Adolescent pregnancy and sexual risk-taking among sexually abused girls. *Family Planning Perspectives, 29*(5), 200–203, 227.

Strober, M., McCracken, J., & Hanna, G. (1989). Affective disorders. In L. K. G. Hsu & M. Hersen (Eds.), *Handbook of child psychiatric diagnosis* (pp. 299–316). New York: Wiley.

Strong, M. (1998). *A bright red scream: Self-mutilation and the language of pain.* New York: Viking.

Substance Abuse and Mental Health Services Administration. (2004). *Results from the 2003 National Survey on Drug Use and Health: National findings* (Office of Applied Studies, NSDUH Series H–25, DHHS Publication No. SMA 04-3964). Rockville, MD: Author.

Sullivan, H. S. (1953). *The interpersonal theory of psychiatry.* New York: Norton.

Sullivan, M. (1988). *What about the boys? Teenage pregnancy prevention strategies.* Washington, DC: Children's Defense Fund.

Substance Abuse and Mental Health Services Administration (2003). *TheDAWN report [on-line].* Available: http://dawninfo.samhsa.gov/pub_94_02/shortreports/files/TDR_ED visits_glance 1994-2001.pdf.Retrieved August 22,2005. Rockville, MD: Department of Health and Human Services

Super, D. E. (1980). A life-span, life-space approach to career development. *Journal of Vocational Behavior, 16,* 282–298.

Suyemoto, K. L., & MacDonald, M. L. (1995). Self-cutting in female adolescents. *Psychotherapy, 32,* 162–171.

Svec, H., & Bechard, J.(1988). An introduction to metabehavioral model with implications for social skills training for aggressive adolescents. *Psychological Report 62,* 19–22.

Sylwester, R. (1995). A celebration of neurons: An educator's guide to the human brain. Alexandria, VA: Association for Supervision and Curriculum Development.

Tannehill, R. L. (1987). Employing a modified positive peer culture treatment approach in a state youth center. *Journal of Offender Counseling, Services and Rehabilitation2*(1), 113–129.

Tasker, F. (1999). Children in lesbian-led families: A review. Clinical Child Psychology and Psychiatry, 4, 153–166.

Tasker, F., & Golombok, S. (1997). *Growing up in a lesbian family.* New York: Guilford Press.

Teachman, J. D., Tedrow, L. M., & Crowder, K. D. (2000). The changing demographics of American families. *Journal of Marriage and Family, 62,* 1234–1246.

Tedesco, L. A., & Gaier, E. L. (1988). Friendship bonds in adolescence. *Adolescence, 23,* 127–136.

Telljohann, S. K., & Price, J. H. (1993). A qualitative examination of adolescent homosexuals' life experiences: Ramifications for secondary school personnel. *Journal of Homosexuality, 26*(1), 41–56.

Telljohann, S. K., Price, J. H., Poureslami, M., & Easton, A. (1995). Teaching about sexual orientation by secondary health teachers. *Journal of School Health, 61*(10), 433–438.

Texas Board of Criminal Justice (1998).*Annual Review.*Austin, Texas

Thomerson, J. (2002, May). Violent acts of sadness: The tragedy of youth suicide. *State Legislatures, 28,* 30–33.

Thompson, E. C., III. (1987). The "yagottawanna" group: Improving students self-perceptions through motivational teaching of study skills. *The School Counselor, 35*(2), 134–142.

Thompson, K. L., Bundy, K. A., & Broncheau, C. (1995). Social skills training for young adults: Symbolic and behavioral components. *Adolescence, 30,* 723–734.

Thompson, K. S. (1980). A comparison of black and white adolescents' beliefs about having children. *Journal of Marriage and the Family, 3*(35), 112–117.

Thompson, M. (1994). *Gay soul: Finding the heart of gay spirit and nature.* San Francisco: HarperCollins.

Thompson, R. A. (1986). The unwed adolescent mother. In D. Capuzzi & L. B. Golden (Eds.), *Helping families help children: Family interventions with schoolrelated problems* (pp. 109–121). New York: Charles C. Thomas.

Thompson, R. A. (1990). Post-traumatic loss debriefing: Providing immediate support for survivors of suicide or sudden loss. In *Highlights: An ERIC/CAPS Digest.* Ann Arbor, MI: Counseling and Personnel Services Clearinghouse.

Thompson, R. A. (1992). *School counseling renewal: Strategies for the twenty-first century.* Muncie, IN: Accelerated Development.

Thompson, R. A. (1993). Post-traumatic stress and post-traumatic loss debriefing: Brief strategic intervention for survivors of sudden loss. *The School Counselor, 36*(1), 22–27.

Thornberry, T. P., Smith, C. A., & Howard, G. J. (1997). Risk factors for teenage fatherhood. *Journal of Marriage & the Family, 59*(3), 505–522.

Thornton, T. N., Craft, C. A., Dahlberg, L. L. Lynch, B. S., & Baer, K. (2000). *Best practices of youth violence prevention: A sourcebook for community action.* Atlanta: Centers for Disease Control and Prevention.

Timmerman, L., Martin, D., & Martin, M. (1990). Augmenting the helping relationship: The use of bibliotherapy. *The School Counselor, 36,* 293–297.

Tisdelle, D. A., & St. Lawrence, J. S. (1988). Adolescent interpersonal problem-solving training: Social validation and generalization. *Behavior Therapy, 19,* 171–182.

Tolan, P. H., Guerra, N. G., & Kendall, P. C. (1995). A developmental-ecological perspective on antisocial behavior in children and adolescents: Toward a unified risk and intervention framework. *Journal of Consulting and Clinical Psychology, 63*(4), 579–584.

Trigg, M., & Wittenstrom, K. (1996). That's the way the world goes: Sexual harassment and New Jersey teenagers. *Initiatives, 57,* 55.

Troiden, R. (1979). Becoming homosexual: a model of gay identity acquisition. *Psychiatry, 42,* 362–373.

Troiden, R. R. (1988). Homosexual identity development. *Journal of Adolescent Health, 9*(2), 105–113.

Troiden, R. R. (1993). The formation of homosexual identities. In L. Garnets & D. Kimmel (Eds.), *Psychological perspectives on lesbian and gay male experiences* (pp. 191–217). New York: Columbia University Press.

Tuma, J. M. (1989). Mental health services for children: The state of the art. *American Psychologist, 44,* 188–199.

Turner, S., Norman, E., & Zunz, S. (1995). Enhancing resiliency in girls and boys: A case for gender-specific adolescent prevention programming. *Journal of Primary Prevention, 16,* 25–38.

Tweed, S. H., & Ryff, C. D. (1991). Adult children of alcoholics: Profiles of wellness amidst distress. *Journal of Studies on Alcohol, 52,* 2.

U.S. Bureau of the Census. (1998). *Current population reports. Marital Status and Living Arrangements: March 1998* (Update). Washington, DC: U.S. Department of Commerce, Economics and Statistics Administration.

U.S. Bureau of the Census. (2000). *Poverty in the United States: 1999.* Retrieved January 10, 2005, from http//www.census.gov/hhes/www/poverty99.html.

U.S. Congress. (1986). *Teen pregnancy: What is being done? A report of the select committee on children, youth, and families.* Washington, DC: U.S. Government Printing Office.

U.S. Department of Education and U.S. Department of Justice. (1999). *1999 Annual Report on School Safety.* Washington, DC: Authors.

U.S. Department of Health and Human Services. (1989). *Report of the Secretary's task force on youth suicide, Volume 3: Preventions and interventions in youth.* Washington, D.C.: Author.

U.S. Department of Health and Human Services. (1996). *Preventing teen pregnancy: Effective programs and their impact on adolescents' risk for pregnancy, HIV, & STIs.* Washington, DC: Author.

U.S. Department of Health and Human Services. (1999). *Child abuse and neglect state statues elements: Reporting laws: Number 6: Reporting procedures* (Report). Washington, DC: National Clearinghouse on Child Abuse and Neglect Information.

U.S. Department of Health and Human Services. (2001). *Youth violence: A report of the Surgeon General.* Washington, DC: Author.

U.S. Department of Health and Human Services, Center for Mental Health Services. (2003). *Bullying is not a fact of life* (CMHS-SCP-0052). Adapted from material prepared by Dan Olweus. Washington, DC: Author.

U.S. Department of Health and Human Services, Children's Bureau. (2004). *Child maltreatment 2002.* Washington, DC: U.S. Government Printing Office.

U.S. Department of Health and Human Services, Substance Abuse and Mental Health Services Administration, Office of Applied Studies. (2002). *The NHSDA Report: Youth violence and substance use: 2001 update.* Washington, DC: Author.

U.S. Department of Health and Human Services, Office of the Surgeon General. (1999). *First Surgeon General's report on adolescent mental health.* Washington, DC: Substance Abuse and Mental Health Services Administration.

U.S. Department of Justice, Office of Juvenile Justice and Delinquency Prevention. (2000). *Children as victims* (NCJ Publications No. 180753). Washington, DC: Author.

U.S. Department Of Education National Center for Education Statistics, (1999). *The condition of education* (NCES 99-022). Washington, DC: U.S. Government Printing Office.

U.S. General Accounting Office. (2002). *School dropouts: Education could play a stronger role in identifying and disseminating promising prevention strategies.* Washington, DC: Author.

U.S. Public Health Service. (1999). *The Surgeon General's call to action to prevent suicide.* Washington, DC:Author.

U.S. Surgeon General. (2000). *Mental health: A report of the Surgeon General.* RetrievedMarch 15,2005 from http://www.surgeongeneral.gov/library/mental/home.html.

U.S. Surgeon General. (2001). *U.S. Public Health Service Report of the Surgeon General's Conference on Children's Mental Health: A national action agenda.* RetrievedMarch 15, 2005from http://www.surgeongeneral.gov/cmh/childreport.htm.

UNICEF Innocenti Research Centre. (2001). *A league table of teenage births in rich nations.* Florence, Italy.

Ventura, S. J., Mathews, T. J., & Hamilton, B. E. (2001). Births to teenagers in the United States, 1940–2000. *National Vital Statistics Report 49*(10).

Ventura, S. J., Mosher, W. D., Curtin, S. C., Abma, J. C., & Henshaw, S. (2000). *Trends in pregnancies and pregnancy rates by outcome: estimates for the United States, 1976–96.* Hyattsville, MD: National Center for Health Statistics.

Ventura, S., Mosher, W. D., Curtin, S. C., Abma, J. C., & Henshaw, S. (2001). Trends in pregnancy rates for the United States, 1976–97: An update. *National Vital Statistics Reports 49*(4), 1–9.

Vermeiren, R., Ruchkin, V., Leckman, P. E., Deboutte, D. C., & Schwab-Stone, M. (2002). Exposure to violence and bringing an end to youth suicide risk in adolescents: A community study. *Journal of Abnormal Child Psychology, 30*, 529–537.

Vernon, A. (1989). *Thinking, feeling, behaving: An emotional education curriculum for children.* Champaign, IL: Research Press.

Viadero, D. (1993). Teaching right from wrong. *Teacher Magazine, 36*(2), 12–17.

Vossekuil, B., Fein, R., Reddy, M., Borum, R., & Modzeleski, W. (2002). *Final report and findings of the safe school initiative: Implications for the prevention of school attacks in the United States.* Washington, DC: U.S. Department of Education, Office of Elementary and Secondary Education, Safe and Drug-Free Schools Program and U.S. Secret Service, National Threat Assessment Center.

Vygotsky, L. (1978). *Society of mind.* Cambridge, MA: Harvard University Press.

Wadsworth, B. (1989). Piaget's theory of cognitive and affective development. New York: Longman.

Waldo, M. (1985). A curative factor framework for conceptualizing group counseling. *Journal of Counseling and Development, 64*(1), p. 58.

Walen, S. R., DiGiuseppe, R., & Wessler, R. L. (1980). *A practitioner's guide to rational emotive therapy.* New York: Oxford University Press.

Walker, E. N. (1989). The Community Intensive Treatment for Youth program: A specialized community-based program for high risk youth in Alabama. *Law Psychology Review, 13,* 175–199.

Wallack, L., & Corbett, K. (1990). *Illicit drug, tobacco, and alcohol use among youth: Trends and promising approaches in prevention.* Office of Substance Abuse Prevention: Monograph 6. Washington, DC: U.S. Department of Health, Human Services, and Public Health Service.

Waller, R. (1992). Cocaine-affected children. *Educational Leadership, 43*(2), 4–8.

Walsh, B. W. & Rosen, P. M. (1988). *Self-mutilation: Theory, research, and treatment.* New York: Guilford Press.

Walters, V. (1981). The living school. *RETwork, 1*(1), 136–144.

Warwick, I., Oliver, C., & Aggleton, P. (2000). Sexuality and mental health promotion: Lesbian and gay young people. In P. Aggleton, J. Hurry, & I. Warwick (Eds.), *Young people and mental health* (pp. 133–146). Toronto: John Wiley & Sons.

Wassmer, A. (1978). *Making contact. A guide to overcoming shyness, making new relationships, and keeping those you have.* New York: Dial Press.

Weed, R. O., & Hernandez, A. M. (1990). Multimodal rehabilitation counseling. *Journal of Applied Rehabilitation Counseling, 1*(4), 27–30.

Weikel, W. J. (1989). A multimodal approach in dealing with chronic Epstein-Barr viral syndrome. *Journal of Counseling and Development, 67* 522–524.

Weikel, W. J. (1990). A multimodal approach in dealing with older clients. *Journal of Mental Health Counseling, 12,* 314–320.

Weiner, I. B. (1980). Psychopathology in adolescence. In J. Adelson (Ed.), *Handbook of adolescent psychology.* New York: Wiley.

Weiner, J. M. (1997). Oppositional defiant disorder. In J. M. Weiner (Ed.), *Textbook of child and adolescent psychiatry* (2nd ed., pp. 459–463). Washington, DC: American Academy of Child and Adolescent Psychiatry, American Psychiatric Press.

Weinfield, N. S., Stroufe, L. A., & Egeland, B. (2000). Attachment from infancy to early adulthood in a high-risk sample: Continuity, discontinuity and their correlates. *Child Development, 71,* 695–702.

Weinstein, C. E., & Mayer, R. F. (1986). The teaching of learning strategies. In M. Wittrock (Ed.), *Handbook of research on teaching* (pp. 120–142). Alexandria, VA: ASCD.

Weinstein, R. S., Marshall, H. H., Sharp, L., & Botkin, M. (1987). Pygmalion and the student: Age and classroom differences in children's awareness of teacher expectations. *Child Development, 58,* 1079–1093.

Weissman, M. M., Warner, V., Wickramaratne, P., Moreau, D., & Olfson, M. (1997). Offspring of depressed parents: 10 years later. *Archives of General Psychiatry, 54,* 932–940.

Werner, E. E. (1982). Resilient children. *Young Children, 40,* 68–72.

Werner, E. E. (1986). The concept of risk from a developmental perspective. *Advances in Special Education, 5,* 1–23.

Werner, E. E. (1990). Protective factors and individual resilience. In S. J. Meisels & J. P. Shonkoff (Eds.), *Handbook of early childhood intervention* (pp. 97–116). New York: Cambridge University Press.

Werner, E. E. (1992). *Vulnerable but invincible: A longitudinal study of resilient children and youth.* New York: McGraw-Hill.

Werner, E. E. (1993). Risk, resilience, and recovery: Perspectives from the Kauai Longitudinal Study. *Development and Psychopathology, 5,* 503–515.

Werner, E. E. (1995). Resilience in development. *Current Directions in Psychological Science, 4*(3), 81–85.

Werner, E. E. (1996). How children become resilient: Observations and cautions. *Resilience in Action*(Winter), 18–28.

Werner, E. E. (1999, September 24). *The children of Kauai: Multiple pathways from birth to midlife.* Paper presented at the Annual Conference of the Life History Research Society, Kauai, HI.

Werner, E. E., Bierman, J. M., & French, F. E. (1971). *The children of Kauai: A longitudinal study from the prenatal period to age ten.* Honolulu: University of Hawaii Press.

Werner, E. E., & Smith, R. S. (1977). *Kauai's children come of age.* Honolulu: University of Hawaii Press.

Werner, E. E., & Smith, R. S. (1982). *Vulnerable but invincible: A longitudinal study of resilient children and youth.* New York: McGraw-Hill.

Werner, E. E., & Smith, R. S. (1992). *Overcoming the odds: High-risk children from birth to adulthood.* Ithaca, NY: Cornell University Press.

West, M. O., & Prinz, R. J. (1987). Parental alcoholism and childhood psychopathology. *Psychological Bulletin, 102,* 201–218.

Whitfield, C. L. (1987). *Healing the child within. A discovery and recovery for adults of dysfunctional families.* Dearfield, Beach, FL: Health Communications

Whitman, J. S., & Boyd, C. J., (2003). *The therapist's notebook for lesbian, gay and bisexual clients: Homework, handouts, and activities for use in psychotherapy.* Binghamton, NY: Haworth Press.

Widmer, E. D. (1997). Influence of older siblings on initiation of sexual intercourse. *Journal of Marriage & the Family, 59*(4), 928–938.

Wilkinson, G. S., & Bleck, R. T. (1977). Children's divorce groups. *Elementary School Guidance and Counseling, 11,* 205–213.

Wilson, J., & Blocher, L. (1990). Personality characteristics of adult children of alcoholics. *Journal of Humanistic Education and Development, 26,* 166–175.

Winbush, R. A. (1988). Growing pains: Explaining adolescent violence with developmental theory. In R. Hayes & R. Aubrey (Eds.), *Counseling and human development.* Denver, CO: Love Publishing.

Windle, M. (1991). Salient issues in the development of alcohol abuse in adolescence. *Alcohol and Alcoholism, Supplement, 1,* 499–504.

Wolin, S. J., & Wolin, S. (1993). *The resilient self: How survivors of troubled families rise above adversity.* New York: Villard Books.

Wong, M. M., Zucker, R. A., Puttler, L. I., & Fitzgerald, H. E. (1999). Heterogeneity of risk aggression for alcohol problems between early and middle childhood: Nesting structure variations. *Development and Psychopathology, 11,* 727–744.

Worchel, F., Nolan, B., & Wilson, V. (1987). New perspectives on child and adolescent depression. *Journal of School Psychology, 25,* 411–414.

Worrell, J., & Stilwell, W. E. (1981). *Psychology for teachers and students.* New York: McGraw-Hill.

Wright, E. E. (1989). *Good morning class—I love you!* Rolling Hill Estates, CA: Jalmar Press.

Yalom, I. (1985).*The theory and practice of group psychotherapy.*New York: Wiley.

Yates, A. (1989). Current perspectives on the eating disorders: History, psychological, and biological aspects. *Journal of American Academy of Child and Adolescent Psychiatry, 28,* 813–828.

Yazigi, R. A., Odem, R. R., & Polakoski, K. L. (1991). Demonstration of specific binding of cocaine to human spermatozoa. *Journal of the American Medical Association, 266*(15), 1956–1959.

Yoshikawa, H. (1995, Winter), Long-term effects of early childhood programs on social outcomes and delinquency. *Future of Children, 5*(3), 51–75.

Youniss, J. (1980). *Parents and peers in social development: A Sullivan-Piaget perspective.* Chicago: University of Chicago Press.

Zabin, L. S., Hirsch, M. B., Smith, E. A., Streett, R., & Hardy, J. B. (1986). Evaluation of a pregnancy prevention program for urban teenagers. *Family Planning Perspectives, 18,* 119–126.

Zavodny, M. (2001). The effect of partners' characteristics on teenage pregnancy and its resolution. *Family Planning Perspectives, 33*(5), 192–199, 205.

Zeanah, C. H. (Ed.). (2000). *Handbook of infant mental health* (2nd ed.). New York: Guilford Press.

Ziegler, S. (1987). *The effects of parent involvement on children's achievement: The significance of home/school links* (ED 304–234). Ontario: Toronto Board of Education.

Zieman, G. L., & Benson, G. P. (1980). School perceptions of truant adolescent boys. *Behavior Disorders, Programs, Trends, and Concerns of Children with Behavioral Problems, 5*(4), 212–222.

Zill, N., & Schoenborn, C. A. (1990). *Developmental, learning, and emotional problems: Health of our nation's children, United States, 1988: Advance data from vital and health statistics* (Report No. 190). Hyattsville, MD: National Center for Health Statistics.

Zimbardo, P. G. (1977). *Shyness: What it is and what to do about it.* Menlo Park, CA: Addison Wesley.

Zitzow, D. (1992). Assessing student stress: School adjustment rating by self-report. *The School Counselor, 40*(1), 20–23.

Zucker, R. A. (2000). Alcohol involvement over the life course. In National Institute on Alcohol Abuse and Alcoholism, *Tenth special report to the U.S. Congress on alcohol and health: Highlights from current research* (pp. 28–53). Bethesda, MD: U.S. Department of Health and Human Services.

Zucker, R. A., Chermack, S. T., & Curran, G. M. (2000). Alcoholism: A lifespan perspective on etiology and course. In A. J. Sameroff, M. Lewis, & S. Miller (Eds.), *Handbook of developmental psychopathology* (2nd ed., pp. 569–587). New York: Plenum.

Index

A

Abandonment, 326
fear of, 329
Abortion rates, in U.S., 166
Absenteeism, suggested interventions, 317
Abstinence-based sexuality education, 180–181
Abstract reasoning, 13
Abuse, xx, 323–327
acts of commission, 326
acts of omission, 326
breaking cycle of, 332–333
characteristics of adult perpetrators, 332–333
collective community initiatives, 354–355
emotional literacy skills for, 359–362
finding safe places/escape routes, 345
against GLBTQ youth, 367–368
guided exercise for retelling story of, 342–345
indicators of, 328–330
life-sized silhouette exercise, 346
long-term effects of, 330–332
multimodal treatment plan for, 346–347
prevention efforts, 333
rape, 333–336
risk and protective factors for, 331–332

and runaways/homeless youth, 336–337
saying no, 340–342
sexual abuse within family, 327
sexual assault prevention, 340
social literacy skills for, 355–359
structured interventions for, 337–355
teacher assistance to children of, 338–340
types of, 329
Academic achievement, 75
academic mentoring program
study habits survey, 311
teacher evaluation form, 316–317
and drug/alcohol abuse, 128
and gang prevention, 255
as predictor of high-risk sexual behaviors, 166–167
as reason for leaving school, 282
and timing of first sex, 164
Academic organization skills, 38
Academic performance, as resiliency factor, 58
Academic skills, for employability, 287
Academic skills enhancement programs, 425
Academically resistant youth, assistance programs for, 299, 302
Accommodation, 267
Achievement orientation, 66
as resiliency factor, 60
Acknowledgment, 194